Institutionalizing Madness

INSTITUTIONALIZING MADNESS

Families, Therapy, and Society

JOEL ELIZUR
SALVADOR MINUCHIN

With a chapter by MORDECAI KAFFMAN

Basic Books, Inc., Publishers *New York*

All names, identifying characteristics, and other details of the case material in this book have been changed.

Library of Congress Cataloging-in-Publication Data
Elizur, Joel, 1952–
Institutionalizing madness: families, therapy, and society / Joel Elizur, Salvador Minuchin; with a chapter by Mordecai Kaffman.
p. cm.
Includes bibliographical references.
ISBN 0-465-03322-9
1. Psychotherapy—Case studies. I. Minuchin, Salvador.
II. Kaffman, Mordecai. III. Title.
[DNLM: 1. Deinstitutionalization. 2. Institutionalization.
3. Psychotherapy—case studies. WM 420 E43i]
RC465.E55 1989
616.89'14—dc20 89-42799 CIP
DNLM/DLC
for Library of Congress

Printed in the United States of America
Designed by Vincent Torre
89 90 91 92 HC 9 8 7 6 5 4 3 2 1

To the memory of my father, Abraham Elizur . . .

—J. E.

And my grandfather, Jose Minuchin

—S. M.

CONTENTS

ACKNOWLEDGMENTS

THE PEOPLE who contributed the most to our work, and to whom we are most grateful, were of course the families whose lives are depicted here. The project could not have existed without their willingness to participate in a most extensive follow-up, and to let others learn from their experience. We would also like to thank the participants in the training workshop and the therapists who worked with these families.

Mordecai Kaffman not only contributed a most important chapter to this book, he was also involved in the project from the beginning. He read many of our drafts, and his feedback and constant support were always helpful. Fran Hitchcock helped with editing and thinking about each draft, and we would also like to thank Jo Ann Miller and Pamela Dailey of Basic Books.

Our wives were both involved with writing this book, and their contributions must be acknowledged here along with our thanks for their support and patience. Akiva Skidel translated some of the transcripts and the early drafts of the book, and we are grateful to Bruce Oppenheimer, Haim Omer, Mark Spivak, and Avraham Elizur, M.D., for their constructive comments. Joel Elizur wishes to express particular appreciation to the Fulbright Program for the fellowhip that helped him come to New York and be free for the writing of this book.

PREFACE

THIS BOOK began as a study of consultation, of how consultation in family therapy can produce changes in the therapeutic system. Its source was a training seminar in family therapy that Salvador Minuchin conducted in Israel several years ago. In the course of that project, he held consultations with a number of families and their therapists, and Joel Elizur conducted a follow-up on some of these consultations, which has now continued for more than five years.

As we analyzed the two-year follow-up interviews, however, we became more and more impressed with the limitations of the consultative process. There was no question that the consultative interview had made an impact on the families and therapists selected for the study. But the subsequent course of therapy, and its effects on the lives of family and therapist, had taken directions that could not have been predicted. Indeed, they could be analyzed only from hindsight. In one case, vital information had never been presented to the consultant because it did not mesh with the curriculum of the seminar or with the therapist's agenda for the family. In several cases plans made on the basis of the consultation had been followed without regard for contextual feedback that should have compelled reevaluation. In some, the attempt to coordinate the efforts of therapists of different disciplines had resulted in the firm demarcation of therapeutic turfs, with the result that therapy planned—and still enthusiastically perceived—as interdisciplinary teamwork had become a far less effective amalgam of uncoordinated efforts.

As we analyzed each case, we saw that the consultant's and therapists' goals and interaction at the time of the consultation were tenable and potentially fruitful. But we were profoundly impressed by the difference between the consultant's, the therapists', and the family's views of the consultation both at the time and two years later. The course taken following the consultation was often not at all what we had expected.

Probably this should not have been so surprising. Consultation is by definition a brief encounter. The information available to the consultant is limited even at the time, and there is no way to encompass the many aspects of the family's and therapists' lives that lie outside the consultant's jurisdiction or that may become important subsequently.

In medicine, a more exact science, a diagnosis usually suggests an appropriate medication or procedure, one that will change the course of the illness. There is enough generalizable information to predict the results with reasonable certainty. In a psychiatric or therapeutic consultation, there are a number of other variables. One is that the "medication" is the idiosyncratic participation of the therapist in the family system. Another is the relationship of the therapist with the consultant. How familiar are they to each other? How familiar is the consultee with the theory and practice of the consultant? How important is the consultant in the social context in which the consultee normally functions?

Therapeutic consultation is modeled on therapeutic supervision, but there are very important differences between the two processes. Supervision entails a prolonged relationship of supervisor and supervisee. The supervisor can identify the therapist as an idiosyncratic part of the therapeutic system and can introduce planned inputs based on knowledge of the therapist, the family, and the therapeutic system. The effects can be observed over time and the inputs modified on the basis of feedback. In consultation, one rarely gets more data over time. Correcting (that is, increasing the complexity of) the view of the therapeutic system is not an option. The consultant is supposed to make interventions, producing a significant shift, by operating in an incomplete frame and without the opportunity to self-correct.

We also realized, as we analyzed these four cases, that their development was profoundly influenced by other circumstances, circumstances that could not be taken into account in mental health practice. Political and institutional issues, to which a therapeutic system is closed, had deeply affected the lives of the patients. Now, as our study of consultation was becoming more and more a study of the limitations of consultation, we began to focus on the limitations of the field itself, exploring the way the mental health system perceives, frames, and labels patients. And we began to speculate: Perhaps madness lies not in the individual, or in the system, but in any structure in which an individual or group is operating as though it existed in isolation.

What had begun as a book on therapy took on a more anthropological tone as we explored the interactions of patients, families, and institutions within their cultural context. In the end, the book has become a study of the partial and culture-bound way the mental health field responds to people labeled patients. Thus the first case, that of Yoav, which began as a study of the use of consultation to introduce a "leaving home" model for an institutionalized adolescent, became a study of diagnosis, more specifically of the fallacy of assuming that in the delivery of mental health services, as in medicine, diagnosis prescribes procedure. The next case, that of Dan, began as the presentation of a hospitalized patient with somatic delusions but went on to explore the mistrust between an outpatient family therapist and the psychiatric inpatient facilities and the way this affected therapy.

Two of the four consultations were with families living in the kibbutz. Their cases—those of Joey and Mickie—are studies in the advantages and disadvantages posed by an environment in which contextual intervention is almost unavoidable. Joey's case, which began as the study of a depressed boy with school problems, became the story of adolescence in a kibbutz and a therapeutic context that encompassed school, individual, and family therapy. In Mickie's case, therapy moved from an individual patient to incorporate the kibbutz and the process of a family's adjustment in this complex society. The idiosyncratic ways in which mental illness can be treated in the framework of the kibbutz community are further explored in a chapter contributed by Mordecai Kaffman.

This book is a joint effort. The four case chapters and chapter

9 were written by both Joel Elizur and Salvador Minuchin. Chapter 1 is by Minuchin, chapters 4 and 5 are by Elizur, and chapter 8 is by Kaffman.

We thought this would be an easy book to write. In the beginning, the idea seemed not only simple but elegant: a study of the beneficent effects of expert consultation with family therapists who were context-oriented, hardworking, and eager to learn and grow. Now what we want to convey is a deep concern with the destructive, dehumanizing force of mental health institutions that insist on maintaining an "objective" stance vis-à-vis the patients in their care. By failing to recognize the culturally bound nature of its organizations, the mental health establishment maintains a pseudoscientific stance that focuses on perhaps the one thing no human has ever been: an entity isolated from culture and context. Diagnostic labels are assigned from this expert stance, with no regard for the power of the labels to organize responses. Patients are separated from the contexts that maintain and confirm them, to be treated as if they were the whole rather than the part.

Everyone knows that the wider focus exists, but somehow it remains unexplored. The blinders with which the mental health field furnishes itself are not culture-specific. Examples can be found across the modern Western cultures and across time. Cases seen in Jerusalem and in the conscientiously responsive and supportive environment of a socialistic kibbutz community find echoes in the homeless of capitalist New York, in deinstitutionalized mental patients in modern Italy, in orphans of eighteenth-century France. The problem is not to find examples. The problem is only to select.

Institutionalizing Madness

1

The Wider Focus: Problems in Context

ONCE UPON A TIME—in fact, in France in the early eighteenth century—unwanted newborns were often abandoned. Left on the porches of churches, private residences, and convents, many died before they were found. Most died soon after.

Concerned experts in the delivery of services operationalized the problem, reducing it to manageable terms in this way: Unwed mothers were abandoning their infants in order to save their families' honor. If a way could be found to preserve the anonymity of these mothers, perhaps the babies could be saved. Technology provided an ingenious solution. A turntable was installed in the door of the foundling hospital. A baby could be placed on the turntable *(la turret)* and passed through an opening in the door into the institution. It was not necessary to open the door, so no one saw the donor. Family honor could be saved, and so could the child.

The results of this humane policy staggered the authorities. The order of St. Vincent DePaul, which sheltered 312 children when *la turret* was established, in 1740 had 3,150. In 1784, there were 40,000, and in 1833, 131,000. This explosion of numbers threatened to overwhelm the available resources.

Grumblings not unknown in the late twentieth century began to be heard. Some said it had been made too easy for wantons to escape their shame. Some asserted that women were abandoning their children under private arrangements in which they were given back their own children to wetnurse, with the sweetening of a stipend from charity. The doors of the foundling hospitals resumed their unbroken shape.

Jacques Donzelot's account* of *la turret* gives an early but familiar example of the problems posed for discussion in this book. The themes are simple, but the questions never are. Like the charitable authorities of those foundling hospitals, we in the mental health field make a habit of proclaiming ourselves experts. We take wide-ranging problems and operationalize them. That is, we first define a manageable piece of the problem as the problem. We then approach that segment as though we had had no hand in its definition. We analyze and ultimately treat it as though we were solving the broader problem, setting aside the knowledge that our segment is not a section of cells that can be stained and made to lie still on a microscope slide but a group of human beings constantly interacting with each other within the social contexts that define them as a group.

It is axiomatic that human beings have to segment in order to cope. We cannot deal with all the inputs of any given moment, let alone of a sequence of events. Given any aggregate, we have to impose an order that makes it graspable. But we know that in highlighting some of its aspects, we are submerging others. We know that there are data we are obscuring even within the data we have chosen to admit, for the sake of order. Why then do mental health experts so often operate as though their constructed truth transcended these human limitations? as though their selected segment were the whole universe? as though it were not their naming that gave definition to the named?

Let us jump roughly three hundred years and see if our wisdom today surpasses that of Donzelot's foundling hospital planners. Our problems now take different shapes, of course. Still, there are some 20,000 children currently in placement under the auspices

*Jacques Donzelot, *The Policing of Families* (New York: Random House, 1979), pp. 26–29.

of New York City's foster care system. How are we coping with this problem?

Foster Care: Is the Solution More of the Same?

Late in the 1980s, New York's Legal Aid Society claimed that hundreds of children in the foster care system were being kept in social services offices during the day and moved to temporary beds night after night because no permanent home could be found for them. In three months, the society contended, one child had received sixty-five different placements. Almost one thousand had been placed five to nine different times. A federal judge ruled that the city had failed in its obligation to provide adequate homes for these children.

The general counsel of the Human Resources Administration, which oversees foster care in New York City, protested that the city was trying to ease the crisis. It had opened nine new group homes.*

The outlines of the problem would not seem unfamiliar to the eighteenth-century overseers of the Foundling Hospital of St. Vincent DePaul. Of course, we have a different concept of the care to be provided. Donzelot's authorities, like social services authorities well into our own day, were concerned with food, clothing, and shelter. But over the past decades, the idea has taken hold that children have to be protected psychologically as well as physically. Accordingly, our solution of choice is foster homes. Therefore the solution to ballooning statistics is, in effect, more turntables: More foster homes. More case workers. Quicker hearings. More placements. No one seems to ask whether a projected 16 percent increase in the number of foster children in the next year could be forestalled. For every child being placed in foster care, there is axiomatically a troubled family group, but

*"New York Faulted for Rights Lapses in Its Foster Care," *New York Times,* September 26, 1987.

since the solution is foster placement, the response to more cases must be restricted to "more homes."

Sometimes there is an attempt to match this complex social phenomenon with a more sophisticated response. But bureaucracy's tendency to survive intact typically defeats the more sophisticated solution. For instance, a commission appointed to recommend changes in New York City's services to children recommended a reorganization that would expand the delivery of preventive social services to include poor *families.* The hope was that such an expansion would lower the rate of disintegration of those families and the resulting tragedies for the children involved.

Andrew Stein, president of the New York City Council, described how the plan was carried out:

> The city accepted the recommendations with great fanfare. . . . But aside from the creation of new organizational charts, little has been done to comply with the call to expand the level of services offered to poor families and their children. The new Family and Children's Services [recommended by the Commission] is in disarray. Its first head resigned last summer after repeatedly having her requests for adequate staffing turned down. She has not yet been replaced.

The city council president concluded:

> Some of the children who ended up in the welfare hotels, or who had to be removed from their homes because their families had disintegrated, could have been spared such fates had there been a more effective, more generous system of preventive social services available to those families. . . .*

The recommendations had been framed as a response to organizational problems. But the report was a philosophical bomb that challenged the total philosophy of services. The bureaucracy therefore responded to the complex resolution in the manner of

*Andrew Stein, "New York's Poor Children: A Tinderbox," *New York Times,* January 17, 1987.

bureaucracies. It created an office with great fanfare and rendered it ineffective. After a year, the problems were the same, the solutions were still simplistic, and the more complex response was still the road not taken.

Under media pressure, the head of the Human Resources Administration tried to lessen the heat by spreading the blame to the private agencies in the city who work within the foster care system. But agency leaders, many of them affiliated with major religious groups, insisted that the problem was the failure of city and state officials to provide firm leadership and adequate resources. The director of child care for the Archdiocese of New York characterized the city's Special Services for Children "an unmanageable circus, where the people don't talk with one another and don't have information about the children."*

The city's response to that criticism was another challenge: the Archdiocese mishandles its own system.

> A fifteen-year-old Protestant girl who had given birth a year earlier was sent to the Mission of the Immaculate Virgin, a foster care center on Staten Island run by the archdiocese. She told administrators there that she was sexually active, but they refused to provide her with birth control services. When she obtained birth control pills on her own, administrators took them away. A few months later, she became pregnant again. . . .
>
> If the girl insists on an abortion, the staff of the Catholic home will not cooperate beyond telephoning the Human Resources Administration to let city officials know of her wish. A city car comes and takes the girl to the hospital for the abortion and then drives her back. In effect, the church looks the other way. . . .†

In other words, even when there was cooperation, it was cooperation without compromise, satisfying nobody, but keeping

*"New York Foster Care: A Public-Private Battleground," *New York Times,* April 9, 1987.

†Ibid.

structures intact. A system that arose from fragmentation was continuing to fragment. A child was defined as separate from her life context. Even a minor and her sexuality were separated, in the service of political polemic. This is the administrative setting within which courts and child care workers have had to make the decisions that would change the lives of thousands of children.

All this information about a nonworking system was not only officially recognized but widely publicized. It is interesting, therefore, that the constant attempts at improvement were confined to doing more of the same. The bureaucratic system remained, and remains, adamant that the same definitions must be preserved. Also preserved, therefore, are the same responses. The only changes ever envisioned are more of the same, somehow rendered more effective. But since the safety of the child is seen only in terms of the individual, the system remains doomed to fail.

Take the case of a mother whose four children were removed eighteen months ago because she was a drug addict. When the city took her children away, she entered a drug treatment program. She has been drug-free now for three months and is anxious to get at least the infant back. But her baby is bonding with her foster mother; she cries if her mother picks her up. The mother's insistence that her baby be returned to her will almost certainly be successful, but in the meantime, as agency practice dictates, the mother sees her baby for two hours every two weeks. "In the best interests of the child," agency practice is moving the baby closer and closer to the foster mother from whom she will soon be separated, leaving her mother upset and uncertain, fearful that the next time she picks her daughter up, the baby will cry again.

Our operationalization of these problems has created a system that takes over the total responsibility for a child removed from the biological family. Families that could be helped are all too often simply written off, as yet another child begins a career of foster placement. In the name of protection, crimes are being committed not only against children but against parents, who are left without authority or responsibility and whose only remaining power is to create more children.

Let us consider a less happy case. A twenty-eight-year-old mother, addicted to crack, delivers a third child. The child demonstrates positive toxicology. The mother is now automatically defined as a child abuser. When she goes home from the hospital, the hospital keeps the infant, ultimately sending him to foster care. A social service agency is mandated to remove the older children, aged two and four, from the room in one of New York City's welfare hotels where they have been living with their mother.

The caseworker assigned calls a police escort and arrives unannounced at the mother's room. Nervous, and with no time to spare, the caseworker can give the distraught mother only the welfare equivalent of her Miranda rights: There will be a hearing; she can appear to oppose the removal of her children. The children are taken to emergency placement, where they stay for a week. Ultimately they are sent to different foster homes.

Meanwhile, the mother, whose room is reserved for families, is evicted. The foster care agency's letter telling her to get in touch with them is returned by the post office, "addressee unknown." The caseworker enters "mother's whereabouts unknown" on the children's records. The odds are high that the children will remain in foster care until, at the age of eighteen, they are dropped from the foster care rolls. Since overwhelming statistics, budgetary requirements, and the realities of poverty still take their toll of the families or group homes where the children are placed, they will probably reappear soon on the welfare and often the police rosters, scarred, undereducated, and unemployable. But the government has acted "in the best interests of the child."

What is the alternative? Ameliorating this situation would not require more services or more funding. It would only require taking a different road, widening the concept of "the best interests of the child" to a view that would include the welfare of the child's family. In many cases the end point could be, not a child removed to a place of safety, but a family able to care for its own.

When Salvador Minuchin was a small child in rural Argentina, his mother grew severely depressed after the death of her mother. In his book *Family Kaleidoscope,* he recalls:

> . . . my infant sister and I were sent for some time to Aunt Sofia, to give my mother space to recover, and quite probably to ensure that we were adequately cared for. During the economic crisis of the thirties my parents farmed us out for a while, again to Aunt Sofia. We were instructed to eat well before returning to our routine of polenta and bread at home.
>
> On neither occasion did my relatives or my parents call this foster care. . . . My aunt didn't think my parents were doing a poor job or that she had to compensate for them; neither did my parents . . . it was taken for granted that relatives functioned as a system of support.*

When government enters the picture, however, it is necessary to formalize. The problem must be segmented and labeled for the use of the law. The simplest way to deal with the problem is to see the child as a separate unit: the victim. The family then becomes the abuser or neglecter. Under the auspices of a legal, and therefore adversarial, system, the government acts *in loco parentis.*

There is, of course, no question whatsoever that some families do abuse their children. There are cases of neglect, sexual abuse, and physical and psychological battering. In these cases, removing the child is the correct response. Nevertheless, the system as a whole is built around a conceptual skew, which is warping and sometimes ending the lives of thousands of children.

Within this adversarial system, which poses the child as the victim, child welfare personnel tend, naturally enough, to see themselves as child saviors. Many have developed a very critical attitude toward biological parents, whom they assume to be neglectful at best. But a research project that investigated alternative approaches found that it was possible, in a relatively short time, to change the attitude of foster parents and case workers while increasing their skills.† Without adding staff, and within the same budget, the investigators were able to encourage a sig-

*Salvador Minuchin, *Family Kaleidoscope* (Cambridge, MA: Harvard University Press, 1984), p. 155.

†"Foster Family Workers," the E. M. Clark Foundation.

nificant number of biological parents to keep in touch with their children, maintain a sense of responsibility for their upbringing, and cooperate with the foster parents and the agency in planning for their return to them.

But as usual when one investigates a segment of an ecological system, changes in that segment demanded systemic changes. As the biological parents began to be kept in the picture, organizational changes in the agencies became necessary. Intake had to take a different shape, so that the biological parents could become part of the planning process. Contacts between biological parents and children required changes in agency policy regarding time and location of visits. The boundaries between biological and foster parents had to become less rigid. The return of the child to the biological family required the participation of all parties during a transitional period in which biological and foster parents pulled together in partnership instead of remaining two warring camps the child would alternately enter or leave.

But now agency changes made it evident that another part of the system was going to feel the pressure to change. Initial assessment of a family after an allegation of neglect or abuse had been based on the presumed "best interests of the child." This is a flag that the media, politicians, and good and concerned citizens use to express justified indignation at the abuse of a child. Therefore assessment of the family is made in an atmosphere of fear and judgment. What will happen if the child is not removed from the home and is subsequently hurt? In this context, the worker takes the only sensible solution, protecting both the child and the worker by removing the child to a place of safety.

But what if the procedure were slowed to include a more thorough investigation of the family? What if there were an investigation of the strengths and flexibility of the family? an exploration of the extended family network and its ability to supplement the biological family's needs? What if caseworkers, taught skills in family intervention, expanded the focus of concern to include family reconstruction as one of the goals of intervention?

The pressure for change would then move to the judicial system, to the family court, where a judge may make decisions on as many as fifty families in the course of a day, and where different lawyers are assigned to represent the child, the agency, and sometimes even the parents, in a system designed to cast people as adversaries and determine who is the victim and who the villain. The judicial system would have to change to work with the stressed *system* of children of families of the poor in the richest country in the world.

But then the culture would have to change. Today a corporate raider is profiled on page one of the financial section when the offer of millions of dollars persuades him to drop a campaign. The state's takeover of children, in their "best interests," may make an occasional human interest story. There is apparently no connection between extreme wealth and extreme poverty. One of the worst problems for ecological thinkers and operationalizers alike is that in pulling one weed, they find themselves tugging at the universe. But is oversimplification really the answer?

Deinstitutionalizing the Mentally Ill: One Solution in Several Contexts

Another example of simplistic operationalization is visible in the homeless "street people" who roam city subways and stake out hot air vents for the winter, surviving on panhandling and bottle returns. Many of the street people are mentally ill, "deinstitutionalized" in a move that was actually a well-meant attempt to improve the quality of their lives, but that left the mayor of New York wondering who's "looney."

Governmental isolation and labeling of the mentally ill has a long history. The French historian, Michel Foucault,* maintains that "the classical experience of madness" can be placed in 1656, with the founding of the *Hospital General.* Before that, he argues, the mentally ill were commonly segregated and interned with a host of undesirables rather than treated. Some-

*Michel Foucault, *Madness and Civilization* (New York: Pantheon Books, 1965).

times the mad were publicly taunted, or whipped, and history records a kind of game in which they were chased in a mock race and driven out of the city. Sometimes they were sent far from the cities in groups, or "delivered to the river" for the voyage that became known as the "ship of fools." It was during the classical period, in Foucault's construction, that the medical (or mental health) establishment stepped in to define itself as expert vis-à-vis the problem and to claim the ownership of pathology and health.

Not everyone agrees with Foucault's radical perspective. Some criticize his history as more elegant than accurate: Peter Sedgwick points out that long before the classical experience of madness postulated in Foucault's timetable insane people had been in custody and undergoing therapy (however primitive) in Europe. There were several hospitals with special accommodation for the mentally ill in towns across the Rhine valley prior to Foucault's classical age. There was a nationwide chain of charitable asylums, especially for the insane, from the fifteenth century, in, of all places, Spain—not a society devoted to modern rationalism. Again, various techniques attesting a crude physiological view of mental illness, which in Foucault's model are attributes of the Age of Reason, were actually common in prerationalist Europe, many stemming from Muslim societies. Klaus Doerner argues that there was no uniform, state-controlled confinement: the English and German patterns, for example, varied greatly from French.*

But even Foucault's critics share his focus on the interdependency of psychiatry and the beliefs of the times, as well as on the temporality of solutions. If 1656 marks the beginning of internment in Foucault's timetable, the 1960s mark the beginning of our process of deinstitutionalizing mental patients as a challenge to the seventeenth-century solution. Deinstitutionalization, in turn, serves as an example of how perceptions of problems and solutions are entangled with the political and emotional tissue of an era.

*J.C. Merquior, *Foucault* (Berkeley: University of California Press, 1985), pp. 26–28 *passim.*

In the 1960s the care of those labeled mentally ill was strongly influenced by the confluence of new methods of pharmacotherapy with that decade's penchant for the revolutionary. The rights of the mentally ill joined other liberation movements—the feminist, the gay, the black, the poor—in a crusade that promised to change institutional control in the Western world. For the psychiatric patient, it was Pinel again—the realization that the hospital itself creates conditions that harm the patients. What had seemed a neutral control, enabling treatment, was seen as an instrument of depersonalization. Some began to equate hospitalization with slavery, and there was a widespread search for alternatives.

Judy Chamberlin, who was herself a psychiatric patient in six different establishments over a period of five months, described the process:

> Mental hospitals have been called "total institutions," in which even such ordinary decisions as when to eat, go to the toilet, and go to bed are made by others. A natural consequence of being subjected to such a regimen is a feeling of depersonalization. Feelings of depersonalization are frequently considered primary symptoms of mental illness. To complete the circle, psychiatrists usually attribute their patients' feelings of depersonalization to their internal state and not to conditions within mental institutions. . . . not only are the lives of patients controlled, but patients are constantly told that such control is for their own good, which they are unable to see because of their mental illness. Patients become unable to trust their own judgment, become indecisive, overly submissive to authority, frightened of the outside world. The antitherapeutic nature of mental hospitalization has long been recognized.*

Chamberlin enrolled in the radical therapist movement, which like other liberation movements promises clear solutions

*Judi Chamberlin, *On Our Own: Patient-Controlled Alternatives to the Mental Health System* (New York: McGraw-Hill, 1978), p. 6.

if one is truthful to the ideology of the movement. But while her criticism of the psychiatric hospital is powerful, her language fades when she tries to describe radical solutions. They are nonspecific and confined essentially to the healing power of human contact.

No movement in the mental health field occurs in a vacuum, and in each country the deinstitutionalization movement took the shape of that country's sociopolitical organization. In England the movement was spearheaded by R. D. Laing, one of the European philosophers who in the 1960s dreamed of giving direction to the generation of the flower children. Accordingly, his experiments in Kingsley Hall took an existentialist bent. In the United States, the sprawling movement became identified with various popular "self-help" movements. In Italy, where nothing apolitical can happen, deinstitutionalization took a political garb.

Deinstitutionalization in England

In 1968, in an article called "Metanoia: Some Experiences at Kingsley Hall, London," Laing defined schizophrenia as "a set of attributes that some people who are experts in making this set of attributions make about other people." He added, "Those people who make this set of attributions have to prove that it refers to something real. My summary of the evidence to date, is that they have not done so."*

For Laing, schizophrenia arises at the moment of labeling, as a function of the diagnosis. He suggested calling it instead a "metanoiac voyage," from the Greek word for a change of mind. Such a voyage might be good or bad. It could be a voyage of self-discovery, and with a liberating outcome. But the hospital setting is designed to turn it into a catastrophe, a pathological process from which the person then must be cured. He proposed instead "to regard what was happening as a potential healing process

*R.D. Laing, "Metanoia: Some Experiences at Kingsley Hall, London," in Ruitenbeck, H., (ed.) *Going Crazy: The Radical Therapy of R. D. Laing and Others* (New York: Bantam Books, 1972), p. 13.

through which the person ideally may be guided and during which he is guarded."*

The American psychiatrist James S. Gordon described Kingsley Hall in this manner:

> Kingsley Hall provided troubled people with an alternative to hospitalization, an opportunity to live and grow through their madness. It was a place for "doctors" and "patients" to shed their restrictive roles and help and learn from one another immediately, without the distorting mediation of a hierarchical medical structure, without coercion. It was a place where people could simply be. It was simultaneously an experiment in psychotherapy and an attempt at communal living.†

Other pioneers of the antipsychiatric movement, however, have criticized Laing's work as still rooted in the British psychiatric establishment. According to Judi Chamberlin: The glamorization by some self-styled radicals of Laing's therapeutic commune—Kingsley Hall—ignores its most glaring contradiction, the unacknowledged separations and distinctions between those who came as healers and those who came to be healed. Mary Barnes, Laing's and Kingsley Hall's most famous "case," was clearly not thought of as an equal by the "well" members of the household, nor did she think of herself as equal.‡

Laing's books were widely read by the sixties generation. He transcended the psychiatric field to become a cult figure—a guru. But his experiment had the hallmark of his period. Although it challenged institutions, psychiatric hospitals, families, and language, and dreamed that human beings could transcend their context, like Icarus, the dream could only self-destruct. The English psychiatric establishment managed to encapsulate the experiment as part of a radical fringe, and while Laing and his ideas are well known, they have not affected either the delivery

*Ibid., p. 12.
†James S. Gordon, "Who Is Mad? Who Is Sane?" In Ruitenbeck, *op. cit.*, p. 78.
‡Chamberlin, *On Our Own*, p. 6.

of services in the psychiatric hospital or its organization and functioning.

Deinstitutionalization in Italy

The Italian movement toward deinstitutionalization took shape amid the struggle for control among Italian political parties. Therefore, it takes the language of politics, and its solutions are the product of legislative procedure. Franco Basaglia, its leader, was the head of an 800-bed mental hospital in Gorizia, a city on the Italian-Yugoslavian border. Sharing with Laing a view that the hierarchical, authoritarian nature of mental hospitals was instrumental in creating conditions that were then attributed to the patient, Basaglia and his co-workers took a political position. They challenged the framing and scientific objectivity of diagnostic labels and declared deviancy, as defined by the psychiatric establishment, to be a tool of oppression of the disenfranchised. With this banner, they joined the political left.

Between 1968 and 1974, Basaglia and his followers were instrumental in moving the Italian Communist Party to include the "liberation of the mental patient" as part of its official platform. In 1978, the Christian Democrats and the Communist Party joined forces to develop a new mental health act. Basaglia was the consultant, and Law 180, passed by the Italian parliament in May, 1978, is frequently called Basaglia's Law. It mandated the phasing out of large psychiatric institutions in favor of community-based mental health centers and placed strict controls over involuntary commitment to general hospital psychiatric wards.

Framing hospitalization as a political act, the Italians through political action stopped the construction of psychiatric hospitals and created a crisis in the delivery system of care of the mentally ill. Suddenly patients released from hospitals were living in the community. What seemed correct in the political and ecological literature did not occur as an orderly process in real life. Italian families who had relied on psychiatric segregation to cope with their psychotic members now experienced the pain and confusion of living with them. The community-based facilities responsible for a prescribed geographical area *(unita sanitaria locale)* were commanded to cope with problems they were not prepared to deal with. Nonetheless, out of the disorder created by political fiat grew an ideological shift in mental health and a chain of community services dealing with extremely difficult patients on an outpatient basis. During the last ten years, the context of most patients has remained part of the focus of therapy, and because patients for the most part live with their families, the establishment can rely on systems-oriented services for the control and healing of identified patients.

Deinstitutionalization in the United States

In the United States the process of deinstitutionalization occurred in a rather different political climate. At the same time that the massive use of tranquilizers in psychiatric hospitals was shaking hands with the liberation movements of the 1960s, fiscal conservatives were heralding tranquilizers as a miracle that would would cut budgets while humanizing psychiatric treatment. Thousands of patients were sent "home" from psychiatric institutions, whose funding was cut to the bone.

The results should have been gratifying to both groups. In New York City, for instance, the number of psychiatric patients in state hospitals declined from 93,000 in 1955 to 19,000 in 1987.* But what happened to the deinstitutionalized patients? Are the solutions of the 1980s less simplistic and more satisfying than the 1656 solutions of Louis XIV?

Again, solutions reflect the ethics of a period and their political implementation. The dreamers of the sixties envisioned a welfare society that would create a chain of halfway houses—community-based services for the mentally ill poor—buttressed by a political system invested in a "Great Society." That dream was replaced by a conservative ethos embodied in a government with an ideology of individual self-reliance and the withdrawal of

***New York Times,* September 12, 1987.

government from welfare concerns. Sent from the closing institutions to the never-developed services of "the community," many of these deinstitutionalized patients simply disappeared from statistical view.

By the late 1980s, the federal government was estimating that there are between 300,000 and two million people homeless in the United States, as many as a third or half of them mentally ill.* This statistical lumping of the homeless, the poor, and the psychotic is reminiscent of the lumping of the Great Internment. The number of psychotics among the homeless may be deliberately exaggerated to disguise the socioeconomic aspects of homelessness. But even taking the lower estimates—figuring one-third of 300,000—yields a staggering number of homeless psychotics in the United States. Once protected in social isolation in psychiatric institutions by the acts of segmenting and labeling, they have now been "protected out" of dehumanizing institutions, released to community services that exist largely in the imagination.

Worse, although thousands of mental patients have been deinstitutionalized, the hospitalization of adolescents is up fourfold. As before, the hospital functions as a total institution. As before, the hospital communicates to the family that the responsibility for the patient's healing is no longer theirs. A transference of responsibilities occurs. The family is supposed to wait, ready to resume its functions when the hospital staff finish theirs. But this punctuation of life occurs only in psychiatric formulations. In real life, the family and other social systems reorganize without the patient. When the adolescent returns, it is to a different social organization. This cutoff of the patient from the significant social environment, this surgical procedure on the life of the patient, in many cases is instrumental in the continuing manufacture of the psychotic homeless. With symptoms masked by tranquilizers, the patient, whose connections to home and family are weakened or even severed, may become part of the population of the shelters or choose to take to the streets.

**New York Times,* November 29, 1987.

Thus we are faced with another problem in mental health: What do we do with our homeless psychotics? Human beings are sleeping in the streets in the cold winters of New York. What can we do?

In November 1987, New York City began a program to remove severely mentally ill homeless people from the streets and parks of Manhattan and forcibly to provide them with medical psychiatric care. Vans staffed by teams consisting of a psychiatrist, a social worker, and a nurse brought to the Bellevue Psychiatric Emergency Room homeless people who were considered to be in need of immediate hospitalization and to pose a danger to themselves or others.

The vice president for mental hygiene in the city hospital system, Dr. Luis Marcos, declared that the program could lead to the reintroduction of long-term care for some people living in the streets. "This is the beginning of the recognition for the need for asylums," he said. "The mental health care system will never be the same. For the first time there is a recognition of the patient's right to treatment [and to] freedom from the prisons of mental illness, rather than the freedom to die in the streets."*

Though undoubtedly sincere, the words of Dr. Marcos are reminiscent of other solutions. One cannot side against the establishment in this: New York winters are bitter, and people should be sheltered, psychotic or not. But the questions history will ask are: Is this a correct solution? What problems does this posing of the problem entail?

As if to give human contours to abstract or global issues, the history of the psychiatric establishment has added to its hall of fame the name of a secretary who called herself Billie Boggs, although her legal name is Joyce Brown. The first street person forcibly hospitalized under project HELP (Homeless Emergency Liaison Project), Ms. Brown challenged the city's right to hospitalize and treat her against her will.

*"Mentally Ill Homeless Taken Off City Streets," *New York Times,* November 8, 1987.

A Drama in Three (or More) Acts

Act I

Joyce Brown is picked up by the project HELP mobile team. For over a year she has been living on a street corner over a hot air vent. She is reported to have shouted obscenities at passersby, shredded money given to her, and urinated on it in a ritualistic fashion that indicates mental illness. She has been observed running out into the traffic and wearing a coat spotted with feces. Ms. Brown sues.

Act II

Justice Lippman rules that the respondent's psychiatrist and the psychiatrist who testified on behalf of Ms. Brown are diametrically opposed in their assessment of her mental condition and in their prognoses as to whether she is likely to cause herself or others harm. The court, deriving little psychiatric guidance, places great weight on the demeanor, behavior, and testimony of Ms. Brown herself, who is lucid and forceful. On the basis of the evidence, the judge decides that Ms. Brown should be released from the hospital.

Act III

The city appeals. The Appellate Division of State Supreme Court in Manhattan rules that Ms. Brown is mentally ill and a danger to herself and others. The court says the trial judge erred by placing too much emphasis on her own testimony and not enough on that of the psychiatrist who treated her.

Ms. Brown is released a month later after refusing to be treated with antipsychotic drugs. A state judge has barred the hospital from treating her against her will. The hospital says that under these conditions it is pointless for her to remain in the hospital. "I was never psychotic," she says. "I was homeless. I am still not psychotic. But I am still homeless." Still, she has been offered a bed in a hotel for homeless women which, according to the city, provides regular meals, social services, activities, and medical care. Psychiatrists predict that, outside the controlled environment of the hospital, her condition may deteriorate.

In this political and human drama, one should highlight the absurdity and humor of the subtle plot. A judge, confused by contradictory psychiatric labels, considers the behavior of the patient as evidence. He is reminded by the Appellate Court that lawyers and psychiatrists have a clear agreement not to challenge each others' jurisdictions. He is reminded that doctors own psychiatric labels and control their assignment. A psychiatrist provided by the American Civil Liberties Union found Ms. Brown not psychotic; the psychiatrists from the City found her clearly psychotic; the experts' disagreement does not invalidate the right of the psychiatric establishment to stake claim to objective knowledge.

The mayor of the city stood with Ms. Brown's four sisters: She should be hospitalized. The family, no longer Ms. Brown's support system, wanted the city to resume responsibility for the "care and cure" of their sibling. On the other side were lawyers for the American Civil Liberties Union, who argued for Ms. Brown's inalienable right to live wherever she wants, including the sidewalk in winter. They were not interested in how it happened that Ms. Brown's connections to her support systems were lost.

The mayor, who said in effect, "I want this woman to get cured fast," might in effect have accomplished that. First, he gave her the opportunity to break the continuity of her homelessness by providing twelve weeks at Bellevue. Second, she was released from the hospital to a known address—a room in a residence for homeless women. Third, he offered himself as a clear target for her grievances and resentment, and fourth, she was given a context of people ready to help her reestablish her life. She was connected to a support system, and perhaps even to her own family. The final results cannot be reported here; after resurfacing several times—accused of possession of a controlled substance, invited to lecture at Harvard University, or found once more on the streets—Joyce Brown has for the moment disappeared from media view.

Ms. Brown was clearly a homeless person; she may or may not be psychotic. Putting her in the limelight, the press gave us the opportunity of looking at larger phenomena: the absurdity of our attempted solutions; the passion with which each side embraces its own segment of truth and defends it against the deceivers, those liars and cheats who defend their own truths; and the interconnectedness between the political, judicial, and moral systems and psychiatric labeling and practices. The cast of characters hasn't changed since 1656. Problems and solutions are still laid out on a seventeenth-century framework.

The point of the story is not about homelessness but about services for the mentally ill. A better framing of the problem could bring profound differences. In fact, this book is written with the hope that we can call attention to alternative ways of responding.

2

Yoav

IN THE BEGINNING was the word. The act of naming was Creation, for it was the label that gave each object its accepted shape and meaning.

"But," Gertrude Stein dissents, "a rose is a rose is a rose." Not so. Speech is a social phenomenon in which speaker and addressee are united by meaning—that is, of course, ideology. In the 1950s, when famine ruled certain areas of China, starving people refused to eat corn, which was plentiful, because corn is pig fodder. Is fodder by any other name food? Certainly not, Ms. Stein. Naming alters both roses and corn: taste, smell, and use.

The psychiatric establishment was born knowing the power of words, and it has been refining its tools ever since. The *Diagnostic and Statistical Manual,* now in its third revision, is its bestiary, and as in Genesis new worlds are created and whole worlds disappear, all in the act of diagnosis. It may be that R. D. Laing failed to achieve his goal of rescuing schizophrenics from the traditional psychiatric hospital because his new naming, *metanoia,* failed to reach an audience educated in other Greek words. Homosexuality was part of the second *DSM* but not of the third; a whole category of psychopathology, recategorized, became normal.

Minorities know the power of words as ideology. In Europe not long ago, the word *Jude* determined your form of death as surely as the yellow Star of David on your jacket. In the United States, the word *nigger* determined the shape of uncounted numbers of lives. Its victims recognized the power of naming when they shed the word *Negro* for *Black* some twenty years ago.

In mental health, naming has similar consequences for the named. Of course, the response to the naming will depend on the ideology of the naming institution. A "phobic" patient may receive behavioral therapy, individual psychoanalysis, family therapy, outpatient treatment, or hospitalization. Some researchers in psychotherapy affirm that statistically the results will be the same. We have never believed that to be true, but, of course, we are family therapists, and we knew Yoav not as a statistic but as an immature sixteen-year-old, some five years and many worlds ago.

After six months of individual therapy in Alpha Psychiatric Hospital, Yoav was functioning well in the ward and in its educational program. A cooperative and well-mannered adolescent, he was clearly not psychotic, and no drug treatment had been needed at any time. The staff thought he was "sufficiently organized" to leave the hospital.

Yoav's parents, however, were strongly resisting his discharge. They complained of highly disturbed behavior during home visits, contending that Yoav was still violent at home, even if he was well behaved at the hospital. The therapist was persuaded that the parents' failure to form a united front to control Yoav's outbursts at home was the obstacle to his discharge and rehabilitation. Accordingly, Minuchin's strategy for the consultation session was to use a broader framing to heighten the involvement of the parents in Yoav's discharge.

The Consultation: "I Don't Think Your Parents Are Ready"

The parents and Yoav's nine-year-old sister, Rona, arrived early. The therapist greeted them, stating that this consultation would be an attempt to evaluate the current situation and ways of treatment. Rona, a plump child, seemed calm and self-assured. Noam, a forty-five-year-old business executive, looked tense and worried. His forty-two-year-old wife, Tamara, a high school teacher, was slim and elegantly dressed, but her mouth worked nervously. Yoav arrived by himself from the hospital a little later and sat between Rona and the therapist. He seemed self-conscious, fidgeting in his chair; he often gave the therapist a nervous smile, as if seeking approval.

The therapist had sketched in the boy's background for Minuchin. Yoav had been hospitalized because his serious conflicts with his mother had become more and more violent. Individual outpatient therapy had failed to help him control his irrational resentment of her, particularly "the way she twitches her mouth—she knows I can't stand that!" The therapist theorized that hospitalization had stabilized the situation by giving Yoav a psychiatric label—"schizotypal personality disorder"—and removing him to the safety of a ward. The parents, absolved of responsibility by having sought the proper treatment for their son, were simply waiting for the experts to do their job.

The therapist began the session by asking the parents if they were ready for Yoav to come home. Noam responded nervously, "Can he control his angry outbursts or express his feelings less violently?" Instantly Yoav began to shout at his father, prompting the therapist to reestablish a rule she had imposed in earlier sessions: Yoav must find a less disruptive way to express his anger. Yoav chose to sneeze, and the conversation thereafter was constantly punctuated with explosive sneezes.

"I've never thought Yoav's clashes with me were all that harsh," Tamara volunteered. "The problem is Noam's anger at me." Less anxious than Noam about Yoav's outbursts, she mostly wanted the assurance that her husband would stand by her if she agreed to Yoav's return home.

NOAM: *[to wife] It's not that I think you've mishandled Yoav. He's got problems, I know that.*
YOAV: *Achoo!*
NOAM: *And I'll back you up. But I just haven't got the psychic strength—*
YOAV: *Achoo!*
TAMARA: *You're still afraid of Yoav's reactions. And I'm afraid because you're afraid.*
THERAPIST: *[challengingly] What if Yoav comes home and argues with you, and your husband is afraid of his reactions?*
TAMARA: *I don't have the strength for that.*

The session became stuck on this theme, both parents and Yoav declaring, one after another, that they could not bear the stresses that arose when Yoav was home. It was clear that Yoav viewed himself as the victim of a problem family that had put him in the hospital (a framing supported by the hospital). Noam thought the problem was Yoav, a framing equally supported by the hospital, while Tamara felt victimized by a father-son coalition. Together they formed a system composed of separate units rigidly structured in a way that made cooperation impossible.

THERAPIST: *Yoav, I really don't think that your parents are ready to have you home. Can you talk with them about that?*
YOAV: *Well, I'm sure not ready to go back.*
THERAPIST: *I don't blame you. I mean, if your own family doesn't want—*
YOAV: *The hell with them!* I'm *not ready.*
THERAPIST: *All right. Talk to them. When will you be ready, and what should they do so you can come home?*
YOAV: *I don't want to talk. I don't want to go back, and I mean it! I'm sick and tired of them! If I hate them, it's no wonder! I don't want them! There must be other places. If I*

go home, I'll only be back in the same place that put me in the hospital.

THERAPIST: *You could stay in the hospital.*

YOAV: *I don't want to stay in the hospital! But I don't want to go home. [weeping] I'm sick and tired of being the problem child. I really don't have problems—hardly at all! My only problems are with my family!*

NOAM: *[softly] Yoav.*

YOAV: *[shouting] Why are you suddenly thinking about family therapy? I've been through six months of hell in a mental hospital, and* now *you're talking about changing? Why should I bother? To go back to school, and get behind again, and—*

NOAM: *I'm not talking about going back to school. I'm talking about coming home.*

YOAV: *If I come home and don't go to school, I'll be bored stiff. There's nothing for me to do there. I'll just annoy you—make you miserable, and ruin your life for you. There are boarding schools. There are—*

TAMARA: *Would you be happy at—?*

YOAV: *Would I be happy at home?*

TAMARA: *I'm hoping we'll all be happy, if you improve.*

YOAV: *Well, I'm not happy when you twist your mouth into that. . . . Damn it, I can't look at you!*

Watching the family's nonverbal behavior from behind the one-way mirror, Minuchin could detect hesitant attempts to connect, the desire to please, and fumbling attempts at accommodation. But as the level of stress increased, Yoav's language became more and more concrete, and his responses were increasingly limited to his preoccupation with his mother's nervously working mouth and his violent sneezing. Minuchin decided to join the session to see if he could help the therapeutic system expand its straitened repertory of transactions.

MINUCHIN: *[entering] This young man acts tough, but he's a gentle, lonely child, very loyal to his family. I think he is capable of doing well in many places. He does well in the hospital. He could do well in my house, and he could do well in a kibbutz.*

YOAV: *Achoo!*

MINUCHIN: *But he couldn't keep sneezing in my house, because that bores me. I'd tell him, "Don't do that," and I'm sure he'd stop in two days. But it's interesting that a person who could do so well in many places is a lot more childish than he should be. You have to grow up a little, Yoav. Sometimes you are affected—*

YOAV: *By small things. Small and silly.*

MINUCHIN: *Yes. But sometimes you are intelligent, and likable, too. It's your family dance that causes you to act more disturbed than you really are.*

Minuchin's first movements were to join with Yoav in a mixture of positives and challenges: Yoav is likable but childish, he is intelligent but boring. This approach usually makes the adolescent curious enough to join the consultant while seeking to elicit more information.

YOAV: *What do you mean by "dance"?*

MINUCHIN: *It's the way you all move about together.*

YOAV: *Family life?*

MINUCHIN: *Yes. I'm an expert on growing up. And I think that before you can leave home successfully, you're going to have to learn to live at home. But this is a job for all of you. And I don't think your parents are ready to take you back.*

YOAV: *What connection is there between my ability to get along well in the house and going out into the world?*

Feeling intellectually challenged, Yoav responded with a counterchallenge entirely normal for an adolescent. But the affect had become neutral; two people were talking together in an atmosphere of reason.

MINUCHIN: *[disapprovingly] If you want me to answer you, you'll have to speak more slowly, and use easier Hebrew.*

Minuchin prolonged the moment by asking Yoav to become easier to understand. Although he didn't realize it at the time, he was responding to Yoav's previous disorganization in the face of stress in his family by creating a simpler context, controlled by Yoav. This strategy proved very significant for a boy who, it turned out, had always doubted his capacity to understand and to learn.

YOAV: *[slowly] For instance, say I don't get along well with my family. Say I quarrel with them. But say when I reach eighteen, I go into the army and out into the world.*

MINUCHIN: *Your Hebrew is still too much for me. You are educated and smart, and your language is beyond my level. Try to help me understand. Use simpler language.*

YOAV: *Well, do I really have to grow up with my mother? I get nervous with her.*

MINUCHIN: *Of course. But each of you has to change. Your mother has to become the mother of an adult. But in order for her to be the mother of an adult, you have to be an adult with her. I want to tell you, I don't understand why you are in the hospital. You seem quite normal to me.*

YOAV: *You are surprised that I'm in the hospital?*

MINUCHIN: *Yes. Why are you? You don't look crazy to me.*

Indeed, how disturbed was Yoav? Different diagnoses appear when different sets of data are emphasized. Yoav's father thought he was simply crazy. The staff at Alpha had made a more benign diagnosis of schizotypal personality disorder. But Minuchin's transactions with Yoav, governed by a search for competence within a developmental-contextual model, were eliciting behavior that fit with a much more hopeful diagnosis of a childish adolescent involved in a dysfunctional family dance. Yoav accommodated to Minuchin's difficulty with the language, not only by speaking slowly and carefully but by asking intelligent questions and completely dispensing with the sneezing that had expressed "unbearable" anger. It almost seems that diagnostic thinking is conducted in a Berkeleian universe, and, since diagnosis is always partial, the best therapeutic policy is to frame some reality that emphasizes adaptive capacities, resources, and possibilities for growth.

YOAV: *I don't know why they brought me to Alpha. I don't think there was even any reason to go to a psychologist. Someone advised me to do it, and I did. From then on—*
MINUCHIN: *And why are you still here? Aren't they ready to have you back home?*
YOAV: *Well, I lost my temper with my mother. She—*
MINUCHIN: *What?*
NOAM: *He said—*
MINUCHIN: *Wait, Noam, please. Yoav, I don't understand. Explain in different words.*
YOAV: *She wasn't fair. She's supposed to help me with my homework. But she didn't want to take the time to help me. She neglected me—*
MINUCHIN: *And you wanted to change her? to make her pay attention to you?*
YOAV: *Well, I don't know if I meant to change her. But she's supposed to help me.*
MINUCHIN: *And for this you went to the hospital?*
YOAV: *I got very angry. I burst out. And because of my display of nerves, they committed me to the hospital.*
MINUCHIN: *Have you overcome your nerves? or not?*
YOAV: *I could control my nerves. But I don't always want to.*

Minuchin blocked Noam's attempt to help in order to maintain Yoav in a framing of competence. Yoav responded to his request for clarification in terms that suggested a young man of skill with language and good control. It seemed clear that in a nonstressful setting that emphasized competence, Yoav could function normally, and Minuchin continued challenging his hospitalization on those grounds. But nobody's world is a steady-state environment, and we would soon see Yoav respond very differently to a different context.

MINUCHIN: *When you get nervous, you get childish. But when you're not nervous, you're really a nice guy. Do you think you can control yourself?*

YOAV: *Yes.*

MINUCHIN: *I want to be convinced. I want you to talk to your parents. And I want you to control yourself the whole time.*

YOAV: *All right. [to his parents] I am really sorry that I reached the state that got me to the hospital. I don't think it was necessary. I know what it's like to be in the hospital, and now I want to get out of here as fast as I can. I want to settle down to life at home. I want to get back in school, so that I have a life of my own and don't feel the emptiness all the time. And if I have trouble with my schoolwork, I want you to be prepared to help me. I want us to get along well together.*

Inwardly, Minuchin was registering a "So far, so good." But now it was time to test. What would happen if the parents failed to accommodate?

MINUCHIN: *[to the parents] Now I want to give you an assignment. Yoav is to talk to you like a grownup, and you are to make normal demands. Don't make it easy for him.*

TAMARA: *All right. I have no intention of helping you with your schoolwork, Yoav. And I don't want to hear any more of your cursing—in fact, I don't want to hear any more demands, period. I mean it! There'll be no more talk about my mouth, or my face, or how I should do this for you, and how I once did that to you. I'll do what I want to do.*

YOAV: *Selfish.*

TAMARA: *Exactly.*

YOAV: *Really selfish.*

TAMARA: *You've got it.*

YOAV: *I hate selfish people.*

TAMARA: *Fine.*

YOAV: *I'm not giving you anything. You're selfish. I hate selfish people.*

TAMARA: *You don't have to give me anything. But you're*

going to respect me. I want you to respect my right to laugh, or not laugh, to help or not help.

YOAV: *When you feel like getting mad at me, get mad at Rona instead.*

TAMARA: *Oh, Yoav, you know I don't* want *to get mad at you. Honestly, honey—*

YOAV: *Oh, shut up! That's it, forget it! Go away and leave me alone!*

MINUCHIN: *You told me that you could control yourself, but it looks as though that's true only with me.*

The reasonable tone and careful language that Yoav had used with Minuchin changed as soon as his mother challenged him. His language became repetitive and impoverished, and his ballooning intensity rendered her helpless; it appeared she had no way of transacting with him in a less engaged fashion.

MINUCHIN: *When you talk to me, you can be an adult, because we have no emotional ties. But when your mother expects you to act like an adult, you turn into a child.*

YOAV: *She's the reason I went to the hospital.*

MINUCHIN: *It's interesting that such a bright kid can suddenly turn so childish.*

YOAV: *I get childish with my mother. I have an emotional problem with her.*

MINUCHIN: *Do you think you could grow up?*

YOAV: *I* am *grown up! I'm tall and strong.*

Looking at the interview with the wisdom of hindsight, it is easy to discern how stress was now causing Yoav to react to Minuchin with concrete thinking and stereotyped speech.

MINUCHIN: *[to Noam] Do you think the hospital can help Yoav grow up?*

NOAM: *Well, I know the home always helps most.*

MINUCHIN: *Would you be ready to change so he can come home?*

NOAM: *The truth is, I don't know in what way we need to change. We need guidance.*

TAMARA: *You do too know! The therapist told us to do what we liked without being afraid of Yoav's reaction. Remember on Saturday when Yoav visited us? For once you didn't spend the whole time worrying about him. Everybody was free to do as he liked. And Yoav wasn't violent. He was perfectly all right.*

Tamara, with Minuchin's support, went on to ask Noam to support her with Yoav. As they talked, Minuchin engaged Yoav, keeping him from interfering. Tamara wanted clear limits and the autonomous functioning of an average adolescent. If Noam could be less sensitive toward Yoav, perhaps Yoav would learn to assume more responsibility for himself.

NOAM: *But can he live up to our demands?*

YOAV: *Achoo!*

NOAM: *Maybe we put too much pressure on him to succeed in school.*

TAMARA: *I was only helping him with his schoolwork. He put the pressure on himself. But we're supposed to talk about ourselves now.*

MINUCHIN: *You will need to change if Yoav is to come home. You have to clarify to yourselves whether you are ready.*

NOAM: *Yes. I'm glad that Yoav will be able to return home.*

MINUCHIN: *[to Tamara] You have a lot of good ideas. It's too bad you can't use them as long as Noam is afraid and anxious with Yoav.*

Working within the framework of a conflictual parental subsystem that triangulates a normal son, Minuchin ended the session with an unbalancing act, supporting Tamara's position. The therapist was left with a blueprint that strengthened her convictions about working for Yoav's return home. She was to help the parents coordinate their concern and their demands of him, while Yoav was to be expected to learn how to reintegrate into his family on a more mature level. The family and the therapist left the session feeling hopeful and confident, important ingredients for any form of therapy.

Therapy at Alpha Hospital: Blaming the Parents

The course of Yoav's treatment subsequent to the consultation is described in the therapist's report:

> *After the consultation, the family decided to take Yoav back in stages. For the next three months, Yoav gradually made the transition to home. He was highly motivated to break loose from the hospital and showed rapid progress. Family therapy continued regularly once a week, mainly conducted according to the "leaving home" model proposed by Haley.* * *The parents were encouraged to clarify their incongruent and sometimes confused communications, and the father was instructed to exercise his authority in setting limits for Yoav.*
>
> *Yoav began visiting home more often. The atmosphere remained relaxed, and conflicts were mediated during the family sessions. Yoav's bizarre behaviors seemed to have disappeared completely. At that point the parents agreed to take Yoav home each evening. He was put in the day program and came to the hospital daily for his lessons, occupational therapy, and individual sessions.*
>
> *At the time, it seemed the family was changing in productive directions. Everyone was enjoying joint family activities, and the father was succeeding in maintaining a firm stand. There was order in the house, and the difficult transition outside of the hospital was handled by the family with the support of the hospital's special school and its day treatment program.*

*Jay Haley, *Leaving Home: The Therapy of Disturbed Young People* (New York: McGraw-Hill, 1980).

Then, against the advice of his teacher in the hospital, Yoav decided to make up the gap in his schooling and sought his mother's help with his studies. I went along with Yoav's request and worked to help him negotiate on a mature level with Tamara. But their renewed closeness led to intense conflicts. When Tamara's father became seriously ill, forcing her to spend more time with him and to curtail her study sessions with Yoav, Yoav felt abandoned. Conflicts escalated to a level that overstressed the family; Yoav became physically threatening, and a few times his father had to restrain him physically. The parents then pressed the hospital to take Yoav back.

We refused to readmit him. As Yoav's behavior in the day sessions showed continuing improvement, there seemed every reason to continue the current course of rehabilitation. We told the parents that they must work through this transitional stress and change so as to accept Yoav back into the family.

Minuchin's consultation had emphasized that the family (including Yoav) was a stressed system that needed the hospital's support for changing. But by now, the impact of his consultation had clearly dissipated. Yoav was once again seen as the victim of his family, and the hospital staff was entirely on his side. Yoav's cooperative attitude and the improvement he had made were reinforcing their protective attitude toward him, making it easier for them to identify with his complaints, while the parents' stress and difficulties were minimized.

Alpha is an advanced teaching hospital, its reputation built on brief, intensive treatment. Success is measured by return to the community; recidivism and transfer to long-term facilities are signs of failure. In this context there was inherent pressure to end Yoav's prolonged hospitalization, as well as stress on the part of the family therapist, who undoubtedly wished to prove the worth of her theories.

At this point a systems approach might have indicated a session including Yoav's teacher, to develop a plan to separate

Tamara from the educational contract. But instead of alleviating stress, the therapist continued to push for increased control, offering the parents only vague and accusatory suggestions to "change" or "accept Yoav back"—an impoverishment of therapy that can occur whenever a therapist adheres too rigidly to one partial construction.

The parents begged me to provide any alternative for Yoav that would alleviate the family's stress; even a foster-care arrangement would do. But we vetoed this request. Our position was that their difficulties in acting as a team were no reason to hospitalize Yoav or take him away from home. If Tamara kept getting into frequent conflicts with Yoav, she needed to learn how to stop reacting to Yoav's provocations. [What would their response have been if the "patient" had been Yoav *and* his family?] *The parents then suggested that Yoav go to live with his uncle Gabriel, a twenty-eight-year-old bachelor, who was willing to room with Yoav and find him a simple job at his own place of work. This seemed a good solution, allowing us to cooperate with the family's needs without retreating from the demand that it accept responsibility for Yoav's reintegration.*

For several months things went well. Yoav found a regular job and was discharged from the hospital, continuing as an outpatient. The parents maintained close contact with him with visits and telephone calls. Then Gabriel changed jobs and was no longer able to keep in close touch with Yoav at work and at home. Yoav grew tense and began to demand that his family take him back. Several times he appeared at their door late at night, making a racket and trying to force them into quarrels. Frantic, the parents called us for help. But we made it clear that it was the parents' responsibility to control Yoav. They tried calling the police. The police declined to interfere, warning them that Yoav was their responsibility. Then Yoav turned himself in to the police, asking for help in safeguarding his rights as a minor. The police threatened to charge the parents with neglect.

It is interesting that here once again Yoav was acting competently outside the family context, convincing the local police department that he was the victim of neglect. And once again an authority reacted by blaming the parents. Institutions charged with social control can become remarkably destructive when they ignore the complexity and interconnectedness of a system.

The family had reacted creatively to the hospital's insistence that they find inner resources, giving the whole system a period of moratorium. Had the hospital not become involved in a power struggle with them, it might have reciprocated with equal flexibility by including Gabriel in its treatment and supporting the expanded family system in the effort to reintegrate Yoav into normal society. But this would have been a long-term, complex process demanding constant availability and attention, and unfortunately a hospital's organization does not generally favor such investment in the aftercare of its patients. Therapists must be available to new inpatients, and here the therapist was pulling away from the case when the new crisis erupted. Instead of noting the failure of a temporary support system, which would have demanded her reinvolvement, she focused on the ineffective parental control. Having found a simple solution, she proceeded to apply it beyond its limits.

Once again the parents asked that Yoav be hospitalized. Yoav, too, took to coming to the emergency room, begging to be admitted. The hospital staff reevaluated Yoav's mental status but found no reason for a change in diagnosis. His psychiatric status did not warrant another hospitalization, which would probably lead to regression. The parents then took Yoav to a consultation with Dr. Rosh, a rather unconventional neurologist, who thought that his brain functioning could be improved with natural cures and drugs. We told them that such steps should be coordinated with us beforehand; otherwise they would sabotage our treatment.

We then tried to accommodate them in some way by suggesting that Yoav be placed in our day treatment program again. But since the parents were acting so manipulatively, we insisted that as a precondition for Yoav's reacceptance, a direct tie with Gabriel be established. The parents refused and told Yoav to stop coming to the hospital. He disobeyed, but I could not continue for long to meet with him without their permission. For a while, Yoav kept coming to the emergency room asking for help, but the hospital director himself had become involved in the case, and our whole staff acted in unity. Yoav was refused admission whenever he came. Some time later I learned by chance that the parents had taken Yoav to Beta Hospital. At that point I lost track of the case.

The therapist's account concludes sadly, but with the righteous indignation of the unappreciated Good Samaritan:

I invested a great deal of intensive work with this family, and the hospital's staff and director worked along with me to convince the family to accept Yoav. We did not want to perpetuate Yoav's status as a mental patient. Looking back at the therapy, I realize the potency of their rejection of Yoav. When he was discharged from the hospital, they had no choice but to try to receive him back. But they kept trying to prove he was a sick boy. They had to hold onto his illness so as to avoid their own problems and reduce their guilt feelings over the family problem. They showed paranoid features, and I would be careful with them.

Because mental health professionals (but only mental health professionals) are empowered to diagnose mental illness, Yoav's symptoms were catalogued to *DSM III* precision. But were the parents paranoid in thinking that the hospital's staff were insensitive to their plight and blamed them for Yoav's behavior? Might not the staff just as well be diagnosed as suffering from paranoid delusions in thinking that these defeated parents were enemies, to be carefully avoided? But that would not be likely to happen. In this paranoid system, only the hospital held the power to label.

Focusing only on the individual, the hospital saw no need for readmission, or even for pharmacotherapy that might have helped the family that had to live with Yoav. The therapist was apparently entirely in tune with the hospital; her version of family therapy included little consideration of the way Yoav's characteristics interacted with family life and the broader context of school and work. Given a theory to work by, she seems to have focused only on the overinvolved mother-child pair and the way the parents detoured their conflict by focusing on the child.

This was much more than a case of lazy therapeutic thinking. The basic flaw lay in the organization of the hospital/family mesosystem and the inability of the hospital to incorporate and process data that did not fit into their ideological schema. Thus the family's information was labeled "manipulative," and even the findings of a neurologist were discounted, apparently because he seemed to be an ally of the parents.

Yoav's History: "A Developmental Lag"

After requesting the therapist's report, quoted in part above, we began to work on the transcript of the consultation session. Reading it made very clear Yoav's tendency to resort to concrete, repetitive, and stereotypic language when stressed. We wanted to have more information, in particular any indication that there might be organic involvement. Elizur went to interview the parents and later, with their permission, he looked at Yoav's hospital files. Here are the findings:

When Yoav was six, psychological tests found him to be impulsive, with poor fine-motor coordination and a concentration level well below that of his peers. The parents were told that this was a developmental lag that would correct itself with time, but it did not. Yoav fell behind in his schoolwork, and he was ridiculed by his peers. Tutoring was arranged, and he was transferred to another school, but at age ten he was still a nonreader. Tamara, herself a teacher, began to help him. Eventually they were working together for four or five hours a day. Yoav grew extremely sensitive to his mother's criticism, but with her help, he kept up with his schoolwork.

Then the family was transferred to Canada for three years. Yoav studied in a yeshiva, where he worked on Hebrew for half a day and English during the second half of the day. While the teachers were understanding of his academic failures, the children did not forgive his clumsiness at learning new rules of conduct. Yoav became a social isolate, often the object of mockery and abuse. Naturally he clung to his mother for help. The mother/son dyad coalesced into a closed system, and Yoav was inhibited from exploring any other context for his development.

When they returned to Israel, he was placed one grade behind. He still had great difficulties in his studies, despite the intensive four to five hours of tutoring with his mother, and he had no friends.

At the end of junior high school the school suggested placing him in a vocational program. Tamara was in favor of that plan; it was a realistic suggestion and a way out of her slavery. But Yoav reacted with overwhelming anxiety, a result of the excessive instability in his developmental context, which had demanded of him adaptation skills that he did not possess. The threat of losing his mother's support was unbearable. He attacked her vehemently for wishing to desert him and pleaded with the school authorities to change their verdict. The school agreed to let him continue with his regular class, and Yoav accepted the suggestion that he go into individual therapy.

The next semester Yoav failed, and he dropped out of school. Now he stayed at home all day, denying that he had a problem yet blaming Tamara for reducing her tutoring time with him. Life at home became hellish when Noam tried to placate both mother and son. Yoav ran away from home several times before being hospitalized.

Hospital files reveal that a psychologist tested Yoav on admission and found neurological dysfunctions. He suggested that Yoav required a well-structured and simplified environment. Yoav had a high intellectual potential, but the effect of his disabilities was to reduce sharply his actual use of it.

That these findings were not revealed to Minuchin at the time of the consultation suggests that the therapist did not think that data about the individual and his rehabilitation were relevant for a family consultation. This illustrates an intrinsic weakness in the consultation process: the consultant must depend on the consultees for relevant data. But it also demonstrates how inevitably the selection of data is influenced by a therapist's biases.

Moreover, the therapist's work in the hospital did not include going out to Yoav's natural milieu in order to explore his failure at school and the possibilities for his social-educational reintegration. There were only two possibilities for cure. One was the hospital's assumption that individual improvement in the controlled environment of the hospital would somehow carry over to the outside world. The other was the model that called for keeping the parents involved and responsible for their son, assuming that the family has all the necessary resources to cope with their situation. Information, and indeed feedback, that did not fit the chosen routes was simply disregarded.

A Follow-Up Visit with the Parents: "He's Very Sick"

On another visit to Israel, two and a half years after the first consultation, Minuchin tried to arrange a follow-up interview, to find out what had happened.

Noam and Tamara were initially hesitant about coming for an

interview. Tamara was suffering from breast cancer; following surgery, she was now receiving chemotherapy, and she was exhausted and weak. They finally agreed to the interview, but they insisted that there was no way to include Yoav: Beta Hospital had said that he was at a difficult point in his treatment.

Tamara seemed pale, and she was obviously thinner, but she was still well groomed and tastefully dressed. Noam looked a little grayer but otherwise unchanged. Minuchin began by asking what had happened after his consultation.

NOAM: *Yoav continued treatment at the hospital, until they told us he wasn't sick any longer and could be discharged. We thought he ought to stay there, and so did Yoav. In fact it became increasingly difficult. He continued accusing my wife, and he broke things in the house. We asked for him to be hospitalized again, but they told us to use force, or call the police. We brought in the police. At one point I even hit him. But nothing did any good.*

TAMARA: *Things got worse and worse. I had to prepare his food for him and then shut myself up in my room; only then would he come out of his room. Later on he wouldn't even come into the house unless I was in my room with the light off. So I had to go to sleep at eight o'clock; I couldn't even read. It was winter, and I didn't want him standing out in the street. And then he'd wake up in the middle of the night complaining that he saw me in his dreams.*

MINUCHIN: *What about you?*

NOAM: *He'd talk to me, but only about her. He kept telling me that she made faces at him. I'd explain to him that none of this was directed against him, and he would seem to agree. Then just a few minutes later he would begin all over again.*

TAMARA: *Sometimes the hospital would send him home again from the day program, for being late, and then he'd just roam the streets all day. When he began to work with his uncle, things were much better for a while, but later his uncle couldn't watch over him, and the hospital told us to take him home again. We explained that we just couldn't have him at home, that he was aggressive and broke things, but things got worse and worse. We asked the hospital to retest him. But they just told us that Yoav was not sick and that his problems were a matter of our educational approach. And all that therapist could do was to tell Yoav if he couldn't get along with me, he shouldn't come home. But where was he supposed to go? He roamed the streets for days. He slept in a classroom in his old school for three nights, and once he was actually on a bench in the street. He went to the hospital again and again, but he was refused admission. So he went to an emergency room, and the night nurse called and asked why we wouldn't let our son come home. He was such a nice boy, she said. I don't know how we made it through all that.*

Whatever Yoav's underlying pathology, there is no doubt that at this point he and his parents were living in a delusional system. Yoav's suspicion and his demands that his mother accommodate to his experience are indeed psychotic. The plight of the parents and the mother's restriction of her own life space to "save" Yoav highlight both the extent of the parents' capacity to sacrifice (in spite of the hospital staff's opinions) and the uselessness of their misguided efforts. Their "solutions" only compounded and maintained the problem. And of course the hospital framing left the family in a cul-de-sac.

NOAM: *I want to add that Yoav was always looking for work. He'd make a good first impression and get hired, and people would try to help him. But after a few days he'd start making trouble. He never held a job on his own for more than a week.*

TAMARA: *I felt terrible, all the time. I slept a lot; as soon as I got home from work, I wanted to go to sleep. I went crying to the family doctor, asking her to help us get him into another hospital. Finally we were granted an appointment with the director of Alpha, and I can see him now, sitting behind this enormous desk, playing with his pipe. It's a small thing, but all the time we were talking I was thinking how much more interesting that pipe must be to him. And suddenly he just picked up the phone to make a call. I don't know how he could behave that way. The last time I was at the hospital—it was after one of Yoav's escapades, when we didn't even know where he'd spent the night—I saw the therapist and cried and cried. After that they wouldn't talk to us anymore. They just locked the door on us. I felt we were sinking in a swamp.*

The therapeutic staff, firm in their belief that one diagnosis is truth and that one treatment is the way, clearly became desensitized to the pain caused by their therapy. Vision narrowed by administrative procedures became hermetic. In this professional context, dehumanized voices could communicate in professional lingo to other professionals, but no one was listening to the parents.

MINUCHIN: *How did you feel within the family?*
TAMARA: *We fought all the time. Especially after family get-togethers. I had the feeling all the time that my husband and Yoav both wished I were dead.*
MINUCHIN: *Did you know how your wife felt?*
NOAM: *Only much later. At the time, we couldn't talk to each other. In our hearts we blamed each other. She made me feel that I couldn't handle Yoav, and I felt bad, as though I were to blame. Sometimes I wondered if she wanted to separate, to be with Yoav but not with me.*
TAMARA: *No, never. I felt that he was blaming me, because he used to tell me that maybe I* was *moving my lips in a way that angered Yoav.*
MINUCHIN: *Both of you experienced tremendous pain and guilt, and you needed a lot of support from each other, which you couldn't find. Has the situation between you changed any?*
NOAM: *Things got much better after Yoav was hospitalized in Beta. We felt that he was finally being taken care of, and that left us more time for ourselves. Instead of being so taken*

up by problems with Yoav all the time, we began talking to each other again, and then we both came to understand that neither of us wished to hurt the other.

TAMARA: *Before he was hospitalized again, it was impossible. We felt we were in some sort of Kafkaesque maze, with no way out.*

The parents' experience at the hands of the mental health profession was indeed Kafkaesque. They were declared guilty by the experts (who, after all, must know). The nature of their crime was amorphous; they knew only that it had to do with parenting. Their sentence was hard labor: "Mend your ways." This punishment was compounded by the constant reminder of their crime and by the certain knowledge that there was no way out—a Sisyphean punishment for a Kafkaesque conviction. Their experience increased their sense of isolation. The mental health teams became the only source of information about themselves, the only providers of meager crumbs of self-esteem. Their attempts to establish a closer relationship with these "benefactors" were interpreted as manipulative; their efforts to correct their behavior were evaluated and found lacking. Intrafamily conflicts increased as each parent saw the other as guilty of mishandling Yoav, and was perhaps anxious to remove the guilty spouse—a situation that was, of course, labeled paranoid ideation by the experts. Beta Hospital brought them relief. A clear diagnosis of Yoav as a paranoid schizophrenic freed both parents from the dock and allowed them to enrich their ways of interacting. It also diminished their anger at Yoav, who was, after all, sick; their guilt toward him could be mixed with pity and concern about his fate. However, in this new constellation it was Yoav who paid the price.

MINUCHIN: *And now? What about your physical condition?*

TAMARA: *They think they got the cancer in time, but the next year is going to be rough. It's a difficult treatment.*

MINUCHIN: *How has cancer influenced your relationship?*

TAMARA: *It's odd, but now for the first time in many years*

I feel sure my husband loves me. I had the feeling before that someone in the family would have to die, and that my husband wanted it to be me. Now I know he never thought such a thing. He's very concerned about me, and he really wants us to be together.

MINUCHIN: *What's happening with Yoav now?*

NOAM: *Well, he likes Beta. When we told Yoav about it, he went over there by himself, and he's been there ever since. But the hospital tells us he's very sick. He's really schizophrenic, not borderline, as Alpha thought. As I understand it, he's going to be there for a long time.*

MINUCHIN: *How does he relate to you when you visit?*

TAMARA: *He's still pretty rough on me. He keeps thinking I'm mocking him.*

MINUCHIN: *How's he doing in the hospital?*

NOAM: *There's no real improvement. In fact, he has intense outbreaks of violence. But at least he's being taken care of. I don't know what's best for him, but I do know that in Alpha everything went downhill. I honestly don't think they saw what was happening with Yoav anymore. The more we tried to talk to them, the more they refused to reexamine his condition. At Beta at least they talk to us and explain what is happening to Yoav, and what they are trying to do with him. We feel they care about Yoav.*

TAMARA: *And they don't put us down. I know it doesn't have as good a reputation at Alpha, but at least the director doesn't think he's God.*

After the session, Minuchin requested permission to visit the hospital. The parents stipulated that he meet only with Yoav's therapists and not try to see Yoav. After their experience with family therapy, they had no wish even to suggest its resumption.

A Visit to Beta Hospital: Yoav's "True Personality"

Several days after the interview, we visited Beta. We had previously reread the transcript of the first session and reviewed Yoav's history, and we had come to the conclusion that he should be evaluated for organic deficit. We hoped to suggest this possibility to the hospital staff.

Entering the grounds of this huge state hospital was like being framed into a Hollywood western. A wide alley was Main Street, and we were the strangers being watched as we moved into a bizarre land of long ago. Here nonreason ruled, and chronicity seemed the hallmark of a bleak world and its long-forgotten inhabitants. An adolescent could not possibly pass a year and a half in such an environment without being negatively affected.

The staff was obviously pleased by our interest in their work and welcomed us as important dignitaries. The chief psychiatrist was trying hard to be helpful. He smiled apologetically when he described the routine of life on the ward. The psychologist was a young woman whose countenance radiated earnestness. Evidently they took pride in being able to provide their adolescent inpatients with long-term psychotherapy.

PSYCHIATRIST: *When I first met Yoav, he wasn't studying or working regularly. In fact, he had no home. I showed him our ward, and I told him I thought he ought to be hospitalized. The next day he arrived at the hospital on his own.*

MINUCHIN: *Is he making any improvement?*

PSYCHIATRIST: *Unfortunately, he's very paranoid. If someone smiles, he thinks he's being made fun of. If his mother moves her lips, it's a sign of contempt. He's also very tense and can break out in fits of violence. During a group therapy session, he is likely to hit someone he thinks has insulted him. The nurses are afraid of him, but the other patients tease him. They call him the dickless dunce and play at getting him mad. One time one of the girls unbuttoned her blouse in front of him. She said he was useless as a man. He had a seizure once that looked epileptic, but he didn't cut his tongue or urinate. We sent him for an EEG and a CAT scan, but the results were negative. He had another seizure another time when he got very excited.*

PSYCHOLOGIST: *I was very surprised to learn that Alpha diagnosed him as borderline, not requiring hospitalization. We recognized him at once as a paranoid schizophrenic. Maybe at Alpha he put up a good front, so they never saw his true personality. But here as he adjusted to life on the ward and grew more at ease, all his characteristic symptoms were gradually exposed. Here he gives expression to his suspicions and his tendency to violence, just as he did at home.*

Both the psychiatrist and the psychologist discounted the effect of the hospital context. The psychologist was probing for Yoav's "true personality," completely unaware of the absurdity of defining deterioration as more accurate self-exposure. There was no recognition that the diagnosis of paranoid schizophrenic had now organized Yoav's life. It seemed that Yoav had quickly become oriented to the rules of living in his new environment, and violent outbursts fit that context. They earned him the fearful respect of the nurses, protected him from the humiliation suffered in the peer group, and gave legitimacy to his new status.

ELIZUR: *Have you met Yoav's parents?*

PSYCHOLOGIST: *At first, Yoav refused to see them. Whenever they came for a visit, he ran away. This made them very angry, and for a while they wouldn't come to visit. They made their feelings known, and after that the nurses couldn't stand them. They felt that if a child runs away from home and the parents won't even come to visit, the parents must be a real disaster area. The psychiatrist who was seeing the parents at the beginning said they were impossible—nearly inhuman. There was a general atmosphere of hatred toward them.*

ELIZUR: *What was your approach?*

PSYCHOLOGIST: *A few months after I began to treat Yoav, I*

arranged a family session, but it was disastrous. Yoav became furious with his mother immediately, and she screamed at him. Noam was more restrained, but he was angry at both Yoav and his wife. There was a general feeling of helplessness. The meeting was awful. Yoav refused to talk to me for a long time afterward. I realized then that Yoav could meet me only within an exclusive relationship. I've been seeing him now for about a year. At first all he could talk about was how his brain and body were degenerating. He didn't do a thing. Most of the time he just lay in bed. But after a while, he began to open up. He tested me a lot, but finally he began to accept me, and I've been careful to safeguard that relationship. For him I'm the good one, and everyone else inside or outside the hospital is bad. I try to serve as a bridge to other things. I see progress in that he now begins to relate to the group, even if it is in a negative, suspicious way.

The therapist's language was familiar. She spoke the language of thousands of young, naive, well-intentioned professionals who have been taught to talk standard professional jargon as a good, clear substitute for the confused descriptions of people's lives as they really are. We felt defeated by the environment, by the good intentions, and by the banalities of psychologese.

MINUCHIN: *What does he do during the day?*
PSYCHIATRIST: *In the morning Yoav may go to class or to occupational therapy, but he does little. Sometimes he sews or embroiders, but it is purely mechanical work, suitable for the retarded. Most of the time he simply stays in bed. I don't want to force him to move—I prefer to give him the chance to be autonomous. But he's preoccupied with his inner world: Who has hurt him? How should he react? Sometimes he plays a little table tennis.*

The sensitivity to subtle nuances in the therapeutic rapport contrasted sharply with the lack of attention to the limited possibilities open to Yoav. Yoav was now eighteen. He did not get along with a group that teased him. He stayed in bed most of the day and sometimes studied a little or performed repetitive tasks in occupational therapy. So he lived inside his own world, allowing his "fairy godmother" therapist special visiting rights.

Minuchin tried to move the staff toward more exploration of Yoav's makeup.

MINUCHIN: *What's his thinking style?*

PSYCHOLOGIST: *It's strange, but he's like someone suffering from organic damage. His thinking is very concrete, and he has difficulty dealing with abstractions. From an intellectual point of view, he does not come up to the other adolescents, though sometimes he uses richer language, and he can be sensitive to nuances.*

MINUCHIN: *Does he read?*

PSYCHOLOGIST: *He seems to have a problem with reading. He claims that the letters keep jumping in front of his eyes. The teacher has been selecting particularly easy books to read, but he still has trouble. Once he made a real effort to read a book after I told him how much I liked it as a young girl. But he couldn't quite manage to tell me its central theme.*

It seems that the diagnosis of schizophrenia was all-encompassing and irrefutable. Data that did not fit this "objective" diagnosis were relegated to the background. The psychologist proceeded with her regular course of psychotherapy, avoiding the implications of her careful observations of Yoav's behavior and cognitive style. The psychiatrist was certainly aware of the diagnostic significance of the seizures that he observed, but he dismissed them. Did the simplicity of the wards rob the staff of complexity?

ELIZUR: *Have you made any more attempts to work with his parents?*

PSYCHOLOGIST: *Some six months ago, when I was sure of the bond between us and Yoav was much quieter, I took the risk of meeting his parents. Tamara was in an emancipation stage, finally deciding that she wanted to live a life of her own and not function as just the mother of a sick child. I saw that they seemed to feel guilty about Yoav's condition, and I gave them a lot of support, expressing understanding for the sorrow and anger parents generally suffer in such a situation. Once they'd told me how very difficult life with Yoav was for them, they began to talk about the beautiful moments they'd shared with him. They brought him a new pair of trousers, and he liked them and thanked them. The mother even got up the courage to give him a kiss. Things are better all around—the staff likes them better, and I think the parents finally feel that the entire burden doesn't rest on them, that the ward is helping them. I think, too, that there has been a change for the better since Yoav doesn't visit at home anymore. Attempts at home visits were always disastrous.*

Diagnosis and long-term hospitalization removed Yoav from a family context that might disturb him, including any context of a possibly constructive crisis. The parents, having handed his care over to the experts, were also given a stable, long-term diagnosis, and the hospital staff could acknowledge their suffering.

MINUCHIN: *What do you think about the future?*
PSYCHOLOGIST: *That's a question I hate to think about. I have no idea how much longer he'll be allowed to stay on the ward. He may be moved to an adult ward, in which case, by the hospital rules, I won't be able to work with him. He'll get no psychotherapy at all. A more hopeful possibility is that he will slowly improve here and learn to relate to others without quarreling. In that case, he may someday manage to lead a fringe existence outside the hospital. But I don't know how realistic that is.*

The staff had not requested consultation, but they were interested in feedback. We thought that by joining, supporting, and suggesting, we could initiate change that would seem to emanate from them and not from us.

PSYCHOLOGIST: *What do you think?*

MINUCHIN: *You've managed to create a world that is safer, more predictable, and better than the world of Yoav's family and the outside. He will want to stay with you, and I don't think you will ever leave him.*

PSYCHOLOGIST: *What do you suggest?*

MINUCHIN: *I believe you have become a bridge to Yoav, but that you've lost the freedom to innovate. You keep doing the same things. You need to think of something new. I can't say what—I don't know you or the patient well enough. But I can see that you are stuck.*

PSYCHIATRIST: *We could begin to look at his interactions in the group and interpret his oversensitivity to criticism and the unrealistic demands he makes on others. There's also the possibility of resuming family sessions.*

MINUCHIN: *With such a limited prognosis, there's little to lose by trying. And a tremendous amount to gain.*

Leaving the hospital, we felt depressed, indignant, and, yes, hopeless and guilty. We couldn't help Yoav in such a context, and the certainty of the psychiatric label had the weight of a tombstone. How could we push the staff toward uncertainty?

Following the visit, we wrote the Beta staff a letter. After thanking them for their cooperation, we added:

We agree with your comments on the symptoms of organic disturbance, such as the difficulties in concentration, the concrete thinking, the tendency to perseveration, and the difficulties in reading, as well as the convulsive occurrences.

It is clear that there is also paranoid ideation, and the interesting question is whether the paranoid reactions are superimposed on a basic structure of a boy with organic difficulties.

Yoav grew up in a family that had expectations of him in

excess of his ability. According to the parents, he had difficulty coping with school, and his failures in his studies created great pressure on him and on his family. Their inability to obtain proper guidance in dealing with his special problems may well account for a large part of the family problems and adjustment difficulties that arose over the years.

These hypotheses, which you brought up in the course of our conversation, may well throw some new light on the case and the ways of handling it.

The letter concluded with a request for further information in the future, particularly about any innovations in working with the family and plans to rehabilitate Yoav as a constitutionally impaired young man.

But when a system closes itself, it develops blinders for information that is dissonant with its diagnosis and treatment. Three months after our visit, we learned through the Beta psychologist that Yoav had hit a fellow patient and a nurse and had been moved back to Alpha, this time to its closed adult ward.

New Treatments at Alpha

The decision to transfer Yoav to Alpha was relayed to Noam and Tamara abruptly, in an authoritative manner that was unusual in their relations with Beta. A few days later, they received a telephone call from Alpha, informing them that Yoav had arrived. When they came, they found him bruised and highly agitated, wearing torn pajamas. A hospital aide had moved him from Beta against his will on a day when the psychologist was not at the hospital. Yoav had had no advance preparation for the move.

Despite their premonitions, the parents found themselves being treated with respect by the new ward psychiatrist. There was no threat of going back to family therapy, and even individual therapy was deemed to be contraindicated for paranoid schizophrenia. Pharmacotherapy was the major mode of treatment, and different phenothiazines were tried. There were no signs of sedation, and the dosages were increased. Careful study revealed that the drug treatment was having a toxic effect on Yoav. Traditional medications for schizophrenia were then discarded, and lithium was tried. After lithium came a series of electroshocks. Nothing worked, and the staff members were becoming increasingly fearful of Yoav's rage. Once this fragile-looking youngster had to be restrained by five of the toughest attendants. The nursing staff began to tie Yoav to his bed whenever they suspected that he was about to explode. The "patient's violent condition" did not remit, and the staff tied him for longer periods of time, on one occasion for two months.

Modern medicine was failing its battle against unreason, and as Yoav's care was increasingly delegated to the attendants, an approach of authoritative control and containment prevailed. Such methods of dealing with madness have been traced to the houses of confinement two centuries ago, when madness was a raging passion of the soul and the most forceful methods for breaking the animal spirit were employed.

Meanwhile, relations with the parents were improving. Yoav was not violent toward them, and whenever he became upset during their visits, he would ask them to leave earlier but to continue their regular visits. When the family celebrated his sister's Bat Mitzvah, Yoav was allowed to go—his first time out after six months in Alpha. The home visit was very successful. Yoav made a little speech at the party and interacted with many of the relatives, showing no signs of disturbance whatsoever. But three days later, at the hospital, he became violent again and was tied up. Yoav claimed that the outburst was brought on by frustration over being forced to return to the drab reality of the mental hospital. The psychiatrist explained to the parents, however, that Yoav had made a tremendous effort to control himself at home, and was now discharging his tension.

When Yoav had been at Alpha for seven months, the psychiatrists told his parents that the staff had tried its best but to no avail. They highly recommended an alternative treatment—a lobotomy. There was a good chance that Yoav's violence could be controlled by surgery. The parents had to decide, and because

Yoav would not be able to stay much longer at Alpha, their refusal would mean a transfer to a chronic hospital.

Dissenting Voices: "A Straightforward Case of Brain Damage"

"One thing we have learned," said Noam, "is not to be afraid of choices, and not to let them make these decisions alone. Yoav is *our* son." Before making a decision on the proposed lobotomy, the parents sought the opinions of outside professionals. They again consulted the neurologist, Dr. Rosh, and then went with Yoav to a senior psychiatrist, Professor Keshet.

Dr. Rosh's report did not mince words:

> *Yoav was a straightforward case of minimal brain damage in the frontal and temporal lobes. I made that diagnosis three years ago, and the epileptic seizures that occurred later confirm it. The EEG and CAT scan are not sensitive enough for such diagnosis. I have examined many such patients who were improperly drugged because their psychiatrists did not know neurology. I never hide my views because of professional etiquette, and that does not make me a favorite of the local establishment.*
>
> *I prescribed carbamazepine and propranolol to increase self-control over the paroxysm. This treatment is not original—it has been described in recent professional literature—and I thought it might also help Yoav contain the paranoid ideations. Royal jelly and Vitamin B complex are supplements to create more favorable inner conditions in the body and mind. All other medications were discarded. The good results are already showing. There has not been a single outburst since Yoav's medications were changed.*

Professor Keshet agreed with Dr. Rosh's approach. Keshet is an eminent Israeli psychiatrist who often disconcerts his colleagues by publicly airing his views that: "many patients are misdiagnosed as schizophrenics because psychiatrists are taught to look for statistical signs instead of relating to the whole person." He is an intellectual speaking with a powerful voice:

> *I did not do much in this case. I am familiar with Rosh's life work, and I am one who respects his expertise. It was clear that Yoav is not a schizophrenic. I spoke directly with the hospital's director to convey my opposition to lobotomy and my support for Rosh's opinions. Personally I believe that what they termed "violence" is a response of a person who feels his territory is constantly being impinged upon without his control.*

Though Yoav knew nothing about the plans for his lobotomy, he was aware that he was a candidate for the chronic hospital. Then, following the change in his medications, his condition took a dramatic turn, and suddenly he asked for his long-forgotten guitar and for books. The staff refused. Yoav continued to be confined in his room. The staff noted the improvement but explained to the parents that Yoav was not ready for such a rapid change. Why? Perhaps, the staff of the ward needed to retain authority by denying Yoav's wishes. Luckily for Yoav there was a reorganization in the hospital and he was transferred to a more open ward. Joel Elizur visited him four months later.It was now four years after the initial consultation with Minuchin.

A Visit to Alpha Hospital: "The Paranoid Core Remains"

Yoav looked well. The eyes of the slim, soft-speaking young man held a glimmer; his fingers nervously shredded a piece of paper. He wanted to get out of the hospital, and he proceeded without delay to substantiate his improvement:

> YOAV: *Now I go regularly to occupational therapy. I have therapy sessions, and I'm working to improve my English. I*

study a lot, and I practice the guitar whenever they let me. The staff says that I'm normal, and we have good relations. It's very different from before, when they tied me for weeks. They didn't understand that I immediately calmed down after a blowup. But now I control myself and don't quarrel with anyone.

ELIZUR: *How do you explain this change?*

YOAV: *I was given a chance in this ward, and I used it. I understand that the hospital can be very tough, and it frightened me. I never want to be tied again, and I'm afraid of being put in a chronic hospital. At home, I know that Mother is sick, and so I don't expect her to take care of me. I don't think the hospital has helped me at all. I was at my best when I stayed with my uncle.*

ELIZUR: *What do you do when you feel insulted? You had violent outbreaks before.*

YOAV: *I'm still pretty sensitive, and sometimes the patients here insult me. I'm also angry at the hospital. But I can control myself.*

The ward's chief psychiatrist was interviewed separately during the visit:

God helped Yoav, and there was a reorganization that brought him here. Nobody had the time to supervise him, so he was able to leave his room. And when we saw that nothing terrible happened, we let him go to occupational therapy. The more things he did without restrictions, the more he improved. The paranoid core remains, but he has developed tools for controlling his behavior.

Probably the entire staff of the hospital dismissed the fact that for the last five years *they* had been attacking Yoav. His fear of attacks was labeled paranoid, an abnormality rather than a response to life circumstances.

ELIZUR: *How do you intend to proceed now?*

PSYCHIATRIST: *If Yoav had somewhere to go, he wouldn't be*

here. He needs to learn a trade and increase his social skills, but to be in a rehabilitation program he needs a place to live. He can't stay at Alpha much longer, and his mother's condition makes it impossible to send him home. The only alternative seems to be a hospital that serves an older chronic population. It's not the most appropriate facility, but they have various programs there to teach different skills. They might give him some work to do, and, more important, there will be no limitation as to how long he can stay inside.

This was the institution's dismal reflection of social reality. Public funds in Israel have been used to build mental hospitals, while the infrastructure of rehabilitation continues wanting.The discussion with the psychiatrist continued into an exploration of private facilities that could work toward Yoav's reintegration into normal society. However, he was reserved and communicated his feelings indirectly.

PSYCHIATRIST: *It depends on the parents. It remains to be seen whether they can and would pay the very high tuition.*

A Home Visit to Noam and Tamara

A few days later, Elizur talked with Noam and Tamara. This time the discussion was mainly with Noam. Tamara, who was terminally ill, stayed in bed. Her face was pale and her body withered.

TAMARA: *Regular medicine has given up on me. I can still hope. But I also think about my death, and I would like to see Yoav settled somewhere out of the hospital before anything happens to me.*

NOAM: *Yoav has been very much improved. He comes to visit us every afternoon. In the evenings he goes to the movies or plays basketball with his uncle. We would not agree to have him placed in a chronic institution, but we can't care for him at home. I would like to visit a private rehabilitation center, and we'll make financial sacrifices if need be.*

Yoav and his family will go on to encounter new tasks in their continuing search. A couple of months after Elizur's visit they called to say that they found sources of public support to pay for the rehabilitation costs in a very good rehabilitation institute that works with young adults. Perhaps there is some light at the end of this long tunnel.

Reflections

The hospital tells us that [Yoav] is very sick. He's really schizophrenic, not borderline, as Alpha thought. As I understand it, he's going to be there for a long time.

Yoav was eighteen when his father gave this sad report. At the time, he had been institutionalized for almost three years. Three more years of institutionalization were to follow, during which Yoav would be returned to the first hospital and transferred to three different wards. His life, like that of Malamud's *The Fixer,* would be increasingly circumscribed. While still in an open ward, he would be given massive doses of tranquilizers. Moved to a closed ward, he would be given electroshock treatments and tied to his bed for months at a time. When nothing seemed to be working, a lobotomy—the ultimate constraint—was seriously proposed.

Only at that point did Yoav's family amass sufficient courage to take the decision back from the experts. When the neurologist repeated a diagnosis he had made years earlier—that Yoav suffered from a neurological dysfunction in the temporal and frontal lobe—that diagnosis now gained enough salience in the world of deviant labels to relabel Yoav and release him into the world of the normal.

Yoav

In four years of follow-up to a consultation, we witnessed Yoav's progressive movement away from his family and life in his community into the narrow and narrowing experience of institutional living. His case is a paradigm of the stages of that unfortunate process. Wrapped in psychiatric labels, he adapted to fit the niches made for him in the labeling/treatment system.

During this process his family was accused, by supposedly nonjudgmental professionals, of nameless crimes somehow clearly causative of Yoav's difficulties. His parents acted out their assigned roles—paranoid, intrusive, and manipulative. The hospital, always protected by the shield of professional neutrality, labeled, relabeled, and relabeled again. Like the Sorcerer's Apprentice, it was always ready to correct error with error. But it never relinquished its magic wand. And it never included itself in the picture of pathology and constraint.

Looking at the family/hospital relationship as a whole system, one can discern patterns that appear to be universal in the process of institutionalization. Once a diagnosis is applied, as Bronfenbrenner notes, "Seldom is attention paid to the person's behavior in more than one setting or to the way in which relationships between settings can affect what happens within them."* Yoav's case gives us a fascinating view of distorting labels, beliefs reigning absolute over unrealistically tiny segments of the whole picture, the struggle of ideologies, and the impact of all this on people: Yoav, his family, and the staff of the psychiatric hospitals.

Psychiatric ideology for the most part assumes that diagnosis is an objective description of organic and intrapsychic realities. Yoav's case challenges this assertion. Throughout his encounters with different therapists and contexts, he constantly blended into his environment, displaying a remarkable ability to behave differently in different circumstances under different diagnoses. Although he could act competently in many ways, the diagnosis of madness organized a rocklike reality that constrained possibilities, restricting his life so that the most morbid expectations were fulfilled.

*Urie Bronfenbrenner, *The Ecology of Human Development by Nature and Design* (Cambridge, MA: Harvard University Press, 1979), p. 18.

Family therapists, who know the governing power of labels, think of diagnosis as a dynamic metaphor: a construction that changes whenever the observer shifts to a new position within the system. Nonetheless, even family therapists who worked with Yoav observed their own grain of sand as if it were the universe.

Yoav's was an ecology fragmented into opposing ideas, and therapists were caught unaware of the way that the structuring of their work dictated their thinking. Consequently, Yoav's case is sprinkled with instances in which crucial information that cast different light on the case was simply glossed over, treated like white noise in a symphony rich with pathology. Resources of healing that could have been available from the start were utilized only after years of suffering and despair.

This story can be useful if it teaches us to increase our awareness of complexity, to recognize that there are always more possibilities than we perceive, and to learn to respect feedback that shows we have exhausted the usefulness of a construction. Family therapists should pay particular attention to the intrinsic bias of overstressing a family with exceedingly high expectations. Systems can transform only in discontinuous movements, and the process may induce stress as a byproduct. But stress is not in itself therapeutic. Furthermore, the major locus of change does not necessarily reside at the family level. Therapy that focuses on the family in isolation is in danger of serving an ideology that values families but resists taking political measures to deal with social factors that overtax them.

3

Dan

IN 1974* Don Jackson declared the death of the individual. It was a marvelously creative statement. Suddenly family therapists could see the invisible connections between the individual and the system. We understood that the decontexted individual was a mythical monster, an illusion created by our psychodynamic blinders. Now, like Castenada's Don Juan, we could see the organic wires that lead from our belly buttons to the other people and things in our universe. The feeling was one of cosmic awareness.

In the same journal† Lyman Wynne sounded a cautionary note about the individual as subsystem and warned us not to throw the baby out with the bathwater. But nobody was interested in caution. These were years of paradigmatic change, and family therapists united against the intellectual chains that had confined the psyche inside human skin. It was Pinel again.

Gregory Bateson's powerful rhetoric opened new vistas for the practice of therapy. The mind was an external process. To a world learning to think of its finite resources, systems theory brought images of harmony and a logic that might transcend human hubris. The period of flower children and Black is Beautiful, of

*Don D. Jackson, "The Individual and the Larger Contexts," *Family Process* 6 (1967): 139–47.

†Lyman Wynne, Untitled discussion, *Family Process* 6 (1967): 153–54.

women's liberation and gay rights, of the war on poverty and the Great Society, was a period of hope. Family therapy was a golden thread in the fabric of ecological awareness. The psychiatric establishment might still be in the hands of the Pharisees, but we knew we were the future.

With time the field divided into a number of practices dressed as schools, though all in all we maintained a collegiate spirit under the flag of systems theory. Around the same time, psychoanalysis, which had overpromised a rose garden, began to see its power erode. Analysts steeped in individual truths began to be replaced by psychiatrists who did not believe in the individual either. The modern individual psyche was reduced to organic fragments, and an array of scientists who found life largely irrelevant began to experiment with chemical components to match and calibrate human emotions.

In time, each group established its own enclave. Psychoanalytic practitioners and psychodynamic therapists retrenched from medical schools and hospitals into powerful bastions of private practice and outpatient clinics. Family therapists, who have seen their field mushroom in the last three decades, remained predominantly outpatient but made significant inroads into working with larger systems: social welfare, schools, hospitals, and even businesses. Organic psychiatrists now have free rein in most medical schools and university hospitals in the United States.

It now seems that the time is ripe for individual and family therapists to unite against new pretenders, and perhaps that is beginning to happen. The transgenerational practitioners/theorists—Bowen, Nagy, and Whitaker—in their exploration of the transmission of patterns and myth, bring echoes of early psychodynamic formulation to their theories of the development of schizophrenia. Maurizio Andolfi speaks about focusing on the individual. For their part, psychodynamic analysts are working with couples and struggling to make sense of the complexity of multiple individual dynamics that they construct as families. Constructivist psychoanalysts, Lacanian therapists, and individual and family therapists talk about the co-construction of narratives in very similar terms.

Nonetheless, so extraordinary is the power of ideologies that each paradigmatic field still claims the whole universe of truth and demands total ownership of the official metaphors. The reflex response is still to put the wagons in a circle. When Jay Haley recently made it clear that he had not deviated from a position he has held for decades—that schizophrenia is a sociopsychological entity and that hospitalization and drug treatment may produce irreversible iatrogenic results—Carol Anderson and Michael Goldstein, who have been in the vanguard of the "psychoeducational approach" of working with families of schizophrenics, responded with a broadside: Haley was blind not to see the importance of joining with a family's pain at having a schizophrenic member. Immediately the lines were drawn, and family therapists of different persuasions chose up sides, joining one of the parties and becoming deaf to what the other was saying.*

In the case that follows, therapists from different ideologies—family therapists working in an outpatient clinic and psychiatric staff working in a hospital—attempted to develop a collaborative therapy. When there was a crisis in the treatment, however, each side retrenched to the fortress of its own ideology, with significant consequences for the family.

The Psychiatric Diagnosis: "A Depleted Internal World"

Dan, eighteen, was a patient at one of Israel's most prestigious hospitals. During his last year in high school, he had begun to complain of pain in his penis and bladder and a frequent need to urinate, for which no medical cause could be found. He had also been experiencing difficulty in concentrating and excessive anxiety about his examinations and upcoming army service. He had

*Jay Haley, "Schizophrenics Deserve Family Therapy, Not Dangerous Drugs and Management," *Family Therapy News* 19, no. 2 (March/April 1988); Carol Anderson, "Psychoeducational Model Different than Paradigm," *Family Therapy News* 19, no. 3 (May/June 1988); Michael Goldstein, "Correction on Views Offered by Awardee," *Family Therapy News* 19, no. 3, (May/June, 1988).

been referred to a psychiatrist, and in individual therapy he had begun talking about suicide, expressing estrangement from his peers. During a pre-military outing, he had experienced an anxiety attack and had been returned home. His suicide threats had become more intense thereafter, and his psychiatrist had suggested that he be hospitalized.

The hospital's psychiatric diagnosis was grim:

> *The patient suffers from a primary personality disorder with schizoid characteristics and somatic delusions. There is a long-term premorbid process that increased in severity as his internal world was gradually depleted. The unavoidable question is whether it is a deep primary disorder in personality development or a schizophrenic process, simple type, with characteristic impoverishment and constriction.*

As always with psychological issues, the words here are constructing what they supposedly describe. Dan's psychiatric diagnosis is a cosmology, describing pathology in a closed system, an "internal world [that has become] gradually depleted." But even the most "depleted" internal world is still complex and exciting, providing a wealth of data to become the building blocks of enticingly coherent and persuasive psychological narrative. Now a story can be built, told in a language familiar only to the other storytellers, a recognition code of the chosen that excludes the uncircumcised. The story will also exclude everything but the inner pathology. The external world, of no small significance to most people, will have no labeling in this expert construction.

Five months after Dan's admission to the hospital, his symptoms were persisting. The staff was puzzled, and Dan's parents were worried, complaining that the longer he was in the hospital the more he was assuming the behavior of inmates. They felt that their son was a bright youngster with some longstanding problems and an encumbering symptom but that he seemed neither psychotic nor organically impaired. They therefore asked that a family therapist be brought into the case.

Dan's History: Regulating the Distance between Parents

The family therapist's subsequent report of what had brought Dan to this point contrasts with the hospital's diagnosis in placing Dan squarely in the external world:

Dan's father, Isaac, is authoritarian and overbearing; he expects to be treated like a king. He's selfish, distant, and cold, and marital relations have long been distant and strained. He's always been hard on Dan, right from the boy's birth. Dan is an inhibited, rather shy child, and Isaac pushes him unmercifully. Dan is very close to his mother, Sara, who pets and protects him. Yes, maybe they're a little too close, but it's a warm, loving relationship that helps make up to Dan for his father's harshness.

This was Sara's story, of course. Like all stories, it was true but partial. From Sara's perspective Dan was shy, Isaac was harsh, and she was warm and loving. With this view of her problem Sara came to the family therapist asking for her support. From the systems perspective of the therapist it was obvious that Isaac's pushiness maintained Sara's protectiveness, which maintained Isaac's pushiness; both were maintained by Dan's behavior, which was maintained by both. Here is her account:

Dan is a very insecure child who was noticeably shy and inhibited even as a toddler. When he began school, his teacher considered him cognitively and emotionally retarded, and he was moved to a special school. Isaac protested, claiming Dan was just immature because of his too-close relations with Sara. He arranged for a battery of tests, which proved Dan had a higher intellectual potential than his performance. Dan went back to the regular school and began getting intensive help from a tutor and an individual therapist. Dan's functioning at school improved, and he actually proved to be a bright student, but he was always a mama's boy. Sam, who was born three years after Dan, became Isaac's child. The brothers fought a good deal, with the active involvement of the parents, who sided with their protégés.

When Dan reached the age of twelve, the tension between the parents reached a new peak, and they separated. Dan complained of sharp stomach pains and was operated on for what turned out to be an imaginary case of appendicitis. The parents reunited to take care of Dan, and they continued living together, though the marriage remained stormy.

Shortly after his operation, Dan began to complain of strong anxiety before each test in school. From then on a fixed pattern emerged. Dan would present problems; his parents would respond. Dan developed into a hesitant, passive, and anxious adolescent, never too competent at home or at school.

The 20/20 vision of a clinical history makes it possible to pinpoint several factors as the precursors of Dan's hospitalization ten years later. Individual therapy confirmed Dan's position as a disturbed child. So identified, he could become the regulator of distance between his parents. They could fight over their differences through him, and they could stay together out of concern for him. Of course, only Dan was given a label.

By the time his parents separated, Dan had learned the language of deficit very well. His symptoms took on a somatic expression, and pediatricians, who generally talk only to the parents and poke only the children, helped transform this psychogenic pain into a somatic symptom. The hard science of physiology forced them to confess their error, but even expert error became another nail in the construction of Dan as a disturbed individual.

Several months before the end of high school Dan began to complain of pain in his penis and bladder and the need to urinate frequently. Extensive medical tests found nothing organic. Dan began pharmacotherapy with supportive individual therapy. In therapy he cried a great deal, and began talking about suicide. He felt estranged from his peers, who were discussing their upcoming army service, while he was unable to leave home and cope with the military regimen. Suicide threats became more intense after Dan had an anxiety attack during a pre-military outing and was returned home. His psychiatrist suggested that he be hospitalized, and the family agreed with a sense of relief.

This clinical history is, of course, the construction of the family therapist. As such it contains the classic dysfunctional family triangle: The spouses' conflicts are negotiated through the first-born. Mother gains competence through mothering, and a strong bond develops between mother and child. Father resents the displacement and attacks the boy, who is defended by his mother. The boy becomes a family healer by being its patient. Rigid family patterns develop, and individual treatments that do not change the patterns achieve limited results.

Of course, stories also reflect the stage on which they are played out. Dan is the identified patient—he is in a mental hospital, after all. So even for the family therapist, he is the star. Father, mother, and brother are supporting players, and circumstance itself takes second billing in the story of the hero.

When Dan was committed to an adolescent ward, the psychiatric staff had this same data, but their construction was completely different (but of course maintained with the same certainty). They traced in detail early deprivations and their effects on the child's personality development. The patient's somatic delusions were carefully described, and an entire premorbid process was lovingly created for a perfect fit to the *DSM III.* The family therapist's history describes Dan's treatment:

Dan did not improve with the usual armementarium of individual, group, and milieu therapy and tranquilizers, so his hospital psychiatrist decided to try a nonconventional approach. He theorized that Dan needed to re-encounter the basic issues of early development through a trip to the past, accompanied by his parents.

Dan was encouraged to regress. Parents and staff were

instructed to attend to his "primal needs." Sara went to the hospital twice daily, bringing food she'd cooked especially for him. The parents tried to occupy Dan's time as if he were a small child. They took him to the seashore and talked with him for long hours. When Dan came home on weekends he sometimes slept in his parents' bed, where he would remain for hours, crying over his condition. Yet there was no improvement, and with time Dan seemed to be even less prepared to go out and meet the world.

Healers and storytellers have always ensnared audiences with the poetry of their metaphors, by the development of their story lines and by the power of their tight logical construction. The hospital psychiatrist's story is one of the favorite myths of all cultures. It is therefore not surprising that the parents accepted this scenario and engaged in this rather strange trip to the past. But did the psychiatrist believe his Ferenczian incantation? Did he think about the complications that a "pre-Oedipal" eighteen-year-old sleeping with his parents might produce by having a normal erection during sleep? What was the mother's response supposed to be?

Sara experienced this period as unbearably stressful. She sought individual therapy. However, I thought that her strain was related to the hospital's approach, with which I disagreed. Therefore, I suggested family therapy. The parents asked the hospital to free Dan for the family sessions and to establish a cooperative relationship with me. The hospital was hesitant; they were not against family therapy if the family wished it, but they wanted a "psychodynamic family therapist" whose thinking would be more in tune with the hospital's.

The Consultation: "Three Years Is Better than Two"

The problem facing the family therapist was how to work with the family *and* the hospital. She was a social worker as well as a family therapist; both handicaps excluded her from the brotherhood. The M.D. talks with medical authority about the treatment of disease, while the M.S.W. seeks to delineate dysfunctional family patterns. Their differences in language seem irreconcilable, but this family's request had harnessed them in tandem. Which way would they pull? The consultation with Minuchin was arranged as an opportunity for the two therapists to meet, to see if they could agree on a joint family diagnosis and treatment.

Dan and Sara entered the room together. Dan's movements were slow and clumsy. During the five months of hospitalization he had put on considerable weight, and his speech revealed sedation. Fifteen-year-old Sam strode into the room full of confidence. His build was like Dan's, but without the fat. He was followed by nine-year-old Rachel, who entered quietly. By her side was Isaac, forty-seven, built large like his sons, his deeply furrowed face radiating authority.

The family therapist conducted the initial part of the meeting. The hospital's psychiatrist, a young woman, sat in as an observer. As the session began, Isaac took over, stating that he had come because the family needed family therapy. Miriam, the therapist, responded by trying to explore the question of what family conditions would allow Dan to go home. She was following Minuchin's guidelines for thinking about ways of involving the family in the treatment of hospitalized adolescents and increasing the family's responsibility for the preparation and timing of discharge.

MIRIAM: *I would like to hear from you, Isaac. Under what conditions in the family could Dan come home?*

ISAAC: *Dan's not in the hospital on account of us! I don't buy that!*

MIRIAM: *I understand that Dan's present condition does not really require that he stay in the hospital.*

ISAAC: *Well, there's nothing wrong with the atmosphere at home! It's Dan. He's the one who won't participate in family activities. And as for his fights with Sam, the only—*
MIRIAM: *Do you have any ideas about how the situation at home could be improved?*
ISAAC: *Well, it's pretty difficult. Right now Dan ignores Sam completely, as if he didn't exist. They used to fight like two normal brothers, but now the tension between them is too high. Dan lets it get to him. I think he actually blames Sam for what happened to him.*
MIRIAM: *Sara, how do you see the situation?*
SARA: *Dan and Sam have always argued. And Isaac has always punished them. It's not fair—Sam's the one who starts it. Isaac favors him, and naturally that hurts Dan's feelings.*

Miriam's probe frightened the family. It is the nature of parents to feel guilty, and in psychiatry's linear assignment of roles, parents do usually get to play the villain. Miriam realized quickly that she must join the family by tracking their story.

MIRIAM: *You think Dan blames Sam?*
ISAAC: *Well, he says Sam used to annoy him. But he also said himself, once, that people's madness is to accuse others and not themselves.*
RACHEL: *Sometimes Dan starts it.*
DAN: *[slowly] I . . . Well, I think Sam likes to quarrel, not just with me. My problem is that I never stood up to him. I'm essentially a passive personality.*

As Miriam elicited exploration of these issues from each of the family members, Minuchin, observing behind the one-way mirror, realized that she was becoming too involved in connecting with the family and the hospital psychiatrist to realize that the discussion was based on images from the family and hospital setting: a normal family in supportive therapy and a psychotic

Dan

Dan in a psychiatric ward. Minuchin joined the session with the goal of moving the therapeutic system away from this division of their reality into mad and normal individuals and toward a transactional view that would seek out the connections among the individuals.

MINUCHIN: *This discussion is interesting, but I'm confused. I see a nice, normal family talking about normal things. I see a boy, Dan, who is talking normally. Normal children, normal parents. Dan, why on earth are you in the hospital?*
DAN: *Well, a few months before the end of the school year I started having to go to the toilet all the time. I felt a lot of pressure to urinate. We decided that I should go to the hospital so that this pressure would go away.*
MINUCHIN: *So it had nothing to do with Sam.*
DAN: *It has a lot to do with him.*
MINUCHIN: *Is he in your bladder?*
DAN: *Yes.*
MINUCHIN: *How did he enter your bladder?*
DAN: *He used to provoke me a lot when we were kids, and he was aggressive. The pains I have are symptoms of my deeper problems.*

Dan had been thoroughly acculturated to the language of inner dynamics and deep psychology that characterized his therapeutic dialogue in the hospital. In this language, interpersonal transactions vanish, and life experiences are transformed into symbols of underlying pathology. Minuchin continued joining with him, trying to encourage the description of normal events.

MINUCHIN: *You're not convincing me. Are you in the hospital because you want to urinate all the time?*
DAN: *I go to the toilet, then a few minutes later I need to go again.*
MINUCHIN: *Have you been urinating like this for five months?*

DAN: *No, it's nearly a year, but I've been hospitalized for five months.*
MINUCHIN: *Do you have a room with a toilet in it?*
DAN: *No.*
MINUCHIN: *How do you manage, then?*
DAN: *I hold it in.*
MINUCHIN: *Do you want to pee now?*
DAN: *Yes.*

Concreteness was creating confusion. There was a symptom symbolic of deep inner troubles, and there was a concrete event: pressure in the bladder. As the event was reduced to absurdity, its connection with the symbolic meaning was broken, and tragic certainty could be replaced with ambiguity, puzzlement, and humor.

MINUCHIN: *You are doing a very good job of holding it in during this session. Can't you pee at home?*
DAN: *Of course I can pee at home. But I'm not a well person. I have to be in the hospital.*
MINUCHIN: *Do you have an infected kidney?*
DAN: *No, it's mental. Don't you understand? There's nothing wrong with me physically.*
MINUCHIN: *So you're in the hospital because you want to pee, and you prefer to pee there.*
DAN: *Well . . . yes.*
MINUCHIN: *How much longer do you want to stay in the hospital?*
DAN: *Until I'm all better.*
MINUCHIN: *A year? Two years? Three? Three is better than two.*
DAN: *I want to get better as quickly as I can and then get out.*

Absurdity can be a can opener to the closed logic of pathology. Here it brought discontinuity by introducing a new perspective that framed the hospital and family's jointly created story as just that—a story that was ludicrous because it was so limited and yet was being played out in deadly earnest.

MINUCHIN: *You present a very interesting puzzle. Why would a normal young man prefer the hospital to his home? Why not a convalescent home? Why not Paris?*
DAN: *Because the hospital—*
MINUCHIN: *How about England? London is a great city, and since you can hold it in, you could enjoy growing up there, away from your family.*
DAN: *But I can't get better there.*
MINUCHIN: *Don't you see? You don't want to be at home, but you don't dare be in any other place. So you chose the hospital as a way of not being anywhere. The hospital is neutral territory.*

Minuchin was forming an alliance with Dan through this slightly ludicrous concrete exploration of his symptom. Dan was aware of the humor and clearly saw that as they were talking about his symptom, they were also exploring his relationship to the hospital and his family. As the level shifted, he joined effortlessly. What was this child doing here? Nothing suggested psychosis. The humor in challenging Dan thus also veiled a challenge to the hospital and anger that this attractive youngster had been hospitalized, a practice at once so lazy and so destructive.

DAN: *Well, I want to learn to be away from the family.*
MINUCHIN: *Okay. So you use the hospital as a way to move away from your family—it's a halfway house.*
DAN: *All right.*
MINUCHIN: *How long do you think you'll stay in the hospital?*
DAN: *[shrugs] A year?*
MINUCHIN: *So you still have seven months to go. [to the psychiatrist] Dan has decided how long he will stay in the hospital. Is he paying for it?*
PSYCHIATRIST: *No, it's a public institution.*

MINUCHIN: *And do you have enough empty beds?*
PSYCHIATRIST: *Sometimes there is pressure for admission.*
MINUCHIN: *But Dan has decided on the progress of his illness and the program of treatment. It's wonderful to have such a patient who can tell you clearly what he needs and knows how to legitimize his treatment. Dan, you can manage very well when you are not at your house or the hospital.*
DAN: *Yes, but it isn't comfortable.*

Logic can be as contagious as madness. Bringing in the family context highlighted normal developmental issues of leaving home that were out of focus when the picture centered on Dan. Zooming away to an even wider perspective by involving the psychiatrist made it obvious that the solution was more absurd than the problem, and certainly more malevolent for Dan.

ISAAC: *May I interrupt for one second? I want to ask Dan. What happened to those pains you were always telling me about? You complained of terrible pains in your penis, but you told the doctor only of your wanting to go to the toilet.*
DAN: *But that* is *the pain—needing to urinate.*
SARA: *I don't understand this. When we talked about it, you were crying, and you told me that you couldn't stay at home with all the pains.*

Minuchin's challenge had threatened the hospital's pathologizing frame, normalized the symptoms of the family's patient, and suggested new directions—all in the space of a few sentences. It was not surprising that the parents, seeking re-equilibration, responded with a wealth of data that anchored their story.

MINUCHIN: *What he was saying was that he could not be competent at home. He needs a halfway house. What we have here is a conflict over leaving home and entering a different world, a conflict that happens to many young people. And your parents listen to the young part of you, instead of to the part that could grow up. Maybe your therapist can help the part of you that wants to grow up. You're a very interesting person, Dan, bright and perceptive. I've enjoyed meeting you.*

DAN: *Thanks.*

[MINUCHIN TAKES LEAVE OF THE FAMILY.]

ISAAC: *I'm all confused. I didn't get to ask him what we can do to help Dan leave the hospital.*

One of the problems of consulting with the family of a hospitalized patient is the power of the focus on the identified patient. The orientation of Minuchin's consultation was to normalize Dan and challenge the hospital. But the context of therapy made the family system almost invisible. Isaac was reestablishing the norm even as Minuchin walked out the door. Nevertheless, in the post-session discussion a plan was developed for coordinating treatment. The psychiatrist accepted the invitation to observe family sessions behind the one-way mirror, and the family therapist scheduled a visit to the hospital. Both sides appeared flexible in the working out of common goals.

Team Therapy: The Honeymoon

Interdisciplinary team therapy is at best like a marriage. Some issues are negotiated openly or resolved in a contract, even if the contract is to agree to disagree. Others lurk beneath the surface, with the constant potential for trouble. In this case, the marriage was to be stormy. The family therapist's report continues:

Right after the consultation, family therapy began on a once-a-week basis. The psychiatrist, who continued to treat Dan on an individual basis in the hospital ward, came to observe many of the family sessions and started to integrate a family perspective in her individual work with Dan. For my part, I went to visit Dan at the hospital and met with the many people involved in his treatment. I also asked a psychiatric colleague to work with me, in order to help retain a clear focus on the family and avoid overfocusing on Dan, which was what everyone else was doing.

The hospital's approach began to change. Instead of acquiescing in Dan's regressive demands, they began to expect him to function in the ward in a more adult fashion, to encourage his going out on family and social visits, and to push for an expeditious return to normal life outside the hospital, even if the pains should continue. It seemed that they had resolved the confusion with respect to Dan's diagnosis, and he was being handled as potentially normal. In line with this approach, the family sessions focused on the ways the family would respond to Dan's return home. In the course of working to change the relations within the family, the following therapeutic goals emerged:

1. *A reduction in the overinvolvement of the mother with Dan. We used a good cop/bad cop approach. My colleague was supportive and understanding of Dan's needs for special care, while I would force confrontations between Dan and his parents. Later I joined with the other children in their complaint about Dan's privileged position.*
2. *Strengthening the positive bond between Isaac and Dan. We encouraged Dan to turn to his father for help in matters that had previously been completely within the mother's area of responsibility.*
3. *Resolving conflicts between the parents and bringing them around to cooperating with each other without Dan's intervening and attempting to mediate between them.*

Standard fare in the family therapy menu. The only problem is that it isn't human. Language reifies the therapeutic encounter and, in making it graspable, robs it of complexity. Let us be active readers, aware of the Scylla of logic.

Within two months there was a marked change, of which Dan was a very sensitive barometer. He lost weight, complained much less frequently about his bladder pains, was taken off medication, and was clearly enjoying the freedom to leave the hospital on home visits. We were invited to participate in a case conference at the hospital, and it turned out to be very interesting. Each side presented its diagnostic understanding and its therapeutic approach using a different language. But the common concern for Dan's rehabilitation as a normal young man, along with his rapid improvement, both at the hospital and at home, helped us connect. Everyone was afraid of what might happen during a regression—specifically, that Dan might prefer the comfortable and by now familiar hospital environment to the difficult realities of the outside.

Such working together across institutional boundaries is unusual in the mental health sector in Israel, and probably in other countries as well. Hospitals have traditionally functioned within their own enclosed contexts, whereas family therapists have tended to shun the institutions, which seem uninterested in reforming their structures and implementing new directions. This institution was showing commendable flexibility by focusing on the family context. Instead of emphasizing pathology, it supported Dan's separation from the family and his active coping with the tasks of independent functioning. But this was to be a fair-weather friendship.

For a couple of months Dan remained an inpatient but was treated as normal. Then he was discharged. He continued with his individual therapist on an outpatient basis, and the whole family came in for family therapy. Shortly thereafter, he began part-time work and came to the day program only four hours a day.

When Dan returned home, the tension between the parents grew. Their disagreements concerning Dan spanned every aspect of his life, and their symmetrical escalations and power struggles transformed simple decisions into critical issues. High-pitched arguments poisoned the atmosphere at home, and threats of divorce abounded. Dan soon began again to complain of debilitating pains and of depression.

Shortly thereafter, Dan, with his parents' agreement, decided to return to the hospital. The hospital psychiatrist thought, just as we did, that recommitment was unnecessary and that the family should try coping with the crisis by leaning on its own resources. But the family knew well how to manipulate its way within the system, and when Dan, as the expert patient he was, went to the medical director talking about his worsening symptoms and suicidal ideations, he was readmitted without even a consultation with us. We were given to understand that this time he would be given "proper" medical care. Under the circumstances, we did not think it useful to continue with family therapy while Dan was hospitalized. In the final meeting with the parents after the rehospitalization, it was obvious that they were interested in discontinuing the stormy family sessions and calming the tensions. We made it clear that we could not take the responsibility for Dan's therapy, and we proposed to the parents that meanwhile they continue in marital therapy. This they rejected, and contact with the family was suspended.

It is interesting that the family therapist's indignant account poses her team as outside observers. She describes "stormy" family sessions as though failing to recognize that a therapeutic system includes a therapist's tactics, strategies, theories, or style. Would a "neutral," Milan-type family therapist have had stormy sessions at this point?

It is interesting too that she perceives herself as outflanked, rendered powerless, and left without options by her patient's clever manipulation. Actually there were many alternatives that could have been open to the therapists at this point, had they framed the process following Dan's discharge as a predictably difficult transitional period. They could have taken Haley's position,* creating a structure in which parents would postpone their conflicts and take a unified hierarchical stance in relation to the adolescent. The grim atmosphere could have been lightened by predicting and normalizing conflicts and temporary flare-ups of symptoms. It could have been detoxified with some humor at the absurdity of Dan's plea to get back into the hospital for another vacation from life or the salvation of his family, and at the ease with which the psychiatric system was manipulated. During the period of crisis, the family therapists could have assumed a more directive approach, providing the family with guidance in creating a more stable structure at home without putting the marriage under the microscope. Dan's stress was initially more visible to them than to the psychiatrist, but they could have consulted with the psychiatrist about using medication to support Dan's coping at this time.

Even the alternative of rehospitalization could have been detoxified. Brief rehospitalization could have been framed as a temporary respite from stress that would allow Dan and his family to explore more functional relationships and plan a second discharge better.

These are only some of the possibilities. The therapists could have thought of them, too, had they understood the increased stress not as failure but as process, and if the therapy had not been so tightly focused on the vicissitudes of the identified patient. But the therapists, naturally enough, were afraid that Dan's recommitment would be used by the "other side" to dismiss their work and their ideology. Their thinking became limited to ways of countering this possibility, and when it happened, they were helpless.

*Jay Haley, *Leaving Home: The Therapy of Disturbed Young People* (New York: McGraw-Hill, 1980).

Family Therapy: A Rescue Operation

It is always difficult for human beings to perceive themselves as parts of larger systems. But in collaborative work with the staff of a psychiatric hospital, a family therapist must recognize himself or herself as a cog in the wheels of family, hospital, and therapeutic systems. In this case the failure of a broader vision was most unfortunate. Possibilities that had emerged in the cooperation within a complex system were lost in what was perceived as a setback, and the divisive process that was then initiated would have momentous consequences on the couple's future and on Isaac's health, as well as on the therapist's thinking.

This time Dan did not like the way he was treated at the hospital at all. He was in a different ward, in which the ideology was not psychodynamic but instead a combination of organicist and milieu therapy with behaviorist techniques. He was put in seclusion because of his suicide threat. Various medications were tried with him: major tranquilizers, antidepressants, and lithium. They did not improve his condition. He was then put on a behavioral program that denied him nearly all freedom of movement and made any privilege conditional upon visible change in his behavior. Dan complained that he was heavily drugged and that he was suffering from serious side effects. Twice he ran away from the hospital and threatened suicide, but his parents brought him back. They felt desperate, and five months after his rehospitalization, they asked us for a consultation.

The meeting was very tense. The parents were disappointed with the hospital and very apprehensive that Dan was on the way to becoming a chronic mental patient. Yet when we probed to see if they could agree on any way to proceed together, they immediately began to blame each other again.

I therefore imposed the following conditions for the resumption of family therapy:

1. *The parents had to go to the hospital and take responsibility for Dan's discharge.*
2. *They were to commit themselves, together with Dan, to making all efforts to cope with the difficult period after discharge without readmitting Dan to the hospital. The parents were to be responsible for watching over Dan very closely during this initial period, to make sure that he did no bodily harm to himself.*
3. *They were all to make a commitment to family therapy combined with individual therapy with Dan. We would be in charge of their case, and a psychiatrist from my clinic would monitor Dan's medication.*

Miriam's strategy was modeled on Haley's. She was clear and firm, and her response was certainly reassuring for Dan and his family. It was obvious, however, that this time family therapy had to triumph. Having thrown down the gauntlet, the family therapist was caught in the absolute necessity to prove her prowess. Dan's success would be validation; rehospitalization would be defeat. Unwittingly, a family perspective was replaced by an individual rescue orientation.

The first family session took place a week after Dan had been discharged from the hospital. Dan had given the family a very hard time for the first five days, but at the meeting it was obvious that he had undergone a marked change. Dan was now highly motivated to rehabilitate himself quickly and asked that individual sessions be held with him, parallel with the family sessions.

The main difficulty continued to be the parental power struggle over Dan. We asked Sara to let Dan and Isaac deal directly with each other, even when she disapproved, and placed the responsibility for Dan's rehabilitation on Isaac's shoulders. Sara accepted the new arrangement, but reluctantly. Isaac was visibly pleased with it. He changed his work schedule in order to have time for "the project" and began mobilizing himself to cope with his assignment.

The technique of putting the disengaged father in charge is frequently used with families with young children. Haley described it as one of the steps in a process, to be followed by a focus on the parents and then on the couple.* But Haley later questioned the need for this sequence, suggesting that if the disengaged parent is put in charge, one may find oneself in the midst of a spouse conflict, while if the overinvolved parent is put in charge, the following stage in the process will probably be a parental conflict.†

In any case, Haley was describing the stages of a process whose goal was family change. Here the goal of resolving parental difficulties was abandoned. At this phase, probably all the therapist's energy was invested in making progress with Dan. There was no overall strategy for family transformation, and expectations for changing the couple were radically lowered. This might have been accommodation to the rigidity in the parental relations, but certainly it was also a change in the therapeutic perspective and the therapeutic goal. In a strange way, family therapy took on the function of the hospital and was submerged under the preoccupation with Dan's individual adjustment.

Isaac and Dan began spending many hours together taking care of Dan's affairs: looking for possible places of employment, settling Dan's status vis-à-vis the army, planning and registering for university studies the following year, learning to drive, and so on. Isaac, who could easily use his many connections to organize Dan's life, tended to be overcontrolling and authoritative, and sometimes they had intense fights. My job was to keep Sara out of it and help them negotiate. After two months, Dan was working successfully as a private swimming teacher and as instructor in a ceramics group and was renewing his previous social contacts. Throughout this period, I kept emphasizing what an important contribution Sara was making to the positive changes in Dan. Sara's

*Jay Haley, *Leaving Home: The Therapy of Disturbed Young People* (New York: McGraw-Hill, 1980).

†Personal communication.

bond with Dan became less intensive, and he on his part stopped seeking to be treated as a baby.

Clearly, even though the focus was on Dan, therapy was producing positive changes. In a very short time, a hospitalized patient became a functioning young man. Nevertheless, the systems therapist might question the therapist's induction into the old family pattern: the use of Dan as a regulator of distance between Sara and Isaac.

By the way, it is important when looking at Dan's progress not to forget the family's social context. Dan was fortunate in this respect. His rapid and smooth rehabilitation after being in the hospital for almost a year owed much to a massive investment of time, financial resources, and an important factor in Israeli society colloquially termed "protection"—the use of personal connections to cut through bureaucratic formalities. In a small country with a large bureaucracy, this factor can substantially increase the available social support and decrease stress. In that sense, Isaac could be a very protective father.

Six months after the end of the second hospitalization, Dan began to look for separate housing. The move was made in a cooperative way. He continued to be dependent on his parents financially, but in regard to his daily work, his social functioning, and his daily care for himself, he had achieved the degree of independence appropriate to his age.

At this stage Isaac was decreasing his participation in therapy and becoming increasingly involved in his work. His interest in therapy was on the wane, and at times he was petulant and resistant, as if he needed to reassert his position of authority in the family after his task with Dan became less necessary. The family meetings were becoming difficult, because the marital tensions were beginning to surface again. The children's condition improved, but this was only eight months after Dan's last hospitalization. I was apprehensive that the opening up and repeated staging of the marital conflict in front of Dan would destabilize his functioning, and so I increased the interval between family sessions, moving toward termination.

During this period Sara asked for individual sessions. She described an overwhelming feeling of emptiness and wished to expand her rather constricted life. She began to look for a job and signed up for a course in computers. Her social circle grew, and she began to attend social functions without Isaac. Before long, she found a good job and plunged into it energetically. Isaac began to feel the change and found it particularly difficult to remain at home by himself in the evenings when Sara was out studying. At about this time, his business affairs took a turn for the worse, and he became depressed. However, he did not feel that therapy was for him. I arranged for an individual session with Isaac, but he was reticent and asked how long the therapy was going to take. When a short while later I suggested suspending the family work and continuing only with Dan, there was a sign of relief in their agreement. Overall, we ended this part of therapy with a sense of having made significant gains.

Individual therapy with Dan continued weekly for about another six months and finally was reduced to an average of one meeting per month. Dan completed his first year in the university successfully and decided to major in psychology. It seemed to me that he was almost ready for therapy to terminate.

The description of Dan's individual therapy has been drastically edited, but even so, the narrative retains the mark of a close therapeutic relationship in a process that was clearly rewarding for the therapist and growth-encouraging for Dan. By any standards, one should consider it a success when a therapeutic process ends with a hospitalized adolescent once diagnosed as schizophrenic preparing himself to return to the psychiatric ward someday as a psychologist. But one of the terrible burdens of systems thinkers is that they are condemned to look forever at larger contexts.

The next year was hard on the family. Isaac was worried,

preoccupied with the economic problems of Israel and their effects on his industry. He suffered an exacerbation of his ulcer, was hospitalized, and underwent surgery. Half a year later, the couple returned to the therapist, requesting couple therapy. They were considering separation. Several days before the scheduled meeting, Isaac had a heart attack. He later underwent open heart surgery, after which he only slowly resumed part-time work and remained rather depressed.

A Follow-Up Visit with Sara and the Children: "Is Illness a Language in This Family?"

Dan's treatment was successful. But something went wrong if Isaac had to pay for his son's freedom with two operations and lasting depression. Was the therapist a participant, and should she feel responsible? Two and a half years after the consultation, when Minuchin was again in Israel, she discussed her concern for Isaac with Minuchin and arranged for another session.

The family willingly accepted the invitation to a follow-up session, but a few weeks before Minuchin's arrival, Isaac called to say that he would be abroad when Minuchin was due to arrive. The session therefore included Sara and the three children, all of whom appeared markedly changed. Sara looked elegant. She appeared harried and tense, but there was a vitality to her tension that suggested accomplishment rather than fear. Sam was now a robust six-footer with a gentle smile. Rachel was a flower about to blossom. But the most striking change was in Dan. He looked healthy, his movements were confident, and his eyes radiated life.

The session began with recollections of the previous consultation. Dan described how Minuchin provoked him by suggesting he stay at the hospital one, two, or perhaps even three years, and Sara added her recollection of how Minuchin pushed the psychiatrist, "implying that all the hospital cared about was having its beds occupied." They described major changes in their family. A closeness had developed between Dan and his father. Where Sara used to intervene, she now knew that Dan could handle conflicts with Isaac. The reorganization also benefited relations between Sam and Sara. He was no longer Isaac's protégé, and when he needed parental help he turned to her just as frequently as to his father. The brothers had for the first time become friends. Parental relations did not seem to have changed, however, even though they no longer fought on account of Dan. It was a sore point, and after obtaining Sara's permission, Minuchin began to explore it by asking the children's views.

SAM: *I don't see much change in the relationship between my parents. Most of the fights in the family used to be between Dan and Dad, and Mom stepped out of their problems. That's the main change that I see.*

MINUCHIN: *Rachel, what do you think?*

RACHEL: *I agree with Sam. Most of the fights between my parents were about Dan, and now they fight with him directly.*

MINUCHIN: *How do you see it, Dan?*

DAN: *Over the years I've seen many conflicts between my parents, and I always tried to help them. I think it's easier for any two people to fight over a third person than to fight just by themselves. That's why I put myself between them. Sometimes it was a conscious decision on my part, but many times I did it unconsciously. I think I felt the need to create problems all through the years.*

MINUCHIN: *You mean to solve problems?*

DAN: *To create and to solve them. I felt that the problems I created were helping my parents in some sort of a way.*

MINUCHIN: *That's interesting. You were like a lightning rod that protects the home by attracting the electricity in the storm.*

DAN: *That's why the balloon popped when it was time for me to go to the army. I was afraid Mom would leave the family, and that's why I chose to go to the hospital rather than going away to the army for three years.*

One of the ways therapy works is by providing family members with language and stories that give new meaning to their behavior. Dan had appropriated the therapist's language and used it as personal insights to support a competent and central position in the family. His reconstructed history appeared now as part of a controlled plan to heal the family.

It is interesting that two and a half years earlier he had used the language of intrapsychic psychology and before that the language of bodily pains. He had had good training in these languages in his family and in various schools of therapy. Now his skill was being used not for gaining entrance to the psychiatric institution but for leaving institutional life in favor of new directions.

MINUCHIN: *That's a fascinating idea, Dan. Did you learn it in therapy, or did it come to you naturally?*
DAN: *First the idea came to me, and then I discussed it in my therapy. I realized also that I did it as a kid. Once I even had an operation on my appendix that didn't have to be done.*
MINUCHIN: *It's extraordinary what children will do for their parents. Do you help them too, Sam?*
SAM: *I do try to help, but not like Dan. When I think something is not right, I come right out and say so.*
MINUCHIN: *Give me an example.*
SAM: *For instance, once we were someplace, and Rachel wanted to stay over at her friend's house. Daddy wanted her to come home, and I told him I thought it would be good for her to stay over, but he got angry and shouted. In the end he took her home. I didn't succeed, and I also got into a quarrel with my father. But I believe that if something is not right I have to say what I think.*
DAN: *I think that helping is a main motif in our family. Rachel, for example, is sick for a day or two nearly every*

other week. If someone wants to help in this family, all he needs to do is say he's not feeling well.

SAM: *No, I think Rachel just doesn't like school and would rather stay home.*

MINUCHIN: *Rachel, is this true?*

RACHEL: *Not recently, but I used to stay home a lot.*

MINUCHIN: *What do you do when you don't want to go to school? You tell your mom that you don't feel well?*

RACHEL: *Yes.*

MINUCHIN: *And what does she say?*

RACHEL: *It depends. If I have a temperature she will leave me be.*

MINUCHIN: *Do you know how to give yourself a temperature?*

RACHEL: *[smiling] I can't create temperature in my body, but I know how to make the thermometer show it.*

MINUCHIN: *Can you do other things? Like produce a stomachache?*

RACHEL: *[dramatically] I always have them!*

MINUCHIN: *Is illness a language in this family?*

DAN: *Sam has migraines a lot.*

MINUCHIN: *Is that true?*

SAM: *Yes.*

DAN: *My father was also sick a lot—in the last year he had two operations. I remember when I was young he used to stay in bed a lot. He used to complain about his pain, and perhaps that was his way of asking for attention.*

The information elicited is typical of many psychosomatic families that we have seen.* These are usually very nice families with very low tolerance for conflict, in which family loyalty and protection for family members are overriding characteristics. In this family, at least four members exhibited psychosomatic symptoms. The fact that Dan was on the way to a diagnosis of schizophrenia illustrates the alarming misuse of

*Salvador Minuchin, Bernice L. Rosman, and Lester Baker, *Psychosomatic Families: Anorexia Nervosa in Context* (Cambridge, MA: Harvard University Press, 1978).

this diagnosis not only in Israel but all over the psychiatric world.

MINUCHIN: *Sam, what are you making faces about? Do you disagree with Dan?*
SAM: *Oh, come on. He's as bad as a psychologist. Can't I have migraines? So my father had a heart attack—every day millions of people have heart attacks. Can't he have a heart attack like a normal person?*
MINUCHIN: *Were you affected by the conflicts between your parents?*
SAM: *Well, yes, but I didn't interfere like Dan.*
DAN: *Most of the conflicts between my parents were not so direct. You needed to be a very sensitive person to see it—their faces, and the words they used. I felt it, but I don't know if Sam was so sensitive.*
SAM: *I also saw what Dan has just been talking about.*
MINUCHIN: *Watching your parents became part of your growing up, but you each responded very differently.*
SAM: *I couldn't interfere if they made faces or something. Only if they fought.*

In a family that hides marital conflicts with good manners and triangulation of the children, the latter learn to fine-tune to subtleties and nuance. This heightened alertness can enhance sensitivity to psychological issues; Dan will use this skill in his career in psychology.

MINUCHIN: *You developed your own direct style of reacting, which I think is healthier than Dan's.*
DAN: *Well, I think Sam's reactions to the family cost him a lot, not only in pain but also in the effect on his schoolwork.*
MINUCHIN: *It's an interesting theory that Dan has. He says it is necessary to sacrifice a part of one's self. It's as if part of growing up is that children must sacrifice themselves to save the parents.*

Focusing on the family demand for loyalty provided the children a cognitive framing with which to look at the relationship between their individual behavior and the family. New meanings were added as the focus shifted from the individual to the social. Minuchin hoped to offer the children a drawbridge by which to leave the family castle.

Minuchin then complimented the children on the change in them and asked them to leave in order to talk with Sara alone. Sara was astounded at the children's stories. She said she had never realized how concerned and protective they felt toward Isaac and her.

MINUCHIN: *How is Isaac?*

SARA: *The situation at home has been very difficult. Isaac stays at home most of the time and feels depressed. He works very little.*

MINUCHIN: *What is happening with his work?*

SARA: *He's really lost interest in it. He only works periodically, and our financial situation has gotten very bad.*

MINUCHIN: *What about you? Do you work?*

SARA: *Yes. This is how I stay sane.*

MINUCHIN: *You feel better at work.*

SARA: *I feel more alive when I'm out of the house. I'm appreciated, and I have a good position at work. I also have good friends.*

MINUCHIN: *Does Isaac have any kind of social activity?*

SARA: *He goes out very little, and only with me.*

MINUCHIN: *Clearly he is under stress. What have you done to help him?*

SARA: *I can't help him, because he rejects my help, and he doesn't want to help himself. There are many complications after the operation, but he's not looking after himself. The way he smokes he's killing himself, and the doctors tell him just that. He acts like an invalid, and he tells me I don't take care of him. But physically, he could function much more than he does now.*

MINUCHIN: *When he talks to you like this, is that his way of asking you for nurturance?*

SARA: *[tearfully] I don't think so. Whenever I try my best to do something for him, he rejects it. He says he doesn't want anything.*

Minuchin was concerned about Isaac, whose behavior, as Sara described it, seemed suicidal. He felt somehow responsible for the family's present crisis, and he remembered Isaac with warmth. In the previous session they had established a good rapport, and he thought that he might be able to help him. He therefore postponed his departure to be able to interview Isaac.

One ingredient of therapy rarely included in therapeutic analysis is the therapist's feelings and thoughts. Minuchin's were particularly pertinent in this situation. His father had died of a heart attack many years before, and his mother had died recently. He was still carrying many powerful images of their farewell. Isaac's plight activated in him many of these feelings, and fantasies of rescuing him were undoubtedly part of his wishful thinking and guilt for not having saved his mother.

A Follow-Up Visit with Isaac and Sara: "Death Is around the Corner"

Isaac had been abroad; he came to the session from the airport. He had a slight fever, and his face was like a drab mask. He slumped in his chair and spoke in a rather low and monotonous tone of voice.

Minuchin began the session slowly by joining with Isaac. Isaac proudly described the significant gains made by Dan and the way he and Dan had been able to connect. He explained, "After I saw you pushing him, I told him he was not sick, and now we'd go ahead, step by step. I expected him to go back to normal, and he responded." His face lit up as he described how Dan came to visit him at the hospital and behaved like an adult son, showing his concern for him and trying to make his hospital stay more comfortable.

When Minuchin began exploring the marital relationship, Isaac and Sara steered him to their traditional path, expressing conflicts in the arena of childrearing. Now that Dan was out of the home, they provided an example of tensions centered around Sam.

ISAAC: *I'll give you an example. What Sara does with Sam is like what she always did with Dan. But I've given up arguing with her, and let things pass. I walked into the kitchen and found a torn passport on the table. It belongs to Sam, and I told him three months ago not to leave it in the car. I scolded him, and right in the middle of our argument Sara piped up and said to Sam that he did a nice job cleaning the aviary. I knew she was trying to pull me away from Sam. It's not Sara who's going to pay for Sam's irresponsibility, but Sam is bright, and he used her intervention to escape. I began to say something to her, but then I thought, What's the use? So I switched off.*

MINUCHIN: *[to Sara] And how do you see that issue?*

SARA: *The argument was over when I came into the kitchen. Sam had already told Isaac that it was an outdated passport and he needed a new one anyway. Isaac had finished shouting and screaming, and I noticed that Sam had cleaned the cages. So I made my remark and did not even think about it afterwards.*

ISAAC: *It's not such a big deal for Sam to clean up the aviary. It's his responsibility anyway. But I was in the middle of an argument with him. Sam should have been more careful with his passport. I told him before that it could be renewed.*

MINUCHIN: *I understand what happened between you and Sam. What happened between you and Sara?*

ISAAC: *What she did was sort of sliding in something to make things sweet.*

MINUCHIN: *Sara?*

SARA: *He still expects me to interfere between him and the children. As much as I have changed, he relates to me in the same old way.*

Nothing had changed here. The two contenders were still searching for the soft underbelly. Neither one believed in the possibility of coming together, and neither was really trying. It was an impossible situation, and the need for a third person to help them make the necessary joint decisions and to deflect some of the tensions was still there. Dan had left, so Sam, his father's old pal, had joined Sara in the game of actualizing his father's authoritarian stance. Isaac could only attack, automatically maintaining an isolation that he did not like.

It was more and more apparent that the marital schism and the current way of handling it might be having a devastating effect on Isaac's health. Isaac was sitting as if in pain; his breathing was shallow, and his face was contorted.

MINUCHIN: *Let me ask you something else. I see you're feeling uncomfortable.*

ISAAC: *Yes. After a year in bed and two operations, I feel worse than ever. Everything is bad—my heart, my digestion, everything. Even on my last trip I got sick overseas. Wherever I go, whatever I do turns into shit. I used to be a fighter, the strong one. Now nothing's worth the battle.*

MINUCHIN: *Could you accept help from Sara?*

ISAAC: *Could I—? Look, I'm begging for anybody's help. Let me tell you about the cigarettes, for instance. I'm a heavy smoker, and I want to give up smoking. The doctors told me if I go back to my normal two packs I'll be dead in two years. But it's a helluva battle. Right now I feel I'm bursting and have to have a cigarette. I tried to explain it to Sara, but she says, "If you smoke, don't come back." She starts an angry chain reaction between us.*

MINUCHIN: *What would you need from her?*

ISAAC: *At the moment I don't know.*

MINUCHIN: *What do you think he needs, Sara?*

SARA: *I don't know.*

MINUCHIN: *Apparently he needs some care. People like him don't know how to accept tenderness, and they have lots of difficulty in being weak.*

SARA: *That's very true of him. He just does not accept tenderness from me, and he shows no need for it.*

ISAAC: *That's not true!*

SARA: *When he's not feeling well, and that's a great percentage of the time, he likes to be left alone.*

ISAAC: *Look, when I feel sick, like I do now, I don't want to sit and make conversation. [to Minuchin] My stomach is upset, I have a pain in my shoulder, and I can't breathe. Every time I pick a leg up it's like lifting lead. I have a high temperature, and I only came here because of you. Damn it, Sara, am I abnormal to want to be left alone? Let me go to bed tonight and knock myself out with something strong.*

At this point it is easy to see Isaac and Sara as two distinct figures, frozen by their own defenses and hidden vulnerabilities, and to lose sight of the transactional dynamic sustaining their immobility. Sara certainly knew how to be supportive, while Isaac could accept and appreciate nurturance when it came from others. But their relationship was not providing for Isaac's immediate needs. At this stage, it was necessary to focus on his suicidal behavior and support him by supplementing the system with additional resources.

MINUCHIN: *But there is something else, Isaac. You are depressed, and you need help to move out of your depression.*

ISAAC: *I know. I've seen it in friends who had heart surgery. I was close to death.*

MINUCHIN: *So you know that death is around the corner, and in that kind of situation one needs to become wise. When my father died a number of years ago, and when my mother died, I rearranged my priorities in life. Their deaths made me realize that I am also going to die and that avoiding this fact is crazy. For a short while I became wiser, but after a few months I went back to believing I'm immortal. You're looking death in the face. Are you any wiser now?*

ISAAC: *It's funny, but you know, even before Dan's sickness I felt that I wanted more out of life with my family. I rear-*

ranged my work so that I could be with them more. Then Dan got sick, and as he got better I got sick.

MINUCHIN: *I am concerned about you. I'll make it short, because I want you to get to bed. You're a mess, and unless you get help you will die. I think you have got to rearrange your priorities. You haven't realized that you are playing with death. Let me tell you straight that I think you're suicidal.*

ISAAC: *No!*

MINUCHIN: *It's the worst type of suicide—people who won't realize that they are killing themselves. And you'll keep right on, unless you realize what you're doing to yourself. When you rearranged your business, you lost something very important in your life. You are a person who feels strong and good when he struggles for success. That's how you grew, but at this point you don't have anything to struggle for, and you sink. I want to advise you to find yourself a therapist who has been in contact with death. Somebody who is not afraid to talk straight to you. Don't go with Sara. Start by yourself, and after a while [to Sara] you join him. Let me tell you, Isaac, that I made a special effort to see you before I leave because I wanted to say to you straight the things that I am saying now. I think that you need special help for the destructive way in which you manipulate your body.*

Four Years after the Initial Consultation with Minuchin

Minuchin's follow-up session with the couple was not the stuff of detached scientific observation, but it apparently opened up new possibilities for Isaac. He stopped smoking immediately. A treatment plan was laid out for the couple and for individual therapy for Isaac. Isaac refused both but plunged himself into preparations for Rachel's Bat Mitzvah. The project put him in high spirits, and at the same time some successful business deals went through.

The Bat Mitzvah was later described by Sara as a farewell; afterwards Isaac proposed that they separate. His financial offer was generous and carefully worked out. Sara accepted, and shortly thereafter Isaac moved out. The psychosomatic nature of many of his symptoms was then clearly demonstrated: they promptly disappeared.

Two months after the separation, Isaac and Sara had a joint session with the therapist. They appeared to be on a "separation honeymoon," feeling that the decision was correct and had even improved their relationship. Isaac was involved in his work, but he had also rejuvenated his social life. Sara was just as satisfied with her private life and feeling competent about her ways of dealing with the children. They had just decided to go ahead with divorce proceedings and asked the therapist to function as their common advisor concerning the children. Over the next eight months, they met irregularly whenever Isaac and Sara felt the need. They were worried that their separation might affect Sam, who was in basic training at the time, or lead to some regression with Dan.

The course of divorce counseling was relatively uneventful. Isaac occasionally complained that Sara's high involvement with her work and social activities did not leave her enough time for thirteen-year-old Rachel. But Sara knew how to draw her boundaries and did not become angry with Isaac as quickly as before. She was dating, and even after the initial high began to fade, she felt much more satisfied with her present life. At this period Isaac was feeling somewhat depressed, although he continued to be active on all fronts. Less than a year after the separation, he moved in with a woman he had been dating steadily. His spirits are high now, and he maintains a warm relationship with the children.

Sam's reaction to the separation was the strongest, probably exacerbated by the stress of his initiation into army life. Four times he sneaked out of camp to visit his mother, risking disciplinary action if caught. He complained of frequent headaches and inability to concentrate. This time it was interesting to observe Sara taking a tough approach toward Sam's complaining. She let him know that she did not need him at home. Isaac was the supportive one, and he and Sam developed a man-to-man bond based on their common army experience. Sam's morale went up markedly after basic training, and he has recently been promoted to corporal.

Rachel, like the other children, accepted the separation with neither surprise nor any overt opposition. She is on good terms with both parents, but her active social life is taking her more and more out of the home. Her school work continues to be below average, but she is careful not to fail. There are no missed days because of stomachaches or other such excuses.

Several months before the separation, Dan transferred to an out-of-town university, which accepted him into its psychology program. When his parents separated, he worried about Sam and encouraged him to stick it out in the army. In one of their talks, he shared with Sam some of the difficulties he experienced in having missed army service for psychiatric reasons and told him of his plans to reapply after college. As it happened, Dan got a job in an agency that works with delinquent adolescents. Though he was successful in his job, he was dismissed a few months later when the administration found out about his psychiatric past. With the backing of his father Dan threatened to take legal action against the agency and promptly thereafter was rehired.

Overall Dan managed to stay relatively distant from the family. He continued to visit the therapist once a month, mostly working on individual issues and ways of maintaining a separate relationship with each of his parents. He now has a steady girlfriend. The therapist recently realized that she has become a part of his life (and he of hers) and that it is time to initiate termination.

Reflections

By all accounts this was a successful case. Five years after the initial consultation, Dan is successfully finishing his bachelor of arts degree. Sara and Isaac have each remarried and collaborate well as parents. They are enthusiastic about family therapy and are grateful to Minuchin for his consultations. The therapists learned from the experience, and the consultants are writing a book about consultation. It is indeed time to close the story with the time-honored "And they lived happily ever after."

Why then the hesitation, the uneasy feelings about the unfolding of this therapy? The case eludes easy handling. Given that the written description of events in therapy never captures the complexity of the experience, there are still too many questions. We don't know why therapy was successful. We could construct a coherent and convincing narrative—in fact, we are very good at it. But it would not convince us.

Was this in fact a case of family therapy? Certainly Dan went through a variety of individual experiences—hospitalization, drug therapy, behavior therapy, regressive therapy, and individual therapy—as well as family therapy. And the regressive therapy he had in the hospital was without doubt a family intervention. But since the therapist was not thinking in terms of family but of individual regression, can we arbitrarily call it family intervention? Shouldn't the therapist's focus label the therapy? But if that is so, should individual therapy done by the family therapist be called family therapy?

We think that Minuchin's consultations were instrumental in the successful outcome. The first certainly changed the direction of Dan's therapy in the hospital, and the second startled Isaac enough to make him stop smoking and pay attention to his destructive somatic responses. But inasmuch as his focus was for the most part on certain family members, were his consultations the structural family therapy identified with his name?

Minuchin's playful teasing of Dan and the hospital psychiatrist bears little resemblance to some of his well-known confrontations. The session looks more like a Whitaker session. The concentration is on Dan, the consultant is central, there is no enactment, and the tool of therapeutic challenge is the absurd. The structural elements reside in the boundary making between patient and hospital and in the use of a developmental frame to normalize the identified patient's experience. In the second consultation, there is an exploration of the children's detouring triangulation of parental conflict, as described in psychosomatic families. But which was significant, his structural thinking or his absurd behavior? We think both.

In his consultation with Isaac and Sara, Minuchin, in mourning his mother's death, indulged in a magical rescue operation that was clearly helpful to Isaac and Sara. The intensity of the session and of the relationship with Isaac increased the distance between the spouses, braking the mutual blame that united them and making Isaac responsible for his suicidal behavior. This approach was clearly structural, but there is no doubt that Minuchin's own emotional state brought this structuralist closer to the work of Norman Paul and Monica McGoldrick in their involvement with grief and mourning. In Miriam's description of the family therapy, one can detect the influence of Minuchin and the structural approach, Haley and his strategies in *Leaving Home,* and Peggy Papp and her colleagues in the organization of the two therapists with different function, one supporting continuity and the other encouraging change. Seeing the sessions instead of reading the narrative would, we are sure, reveal the influence of many others—Freud and Bateson, for example, and certainly the feminist movement.

What, then, is the message? Beware of well-constructed stories. They are useful in theory construction and necessary in the development of the soft science of therapy. They are important to each beginning therapist who needs guidelines and signposts. But teaching, like the goddess Siva, must destroy as it constructs. When coherence develops, when you know where you're going—in short, just as it's getting good—that's when you must stop and realize that you may be pulling too far in one direction or another.

4

Families Caught between Hospital and Community

CASE HISTORIES are usually recounted in a condensed, professionally distant manner, in terms of the "facts" of mental illness and premorbid pathology. As such they do not usually create much emotional resonance in the reader. These cases end up forgotten, filed away, like Yoav and the many other institutionalized patients whose road to chronicity is documented in the records of most clinics and hospitals. Obviously our point of view is different. Our analyses of the cases of Yoav and Dan were written with an attempt to show that a different understanding of such cases is possible, that on a personal level these families can be approached with compassion for their tragedy and an emphasis on the similarities instead of the differences between "them and us." On a more general level, we have tried to show that from these life stories we can learn about how families are affected by their encounter with therapists and hospitals, especially about the effects of the biases and failures that occur in the practice of individual and family therapy alike, in private practice as well as in public institutions.

In this chapter, we will look more closely at what we can learn from therapy failures, in particular at the relationship between common types of failure and the organization of our hospital and community mental health facilities. Such failures have become built into the system, because the therapeutic package that is offered does not take into account the malevolent influence that some families experience in therapy, beginning when they reach out for help during a crisis and continuing to the end point in chronic disability.

Since 1952, when Eysenck published his evaluation of the effects of psychotherapy,* it has been well known that a significant proportion of those who come to therapy do not improve. Furthermore, many of those who do improve are actually affected by extra-therapeutic factors and would have been changed without therapy at all. More than thirty-five years later, we have many new tools, a multitude of different schools, and more refined methods of research with which to study not just the end results but also the process of our cures. Paradoxically, we have learned to appreciate the impact of the factors of therapy that are not specific to any one school; many patients in different forms of therapy are helped by these factors, although the duration of their therapy and their understanding of the cure will vary markedly. In this respect the "dodo bird verdict" is applicable to psychotherapy: "Everybody has won, and all must have prizes."† But there are other patients who are better helped by specific types of interventions. When there is a mismatch between their needs and the therapy they undergo, they may fail in therapy. The effects of such a failure are described by one mother:

> I think we all felt such a tremendous let-down that things could have happened but didn't. . . . our inadequacies were exaggerated as a consequence of that single session. Although we probably would have liked to blame the therapist and the Center, we really could not. After all, they were the experts and we were the failure.‡

*H. J. Eysenck, "The Effects of Psychotherapy: An Evaluation," *Journal of Consulting Psychology* 16 (1952): 319–24.

†L. Luborsky, B. Singer, and L. Luborsky, "Comparative Studies of Psychotherapies," *Archives of General Psychiatry* 32 (1975): 995–1008.

‡Anonymous with S. B. Coleman, "We Were Somebody's Failure," in S. B. Coleman, (ed.), *Failures in Family Therapy* (New York: Guilford Press, 1985), pp. 274–83.

This mother makes a simple point about treatment failures that has been surprisingly lacking in most studies of therapy: Failure is much more than is suggested by the research category of "no improvement"; it is also painful and damaging. But even though we know that there are patients who are adversely affected by their experience in therapy, we do not know much about the nonspecific and specific factors that contribute to this deterioration.

If the effects of failure described by this mother were felt after one unsuccessful encounter with a therapist, how much greater must be the effect on those patients who fail in many sessions and with many therapists, patients who have tried many approaches and failed to respond to a wide range of interventions, whether biological, individual, or family-oriented. We have become well aware of the cost and the inefficiency of our current system. Even so, it takes a mental jump to admit that the help of mental health agents has become a part of the pathology and that the field of therapy itself is continuing to apply methods that have been shown to fail and to damage.

Yoav is not an extreme example of those patients whose cases demonstrate the deterioration that takes place between families and therapists within the context of therapeutic institutions. After six years in institutions, Yoav still leads a semi-institutional life and at best can be expected to need a protected environment for a few more years. More than twenty professional therapists have been involved in this case, and if one also counts paraprofessionals, the number of helpers swells to well over fifty. Most of them were dedicated, and a few contributed substantially to his therapy. Obviously, Yoav's deterioration cannot be attributed to one therapist's mistake, to lack of trying, or to a bias of a particular theory. But neither is it reasonable to attribute the thickness of his folder to his illness, his personality, or his family.

To what degree is Yoav's thick folder a product of his coming of age within the hospital context? There is an extensive literature documenting the ill effects of hospitalization and criticizing the paradigm of mental illness. Let us draw on these critiques in order to delineate the iatrogenic processes that are initiated once a patient like Yoav is labeled and confined. These processes affect patients and their families on many different levels, but in the end it is their combined impact that we need to appreciate.

The Iatrogenic Effects of Hospitalization

Effects at the Societal Level

When we look at diagnosis as a culture-bound act, it appears that one of its main social functions is the labeling of deviancy. Labeling initiates the patient into a new role. The first hospitalization in particular has the dramatic characteristics of a rite of passage. It creates a discontinuity with the life before and thereby announces the appearance of a new developmental stage. Subsequently, there is a change of social expectations of the patient as well as a change in the way people behave with him or her. Possibilities for finding work and being reintegrated into normal social life may be curtailed. At the same time there is a greater social acceptance of low levels of functioning, and patients may become eligible for disability benefits. The act of confining a patient retains many of its historical associations with punishment, exclusion, and moral condemnation. These oppressive attitudes produce their own problems for patients and families.

Once a patient has been labeled, the societal reaction stabilizes the deviancy and launches the offenders on their careers as mental patients. One does not need to subscribe to this theory in its entirety in order to appreciate the evidence concerning the impact of the stigma of mental illness.* Professionals who wish to help people like Joyce Brown by hospitalizing them may well hesitate.

> Sometimes I ain't so sure who's got ere a right to say when a man is crazy and when he ain't. Sometimes I think it ain't none of us pure crazy and ain't none of us pure sane until the balance of us talks him that-a-way. It's like it ain't so

*T. J. Scheff, *Being Mentally Ill* (Chicago: Aldine, 1966).

> much what a fellow does, but it's the way the majority of folks is looking at him when he does it.*

The social effects of being stigmatized with mental illness are reinforced by a degradation in patients' civil rights that affects their social adjustment well past their release from the hospital. In Israel, for instance, there is a centralized psychiatric case register that records all inpatient commitments. The privacy of mental patients is poorly protected, and various social agencies have access to these records. Once patients coming for treatment are registered, they never lose their status as mental patients. They will be discriminated against when they try to get jobs as soldier, driver, or security guard, even though a careful assessment of their files often shows that exclusion from these roles is unjustified. M. Rahav, who examined these social practices in Israel, concluded:

> the present use of psychiatric records is not warranted by any empirical evidence, and stems from stereotypes of the mentally ill as dangerous and unpredictable. Continuing this practice discriminates against the mentally ill, prevents them from full, total recovery, and undermines the entire ethic on which psychiatry is based.†

Dan's case provides many illustrations of the powerful effect that social reactions have on patients. While Minuchin could normalize Dan's symptoms and parody the accommodation of the environment to them, the effectiveness of his consultation depended on whether it led to a different environmental response to Dan. When the hospital adopted Minuchin's model, it construed Dan's symptoms as an inappropriate attempt to use its services in order to avoid coping with problems of leaving home. The institutional response to Dan was then based on the assumption that he was "normal," and consequently he was discharged.

*William Faulkner, *As I Lay Dying* (New York, Modern Library, 1957), p. 510.

†M. Rahav, "Labeling the Mentally Ill Through Psychiatric Records: The Israeli Case," *Israel Journal of Psychiatry and Related Sciences,* 22(3) (1985): 221–31.

But when the hospital, faced with a new crisis, reapplied the traditional medical model, Dan was rehospitalized for more than half a year. He would have stayed longer had there not been an intervention by the family therapist. At that point, when the family was organized to respond differently to Dan's deviant behavior, Dan left the territory of the mentally ill, and not long afterwards, he entered the university.

One decision to hospitalize was not erased by another decision to discharge, however. The consequences of hospitalization were continuous and manifold, and part of the outpatient therapy had to deal with them. In fact, had Dan not had a powerful and affluent family behind him, he would have found it much more difficult to get a job, get settled on his own, and deal with all the discriminatory practices that in Israel are related to being rejected by the draft for psychiatric reasons.

Effects at the Hospital Level

In order to study the hospital milieu, the anthropologist E. Goffman assumed the role of an assistant athletic director in a large federal hospital in the United States. Out of this experience he developed his characterization of the hospital as a "total institution," a place where people are segregated from society for a considerable period of time. It operates as a prison in that it organizes in an authoritarian manner an ordered life for its inmates. Goffman* re-created the experience of patients as they go through the many rituals and routines that have become integrated into the daily functioning of the mental hospital. His essays expose the degradation of patients and the means employed by the staff to socialize newcomers in the career of mental patients. Although they were written twenty years before Yoav began his hospital treatment and in a different country, they depict institutional experiences surprisingly close to his, including the violent outbursts that almost led to his lobotomy. In Goffman's words, "If you rob people of all customary means of

*E. Goffman, *Asylums: Essays on the Social Situation of Mental Patients and Other Inmates* (Harmondsworth, England: Pelican, 1968).

expressing anger and alienation and put them in a place where they have never had better reason for these feelings, then the natural recourse will be to seize upon what remains."* Only by developing blinders with respect to the institutional context could Yoav's helpers narrow their thinking to the terms of inner illness, as though his anger could be disconnected from the experience of being subjected to various treatments against his will, of being turned into a forced patient even though he had entered Beta Hospital freely, and of being tied and handled like a wild beast.

Regardless of the type of disorder for which patients are committed, the hospital context organizes their behaviors, their language, and their experience of reality. During their stay in the hospital, patients unlearn many of their social skills and learn how to adapt themselves to the rules of the new environment. Of necessity they learn how to become "good patients" in the eyes of the staff. Yoav's therapists, for example, thought that he was not yet healthy enough to play the guitar, and of course they had the power to decide. This is neither a unique nor an extreme example. In a well-known study by Rosenhan,† eight researchers gained admission to twelve different hospitals by feigning to hear voices. Although they behaved normally once they were admitted, all but one were diagnosed as schizophrenics and on discharge were labeled schizophrenics in remission. Their histories were distorted by the staff and made to fit the theory that they were ill, and their notetaking was interpreted as pathological behavior. Moreover, in the institutional "Catch 22," these voluntary patients could not get themselves discharged on short notice without outside help. Because they could not convince the staff of their normality by behaving normally in the hospital, they found it necessary to employ an attorney to prepare a writ of habeas corpus for each pseudopatient. All in all, it was a deeply unsettling experience of powerlessness and depersonalization.

Hospitalization results in a major loss of civil liberties. Even

*E. Goffman *Interaction Ritual: Essays on Face-to-Face Behaviour* (Harmondsworth, England: Penguin, 1972), p. 147.

†D. L. Rosenhan, "On Being Sane in Insane Places," *Science,* 179, 19 (1973): 250–58.

where state law supports the freedom of hospital patients, studies such as Rosenhan's expose the different reality of institutional practices. In Israel, patients entering the psychiatric wards voluntarily rarely know in advance that they will not be able to discharge themselves without permission. In effect they become involuntary patients who have no right to refuse treatments, including the use of psychotropic drugs, and can be held indefinitely even if the hospital cannot provide adequate treatment. Their only rights are to communicate in writing with the outside world and to have visits, but even these rights can be taken away easily by the hospital's director.* In a study of over 1,300 hospitalizations in Israel, it was found that for more than 75 percent of the involuntary patients, no commitment orders were issued. The attorney general either did not receive information about these patients or, if he did, took no action on their cases. Not surprisingly, the right of mental patients to appeal their involuntary incarceration was almost never exercised, and the study concluded:

> As matters stand today, individuals are being involuntarily hospitalized without the proper supervision and control provided for by law. The patient who must undergo commitment is not being treated to the full measure of civil liberties to which he is entitled by right.†

In the United States, civil commitment laws have been changed by many states, and due-process proceedings involving the judiciary system have been implemented in order to protect the rights of mental patients. Medical-paternalistic standards have been replaced by more restrictive criteria based on the requirement that the patient be shown to be dangerous either to himself or to others. Furthermore, in O'Connor v. Donaldson, the Florida Court of Appeals ruled that patients cannot be held against their

*D. Shnit, "Civil Commitment of Mental Patients in Israel," in U. Aviram and Y. Levav, (eds.), *Community Mental Health in Israel* (Hebrew, Tel Aviv: Cherikover, 1981), pp. 317–45.

†U. Aviram and D. Shnit, "Psychiatric Treatment and Civil Liberties in Israel: The Need for a Reform," *Israel Journal of Psychiatry and Related Sciences,* 21(1) (1984): 4.

will unless the hospital can provide them with individual treatment that gives them a reasonable opportunity for cure or improvement. In practice, American psychiatrists can usually find ways to enforce treatments without asking permission from the court. Despite the significant progress made by the rights movement, hospital patients are still controlled by coercive mechanisms. One of the main reasons why the greater recognition of their legal rights has been of limited benefit to patients is that legal progress has not been followed by widespread creation of alternative community facilities.* The choice for many of the poor inmates of public institutions is between the freedom to wander the streets, homeless and living a substandard life, and a restricted life in the hospital.

The situation is particularly grim for chronic hospital patients, who do not usually fight their incarceration but rather fear the loss of their protected environment. Staying in the hospital becomes a matter of survival once a patient has become habituated to a life style characterized by a low level of functioning, a lack of personal responsibility, a high dependency on professional helpers, predictable routines that are maintained from the outside, and the provision of food, shelter, and entertainment. Even if they wish to live outside, they have little chance for success on their own. In a way, they have been desocialized from normal life, and their status as mental patients becomes their greatest source of security. They adapt to a hothouse that breeds strange growths. Bizarre behaviors are not only the means to institutional certification, but also a way out of oblivion. Aya Kanyuk, after five years of experience in four different institutions, explained in a newspaper interview how she learned this simple lesson:

> I was afraid that they would find out about the real me and so I began to invent lies. It was fitting, because there were expectations that I would be muddle-headed. . . . Once I tried to explain myself by using an image. I said that I have ghosts

*M. S. Lottman, "Enforcement of Judicial Decrees: Now Comes the Hard Part," *Mental Disability Law Reporter* 1 (1976): 69–76.

in my head. But in the mental hospital they accept things concretely. When I saw that they were interested in ghosts I elaborated these stories. I made them theatrical; in my confinement and isolation they were the only creative thing that I could do. The lying kind of gave me a sense of control over my situation. The funny thing is that they did not see that some of my images were taken directly out of *I Never Promised You a Rose Garden.*"*

Effects at the Family Level

Hospitalization often provides a badly needed respite for family members who feel overburdened and demoralized. Unfortunately, the tensions tend to reappear when the patient is discharged. Drug treatment helps, but it does not resolve the stressful problems that patients and their families have to face in their natural environment. When the iatrogenic effects of life in the hospital and of the meanings attributed to hospitalization are added to the accumulated family stress, the problems often become even more difficult to manage.

Initially, hospitalization is often experienced as a defeat, before it becomes an accepted family pattern for dealing with stress. Most families attempt to work out the problems without sending the patient away, and success in avoiding hospitalization can give a positive meaning to the suffering and stress they have endured. Failure brings about a devaluation in the family's worth, accompanied by feelings of inadequacy, guilt, anger, and depression. Families are well aware of the common belief that they played a role in causing the mental illness. Like the patient, they feel stigmatized, and they attempt to conceal "the illness" from friends and relations, thus increasing their isolation.† In this situation the relationship with the hospital becomes very complex; disappointments and anger over the results of treatment are mixed with a great dependence on its services.

*T. Maroz, "The Other Side of the Night; An Interview with Aya Kanyuk," *Haaretz* (Hebrew), March 15, 1985.

†M. Yarrow, J. Clausen, and P. Robbins, "The Social Meaning of Mental Illness," *Journal of Social Issues,* 11 (1955): 33–48.

In the division of roles between the family and the hospital, the family hands over much its responsibility for the patient. Parents lose power, and the medical framing given to their problems increases their dependence on professional guidance, inasmuch as only professionals are supposed to know how to handle mental patients. The boundaries of the family become less well defined. Professionals often function as if they have become a part of the family, and the patient appears to move away from the family and become a part of the "hospital family." At first the hospital functions as a foster family, trying to correct what was wrong or lacking in the family (for example, providing increased structure and control for the disorganized patient). It may use its power to block the family from entering and intervening in its handling of the patient. In such episodes the family, highly sensitive to any criticism of its functioning or to the message that it stay away, finds its experiences with the hospital humiliating and guilt-producing. But at this point there is still the hopeful expectation that the ill member will be healed and promptly returned to the family. As long as the family experiences its suffering as meaningful, there is strength to continue and work with the hospital.

Families are usually very involved when they first make contact with the hospital, and the hospital's response to them in large part determines whether or not they stay involved and for how long. Most hospitals are not interested in having families on their backs. They do not have personnel trained to work with families, and they are not organized for this work. Hence, they are not very interested in learning about the difficulties faced by the families of their patients.

Clare Creer,* an English social worker who interviewed the families of mental patients, found that their lives, in and out of the family sphere, were often severely disrupted. One half of these relatives reported serious effects on their health and general well-being. They were frustrated, helpless, angry, guilty, and depressed. They had neither the tools nor the guidance and support to deal with behavior disturbances that ranged from severe

*C. Creer and J. K. Wing, *Schizophrenia at Home.* (Surrey, Eng.: National Schizophrenia Fellowship, 1974).

social withdrawal to uncontrolled, socially embarrassing behaviors. Creer found that 80 percent of the patients behaved in these disruptive ways, and that when they were seen by mental health professionals, the families' sense of worthlessness and guilt was further increased. Agnes Hatfield,* who has also studied the stress and the needs of families of mental patients, emphasized that most families prefer the patient to live with them. She is critical of professionals, whom she finds unprepared to provide families with appropriate help.

Eventually, the family responds with alienation and withdrawal. Demoralized and weak, they feel powerless to change institutional practices. Certainly they cannot tell professionals how to work. In general, the more prolonged the hospitalization, the more distance is created between the family and the patient. The family reorganizes, and there is a closure of boundaries,† for life in the family must go on, even at the price of leaving one member behind. At that point, the hospital assumes the functions of an adoptive family, and the boundaries surrounding the biological family become once again clearly defined; the movement of the patient from one home to another has been completed.

Effects at the Level of the Individual Patient

The first hospitalization has been depicted as an initiation ceremony that marks a point of change in the relations among the patient, the family, and the society. Once initiated, patients are enveloped by a total institution that seeks to indoctrinate its inmates with the ideology of mental illness and to rewrite their life scripts. Again, the description by Goffman can be applied to current conditions:

> The new inpatient finds himself cleanly stripped of many of his accustomed affirmations, satisfactions, and defences, and is subjected to a rather full set of mortifying experiences:

*A. Hatfield "What families Want of Family Therapy," in W. R. McFarlane (ed.), *Family Therapy in Schizophrenia* (New York: Guilford Press, 1983), pp. 41–65.

†R. D. Scott, "Closure in Family Relationships and the First Official Diagnosis," in J. Jorstad and E. Ugelstad, (eds.), *Schizophrenia 75* (Oslo: Universtitetsforlaget, 1976).

> restrictions of free movement, communal living, diffuse authority of a whole echelon of people, and so on. Here one begins to learn about the limited extent to which a conception of oneself can be sustained when the usual setting of supports for it are suddenly removed.*

When therapists work in this coercive environment to change the self-concept of their patients, their chances of success are obviously very high. Self-labeling is one outcome of this process, which has been compared to brainwashing.

Some understanding of the quality of life in the psychiatric hospital and its effects on the individual patient was provided by the researchers who had themselves admitted and concealed their identities. One of the strongest experiences, mentioned repeatedly, is the feeling of boredom and ennui on the ward.† The life that is protected is also a life stripped of challenges. Occupational therapy cannot substitute for functioning and coping, and time in the hospital has the effect of increasing the gap between the patient and the world outside. Furthermore, it appears that many hospital patients are especially vulnerable to the effects of low functioning and understimulation. Those with a low level of social skills and functioning prior to their admission deteriorate rapidly in the hospital environment. There is a correlation between a life of restriction and understimulation on the ward and the likelihood that patients will be withdrawn and affectively blunted.‡ A significant part of what has been described as "the end state shown by schizophrenics in mental hospitals" can be directly attributed to the effects of institutionalization on these patients.

The hospital affects not only patients' behavior and inner life but also their physiological functioning. One justification given

*E. Goffman, *Asylums: Essays on the Social Situation of Mental Patients and Other Inmates* (Harmondsworth, England: Pelican, 1968), p. 137.

†W. Caudill, F. C. Redlich, H. R. Gilmore, and E. B. Brody, "Social Structure and Interaction Processes on a Psychiatric Ward," in H. Wechsler, L. Solomon, and B. M. Kramer, (eds.), *Social Psychology and Mental Health* (New York: Holt, Rinehart & Winston, 1970), pp. 351–86.

‡J. K. Wing, "Social Treatments of Mental Illness," in M. Shepherd and D. L. Davies, (eds.), *Studies in Psychiatry* (London: Oxford University Press, 1968).

for hospitalization is that the management of acute episodes with high doses of medication requires close supervision. The relative ease with which a high dose can be prescribed—sometimes forced—can, however, lead to the use of such treatment too early and for too long a period. In a research setting, it was found that an initial medication-free period allows for better observation of patients and for some patients is of more benefit than the use of drugs.* But such flexibility in the use of medication is not commonly found in mental hospitals. Too often, drugs are used to control unruly patients and become another tool in the management of the ward. Large doses are sometimes given even before assessment has been completed, to alleviate staff anxieties over the acute manifestations of psychotic episodes.† These criticisms do not discount the efficiency of psychotropic drugs, but as in the case of *la turret* they point to the new set of problems that have been produced by the solution.

The ill effects of forcing organic treatments with little consideration for either their toxicity or the violation of the patients' sense of autonomy featured prominently in the cases of Yoav and Dan. Both of them ran away from the hospital in response to the forced medication and were punished by being put in seclusion. In addition to the trial of many different drugs, Yoav experienced the suffering of electroshocks. The toxic effects of this management on Yoav were most significant, and only the very active reinvolvement of his parents saved him from the next stage of lobotomy. Many patients are less fortunate, and their functioning deteriorates as a result of electroshocks, psychosurgery, and the debilitating and irreversible side effects produced by psychiatric drugs.

*W. T. Carpenter, T. H. McGlashan, and J. S. Strauss, "The Treatment of Acute Schizophrenia Without Drugs: An Investigation of Some Current Assumptions," *American Journal of Psychiatry,* 134 (1977): 14–20.

†L. C. Wynne, "A Phase-Oriented Approach to Treatment with Schizophrenics and Their Families," in W. R. McFarlane, (ed.), *Family Therapy in Schizophrenia* (New York: Guilford Press, 1983), pp. 251–65.

Alternative Pathways among the Family, the Community, and the Hospital

If families find that they need to pay such a high price for hospitalizing one of their members, why do they continue to use hospitals? Could they not take a risk, as Dan's parents did, and cope with the problems on an outpatient basis? There is no one answer to these questions, but whatever one's thinking about families, there is a need to listen to parents like Yoav's when they say, after his hospitalization for more than a year in Beta, "There is no real improvement but at least he's being taken care of. . . . We feel they care about Yoav." The point is that they would have turned to a better alternative had it been available.

The unavailability of alternatives, the great dependence of the families on the hospitals, even the functions assumed by the hospitals, are all part of a mesosystem characterized by the following factors:

1. The paucity of social resources to support either families in distress or unattached, low-functioning individuals results in an overburdening of the family, the hospital, and the community.
2. Organizational dysfunctions, conflicts, traditional mistrust, and other barriers limit cooperation among community agencies, hospitals, and families. When the mesosystem is governed by such a set of interrelationships, it functions like a *golem:* there is no effective leadership to maximize therapeutic gains, and underfunctioning becomes the rule rather than the exception.

Changing the mesosystem to create alternative pathways for patients and their families is not an impossible mission. The following examples do not present an all-encompassing overview of the field, but they can help by pointing to some possibilities for cooperation among the family, the hospital, and the community.

Coping with the Crisis of Hospitalization

Hospital admissions usually occur when there is a crisis with the patient and his natural support system. Various programs have been created to alleviate stress in the system by providing crisis intervention and supporting services. The attempt was to provide alternatives to hospitalization, though the programs did rely on back-up from hospitals when necessary. One such project was initiated more than twenty years ago at the University of Colorado Medical Center.* Langsley and his colleagues applied their model of family crisis therapy to 150 randomly selected families, comparing them to a control group of 150 matched cases in which the patient had been hospitalized. Their research confirmed that intensive family interventions during the emergency period can substitute for hospitalization. Furthermore, measures of psychiatric status during an eighteen-month follow-up showed that the study group was less impaired and continued to use the hospital much less often than the control subjects.†

A different approach to dealing with the crisis of admission was the Training in Community Living program developed by Stein and Test.‡ They worked with an unselected group of patients who came to the hospital, providing them with basic material resources and teaching them coping skills for meeting the demands of independent community life. The program included support and education for family members and others involved with the patients, as well as crisis intervention, drug treatment, and anything else that compensated for deficits, developed strengths, and enabled patients to live in their natural milieu. The program continued for fourteen months, and the results showed its effectiveness in terms of patients' adaptation to community life, including their greater ability to cope with crises without relying on the hospital. Furthermore, it was also found that the

*D. G. Langsley, D. M. Kaplan, F. S. Pittman, R. Machotka, K. Flomenhaft, and C. D. DeYoung, *The Treatment of Families in Crisis* (New York: Grune & Stratton, 1968).

†D. G. Langsley, R. Machotka, and K. Flomenhaft, "Avoiding Mental Hospital Admission: A Follow-Up Study," *American Journal of Psychiatry,* 127 (1971): 1391–94.

‡L. I. Stein, and M. A. Test, "An Alternative to Mental Hospital Treatment: I. Conceptual Model, Treatment Program, and Clinical Evaluation," *Archives of General Psychiatry,* 37 (1980): 392–99.

patients' functioning was enhanced, and that they reported less distress and more satisfaction in life in comparison with a control group of hospitalized patients.

After the Discharge

One of the effects of deinstitutionalization has been the creation of the "revolving-door syndrome," a pattern in which the patient moves back and forth between the mental institution and the community. Length of hospitalization has been shortened, but relapse is frequent. In one review of research, 41 percent of all the drug-treated patients were found to have relapsed within one year following discharge.* Another study concluded that approximately one out of two patients diagnosed as schizophrenic is rehospitalized within half a year following discharge.† Patients who are involved in the revolving-door pattern continue to be labelled and trained by institutional life to enter the modified career path of the chronic mental patient. In this system of treatment little can be done either to resolve stress-producing problems or to increase the families' competence to handle them without the hospital.

Since most patients return to their families following discharge, and since family dynamics have been shown to affect the rate of relapse, the logical step was to create a link between hospital psychiatry and family therapy. One such program for family work with schizophrenia has been implemented and evaluated by Falloon, Boyd, and McGill.‡ The therapeutic package included family therapy with a behavioral emphasis, education, the training of patients and families with problem-solving skills, medication, rehabilitation counseling, crisis intervention, and other forms of help that could be integrated within a community-based approach. This work has been found to be effective on a variety

*G. E. Hogarty, "Depot Neuroleptics: The Relevance of Psycho-Social Factors," *Journal of Clinical Psychiatry,* 45(sec. 2) (1984): 36–42.

†C. A. Taube, *Readmissions to Inpatient Services of State and Community Mental Hospital 1972* (statistical note 110). (Rockville, Md.: National Institute of Mental Health, Biometry Branch, 1974).

‡I. R. Falloon, J. L. Boyd, and C. W. McGill, *Family Care of Schizophrenia* (New York: Guilford Press, 1984).

of measures, including the need for hospitalizations, patients' functioning in the community, and their freedom from disabling symptoms. It was also less expensive to implement than traditional forms of treatment, and the comparison of family with individual interventions showed the former to be clearly superior.

The main emphasis of Falloon and his co-workers was on working with patients and their families, but the success of their program was also related to the input of the hospital and the community. They found that their ability to help patients make the transition from a state of nonfunctioning into becoming fully functional members of society, depended on the availability of rehabilitation resources in the community. Moreover, the hospital and other residential facilities, even though the use of their services was substantially reduced, remained a vital component of the community care program.

Caring for the Chronic Patient

It is estimated that approximately two thirds of all psychiatric beds in Israel are occupied by chronic patients. Expectations for their discharge are low, and most of them will probably remain in the hospital for the rest of their lives. They have security, but their living conditions are for the most part abominable.

Chronic patients have fared much worse in America. The policies of deinstitutionalization resulted in a decrease in the number of patients in psychiatric hospitals. Many chronic patients have been warehoused in the community with very little effort made toward their care and rehabilitation.* They joined the ranks of the homeless or returned to their families, depending on circumstances which they did not control. Others have found a place in nursing homes.† In fact, most of the savings in mental health

*H. R. Lamb, and V. Goertzel, "Discharged Mental Patients—Are They Really in the Community?" *Archives of General Psychiatry* 24 (1971): 29–34.

†H. H. Goldman, J. Feder, and W. Scanlon, "Chronic Mental Patients in Nursing Homes: Reexamining Data from the National Home Survey," *Hospital and Community Psychiatry,* 37 (1986): 269–72.

budgets have been made by decreasing services for chronic patients.*

Against such a dismal background it is interesting to take a look at the Shalom Club, a community rehabilitation project in Israel. This club attempted to meet the needs of patients with the poorest rehabilitation potential, those who have stayed many times and many years in hospitals, who have a fragmentary or nonexistent work history and no secure housing beyond the hospital or the parental home. The main thrust of the program was to resocialize these chronic patients by teaching them basic social skills, to help them to organize their lives in the community, and to engage them in a continuing framework that provided professional and social support. The major difficulty for the patients was to make the fearful transition into the community—a process that could be actualized only with the collaboration and support of the local hospitals and community agencies. A five-year follow-up showed that these chronic patients, who have previously spent an average of over 70 percent of their time in hospitals, succeeded in breaking this stable pattern and learning to live in the community. The direct cost per patient was 35 percent of the cost of hospitalization.†

So What? The Political Challenge

There are many other programs which have not been mentioned here. Taken together they demonstrate that hospitals and community agencies *can* cooperate to support the normal functioning of patients and their families during periods of acute distress and afterwards. However, such coordination depends on dynamics at the level of the macrosystem, where therapeutic considerations, even proofs of cost effectiveness, are not the most important criteria. As a result of such dynamics, the program

*S. S. Sharfstein, "Reimbursement Resistance to Treatment and Support for the Long Term Mental Patient," in S. T. Meyerson, (ed.), *Barriers to Treating the Chronic Mentally Ill* (New Directions for Mental Health Services, no. 33) (San Francisco: Jossey Bass, 1987).

†M. Spivak, "Community Rehabilitation of People in a State of Desocialization," in U. Aviram and Y. Levav, (eds.), *Community Mental Health in Israel* (Hebrew, Tel Aviv: Cherikover, 1981), pp. 347–63.

described by Stein and Test operated for fourteen months only to be discontinued, like many other experimental projects of its kind. Consequently, many of the project's patients "regressed," and their use of the hospital increased.

The fate of the Shalom Club in Israel has not been different. After operating long enough to demonstrate its effectiveness, it was closed down for lack of funding. Many of the patients went back to their hospitals, their lives continuing as if the center had never existed.

Yoav and Dan: A Summing-Up

The lives of Yoav and Dan provide clear examples of the way that madness evolves in human systems. In each case there were points of discontinuity at which crucial decisions were made. The direction taken at each of these points was to have major, long-term consequences. These decisions were not taken alone by the patients and their families; therapists, teachers, and others were always directly involved, and in that sense they too are a part of their stories. And as we broaden our view to include the effects of treatment institutions and the social system, it becomes apparent that they too were part of the cases, powerful sources of bias and constraint that influenced the choice made at each critical juncture.

The implication for mental patients is that their lives are shaped to a large degree by community decisions concerning the allocation of resources, as well as by the organization of the social and medical institutions that families turn to when they need outside support. Madness is a multileveled process; it may be initiated during a particular crisis, but its full unfolding is made possible by the involvement of individuals, families, and communities in destructive transactions. It is a long slide down, with few stations on the way, from the unresolved problems in people's lives to acute breakdowns in adaptation, which for some unfortunate gliders continue into mental patienthood and chronicity. At some point on the way, the concept of madness emerges as an epiphenomenon; once it is identified, it becomes a powerful, autonomous image that adds its share to the process.

This perspective makes it clear that professionals have contributed to the masking of dysfunctional social processes with their traditional emphasis on individual, and lately on familial, vulnerabilities. It is not hard to find psychopathology and brain dysfunction among those who inhabit our hospitals, and the findings are significant. But too often their existence is used to excuse the failure to change problem areas on other levels of organization.

The cases of Yoav and Dan have provided many concrete illustrations of the effects of organizational dysfunctions on the life course of patients. In a way they are like random snapshots of current conditions, calling our attention to the gap between the hopes for reforming traditional hospital practices and everyday reality. For example, in Alpha's initial dealing with Yoav, one can observe how the revolving door syndrome is created and how family work can be corrupted when it is implemented by a hospital that does not change its basic structure and ideology. Yoav's experience at Beta and later his rehospitalization at Alpha demonstrate how hospitals contribute to the creation of chronic disability. At other points during these cases we can observe the need for hospital support during periods of crisis and the way that poor community resources for rehabilitation create an overuse of the hospital, overburden the family, and ultimately push patients into the sick role.

The cases of Yoav and Dan are not only the stories of patients, families, and hospitals; they are also the stories of therapists. They show that therapists, together with their biases, their strengths, and their weaknesses, are always a part of the family and institutional systems and that their position within these systems always has an influence. Consultations from outside the system were found to be a source of new information that helped therapists gain some awareness of their biases and increase their flexibility, so that they could change roles and correct biases. When therapists operated from a rigid position, they entered into power struggles with patients, families, or hospitals, narrowing the possibilities of helping and even producing some harmful effects. Fortunately, the case of Dan also demonstrated the power of working with the family in the community to create a healing context, with possibilities for recuperation, a return to full functioning, and a continuing of development within the sphere of normality.

Could the hospitalization of Yoav and Dan have been avoided, and would the course of their lives have been different if they had been treated differently? In "The Garden of Forking Paths," Jorge Luis Borges describes an ancient Chinese concept of a garden in which one does not have to choose one alternative and eliminate the others; it is possible to choose all ways and thus to create diverse futures that proliferate and fork into infinite possibilities.* We cannot follow this image here; we can only make some imperfect comparisons between cases that have been treated differently, comparisons that may help us learn about ways of providing more and better alternatives to people.

Chapters 6, 7, and 8 are devoted to just such comparisons. Chapters 6 and 7 describe our consultations and follow-ups in two cases in which the identified patients had never been hospitalized. Rather than being removed from their family and social contexts, they were being treated by teams of helpers who, however imperfectly, were working not only with them but with their families and with significant others in the community. The model for this form of community management of mental illness is described in detail in chapter 8 by Mordecai Kaffman, director of the Kibbutz Child and Family Clinic. He not only presents an alternative mode of therapy but introduces us to a new social context and the possibilities that are created when a comprehensive program of therapy is supported by the community and is implemented in close collaboration with its agents.

The successful use of Kaffman's model of treatment is closely linked to the very special characteristics of the communities in which it is used, the Israeli kibbutzim. In the following chapter, Joel Elizur provides a brief overview of the structure and culture of the kibbutz to set the scene for the cases that follow.

*Jorge Luis Borges, "The Garden of the Forking Paths," in *Labyrinths* (New York: New Directions, 1962), pp. 19–29.

5

Ecological Therapy in the Kibbutz

IN THE CASES described in the following two chapters, the identified patients had never been institutionalized. Throughout their labeling and treatment, they remained part of the relatively small and highly interdependent society of the kibbutz. In contrast to the hospital, where all problems belong to the patients, here there was no attempt to hide from our view the problems that were troubling the kibbutz system or to deny the dysfunctional relations that we observed between kibbutz institutions and families. On the contrary, kibbutz representatives were involved in therapy and could be challenged to change their functioning vis-à-vis the families.

It therefore became possible to use the follow-ups of the kibbutz cases for asking questions that could not be applied to the hospital cases. What can be achieved by an ecologically oriented therapist who can collaborate with the community in applying this approach? What are the limitations of this type of therapy, and what biases does it create in the therapist?

One of the prime objectives of therapy in the kibbutz community is to contain crisis situations within the normal family and social environment of the patient. To that end, the Kibbutz Clinic regards the patient as a complex entity made up of biological, social, and psychological aspects, and treatment involves the development of a multitiered set of therapeutic responses designed to deal with all those aspects. In a very severe case, this might include medication, individual therapy, family therapy, the creation of support groups to integrate the patient into the community, and explanation to the community of the patient's problems and the need for a depathologized community response. To prevent this array of people and services from fragmenting, a single coordinator is appointed, who devotes considerable time to working with the patient and significant others in the community.

The kibbutz therapists were thus working in a clinical context that provided them with a steady foundation, unlike the attempts to implement an ecological approach with hospitals. Because of this context, they could react to a setback by rethinking what had gone wrong in the way they applied their model; their work could maintain its ecological orientation despite mistakes and deadlocks.

At the same time, just as in the hospital cases, the work of the kibbutz therapists revealed blindspots that were related to the ways in which they were influenced by the family and the social system. We could observe biases in their thinking and gaps and other labored parts in their therapy. While Minuchin did not need to introduce kibbutz therapists to ecological work, he did find it necessary to challenge some of their adaptations to kibbutz society.

The Ecology of the Kibbutz

Kibbutz in Hebrew means "group"—any group—but the word has come to stand for a voluntary collective community whose founders, coming to Palestine more than seventy-five years ago, organized according to ideals of democratic socialism. The first kibbutz was formed by a handful of people; today, more than

120,000 people live in 250 kibbutzim throughout the country. Each kibbutz is self-administered. A weekly meeting of the entire membership discusses community issues and votes on policies, budgets, admission of new members, and election of committees to handle the daily affairs of the kibbutz. The principal committee is the secretariat, whose membership includes the general secretary of the kibbutz, the economic manager, the treasurer, and the coordinators of the work and education committees. Other committees deal with various aspects of kibbutz life, such as health, cultural activities, personal problems, and the organizational and ideological principles of kibbutz life. To prevent the emergence of a managerial class, the elected officers, as well as the managers of the various agricultural and industrial branches, rotate every few years.

Work is an ideological principle in the kibbutz. All kinds of work are of equal value, and members work wherever they have been assigned, according to the needs of the community. Most people eventually end up doing the work they like to do and are trained in their chosen field. Some menial jobs, such as dining room service, are considered temporary and are filled by all members in turn. Some members, usually trained professionals, may work outside the kibbutz, with their salaries going directly into the community fund. There are no monetary rewards; in this social atmosphere some of the severest criticisms that can be made are that a member does not work well, has materialistic ambitions, or is preoccupied with his or her own needs, insensitive to those of others. A business tycoon would be made to feel like a leper in the kibbutz.

Aside from personal belongings, property in the kibbutz is communally owned. There is equality in all major items of consumption; all members are entitled to housing, kibbutz education for the children, clothes, food, medical care, a budget for purchasing personal articles, cultural activities, and opportunities for self-expression. Generally, the kibbutz as a whole assumes complete responsibility for all the needs of its members. The material standard depends on the financial state of the particular kibbutz, while the standard of services depends on the dedication of its members to their work. The kibbutz cannot provide material comforts equal to middle-class city standards, but it allocates a higher proportion of its resources for social services. The resulting high quality of service is seen in such diverse areas as education, cultural activities, and care of the sick, old, and disabled. There are high expectations of those who provide vital services, and everyone observes what they do, feels free to criticize, and can lobby for their removal from office. Understandably, being a kibbutz secretary or a coordinator of its school is not easy. Although these positions carry high social status, it is sometimes difficult for the kibbutz to find a suitable member to take the role.

The principle of equality notwithstanding, there is an informal social stratification. Some members become leaders by virtue of their qualities, experience, and commitment. They often rotate from one responsible position to another. At the other extreme are the fringe members. Their work is usually routine and of low status, and their functioning is minimal. Socially, they tend to be isolated, and they are at risk of becoming the community's identified patients. Those who become recognized as "weak" may receive special consideration from the kibbutz. This practice is consonant with kibbutz ideals, yet it is not uncommon to hear cries of resentment from some of the more productive members. The benefits associated with managerial positions, such as the use of a car, may spark similar reactions.

There is collaboration and mutual help among kibbutzim, both in times of trouble and in carrying out the tasks of daily life. Groups of kibbutzim have formed several federations, which provide their members with financial help, educational institutions, cultural services, and central purchasing and marketing facilities. These federations also run their own psychological clinics, the largest of which is the Kibbutz Child and Family Clinic.

Individuation in the Kibbutz

Communal life has its own strains and systems therapists working with the kibbutz need to learn the rules of this social system, its special resources, and its specific vulnerabilities. In this highly interconnected community family problems are often intertwined with larger social issues. This point can be illustrated by taking up the issue of the individuation of young adults in the kibbutz. Three different perspectives will be employed in order to highlight the major dilemmas of individuation in the kibbutz.

1. *The individuating young adult*

   Individuation is a relatively new concern in kibbutz life. For kibbutz founders individuation was intrinsic to the process of building together a new society. Their separation from their homes was, for the most part, a drastic step—moving far from their families and breaking away from a middle-class life. Naturally they expected to pass the torch to their own children. Indeed, the first generation of kibbutz children continued in the footsteps of their parents. Leaving the kibbutz was felt to be an act of treason, and the great majority stayed without questioning kibbutz values and ways of life. They developed the kibbutz economy and were, in general, more pragmatic and less ideological than the founding generation.

   In contrast, young adults of today's kibbutzim are faced with more complex issues of self-identity. It was with this generation that the kibbutz experienced for the first time the turmoils of adolescent rebellion and the generation gap. About 65 percent of this generation leave the kibbutz as they reach adulthood. Those who stay generally do so after trying different ways of life outside the kibbutz. The norms and conditions of kibbutz life have changed so much that young people usually try to prove to themselves that they can leave their home community and cope with the difficulties of life before deciding whether to return to the comfort and security of kibbutz life. For many of them this process has become a modern rite of passage. Those who fail in it feel degraded since their return to the kibbutz is not a choice they have made freely. Rather, it is almost as if they are asking their family to bail them out.

2. *The dilemma of the community*

The change in values and norms with respect to individuation has also led to complex new questions for the community. To what extent should the kibbutz use its resources to provide for the self-fulfillment of its grown children in order to attract them into adopting its way of life? On the one hand, kibbutz members are attached to the children, and their decision to stay and carry on with kibbutz life seems like an affirmation of the community. Moreover, in staying on, the young adults support the kibbutz's economic and social life. There is the fear that if too many children leave, the kibbutz would eventually become depleted. On the other hand, no kibbutz would want to bribe its children into staying. Decisions concerning the use of community resources need also to consider the veteran members and their needs for education, travel, material comfort, and so forth.

It is a delicate balance, and there is an unwritten code of values which helps to reduce tensions and conflicts—do not be pesky, show consideration for others, wait patiently for your turn. However, that balance is upset by those who push for more, be they kibbutz children who act out of line or their mates, brought in from outside the kibbutz. Such newcomers are at risk of becoming the "difficult outsiders." Not only are they not socialized to respect kibbutz values, they do not join the kibbutz with an ideology that prepares them for the great degree of mutual accommodation that kibbutz life demands. In such situations the kibbutz can exert a great pressure for conformity. It has an informal system of social control, like that of a tribe or a close-knit extended family, whose functioning is much more effective than any modern police force. The deviant member experiences a general rejection, and unless there is some resolution of the conflict, life together becomes impossible.

3. *The multiple loyalties of the founder's family*

Parents in the kibbutz usually wish their children to continue their way of life, insuring in this way—among other things—that they are in close touch with their children and future grandchildren. Today's kibbutz is no longer the primary one-generational group of the pioneers, and life there without an extended family feels lonesome. Hence, the developmental transition of leaving home is affected significantly by the decision whether to stay in the kibbutz. Whatever that decision is, kibbutz families experience all of the regular issues of separation. There are additional complications, however, that are specific to kibbutz life.

One of the problems of individuation in the kibbutz is that the family of origin, the young adult, and the community can become entangled in a triangle of conflicting loyalties. In a typical constellation there is a conflict between the young adult and the kibbutz, and the parents become overly involved. In such situations the parents may try to act as mediators or lobbyists. When they fail, for example, when a committee or the membership turns down their child's request, the parents can react with intense feelings of hurt and resentment.

Problems of triangulations at this level may take many other forms as well. They may also crop up at other phases of the life cycle. Parents of a child who acts in clearly deviant ways with respect to community rules, feel not only a need to protect her. They also feel shamed vis-à-vis the kibbutz and responsible for making amends and correcting their child. In such cases a critical overinvolvment will develop between the generations, adding a new layer of problems to the original issue. Kibbutz therapists often find that their work involves dealing with such complexities. Consequently, the system that they evaluate, and in which they intervene, is usually larger than the family.

Education in the Kibbutz

A major characteristic of the kibbutz cases discussed in the next two chapters was that the patients remained in school throughout most of their therapy. Minuchin's consultations took place during periods of crisis that involved both the family and the school systems. Furthermore, the presenting problems and the course of treatment were very much influenced by the family-school relations.

The continuation of the kibbutz way of life depends very much upon its education. Will the kibbutz children wish to continue to live there as they grow up? Will they maintain the basic values of the kibbutz and yet succeed in adapting to new social and economic realities? These questions are asked of every educational system, but the intensity with which they are asked in the kibbutz is family-like. The analogy can be extended further by noting that educational teams are expected to be teachers, tutors, toilet trainers, counselors, and enlightened pedagogues. The community has delegated to them many family functions, and consequently they are very much involved with the personality development of the children.

Kibbutz children become involved with the educational system at an early age. Most children live in special children's houses from the age of six months onward. This arrangement was originally a pragmatic solution, enabling both parents to work full-time and participate in community life while providing the best physical and security conditions for the children. As time went on, this system of childrearing became integrated in the kibbutz educational philosophy, providing a developmental context for learning cooperation and community life from an early age. The children live in small groups, according to age. Each group is supervised by a homeroom teacher and a *metapelet,* a caretaker who is usually in charge of all activities outside of formal studies. Their houses include sleeping quarters, play areas, dining facilities, and washrooms. The children come to their families' homes at four in the afternoon, as well as on holidays and Saturdays, and remain with their families until bedtime, when their parents accompany them back to the children's house. Work hours are organized to allow both parents to be free during the afternoon. Nursing mothers work less and are with their children for a good part of the day.

As the children grow up, they are given more responsibility in the conduct of their affairs, such as tidying up their rooms and running the "Children's Farm." Each group forms something like an executive committee, similar in some ways to the adult society. When they reach the seventh grade, the children move to the *mossad,* the regional junior and senior high school that serves several kibbutzim. Essentially the mossad functions as a semiautonomous youth community. The students take an active part in committees that manage many aspects of their life. They have a busy program that includes work, the youth movement, and social and recreational activities. Their sleeping quarters are in the mossad, but they come to their kibbutzim regularly to visit their families and to work.

Today, changes in the kibbutz and in Israel at large are creating crisis in the education of kibbutz adolescents. Kibbutz adolescents grow up in a more comfortable and secure community, whose boundaries have opened considerably to outside influence. The ideology of their parents has lost much of its fervor and single-mindedness, and the kibbutz has become a more diversified and tolerant society. During the last two decades a generation gap has opened up for the first time, with teenagers expressing many of the typical challenges to adult authority that appeared in the West in the 1960s. At the same time, the generation of teachers has also changed. Unlike the founding fathers of the youth communities, teachers today do not accept their work as a consuming mission at the center of their existence. In line with a general trend in the kibbutz, they are more involved with their own families. In a situation where the old ideological blueprints for the school no longer fit present realities, they often feel bewildered as they confront the question of what it means to be a kibbutz educator today.

The modern mossad has become one of the screens on which the doubts and conflicts of adult society are projected, and the teachers are catching the fire from both sides. On the one hand, the adolescents complain of adult repression of individual freedoms, a rather general banner that may cover such diverse topics as dress codes, study programs, and drugs. Unconvinced by the truisms of the past, they may even use the old slogans to confront their educators with the compromising realities of kibbutz life today. On the other hand, parents complain of lack of discipline in the mossad. They expect teachers to assume more authority and to be able to control the group as they had done in the past.

Adolescents bring to the fore the unresolved issues of adult society. Their challenge of adult authority in the kibbutz has demonstrated that its teachers did not have proper means of control and has forced them to face up to the fact that such means are necessary, even in a system of "progressive education" that until recent years did not need to think much about control. And once the issue of control was brought up, it became clear that kibbutz teachers cannot solve the problem on their own, taking for granted that the parents will back them. There needs to be a collaboration, with a clarification of boundaries and lines of authority between family and school. These issues played a major part in the kibbutz case presented in the next chapter.

6

Joey

SALVADOR MINUCHIN once interviewed representatives of seven agencies working with a family in which there was incest among four siblings. The "perpetrator," a sixteen-year-old boy, was receiving individual and group therapy at a residential institution. The school counselor was also working with him, and the art therapist provided *ad hoc* counseling. The two adolescent girls were receiving therapy from an agency that conducted groups for victims; the girls were in different groups, which were organized by age. The youngest child was in a group for boys conducted by a different agency. The family as a group was being treated by still another agency. The mother was in a mother's group at yet another agency and was also meeting weekly with her minister's wife. Counting hours of direct formal therapy, the boy had eighteen hours weekly, the mother six to eight, and the siblings two to four each. The seven agencies had no direct contact with one another. In fairness, each was doing its job well. But the psychological sum of their efforts was, of course, a disaster.

In Western culture, the boundaries that separate the families of the urban poor from the "helping" systems are often very weak. These families do not construct their own stories. Social agencies, the judicial system, the medical establishment, and the schools intrude in their lives, creating, recording, and handing on a family story of dependency and powerlessness. This symbiotic relationship is not explicitly acknowledged, so the disenfranchised families are charged with the task of changing the reality that is only partially of their making. They are given the task, but not the tools.

This orgy of uncoordinated effort is not limited to poor families. A very wealthy husband and wife were recently referred to Minuchin by their individual psychoanalysts, with whom they have had a combined total of twenty-three years of treatment. Their only son has had six years of analysis. The spouses did not talk with each other, but they were united in concern for their triangulated son, who was the identified patient. Of course, each family member talked to his or her own analyst. With pseudo-naive malevolence, Minuchin suggested a meeting of the analysts, the family members, and himself. Each of them rejected the arrangement, preferring the fragmented isolation of their own psyches (which includes, of course, the psyches of the interveners). But without an integration of the "services," this rich family will fare no better than the poor ones.

Apparently membership in a higher social class is no guarantee against therapeutic solutions that compound and stabilize family problems. However, money, good connections, education, and other resources do make a difference in a family's possibilities for treatment. They enable families to choose their own solutions rather than being intimidated by the interventions of public institutions. Social agents tend to be particularly coercive in their contact with the poor. They often decide not only when outside intervention is necessary but what form it will take. This meshing between therapy and social control, justified as it is by social values, is a fertile ground for the creation of imperious policies, policies that ultimately affect all families who depend on institutional support.

Middle-class families do not usually think that such social issues are directly relevant to their lives. However, they too may find themselves in situations where the soft voices of their professional helpers are transformed into strong-arm tactics. "Lobotomy or the chronic hospital," said the experts to Yoav's parents, letting them know that disobedience would be punished by withholding services for which they had no alternative.

Kibbutz families are certainly middle class if we measure them in terms of education and standard of living. However, they live in a very tightly knit community, with interdependence at the core of its ideology. Consequently, the psychosocial boundaries surrounding a kibbutz family are relatively permeable, leaving them vulnerable to the intrusion and confusion that occur between social services and the urban poor. Some kibbutz families are particularly at risk for these effects. Usually these families are low in social status, or they are in a crisis that makes them greatly dependent on community help.

It should also be mentioned that the kibbutz is owned by its members. They constantly observe its governing body, school, and other kibbutz institutions, and they demand accountability. Hence, we can also find in the kibbutz the type of interactions that are usually found between the very rich and the institutions, like private schools, that depend on their support. Dysfunction in such situations is typically related to the powerful intrusion of the family into the institution's proceedings.

In the following two kibbutz cases, it will be possible to observe both the clinical importance of transactions at this level of systems and their complexity, a complexity that defies any simple thinking about the kibbutz in terms of social classes. Since kibbutz therapists are actively involved at this level, their contributions and their difficulties will be important ingredients in the drama. The fact that some are kibbutz members, and that all work in a family clinic owned by the kibbutzim, is also a significant element in the story.

In the 1960s, Edgar Auerswald highlighted the problems that occur when multiple agencies express their benign concern for a single family.* Focusing on the response of social services to what we then called multiproblem families, he called attention to the destructive aspects of specialized social service agencies, which respond selectively to one particular problem by providing *their*

*E. H. Auerswald, "Interdisciplinary versus Ecological Approach," *Family Process* 7 (1968): 202–15.

service. Auerswald called for a "Chairman of the Board" to coordinate these fragmented services.*

In the kibbutz, that can happen. As Mordecai Kaffman spells out in chapter 8, an essential component of the multitiered set of therapeutic responses that the Kibbutz Clinic develops for each case is a coordinator, who is given the job of making all the resources flow in the needed direction. Unfortunately, however, it does not always happen.

The case described in this chapter shows the destructive effect of such a fragmentation of services. The fact that it occurred in the kibbutz and, in particular, as part of the Kibbutz Clinic program shows the strength of accepted models of service delivery. We continue doing what we have done previously, even when we know better. Institutional organization demands respect for its own survival, in the kibbutz society as well as the sidewalks of Tel Aviv and Los Angeles.

Early in the history of the family described here, a child with organic brain damage was born. The kibbutz believes itself to be an optimal setting for a family faced with such a tragic and difficult situation. The kibbutz offers maximum medical and educational help and is constantly supportive to the family. What is less obvious is that the family and the larger system may establish patterns of interaction that are appropriate to the crisis but that then become the dominant style of functioning, both for the family and for the kibbutz in relation to the family. In this case, these patterns extended to the rearing of the youngest child in the family and became dysfunctional.

A Family-School Interface

Thirteen-year-old Joey was an intelligent boy and a natural leader, but he had been functioning marginally ever since he entered the mossad. Now in eighth grade, he attended irregularly,

*Personal communication.

was often very late for class, avoided some subjects entirely, and rarely did his homework. Efforts by his homeroom teacher, Ran, to interest him in his studies and then to control him had no effect. Joey became more and more disruptive, and the other students seemed ready to follow his example. In a school already uneasy about educational and generational issues, the students' response signified more than a disruption of studies: It seemed a frontal attack on mossad norms, perhaps an adolescent rebellion against all forms of adult supervision.

The problem came to a head when Ran suspended Joey for three days.

RAN: *We couldn't hold our weekly discussion hour because of the way the kids laughed at his sarcastic remarks. Honestly, the more outrageously he acts, the more the kids admire him!*

ADA (METAPELET): *You react to everything he does as provocation. Think of it as his way of asking for attention. Try to talk with him, to understand his problems.*

RAN: *I have! He acts as though I'm trying to buy him off. And his parents back him up. I tried to talk with them, but his father just told me that he "believes Joey."*

ADA: *I know the family very well. They have a lot of problems with a brain-damaged daughter. Expelling Joey won't help anybody.*

RAN: *It will help my class!*

Problems in an organization often bring out both the "heavy" and the "understanding" styles of responding. Each contains some truth; each feels intuitively correct. In this case the two positions were related to different perspectives: The teacher was focused on behavioral and cognitive issues in the class, while the metapelet, knowing Joey's family, was more involved with Joey's emotional life. The interveners in this case were already marking out territories, a process that was to recur.

The group calmed down in Joey's absence, but as soon as he returned, the situation got worse. Joey's parents, blaming Ran for the entire problem, demanded his dismissal. They were a family whose views carried considerable weight, partly because of their position as members of a highly esteemed founding family of the kibbutz, and partly because of the father's important position in the kibbutz structure. The school board was caught between the need to support the teacher and its reluctance to tackle this powerful family. The consensus was that Joey was deeply disturbed, but other families were also raising questions about Ran's teaching.

The board decided to suspend Joey indefinitely. His case would be reconsidered only if he entered therapy and showed evidence that he would accommodate to school rules. The question of Ran's continued employment was left open for a more comprehensive end-of-year evaluation.

A similar cast of characters can be found in any school, and the usual solution is to turn to the school psychologist. The psychologist may recognize the problems as a systems phenomenon and the disturbed adolescent as the field where multilevel battles are being fought. But such consultants usually have many constraints on their maneuverability, and the bottom line is usually the same: Just work with this student on adjusting to classroom demands.

Shortly after the school board meeting, Joey's mother, Ruth, called Devra, the school psychologist, to set an appointment for Joey. Devra suggested a family consultation, and the family agreed to meet with Devra and Minuchin.

The Consultation: "He Has to Yell to Be Heard"

The family included Nathan, forty-eight and his wife, Ruth, forty-seven. The couple had been married for twenty years and had spent their entire married life as members of the kibbutz. They had three children. Gad, eighteen, had been drafted into the army a few months earlier. Gad came home only once every two weeks, but he made a special trip to be present at the consultation. Doris, fifteen, though of normal intelligence, was wheelchair-bound by extreme spasticity, complicated by epilepsy. Her condition was currently stable, but she had suffered sudden uncontrollable deteriorations, which could be expected to recur. Despite her handicaps, Doris was pursuing the academic program of the mossad. A special metapelet accompanied her at school, but the main responsibility fell on Ruth, whose kibbutz work assignment was the care of her daughter. Ruth and Doris were together constantly, and neither had much social contact outside the family. Attempts to have others attend to Doris for part of the day had failed; it was difficult to compete with Ruth's total devotion to Doris.

As the meeting began, Nathan, a tall, powerful man, sat down next to Gad, a similarly sturdy young man. Ruth wheeled Doris in and sat down next to her. The mother moved quietly and efficiently, but her face showed clear signs of fatigue. Doris's head was tilted sideways in her mother's direction, and she moved about in the chair with broken, uncoordinated movements. The parents were seated at opposite ends of the semicircle. Joey, seated between the two groups, stared at the floor. He was a good-looking boy with sensitive features, but his long hair covered his face. He informed Devra that he intended to say nothing at this meeting.

After the introductions, Ruth explained the special situation in the family: Doris needed help with everything she did, and Ruth devoted all her time and energy to helping her daughter. As she finished a presentation she had clearly made often, Nathan took the floor.

NATHAN: *Ran has explained everything. I am the problem! [The family laughs.] He thinks that I back Joey up in anything he does, that I'm used to having things my own way, and Joey is like me. He advised me to seek psychological treatment [laughter].*

RUTH: *The problem is that Joey and Ran don't get on together. Obviously, a teacher is stronger than a student, and so Joey was expelled from school.*

DEVRA: *[to Nathan] If that is your feeling, then you must have been hesitant about coming here.*
RUTH: *I have a feeling the present problem goes back to an old, old story. [She winks at Gad, who begins to laugh.] When Gad was in school, he also had conflicts with his homeroom teacher, and things worked out that . . . well, the teacher was thrown out of school. This is a well-known story in our community. I have the feeling that Ran came into the class with the preconceived—*
NATHAN: *[interrupting decisively] He said it.*
GAD: *He said, "Nathan, you want to solve Joey's problems the way you did with Gad, but you're not going to get me that way."*

This was the tale of an embattled family joined together to defend against the enemies outside. Devra was expected to join the united front instead of exploring possibilities for change; almost any other intervention she made would be interpreted as a hostile act.

Calling in from behind the one-way mirror, Minuchin suggested that Devra push the parents to discuss the problems with Joey. A sharp conflict developed: Joey refused to talk, and the parents refrained from pressing him. Minuchin joined the session, insisting that it was impossible to understand Joey's situation if he refused to talk. He pointed out the analogy between the situation at the school and the power struggle Joey was now carrying out against his parents by refusing to speak.

MINUCHIN: *[to Ruth] Please talk to your son and find out what's happening—how he engages you as well as his teacher in a battle for authority.*
RUTH: *But I want to speak with you, not him.*
NATHAN: *[interrupting] I'll tell Joey, all right. [Gad moves closer to Joey, putting his hand on his shoulder.]*
NATHAN: *[with tenderness] Joey. . . . May I say something, Joey?*
JOEY: *Yeah.*

NATHAN: *We very much wanted to come here, and I made you a promise that I can't break. The only one who can break it is yourself.*
JOEY: *But I don't want to.*
NATHAN: *But this fellow is awfully nice—both of them.*
JOEY: *That doesn't make any difference.*
NATHAN: *They say that if you refuse to talk, we won't be able to make any progress. At least tell us why you won't speak.*
DORIS: *If you . . . if you aren't able . . . to stay in school . . . what if you . . . is it worth it?*
JOEY: *[snaps] I don't want to, and that's that.*

Precipitating a conflict between family members allows a therapist to observe the ways in which the family negotiates issues. Who participates? Whose voices prevail? This family's language was very interesting. For the outsider, their language was negotiation from a position of power, but within the family they spoke in words of accommodation, protection, and avoidance of stress and conflict.

Minuchin's understanding of family hierarchies has been developed through working with nuclear families in which these issues have to be calibrated and recalibrated as children and parents move through the stages of individual and family development. In the kibbutz, however, family development is influenced differently, and issues of family hierarchies may be detoured through other parental subsystems, particularly the educational staff. In the case of Joey's family, Doris's extremely difficult childhood had resulted in the establishment of an elaborate network of helpers that further compromised parental authority. Executive parental functions had become a matter of committee.

MINUCHIN: *[to Devra] I think if his family can't help Joey, then your hands are tied.*
NATHAN: *But the problem is between Joey and his teacher. What can we possibly—*

MINUCHIN: *What's happening between you and Joey and between Joey and me is that he has converted this situation into a power struggle that he is winning.*

RUTH: *That's not fair! Joey didn't even know why we brought him here.*

NATHAN: *We asked him to come, and he agreed, after I brought up the idea that he wouldn't have to talk.*

MINUCHIN: *A boy of thirteen cannot have that much power without some help. He has the family behind him. That's why he thinks he can win out against the school. With that kind of help, he'll break his nose against doors. You are helping him in a way that will make life very difficult for him.*

RUTH: *He has power, and we don't. What can we do? Is he done for? [Everyone in the family laughs.]*

MINUCHIN: *[to Devra] It is very interesting that Joey is much stronger than everyone else. They have given him control over the session. So we will fail [leaves the room].*

Minuchin's dramatic exit startled a family that expected helpers to help. They continued their battle with Devra, but now with the nagging uncertainty that their struggle, however just the cause, might be hurting Joey.

DEVRA: *You give in to him?*

NATHAN: *Most of the time, yes.*

RUTH: *I think so. I can't recall cases very well.*

NATHAN: *Most of the time, we give in. [to Joey] In our arguments with you, we give in?*

JOEY: *Yeah.*

RUTH: *[to Nathan] Can you recall what we argue with him about?*

GAD: *How late he should stay out. . . .*

NATHAN: *There are arguments about all sorts of routine matters: putting his things in order, doing homework, coming home, not staying out late with friends. Most of the time, he does as he pleases.*

The mother's vague answers highlighted once again the skewed family organization that had developed around her care of her handicapped child. The overinvolved mother/child dyad was the center of the family. The closed dyad left little room for marital interaction and little room for Joey. Since Joey's movements were only vaguely noticed, his misbehavior was invisible. The father also seemed engaged elsewhere, in the world of work.

Joey was testing hierarchy in the school, trying to apply his family's lack of hierarchical organization there. It seems that family patterns have great power, even in this social context. Although Joey was a kibbutz child, had grown up in the kibbutz children's house, and had had parenting relationships not only with his parents but with his grandparents, his metapelet, and his teachers, in addition to the group of peers (which has a strong socializing influence in the kibbutz), he seemed to model his style of relating to school authorities on family patterns, just as adolescents from other social contexts do.

Minuchin later rejoined the session to continue the exploration.

MINUCHIN: *Are you telling me that Joey grew up like a wild animal?*

NATHAN: *Well, yes.*

GAD: *Something like that. [shrugging, with a rueful smile] He was alone very early, because Mother was tied up taking care of Doris, and Father was always busy with his work. He grew up something of an orphan.*

MINUCHIN: *Then he has to yell to be heard. He can't just say, "I am here." It has to be "I AM HERE!" [The family jump, then they begin to laugh.]*

RUTH: *I am not at all sure that this is so. . . .*

NATHAN: *Just a minute, listen to what he has to say.*

MINUCHIN: *This is what Gad said, and I think he's right. You have to understand why Joey has to keep fighting on the outside.*

RUTH: *I don't think he's. . . .*

MINUCHIN: *[to Devra] The family says that others have to*

change—you or the teacher or the school. It doesn't work. It will not work.

RUTH: *We do the best we can!*

Ruth again was framing the family in their usual position: We are helpless; you have to help us. In relation to Doris, this was simple reality, but it also protected the family against criticism and self-examination. Note, too, that the resentment inherent in the down position had fueled the power the family had over its helpers. If the family rejected help as insufficient, unsatisfactory, or uncaring, it would be the helpers who were at fault.

Still, a difference in the family was beginning to appear. Responding to Minuchin's support, Gad began to act as a co-therapist.

GAD: *If we follow this line, there are some very unpleasant implications for all of us, and it's difficult to accept that. I know, because I was talking about this with my father before I left for the army. It has always been very hard for us.*

MINUCHIN: *But it's easier not to listen to you, Gad. If the family hears what you have to say, they'll have to do something about it. But as long as you are not heard, your father can go on with the minimizing and the laughter, and your mother can continue caring for one child.*

Doris began to cry in a very dramatic way. Because of her condition, the crying quickly escalated into an uncontrollable outburst with spasms and convulsions of her whole body.

RUTH: *[sternly] Doris, don't start crying here!*

Ruth turned to Doris and forcibly held her body still. Gad put a hand on Joey's shoulder. Nathan looked at Devra with a helpless shrug. As in a tableau, the family movement froze: the mother's pain and frustration, combined with Doris' uncontrolled spasms, counterbalanced Gad's helpless attention to Joey and the father's forlorn incompetence.

MINUCHIN: *What do you want to be for Joey, Gad? A substitute father?*
GAD: *No. My relationship with him is different. But we have always been close. I know how stressed he was before this meeting.*

Minuchin was finding it almost impossible to concentrate with Doris screaming. Her needs were taking over the session, and even the room itself. He decided not to "hear" her, to accept her crying as a normal response to her pain and to "listen" instead to Joey's silence. It was an artificial response, which he knew he would not be able to maintain for long.

MINUCHIN: *You try to give him the attention that he doesn't get from his parents.*
GAD: *I want to give him all the attention I can. Yes, certainly.*
MINUCHIN: *Will it be enough?*

Gad, a "budding systems analyst," called the family's attention to their interconnectedness. Joey's experience is common to siblings of chronically ill children. The intensity of Doris's need had not diminished his developmental needs, but Joey had learned to accept that he would be alone and uncared for unless he made himself a problem. What Doris had to accept was guilt. She knew she was taking up too much space.

MINUCHIN: *[to the the parents] Joey demands his teacher's full attention. He gets none from his mother and none from his father, so—*
GAD: *[quietly] That may really be so.*
MINUCHIN: *His situation is very difficult. But every time he thinks he wins a battle, he is actually being defeated. And the family is helping him in that.*
RUTH: *I don't understand.*
GAD: *Every time he fights the teacher—*
MINUCHIN: *[interrupting] Ruth, can you say to Doris that I think Joey has to compete with her?*

RUTH: *Did you follow? [Doris begins to shriek.]*
MINUCHIN: *Did she understand?*
RUTH: *Yes. She was afraid of this meeting before it started. She is very much afraid of guilt feelings.*
MINUCHIN: *Joey, did you understand what I said? [Joey nods.] Sometimes you want more space in the family, but everyone is busy—*
JOEY: *Yes. I don't know. Well, sometimes.*

Joey needed help in learning to express his needs more directly in the family. He also needed to have his parents respond to him without compromising their authority out of guilt. They needed to learn that caring for him must not be confused with inappropriate support against authority or with becoming involved in fighting the mossad.

As Doris continued to scream, Minuchin found it almost impossible to continue the session. He couldn't bear to tell Doris what she already knew: that she had no right to take over Ruth's life, or even to disrupt a meeting to help Joey. He felt boxed in by her distorted body. She had no right to cry so grotesquely, but by rights she should not have been in that wheelchair. For a moment, he experienced what it was to be trapped in the family's private hell.

MINUCHIN: *You have a tragic reality, to which you respond in a certain way.*
NATHAN: *As matter of fact, I've been home very little since Joey was about a year and a half. When I was going to the university, I came to the kibbutz only on weekends. My work still takes me outside the kibbutz sometimes, so I haven't been with my children very much. Ruth took care of Doris, and Doris feels guilty. This, more or less, is the situation. Joey suffers most.*
RUTH: *[interrupting] The problem is, what are we to do? We know about it, we talk about it, we think about it all the time. We don't know how to do it better. By ourselves, this is the best we can do.*
MINUCHIN: *[to the parents] I really think you must talk it*

over by yourselves. You see how Joey succeeds in the process of defeating himself. Please don't help him in this. When you tell Joey that the problem is the conflict with the teacher, you are not helping him. You should talk this over with Joey.
RUTH: *And what if the parents are not in a position to help? if the parents don't know how to help?*
MINUCHIN: *This is something you have to talk over together. [Doris begins to sob again, and Ruth goes to her.]*

For several minutes the parents repeated their demands for advice on more specific ways to change their ways with Joey. Minuchin ended the session, deliberately leaving them in a state of nonresolution. He suggested they could call the clinic and arrange for therapy if they decided to after discussing the problem at home.

What did we learn in the consultation? Not surprisingly, we found that the obvious explanation is partial and simplistic. Starting with Joey and his problems at school, we found a web of dysfunctional interconnections: a closed family, fatigued and depleted of resources, with a seriously handicapped member; Ruth and Doris caught in a seemingly indivisible complementarity that for each of them narrowed the possibilities for independent life; Nathan unavailable in his escape into the world of work; Gad offering substitute parenting that does not suffice; and, of course, Joey—invisible at home and manifesting himself at school as a vengeful powderkeg.

In focusing on the family, however, the consultant failed to appreciate that the family's style of response was strongly maintained by their network of helpers. As often happens with families with chronically ill members, the kibbutz helpers and Joey's family were caught in a relationship that frequently failed to take account of the family's own capacity for growth, leaving them resentful of the intrusive protectors but also dependent on them.

A Parallel Process in the Family and the Mossad

Before the consultation, the family had resisted suggestions for family therapy. After it, they made two decisions that had a major influence on events that followed: They stopped attacking the teacher, both in private and in public, and they decided to seek therapy in a private setting. Although it was an unusual step—the kibbutz generally requires that therapy be provided by the Kibbutz Clinic—they insisted that they needed a therapist not involved with the kibbutz. The request, clearly rooted in their feeling that they were overly visible in the kibbutz and needed to protect themselves against the intrusion of helpers, was approved, and shortly thereafter Joey went back to the mossad. With this decision, they initiated a therapeutic process that focused on Joey and the family alone, while the interactions among the family and the mossad and kibbutz faded out of focus.

In American school systems, psychologists might likewise concentrate on Joey and avoid dealing with the rigidities of school organization, the difficulties of discipline, the organization of the classroom curriculum, and the relations between the school and the community. The consequences of this approach are evident in the failure of most American public schools located in poor neighborhoods, where social issues of poverty and the institutional control of the poor interfere with the school's functioning and students' achievements. But Joey's case is interesting because of the way two therapists selected different territories and each worked within her territory with respectful avoidance of the other.

Judith, who became Joey's therapist, was an outsider, unfamiliar with the culture and organization of the kibbutz. She did not appreciate the permeable membrane between kibbutz parents and teachers and the way they can collaborate or fail to collaborate toward common educational goals. Devra, who was working with the mossad, ceded the individual and family work to Judith. There was little contact between the two therapists.

Family Therapy: Filling a Vacuum

Judith's major goal was to reconnect Joey with his nuclear family and have his parents take responsibility for him, but she accepted their wish that she begin meeting with Joey individually. She felt that what they really wanted was to have someone take over the care of their son. She worked with him in formulating and expressing his frustrated needs and his rage at being abandoned by his parents.

Gradually the therapist incorporated a variety of strategies into her work:

> *I met the parents alone to try to get them to make joint parenting decisions about Joey. I also tried to do some marital therapy, but Nathan resisted, and subsequently I worked with Ruth alone. I hoped to help Ruth air her feelings about the loss of her private life, her sadness and anger about aging with a daughter who would always be dependent on her.*
>
> *There were some joint sessions, where Joey was encouraged to express his anger at his parents and develop a more open relationship with them. He was especially successful in improving his relationship to his father, whom he had previously seen only rarely. He also improved his communication with his mother, although he seemed to have less in common with her. But when I tried to get the parents to use their work in therapy to regain authority over Joey, they continued to avoid any confrontation. As long as Joey was minimally functioning, they were unwilling to change their relation with him.*

This was a therapy of low intensity in a family where a strong voice was needed in order to be heard. Limiting her work to the expression of affect and improved communication, the therapist became another helper complementing the family's needs.

One of the strange and interesting features of the practice of psychotherapy is the assumed discontinuity between the process of therapy and the reality of the patient's life. Joey was considered by Judith as improving when there was more open communication during family sessions, while he was still a marginal student in school, was avoiding after-school activities, and was becoming more and more isolated from his own group.

For a long time, the therapist was not aware that she was stabilizing the system rather than changing it. Gradually she perceived that in her gentle guidance and in the close relationship that she had established with Joey, she was filling a vacuum created by the missing parents. They had trained her to meet their needs without requiring them to change. Before Judith, the family had had a large number of helpers who participated in Doris's upbringing. Judith was simply added to that group, probably taking the role of Joey's teacher in the family's scheme of things. She had no way of realizing that, because the family-school relations were never a part of her therapy.

The family's commentary at a follow-up session about their therapy shows clearly their perception of the therapist's role within the family-school relationship.

NATHAN: *Most of the therapy was with Joey alone. He liked Judith, and we thought that it would help him.*

JOEY: *I think my meetings with her helped me, but I can't explain exactly how.*

NATHAN: *When we began therapy, it was decided that Judith would handle anything concerning Joey's behavior. Judith explained to Ran that this way the friction between him and Joey would have a chance to cool down. And in fact her work with Joey proved that problems can't be solved by force but only by understanding. There were still a few incidents between him and Ran, but Judith managed to make it up to Ran. Finally, Ran understood that Joey had emotional problems and that we weren't out to get him, and our relations became friendly.*

JOEY: *I didn't much care about regulations, but I wanted to stay with my friends in the mossad. Whenever Ran found something to get on my back about, Judith and I talked it over. Sometimes we even thought up what my punishment should be, and usually Ran did what we had decided.*

Knowing that he no longer had parental support for challenging Ran's authority, Joey could work out with Judith alternative ways for resolving his conflicts with adults. But without a change in family dynamics, and with no collaboration between parents and teachers, the whole burden of maintaining this unstable equilibrium rested on Judith's shoulders. It could not last long, especially because the school itself was in a process of change.

Changes at the Mossad

Devra was at the center of this process. Her account has much to say about the teachers, the class, and the organization of the mossad. She might also have observed how the family and school processes were intertwined, but since Judith and Devra were working in parallel instead of collaborating, Devra's information on the mossad, the school, and Joey and his family were not part of what Judith was doing with Joey and his parents. Devra's account describes what was happening:

In the first half year that Joey was in therapy with Judith, everyone was satisfied, and Joey was no longer the focus of attention whenever there was trouble at school. I was working with Ran and Ada, at first helping them to bridge their differences. Later we discussed ways to improve the group's spirit. Ran was becoming more confident in his authority and less argumentative with the class. Gradually, a more positive classroom atmosphere was emerging. At the end of the school year, the mossad's board had a better opinion of Ran's work and decided that he would continue with the group for a third year, as originally planned. It was good for the class, but I think that class dynamics and the improved relationship between Ran and the group pushed Joey to the sidelines. He lost his position in the group and became withdrawn.

Joey entered ninth grade very much on the wrong foot. By then, his friends were mostly older students, the fringe group of the mossad, who were experimenting with drugs. Although it appears from Devra's account that there were positive changes in the mossad, nobody was observing how they affected Joey. Except for his one hour of weekly support with Judith, Joey had become a forlorn boy, without much contact with his parents and increasingly on his own in class. He seemed uninterested in his studies and in all other mossad activities, with which his peers were becoming increasingly involved. Adults tended to treat him as a special case because he was in therapy, so his classmates began to think of him as disturbed. Joey was no longer a James Dean, and although he could "float" in the mossad, he was shunned more and more. Interestingly, the group's reaction toward Joey reflected ways of the adult community; in a society where the use of authority in dealing with members is avoided and where work is performed independently of material incentives, informal group pressures become an important way of penalizing a deviant member who seems to be taking advantage of the kibbutz.

Ran and Ada were experiencing mounting pressure to deal more vigorously with Joey's suspected use of marijuana and with his deteriorated condition, and they passed the pressure on to the therapist. Judith, however, had neither the influence nor the authority over Joey to fulfill their expectations. In her thinking, it was time for the parents to assume responsibility for controlling their son. A stormy session ensued, and the family terminated therapy.

The End of Family Therapy

The family's version of the end of therapy, given in the follow-up interview, again reveals that they perceived the therapist as part of their extended network, not as a changer of family dynamics.

> NATHAN: *Joey stopped going to school regularly and would stay in bed for whole days at a time. Judith was under great*

stress. She put a lot of pressure on us to solve the problem, but we didn't know what to do. Her central argument was that we do not demand enough of Joey, because of our guilt feelings over being occupied with Doris. But it wasn't long before Judith reached a dead end with this idea. She thought of us like a family in the city; for example, she told us that if Joey misbehaved, we shouldn't allow him to go out in the evening as punishment. But that's impossible in the kibbutz. He has his own room in the school building and can come and go as he pleases. I remember the discussion I had with Joey on our way home after the last family session. We talked all the way home, but we couldn't find any real system of rewards and punishments that would work. I then told Judith that she didn't understand the nature of our problem, that her way of handling it wouldn't solve anything, and there was really no point in coming again. I saw that we'd gotten all we could out of her, and anyhow, she was just blaming the victim.

JOEY: *She was way off base in thinking my parents could keep me on a tight leash.*

So therapy was terminated in a power struggle, and the family lost their trust in the therapeutic relationship. For Joey, it was another "victory": he gained freedom for self-destructive behaviors that ultimately left him isolated in the mossad as well as forsaken by his family. Early in his life, he had fallen in the crack between his preoccupied parents, and at this point, he fell again, this time between a well-functioning classroom that excluded him and his disempowered parents.

What went wrong with the therapy? Why didn't Devra include the family, Joey, the teacher, and possibly Judith in her work? It might have been possible to have a conference in the school with all the people involved in Joey's life. Joey's peers could have been included, as well as school personnel, Joey's grandparents, and other segments of his significant world. This type of group work was familiar to Devra and wholly in keeping with kibbutz philosophy and ways of addressing problems in the Kibbutz Clinic.

The answer to this puzzle seems to be pure respect for professional boundaries. Once Joey's psychological repair had been assigned to Judith, Devra refrained from intruding. Judith helped smooth Joey's contacts with Ran, but otherwise she left the unfamiliar school and mossad context to Devra. Once the lines had been drawn, all parties kept to their own turf—much to Joey's detriment.

An Attempt at Filial Therapy

Ironically, the termination of Judith's involvement with the family was followed by a change that she had pursued unsuccessfully for a year: Nathan sought a closer relationship with Joey. He found a new private therapist who agreed to help him build communication with Joey. Nathan began to meet with Joey regularly, three times a week. In Nathan's words,

> *The advisor kind of supervised me in how to talk about his life and the problems that were bothering him. It all worked well for a few months, and we enjoyed having Joey visit home more frequently.*

Families have resources that therapists frequently overlook but that in situations of crisis may lead to change. Left to his own devices, Nathan spontaneously reinvented the technique that Freud used in the treatment of Little Hans. But like Hans's father, he was being advised on how to treat his son while all other family problems were put aside, as though there were no connection between individual psychodynamics and the interpersonal world.

To Nathan, it seemed that Joey was in better spirits during these months, but again Nathan's effort was a partial solution. His advisor explicitly stated that he would be responsible only to Nathan and could not work on school-related problems. Furthermore, the technique of father-counselor does not work very well with adolescents. It was clear that Nathan's need for proximity with Joey came at a point when Joey's needs were for autonomy.

Nathan was surprised when Joey came to him and said that he could not talk to his father as he could to a psychologist. Joey would run to Ruth's parents whenever he and his father had disagreements, and they stopped having regular meetings. Concerning his in-laws, Nathan later noted,

I was angry that they let him smoke in their room and do things that other mossad kids weren't allowed to do. I think it was then that I had a major fight with them. Afterwards, Joey visited them more often, and the problem just kept mounting uncontrollably.

The fragmented world in which Joey grew demanded that he develop the skills often found among children of divorce: maneuvering between factions, coping with conflicting loyalties, and dealing with the always-complicated relations between adult caretakers. He took advantage of the feelings of guilt concerning him and easily avoided conflict by moving from parents to teacher to grandparents. Later he tried to transfer his learning to the new context of the mossad, and he was surprisingly successful in exploiting the multiple divisions within his complicated world. There were no adult authorities in his life; each disqualified the other.

A Crisis in the Mossad, and Coordination at Last

At the time that Joey entered ninth grade, while he was still in therapy with Judith and was getting deeper into trouble at school, Devra was asked to carry the work that she had begun with Ran and Ada into other classrooms. The mossad was then at its lowest ebb, and there were many symptoms of crisis: an extremely high turnover of homeroom teachers; dissatisfaction on the part of many parents, who thought the teachers had lost control over the mossad and were not involving the parents sufficiently; an increasing concern with drug and alcohol abuse; complaints by a growing majority of students, who experienced many regulations as too restrictive, denying them the right to their own tastes and opinions; and a study program that seemed too inflexible to meet the needs of both the fast and the slow learners. It was a big list of troubles for a 300-student school that was trying to provide top education and much more by stretching its staff beyond their limits.

These and other problems kept reappearing in Devra's work with students and staff, and she held a meeting with the mossad's board about the overall situation.

It was clear to me that the mossad needed to take a hard look at itself. The teachers needed to reevaluate their assigned roles, their dialogue with the students, and their relation to the larger kibbutz community. There was a need for new educational programs, for some new and capable staff brought in from the kibbutzim, and most of all for a spirit of transformation and hope. My role in this situation was not clearly defined, and I sensed some expectations that I would provide specific guidelines, particularly in domains that were confused and conflictual, such as the rules concerning smoking and regulation of after-study hours. I thought it would be wrong for me to assume this function; it would keep the teachers dependent on me and confuse our roles. My function was to help them use their strengths and develop their ability to change their school. I accepted a role as moderator of a group of homeroom teachers who began to meet regularly. I supported their attempts to try out new ways and worked with them on developing communication skills and ways of collaborating in small and large groups. Leadership among the young teachers began to form, and the group learned to organize itself better. Basic rules were clarified, a learning center for slow learners was established alongside an expanded vocational training program, higher professional standards in the recruitment of new staff were agreed on with the kibbutzim: These are some examples of the changes. The prevailing sense of confusion and doubt was changing into a more spirited atmosphere of positive expectations and active confrontation of the problems.

At this period I did not have direct contact with Joey. I made a point of asking Ada and Ran about him whenever we met, however. Their message was that although Joey was in therapy and was not acting in a disruptive way, his functioning at school was becoming more and more minimal.

Invested as she was in a total reorganization of the mossad, Devra had little to do with Joey, who after all was "in therapy."

That spring, a major crisis occurred. Late one night, a group of juveniles, apparently drunk, took hundreds of tiles that had been bought for the school's dining room, carried them to the roof, and hurled them to the ground. Most of the adolescents involved had long been known as problem students, but there were also some surprising discoveries of "good" youngsters. Raw nerves were touched when individual questioning of many of the participants revealed a lack of respect toward community property and no sense that it belonged to them. In heated discussions, inside the mossad and in the kibbutzim, such phrases as "a failure of kibbutz education" and "the erosion of social values among adolescents today" were commonly heard.

Joey was one of the tile throwers. By now it seemed he was certainly headed toward delinquency or patienthood, probably both. He was depressed, alienated from any meaningful contact with the world, abusing drugs. Again he needed to yell in order be heard. Ada and Ran asked Devra for a consultation, and Devra arranged to meet Joey.

I was supportive with him, and we developed a good rapport. He agreed with me that at this point it would be best to try to change his environment. He had become involved socially with a deviant group in the mossad and found it hard to resist their pressure for conformity. I pointed out that he was depressed, with nothing interesting or satisfying for him in the mossad. Doing some physical work in the fields might be an alternative that would improve his mood and put him in contact with people he liked in the kibbutz. Joey agreed readily to this suggestion. There were not many alternatives at this point in the school year, and the critical thing was to organize this change in a way that would be therapeutic: supporting Joey, yet placing firm limits.

After meeting Joey Devra had another session with the parents, the teachers, and a representative of the kibbutz. Together they worked out the details of Joey's program and divided the responsibilities. Three decisive months followed. Joey seemed motivated and cooperative, working regularly and well. His foreman took care to provide him with challenges and tasks that would be educational, but even when the work was repetitive and uninspiring, Joey did not complain. There was a tightening of his relationship with his parents, especially with Nathan, who was making great efforts to be at home more.

In September, Joey asked to be readmitted to the mossad and placed in a special class that was being formed, a small group of students who were to learn semiskilled trades and work as apprentices in their kibbutzim. He was interested in studying agricultural mechanics and wanted to be with friends from other kibbutzim who were studying there. The mossad was willing to accept him on a trial basis, and Joey and his new teacher agreed that it would be best if he began as a day student. There was a question of who would supervise Joey's after-school hours, and the answer was provided by Nathan; he was ending his term as a manager, and he decided to come back to work in his kibbutz.

Nothing in the remedy was new: clear limits, work, friendly support, responsibility, removal from bad company—a homely medicine indeed. But for the first time there was a cooperative effort among Joey, his parents, the teachers, and the kibbutz. And as they did their parts, there was less need for therapists. Or rather, as one therapist and then another exited, the father and later the teachers moved into a more active and competent role, confronting the problems themselves. These movements can teach us about the art of therapy: There are times when being minimal can be more effective than being "helpful."

The Follow-Up: "Both of Us Returned Home at the Same Time"

Two and a half years after the initial consultation we met the family for a follow-up interview.

NATHAN: *I think Joey was greatly shaken up by being thrown out of the mossad. He drew closer to me and realized that my approach to life is more realistic. I keep saying to him that if a person does only what he feels like doing, he's not really as free as he thinks he is, because he doesn't know how to adjust to society.*

JOEY: *Way down deep I always wanted to stop studying and just work. I know my father did that; all his serious studies came much later. Anyway, after working in the fields for a while, I guess I just became more serious about life. But when I began to work, I knew that it wasn't really a choice but a necessity. I was in a mess, and I actually had fears of losing my mind. But I don't want to talk about that.*

NATHAN: *I came back to the kibbutz for a tour of duty in the dining hall that I'd been postponing for years. It turned about to be a wonderful year—I think I was lucky to be rid of all the worries and pressures that my outside job involved, and also to find the family as I did. At this stage, Joey, too, began to spend more time in the house. It was as if both of us returned home at the same time.*

JOEY: *There was a natural change on my part. I simply felt more comfortable at my parents' home, and I began to go there more often. I think that the fact that my father came back to be with the family made a big difference.*

NATHAN: *Today I am a family man, whereas before I wasn't*

around. Some significant changes occurred in the family as a result.

RUTH: *I knew it wouldn't be easy for him to leave his work. I could give him my support, and I felt that he needed me. For a while, he was weak, depressed. We got closer, and the atmosphere in the family became more open and relaxed. It's like we got married all over again.*

NATHAN: *We have a special situation. My wife is free mornings, because the kibbutz has assigned her to help Doris in the after-school hours. So when I returned to the kibbutz, we had the mornings to talk to each other. During this one year, I talked to her more than I had during the ten years previously, and as far as I am concerned, it has been an extraordinary experience. In the beginning, we talked about Joey. As he improved, we found there were many other subjects. I discovered my wife all over again.*

RUTH: *I feel that the children have matured this year. An interesting thing that happened is that Doris has asked to visit my parents more regularly. She wants to keep a diary, and she asked my mother to write for her. Of course I'm not allowed to know what's in it, and I respect her privacy. She has just finished some of the matriculation exams, and she'll continue to study next year in order to get a full diploma. Joey isn't home as much now as he was six months ago, but that's normal for his age, and the teachers tell us he is a good student.*

JOEY: *It used to be that Doris was only with Mother and I was only with Father. It's much less like that today. I also talk more with Doris than I used to. I think the fact that my father came back to be with the family made a big difference.*

Even in the kibbutz, with all the substituting and supportive parental figures, the fact that a family of three reorganized into a family of four, with two leaders who feel competent to provide their son with the combination of limits and supportive attention that he needs, is a tremendously important change. When this change was combined with a collaboration among school, parents, and student that had never before existed, Joey's life at home and at school could move forward.

Four Years after the Initial Consultation with Minuchin

The last two years have been a period of relative tranquillity for this family. Joey has completed grade eleven with marked success and no disciplinary problems. He has a good social standing and has begun dating girls.

Gad finished his army service, left the kibbutz and is currently traveling in South America, following a path that has become almost a norm among kibbutz children of his age.

Nathan has organized a new project in his kibbutz, something he began to plan after completing his tour of duty in the dining hall. Although he works longer hours, he has continued to be very much involved in the affairs of the family. Ruth reports that the relations between them continue to be close but that a change has occurred: After Nathan left his previous job, she felt she needed to stand behind him; this last year, she feels she has stood at his side.

Doris completed her final high school examinations successfully and signed up this year for a university correspondence course. Since there is no work for her in the kibbutz, she has become totally dependent on her mother, and the two of them are almost constantly together. Ruth feels weighed down by this situation. The renewed contact between Doris and the grandparents helps, but not enough. The family recently began to discuss with the kibbutz ways of sharing Doris's care that would allow Ruth to work part-time outside the home. There is an attempt to create a special working role for Doris in the kibbutz. In the background is the sad realization that Doris's condition can only worsen over the years.

Reflections

For decades, the therapist was viewed as a wise observer, whose interpretations were merely an Ariadne's thread to guide the patient in a trip of discovery. But as scientists have come to see that the observer is part of the observed, the therapist has become visible in his interventions. Even among psychoanalysts, the image of the objective mirror-like therapist has been replaced. Countertransference, once the unforgivable sin, has been accepted as a tool in the therapeutic process. Among some, the idea is taking hold that therapy is a conjoint trip, in which patient and therapist co-construct the therapeutic narrative. As early as the 1950s, when the pipe-smoking, detached, neutral therapist was the ideal, C. Whitaker conceptualized the patient and therapist together as an organism in which the therapist's growth was part of the process of the patient's recovery. In family therapy, the therapist has always been more or less part of the system, but the division between "conductors" and "neutral therapists" became a theoretical and political issue that highlighted the reluctance of family therapists to acknowledge that they shape the territory that they map.

The idea of co-construction of the therapeutic narrative in family therapy has brought a renewed interest in what happens in the session—both the process by which the therapist influences direction and meaning and the significance of the therapist as a fallible human instrument. To understand the latter, we must look at the therapist's own context, including history, style, culture, stage in life, and professional context—whether hospital, kibbutz, court, or social welfare—as well as the salient words and values that may direct the therapist's observations and meanings. Minuchin's lack of knowledge of the kibbutz social organization made him map a nuclear family with parents in an executive function, which did not resemble the complex organism that had been formed around Joey's family in response to Doris's disability. Joey's psychologist shared Minuchin's bias for focusing on the nuclear family rather than on a child's functioning. Working in the kibbutz, the school psychologist was unaware of the process by which respect for Joey's therapist and acceptance of the school boundaries on her work made Joey's behavior invisible to her. All three interveners put brackets around the segments of Joey's ecology that they felt they could most comfortably or efficiently manage.

This same kind of bracketing is happening on a wide scale with welfare families in American cities. The interveners—the human resource administrator, the social service workers, the caseworkers in foster care—all categorize families in accordance with value-laden imperatives, or perhaps simply practice-sanctioned priorities, without awareness of the effects of their biases in this labeling. The consequences are all too often a fragmentation of services, services organized with an unwitting bias toward preserving themselves unchanged, and depowered families.

7

Mickie

DO FAMILY THERAPISTS actually deal with the "family" that family members experience? If we ask, "Who is your family?" we are not likely to be told, "I am the assistant vice president of X Corporation, and my life design is governed by my loyalty to X." Yet, what of the spouse who is married to the job, the kitchen, the children, the military, AA, the golf club, the church, or his or her analyst? What if the couple functions like a confused reconstituted family, each attached to another network, unable either to integrate or to separate? What if the judicial system is involved in the marriage of the poverty-stricken couple we are seeing in our practice?

Do we tackle these larger systems, or do we insist on separating family members from their nonparadigmatic significant others? Yes, often. When we enter the territory of larger systems, we feel dwarfed. We understand concepts of the nuclear family, but for the most part we are ignorant of the complex social, political, and economic laws that undergird subsystems like schools, courts, hospitals, and social welfare. Few of us, for example, could have anticipated the connections between deinstitutionalization and the labor unions that fought the closing of psychiatric hospitals in the United States.

The City of New York spends over $300 million a year on its

protective services for children and averages a 60 to 80 percent staff turnover every year because workers soon experience depletion, guilt, and hopelessness in their work. One would think, therefore, that this subsystem would be ripe for ecological intervention, that it would realize the necessity of taking into account the systemic interconnection of child, family, poverty, homelessness, racism, drugs, neglect, and violence. That, of course, would be a naive underestimation of the powerful social and political forces that maintain a bureaucracy doing more and more of the same. The larger the social system, the more it is a prisoner, engaged primarily in the task of surviving intact. With the simpler systems of families, family therapists can at least feel masterful. So a family therapy consultant is usually dealing with a paradigmatic therapeutic system, both family and therapist divorced from the social context, quite possibly to everyone's detriment, as in the case of Yoav.

What about the kibbutz? That small society, so intensely aware of its interconnectedness, is an ideal laboratory for ecological intervention, as Kaffman points out in chapter 8. Kibbutz Clinic staff, many of whom are also kibbutz members and therefore parts of a social system that they need to manipulate, are always aware of the complexity of their task. Or are they?

A Family "Rashomon"

Family members though living a common history do nonetheless construct a different story out of their shared experiences. As in Ryonosuké Akutagawa's "Rashomon" they are all true.

Shaul's Story

I grew up in Kibbutz Ramot. My whole family is there. I was competent, good in sports, well liked in my peer group. Everybody, including me, was sure that I would return to the kibbutz after my army service. But in the army, I met Hagar, a Tel Aviv girl. Maybe I was attracted by the fact that she always had the courage of her convictions. But we left the kibbutz on account of her. She could not adjust to the work, was not ready to compromise, and never had the patience to let people get to know her. So we left.

Several months ago, we had to come back on account of our daughter Mickie, who had been thrown out of school. Mickie's had a lot of problems. My company has transferred me three times in the last four years, so she's had to adjust to one school after another. Finally, I guess, something just snapped. She stopped studying and had no friends. It was the middle of the year. The school suggested we put her in a residential school! We thought that was way out of line, but no regular school would take her. We practically had to beg to come back here to the kibbutz. My family used its influence, and we were accepted as a special favor. The kibbutz has really been trying to help us integrate. But Hagar! It's not just that's she's pushy. It's the way she treats Mickie. Yesterday she slapped her. Of course Mickie ran out and was roaming around during family hours. The whole kibbutz is talking about it.

We tried living outside the kibbutz. It didn't work. Now we're back, and it has to work. Hagar's got to learn that everyone doesn't dance to her tune.

Hagar's Story

The kibbutz is not my home. I came back for Mickie's sake. All her problems are the result of our moving around. But she's driving me crazy. She rejects me, no matter how hard I try. And Shaul's always on her side, trying to be her pal. He and the whole damned clan—nobody thinks of me. I'm a licensed nurse, but I'm forbidden even to ask to work at the kibbutz. Who are they to pass judgment on me? They've labeled me a selfish monster, a "child abuser." I have no one to turn to; even my parents are on Shaul's side.

Naomi's Story

I am Shaul's eldest sister. We are a central family in the kibbutz; my parents are among the founders. So Shaul's leaving came as a surprise to all of us. We understood it was because of Hagar. She is a strongly individualistic person, with an explosive temper. Our form of life doesn't suit her very well. Still, we supported their decision to come back; Mickie needed good care and a stable home. There was a pretty heated discussion at the secretariat: There's a shortage of housing, the group Mickie was to enter was already considered problematic, and Hagar's past work record raised a lot of questions. But finally the committee recommended accepting them and it was passed at the general meeting. But the atmosphere was very unpleasant. In situations like this, you really feel how painful gossip can be, with all that talk about favoritism. And the people who remember Hagar from before are having a field day. Only yesterday, I saw Mickie wandering about during the afternoon, like an abandoned child. Everybody is talking. We need professional help at once.

The Consultation: "I Don't Think You Know How to Listen"

Galia, the Kibbutz Clinic therapist, was waiting in the office as the family arrived. The first to come in was Mickie, a plump girl with an alert look. She immediately surveyed the room, tried to peek into the one-way mirror, and began making faces in front of it. From time to time, she would look around to assess the adults' reaction to her behavior. Sheila, a pretty child, seated herself quietly. Hagar, thirty-five, was overweight, dressed plainly, and ill groomed. Shaul, thirty-four, smiled in a friendly manner and shook Galia's hand. Young for his age, thin and wiry, he was dressed in sporty clothes and looked relaxed.

GALIA: *What is happening in the family now?*

HAGAR: *Mickie is impossible, as usual. The day before yesterday—*

MICKIE: *No, Mommy!*

HAGAR: *I went into the bathroom and found dirty pants on the floor—*

MICKIE: *No, Mommy! Don't tell! Daddy, make her stop! [She gets up and tries to leave the room.]*

SHAUL: *Stay here, sweetie. You don't have to listen.*

HAGAR: *The floor was dirty, there were marks on the wall—it was disgusting.*

SHAUL: *Don't cry, Mickie. Sit over here and shut your ears.*

HAGAR: *I'm finished. Now Shaul is dealing with her.*

SHAUL: *Hagar tells me to handle her, but something always happens. Mickie gets home at four. Something blows, so Hagar throws her out, and she goes back to the children's house and doesn't come home till supper.*

HAGAR: *What kind of girl could make such a mess? She knows how hard I work to keep the house clean, and—*

SHAUL: *I don't think it matters what Mickie does. Even when she sits quietly, watching television, Hagar shouts, "No! Go away!" Any little thing—*

HAGAR: *But you're not telling your part in this story. Why don't you ever back me up? You argue with me, and all the time Mickie. . . .*

"How can Mommy shame me in front of strangers?" "How can Shaul side with Mickie against me?" "How can Hagar be so insensitive to our daughter's pain?" Each family member was isolated, closed in by his or her own emotions and unable to receive new information. Each one was the victim; each of the others was the enemy.

Of course, Shaul had the advantage. He had the educational establishment as his ally against the abusive mother. Mickie was caught in the middle of a struggle not of her own making. Her behavior was a battlefield marked out by the combatants: Her mother labeled her impossible, her father labeled her the victim—only a narrow band of behavior was possible.

The therapist tried to get the parents to discuss and agree on any one issue with respect to handling Mickie. They continued to sling accusations at each other, however, making Galia their judge. At this point, Minuchin entered the room from behind the one-way mirror and talked to Galia, remaining standing as if making a pronouncement.

MINUCHIN: *These people do not hear each other: Shaul says, "I am right," and Hagar says, "I am right," and this is their priority. [He goes over to Mickie and sits down on the rug.] Come here, young lady, I want to talk to you. How old are you?*
MICKIE: *[smiling shyly] Nine.*
SHEILA: *And my name is Sheila, and I'm six.*

Minuchin talked with the children for some ten minutes, chatting with them about their lives, then turned to the parents.

MINUCHIN: *You have lovely children. I think they will develop very well, if you can give up your fight for control.*
HAGAR: *I agree with you. It's just what I've been saying all along, Shaul. You try to be the one who's right, and so do I. We keep fighting all the time about who's right, and the children get lost in the shuffle.*

A consultant has the power to relabel and thereby offer alternatives to the family, at least temporarily. Minuchin arbitrarily declared the children nondeviant in order to focus on the "I am right and you are wrong" parental subsystem, which was displaying itself at its most irrational. This focus was only a partial truth, introduced as a therapeutic provocation. It was also a working framework.

Minuchin asked the parents to discuss this point between them and left the room. Before long, the couple was back to the old pattern: a struggle about the right way of handling Mickie. Galia could not avoid being triangulated. Minuchin therefore suggested that Galia simply remove herself until the parents reached agreement on some topic. She assigned them this task and joined him in the observation room.

Alone now, the parents rigidly maintained their pattern of mutual blaming. Finally, Minuchin suggested that the therapist call through the intercom and tell whoever answered to agree with anything the spouse said—a unilateral disarmament. It happened that Hagar answered, so she was the one who got the message.

HAGAR: *Galia has asked that I agree to whatever you say as we discuss our ways with Mickie.*

SHAUL: *Oh. Well, all right, in my opinion, part of the problem comes from the rules you set. Mickie would feel at home if you'd just relax your rules.*

HAGAR: *I agree.*

SHAUL: *At some point, we must close our eyes.*

HAGAR: *I agree. I really have no problem with this. That's how it used to be.*

SHAUL: *It was never like that. She's always asking me to turn on the TV, because she's afraid of how you'll react if she turns it on.*

HAGAR: *[angrily] Why does she always turn to you? Did you ever think about that?*

SHAUL: *Because she's afraid of you. I think I treat her more tenderly.*

HAGAR: *[very angrily]* She *gets the tenderness that's lacking in our relationship. You don't seem to understand that we are the kind of parents whose connection with each other goes through the children. This is a terrible situation! [Minuchin and Galia return.]*

MINUCHIN: *What kind of family hypnosis is active here? Shaul, you must be doing something very interesting in the family, which makes everyone think that you're the good man and she's the bad woman.*

SHAUL: *Well, I guess I understand what you're saying. But when it comes to the way Hagar handles Mickie—*

MINUCHIN: *The problem is not Mickie! Both of you keep*

insisting that only one of you owns the total truth. If you change that, Mickie will make progress.

HAGAR: *I really feel it's just as you put it. In Ramot, my life has become like a trial. Shaul is constantly judging me, and he always finds me guilty.*

Shaul responded to Minuchin's opening tactic ("Your behavior frames and creates Hagar's") with "Hagar's mothering is terrible," moving the situation back to blaming. When Minuchin restated his belief in complementarity, Hagar used his statement to blame Shaul. On the face of it, no change had occurred. But in the therapeutic dialogue there was now an alliance with Hagar, which created an opportunity for new exploration.

MINUCHIN: *When you ask Shaul for his support, are you aware of the moment when he stops listening to you?*

HAGAR: *Yes.*

MINUCHIN: *Fine. Talk to him, but try to make him listen.*

HAGAR: *Last evening—do you remember, Shaul?—I told you I was feeling low. It didn't bother you one bit. Were you listening?*

SHAUL: *Well, did you tell me that because you wanted me to help?*

HAGAR: *I was trying to make you realize that I feel criticized by the whole family! I feel very lonely and terribly aware of the kibbutz gossip. I'm falling apart! All the good feelings of coming home have disappeared, and I feel very insecure. But you're like a blank wall.*

SHAUL: *You never said that.*

HAGAR: *You dozed off! And I lay in bed wide awake, thinking maybe we could still talk! [Her voice quivers.]*

The mood changed. Accepting Minuchin's support, Hagar communicated her pain instead of yelling in impotent anger. This made it much easier to like her. Minuchin continued to expand the exploration of "her" truth. He suggested that Mickie and Sheila go to the playroom and returned to Hagar.

MINUCHIN: *[going to Hagar] You were married ten years ago. When did the marriage die?*

HAGAR: *I don't think it's altogether dead. I will say it's been asleep for two years. And it's worse here. They just won't accept me. But when I try to talk to him about it, he says I'm just imagining things.*

MINUCHIN: *Do you think you could wake your husband up?*

HAGAR: *He's asleep sexually, too. I keep telling him, "I guess I no longer attract you," but he says I'm always the one who's too tired.*

MINUCHIN: *Is he impotent?*

HAGAR: *No, but he's not the way he used to be. I thought that maybe—*

SHAUL: *[jokingly] The crisis of the thirties.*

HAGAR: *I thought that maybe because I've gained weight. . . . I used to be better looking and more attractive.*

MINUCHIN: *And why did you start neglecting yourself? Are you bored with him, too?*

HAGAR: *He doesn't bore me, he depresses me. And he's critical, like my father. When my parents come, Dad will say to Shaul, "What's the matter with you? Why don't you keep her in line?" I stand all alone, on my own.*

MINUCHIN: *It means that Mickie is the only one who supports you.*

HAGAR: Mickie *supports me?!*

MINUCHIN: *If she didn't keep engaging your attention, you'd feel even lonelier.*

SHAUL: *You mean Hagar discharges some of her tension on Mickie.*

MINUCHIN: *He simply does not want to understand, does he, Hagar? I said the opposite of what he is now saying.*

HAGAR: *I understood exactly what you said.*

MINUCHIN: *Since your husband is asleep, Mickie is helping you not to feel so isolated and not to become depressed.*

HAGAR: *Which means we shouldn't send her away. But if she stays with us, she'll always be in the middle.*

The unfolding of a story depends on the audience, and Minuchin had provided Hagar with a listener. This enhanced Hagar's position and provoked Shaul to woo her back.

The family function Minuchin assigned to Mickie was nothing more than a therapeutic construction that supported his strategy. Framing the confrontation between Mickie and Hagar as part of a three-person phenomenon highlighted the spouse conflict in a way that demanded a new response from Shaul.

MINUCHIN: *You've both been killing your marriage. Now I am giving you the job of rebuilding it. It's up to you, Hagar. You've got to help him.*
HAGAR: *You've got to be kidding! He doesn't listen to me. And I'd have to change the entire family. They don't respect me, and he listens to them, not me.*
MINUCHIN: *So you have your work cut out for you. Is Shaul an only child?*
HAGAR: *Well, in some ways he was like an only child. He was their fair-haired boy, and the family has always paid special attention to him.*
MINUCHIN: *No wonder you have to help him. He's got to learn he's not so special. And you've got to rebuild your marriage. Otherwise, you may end in divorce.*
HAGAR: *He's told me many times that we may need to divorce. But how can I change him?*
MINUCHIN: *I think it will be important to meet with the entire family to see how it can be done. Let's stop here now and meet again next week.*
SHAUL: *But you've barely spoken to me! Only to her.*
MINUCHIN: *Yes, because I do not think you know how to listen to anyone talking to you directly. Perhaps you heard me as I talked to her.*

The session ended in a surprising way for the family. Hagar found herself defined as the stronger member of the couple, with the task of changing Shaul, while Shaul found himself devalued—a very unfamiliar situation for him. Had they been a family with well-defined boundaries, this strategy might have created a movement to decrease their involvement of Mickie in the marital battle and supported a direct discussion of differences on more equal footing. But in the kibbutz, the boundaries between family and context are more permeable, and conflicts between Hagar and the larger family and social systems were enhancing Shaul's position and adding fuel to the marital strife. Minuchin therefore suggested that Galia include as many members of the extended family as possible in the next session.

A Meeting with the Extended Family: "Hagar Has Horns"

The second meeting, the following week, included Shaul's sister, Naomi, and Rivka, his brother's wife. Naomi was then chairing the guidance committee of the kibbutz. Although they were the only two members of the extended family present, we could assume that they had been delegated authority and that the information and decisions made in the session would be communicated immediately to the rest of the family and to the resonating chambers of the kibbutz.

Minuchin had decided to focus the session on assimilation to the kibbutz—an important word in the language of a communal group. This framing would be used to move Hagar out of the position of identified patient.

GALIA: *[to Naomi and Rivka] I appreciate the effort you made to get here. I think there is a crisis situation in Shaul and Hagar's family, and your extended family in the kibbutz made a valiant effort to accept them.*

NAOMI: *[clearly taking the role of spokesperson for the family as she reports to the therapist] Shaul and Hagar have been very unstable, moving about from place to place for years.*

The family thought it best for them to return, and Ramot will do what it can to help.

SHAUL: *Well, I always thought we would return, but it never crossed my mind that it would happen this way. I didn't want charity. It was Hagar who thought—*

HAGAR: *I felt it was time to return, because our problems stem from all our wandering about. In the kibbutz, we have a stable home. All the problems can be faced here more easily.*

GALIA: *And how is this "home" helping you now?*

RIVKA: *The kibbutz is doing its utmost. But I think Hagar expects too much of the family.*

SHAUL: *The kibbutz asked the family—it was almost a condition for acceptance—to take responsibility for helping us rejoin. So we meet with Naomi regularly every week. Rivka was a great help with Mickie in the school. Our situation was very difficult, and we were made to understand that if I hadn't been born in the kibbutz, we wouldn't have been accepted. Hagar doesn't understand how obliged we are to the kibbutz.*

Coming from a different background and not sharing some of the kibbutz values, Hagar was both less sensitive and less bound than Shaul to the many informal duties and rules of the kibbutz. Shaul was moving gracefully on home territory, but Hagar's experience was that of the immigrant: devaluation of worth, social isolation, and loss of supports. Her husband had joined a cross-generational coalition against her and denied it. She felt she was fighting for survival, while to the others she appeared rigid and paranoid.

MINUCHIN: *These are very difficult conditions for successful integration. Can you talk about it?*

HAGAR: *They sure are. I'm expected to report on my behavior all the time. Why? Damn it, I'm mature enough to know how and with whom to talk! And the health committee treats me like dirt. I'm a nurse! But I'm doing menial work.*

I know I had problems before, but that was years ago. I'm not the same Hagar.

NAOMI: *We've already told you that it's not enough for you to say that you have changed. Your behavior hasn't.*

GALIA: *Rivka, as a sister-in-law, how do you see the situation?*

RIVKA: *There is no doubt that Hagar is under observation. But if she had really changed the way she says she has, she'd be able to cope.*

MINUCHIN: *Why aren't you under observation, Shaul?*

SHAUL: *Well, I was born in the kibbutz. They've known me since I was a child, and they trust me.*

MINUCHIN: *And how would the kibbutz like Hagar to change? Should she lose some weight, or smile more often? Should her eyes turn blue?*

Since the ploy to move Rivka to support Hagar had failed, Minuchin returned to his challenge of Shaul, using concreteness to the point of absurdity to challenge the logic and order of the institutional language.

SHAUL: *Well, the kibbutz didn't assign Hagar to work in nursing. She should accept this.*

MINUCHIN: *Is that all they mean when they say that Hagar must change?*

SHAUL: *It's one thing. Another is Hagar's overdependence on the family. Neither Rivka nor Naomi sees any change in this respect.*

MINUCHIN: *Where were you born, Hagar?*

HAGAR: *In town—Tel Aviv.*

MINUCHIN: *Which means you are not a Bantu.*

HAGAR: *[laughs] No, I am from here, a native of this country.*

MINUCHIN: *But not from this tribe.*

HAGAR: *Not from this tribe, no.*

MINUCHIN: *I was also an immigrant, and not just once. I was born in Argentina, then I lived in Israel for a time, and now I am living in the United States.*

HAGAR: *You move about, the way I do.*
MINUCHIN: *That is how we are. [Hagar smiles.] And I understand the difficulties of the immigrant.*

By defining himself as an immigrant, and labeling Hagar the same, Minuchin gave different meaning to her behavior and joined her in the culprit dock. In the same move, he highlighted the roles of the others as the accusers, who were creating confusion and tension.

MINUCHIN: *Shaul, you seem to be closer to your tribe than you are to your wife.*
SHAUL: *I guess she feels that way sometimes.*
MINUCHIN: *You side with your family against Hagar. That's why she feels so lonely.*
SHAUL: *I don't side with the family against Hagar! I'm trying to follow kibbutz norms. Hagar doesn't understand—*
RIVKA: *I must say on Shaul's behalf that things are very difficult for him. He takes care of the children much more than Hagar does. I understand that Shaul should support Hagar, but—*
MINUCHIN: *[getting up and looking at Hagar as though through a magnifying glass] Shaul is all right, but you have horns. [Hagar laughs.] What is going on here?*

Standing up, talking to Naomi and Rivka, Minuchin felt and acted like a public defender, making his summation to the jury. He was establishing distance so they could look at Shaul and Hagar as a joint social system.

MINUCHIN: *Because you are too intent on Hagar's horns, you forget that the major family issue is their integration in the kibbutz. We invited you because you are involved in helping them integrate, and we wanted you to know that joining with Shaul alone will not help the family.*
SHAUL: *Well, for the sake of argument. . . . But how do Hagar and I get out of it?*
MINUCHIN: *Your family is in the midst of a transition from culture to culture. You were born in the kibbutz. You're well*

acquainted with the laws governing the place, so you could be of great help and support to your wife in her efforts to integrate into this society. She needs to feel you're on her side.

SHAUL: *We have problems. We're very different.*

MINUCHIN: *That's a job for you and your wife, without the family. You will have to work with your therapist on it.*

The session continued a while longer with an exploration of how Naomi's husband and Rivka, who both began kibbutz life when they married, had experienced this absorption. Naomi and Rivka held to their general criticism of Hagar's personality, but Minuchin persevered in demarcating clearer boundary lines for the couple. By the end of the session, Shaul had acknowledged that he was part of the problem, and the therapeutic contract had expanded to include him as a patient instead of as protector of Mickie.

Ecological Therapy: Working with Family, School, and Community

Galia had previously established herself as liaison and adviser to the school system and to the absorption committee. Consequently, the impact of Minuchin's consultations could be combined with the opportunities afforded by her position in the family and community systems to produce change not only in the family but also in the relations between the family and the community. Her account describes the several directions her work took.

Mickie

The first half-year of therapy was focused primarily on Mickie's crisis at school and in the family. The objective was to help her adjust within the normal educational framework.

I worked with the principal, the group's homeroom teacher, the metapelet, a teacher for remedial work, and the education committee of the kibbutz. I asked a learning disability expert from the clinic to evaluate Mickie and supervise the teachers in the development of her learning program. Mickie was making progress, but periodically she was involved in intense incidents during which everything seemed to be falling apart.

About a month after the consultation, Mickie threw a fit in front of the class, shouting and pounding the floor with her fists. Both teachers and students were very upset. The school principal convened a major meeting, with all the staff involved with Mickie present. The school's position was that Mickie was profoundly disturbed in a way that made it impossible for her to continue within the regular educational framework. Because of Hagar's rejection of her, a residential school for children might provide her with a more "accepting and supporting milieu."

As a kibbutz member, I found it easy to understand the teachers' frustration; they were doing their utmost to help Mickie and feeling that Hagar was ungrateful and uncooperative. But I was able to insist that the school give Mickie some time. I said that Mickie needed a secure and stable environment in order to adjust gradually to school. I asked the principal to give therapy a chance and, for a limited time, to assign a special person to work with Mickie at close range. Fortunately, the metapelet volunteered to take on this special responsibility. She appeared competent with the children and more than the others was able to respond to Mickie's outbreaks of temper matter-of-factly. She came to the clinic for supervision, and the principal agreed to arrange for a substitute for her on those days, as well as during the hours when her time would be taken up with Mickie.

Anyone who has worked within an educational system knows that this was not a routine matter. Vast willingness to mobilize manpower for the needs of members in distress is a characteristic of the kibbutz, and in this example we can observe its effects on therapy.

Unfortunately, Hagar kept receiving any reports from the school about Mickie's misbehaviors as criticisms of her. She was anxiously attempting to discipline Mickey by using various punishments, and it was not working.

I decided to separate the issues at school from the family. The school context belonged to the teachers and Mickie, and I urged Hagar to let them work at it, respecting the home/school boundary. The educational staff helped by agreeing to refrain from telling the parents about each incident with Mickie.

Tensions between Mickie, the metapelet, the school, and Hagar began to decrease as they all kept their parts in the agreement. The metapelet, combining support with firm demands, formed a good relationship with Mickie. The whole staff accepted the therapeutic line: If Mickie felt that she could not concentrate or was on the verge of an outburst, she could leave the classroom and visit the metapelet. The metapelet would then accompany Mickie back to the classroom and sit down next to her as long as necessary. Her task was to resolve with Mickie the source of trouble and then help her to organize herself into a frame of studying. Her presence enabled the teacher and the group to go on with their work, while Mickie received less negative attention.

The mood of the group toward Mickie changed significantly after the teacher and the metapelet dedicated some of the weekly "educator's hour" to discussing the difficulties of integration and group rejection. I instructed them in some nonverbal group games that illustrate these themes, and once the children opened up it was found that Mickie was not the only one to have suffered from the experience of being the group's scapegoat. Subsequently there was a general improvement in relations in the group, and the children became significant supporters of Mickie's attempts to integrate. Very soon, assistance to Mickie consisted mainly of helping her organize herself in the morning. It was enough for her and for the teachers to know that they could turn to the metapelet.

As the pressures around Mickie's adjustment to the school and to her social setting lessened, the tension between the parents and their arguments over questions of education lost most of their sharpness. Both the educational personnel and the parents felt they shared in the efforts to absorb Mickie into the regular kibbutz framework and experienced with her a sense of success.

It is interesting to note the effect of this changed situation on the marriage. There is a plethora of concepts in family therapy to describe the process by which spouses displace their inner tensions onto their child-patient. The experience of Mickie's parents showed that although marital differences needed to be worked through—are they ever absent in normal families?—the rigidity seen by Minuchin owed much to the impingement of other systems upon the couple. The similarity with Yoav's case is striking, but fortunately the tensions surrounding Mickie were resolved in a more benign way. Instead of scapegoating the family as completely responsible for the problems and overloading it with demands, the therapist in this case could use the kibbutz resources for problem solving and the support of normal family functioning.

Family Boundaries

Meanwhile, complaints about Hagar's behavior had not abated, whether in connection with Mickie or her work or family relations. Galia and another therapist, David, began to work with the couple as a team.

David and I focused on the integration problems in the kibbutz and the return of the prodigal son to his clan. We continually supported Hagar and sought to enhance her position in the family.

Another prominent issue was the way Shaul's family monitored Hagar. We suggested that it would be better if neither Naomi nor anyone else of the extended family were charged with representing the kibbutz and supervising the family's integration. Shaul and Hagar presented this argument to the kibbutz's secretary, and another member of the guidance committee became their sponsor.

Hagar and the Community

Hagar's integration with the kibbutz proved to be a thorny issue. She felt publicly humiliated by the conditions of her acceptance, which forbade her to nurse in the kibbutz, although the kibbutz was suffering from a shortage of trained nursing personnel, and Hagar had no permanent assignment anywhere else. We therefore proposed that Hagar go out for a year's assignment to work in a neighboring kibbutz, with our staff supporting her by way of supervision. We met with the kibbutz secretary and the absorption committees, and finally the kibbutz agreed. It was more difficult to convince Hagar to take the opportunity, and we perceived how fearful she was of failing.

Yet with our support, she completed her year in a minimally adequate manner and succeeded in no longer being the subject of gossip. The crisis came the following year, when she asked Ramot's committee for a nursing appointment and was refused. As usual, her reaction was intense anger, anxiety, and constant preoccupation with the wrongs done to her. Now everybody thought she was paranoid. She had a social label, and the kibbutz would neither forget nor forgive her past.

Galia's language conveys her intense involvement and her protection of Hagar. We don't hear the modulating language of objective distance that characterizes therapeutic reports. In the complex territory of the kibbutz, Hagar's public behavior became a benchmark for measuring Galia's competence.

Because of her closeness to the kibbutz, Galia was now under the microscope, entangled in a social conflict. Hagar expected her to lobby actively on her behalf. The kibbutz expected her to produce social quiet. Obviously, the more Galia became involved in issues of social functioning, the less clear it was who she was responsible to. This is also the experience of therapists who work for other types of institutions—the welfare agency, the hospital, the court—and who become involved in arbitration, social control, or protective care. The issue then is to recognize the limitations of continued involvement, to know when and how to disengage.

Therapy: Terminable or Interminable?

Most of the marital and family therapy was carried on the year that Hagar was working in the neighboring kibbutz. As the atmosphere in the meetings with the couple turned positive and more intimate, Hagar brought up the subject of her excess weight. The couple explored the symbolic meaning of her losing weight. Hagar set a reasonable goal for herself, and she reached it with the help of individual hypnotic sessions. The relations between the couple reached a new high at this stage. We decided that the time had come to bring an end to the therapy, a year and a half after the consultation with Minuchin.

Four months later, I got a telephone call from the kibbutz nurse. It appeared that Hagar had consulted her about dizzy spells she sometimes experienced at work. The nurse "had a good ear for listening," and Hagar became a regular visitor in the infirmary, with various complaints of somatic distress. The visiting kibbutz physician then did a check-up and suggested a psychiatric consultation.

Hagar was again referred to me, and she called to request resumption of therapy. I decided to work with the couple from the beginning. Shaul agreed, and we had a few sessions in which Hagar expressed her dissatisfaction with her life in the kibbutz, all the more now because Shaul had assumed an important position at work and was less available to the family. Within a short time, Hagar reported an improvement in her symptoms of anxiety. I was impressed with the improvement in the couple's communication and flexibility, but the unresolved issues made it difficult to terminate treatment. Hagar continues to be something of an outsider within her society. From time to time, she explodes with anger and again becomes the subject of criticism in the kibbutz. At such times I feel the kibbutz expects me to change Hagar's personality.

A family therapist working with a nuclear family in an office may be impressed with the scope of this example of kibbutz therapy and at the same time find it imperialistic. Here we have a combination of family therapy, individual therapy, hypnosis, educational counseling, social organization, group dynamics, propaganda, lobbying, and exhortation conducted at the clinic and in the kibbutz. The selections for intervention vary from individual sessions to meetings with the secretariat to work with the extended family to intercession with the education committee to supervision of the metapelet and consultation with the nurse.

The unusual flexibility of kibbutz institutions is reflected in the Kibbutz Clinic's approach, but there are always demands to increase the scope of treatment. The kibbutz has become a sophisticated consumer of therapy, challenging any fixed theoretical orientation on the part of the clinic's staff. If there are cognitive-behavioral techniques for working with impulsive individuals, why not use them with Hagar? And what about hypnosis, drug therapy, long-term psychodynamic treatment, and so on? And if the Kibbutz Clinic cannot provide a technique, then there are always private practitioners eager to work with kibbutzim. These are problems that occur in small, highly involved communities, but they are also experienced by private consumers of therapy, insurance companies, and health care organizations. And as psychological needs seem ever to increase, so does the number of "alternative" therapists and enlightened referral sources.

When does the demand for flexibility become a form of irrationality that does not respect individual constitution, pushing therapists and nonadjusting members to achieve some ideal preconceived standards? One's answer to that question will reflect one's clinical orientation and philosophy of life. In this particular case, the attempt to make Hagar a better human being became part of the conflict between her and the kibbutz.

The Follow-Up: "They Were Always Experts at Balancing"

Two and a half years later, Hagar and Shaul gladly agreed to come to a follow-up session with Minuchin and the two therapists. As the family entered the room, Mickie, who had grown tall and begun to show signs of sexual development, greeted Minuchin demurely and sat down next to her parents. There were no signs of the restlessness that she had displayed in the past. Sheila sat down next to Mickie, surveying the room. Hagar and Shaul seemed proud to present their children to Minuchin. At the beginning of the session, Minuchin asked the parents to engage Mickie and Sheila in a description of their life in the last four years. As they responded in the usual monosyllabic, bored way in which polite children respond to adults' queries, Minuchin declared them normal, and they left the room.

MINUCHIN: *Shaul, perhaps you can give me a picture of what's happened since our last meeting.*

SHAUL: *I think that, all in all, Hagar and I have learned to live with each other's weaknesses and idiosyncrasies. Sometimes we have differences over educational approaches.*

MINUCHIN: *What are the differences?*

SHAUL: *Well, I grew up in a very permissive household, with no fixed rules. We were all free to decide for ourselves what we would do in our free time. Hagar thinks we should interfere more and guide the children toward all sorts of activities.*

MINUCHIN: *I see great changes in Mickie. How did you succeed in helping her make such great progress?*

HAGAR: *Well, the combination of our two styles was important. I tend to worry more, and I want to give a lot to the children. Sometimes I am too concerned and a bit hard on them, but I think that our having been able to talk things out, and even to quarrel, has helped us. We could decide about new things, and the improved atmosphere at home helped Mickie.*

SHAUL: *I think the main thing that's helped Mickie is stability. We used to move a lot, but now we've been in the same place for three years. Of course, there are also things we did and things that were done in the children's house.*

HAGAR: *Sometimes you drive me to despair, the way you belittle everything we've done.*

MINUCHIN: *There are things that did not change. Shaul is an engineer, used to looking at blueprints and seeing things in large patterns. You, on the other hand, are a nurse, who looks at the way things develop and examines the details of everyday life. I think you are both right, each from your own perspective.*

As usual in a follow-up, Minuchin tried to use descriptive language that would frame the family as nondeviant.

HAGAR: *I think you're right. But we shouldn't try to convert each other. Things can be seen in different ways.*

SHAUL: *There were a lot of difficulties and confrontations before we learned to live with each other. Then we broke off the therapy. But later on, we renewed it.*

MINUCHIN: *You really do talk like an engineer. You get into the car, turn the key, and start moving. But I am interested in more details.*

SHAUL: *There were many times when we reached a state of*

high tension. The therapists helped us find a way out. Even after we discontinued therapy, they were like a safety valve. You may not have to use it, but it's good to know that it's there.

MINUCHIN: *[to Hagar] Perhaps you can give more details about the therapy.*

HAGAR: *I don't remember the details any too well, either. At first, we had many arguments, and Shaul's family used to intervene, as if they were the judges. We felt that this wasn't good, and we stopped it. We saw that we were able to solve our problems, at first with the help of the therapists but later without much intervention on their part.*

One of the signs of effective therapy is that the therapists' interventions have become homogenized with other family experience's and have lost sharpness. This phenomenon creates havoc with therapists' egos.

MINUCHIN: *Earlier, I noticed a big change in Shaul: the way he took control of handling the children and showed respect for you. I think that's very nice.*

SHAUL: *It is fine when it happens, but I think there should be more of a balance between the two of us. Hagar represents authority to the children; you are the one who decides on the rules of behavior. If they want to ask for something, they turn to me. It's not good for the children to think of us as a "bad guy" and a "good guy."*

MINUCHIN: *How did it come about that Hagar is the one who makes the rules and you are the "good guy"?*

SHAUL: *We come from different family backgrounds. . . .*

GALIA: *I think Hagar is still fighting for her place in the family, and she's trying to add some explicit rules that will become part of your family culture. [Hagar smiles.]*

MINUCHIN: *[to Galia] I saw just now how happy Hagar was with what you said, while Shaul took your words as criticism. You are still involved as an arbiter between them.*

HAGAR: *Look, Galia takes good care of me. For instance, when I got here after the long trip, she made me a cup of coffee. It never occurred to Shaul to do that. She has the heart of a woman, and this may be the reason I feel so good when I hear her speak. But I live with Shaul, not with her. Our relationship must improve.*

MINUCHIN: *Shaul, how come the therapists arbitrate between the two of you?*

SHAUL: *In our meetings with them, we each seek support for the way we feel. I think Galia supports Hagar, and David supports me.*

MINUCHIN: *[to therapists] They were always experts at balancing, and you are helping them. [taking a pencil and holding it horizontal between his fingers] You see, in some families things go like this [tilting the pencil] for a while, and people endure it. But this family finds it difficult to cope when things become unbalanced.*

Minuchin found himself changing the follow-up into a consultation session. The therapists' interventions had stabilized the couple's transactions in a narrow range. The balancing act with the pencil was a challenge to the therapists as much as to the couple.

HAGAR: *But for me this is a difficult period.*

MINUCHIN: *Of course. But I think in general the changes you've made in these past two years are extraordinary.*

SHAUL: *What do you see that's happened during this time?*

MINUCHIN: *Two years ago, as I recall, there was an agreement between you and Hagar: She talked 90 percent of the time, and you 10 percent. So Hagar was 90 percent anxious and you were 90 percent indifferent.*

SHAUL: *Now it's 50–50.*

MINUCHIN: *I see many other changes. You, Hagar, demand attention much less than before. He talked a lot today, and you listened. You waited for the moment when you would have your say. This is a big change for both of you.*

GALIA: *I want to ask you whether this family still needs us as arbiters in order to continue to be in balance.*

MINUCHIN: *I expect them to learn to accept periods in which he is right and she is wrong, as well as periods in which she is the star. They haven't yet developed this mechanism. In some ways you, Shaul, have succeeded in making this couple a precisely balanced machine, and I congratulate you on that. [Minuchin shakes his hand and Shaul laughs.]*

SHAUL: *In order to keep the balance, you must shake Hagar's hand twice.*

MINUCHIN: *I like your humor. But I don't have to shake Hagar's hand twice. I can tell you that I like you without at the same time having to like Hagar. [to therapists] I think you have developed a pattern with this couple that supports symmetry.*

GALIA: *But I see Hagar suffer and the effect this has on the family. In particular, I notice her difficulties over work in the kibbutz and her social standing there. I feel I must intervene.*

MINUCHIN: *Maybe by supporting Hagar you have also created a balanced system that includes you, Hagar, and the kibbutz.*

GALIA: *That may very well be true. I think I was cautious and tried to avoid a crisis, knowing how reactive kibbutz society is. I would have liked more distance from kibbutz pressures.*

MINUCHIN: *Galia, your close contact with the kibbutz helped at the beginning of treatment, but now things have changed. I think Shaul and Hagar can learn to cope with unbalanced situations.*

At some point, this follow-up was transformed into a consultation, challenging the therapists to cease their balancing function, declare their inability to transform Hagar into a different person—as well as the absurdity of such demands—and help her face her social reality. As with any long-term process of therapy, undue protection can only postpone clients' struggle to secure their own niche in society and make whatever peace they can with the unfairness of life. It seemed that Hagar, after a three-year moratorium on working in kibbutz health care, was going to have to learn to compromise and find some source of self-esteem other than as a nurse in Kibbutz Ramot.

To implement Minuchin's new input, the therapist would need to translate general suggestions into specific steps that fit the social context of her therapy. In order to withdraw from her function of supporting Hagar, she could coach Hagar in ways of dealing with kibbutz authorities. In order to reinforce her boundaries with the kibbutz concerning Hagar, she could frame the conflict about work as a nontherapeutic issue and declare an end to Hagar's patienthood.

Five Years after the Initial Consultation with Minuchin

The process of terminating therapy was not smooth, as Galia's account of the next two and a half years reveals:

> *After the second consultation, there were only a few sessions with the couple, at irregular intervals. Hagar asked Shaul to take care of their garden and to plant a hedgerow around the house. He did, and the hedgerow came to be a symbol of their privacy and a guard against the critical intrusion of others. Hagar was appreciative of his support, and in our last meetings she listened to Shaul's wish to be more separate and invest himself in the challenges of his work. It was difficult for her to experience our support of Shaul, yet she was not reacting defensively, and the couple negotiated an agreement on this issue. At this point, we decided to discontinue our regular meetings.*
>
> *However, termination was not so easy. A couple of months later, we began to hear complaints from the kibbutz about our "premature termination." At that time Hagar did not have any permanent working position in the kibbutz, and she felt victimized. The explosive incidents between her and other kibbutz members were rapidly escalating in their intensity and frequency. Hagar was restless, slept badly, neglected her appearance, and was barely functioning at home and at work. Shaul, feeling unable to help her, went to the*

kibbutz physician who asked for a psychiatric consultation. The pressure on me was very high, and despite my intention to stay uninvolved and let Hagar and the kibbutz solve their differences directly, I thought that a breakdown had to be averted. I met Hagar with a consulting psychiatrist, who suggested she use some medication during this period, but Hagar refused. She did try, though, to increase her self-control and accepted the view that she was harming herself by this behavior. Gradually her condition began to improve.

With the overview we have of the therapeutic process, we can see this as one more crisis that tested the therapists' views and decision to disengage. Their position is an interesting example of providing support, including psychopharmacology, for a person in acute distress while still framing the person as normal.

There were a few more meetings with Hagar, as well as a meeting with her and the kibbutz representatives together. In this meeting, Hagar spoke competently, and we explained that therapy with the family was no longer necessary and that the issue of work should be discussed directly between Hagar and kibbutz representatives in order to make clear decisions about her place of work. Following that, the working committee decided that Hagar would not work in kibbutz health care, including temporary duties, unless a permanent position were found for her. The current and near-future situations were explained in order to dispel any unrealistic expectation. Hagar then asked to meet with the kibbutz secretary, coming up with the idea of working as a nurse in the nearby town. It's an unusual arrangement, but the kibbutz agreed if Hagar could find a job.

Hagar was resentful, but her feelings improved as she actively searched for a job during the next couple of months. She found one in a hospital at a developmental town. She likes her work, although she complains about the difficulties of commuting. We moved into the more distant role of advisor to the whole system. Recently we were invited to the kibbutz's celebration of Bar Mitzvah (it is a communal event for all thirteen-year-old children of both sexes, who organize the ceremony and stage a play). Shaul and Hagar were proud of Mickie's performance. They seemed content with their life.

Four years after the initial consultation with Minuchin Galia terminated her therapy. The last year has been a relatively stable one for the family. Shaul became the kibbutz's economic manager while Hagar continued to work outside the kibbutz. There was one crisis between Hagar and the kibbutz during the year, and again Hagar had a very strong and sensitive reaction. The relations with Galia were resumed briefly, and Galia realized that even though therapy was terminated, she will continue to be a source of support to this family whenever she is needed.

Reflections

The therapy with this family demonstrates the possibilities and the risks of implementing systemic work with individuals, families, and social systems. This treatment model puts high demands on clinicians. They have to address themselves to a wide array of issues spanning the life cycle—to become general practitioners in a world that is being increasing divided into special services. This family, which is not an extreme example, could have been treated by an unconnected assortment of helpers, including a school psychologist, a marital therapist, individual child and adult therapists, a medical psychologist, and a psychiatrist, as well as specialists in weight control and group dynamics. Therapists who wish to coordinate these elements need a supportive framework, a clinical organization that will invest in the training of generalists and supplement their work with specialists who will work in teams under the guidelines of a systemic approach. A high degree of organizational complexity is necessary, for sustaining the common-sensical application of a systemic approach is not simple.

The possibility of employing a systemic model of therapy is thus linked to the leadership position of the therapist with the most comprehensive overview of the problem. This is often a complicated issue between professionals; the possibilities for rivalries and lack of communication were observed during the follow-up of our city cases. In the model employed by the Kibbutz Clinic, to be described in greater detail in the following chapter, this issue is resolved by designating one clinician to be responsible for all therapy-related issues of the family.

Most therapists do not have such a degree of support for a holistic therapy; negotiating with other professionals involved in their cases requires much energy. More usually they demarcate their territorial fragment, be it the intrapsychic world, family relations, school adjustment, sexual performance, or any other aspect of human life.

Clearly there is much to gain by developing holistic therapies and the institutional patterns that would support them. Multi-problem families involved in an uncoordinated multiagency treatment, drug addicts and alcoholics who need to internalize a sick label in order to be helped, the institutionalized psychiatric patient or juvenile delinquent—these are examples of life conditions for which comprehensive programs are needed. At the same time, we need to learn with Shaul and Hagar and their therapists that expectations concerning the scope and magnitude of change can easily be overextended. The more involved ecological therapists become, the greater is the risk that they may become substituting figures, responsible for maintaining the stability of the clients, the homeostasis of families, and the smoothness of the social process.

8

Community Management of Mental Illness: An Alternative to Hospitalization

By Mordecai Kaffman*

THE CASE of Yoav shows clearly the dilemma of parents who, without adequate social supports and a structured program of daily activities, are asked to deal with and contain at home the intolerably disruptive behavior of an acutely or chronically mentally ill patient. When Yoav's parents declared themselves defeated in their effort to cope with their son's disorganized behavior, they were not pretending or putting on a show of helplessness. In the hope of getting help, they turned alternately

*Mordecai Kaffman is Medical Director of the Kibbutz Child and Family Clinic, Derech Haifa 147, Tel Aviv, Israel.

to the psychiatric hospital, to their family therapist, and to the police, but each of these social agents proved a disappointment. (It is perhaps ironic that the nonprofessional support of Yoav's uncle was more effective than any of these established institutions in achieving the dual aim of relieving the boy's parents of their heavy burden and finding a way of improving his functioning, if only for a limited period.)

For a number of years, Yoav's parents turned for relief to psychiatric hospitals, which they expected would isolate him temporarily until he was able to carry on an independent and socially productive life and rejoin "normal society." What Yoav's parents did not know was that the prospects of achieving such positive results by way of the mental hospital alone were far from bright. Currently more than 60 percent of admissions to psychiatric hospitals are in fact readmissions.* Relapse occurs in 30 to 50 percent of schizophrenic patients as early as during their first year of release from hospital, even if they are under controlled medication and psychiatric follow-up.† A pattern of movement back and forth between the hospital and the community, the so-called revolving door syndrome, develops among many psychiatric patients, who, according to Stein and Test, "continue to spend considerable time in mental institutions, function poorly between admissions, and experience high readmission rates."‡

This situation is hardly flattering to the psychiatric establishment. It offers a very discouraging prognosis and calls for great care in determining which patients have a reasonable chance of improvement and functional reintegration into society following psychiatric hospitalization. The person or group with the power to determine whether a given patient should be hospitalized bears a heavy responsibility, for on that decision may hang the entire course of a patient's life. Unfortunately, this fateful decision is often based not on an objective evaluation of the patient's situa-

*J. Talbott, "The Chronic Mentally Ill," in S. Arieti, (ed.), *American Handbook of Psychiatry*, vol. 7 (New York: Basic Books, 1981), p. 372.

†L. Falloon, J. Boyd, and C. McGill, *Family Care of Schizophrenics* (New York: Guilford Press, 1984), p. 17.

‡L. Stein and M. Test, "A State Hospital–Initiated Community Program," in John Talbott, (ed.), *The Chronic Mentally Ill: Treatment, Progress, Systems* (New York: Human Science Press, 1981), p. 160.

tion but on lack of choice. The medical authorities may be well aware that theoretically there are better alternatives to hospitalization, but in practice these are, alas, unavailable.

Even without resorting to statistical data (of which there is a great deal in the professional literature) on the unsatisfactory long-range results of hospital care, one can easily point out the weaknesses and internal inconsistencies of the hospital system. Can a mode of therapy based on seclusion and forced contact with an insane world possibly be conducive to restoring the mentally ill to "normal" patterns of behavior and social interaction? Rather, everything invites the patient to continue playing the role of a mentally ill person: the hospital climate, with its emphasis on deviant social norms in all spheres of life; the constant contact with people who carry the official designation of mentally ill; the observant eye of the psychiatrist, who has been trained to look for and record every sign of mental illness that can be included in the *Diagnostic and Statistical Manual of Mental Disorders (DSM-III).* In the interesting phenomenon called *psychiatric mimesis,* patients have been known to volunteer, for the benefit of their psychiatrist, bizarre responses to the never-ending questions about hallucinations and delusions. There are even compliant patients who are prepared to put upon themselves the stamp of schizophrenia, partly under the influence of the abnormal surroundings and partly out of fear of losing the status of mental patient. In the atmosphere of complete dependence that prevails in the mental hospital, the threat of having to go back to ordinary life and face its many challenges becomes intolerable, and the patient is encouraged to continue playing the sick role, free of all responsibility. Indeed, one must always take into account the possibility that the mental institution will play an iatrogenic role, contributing to the perpetuation of chronicity through low expectations for the patient's level of functioning and sense of personal responsibility, as well as the institutional climate of existential emptiness. It goes without saying that psychiatric hospitals, in the nature of things, have very limited opportunities for developing the patient's skills and capacities to solve the real problems of life.

Avoiding the Revolving Door Pattern: The Importance of Preventing the First Hospitalization

The first commitment to a mental hospital may serve as a crucial imprinting and learning experience for the mentally ill patient. It offers a socially sanctioned way of escaping from difficulties and pressures and teaches the lesson that a certain style of insane behavior will produce a haven in the hospital. After the first hospitalization, the patient is generally brought back into exactly the same conditions and life stresses that had given rise to or intensified the mental illness in the first place, and not surprisingly, the revolving door syndrome sets in. For this reason, the possibility of avoiding the first commitment should be seen as a question of cardinal importance, encouraging a very serious search for any possible alternative.

This is the guiding policy in the Kibbutz Child and Family Clinic. Using the means provided by a well-organized community like the kibbutz (in terms of manpower, facilities, and financial resources), the clinic has developed a model of community care designed to avoid hospitalization, particularly a first commitment to a mental hospital.

The cases of two kibbutz members, each referred to the clinic with an acute psychotic clinical picture, exemplify the method and point to the problems that its practical applications entails. In both cases, the psychiatrists who dealt with the patients through the outpatient services of a mental hospital saw no way of continuing with the therapy other than by full hospitalization.

The Case of Leon: Ambulatory Treatment of a Paranoid Patient

Leon, twenty-nine years old and the oldest of three children, was born at Kibbutz Aviv. His sisters (twenty-two and twenty-five, respectively) were described by the referring psychiatrist as "not problematic." Both Leon's parents and the representatives of the kibbutz institutions involved described his condition as very serious. Because Leon refused to come to the Kibbutz Clinic, they requested an urgent consultation in his absence, the meeting to be attended by the secretary of the kibbutz, the chairman of the kibbutz health committee, the nurse in charge of the infirmary, and of course the parents.

I first met with the parents alone. Both are among the founders of the kibbutz, extremely conscientious and diligent people who fulfill all the obligations of kibbutz members. Socially they are quite isolated, however, and not surprisingly: Both were full of criticism of everything that went on around them in the kibbutz—the indolence of many members, the inadequacies of the educational establishment, which in their opinion hindered full development of their children's capabilities, and the preferential treatment some members received from the kibbutz institutions. Clearly, the father was the leading voice in this campaign, with the mother following along, very much under his influence.

According to the parents and the representatives of the kibbutz institutions, Leon spent considerably more time in his parents' quarters than was customary among his peers. Since early adolescence, however, he had had a strained relationship with his father, who was never short of reasons to criticize Leon. In school the boy was considered an average student, and there were never any specific complaints about his conduct, but his father never missed an opportunity to point out that he was wasting his life away, without realizing all his potential. At the end of high school, Leon joined the army. He participated in the Lebanese war in the infantry, although he did not achieve any distinction and in contrast to most of his peers from the kibbutz did not become an officer. At the end of his military service, Leon took a year's leave from the kibbutz in order to earn some money for a trip to the Far East, something he had dreamed of for many years. Since he had learned no skill in the kibbutz, he was able to get only a low-paying job as a waiter in a restaurant, but he nevertheless managed to collect the money needed for the trip. He found great enjoyment in his travels abroad and wrote enthusiastic letters to his parents describing his experiences in Nepal and Thailand. When he returned to the kibbutz, he felt humiliated and insulted to be offered a tedious routine job in the factory where his father worked, but he raised no objections and accepted the work. Shortly after his return, he became involved in a passionate romance with Rachel, a pretty, vivacious girl of a neighboring kibbutz, three years his junior.

The turning point came when after five months Rachel suddenly ended the relationship. This came as a very severe blow to Leon, who was hurt and humiliated. He became uncharacteristically aggressive, pressuring Rachel and even threatening her in an effort to continue the relationship. From that point on, Leon's condition began to deteriorate. He developed delusions of reference and insisted that people in the kibbutz were making fun of his manhood, even making oblique references to him in the internal bulletin of the kibbutz. He was sent to the psychiatric outpatient clinic of the nearby Gamma Hospital, where he was treated with drug therapy and weekly individual psychotherapy. His condition continued to worsen, however, and he displayed persecutory delusions, convinced he was being followed by army intelligence agents and even by people of the broadcasting services, who were accusing him of responsibility for the death of soldiers in Lebanon.

After two months of outpatient therapy, Leon broke off all ties with his psychiatrist, refused to take the medication, stopped working, and devoted his entire energies to bringing formal complaints that the kibbutz was doing nothing to defend him against the conspirators who were out to blacken his name and ruin him. He related his story in endless conversations with several kibbutz members, who listened to him patiently and tried to persuade him that his allegations were groundless. He even wrote a detailed letter to the chief of the general staff of the Israel Defence Army, complaining that he was being molested by the army and asking him to intervene on his behalf. The list of those who were out to get him kept growing, including his father and his two sisters. People began to shy away from him, and even though he showed no signs of violent behavior, they expected a dangerous outburst to occur sooner or later. The kibbutz secretary informed the army of Leon's condition and recommended that he not be called up for reserve duty, which would put a gun into his hands. His social isolation became unbearable. He broke all ties with his family, and the kibbutz members increasingly avoided him, rather than listen to his claims yet again. At this point, his parents and the representatives of the kibbutz institutions turned to the Kibbutz Clinic to discuss with us the unequivocal recommendation of the psychiatrist from Gamma Hospital that Leon be committed to a mental institution. In the psychiatrist's opinion, Leon had a schizophrenic disorder with prominent paranoid features, which could only be handled in a closed psychiatric ward, especially in light of Leon's absolute refusal to cooperate in any kind of treatment.

At the end of the consultation, I made it clear that I was reluctant to give my immediate approval to involuntary commitment. I suggested that we try a different option before we decided on hospitalization that would label Leon forever as a schizophrenic and start him on a lifelong psychiatric career. Rather than giving him a permanent psychiatric label, I preferred to depict Leon's condition as the aftermath of a series of stresses, including a delayed psychological reaction to the traumatic events of the war in Lebanon. I defined his condition as an extreme sensitivity to criticism and an inability to deal with rejection and failure, as evidenced by his handling of his failed relationship with Rachel. The extreme responses of alarm, suspicion, and reserve that he experienced on the part of his social environment, after he had been labelled mentally ill and dangerous because of his bizarre delusional ideas, served to strengthen his belief in the authenticity of his delusional thoughts.

In place of hospitalization, I proposed a community care program appropriate to the circumstances of the case. As a first step in the direction of a change in the strained relations between Leon and his environment, I suggested that the kibbutz secretary hold a friendly conversation with Leon. He would tell Leon that upon reconsideration he had concluded that there was some merit in Leon's complaints against the army, the radio, and the newspapers, but that the the case was rather serious and delicate, beyond the capacity of the kibbutz members or their elected representatives to handle. He would advise Leon to put down all his grievances in writing, so that the kibbutz authorities (with his participation, if he so desired) could turn the material over to the legal department of the kibbutz movement. The kibbutz secretary would also make clear to all concerned that until legal advisors had gone over the material and submitted their conclusions and recommendation, the entire subject (referred to as "the Affair") should remain off limits for discussion in the kibbutz. He would officially notify the full kibbutz membership (about 250 people) that the whole matter had been turned over to the proper department, and that the members, who lacked the necessary expertise to act on the matter, should refrain from talking about it or allowing any information whatever to leak out.

To make the idea more acceptable to Leon, I suggested that the kibbutz nominate a special person, someone who enjoyed Leon's full confidence to coordinate all the work involved. That coordinator, together with the kibbutz secretary, would inform Leon at an appropriate time that they had decided to consult me, as someone neutral and reliable, about how to proceed with the matter beyond turning it over for a legal examination. They would then tell Leon that in the course of our discussion I had expressed my regret that because of his perceived persecution, Leon had neglected to carry out many plans that might prove vital for his future, for instance, that at the age of twenty-nine he had acquired no occupational skill and had not secured permanent work. They would convey a clear message that, of course, it was understandably difficult for Leon to concern himself with his vocational advancement in view of all the stresses he was under. Therefore, it would be well for him to consult some competent person to help him with all these problems, so that he could devote part of his energies to realizing some of his personal plans, rather than allow the time to pass in aimless activity until after the legal investigation brought in its report. At that point my name could be suggested as the most suitable person for him to consult.

In addition, I proposed that a support network be organized of kibbutz members who would be ready to meet with Leon frequently in a completely free and unofficial manner. Their role would be a social and recreational one, with the goal of normalizing Leon's relationship with the kibbutz. It would be clearly understood that discussion of "the Affair" or any of its ramifications would be taboo, except perhaps for an occasional mention that the matter was now in the hands of the kibbutz movement's legal advisors.

This was the outline of the first phase of the treatment as we discussed it with the representatives of the kibbutz. It contains the basic elements of the community care program for the mentally ill recommended by us at the Kibbutz Clinic. In the first place, the program calls for the organization of a large number of people who are ready to volunteer time and effort for a support network. The number of people in this broad network and the division of functions among them vary from case to case. The network has several aims: to spend as much time as possible with the patient, helping replace pathological self-engagement with constructive content of conversation or occupation; to encourage the patient, without direct confrontation, to fill the gaps that have been created in daily functioning; to help improve the patient's work performance and foster better relations with the work team; to invite and accompany the patient to social gatherings and the various communal events in the kibbutz, such as cultural events and general meetings of the membership; to encourage physical activity in games and sports; and to share in pursuing the patient's hobbies. The community care program involves a strongly structured schedule of daily activities, planned jointly by the treatment team, the patient, the coordinator, the family, and members of the support network. The individually tailored schedule includes work, leisure activities, and social and family life. The coordinator receives daily reports from everyone involved in the program and in turn reports to the treatment team, to enable prompt intervention if it should be required. A medical nurse, a physiotherapist, and frequently the local physician as well are important participants in the network, in charge of monitoring compliance with and detecting any adverse reactions to the psychotropic medication as well as any other issues involving health and physical exercise.

An essential element in our community program for acute or

chronic psychotic patients is the coordinator, whose central task is to maintain regular contact, on the one hand, with the treatment team (composed of two staff members of the Kibbutz Clinic, a psychologist or psychiatric social worker and a psychiatrist, both experienced in community and family therapy), and, on the other hand, with the patient, the family, the kibbutz institutions, and the various members of the kibbutz support network. The coordinator becomes something like a guardian for the patient, devoting anywhere from two to six hours a day to the implementation of the therapist's recommendations and to the execution of the agreed program of daily routines, in work, social, and recreational spheres.

In the course of the consultation regarding Leon, we also impressed upon Leon's parents the importance of holding family therapy sessions, in order to find ways of coping with the chronic conflict between Leon and the rest of the family, particularly between father and son. We saw as a further topic of the family meetings the need for the parents and sisters to reach a deeper understanding of the nature of Leon's mental illness. Ever since the word *schizophrenia* appeared in connection with Leon, the parents had been reading material on the genetic influences involved in the development of the illness and the poor long-term prognosis of the disease.

This first consultation, without Leon present, took more than four hours and consisted of three parts: a meeting with the parents alone, a meeting with the kibbutz representatives alone, and a joint session to summarize the conclusions. All concerned accepted the proposal and decided to begin its implementation. Within a few days, a support network was organized and Reuven, a very dynamic and cooperative kibbutz member, was appointed coordinator. A month later, Reuven reported that Leon had calmed down considerably once he became convinced that his claims were being taken seriously, especially after he received official proof that the various documents and testimonies had been turned over to the legal department of the kibbutz movement. In response to the more positive attitude toward him on the part of the various kibbutz members, who refrained from arguing about his paranoid claims, he talked considerably less about "the Affair." Generally his daily meetings with Reuven were conducted in an atmosphere of complete trust and comradeship.

Leon continued to close himself up in his own apartment, but he agreed to come to the Clinic if Reuven would accompany him. He requested that at the first meeting neither members of his family nor any other kibbutz member be present. In principle we try our best to avoid any arguments with paranoid patients, so I accepted Leon's conditions. Present at the session, then, were Leon, Reuven, I as the psychiatrist, and a co-therapist, Peter.

Leon told us of his childhood days, then of his adolescence, which had been very difficult. Both his parents and his educators had been displeased with his progress and kept telling him that he was capable of achieving more. He would compare himself with his peers and conclude that he was an incompetent ne'er-do-well. The first time he felt good about himself was during his trip abroad, which he had accomplished after coping successfully with both the financial difficulties and the anxieties of going abroad on his own. He had then experienced high-spirited self-fulfillment, and his sense of personal value was at a peak. He came back to the kibbutz full of ambitious plans, but he was deeply hurt when he realized—or felt—that the people in charge of work assignment in the kibbutz were hostile toward him and were forcing him to become a tiny screw in the big kibbutz machine, assigning him to a job that had caused his father to fall to pieces some years previously. When his love affair with Rachel fell apart—for no good reason, he felt—his entire world collapsed.

At the end of this narration, presented in a well-ordered and logical manner, Leon immediately moved on to clearly paranoid thinking, uncontrolled and totally lacking in self-criticism. People in the kibbutz had exploited his love affair to accuse him of all sorts of evil doings. Both the army and the broadcasting service were persecuting him, using secret listening devices to listen in on his conversations and interfere with his privacy. As evidence he brought up, among other things, some newspaper clippings describing cases of murderers whose names bore some remote similarity to his own. He also described a recent television story on the war in Lebanon that in his view told of illegal acts he had perpetrated and would have to account for in military court. This conspiracy to incriminate him in acts of murder called for an incessant counterattack on his part, he concluded.

Reuven reminded Leon that his complaints had been turned over to the legal department and that they had to await patiently the results of the investigation. I added a word of praise of Leon for directing his grievances to the proper authorities rather than wasting his time by talking about them to one and all. I added that all such investigations take time, and I recommended that he try to utilize the interim properly: He ought to take up his free time with some worthwhile activities that would give him more satisfaction than continued fruitless mulling over "the Affair." Leon replied that he doubted he could seriously devote his time and energy to other matters as long as the issue of "the Affair" remained pending, since for him this was a matter of life and death, and his mind was not free for anything else.

The co-therapist and I made it clear to Leon that we understood clearly how he felt: As long as he was involved in his struggle to clear his name, he had no spare energy left for anything else. Nevertheless, he must not forget that a qualified group of experts was looking into the facts, and there was therefore no reason for him to neglect himself, in this way actually serving his enemies. We at the Clinic would be only too glad to help him find ways to advance his own plans and to try to restore his mental energy. I mentioned that the co-therapist had actually specialized in this very matter—the restoration of mental energy. At first it would not be easy, as Leon would have to make a real effort to recoup the energy he had lost, but fortunately, he had some excellent allies fighting on his side, namely Reuven and some very good kibbutz members who were willing to help Reuven in Leon's behalf. He could be sure that this group of friends would do anything to help him return gradually to physical, social, and cultural activity, including changing his place of work to one that he would find satisfactory. I also recommended that he take a psychotropic agent (Pimozide) that, I said, was different from any other medicine he had received so far in creating energy, dispelling anxieties, raising morale, and insuring restful sleep. The antipsychotic medication was also presented as a means of strengthening Leon in both body and spirit, to prepare him better for his personal struggle once the results of the investigation were known.

Throughout the session it was emphasized to Leon that he must agree to a moratorium regarding "the Affair," until such time as the investigation had ended and the legal advisors had presented their recommendations. At the end of the session I added that I had one more irrefutable argument that ought to convince him to cooperate with the clinic: He would no doubt agree that all the efforts so far to improve his condition had borne no fruit; on the contrary, here he was, twenty-nine years of age, shiftless, with no skills, nearly detached from the social life around him, on bad terms even with his own family. This being the case, why should he not try a different type of treatment, at least for a period of, say, two months? Leon finally agreed to cooperate with the Kibbutz Clinic, thanks in large part to the efforts of Reuven, who played a decisive role in persuading him to cooperate with the suggested program.

During the first three weeks of treatment, Leon and Reuven met the therapists by themselves; Leon insisted on keeping the family out of these meetings. The conversations revolved around two main themes: Leon's return to work and the content of the conversations between Leon and the members of the support network. The treatment team expressed disappointment that Leon and Reuven had not yet agreed on Leon's place and conditions of work. It was made clear to him that he was right in feeling that some members in the kibbutz treated him disparagingly and were critical of him. But, he was asked, how could he expect to be treated with appreciation and respect if he stopped working, when it is well known that in the kibbutz a member's contribution to the collective through work is perhaps the most important factor in determining that person's worth? It was therefore decided, largely with Reuven's help, that a proper place of work must be found very quickly. Leon had in mind the garage, since he always had an interest in motor vehicles and the way they worked.

The second topic of these first meetings concerned Leon's awareness that in accordance with the guidelines of the treatment team, people he talked to paid no attention to and never reacted to what he had to say about "the Affair." It was made clear to him that here was another matter that harmed his standing in the kibbutz; someone who talks on one subject only is never considered an interesting partner for conversation, but rather a person of limited horizons. If he kept coming back to himself and his grievances, he could not expect continuing attention and sympathy. In fact, we reminded him, he was very wise in turning over the entire matter to an objective authority outside the kibbutz, instead of repeating his story to his fellow-members, like a broken record. To illustrate the point, one of the therapists gave Leon a long and tedious lecture on the subject of the backache he gets every time he sits for some time in an uncomfortable armchair. Leon was then asked to give a five-minute talk on his occasional headaches, while Reuven and the therapists displayed signs of total boredom (yawning, restlessness, and so on). Leon received this type of humorous role-playing very well.

At the end of the first month of therapy, Leon agreed to having his parents and sisters attend the sessions as well. From then on, the regular weekly meetings alternated between individual and family sessions, sometimes in the kibbutz but usually at the Clinic. In addition, we held regular meetings with the coordinator and relevant members of the community support system.

For three months, the meetings continued to be held weekly, and then they took place less and less frequently. The main components of the therapy were these:

1. An explanation of the essence of the paranoid phenomena, addressed to both the family and the members of the community who were in any way involved with Leon. The delusions were explained not in pathological terms but as a quite common response of a very sensitive person under conditions of stress. In this way reactions

of fear or fatalistic helplessness on the part of the family and others were reduced or eliminated.

2. Renewal of contact between the patient and the community as a whole, with the help of the support system. Through their assistance in carrying out the daily program of activities, Leon little by little freed himself of his social isolation and the total absence of stimuli from the outside world. The idea was to overcome the state of existential emptiness and sensory deprivation that had undoubtedly aggravated his ruminative self-engagement and delusional thinking.
3. Clear instructions to anyone who had any contact with Leon, especially the members of the support network, about how to keep up the moratorium by total avoiding any conversation or arguments relating to his delusions and raising alternative topics for conversation or activity.
4. Relieving the sources of pressure that came from within the family. In the first phase of the family therapy, it was necessary to overcome reactions of confusion, anger, and guilt. We then moved on to the conflict that had existed for years between Leon and his family, especially with his father. We explored both causes and possible solutions, and made efforts at constructive separation and individuation between Leon and his parents, encouraging as much independent functioning as possible. In a parallel endeavor, we tried to end the parents' virtual isolation within the kibbutz by getting them at least partially involved in the community's affairs.
5. Proper supervision by the kibbutz infirmary of Leon's prescribed neuroleptic medication. With every patient in need of psychoactive drugs, we prescribe what we considered to be the lowest effective dose of antipsychotic medication. Leon received a single daily dose of Pimozide, which, in our own experience and that of others, is very effective for monoideistic conditions.*

*A. Munro, "Pathological Jealousy: An Excellent Response to Pimozide," *Canadian Medical Association Journal* 131 (1984): 852–53.

The treatment brought excellent results: The delusional paranoid symptoms that had occupied Leon, his family, and indeed the entire kibbutz for nearly a year disappeared completely within two months after the community care program was initiated. Leon very quickly found his proper place at work in the garage, and with the aid of a good technical instructor he soon reached a satisfactory level of technical knowledge and productivity. Relations between him and the family, especially his sisters, improved markedly. His daily routine was filled with varied activities. His style of interpersonal communication improved considerably as the result of a social skills training program, carried on in the course of therapy, that included appropriate ways of giving and receiving criticism. Six months after the start of therapy, Leon continued to be in very good condition. His general functioning and behavior were perfectly normal, there was great improvement in his social skills, and the persecutory delusions disappeared entirely. At that point a part of the therapy revolved around freeing Leon of the fear that his unsound state at the time of his illness might remain imprinted for all time on the memory of the community.

Eighteen months later, Leon was described in the follow-up report as follows:

> *Leon is feeling well, he works in the garage a full day every day, doing a responsible job in an independent and productive manner. In preparation for the Children's Day, about to be observed in the kibbutz, he volunteered to put up all sorts of games in the yards of the children's houses. He is at present taking a basic course in computers, and next year he intends to take a regular course in computer programming. He has begun to take part in the social gatherings organized by the so-called Singles Department of the kibbutz movement, in the hope of meeting a suitable mate.*
>
> *From a psychiatric point of view, there are no special symptoms. Leon remembers clearly the persecutory delusions that had plagued him in the past and refers to them as "fantasies" or "false day-dreams." He also remembers that he had agreed to an investigation of "the Affair," but he is*

> *not interested in knowing whether or not that investigation was ever held. In fact, he is still somewhat ashamed that the entire kibbutz saw and heard him steeped in his fantasies and groundless accusations. He realizes that he was ill at the time and wonders whether there are still some members in the kibbutz who look upon him today as mentally ill.*

In the final stage of therapy we held a review of the main conclusions: how the paranoid reaction came into being, and what would bring about a relapse or recrudescence of the psychotic symptoms. The therapeutic team reconstructed Leon's psychological biography from the raw material that had come from the individual and family sessions. It described how Leon had absorbed and internalized his father's critical approach toward him. In the past, it seemed natural for the father to realize his unfulfilled dreams by proxy, through his son. With the best of intentions, he put pressure on Leon, constantly criticizing him for his low achievements. A vicious circle was soon formed, in which the father pressed Leon harder and harder to realize his full potential and Leon became more and more resentful and enraged at his father for confronting him morning and night with his own failures and inferiority. Toward the end of adolescence, Leon removed himself physically from his father, but the sense of guilt over his failure to fulfill his father's, his teachers', and especially his own expectations never left him.

Things were no better for him in the army, where he served in various inferior posts, whereas most of the kibbutz-born soldiers assumed responsible positions and many achieved officer rank. The trip abroad brought on the illusion that things had changed: For the first time in his life, Leon felt free to do what he liked. But when he came back to the kibbutz, all his dreams were shattered. He was again given unskilled work, mostly routine and boring chores in physical proximity to his father. Once again he was forced to listen to his father's repeated criticism of the kibbutz authorities responsible for what in his eyes was a discriminatory work assignment. On top of all this came the failed love affair.

At this point, Leon's self-criticism and sense of total failure grew and could no longer be contained within himself. Following the parental model, Leon projected this self-criticism and the blame for his own failures onto the shoulders of others, whom he blamed for either making fun of him or constantly pointing an accusing finger at him. Slowly but steadily, the circle of his accusers kept widening: Wherever he turned, he found people who held him responsible for past failures, in the kibbutz as in the army. The accusations against him became more and more severe from one day to the next, as his assumed accusers used the various information media to disclose publicly his misdeeds.

Today, the report concluded, Leon has grown not only in years but also in his ability to free himself from his dependence on his father. At present, therefore, he is capable of going outside the closed circle of mutual recriminations and unsatisfactory relations between the two of them, capable of talking freely to his father without any tension, of seeing in him a man—flesh and blood—who did not achieve in life all he hoped for and therefore sounded at times bitter and unhappy. Now each of them has learned the lesson that he, and he alone, is responsible for reaching his share of happiness by his own efforts.

Leon confirmed the accuracy of this biographical sketch of himself. His verification may be essentially similar to the experience of patients who bring up Freudian, Jungian, or Gestalt dreams—or else no dreams at all—in the course of their therapy depending on the school of therapy their psychotherapist belongs to. Be that as it may, Leon agreed that this was his present view of the developments that led to the birth of his paranoid ideas. On the basis of the newly acquired insight, Leon was able to draw reasonable conclusions as to the factors, the circumstances, and reactions that could return him to the psychotic condition.

Indeed, the case of Leon illustrates well the three interacting etiopathogenic factors usually found in the genesis of paranoid disorders:*

1. The family roots, which included in this particular case (a) a parental message—particularly on the part of the

*Mordecai Kaffman, "The Core of Truth Behind the Delusional System," *International Journal of Family Therapy* 3(1981): 29–41; idem, "Paranoid Disorders: The Interpersonal Perspective," *Journal of Family Therapy* 3(1981): 21–30; idem, "Paranoid Disorders: Family Sources of the Delusional System," *Journal of Family Therapy* 5(1983): 107–16.

father, the dominant figure in the family—of dissatisfaction, excessive criticism, embitterment over the half-empty glass in life, and unwillingness to put up with the half-full glass; (b) the recurrent projectional family message of blaming personal failure on environmental factors; and (c) placing on Leon's shoulders the very difficult task of carrying out the family's unfulfilled dreams and the responsibility for reaching goals that were determined by his father, but not by him.

2. The kernel of truth in the paranoid thinking: No doubt Leon's highly sensitive antennae accurately received the message of the generally disapproving attitude of the kibbutz members toward a family that was continually closed up and embittered, occupied in spitting into the well whose water they had to drink. Leon and his family were right in their recognition of the negative attitude toward them building up in the community, the accusing finger of kibbutz public opinion (sometimes called "the kibbutz police force") pointing to the meager contribution the family was making toward the community's well-being and progress. Thus the feelings of social isolation within the kibbutz that the family felt were totally founded on facts. Moreover, the insignificant jobs that were assigned to Leon in the army while many of his peers were risking their lives in front-line assignments did nothing to enhance his stature in the eyes of the community.
3. Factors that perpetuate the illness: Leon's social isolation and stopping all normal activities in the pursuit of "the Affair" contributed toward a concentration on the reference ideas and the creation of an existential emptiness that was filled by the paranoid ideation that became the crux of his entire life. The monoideistic theme was fuelled by the constant arguments and discussions with the growing number of kibbutz members about "the Affair." These never-ending arguments could lead to no reasonable resolution, as long as Leon continued, with the aid of some of his audience, his detective work in

> search of his imaginary accusers, who in fact were inside Leon himself.

After eighteen months of therapy, it was decided to discontinue the regular meetings that had been taking place every two to four weeks. Follow-up meetings were then held every three months. The support network, which had no further work to do, stopped functioning, but Reuven continued as coordinator, maintaining regular contact with Leon and the treatment team.

Of course, we have no way of knowing what might have happened to Leon if, instead of entering the community care program, he had been committed to a mental hospital, as the regional psychiatrist recommended. Our experience with paranoid patients committed to hospital against their will has been that in most cases they fail to cooperate in the therapy and reach chronicity. The enforced commitment usually provides the patient with additional weighty justification for his persecutory delusions. It seems to us that therapy conducted within the patient's community, avoiding a head-on confrontation with the delusional system, offers a better chance of a positive outcome. At any rate, the case of Leon, which illustrates our comprehensive method of work within the community, is by no means exceptional as far as the outcome is concerned, and it points up clearly the substantive differences between the community program and the conventional psychiatric therapy based on hospital care.

The Case of Yitzhak: A Home Care Program for Acute Psychosis

Yitzhak, aged twenty-seven and single, is the firstborn in a family that is considered one of the superior families in the kibbutz. His father, a publicist, is a very active man, a man of ideas and one of the leading figures in the kibbutz movement. His mother is an educator, active in cultural activities, and a successful principal of the regional kibbutz high school. Yitzhak's brother, two years his junior, is studying literature at a prestigious American university and a few months ago published his first novel, which was received very enthusiastically in literary circles in Israel. Yitzhak also has a sister, who is nineteen and at present is serving in the army. She too has excelled in whatever she tried her hand at; an excellent student, she was considered the queen of her class and was placed in charge of the cultural program of the high-school-age group in the kibbutz.

Against the background of such a brilliant family, Yitzhak contrasted as a person of only average ability. Although his school record was not at all bad, there was no field in which he excelled. He was a loner and spent long hours in his room, reading or listening to Oriental popular music—a far cry from the musical taste of the rest of the family. Unlike his family, with its ethos of active, down-to-earth contribution to the community in the social sphere, Yitzhak appeared to be somewhere up in the clouds. In his reading, he kept going back to the writings of Carlos Castaneda, at the same time trying out various forms of meditation. The latter was the source of many arguments in the family, especially between Yitzhak and his father, who critically rejected any form of "irrational and esoteric occupation" at the expense of pursuits that he considered socially more useful.

When Yitzhak went into the army, to his parents' disappointment he did not volunteer for one of the select commando units and showed no interest at all in advancing in the military hierarchy. After completing his army service, he returned to the kibbutz, and for a year-and-a-half he worked in the kibbutz barn, until his turn came to go out for academic studies. Once again, counter to his parents' expectations, Yitzhak chose to study subjects—such as mystical Oriental religions—that seemed to them to be of no possible ideological or practical value for the kibbutz. At the end of his first year, when Yitzhak was required to write a final paper, he immersed himself day and night in preparing a paper on the secrets of the Cabala. At about this time, his parents and friends began to notice a radical change in Yitzhak's character and his typical behavior. Contrary to habit, he began to seek the company of people, even of strangers, to whom he would expound, at great length and in vague language, on what he claimed to be his own marvellous discoveries about some heretofore obscure passages in the *Book of Zohar,* by Rabbi Shimeon bar Yohai. It was becoming increasingly difficult to hold an ordinary conversation with him because of the marked loosening of association with obscure neologisms and illogical thinking. Gradually he developed fragmented megalomanic delusions about—among other things—being able to influence the course of the stars, uncover any secret anywhere in the cosmos, and cure any malignant disease. He hardly slept at night, and he generally exhibited global functioning impairment, bizarre ideation, blunting of affect, and grossly disorganized behavior.

After about four months, as these psychotic symptoms became more and more prominent, it became clear that Yitzhak was in urgent need of psychiatric help. On his father's initiative, he was seen by one of Israel's leading psychiatrists, who diagnosed the disease as "schizophrenic disorder, paranoid type, with grandiose delusions." The psychiatrist recommended treatment in a day-hospital setting, and Yitzhak was brought there every day for a three-month period. He was treated with medication (thioridazine and perphenazine) together with psychodynamic and milieu therapies. No improvement whatever was observed, and there was no cooperation on the part of Yitzhak, who kept claiming that he was not mentally ill. The psychiatrist in charge finally recommended full inpatient care in a closed psychiatric ward. At this point, the family turned to the Kibbutz Clinic for a second opinion.

In line with the Clinic's accepted practice in cases of this nature, we recommended that a home care program be tried before any decision was made about commitment to hospital. It was explained to the parents and the representatives of the kibbutz that in the first stages of treatment Yitzhak would have to remain confined to his quarters, in an empathic, supportive, and nonconfrontative milieu. As soon as we obtained the approval of the kibbutz representatives, arrangements were made for an around-the-clock social support network that was to accompany Yitzhak during the acute phase of the home management program. Because the patient was in a highly excited state, relatively large doses of antipsychotic drugs were administered for the first six weeks (chlorpromazine and fluphenazine deconoate in weekly parenteral doses). Intensive medical nursing was also provided.

Although Yitzhak objected to being treated with medication, in practice he was quite cooperative. Six weeks after the beginning of the home care program, there was no trace of the delusional thinking, and his reality testing, his behavior, and his affect all were within the norm. At the end of the second month of therapy, Yitzhak was able to return to normal community living with good insight and right critical judgment regarding the abnormal nature of the psychotic symptoms. In the individual therapy sessions, he admitted that in the two weeks preceding the psychotic crisis he had smoked marijuana every day, for the first time in his life, believing that in this way he was reaching an outstanding degree of awareness and developing supernatural power in his intensive dealings with the mysteries of the Cabala. During the psychosis, he felt completely free from the feelings of inferiority that had troubled him for years; instead, his spirits were very high, and he felt omnipotent in his ability to fulfill all his aims and desires. Right then he was eager to involve everyone around him in the wonderful experience of a man who, having cast off his chains, was capable of solving all the world's problems.

Beginning with the fourth week of treatment, Yitzhak was permitted to leave his quarters in a supervised manner. Simultaneously, his contacts with fellow kibbutz members kept widening, and the care of the support network became less and less stringent. Gradually he assumed responsibility for taking care of his personal needs as well as for his quarters. At the beginning of the second month of the community program, Yitzhak was given work in the kibbutz barn, where he had successfully worked before. At first he worked only an hour a day, but within a few weeks he was working six hours a day and performing in a responsible manner. It was recommended that, at least for the time being, Yitzhak discontinue his studies and his involvement with mysticism.

About three months after the clinical remission of the florid psychotic symptoms, characteristic symptoms of a major depression quite unexpectedly began to appear. The depressive episode was marked by social withdrawal, continuous sadness, decreased energy, loss of interest and pleasure in all usual activities, and a sense of worthlessness. Although I as his psychiatrist considered various diagnostic possibilities, such as schizo-affective or bipolar affective disorder, I chose to explain the depressive episode to the patient and to significant others as an expected reaction, the swing of the pendulum—that is, a temporary swing toward the other extreme of the range of moods, resulting from Yitzhak's reluctance to part with the psychotic world of megalomanic omnipotence and to return to the cold, gray world of reality. Under the guidance of the therapeutic team, the support network was reinstalled, organizing social interactions and physical activities and accompanying Yitzhak to kibbutz events, theatrical and musical performances, and the like. Yitzhak began to complain that the antipsychotic medication was causing greater fatigue and difficulties in concentration, so it was decided to discontinue this medication altogether and replace it with an antidepressive drug (clomipramine), which Yitzhak received for three months. After four or five weeks, the depressive syndrome began to disappear, and Yitzhak eventually returned to full normal activity.

In all, the therapy took over two years, in the form of combined individual and family sessions. There were biweekly meetings, alternately with Yitzhak alone and with Yitzhak together with his parents and his sister. The family therapy helped Yitzhak free himself from his belief that he had to excel in some special original way in order to realize the mission of perfection resting on the shoulders of his family. In the family meetings, Yitzhak came to realize that his parents too were prone to err and had failed in the realization of many of their dreams. His parents admitted that in the past they had erred in not being sufficiently tolerant of Yitzhak's different character and his chosen way of life. The psychotic crisis and the therapy clearly helped all members of the family to be more respectful of the differences among them and to see that the earth would continue turning on its axis even if they failed to reach perfection.

In the third year of therapy, Yitzhak went back to the university. He graduated in history and began successfully teaching the subject in the regional kibbutz high school. He married and became the father of a baby. Four years have gone by with no noteworthy events from a psychiatric point of view.

What was it that brought about Yitzhak's psychotic breakdown, which several psychiatrists diagnosed as a schizophrenic disorder? Of course, to this question we have no unequivocal answer that will be equally acceptable to the wide range of investigators who are looking, each from a different point of departure, for the genetic, biochemical, neurological, family, or psychosocial factors that, singly or together, would account for the development of a schizophrenic disorder. In the explanation we offered to Yitzhak and to significant others, we decided to avoid scientific language and focus on the effects of an overwhelming drive to achieve exceptional results at the university, probably reinforced by harmful reactions to the increased use of marijuana. Under the influence of these stressful factors, a psychotic megalomanic compensation emerged to balance Yitzhak's underlying chronic dissatisfaction with himself as, in his own eyes, the black sheep of a prominent family accustomed to extraordinary achievement. In giving this explanation, we were not negating or contradicting any other hypothesis for schizophrenia, whether as a constitutional predisposition, or a neuropathological condition with enhanced dopamine activity, or an error in the genetic code. We were simply following our general policy of trying to construct our etiological and diagnostic explanations in terms of practical considerations and with recommendations for the shortest and most promising way of returning the psychotic patient to normal functioning in the community.

Conditions Needed for Home Treatment of Acute Psychosis

The cases of Leon and Yitzhak demonstrate how a program of short-term, comprehensive, twenty-four-hour-a-day home care can offer an effective alternative to hospitalization. These two patients are typical of a group of more than fifty acute psychotics who have been similarly treated with home confinement in the kibbutz. In the vast majority of these cases, their treatment resulted in relatively prompt control of psychotic symptoms, such as psychomotor agitation, disorganized bizarre behavior, incoherence, delusions, and hallucinations.

A variety of acute conditions, including schizophrenic and manic episodes, paranoid disorders, major affective disorders, and unspecified psychoses, can be handled at home if the community is able to provide the conditions indispensable for home confinement treatment and if a thorough examination of the case does not show that hospitalization is unavoidable. In spite of our general reservations regarding the efficacy of psychiatric inpatient treatment, we find commitment to a hospital to be mandatory under certain conditions: when suicidal or homicidal behavior presents a serious physical threat to the patient or to others; when there is disruptive, disorganized behavior that is intolerable to the patient's environment, with total refusal of the patient to cooperate with the program; or when a physical illness accompanies the psychiatric symptoms, requiring diagnostic evaluation and appropriate treatment in an inpatient setting.

Before we will recommend the home-care program, the following preconditions must be met:

1. There must be absolute assurance that for at least the first four weeks of the program, the patient will be provided with intensive nursing care, in full cooperation with the local family physician and the medical nurses. The physician and nurses must be willing to receive the necessary instructions regarding medical management and medications from the Kibbutz Clinic's therapeutic team, which is usually composed of a psychiatrist and a family therapist.
2. Constant close contact between the therapeutic team and the local medical team, both in frequent regular meetings and by telephone, must be assured.
3. The patient's family must be totally committed to carrying out the program and to family therapy. It is, after all,

the family that will be most directly involved in the daily care of the patient.

4. There must be an iron-clad commitment by the kibbutz to make available a suitable coordinator. The coordinator must be relieved of regular work obligations for an adequate number of hours every day in order to maintain daily contact with the patient and, as the need arises, to work with the family, the treatment team, the kibbutz institutions, and the kibbutz members in the support network.

It is by no means simple to fulfill all the conditions for the proper execution of a comprehensive home-care program of this type. Such a program is much more complicated and expensive than the so-called home-care programs in which a nurse makes short visits to the patient's home, dispensing drugs and giving an occasional bit of advice on managing problems. Our model is based on close and continuous medical surveillance, nursing care around the clock, continuous psychosocial support, and the careful adjustment of drugs to observed changes in the clinical condition.

The kibbutz, as a tightly organized and strongly structured society, offers exceptional and unrivalled conditions for such community treatment. It is backed up by a mental health clinic with professional personnel specially trained to design and supervise the appropriate community health program, and it offers ample possibilities to mobilize a suitable support network as well as a qualified person to act as coordinator, able to devote several hours of work a day to the project. Undoubtedly, finding or creating such conditions in other types of community is far more difficult, for lack of adequate personnel, both professional and paraprofessional, as well as for budgetary reasons. It is worth recalling, however, that until about twenty years ago, the kibbutz had no community-care program for the mentally ill; the conditions for implementation of the model had to be developed step by step, with great expenditure of effort and adequate investment in community mental health education. Even today there are a good number of kibbutzim where, for various reasons, the program has not been tried. In our view, the proper conditions for a community program can be created in any social framework, if the authorities responsible for mental health in the community realize that the human and financial resources available for mental health care can be used in a more effective manner. Judging by results, we believe that our model of care, as applied in the kibbutz, is in the long run less expensive than hospital treatment or fragmentary community care. In Israel today there is a crying need for more adequate community mental health services. In the early 1970s the Israel Ministry of Health—in line with similar steps in many Western countries—announced the decision to develop a series of community programs at an accelerated pace. Unfortunately this declaration remained in the realm of good intentions. In 1972, when the decision about the revolution in community services was first made known, the government's share in the total expenditure on community mental health services was 3.2 percent, and in 1987, the share of the government allocation to these services was about the same. At the same time, the government's share in the budgets of psychiatric hospitals kept growing at an accelerated pace (a growth of 35 percent in the past eight years). Likewise, the professional staff in mental hospitals grew at a pace four times as fast as the parallel growth in community health services.*

Even those few community mental health centers that were established in Israel in the past fifteen years do not meet the criteria we expect to find in an authentic community-care service. Most of them are outpatient clinics (directly connected with mental health hospitals) that do individual follow-ups and base their treatment program on the administration of medication to discharged patients, in the hope of preventing further relapse. In this type of "community" service there is very little contact, if any, with the surroundings, with the family, and with the significant others.

*U. Aviram and Y. Levav. "Trends and Issues in Community Mental Health in Israel," in U. Aviram and Y. Levav, (eds.), *Community Mental Health in Israel* (Tel Aviv: Cherikover, 1981), pp. 129–45.

Breaking the Revolving Door Pattern: Community-Based Care for the Chronic Mentally Ill

The cases of Leon and Yitzhak have demonstrated how treatment with our program of home care during a first episode of acute psychosis can substantially reduce the duration of the illness, return the patient to an adequate level of functioning with no complications, and by avoiding hospitalization reduce the danger of the subsequent revolving door syndrome. For some patients, however, it is too late to avoid the revolving door; they are already in it. In these cases, the myth of the mental hospital as the only—or the preferred—therapy solution for the severely ill mental patient and the general ignorance of the existing alternatives have served to perpetuate the indescribable suffering of all the actors in the drama called "The Chronic Mentally Ill." With these patients, as with those who have never been hospitalized, the model of community-based treatment described above has proved highly successful, in their case breaking the cycle of repeated hospitalizations and leading them to long-term improvement in functioning in the community.

Two clinical examples will illustrate the basic ingredients of the community management program for the chronic mentally ill patient at the Kibbutz Clinic. In both cases, the patients were referred to us after several years of unsuccessful conventional hospital-centered treatment.

The Case of Betty: Resocializing a Restricted Life

The case of Betty is characteristic of the low expectations of the hospital mode of treatment. Betty came to us at the peak of a lifelong career of psychiatric illness: By the age of thirty-three she had had five hospitalizations, each followed by continuous psychiatric outpatient care and administration of intensive neuroleptic medication. She had reached what the psychiatrist in charge considered to be the optimal expected condition, although by even the most minimal criteria her objective condition was very poor. An obese woman with the face of a child, she spent most of the day in her room, totally dependent on outside help. So passive was her attitude to life that even her suicide threats were not taken seriously and only provided the people around her, exhausted from having to care for her day after day, with the justification for committing her to hospital yet again. After several months, Betty would return to the kibbutz and to her previous condition of chronic hibernation, with a letter from the hospital that once again confirmed the never-changing diagnosis of residual schizophrenia and gave instructions for the continued administration of antipsychotic medication.

When Betty was fourteen, her parents, members of Kibbutz Galim, divorced. Her father left the country and was never heard from again. During this period, her mother stopped working, partly because of her health—she was diagnosed as suffering from ulcerative colitis in a state of remission—but mainly to take care of Betty, who was considered a problem child even prior to the divorce. At the age of twelve, Betty refused to sleep in the children's house and instead slept in her parents' quarters. She became overattached to her mother, frequently running away from school to seek her out in her place of work. She lived on the fringe of her peer group, did poorly in school, and overate grossly.

When Betty turned eighteen, she went into the army, where she served as a minor clerk of whom very little responsibility and effort were required. Her army camp was located not far from the kibbutz, so she was able to get home quite frequently. During these visits, she spent most of the time in her mother's quarters, endlessly lamenting her sad fate as the only child of a broken family, with no contact with her father and her mother limited by ill health, unable to take proper care of her. The mother would respond that she herself could hardly be said to be "sleeping in a bed of roses," thereby reinforcing the cycle of self-pity and helplessness between the two women.

At the age of twenty-one, Betty completed her army service and came back to the kibbutz, where she was given quarters of her own. She still had no friends, and her mother was her only gateway to the outside world. She kept switching from one job to another, unable to cope with the demands of a responsible job, most of the time daydreaming and often leaving her workplace in the middle of the day with no explanation.

Betty's condition kept deteriorating. She spent most of her time lying on her bed or watching television, neglecting her personal cleanliness and paying no attention at all to the growing disorder in her room. She ate without restraint, with recurrent episodes of binge-eating. Her mother was very critical of her indolence but at the same time continued to take care of all her needs. Betty refused to go for treatment to the regional mental health clinic, claiming that psychiatric treatment was bound to affect her brain and would lead her to commit suicide. The family physician at the kibbutz discussed the subject with the kibbutz health authorities and with her mother, and all agreed that she should be committed to a mental hospital. At about age twenty-two, therefore, Betty was committed, for the first time, to a closed ward of a mental institution. She was treated mainly with antipsychotic medication (perphenazine, fluphenazine, and trifluoperazine), but she refused to participate in the occupational therapy program and remained passive and uncooperative in the individual and group therapy meetings. She was discharged after seven months with a diagnosis of chronic schizophrenia, residual type; a very poor prognosis; and a recommendation to continue intensive drug treatment.

As was to be expected, Betty returned to her previous state of isolation, inactivity, and dependence on help from her mother and the various kibbutz institutions. She became generally known as suffering from an incurable chronic mental illness. During the ten years that followed, she was hospitalized four more times, whenever the tension and quarrels with her mother became aggravated. During these crisis periods, she manifested clear psychotic symptoms, including delusionary talk about some strange powers that were taking possession of her, dictating what she was to do and what she was forbidden to do during her waking hours and telling her that she would soon receive information on the time and manner of her death. In such situations the psychiatrist in charge would further increase the dosage of her medication, hoping—in vain—to avoid rehospitalization. When the psychiatrist proposed that she be hospitalized for the sixth time, the kibbutz nurse, who had recently participated in a training program in the Kibbutz Clinic and had heard of our therapy model, succeeded in convincing Betty's mother (who at the time was far from well) to turn for help to the unit in our clinic dealing with chronic psychiatric diseases.

In accordance with our model, the first consultation at the Clinic included, in addition to Betty and her mother, several kibbutz members who had volunteered to serve as a support group for Betty. The network consisted of representatives of the kibbutz committees on health and on work, a neighbor, and the nurse who had taken the initiative in bringing about the meeting. The coordinator appointed at our request was a middle-aged woman of the kibbutz who was freed from work responsibility for four hours a day in order to maintain daily contact with Betty, help carry out the therapist's instructions, and follow up closely on the activity of the support group.

In my psychiatric evaluation of Betty's condition, I observed no symptoms whatsoever of schizophrenic or any other psychotic disorder. What I saw was an undifferentiated type of chronic psychiatric disturbance in an individual with very restricted social experience in life, tied to her mother by symbiotic dependence, scared by and trying to run away from life's challenges, and therefore habitually presenting herself as crazy to anyone who would demand that she leave her sanctuary. In the course of the consultation, Betty admitted that when she felt threatened by attempts by her mother or the kibbutz representatives to push her out of her state of seclusion, she would invent all sorts of "strange" answers, which she elaborated on during her periods of hospitalization. She also admitted that she used to answer all the hospital psychiatrist's questions in the affirmative, in the hope of confirming the diagnosis of bizarre delusional ideas.

It was clear to us that only a structured and systematic resocialization program, in close contact with the support group, would encourage Betty to cross the narrow bridge that still linked her with what was in her eyes an alien society, fraught with serious danger. Betty would have to call upon more courage and strength than she now had if she were to give up her bill of rights as a mentally ill person of long standing, recognized as such by the kibbutz as well as by the psychiatric establishment. She showed great ambivalence in her motivation to cooperate with the rehabilitation program. On the one hand, she wanted to change her condition of a meaningless life and continuous boredom; but on the other hand, she expressed openly how convenient it was to be under no pressure to work and to be able to stay in bed as long as she wished; she required many hours of sleep because of the huge amounts of medication she was taking. We discussed the pros and cons of the situation for a full two hours before Betty finally agreed that she would join in a process to change her present status, step by step, always with her full agreement. This conclusion was conveyed, in the presence of Betty and her mother, to the coordinator and to the network, with repeated emphasis that no one should expect any revolutions; a baby who is just at the brink of walking cannot be pushed to start running or riding a bicycle. At the same time, we conveyed a message of hope, pointing out two favorable factors in Betty's crippling condition: first, that Betty was aware of her condition and did not deny that her present life was far from satisfactory, was in fact filled with suffering, misery, and boredom; and second, that there were a number of people around Betty who were ready to help her, prepared to adjust to her slow pace as she tried to break out of her prolonged state of seclusion.

With Betty's agreement, it was decided that as a first step in going out into the world she would leave her room for ten minutes every day at a predetermined hour. Accompanied by the coordinator, she would visit the physiotherapist at the kibbutz and carry out a few simple exercises. It was also decided to reduce gradually the dosage of her medicines, which doubtless were contributing no little to the perpetuation of a chronic state of apathy, sluggishness, and drowsiness. Betty's mother was released from her role as Betty's permanent caregiver. Instead she was given another assignment in the kibbutz—to act as companion to a child who had cerebral palsy and was permanently confined to a wheelchair. She was to talk to the handicapped girl about the news of the day, culled from the daily newspaper, and the same topics were to serve as the central matter in her daily talks with Betty.

The therapeutic team (the psychologist in charge and the psychiatrist) met with Betty, her mother, and the coordinator every three weeks. Sometimes the various members of the support system were also invited to these meetings, held either at the kibbutz or in the regional Kibbutz Clinic.

Betty immediately broadened the range of her activities: After the walks and the physical exercise, she began working for part of the day in the kibbutz laundry, doing some responsible work and performing well at it. She also began to take care of her room and her personal cleanliness. For the first time in her life, she was ready to acknowledge that working more than the absolute minimum gave her a feeling of satisfaction. Gradually she began taking a more active part in her own therapy, rather than allowing herself to be "pushed around," as she said of the early stages. On her initiative, a new item was added to the therapy: She expressed a wish to improve her conversational skills, having come to feel that her conversation was boring and very limited, because she could not continue a topic of interest beyond the first two sentences. A lot of role rehearsal within a structured conversational skills training program in the therapy sessions followed, accompanied by homework with the social support group. As a result, her social and conversational competence improved considerably.

One year after the therapy program was initiated, the coordinator summed up the situation:

> *Betty's condition is better than it has ever been. She is alert and active. She works three hours a day in the laundry and two hours in the library. Her performance is very satisfactory. She does physical exercises for half an hour a day and showers daily. Two months ago, she began attending a course in the regional community college on the history of Jerusalem. She has already participated in a study trip that is part of the course. After work she takes a rest for two*

hours. She has begun reading some popular books and is enjoying it. (For many years she did not read at all.) After her rest, she generally goes visiting, either at her mother's or at the home of some kibbutz member: as many as seventeen members in the kibbutz have expressed their readiness to play host to her about once every three weeks. Before she goes out visiting, she makes sure to coordinate the time of the visit with the host family. After this social activity, she takes herself for a walk around the kibbutz and then goes into the dining hall for her evening meal. Recently she took part for the first time in a discussion at the kibbutz general meeting on the problems of the second generation. She was listened to attentively, and that gave her a lot of satisfaction. Last week, for the first time in her life, she invited one of the families that she visits regularly for a return visit in her quarters. For the occasion she gave her room a very thorough cleaning and prepared some light refreshments. She has also joined a Weight Watchers group in the kibbutz, and she is gradually reducing her weight. In about a month she is to go out to study bookbinding, at the behest of the kibbutz library.

Clearly, there are still many problems. In talking with her it is obvious that she lacks self-confidence and generally leaves the initiative for the conversation to others, although she is able to take an active part. Her approach to life is a bit childish, and she is still interested to know whether there are people in the kibbutz who consider her "crazy." But all in all, her progress is astounding and beyond all expectations. As to the mother, she continues to work two hours a day and feels much relieved in her relations with her daughter, but her general physical condition is not good. She is probably going to have to undergo an operation. . . .

Two years have passed since the writing of this positive report. Betty's condition is stable, and her functioning has continued to improve. The help of the support network is still required, but less frequently and less intensively. Once a month Betty comes to the Clinic for a meeting with the treatment team, accompanied by the coordinator, who continues to maintain steady contact with Betty, her mother, and the therapists, ready to intervene or to help as the need arises.

As soon as therapy began, Betty's delusional constructs disappeared altogether. In the course of the three-year follow-up, there was never any reason to consider rehospitalization: the revolving door syndrome seems to have come to an end.

It may well be that psychiatrists who are faithful followers of the descriptive psychiatry officially represented by *DSM-III* will continue to see Betty's case as a typical example of chronic schizophrenia, but in temporary remission. We, on our part, view the long history of social withdrawal, exceptional behavior, poor functioning, and delusions as the reaction of a constitutionally weak personality to the conditions of life in the presence of dysfunctional family and social patterns of interaction. This is first and foremost a case of a social-interpersonal type of illness, and a model of therapy such as the community psychosocial program described above appears more promising than a traditional medical model of treatment, which in Betty's case had led to chronic invalidism, repeated hospitalization, and massive use of medication with subsequent oversedation.

The case of Betty is one of many cases of chronic mentally ill patients for whom the community-based program led to a successful outcome. As we have reported elsewhere,* in 53 percent of the chronic mentally ill patients treated at the Kibbutz Clinic with a community-care program, the results were more than satisfactory, and the stated goals of the program were reached. Our criteria for determining the efficacy and success of the treatment include:

1. Improved psychosocial functioning, as expressed in the ability to participate in the community at an acceptable level of self-sufficiency and independence in day-to-day functioning (grooming, cleanliness, meals, laundry, homemaking).

*Mordecai Kaffman, "Management of Kibbutz Chronic Mental Patients: Factors Influencing Failure in the Community," *Israel Journal of Psychiatry* 19(1982): 263–78.

2. Improved social competence, including better use of leisure-time activities (newspapers, books, sports, music, radio, television, hobbies, study groups) and participation in at least some of the activities organized by the kibbutz for the whole community.
3. Extension of interpersonal communication and social relations with friends, coworkers, and members of the support network.
4. Working every day, in a responsible manner, for at least six hours, thereby becoming a productive member of the community.
5. Staying out of mental hospitals for at least three consecutive years.

In sum, even for a chronic mental patient such as Betty with an established "psychiatric career," there is hope. In a considerable number of cases, a program of adequate community care makes it possible to reach the desired aims of enhanced social functioning, vocational progress, changes for the better in the dependent life style, and a better quality of life within the community.

We were reassured in our conclusions by the recent report on the Vermont Longitudinal Study of persons with severe mental illness who after deinstitutionalization had received a long-term community treatment program.* Two or three decades later, more than one-half the patients were found to have considerably improved or recovered. In their excellent study, Harding and collaborators point out that "the data give evidence that, contrary to the expected downward and deteriorating course for schizophrenia or for other severe and chronic psychiatric disorders, symptoms can be ameliorated over time and functioning can be restored."†

Obviously we do not claim that community treatment offers a panacea for all cases of chronic mental illness. There are, of course, patients who remain functionally handicapped, totally

*C. Harding et al., "The Vermont Longitudinal Study of Persons with Severe Mental Illness, I: Methodology, Study Sample, and Overall Status 32 Years Later," *American Journal of Psychiatry* 144(1987): 718–26.

†Ibid., p. 724.

dependent on a permanent support system and far removed from society's mainstream. No therapeutic system has so far been devised that can wipe out the effects of diverse neurologically handicapping conditions, severe brain damage, inborn personality defects, or lifelong symbiotic parent-child relationships that totally lack motivation for mutual autonomy. Moreover, no successful community program can be implemented unless the community can mobilize the required resources for the type of program we have described. In our experience we have found vast differences among kibbutzim in their willingness and capacity to implement a long-term program that calls for considerable personal sacrifice and a large outlay of funds (the government mental health services do not contribute anything to cover the cost of the program). One must admire those kibbutzim that have succeeded in overcoming the obstacles. They have had to solve difficult logistic problems, such as finding and freeing from current responsibility a suitable person to act as coordinator of the project and organizing an extended comprehensive support system. Furthermore, it sometimes takes a special effort to convince the local medical staff—the family physician and the nurse in charge—to cooperate with the proposed plan. Thus one must not wonder that in some cases, especially in a small kibbutz or in one heavily burdened by a variety of financial or manpower problems, the hospitalization alternative is preferred to a community care program.

The Case of Alice: A Trio of Treatments

The case of Alice,* who came to us with a diagnosis of chronic schizophrenia, is of particular interest because it enabled us to compare her state during three different periods of her life, when she underwent different forms of treatment. Alice lived in the kibbutz for nineteen years. In the course of the first nine years from the onset of the illness, she was treated according to the medical model of a psychiatric institution. During those years,

*A partial description of Alice's treatment appeared in Mordecai Kaffman, "Community Care for the Kibbutz Chronic Psychiatric-Patient," *International Journal of Family Therapy* 3(1981):193–204.

she was periodically institutionalized because of episodes of acute psychotic exacerbation. Her treatment was then transferred to the Kibbutz Clinic, where she received treatment according to our community-based management program for a period of ten years. During this latter period, the treatment was carried on entirely within the kibbutz, without resort to mental hospital treatment.

Alice, married and mother of a fifteen-year-old daughter, was thirty-eight years old when she was first referred to the Kibbutz Clinic. She and her family had immigrated from the United States and had joined the kibbutz nine years before the application to our clinic. People who came in contact with Alice soon learned that she had good intellectual potential but was passive and withdrawn, lacking self-confidence and independence. At work she requested guidance and instructions for every move, and she showed helplessness in everyday situations. Her husband was the dominant figure in the family, very sure of himself and responsible for all the decisions. He openly displayed a superior and pitying attitude toward his wife and considered himself responsible for teaching and guiding her in all the problems of life. Similarly, her daughter did not conceal her contempt for her. She was ashamed of her mother, rejected her rudely in the presence of her peers, and tried to reduce her relationship with her to a minimum.

During the nine years Alice had been in the kibbutz, she had been hospitalized in a psychiatric ward four times, each time for a period of two to five months. Between hospitalizations, she remained in the community for average periods of one-and-a-half years, functioning marginally in all spheres of life. As time went on, she would spend more and more time at home, mostly lying in bed, and occasionally getting up to do some superfluous work thought up especially for her, a sort of occupational therapy of no practical use to the kibbutz.

The recurring hospitalizations were occasioned by the appearance of acute psychotic symptoms, characterized by extreme psychomotor agitation and lengthy talks about plans to write a book and to teach literature at the university. In such a state of acute psychosis, Alice would be committed to a psychiatric hospital, where she would be given the diagnostic label of "chronic schizophrenic disorder, paranoid type." The hospital treatment would include the usual elements of institutional care: antipsychotic drug medication with the addition of some type of inpatient milieu therapy. The aftercare treatment was determined by the institutional psychiatrist and was based mainly on monthly follow-up visits to adjust the drug therapy to her clinical condition. The kibbutz nurse was instructed to accept the patient's failure to function in her daily life, which was considered by the psychiatrist in charge to be all that could be expected; here was a case, in his opinion, of a chronic schizophrenic with permanent functional incapacity. All parties involved in her care could see no other way but to go along with the inevitability of intermittent institutional treatment. Alice became totally dependent on her husband, seemingly unable to lead an autonomous and meaningful life. She was apathetic, lacked initiative, and took no interest in anything in her surroundings.

When Alice's husband announced his intention to begin divorce proceedings in order to marry a woman he had been having an affair with for over a year, Alice's psychotic behavior was once more exacerbated. At this point, it was decided to transfer her treatment from the hospital to the Kibbutz Clinic. The Kibbutz Clinic appointed a psychologist in charge of continuation of Alice's treatment. In our eyes, Alice exhibited all the characteristics of an "institutional syndrome within the community"—that is, a life style of helplessness, an inadequate social life, nonresponsible behavior, and a recognized status as a chronic patient. The therapist, in accordance with our model, worked in full cooperation with me as the psychiatrist. At later stages, the therapist in charge alone managed the treatment plan, mostly on the basis of weekly meetings with the patient and the coordinator of the social support network; I continued to meet with Alice, but no more than once every four to six weeks, either to check the effects of the prescribed antipsychotic medication or at the initiative of her regular therapist in periods of crisis or when special problems arose. In the case of Alice, as with other patients like her, our policy regarding medication was to use the lowest effective therapeutic dose of antipsychotic drugs and to avoid the use of multiple drugs. The high-dose regimen of neuroleptics that Alice had been receiving on the instructions of the hospital was therefore gradually decreased until she was sufficiently stabilized with a low-maintenance dose of fluphenazine decanoate (10 mg. i.m. every four weeks).

In the beginning, the treatment program had three main components:

1. Family therapy, initially involving joint sessions attended by Alice, her husband, and their daughter. The goals of these meetings were chiefly to work out conditions for a constructive divorce, to raise the patient's faith in her ability to deal with problems of daily life without her husband's help, and to encourage her to behave more assertively toward her daughter. At a later stage, when the divorce proceedings were over, the meetings continued once a week, usually with the patient alone but sometimes together with the coordinator or, less frequently, with Alice's daughter.
2. A community support system, set up with the aid of the kibbutz mental health committee. The ten to twelve people in this group consented to cooperate in a program whose initial aim was defined as preventing social isolation and further hospitalization following the divorce crisis. Among those who volunteered to be part of the support network were representatives of the health and work committees, a medical nurse, two workers in the communal kitchen (which was then considered by all to be the most suitable place of work for Alice), two of her neighbors, and a few other volunteers who were willing to invite her to social gatherings from time to time. A member of the kibbutz trained as a social worker was chosen to be coordinator of the network. A single meeting was held with all members of the support network, together with the psychologist and psychiatrist in charge. The goals of the program were discussed, opin-

ions were exchanged, and practical suggestions were made for working out the agreed treatment plan. Afterwards, contact between the therapist and members of the support network took place almost exclusively through the coordinator at regularly scheduled meetings, in addition to unplanned consultation by telephone in unexpected situations.

3. A very structured program, suited to Alice's abilities and limitations and taking into consideration her low level of concentration, lack of initiative and independence, and poor capacity for meaningful social contact. A series of simple chores was arranged for her in the kibbutz kitchen, at first within a framework of five work-hours a day. In addition, a daily schedule of various leisure-hour activities was planned (physical exercises, lessons to improve her spoken Hebrew, cake baking, interior decoration of her room, and flower arrangement). A number of volunteers saw to it that she would be taken from her apartment, according to a preplanned schedule, for casual social visits or to organized entertainment activities of the kibbutz.

As time passed, this comprehensive plan proved a success far beyond expectation, although Alice's progress and achievements did not follow a straight and steady course. There were indeed unexpected problems, temporary failures, and periods of regression. When she began working in the kibbutz kitchen, Alice presented the clinical picture characteristic of chronic mental patients. Her helplessness was expressed by periods of inactivity, childish questions to members of the kitchen staff, and continual requests for superfluous instruction in carrying out her chores. This behavior proved burdensome and irritating to the rest of the workers, especially since her output was very low, partly because she frequently left work for no justifiable reason. She seemed not to understand her special situation, and instead of fulfilling her duties in the kitchen, she constantly complained about the boring work, persistently but unrealistically demanding to do responsible educational work in one of the children's homes. There were also problems in the social sphere. Volunteers who invited Alice to social gatherings complained that not only would she remain much longer than was acceptable but that she would appear at their homes as an uninvited guest on repeated occasions and with various excuses. They frankly expressed their feeling that the task they had undertaken most willingly was now complicating their private lives and becoming burdensome.

A prompt clarification of each of these problems was held between the therapist and the coordinator, and their conclusions were discussed in talks between the coordinator and pertinent members of the network. At the same time, the problems were raised in therapy sessions with Alice, where techniques such as role-playing, modeling, and homework assignments were utilized to improve her awareness of others and promote more responsible and acceptable social behavior. Members of the support system and significant others in the community were encouraged to demand, in a positive but forceful manner, that she fulfill her work duty more adequately. It was decided that rather than ease her duties, the kitchen staff would set aside a separate corner for her in the kitchen and assign her more responsible tasks, with very clear instructions and emphasis on the value of her work. Arrangements were made to reduce sharply the number of kitchen staff she could turn to for guidance. To improve her social functioning, people whose task it was to help keep her from social isolation received explicit directions to set limitations on the time and duration of visits. They were shown how to put this as a positive message, called for by reality and the need to respect the privacy of others, without any implication of rejection.

To the surprise of members of the network, Alice listened to their complaints, improved her behavior at work considerably, adjusted to the conditions set for social activities with network volunteers, and gradually achieved a noticeable degree of independence at work and in leisure-time activities. About a year after the community-based program began, it was possible to transfer her to more interesting work, assisting the kibbutz nurses in caring for elderly and bedridden patients.

During the ten years that followed the inception of the community treatment program, Alice remained in the kibbutz with no need for hospitalization. She worked daily at an occupation that is needed and valued in the kibbutz. The relations with her daughter improved considerably. She seemed reasonably happy, participated in most of the social activities of the kibbutz, and was able to occupy herself independently in leisure hours and to maintain social contacts with a number of persons without the need of any special support system. Only once, a year and a half after the community program began, did she have an episode of acute psychotic relapse, which seemed to be related to a series of stressful situations and disappointments. The relapse was successfully treated within the community through home confinement. Rapid control of the acute symptoms was obtained by an increased parenteral dose of fluphenazine decanoate; Alice calmed down and achieved symptomatic improvement within a few days. During and immediately after this critical period, members of the network were encouraged to intensify their contacts with Alice by visiting her more frequently, expressing their hope for a speedy recovery, and displaying great interest in her return to her ordinary routine. Alice did return to work shortly thereafter, and after that no symptoms of psychotic exacerbation reappeared as long as she remained in the kibbutz.

Unfortunately, Alice's story does not have this happy ending. She met and subsequently married a widower, fifteen years her senior, who lived in a small town in the south of Israel with his mentally retarded son. Alice decided to leave the kibbutz, so that she could—in her own words—"turn a new leaf in life in the company of my husband and his son, far away from the bitter memories of the past." For about a year she managed to cope with the difficulties and stresses of her renewed family life. But then once again symptoms of acute psychotic exacerbation began to appear, with psychomotor restlessness, clear deterioration in functioning, illogical thinking, and bizarre delusions. This time, as a member of a private family in town, far away from the social setting of the kibbutz, she had no choice but to have herself admitted to the nearest mental hospital. There she was assigned to a closed ward, with no social contact other than with other psychotic patients. Her husband, strongly alarmed by this development, felt cheated, stopped visiting Alice at the hospital, and expressed his deep regret over the unfortunate marriage and his wish for a divorce. Under these aggravating circumstances, the combined use of high-potency antipsychotic drug therapy, individual therapy, and some occupational therapy produced no improvement whatsoever in the psychotic episode. At this point, when all her dreams of rehabilitating her life had evaporated, the hospital constituted her only refuge; she was left with no place to go, and no reason to go anywhere. When her condition did not improve, she was given a higher dosage of antipsychotic drugs, which brought on marked neurologic side effects.

At that time, I visited her in her closed ward. I barely recognized her, and it was hard not to be repelled by her bizarre looks and behavior, her masked facies with its idiotic expression, her drowsiness and inattention, and her physical rigidity and postural instability, caused mainly by the massive medication and by institutional adaptation. No doubt her repellent external appearance was a weighty factor in her husband's decision to go through with the divorce as soon as Alice was discharged from the hospital. After three years of hospitalization, Alice was put in the ward for the chronically ill, and no hope was held out for her recovery. She is now waiting to be admitted to a sheltered home program for the mentally incurable.

The case of Alice may serve as a good example of the chronic vulnerable psychiatric patient, with recurrent episodes of acute psychotic exacerbation, who has been treated by two different therapeutic programs with sharply different outcomes. We have no doubt that with patients like Alice, there is a clear preference for the community alternative rather than treatment at a mental hospital. Unfortunately, after she left the kibbutz, Alice had no alternative other than recommitment to a mental hospital.

Hospital Care Versus Community Care

The cases described in this chapter, and many other cases like them, have demonstrated clearly that far from providing the best treatment for most mentally ill patients, the psychiatric hospital often acts to perpetuate the patient's social inadequacy. Moreover, by labeling patients with frightening diagnoses, especially of schizophrenia with its severe connotation of a future of insuperable problems, the hospital ties the patient's prognosis to the psychiatric diagnosis—which may turn out to be right or wrong—rather than to the quality of treatment, an essential factor in determining the patient's outcome.

If a community-based model of care for the mentally disabled has been seen to have clear advantages over hospital-based care, it might be expected that mental health services would be rapidly moving toward increased emphasis on community programs and away from the use of hospitalization in treating mental illness. Yet this is not the case. In Israel and in most countries throughout the Western world—Italy is the notable exception—most of the mental health resources continue to be poured into the one-track road of the inpatient setting, despite its proven ineffectiveness in a large percentage of cases.

How is one to account for the preference for mental hospital treatment over other alternatives? In part, the answer is that myths die hard. It is a popular myth that the hospital is the most refined instrument for diagnosis and treatment of all serious and complicated illnesses, and for hundreds of years mental illness has been considered the most intricate and mysterious of human disorders. Dogmatic concepts regarding the mentally ill and a deep-rooted belief that they require treatment in a separate institution, away from "normal" people, are not easily changed. Similarly, it is almost impossible to counter the pessimistic attitude fostered by the use of some psychiatric labels, particularly schizophrenia, which in the eyes of the general public leave little room for faith in any treatment but a medical model with the mental hospital at its core.

Another reason for the dependence on the hospital setting is the need for respite on the part of the chronic mental patient's family. In general the family of the chronic mental patient living at home must bear the intolerable burden of round-the-clock care. Such families often feel trapped; they suffer guilt, fear, anger, frustration, and hopelessness. In the absence of psychiatric outreach support, they may burn out. If they have no other resources to turn to for substitute care and assistance when the inevitable crises occur, hospitalization begins to appear as the only available solution. The mental institution then takes over the care for several months, until the patient reaches a level of conduct that meets the standards of the hospital and the family is once more ready to take over the full-time job of daily care. This cycle turns the hospital into a vitally necessary institution unless the family manages to find some extra-professional support to enable it to cope.

Yet another obstacle to a shift from the accepted hospital treatment to community psychiatry can be found in the revolutionary nature of the changes that are required on the part of mental health professionals. In the hospital-based model, the mentally ill are separated from the rest of society and brought into the territory of the psychiatrists under strictly stipulated new living conditions. In community health programs, the mental health workers must radically change their habits and work within the milieu of their patients. To accomplish this, reversal will require changing not only how mental health professionals are trained and supervised but how they traditionally see themselves.

It is small wonder, then, that community treatment runs a poor second to hospital treatment of mental health patients, despite the hospital's unsatisfactory record of achieving successful outcomes. In John Talbott's words, "Treatment in the community is . . . still a national disgrace . . . with only isolated examples of programs providing comprehensive care."*

No form of psychotherapy that is not supported by a comprehensive community help program can possibly cover the complex

*John Talbott, "Care of the Chronically Mentally Ill—Still a National Disgrace," *American Journal of Psychiatry* 136(1979):688–89.

needs of the patient and the patient's family. It goes far beyond what is usually offered in the outpatient clinic, connected to a psychiatric hospital, whose role is to follow up and administer medication to discharged patients, in the hope of preventing relapses. Such services have little or no contact with the family and significant others. Similarly, it goes beyond the individual and family therapy offered by the majority of therapists in mental health centers. Family therapy that is not tied in with a larger system of care is in most cases bound to fail. The family therapist must take into account that every family, even the most competent, that carries the heavy burden for care for a patient with a crippling psychiatric illness is in constant danger of breaking. In most cases it is unable to cope with the stressful situation for very long without social support and outside helpers. To the best of our knowledge, there is so far no therapy in existence that can improve the dysfunctional psychosocial patterns of chronic mentally ill patients, functioning away from the mainstream, without the support of the appropriate social institutions. Neither confinement in a mental hospital nor family therapy alone will perform the miracle of community adjustment in the absence of additional support systems.

9

If You Ask the Right Questions . . .

WE BEGAN THIS BOOK with a seminar in family therapy. It was a successful program: The teacher and the professional students finished their five days together with a satisfying sense of having covered concepts and techniques that are useful in professional practice.

Unfortunately, we decided to follow up on four of the cases presented in the seminar, and we ran head on into life—not life with a capital L, just life, simple events. The social contexts in which the dramas of our cases had been staged had not attended the seminar. Institutions insisted on being institutions. The power of labeling to elicit images and behaviors and to obliterate perspectives remained. The control of ideologies over the hierarchy of values, esthetics, and behavior remained. The search for logic and coherence in discourse imposed an order that failed to match the disorder of real life. The wires that connect people—that complex web of connective tissue that imprisons patients, families, therapists, and consultants in a social ecology governed by pervasive invisible rules—still remained largely invisible. And in the midst of it all, with the fantasies of Gulliver, were a lightweight family consultant and a psychologist who still cannot resist challenging families with the bright rhetoric of storytelling. We cannot believe that this is totally useless. But as soon as we change a framing that makes us central, the limitations of our power become very clear.

Still, it is often said that if you ask the right questions, you are at least partway to the answers. So let us end this book as we began, with some questions about consultation in family therapy and the role of family therapy consultation vis-à-vis the family and larger systems.

The Creation of Discontinuity and Mobilization of Resources

From a systems perspective, consultation is a process of increasing the complexity of the therapeutic process in such a way that it opens new alternatives for therapy. To achieve this goal, the consultant interrupts the established patterns in the therapeutic system, creating discontinuity that is often followed by a reconceptualization of problems and an exploration of new pathways for change. When this step is successful, it is followed by a mobilization of resources. The consultant and therapeutic team join in co-authoring an alternative way of constructing the bits of the family story, one that allows family members to find different ways of positioning themselves with respect to each other and to the significant social system.

Consultations often begin with an impasse, a situation in which both the family and the therapists are entangled in a stuck system. The healing process begins even before the consultation, with the participants' expectations that the consultation will help, their faith in the competence of the expert, and their respect for the expert's authority. The system becomes more open to new directions, and the consultant is empowered to an unusual degree. Much of the consultant's ability to disrupt previous processes and gain access to the system's healing potentials is a consequence of this preparation.

Again and again in the follow-ups, we were impressed with how little the families remembered the actual content of the consultations. Sometimes they simply could not recall what had happened; sometimes they blithely misquoted. But it is clear that consultation was a kind of ritual that sparked the family to seek its own healing resources. There was not just a rational understanding but an emotional experiencing of a different reality, a reality founded on a reorganized matrix of relationships inside the family and between the family and the social system. In Minuchin's constructions, competence was emphasized instead of pathology, supportive collaboration replaced mutual blaming, and family and therapist were transformed into a healing context.

But unless the system is able to use a consultation to expand and grow, there will be a strong tendency for the therapeutic system to return to equilibrium. Unfortunately, most consultations do focus tightly on family change, and because the consultant is then no longer on the scene, this narrow focus on the family distorts the understanding of the relationships within the therapeutic context. Therefore the consultation's effectiveness is very much a function of the extent to which the consultant's theories are grafted into the therapeutic system. If that doesn't happen, any momentum will quickly be lost.

We also saw that the consultant was unable to modify the context in the cases in the psychiatric hospital. Consultations with hospitalized patients should be done in the hospital only when the consultant fully understands how the hospital functions and the inpatient staff is committed to a dialogue with the therapist. In both Dan's and Yoav's cases, for example, the family therapist presented the case as a problem of transition from the hospital to the home. In effect that was not the issue. Dan remained in the hospital for a year after the consultation, and Yoav five. In retrospect, Minuchin's reliance on information from members of the hospital staff who were not decision makers was a counterproductive framing.

In the two kibbutz cases, there was more chance for continuity. Practice and theory in the Kibbutz Clinic are part of a long dialogue involving ecological systems therapy. But even under these more promising conditions, the impact of the consultation tended to fade quickly. In fact, we have come to believe that family therapy consultation has a tremendous number of unknowns. The practice of a single consultation is itself questionable. In an unknown therapeutic system, at least two consultations are necessary. The first half of the first session should be run largely by the consultee, so that the consultant can intervene in the whole therapeutic system.

The Erosion of Impact

Right after the consultations, a honeymoon period ensued. There were feelings of unity and a bonding typical of people who are working together toward a common goal. The level of energy was high, and a variety of important changes were made. Some of these changes held up over time, but others were dissipated when a setback occurred and conflicts between members or the system resurfaced. This is a universal reaction that occurs after any session with a consultant, and as such it is as much a part of the consultative process as the preparation prior to the session. Sometimes it is defined as resistance, when helpers are convinced that their intervention is correct and that they are observing a system with a stake in staying unchanged.

Consultants who perceive themselves as part of the system, however, think of the reaction to their intervention as feedback from another part of the system. They make use of this feedback to ensure that the gap between them and the therapeutic system will not be too wide for working together. In doing so, they may correct some of their perceptions and surpass some of the limitations of their initial interventions. They do not have to respect any consistent theoretical framework of family therapy, and the focus of their work does not even have to stay on the family.

Obviously, when there is a single consultation this process of mutual adaptation is limited. The family continues working with the therapist, and those parts of the consultation that are too incongruent with the ongoing therapy are left behind. Such incongruities may occur on all levels of the system.

Another important factor influencing the impact of the consultation is the fit between the consultant and the therapist. Consultation is first of all a collaboration between a therapist and a consultant, a form of co-therapy in which there are clearly defined therapeutic roles. The consultant is supposed to provide a knowledgeable perspective, while the consultee, who maintains control over the case, is expected to implement any new insights gained. Systems consultants function in varied ways during consultations. They may intervene actively, using a variety of techniques as they search for a way to perturb the homeostatic cycles. Some consultants seek to create some change during the actual session, while others give homework assignments or use other means for creating a change after the session. But whatever the specific approach of the consultant, the therapist must continue the work if the change is to be stabilized. It is a complex collaboration, and if there is too wide a gap between the consultant and the consultee, the effects of the consultant's work with the family will be negated.

One source of incongruities on this level is the fact that family consultants usually meet only with the family. A family consultation is therefore particularly suitable in cases where therapists have become stuck in their family work. When the problems at the heart of a therapeutic impasse are on a different level of the system, however, the bias of family consultation is to miss or to underestimate their significance. In such cases, therapists will have trouble continuing the work that was demonstrated in the family consultation. They may push in the direction of more intensive family work without being aware of other factors hindering their work, such as a misunderstanding of the individual patient or a lack of collaboration between the family therapy and other social systems such as the school.

The general problem in these situations is that the consultant depends too much on the stuck therapist for information and for organization of the consultation. To avoid the effects of those biases on the consultation, some systems consultants invest much time in learning about each case and planning the arrangement of the consultation. Another possibility is to have a follow-up consultation, to explore and work with issues that could not be taken up the first time. It is interesting to note that in the two cases in this book in which Minuchin made a second consultation, his work moved away from its original focus on family dynamics.

Another type of problem in the collaboration between consultants and therapists is simply a lack of understanding. We use words and gestures to communicate, and we assume that they have the same meaning for other people. We think we have understood each other, and we deem the discourse successful, but all too frequently we are surprised. Such a surprise occurred in the follow-up of Yoav's therapy. Minuchin concluded his original consultation believing that he had communicated successfully to the therapist his model for inpatient family therapy. The therapist, however, paid attention to only a fragment of this model—the particular family interventions that occurred during the session—as though it were the whole. What was a construction for Minuchin was treated by the therapist as truth, and what was a technique chosen for the one session became a fixed therapeutic posture. Such examples point again at the limitations of single consultations, particularly when the consultant and the consultee have not previously worked together.

The Challenge of Larger Systems

The feedback that we got from the follow-ups showed that the sense of completion we had gotten from studying these cases as cases in family therapy consultation was a mirage. After a while, we could not even enjoy the pyrotechnics of therapy, because no matter how exciting the family therapy intervention was, the power of the organizations in which these families were embedded was even more exciting and frightening.

The four families offered an opportunity to look at the context of treatment. The first two cases demonstrated the capacity of psychiatric hospitals to maintain themselves unchanged, responding to historical determinants to support the psychiatric establishment, maintain the illusion of scientific truth, and create a language that validates the narrowness of their data. We saw their capacity to maintain madness. Of course, not all psychiatric institutions are like Alpha and Beta hospitals, but the majority are, and the conceptual model is shared by all.

There are other models. In the late 1960s John Elderkin Bell, armed with a camera and a grant from the National Institute of Mental Health, traveled through Africa and Asia to study the organization of hospitals (medical and psychiatric) in non-Western cultures and published his experiences in a book, *The Family in the Hospital: Lessons from Developing Countries.** The hospitals he described bear little resemblance to the image we carry in our minds. The photographs show scenes strange to our eyes: next to a bed, a pallet on the floor where the patient's mother or wife sleeps; whole families moving from their home and camping near the hospital to provide food for the hospitalized patient; a village created around the hospital to provide accommodation to the patients' families; the family being used to provide auxiliary services in the hospital. One wonders what cultural blinders have limited our sight. How is it that in our image of the hospital, we can see only rows of sterile beds, clean sheets, empty, boring spaces, nurses in white or blue uniforms, doctors in white tunics and stethoscopes, sterile people forming a tight, impermeable barrier against the noisy, germ-ridden humanity of families?

For a while, Bell gave workshops in hospitals, focusing on the context of the hospital as a container of people and contrasting it with the non-Western model to highlight the different views of illness and cure in different cultures. But there were not many buyers for this kind of exploration. The hospital is an institution as sacred as motherhood and falafel. Nobody plays around with symbols—certainly not with symbols that are a growth industry

*John Elderkin Bell, *The Family in the Hospital: Lessons from Developing Countries* (Chevy Chase, MD: National Institute of Mental Health, 1969).

of billions of dollars, employing hundreds of thousands of people. So we keep overlooking the impact that the organization of hospitals has in the life of the physically ill and the power of psychiatric hospitals to institutionalize madness.

Consultations of hospitalized patients that do not take into account the hospital's relationship with patients and their families are a mistake. Let us underline that fact: They shouldn't happen. In the two hospital cases in which we consulted, Minuchin operated with partial and misleading information, and because the consultation was away from the hospital, he had no impact on the organization. One assumes that the consultant works on the therapeutic system, but that was not so in these cases, where only the family and the consultee were present.

The kibbutz cases show the possibilities inherent in well-run mental health clinics, but they also highlight the difficulties. The well-being of difficult patients requires a commitment of resources that the kibbutz society is willing to spend; others are not.

We would like to end by reflecting on Yoav's nightmare. Our last follow-up shows that the hope of finding a place for Yoav outside the hospital sustained his family through a very difficult bureaucratic struggle. But even with the help of the hospital and of Joel Elizur, the battle lasted for over a year. First, public funding had to be found to help defray the costs of placement in a community-based program with a halfway house. That took over six months. When funding had finally been secured and Yoav's records were sent to the rehabilitation program, the program flatly refused even to interview this "paranoid schizophrenic with tendencies to extreme violence." They refused his application twice, and Yoav was moved to a chronic hospital because the length of his hospitalization at Alpha had been much greater than is customary at a hospital that deals with acute psychiatric conditions only. Noam persevered, and finally, at the age of twenty-two, Yoav left the hospital. He entered the private rehabilitation center and lives in an apartment with two other former patients. He is holding a job that takes care of his basic needs. How far he will be able to move toward being an independent adult remains to be seen.

Yoav is a young man in the prime of life. But a halfway house is clearly the appropriate environment for him. The five years he spent in institutions have impoverished him, making this half-life inevitable. In those five years, not only was his development restricted but his social connections were cut. His mother is dead. He knows almost no one in his age group, and even his sister seems a stranger. His main contact with life outside the halfway house is his aging father. Like New York City's Joyce Brown, he has been made a social isolate by the interventions that were supposed to help him.

We cannot give him back those years or correct the results of our ignorance and lack of effectiveness. But we can ask our colleagues, when they are certain of their diagnosis of a sixteen-year-old, to think of him.

INDEX

Index

P9-ECX-380

THE BLACK MARBLE

Joseph Wambaugh

THE BLACK MARBLE

DELACORTE PRESS/NEW YORK

Published by
Delacorte Press
1 Dag Hammarskjold Plaza
New York, New York 10017

"Starinye Vals," "Kak U Duba Starovo," and
"Kogda Ya Pyan" lyrics from
Alexander Zelkin Sings Russian Songs, Old & New;
"Ochi Chornyia" lyrics from
Marusia Sings Russian Gypsy Songs
(Vol. 1) on Monitor Records.
Used by permission.

Manufactured in the United States of America

For the sterling of Pasadena,
Beverly and John Tarr,

and

For Peter J. Monahan,
Sensitive soul,
Compassionate confessor,
Rhapsodical saloon keeper!

1

The *Batushka*

An explosion of chrysanthemums, candlelight, Oriental carpets, Byzantine eyes. Plumes of incense rising between two a cappella choirs, blown heavenward by chanting voices.

The man in the yellow rubber raincoat swayed unsteadily and raised his sturdy arms toward those marbling clouds of incense enveloping the Holy Virgin. Her eyes were sweet.

Other eyes were reproachful, severe. Byzantine eyes. A kaleidoscope of ikons, small and large: saints, holy men, madonnas. All around him the faces on the ikons stared with great, dark, unrelenting eyes.

From time to time the man in the yellow rubber raincoat would wobble against the burly woman standing next to him.

Finally she'd had enough. "*Zhopa!*" she muttered.

He answered her in English: "Yes, I'm terribly sorry."

Then both choirs burst forth with the tragic, timeless, Slavonic invocation: "Blessed art thou, Lord God of our Father . . . have *mercy* on us."

The man in the yellow rubber raincoat was overwhelmed by the enduring pathos in those Russian voices, and by the clouds of incense he breathed gratefully, and by the low gilded ceiling and the throngs of believers standing shoulder to shoulder. He kept looking about at the quixotic tapestry of ikons, and the huge ikonostasis screen. Great dark sad eyes. The ikon of the Virgin and Child nestled among apricot and butter and salmon carnations. The *batushka* raised the *pomazok* to brush the sign of the cross on the forehead of the first in a long queue of communicants.

The communicant was sleek and feline. Her gray coat was damp from the rain. It flared from a belted waist, and the fur cuffs and hem matched the fur in her hat. She wore calf-molded, gray leather boots. The man in the yellow rubber raincoat was overcome by her beauty when the *batushka* brushed a cross of holy oil on her forehead. She could have stepped from the stage of an opera by Glinka or Borodin: a maiden fallen from a troika in the forest. The man in the yellow rubber raincoat could almost imagine flakes of luminescent snow on the fur of her collar.

But it wasn't fur, not real fur anyway. And she wasn't Russian, and she certainly wasn't a maiden. She was third-generation Anglo-Irish, currently living with a second-generation Ukrainian, in church on Russian Christmas only to please his great-aunt, who was going to loan them fourteen thousand dollars unsecured for a Jaguar X-J-12, which she needed about as much as she needed those tight boots cutting off her circulation.

The room capacity was limited to three hundred. There were four hundred souls crowded into that modest cathedral for vesper service. Yet few residents of Los Angeles knew that this holy night, Thursday, January 6th, was the eve of Russian Christmas. There was a far holier day to anticipate on Sunday. They *all* knew about that one. And this year, praise God, it would be celebrated in nearby Pasadena! Super Bowl XI.

The voices: "Blessed art thou . . . have *mercy* on us."

The man in the yellow rubber raincoat felt a bubble of sourness in his throat, swallowed it back, belched, and staggered sideways into the burly woman.

This time she wanted to make sure he understood. In accented English, she said, "Asshole!" And jolted him with a plump elbow to the ribs.

"Uh!" the man in the raincoat gasped, his wet cinnamon hair whipping across his eyes.

"Go home!" she whispered. "You damn dronk. Go home!" And she gave him another jab in the belly.

"Uh!" he belched. "Yes, I'm terribly sorry."

Then he turned, holding his stomach, and staggered toward the door, through the press of standing believers, out of this pewless teeming house of God.

When he got to the door, something clashed at his feet. A small boy said, "Hey," and grabbed his raincoat.

"Here," the boy said, handing the man a set of glinting handcuffs, one steel ratchet dangling open.

"Yes, I'm terribly sorry," the man in the yellow rubber raincoat said, taking the handcuffs and shoving them down inside the front of his belt.

One moment, candlelight and incense and color. The next, darkness cold and wet. But then, always just beyond, was black and cold and rainy night.

"Lord God, have mercy."

The man in the yellow rubber raincoat couldn't get the handcuffs tucked inside his belt. He didn't understand that the belt buckle had slid around to his hip. He groped and pulled at the belt, causing the handcuffs to fall down inside his underwear. The steel was cold, and he cried out as the open ratchet gouged his genitals.

The man in the yellow rubber raincoat struggled. He leaned against the wall of the cathedral, in the shadows, and thought about it. If he was logical and calm it should be very easy to extricate the handcuffs. But he was shivering in the rain. He lurked deeper in the shadows and stealthily withdrew the bottle of Stolichnaya from the pocket of his raincoat. He tipped it up, swaying, and in just seconds the silky flood of Russian vodka warmed him to the toes.

Now he stopped shivering. Now he could think. Except that he was reeling and had to sit. He plopped down on the front step of the cathedral. Right on the tip of the serrated edge of the steel ratchet, lined up directly with his scrotum.

A bent and withered usher inside the cathedral thought for a moment he heard a man scream. Impossible, he shrugged.

Now the man in the yellow rubber raincoat had totally lost the belt buckle. It was all the way around the back, as was the holster and bullet clip. The fly on the old loose poplins was pulled six inches off center. He groped and tugged. He pulled upward, which was the wrong way. The harder he pulled the harder the steel ratchet gouged deep into the wounded sac. He couldn't find the fly. It too had disappeared. He thought he had his pants on backward.

The bent and withered usher inside the cathedral cocked his head and looked toward the ikon of St. Isaac high on the wall. This time he was certain he heard a man scream.

Three women arrived late for Christmas vesper service. One was seventy-three years old, an immigrant and monarchist who had never stopped bemoaning immorality and anarchy in America, who dreamed of her bones being buried in Russian soil. She crossed herself and threw her arms around her two daughters and shrieked in horror. There, by the old monastery garden, framed by the onion dome of the Holy Virgin Mary Russian Orthodox Cathedral, a howling dervish, a phantom with matted soppy hair, was twirling in the shadow of the golden cupola. His yellow rubber raincoat was spread wide. His dripping pants were torn down around his ankles. Both hands held his genitals. He moaned ghostlike, doing a lonely mad waltz in the rain.

Now, over the heartbreaking Slavonic chorus, the bent and withered usher thought he heard a *woman* screaming. He cocked his head and offered a prayer to St. Isaac about the baffling indignities of advanced age.

The man in the yellow rubber raincoat was exhausted from the tremendous battle. His handcuffs were on the pavement, as was his four-inch Smith and Wesson .38 caliber revolver, as was a set of keys and a dirty handkerchief. Now he was sitting, bare buttocks in a rain puddle, pulling his underwear back up over his knees, realizing that his pants had not been on backward after all.

Five minutes later, he had all his equipment stuffed into the pockets of his raincoat along with the bottle of Stolichnaya. His fly zipper was torn completely off his baggy poplins and dangled between his legs. He stumbled thankfully back into the church.

"Have mercy on us . . . Holy God Immortal . . . Have mercy on us."

He was once again hot and smothering in the damp press of communicants, watching a slender erect man at least eighty years of age, wearing a threadbare olive topcoat, drop to both knees before the ikon of the Virgin and Child. The old man bowed with grave reverence and stood unassisted before the *batushka,* aglow in the candlelight. The old man bent to the cross in the hand of the priest and kissed the golden bas-relief of the crucified Christ.

The *batushka* smiled in recognition. The old man was of the First Immigration, a brick mason from Rostov who had in years past donated his skill to his church. The man in the yellow rubber raincoat didn't know the brick mason. He saw instead a gallant old White Russian soldier, perhaps a Cossack colonel, now standing at attention before the *diakon* to receive the body of Christ as reverently as he may have stood before the czar himself before boarding a train for The Front.

It became too much for the man in the yellow rubber raincoat. He couldn't stifle the wet drunken sob. It escaped his mouth like the bark of a seal. The communicant in front of him was startled. He turned and looked at the flushed, tear-streaked face, the soppy strings of cinnamon hair flopping in his eyes.

"Yes, I'm terribly sorry," the man in the yellow rubber raincoat said in answer to the silent gaping communicant.

Now the man in the yellow rubber raincoat was himself kneeling before the holy ikon. He pressed his lips grimly, but to no avail. A great sob welled and he barked. The *batushka* looked up sharply.

Two altar boys assisting the *diakon* snickered and whispered to each other. The man in the yellow rubber raincoat had to be helped to his feet by two communicants. He turned and grinned foolishly at his benefactors and said, "Yes, I'm terribly sorry."

"Go on," the man behind him whispered. "Go on, you're next."

The man in the yellow rubber raincoat was swaying before the bearded *batushka,* who looked as though he'd rather give the drunk his fist than his blessing.

Then it simply became too much for the man in the yellow rubber raincoat. All of it: the holy Slavonic chants, the enveloping clouds of blessed incense, the myriads of candles and the rainbow sprays and bursts of carnation and chrysanthemum, the gallant old soldier–brick mason, the omnipresent ikons, and those suffering reproachful Byzantine eyes. He slouched humbly before the priest. And then it all came. His brawny shoulders heaved and he bowed his head and let the scalding waters run. He wept.

His raincoat was open and with each shuddering heave of his shoulders the torn fragment of flyfront jumped and bounced between his knees, a sad rag of a puppet hopping gracelessly on a single wire.

It was unspeakably offensive in this holy place, on this holy day, yet so pathetic the old priest was touched.

"It's all right, my son," he said, and brushed the wand on the weeping man's forehead.

The man in the yellow rubber raincoat felt the warm oil trickle down between his eyes and he grabbed the hand of the bearded priest and said, "Father, I'm terribly sorry. I'm *so* sorry, *Batushka.*"

"It's all right, my son. *S Rozhdeniem Khristovym.*"

When he heard that ancient Christmas greeting, he kissed the hand of the *batushka.* Then he lunged past the communion basket and swayed toward the door, scarcely able to breathe.

The bent and withered usher shook his head in disgust and threw open the door for the drunk in the yellow rubber raincoat. The rubber raincoat was old, a dirty canary yellow with a blue collar. The usher looked curiously at the raincoat. It was one of those long, high-visibility slickers worn by men who worked in auto traffic. The usher looked more closely. The raincoat bore an oval patch over the heart. As though for a badge!

"You *can't* be a policeman!" the usher sputtered.

"Yes, I'm terribly sorry," the man in the yellow rubber raincoat belched. Then he staggered into the night.

The last thing he heard before the rain struck his face was the eternal Slavonic chant: "Have mercy on us . . . Holy God Immortal . . . Have *mercy* on us."

2

La Buena Vida

Victoria's redolent warm puffs hinted of the pâté they had shared that night. Madeline Dills Whitfield lay awake listening to the rain. She snagged a lacquered Juliette fingernail on pearl satin sheets sliding closer to Victoria without waking her. Vickie whimpered in enviable sleep as Madeline waited for three Dalmanes and six ounces of Chivas Regal to release her.

Now their mouths were almost touching. Vickie's tongue flicked wet and Madeline ached to stroke the incredible arch of her neck. It was a marvelous neck, now carrying a faint scent of Bellodgia, a neck that lent great hauteur to her movements.

Hauteur. Madeline remembered last Monday afternoon when she and Vickie had strolled across the grounds of the Huntington Sheraton, that once-opulent old dowager of a hotel. That relic of the days when Pasadena was the cultural and social center of the entire Los Angeles area. When old bewhiskered Henry Huntington would don a homburg and waistcoat and ride from his San Marino mansion to Los Angeles in his own railroad car. On a private spur laid by Mexicans and Chinese to his very door.

It hurt to see her so seedy, time-ravaged and mutilated by a grotesque porte cochere of gray concrete, grafted onto the entrance of the hotel where Madeline's mother had been presented at a debutante ball in 1923. And it hurt more when she walked with Vickie by the Bell Tower, toward the hotel's Ship Room, where "Old" Pasadena society had enjoyed dance music virtually unchanged for thirty-five years.

Before she died, Madeline's mother said she was glad her husband had not lived to see the foreigners buy the dear grande dame. Old Pasadena feared the investors from the Far East would tear her down and cover the grounds with cherry trees and high-rise condos.

Madeline and Vickie had stopped in the lobby for a moment, and impulsively, Madeline had turned toward the creaky Picture Bridge which linked the old building with the homely new wing and overlooked the swimming pool where an Oriental waitress served cocktails. Madeline wanted a Scotch and water, but she paused on the footbridge and looked up at the rustic timbered roof, at the painted murals on the gables. The murals suggested pastoral early California. As it never was. Mexicans, Indians, Americans, padre, peasant, landowner: brothers all, in the ubiquitous vineyards and groves.

Then the too familiar empty thud in her chest. A rush of heat to her temples. The price for daring to wax nostalgic, for lingering on this Picture Bridge. Where she had so often stood as a girl and made wishes she had never been given reason to doubt would come true. Then she turned toward South Pasadena and saw the layers of mauve and azure gasses heaving in from the west, and remembered that this lovely vapor blanket made the San Gabriel Valley air perhaps the deadliest in Southern California.

But it wasn't just the smog that was killing Old Pasadena. It was *la buena vida* of the past coupled with the frugality of the old social order. When white domestics would not work for the wages offered, there were others who would. The blacks were enticed to Pasadena in large numbers and they prospered and multiplied. And then more came and prospered less but still multiplied. Until a day when fourth-generation Old Pasadenans were troubled to discover that twenty-five percent of their school district was composed of children black and brown. And in another ten years they were shocked to discover that thirty-five percent of their public school children were black and brown. And then one day they were outraged and bewildered to discover that over fifty percent of the children in Pasadena public schools were black and brown! Then the white flight began in earnest.

A nine-thousand-square-foot mansion with guest house, tennis court, swimming pool, and two verdant acres of hundred-year-old twisted oak sold for one-fifth the price of what it would bring "over the hill," or "on the west side," on the beaten path of *nouveau riche:* Beverly Hills, Holmby Hills, Bel-Air, Brentwood. Henceforth, Old Pasadena was under siege and near panic. Some were old enough to have children grown and need not fear ghetto busing. Others dropped all democratic pretext, and prep schools quickly became overcrowded. Others moved a few blocks away into the tiny bedroom community of San Marino which had its own public school district. All white.

Madeline Whitfield now needed that drink very badly. She and Vickie left the bridge and walked quickly down to poolside. Then she heard it. The man was unmistakably a Minnesota tourist in for the Super Bowl. Who else would be reeking of coconut oil, white-legged in Aloha print shorts, red socks, black-and-white patent-leather loafers? A hairy belly glistening oil in sunlight which any Californian knew was not hot enough to burn even this flabby outlander. But then he was probably using the pool and the sunshine as an excuse to get drunk at one o'clock in the afternoon. As if an excuse was needed during Rose Bowl and Super Bowl weeks in Pasadena.

The man's voice was bourbon thick. He said, "That bitch moves like a stallion!"

And Madeline Dills Whitfield, who had been forced into inactive, sustaining membership in the Pasadena Junior League three years before for being too old. Madeline Dills Whitfield, only twenty-five pounds past her prime, never considered pretty, but damn it, not homely. Four years divorced, childless, two-year analysand, three-year patient of a dermatologist (I *know* that middle-age fat is just excess adipose tissue, Doctor, but *why* did I have to grow a moustache!). Madeline Dills Whitfield, who dutifully spent more than she could afford in Beverly Hills high-fashion shops like Giorgio's—which boasted a billiard table, and a full-time bartender serving free drinks to patrons—where Pasadena matrons invariably shopped for clothing with exclusive labels but basic lines. Madeline Dills Whitfield, who cared enough to have her nails done at Ménage à Trois. (Also over the hill in Lotus Land—thirteen bucks, tip included, for a Juliette, forty-five to make hair look more natural, sixty-five bucks to look like you just got out of bed—and you better know the license number of your Mercedes because all the parking attendant has are Mercedes keys in *that* key box, lady.) Madeline Dills Whitfield, who had not seen male genitalia for five years, yet who was just peaking sexually at the age of forty-three, unsheathed a smile like a knife blade.

The kind of abandoned smile seldom seen on Pasadena Junior Leaguers, unless they were ignited by Bombay martinis at Annandale Country Club. A smile which would unquestionably be deemed provocative by the socially wed and nearly dead at the all-woman Town Club. Oh God, she dreaded the day she'd be old enough to *want* to join. Madeline Dills Whitfield unleashed a smile she had reserved for

Mason Whitfield on those rare occasions he bedded her in the last dreadful years of their marriage.

A smile which carried a promise made instantly, consciously, irrevocably—to screw the patent-leather loafers right off this Minnesota greaseball.

A smile which was not even *seen* by the hairy stranger. Because he was admiring Vickie. Staring after *Vickie.*

The oily stranger turned again to his friend and said: "Look at the muscles in her legs. She moves like a stallion, I tell you!"

Then Madeline felt loneliness all right. And *real* fear. The kind that choked her awake in those first months after Mason had gone. The worst kind of fear, born of loneliness, which only became manageable when Vickie came.

Vickie. Madeline sat there with Vickie by the pool and drank three double Chivas with water-back, and controlled that fear and looked at the hairy stranger scornfully. She wasn't jealous, she was *proud.* Vickie belonged to *her,* and Madeline loved her obsessively.

The rain was steady. She wondered if she'd be awake the entire night. Probably, if she insisted on these tormenting thoughts. But as she lay in the dark and looked at Vickie's elegant jaw, she couldn't help admitting that she would have given a healthy chunk of a secretly unhealthy trust fund if that oily man had said drunkenly to Madeline: "You bitch, you carry yourself like a *stallion!*"

Madeline wryly wondered if, in the history of the old Huntington Hotel, any "sustaining" Junior Leaguer had sat by the Picture Bridge and yearned for a man to look at her thighs and arouse her with an antiquated, vulgar, erotic cliché. By comparing her to a male horse.

Victoria stirred in her sleep. Madeline touched her lovingly and risked awakening her by snuggling closer until her mouth was touching Vickie's ear.

"Sleep, love, sleep," Madeline whispered. She stroked that arched neck and said, "Sleep, my darling."

But Vickie opened her eyes: perfect ovals, blinking in momentary confusion. Madeline kissed each eye, marveling at the luster: wet chocolate irises, whites like lapis lazuli in the moonlight.

"Sleep, love, sleep."

Vickie sighed and turned just enough for Madeline to see how deep those eyes were set, how shaded by brows of silver white. Madeline wanted to touch her face and kiss that lovely ear.

Like most insomniacs, Madeline toyed masochistically with her devils in the night. Today's tennis exhibition at the Valley Hunt Club.

It is the oldest social club in the Los Angeles area. Where ladies still sit courtside and worry over coming-out parties. Where Old Pasadena strives to nourish its moldering roots by presenting the family flowers at frantic and archaic debutante balls.

Madeline had been courtside at the Valley Hunt Club, ostensibly watching a listless college tennis exhibition while downing the third double Scotch and water of the afternoon. She had waited an appropriate time to order her fourth because of the presence of Edna Lofton, an obtrusive bitch Madeline had known since Kappa House days at the University of Southern California, when Edna was a smartass sorority viper.

Edna Lofton, another "sustaining" Junior Leaguer, also active with Madeline in the Junior Philharmonic and the Huntington Library Docents, seldom missed the opportunity to grin knowingly whenever Madeline ordered more than three or four afternoon cocktails at the club.

Like other "younger" Valley Hunt Club members, Edna had switched from Yves St. Laurent sunglasses to the latest from over the hill: oversized sunglasses with logograms engraved on the lower lens. In Edna's case it was a little white tennis racquet. It should have been a spider and a web, Madeline thought. Madeline herself had bought a pair in Beverly Hills at the Optique Boutique. She had wanted the tennis racquet too, but resisted because Edna had beaten her to it, so she settled for a white flower. Madeline thought the glasses chic and becoming, though the little speck was annoying when she looked at anything below eye level. The price tag annoyed her even more.

One day while shopping on Lake Avenue in Pasadena she had encountered something considerably below eye level: a barefoot black girl about seven years of age. The child stopped her skateboard. "Lady?" She was licking a green Popsicle, gawking at Madeline's ninety-dollar, double-gradient sunglasses.

"Yes, dear, what can I do for you?" Madeline smiled.

The girl stopped licking and said, "I was wonderin. How come you don't jist wipe the bird shit off them funny glasses?"

The following Sunday, Madeline's Mexican housekeeper, Yolanda, wore those glasses proudly to a picnic in Elysian Park.

Edna flipped up her sunglasses with the little tennis racquet on the lens, and said sweetly: "Madeline, go easy, we're playing doubles later and may need you as a fourth."

Madeline tried a sassy, nose-wrinkling grin. She stuck out her tongue at Edna, but given the pain and the fear and the Chivas Regal flush in her face, it didn't come off.

"Put your tongue in, dear," Edna purred. "You look like the victim of a hanging."

The second set was as dilatory as the first. Most of the spectators were of course U.S.C. rooters. Old Pasadena, if the money was still intact, seldom attended state-supported institutions like U.C.L.A. It was impossible to concentrate. She imagined Edna's vindictive gaze on her back.

Madeline was in tennis whites and hated it. She was considering trying tennis pants, but was fearful that the club would disapprove if she played in anything but a skirt. Actually she didn't want to play at all anymore. She had always hated the game, but without some exercise she'd probably look like a medicine ball. (Why the continual weight gain, Doctor? I don't drink *that* much. I haven't eaten a really full meal since my husband left me, I swear!)

Mason Whitfield. Stanford, class of '48. Infantry officer in Korea. Decorated for typing a report in a tent near Seoul in freezing weather after the company clerk was evacuated with the clap. He had typed for six hours without gloves and was frostbitten. Mason returned to Pasadena wearing a Bronze Star and a Purple Heart.

Like his father before him, Mason had gone to Harvard for his LL.B. and joined a law firm in downtown Los Angeles. One of those giant firms where the lawyers in Probate don't even know the guys in Corporate. He managed to work ten years without ever setting foot in a courtroom. He made big bucks. He was a near-perfect, Old Pasadena scion. He and Madeline prospered. But they didn't multiply. He had a flaw or two.

Madeline felt Edna's eyes on her back, and self-consciously tucked a roll of cellulite under the tennis panty which was cutting into her flesh. Madeline just knew Edna was still telling the Filthy Story about Mason Whitfield, when he made a boozy revelation to the barman at the Hunt Club: "Wanna know why I left my wife? Zero sex appeal, that's why. And I just came back from a wonderful holiday in Acapulco. Wanna know what I like best about my secretary? The moustache doesn't scratch my balls as much as Madeline's did."

The secretary's name was Herbert.

Madeline was sure it was a rotten lie, because within a year Mason fired Herbert and married a San Marino widow without a moustache.

"Mrs. Whitfield? You probably don't remember me? We met at dinner? At the Cal Tech Atheneum?"

Madeline looked up, blankly. She was feeling the Chivas Regal more than usual.

"Remember? I was with Dr. Harry Gray?"

He was a balding little man in a lumpy warm-up suit and dirty canvas Tretorns. He made every statement a question.

"Oh, yes," Madeline lied, "of course, you're . . ."

"Irwin Berg? Remember?"

"Oh, yes, Dr. Berg! Of course!"

Now she knew him. She had enjoyed talking with him at a Cal Tech dinner party to raise funds for foreign students. He was said to be an extraordinary astrophysicist and a candidate for Big Casino: a hot prospect for a Nobel Prize.

"May I buy you a drink?" His round, steel-rimmed eyeglasses were fogging and slipping over his perspiring nose.

"I'd *love* a drink," Madeline said. She was settling down, the last Scotch working nicely now. She leaned closer and whispered, "The barman probably couldn't make change for you anyway. Since I'm a member and you're a guest, I'll buy."

Then Madeline took the little scientist by the arm and walked him into the Hunt Room, where Edna Lofton was ordering a Virgin Mary, her muscular lacy bottom pressed against the mahogany.

Edna was laughing uproariously at one of Wendell Hargrove's dreadful jokes. Hargrove was a third-generation stockbroker and an "A" tennis player, which was the only thing keeping his fifty-year-old body intact, what with the fifth of booze he consumed at noon luncheons at the California Club in downtown Los Angeles. Were it not for his daily tennis, everyone knew that his fierce aging body could never withstand the massive bourbon dosage.

"Guess we won't need that fourth for mixed doubles, Madeline," Edna Lofton smiled. "Marcie's going to play again. So you can go ahead."

"Go ahead what?" Wendell Hargrove asked.

"Go ahead and have another double Scotch," Edna laughed. Then she added: "I might even have one."

But the damage was done. Madeline blushed painfully. Edna looked with curiosity at Madeline's companion and thrust out her hand: "Hi, I'm Edna Lofton."

"Oh? Pleased to meet you. I'm Irwin Berg."

Madeline said, "Dr. Berg's a guest of . . . who are you a guest of?"

"Mr. and Mrs. Bates. I met them at the Atheneum. They're watching the match."

"You an M.D.?" Hargrove asked thickly and Madeline saw that he was well past any more tennis this day.

"Dr. Berg teaches at Cal Tech. He's an astrophysicist," Madeline offered, subtly eyeing the barman, who nodded and reached discreetly for the Chivas Regal.

"Really?" Edna said. "Don't get many astrophysicists in the Hunt Club."

Later that evening, Madeline, showered and dressed in a basic dark pantsuit, was standing alone at the dessert table deciding to pass the entrée in favor of some strudel and chocolate mousse when Edna Lofton got up from her table and crossed the dining room to talk to her.

"Is Dr. Goldberg with you, Madeline?" she asked, walking Madeline toward the empty drawing room.

"Dr. Berg. No, he's not with me. Why?"

"He's sure a cute little fellow," Edna winked, batting her evening eyelashes.

"I suppose so," Madeline said cautiously.

"Play your cards right, Mad, and he might invite you to some of those *fun* Cal Tech science parties at the Atheneum. A lot of *mature*, visiting professors must be awfully lonely for one of the few available *single ladies* they'd be proud to take just anywhere!"

"Edna . . ." Madeline sputtered, but too late. Edna Lofton had turned and was hurrying toward her guests in the dining room.

Madeline Dills Whitfield had stood alone in the empty drawing room and looked vacantly at the landscape painting as though she had never seen it before. She had seen it all her life. She suddenly longed for the paintings of hunters and hounds. In the *bar*.

A *single* lady. As though it were Madeline's fault. As though she had planned to be a single lady. She had never known *anyone* who had planned to be a single lady. Madeline Dills had never even lived away from her parents except for college terms at U.S.C., ten miles from Pasadena. Had never lived anywhere else except for six months in Europe with her parents when her father sold his interest in the orthopedic clinic and took a long vacation. She had never in her life given a *single* thought to being a single lady.

She was the daughter of Dr. Corey Dills and the wife of Mason Whitfield. She had willingly surrendered her Christian as well as her maiden name.

It had always been: "Mrs. Mason Whitfield is giving a tea Wednesday afternoon . . ."

Madeline Dills, by Dr. Corey Dills out of Mrs. Corey Dills. Edna

Lofton, by Mr. Bradford Lofton out of Mrs. Bradford Lofton. They had to give up *both* names. Androgynous. *Mr.* Mason Whitfield and *Mrs.* Mason Whitfield. Hermaphroditic!

The stag ruled. It was her heritage and she accepted it. Which is perhaps why she didn't make a fuss during the divorce. Her family trust fund was much larger than his. *She* paid *him* for his share in the home and furnishings bought as community property. No alimony. She didn't need or want his money. Her mother was hale and hearty then. Madeline didn't make a fuss and Mason said he appreciated it. He said she was a perfect lady.

Now there was the new Mrs. Mason Whitfield living in San Marino. He hadn't the decency to give up his Annandale Country Club membership. So how does one address invitations? Mrs. Madeline Dills Whitfield? The return of her names was . . . awkward. As awkward as having *single* ladies at dinner parties. How does one seat them? And the clubs where *single* ladies were never meant to be? It wasn't awkward, it was *horrible.*

Thank God for Marian Milford's homosexual brother, Lance. He danced beautifully, had impeccable manners, and for ten years had eased dinner problems in Old Pasadena society by escorting half the widows and divorcées in town to social and charitable gatherings. Old Pasadena and San Marino had an exceedingly low divorce rate thanks to the continuity and tradition of society. And thanks to disapproving parents who structured wills and trusts which pauperized many a misbehaving daughter who opted to take the bit in her teeth like less constant, free-spirited sisters over the hill, on the west side.

• ● •

The Dalmanes and Chivas were interacting. Madeline was about to drift asleep when Victoria sat up.

"Oh, no, Vickie!" Madeline groaned. "Not now. I'm dead!"

But Vickie yawned and stretched languorously and got out of bed. Madeline moaned, got up reeling, and stood naked in the moonlight, reviving when she threw open the French doors to the cold January air.

Suddenly she hoped that someone, anyone—man or woman—would see her through the rain and white oak trees and Canary Island pines. Perhaps someone higher up San Rafael, in a hillside mansion, a gardener, a maid, anyone. She was dizzy, yet she stood defiantly naked under a leering moon, convinced that if someone *could* see her through the wall of camellias that someone would be aroused by *her* naked body.

Then she looked down into the valley and saw that the rain had cleared the smog from the Rose Bowl. It would be an ugly carnival on Sunday when Super Bowl XI hit Pasadena, but she and Vickie would be across town winning the Beverly Hills Winter Show. She and Vickie would be basking in attention, glory, *celebrity*.

Vickie looked at Madeline for a moment, then turned and trotted over to an American Beauty. She squatted beside a puddle of fallen rose petals and emptied her bladder. Then she shook herself, scampered across the lawn, in through the French doors, and leaped up onto the bed.

The Dalmanes and Chivas turned Madeline's legs gelatinous. She closed the doors and threw herself into bed, hardly noticing the crumbs of mud and garden mulch on the pearly sheets.

"You're impossible, Vickie," she scolded. "Impossible!" Then she stroked Vickie's neck once, twice, and her hand fell limp.

Madeline had a wonderful dream that night. Vickie won best in show, easily earning the last of fifteen major points she needed to become a champion. And then she went on to Madison Square Garden to win. She became the unquestioned grand champion—the finest miniature schnauzer in America.

Vickie grunted uncomfortably for a moment. She growled and squirmed until she managed a puffy fart. Then another. Now she sighed happily and licked Madeline's face. Then she snuggled, and snored, and slept as deeply as her drugged mistress.

3

The Terrier King

The natural mascara around the eyes of the Dandie Dinmont was the blackest he had ever seen.

"Look at those saucers," he said, admiring their roundness. Then he turned to the girl, looked at her breasts and grinned. "Your saucers are beautiful too."

The girl feigned naïveté and said, "Not as pretty as the Dandie's, Mr. Skinner."

Then Philo Skinner turned his critical eye back to the Dandie Dinmont and startled the girl by flashing the straight razor so quickly in the face of the terrier. She was glad she hadn't gasped. He was mercurial, but with good cause. Philo Skinner was a top terrier man on the West Coast. In the past six years he had big wins at Madison Square Garden, Chicago International and Beverly Hills. With a Lakeland, a Kerry blue and a Dandie. The girl knew that if she could survive his temperamental eruptions, like the one earlier in the evening when she left a tassel 1⅛ inches from the bottom of the ear leather in a Bedlington terrier (he measured it), and if she could get used to never being paid on time and having a few "clerical errors" in her paycheck (always errors which made her check *short*), and if she could repel his sporadic sexual advances, well, Philo Skinner was a champion dog handler. A *champion*. And she could learn.

"Don't ever let me see *you* trying this," Philo Skinner said, holding the Dandie firmly under the chin with the long fingers of his left hand while the straight razor in his right stripped the nose from the top to the tip. The Dandie's white topknot was electric from back-combing.

"I'd be scared to death to do that," the girl said. "Those barber razors are scary."

"Well, careless people can misuse a stripping knife as well. You ever hurt an animal here and you'll find your little fanny out in the street."

He deliberately let his gaze drop to her little fanny, which was pointed up nicely through the gap in her white smock as she leaned across the grooming table.

"I'll be real careful always, Mr. Skinner," she said.

"Never use the knife when working under the eyes," he said, looking back to the patient little terrier. "Roll the finger and thumb together the way the hair grows. See? How old are you, Pattie Mae?"

"I'm nineteen, Mr. Skinner," the girl said, marveling at those darting, tobacco-stained fingers.

He plucked the eyes clean, even to the lashes. He was so expert and quick the dog almost dozed through it.

"Can you guess how old *I* am, Pattie Mae?" he asked, releasing the dog's chin and stroking the little animal behind the ears.

Oh, shit! She hated it when these old guys started that crap. It was impossible for her to guess the age of anybody over thirty let alone an old turkey like Mr. Skinner. His dyed black hair was all thin and scraggly. And he was all wrinkly around his droopy eyes and mouth. And those crappy gold chains around his neck and those Dacron leisure suits didn't fool nobody. Shit! Those nylon shirts open clear to his belly button, she could see the gray hairs all over his bony old chest! He could play all the Elton John tapes he wanted to, he was still just an old fart.

"I'd say you're about forty, Mr. Skinner," she lied.

"Not too good a guess, Pattie Mae," he grinned, teeth yellowed from three packs of Camels a day. "I'm fifty-two years old."

"Really!" the girl said. "I'd never . . ."

"You know, Pattie Mae, handlers are like jockeys. An owner can't show a dog in real competition any more than a horse owner can ride his horse. I'm a jockey and I can *ride,* baby. I can *ride.*"

"Uh-huh," the girl said, mesmerized by his fleet plucking gentle fingers.

"I'm glad you came to me to learn. I can teach you lots a things. You're talented. It takes much more talent to show *little* dogs. You like the terriers, don't you?"

"Yes, I love them, Mr. Skinner."

Philo Skinner was still stripping. Fingers rolling, kneading, plucking, stripping. The dog sighed luxuriously. "Be glad you don't handle poodles. All those fag handlers. No action for a young thing like you. It's tough enough to find some action when you're out on the road showing dogs. Lots a fag handlers."

"Uh-huh," the girl said, sucking on a broken fingernail.

"Oh, you'll be a popular handler someday with the real men on the show tours. There's one woman handler, named Wilma. A punchboard. What the hell, she's a little dumpy, but when you been looking at dogs all day . . ."

"Uh-huh," the girl said, the joke wasted. "You sure got the touch, Mr. Skinner!"

"Wanna strip the ears?" He took her arm gently, nudging her in front of him at the grooming table.

"Okay, Mr. Skinner," she said, a bit edgy, wondering if tonight was the night. The other girls said he made his big move after you'd worked there about a month. She'd been working for Skinner Kennels three weeks.

Philo Skinner was standing behind the girl now, admiring how her bottom stretched the exotic orchid patches on the jeans. None of these young girls wore underpants anymore, he thought. Not a goddamn one of them! And they didn't bathe any too often either. This one had dust and lint in her scruffy brown hair and her dirty fingernails were bitten to the quick. But damn, she had tits like mangoes!

"Strip exactly one inch from the top to exactly one inch from the bottom. Understand?"

"Yes, sir," she said uneasily, feeling him press in behind her as he pretended to guide her hand to the tassel of the terrier's ear.

"The ears can't be clipped," he said and she smelled his tobacco-sour breath on her face. "It doesn't look natural. It has to be stripped to be natural."

He moved in very close, leaning on her leg. Oh, gross! The old fart had a hard-on!

"That's it, Pattie Mae," he whispered, rubbing it against her. "Strip all the hair away. Strip, Pattie Mae. *Strip!*"

The door opened and Philo Skinner leaped back, turning his body away from a squinting smock-clad woman dragging a reluctant Airedale through the door.

"Pattie Mae, why the hell're you still here?" she demanded, looking at Philo Skinner suspiciously. He adjusted his own white smock to hide the telltale bulge, and began fiddling with the cage dryer.

"Gotta be a goddamn electrician to keep things working around here," Philo Skinner grumbled. "Mavis, who the hell used this thing last, anyway?"

"I dunno," she said, still squinting from Philo to his new apprentice. "Pattie Mae, why you working so late?"

"Well, uh, Mr. Skinner said he needed . . ."

"Mavis, you know goddamn well we gotta get this Dandie ready. Christ, Pilkington's our best client these days. I gotta be free to devote the next couple days to the Beverly Hills Show, don't I? Christ, it's pouring outside!"

Philo Skinner was eminently thankful for the Thursday night rain, his excuse to turn to the window and let the tumescence subside. "Goddamn cold rainy night," he said gratefully.

"Well, since I don't really think Mr. Skinner intends paying you time-and-a-half, I think you should go home now."

"Yes, Mrs. Skinner. I'll just put the Dandie to bed," the girl said, slipping the smock down over her breasts, braless under a jersey which said: "I love puppies and cuddly things."

Goddamn, Philo Skinner thought. Cuddly things. Goddamn. Then he looked at Mavis, fifty-one years old going on sixty. Skin like sizzling pancake batter. Two eye jobs already. Hair dyed the color of puppy shit, with enough spray to do a whole platoon of goddamn terriers. I love puppies and cuddly things. Oh, God! And then it swept him away: an overwhelming emptiness and yearning.

After the girl scurried out the door with the Dandie Dinmont, Mavis Skinner said, "Well, Philo, I hope this one stays a little longer than most. Think you can keep from running her off like all the others?"

Philo Skinner lit his sixty-third cigarette of that calendar day and sat on the grooming table and stared outside at the night rain. Emptiness, loss. Yearning for . . . for a chance. Just a goddamn *chance,* is all he asked.

"If I ever knew for sure what I suspect about you, Philo, it'd be sayonara, baby. I ain't Betsy or that other bitch you were married to. I won't put up with that shit."

Philo Skinner heard not a word. He dragged deeply on the Camel, exhaled up through his nose, back down into his tortured lungs, and stared at the rain. Yearning.

"It's been a rocky go, Philo. I mean it's been tougher being married to you for two years than it was to Milton for twenty-five years, I can tell you. I'll try to make it work, you know that. But I'm not gonna put up with any screwing around. You were thinking about nesting with that little bird, weren't you?"

And as he would look back on this moment for the rest of his life, Philo Skinner would always wonder precisely what event inspired him. Was it that pathetic fifty-two-year-old erection which died aborning? Was it Mavis' tongue, sharp as a grooming knife? Stripping away the little he had left the way you'd strip the loins of a schnauzer? Was it that he wanted to cry because Pattie Mae was only nineteen years old? He would always wonder.

"Philo, *were* you?"

But he was already through the door of the grooming room, heading for the kennel, heart thumping, hands and feet and armpits slimy. Philo switched on the light and stood in the center of the 175-foot concrete aisle which dissected the building. There were thirty floor-to-ceiling, chain-link dog pens on each side of the long aisle. Each four-by-eight-foot pen boasted running water, an easy-clean feeding trough, and a warm soft bed off the floor. In addition, each dog pen had a slit-rubber doggie door allowing easy access to outside dog runs twice the size of the inside pens, covered with gravel for the pleasure of the animal and to prevent splayed feet. The outside runs were protected by chain link, ten feet high—completely enclosed on top—not to keep dogs in but to keep thieves out. There were high-wattage security lights and a burglar alarm as well, to safeguard Skinner Kennels from prowling dognappers.

The inside lights woke several of the more nervous animals who whined when Philo walked to the pen containing Rutherford's bitch.

"Hello, honey," he whispered to the miniature schnauzer. The dog opened her eyes, wagged her stubby tail a few times and fell back asleep on her foam mattress.

Rutherford's bitch wasn't nearly right. Too cowhocked. Way too throaty. But he knew one that was exactly right.

"Goddamn!" Philo whispered. Then he dropped his cigarette on the kennel floor, stepped on it and went back into the grooming room.

Philo arrived home that night, during the same hour that Madeline Dills Whitfield was being mercifully rendered unconscious by Chivas Regal and four Dalmanes, during the same hour that a drunken man in a yellow rubber raincoat was reeling through the door of his furnished apartment, dripping wet, eyes raw from vodka and incense and memories of other Russian Christmas Eves.

Philo made a telephone call to a man who owned a fashionable dress shop on Wilshire Boulevard. Who did other business more profitably.

"Hello, Arnold?" Philo whispered into the phone.

"Who's this?" an irritated voice answered.

"Philo Skinner."

"Why the hell you calling me at home? I told you to forget my home number. What I gotta do, get the fucking number changed?"

"Arnold, this is important."

"I told you, Philo, it's outta my hands. You owe almost eight dimes. You never shoulda got in so deep, but you did. So you gotta pay and you got two weeks more to do it. Now good night."

"Arnold, wait!" Philo begged. "I wanna pay you sooner. I wanna pay you Monday morning."

"Well that's different," the voice said, considerably more congenial.

"I can pay you all of it, Arnold. On Monday. But you just gotta get me down on Minnesota in the Super Bowl."

"Good night, Philo."

"Wait! Wait, goddamnit!" Philo pleaded. "I been a good customer, Arnold. I been good. I been a friend!"

"Philo, you can't pay the eight K. Some guys are gonna be awful upset, and now you wanna get down some more?"

"Arnold, remember I told you Mavis has this property? It's an apartment building in Covina. Remember I told you? Well we sold it. We're netting eighty-five thousand! Christ, the escrow closes in ten days! Even if Minnesota loses Sunday and my markers go higher, I can pay *all* of it in ten days!"

There was silence on the line and then the voice said: "Come see me tomorrow. *With* the escrow papers. Prove you got the property. You got it, you sold it, you prove it, Philo."

"Arnold, please! Mavis can't know about this. Goddamnit, it's technically *her* property from her first husband! I can't take a chance on Mavis finding out about the markers. *Trust* me! Please, Arnold!"

There was silence again and the voice said, "How much you wanna get down?"

"What's the best you can get me this late?"

"Six points."

"Okay, get me down for seven thousand."

"You're fucking *crazy*, Philo. Good night."

"Wait! Wait! Lay it off, you don't wanna cover it!"

"Philo, Minnesota is gonna *lose*. I tell you as a friend, Oakland's gonna win by ten at least."

"So what! I'm gonna have eighty-five thousand in ten days!"

Silence, and then: "Okay, and if you're wrong, your bill is gonna be fifteen thousand with our little store, counting the vigorish. That's outta my hands, Philo. You don't pay and it's *outta* my hands."

That night, while a tortured woman in a Pasadena mansion slept thanks to Scotch and drugs, and a tortured man in a furnished Hollywood apartment slept thanks to Russian vodka, Philo Skinner, cold sober and electrified, slept not at all.

Minnesota would *win.* Win, goddamnit! And then it would all be academic. There'd be no *need* to do it. He could maybe even laugh about it. To himself. But if Minnesota lost. If they lost . . . And then, the epiphany: He *knew* Minnesota would lose. He *wanted* Minnesota to lose. And he was betting on them.

If Minnesota won he'd merely be covering his losses. His miserable life would be essentially unchanged. But if Minnesota lost . . . if they *lost,* he'd *have* to do it. And it would *work.* And he'd have eighty-five thousand dollars. Seventy thousand after paying his gambling losses. Seventy thousand tax-free dollars! But not from an escrow.

There was no escrow. There was no apartment house. He owned nothing but his business, and Skinner Kennels was hopelessly in the red. His house *might* net five thousand after the second mortgage was paid off. His four-year-old white El Dorado wasn't worth what he still owed on it.

The way out had come to him tonight, there in the grooming room, while Mavis was poor-mouthing him. Stripping, stripping it all away. But like most neophytes, Philo Skinner needed impetus to commit a serious crime.

Fear. He smoked, and sweated the length of his six-foot-three-inch frame. He listened to Mavis snore, and rain patter, and *welcomed* the rush of fear. That's what he *needed.* He even helped it along. He tried to imagine what they'd do to him if Minnesota lost. *When* Minnesota lost. If he phoned Arnold and told him it was a lie about owning an apartment house, that he couldn't pay.

Someone would come to the kennel when he was alone, at night. It wouldn't be Arnold of course. He tried to imagine the man. Two men, probably. Maybe one of them a big nigger. Philo Skinner had always feared black men. Maybe the other, some sleazy little kike friend of Arnold's. He would try to run but they'd corner him in the kennel. The dogs would bark wildly at the implacable strangers. They'd find Philo's grooming shears. The spook would want to castrate the honkie. The Jew would decide they should leave him in condition to sell and borrow and come up with the coin. The Jew would smile and say: "Let's *circumcise* this schmuck." Or maybe . . .

But it was enough. His side of the bed was soaked. He'd have to get up in a minute and change pajamas. His teeth and jaws ached from gnashing and clenching. This kind of sweat wasn't work sweat. It smelled entirely different. Now he had the impetus to do what he *wanted* to do. Philo Skinner learned what so many lawbreakers learn, and often admit, but not to judge and jury. It was a goddamn *thrill.* He was high! Philo Skinner drank moderately and despised the effect of drugs. He smoked grass and hash only to impress any young women he met in bars. Now, listening to the rain in the night, he was *flying.*

Fifty-two years of obeying every goddamn law on the books whether it made sense or not. Just this once he'd do it. And it wouldn't hurt anybody. Not very much, anyway. And not for very long. He'd never felt so alive.

Before he changed his sweaty pajamas, Philo Skinner lit his seventy-fourth cigarette of a very long day. He lay in the darkness, smiling. He was betting seven thousand dollars on the Minnesota Vikings. And they were going to lose. And then he would *have* to do it. And he would be rich. And free! He knew a former handler who had become a Mexican national and was doing all right as a partner in a Mexican hotel. Puerto Vallarta. Margaritas at sunset. White teeth. Brown bodies. *All* willing. Seventy thousand tax-free American dollars. Good-bye, Mavis. Good-bye to *all* the dogs.

He thought of the feisty Minnesota quarterback. Fran Tarkenton, I hope they break your fucking arm.

4

The Rabbit

Valnikov slept in the yellow rubber raincoat. He slept crossways on the daybed, one shoe on, one shoe off. He slept on his back, head tilted, face florid. His eyes were almost stuck shut from sour vomitus belches.

Valnikov snored and wheezed, and as usual, dreamed of the rabbit. He cried out in his sleep and awoke when the hunter cut the rabbit's throat, broke the rabbit's jaws, and began peeling the skin back over the rabbit's face. The tearing muscle hissed and jawbones crackled in the powerful hands.

"Lord God!" he sobbed and awoke himself.

It was hard to tell where he hurt most. His head felt like a huge festering sponge. His back felt hinged. If he tried to straighten, the crusted rusty hinges would scream.

He almost screamed when he stood. Now at least he knew what hurt most: the festering sponge. His head was mushy. Lord God, have mercy. He fell back on the bed, moaning. Then Misha said, *"Gavno."*

"Please, Misha," Valnikov pleaded. "Oh, my head!"

But Misha repeated, *"Gavno, gavno, gavno."*

Misha only knew one Russian word and it meant *shit*. In fact, it was the only *human* word he could say.

Valnikov glared with one blazing eye and saw that Misha was standing on Grisha's head. Misha twittered and chirped and sang for his master, who held his ears and cried: "Please, Misha, please. Noise *hurts*."

But Misha just tossed his lovely emerald head, preened, and said: "*Gavno.*"

Shit.

Then Valnikov became aware that he was soaked by the perspiration from the oppressive rubber raincoat, and by the dream of the rabbit, which always brought night sweats.

Misha yelled: "*Gavno!*" like a challenge and through the agonizing mist of the vodka hangover Valnikov was amazed to see that Misha had just crapped on Grisha's head. As though he truly understood what the word meant! Well maybe he did. Who could say what a bird or a man understood.

It wasn't the shit, it was the noisy "*gavno*" which angered Grisha. The little rodent lunged at Misha, who squawked and flew to the trapeze at the top of the seven-foot cage. The furious little animal then sulked around the floor of the enormous cage until he found a comfortable place to settle down again. His head was covered with *gavno.*

The furnished bachelor apartment on Franklin Avenue was crisscrossed with clothesline which ran from the top of the giant animal cage to a nail pounded over the bathroom door frame. Three pairs of underwear and two pairs of socks were hung on that indoor clothesline, thanks to the endless queue of women at the apartment building's coin-operated clothes dryer.

There were unwashed glasses and dishes and empty vodka bottles on the formica table, on the plastic chairs, on the kitchen sink, in the kitchen sink.

Stacked higher than the dishes and glasses was a vast collection of recordings, in and out of album covers. The records were on the kitchen table, on the chairs, on the sink. And two were *in* the sink—which puzzled him this morning. At least they weren't damaged by water since he only washed dishes one at a time when necessary.

The tiny cluttered apartment boasted one great luxury, aside from the large record collection: a Micro Seike turntable and two Epicure speakers worth a thousand dollars each, capable of making the whole apartment house thump and vibrate.

Valnikov stood, stripped off the rubber raincoat and all of his wet outer clothing. He forced himself to march to the bathroom and showered in icy water, unaware for the moment that he had forgotten to remove his underwear and one sock.

His broad red face was bleeding in three places after he shaved. He spilled tea on his blue necktie when he drank, unable to hold the shaking glass of tea with both hands. Then he put the gerbil's food in

Misha's dish and the parakeet's food in Grisha's dish. He was halfway out the door before he thought that he had possibly made a mistake. He returned and saw that he had.

He groaned, and shooed Misha away from the rodent's dish.

"Please, Misha, eat your own food."

His voice thundered in his ears, through the flaming mush of his brain, through the infected tissue.

"Oh, never mind," he said. "Go ahead and eat Grisha's food. Grisha, you eat Misha's food today."

He hobbled toward the door again, looking at his watch, listing from side to side. Then he realized that a burrowing rodent from southern Russia could never jump high enough to eat a parakeet's food in a feeding tray five feet above his head.

Valnikov managed to switch the food. Corn and barley for the gerbil, gravel and seed for the parakeet. Then he gave the little creatures water and looked at them.

"Are you two even slightly appreciative," he moaned, "of the pain this is giving me?"

Misha answered him. The parakeet had been swinging on his trapeze, his back to Valnikov. The emerald bird did a deliberate forward fall, gripping the tiny bar in his claws. When he was hanging upside down, staring directly into Valnikov's wet fiery eyes, Misha said: "*Gavno.*"

Fifteen minutes later, Valnikov had parked his car and was weaving painfully toward the front door of Hollywood Police Station.

The caseload for business burglary was never too bad on Friday. Monday, after the channel-lock and pry-bar thieves had plundered during the two days businesses were closed, Valnikov would have his table littered with burglary reports. But today would be all right. Except for the merciless throbbing in his skull.

Two youngish homicide investigators the others called Frick and Frack were amusing themselves by telling ghoul stories to Irma Thebes, the foxy little investigator who worked the sex detail.

"Irma," Frick grinned, "take a look at this suicide report."

Irma grimaced, pretending she wasn't interested, but as always she read the report with abandon.

"Dude severed both wrists, then turned on the gas jets in his walk-up, then hit himself in the head three times with a hatchet. The third time he managed to pierce his skull."

"That ain't nothing," Frack said, leaning over her desk. "I had a broad last month cuts both wrists, then drinks D.D.T., then, get this, she tried to *choke* herself with a nylon stocking, using a wooden spoon for a tourniquet!"

"Awful, that's awful," Irma grimaced, dying for more.

Their unsmiling lieutenant, Woodenlips Mockett, interrupted by saying: "How's that murder from over on La Brea? Any progress?"

"Naw, the victim ain't talking," Frick said, wanting to continue the game of Can You Top This for Irma Thebes.

"What is this, amateur night?" Woodenlips Mockett snarled. "You getting anywhere or not?" Then he looked at Irma. "I mean on the *murder case.*"

"Well no, Lieutenant," the young detective said. "But that dude's a black militant and an ex-con. I think we find the guy done it we oughtta give him an ecology award."

Dudley Knebel, a robbery detective, then said, "Got a suspect? I got a victim who'll I.D. anybody I show him. Owns the burrito stand over on Western."

"*That* dingaling!" said a burglary dick they called Montezuma Montez. "Him and his wife, Hamhocks Hilda, they'll pick your *partner* out of a lineup, give them a chance."

"Hey, is it true about Hamhocks Hilda, the way she makes hamburgers?" asked Frick.

"It *is* the gospel, Jack," Montezuma Montez answered, grinning. "Captain Hooker *seen* it."

"What's true?" asked Woodenlips Mockett, nervously.

"Well, she's *always* pissed off at cops," Frick said. "Cause she gets robbed, oh, two, three times a month. And we never catch nobody. So you order a hamburger, she takes the meat and mashes it right up between her legs, right up on her greasy old Brillo pad."

"I don't believe that!" cried Woodenlips Mockett, who had mooched two burgers from Hamhocks Hilda just the day before.

"I swear, Lieutenant," Frack said. "When I busted her old man that time he went upside her head with a meat mallet, he told me what you gotta do is, you gotta always check the hamburger patty. See there's any little black curly hairs sticking out."

"Well, that ain't no big thing," said Clarence Cromwell, one of two black detectives at Hollywood. "She *cooks* it, don't she? Ain't so bad anyways, less he tuned Hilda's greasy old organ *jist* before she made your burger, Lieutenant."

Woodenlips Mockett waited a decent interval before hurrying out of the office to check with Captain Hooker to see if the men were lying to him again.

Then a voice boomed through the slightly open door of the interrogation room. Nate Farmer, the other black detective unwillingly transferred to the sex detail from auto theft, was interviewing a rape victim who lacked credibility.

She too was black. So was the alleged suspect. Blacks robbed, raped and murdered other blacks, more often than not. Same with whites. Hoodlums rarely bothered to discriminate.

His voice thundered through the room: "So he's been takin a piece for six months, and you been enjoyin it, and now all of a sudden you find your little belly gettin big and you're all of a sudden a *child* a seventeen, and your social worker says the county'll pay for your little whelp if you put your boyfriend in jail for rape! Well I ain't gonna go for it!"

"Last rape victim I handled turned out to be a call girl with twenty-two arrests," Irma Thebes observed.

"Didn't know she was raped till the check bounced, huh?" said Frick.

A Cuban boy, eleven years of age, was sitting in the squad room listening wide-eyed to the raging black detective. The boy was a renowned Hollywood bicycle thief. They called him Earl Scheib Lopez, in honor of the auto painter who could paint any car for $49.95. Earl Scheib Lopez boasted that he could paint any hot bike for a buck and a quarter, in *ten* minutes, and have enough sniffable paint left to get three of his pals loaded.

Earl Scheib Lopez always had his jeans stuffed with coins and he was now playing nickel-dime blackjack with Fuzzy Spinks, of auto theft, who could tolerate the little bike bandit ever since the day he rolled over (for a fifty-buck snitch fee) on a Cuban gang who had hijacked a load of Ferraris, and Fuzzy got a leg up toward Investigator III. Earl Scheib Lopez used the fifty scoots to buy two cases of aerosol paint cans and there were three hundred bikes stolen in Hollywood in the next two weeks.

His latest arrest was for a bit of derring-do: On a whim, the little crook had jumped on a display bike in a department store downtown, ridden it through five screaming sales clerks, down the *escalator,* and out on the street making a getaway clear to Hollywood in twenty minutes. But he had underestimated his fame. The Central Division investigators had no trouble identifying the bike bandit: only Earl Scheib Lopez was *that* kind of swashbuckler.

But he wasn't swashbuckling now. He was playing blackjack very quietly with Fuzzy Spinks, who was baby-sitting him until they could release him to grandma, who was getting sick and tired of taking a bus to police stations and courtrooms for Earl Scheib Lopez. One day, after his third arrest in one month, she had made an extra bus trip. This one to the "Glass House," Parker Center downtown, to the office of the chief of police. The old woman waited patiently for two hours to see the chief's adjutant and then explained through an interpreter in polite and formal Spanish that she had come to sign the necessary American documents—to put Earl Scheib Lopez in the gas chamber.

Fuzzy could see that the little thug was very anxiously listening to the mean-looking black detective yelling at his "rape victim."

"You ever pull any rapes yet, Earl?" Fuzzy asked, peering at the boy over his bifocals, actually trying to get a peek at Earl's cards because the ante was up to thirty-five cents.

"No way!" Earl said, staying on fourteen while Fuzzy busted.

"Yeah, well don't ever try it. These detectives here can look right up a broad's unit and check her lands and grooves. Just like the muzzle of a gun. Understand?"

"Yeah?" Earl Scheib Lopez said, pretty damned impressed for once.

"They match em up with the marks on *your* rape tool, and you get twenty goddamn years. Get me?"

"Yes, *sir!*" Earl Scheib Lopez said. He was showing a king of diamonds.

"You hitting?" the old cop asked hopefully, since he had to hit sixteen and was down to his last ninety cents.

"Damn it!" Max Haffenkamp, from residential burglary, slammed the phone down. "Hollywood's turned into a frigging ghetto! People're so evasive they won't even say hello, they think it's a cop."

"Tell em you found their welfare check," Clarence Cromwell said. "*Then* they'll talk to you honkies."

"Lord, I hope there's a gang killing tonight," said Frick. "I need some overtime, make my car payment."

"I'm losing weight, Irma," Frack leered, sucking in his chest. "Stomach like a washboard. You could wash your lace underwear on my tummy. Anytime."

Just then the rape victim stormed out of the interrogation room yelling: "Well if you won't bust that sucker, I'm goin to the F.B.I. cause I ain't his escape goat. And *you* nigger!" She aimed a skinny finger at Nate Farmer. "You I'm suin for defecation of character!"

All the yelling was interrupted when a radio voice came over the monitor. It was the police helicopter.

"This is Air Six," the radio voice said. "Anything for us?"

And then, as always, three or four ex-vice cops called out suggestions:

"Yeah, bomb the dopers on Sunset."

"Strafe the pimps on Hollywood Boulevard."

"Napalm the fruits on Selma Avenue."

And so forth.

Suddenly Frick threw his arrest reports to Frack. "Rape and murder. Rape and murder. I'm getting sick of it!" Frick cried.

"Hmph," Clarence Cromwell snorted. "You the one doin all the rape and murder, chump. Killin time and screwin the city."

All conversations, bitching, and dramatic outcries were suddenly interrupted. It became breathlessly still.

Dora Simpson, the record clerk from downstairs, sashayed into the squad room, dropped some reports on the desk of Woodenlips Mockett, and wriggled out again.

"With those lungs, that girl could stay underwater for *days,*" Fuzzy Spinks sighed.

Dora Simpson had gone unnoticed during ten years of employment with the Los Angeles Police Department, until she transferred from Northeast Station to Hollywood Station. Then she had begun dating a retired plastic surgeon with a Pygmalion complex.

Dr. Henry Sprackle took a centimeter off the bridge of her nose and two off the tip. He implanted nearly a *pound* of foam in her sagging breasts and buttocks. He whacked away the loose flesh from under her chin and eyes and hacked off two and a half inches of belly fat.

Finally, he threw away her cat's-eye horn-rims and had her fitted with tinted contact lenses. He took her to Elizabeth Arden's for a Farrah Fawcett feather-cut and she was *almost* perfect. Then he took her to Frederick's of Hollywood and bought her ten pairs of crotchless black underwear and she *was* perfect.

Dora Simpson was born again, but no Baptist preacher had a hand in it. A former ugly duckling was now the object of many a wet dream at Hollywood Station, and indeed all over the Los Angeles Police Department. They said that Deputy Chief Digby Bates, the most notorious swain among the ranking brass, had offered the area commander *four* additional patrol officers if he would release Dora Simpson for a transfer.

Frick and Frack were insane over her. The two young cops had worked together six years, both in patrol and detectives, and they'd bedded the same station house groupies for so long they'd begun to have similar erotic fantasies. Most of them these days involved Dora Simpson because they thought of her as an android. She wasn't human. She was sculpted in the laboratory of Dr. Henry Sprackle.

All that jiggly stuffing in there! Imagine searching for the surgical scars! Would she do *anything* her master told her? It was wildly decadent and perverse. Frick said that as soon as his second divorce was final he was going to propose to her. Frack said that *he* was going to propose to Dr. Sprackle, since Dora Simpson as an android was not in a position to accept on her own behalf.

She was the station house celebrity for sure. Everyone called her Spareparts Simpson.

"Looks like you're goin to a funeral, and it's yours," Clarence Cromwell said when Valnikov weaved through the maze of tables and coffee-drinking detectives with his second cup of tea.

The voices. The noise. The painful cacophony of two dozen detectives wearing out the only essential tools of an investigator: pencil and telephone.

"Light workload, Clarence?" Valnikov asked.

"Nothin to it," Clarence Cromwell said. Broad-chested with a face as creased and shiny as old leather, he was a twenty-five-year cop who had also worked "downtown" in better days.

Covering for a high-rolling girlfriend who passed some bad checks had been Clarence's downfall and earned him a transfer ("There is *no such thing* as a disciplinary transfer in the Los Angeles Police Department. Of course, you understand that, Sergeant Cromwell? This is merely an administrative readjustment.") back to where he started, Hollywood Station. But if one saw the glass half full, well, it wasn't as bad as 77th Street Station, which policed Watts, and was the armpit of detective duty. Hollywood dicks wasn't such bad duty, considering.

But poor Clarence Cromwell was withering on the vine. He wore a big moustache and a medium Afro and Italian suits. He was rushing resentfully into middle age, drinking too much, but not nearly like Valnikov. He was still wearing two shoulder holsters which thrilled the hell out of cop groupies but weren't much better than ballast these days. When Clarence had worked robbery-homicide downtown, those twin Colt magnums had blown away four bandits in six short happy years.

On the night following the last shoot-out, a Chinatown groupie sidled up to the still shaking detective at a bar and grabbed him by the crotch and said, "I wanna see your *other* magnum, Clarence. Baby, you look like Sidney Poitier *wishes* he looked."

Those were the days.

"You okay?" Clarence Cromwell asked when he saw Valnikov's trembling hands.

"I'm all right, Clarence," Valnikov smiled, losing the thread of what the burglary report was all about.

"Got any bodies in jail today, Val?"

Valnikov looked at Clarence Cromwell and just shrugged pathetically. Clarence Cromwell lit a cigarette and looked at Valnikov's hands again.

Clarence Cromwell had been there many many times. Valnikov was one of four or five detectives Clarence Cromwell would bother with. First, because he knew Valnikov from robbery-homicide in better days. And secondly, because Valnikov was a veteran with more than twenty years' service, most of it in the detective bureau. If there was anything Clarence Cromwell despised more than the police brass it was RE-cruits.

Clarence Cromwell looked around in disgust. Fuckin RE-cruits. Add up the total service of the whole burglary detail and there wouldn't be three hashmarks total. Except for himself and Valnikov. Fuzz-nutted kids. Like that little brother, Nate Farmer, always hollerin. Thinks he's some kind a black Kojak, or somethin. And those two kids Frick and Frack. All they ever thought about was their cocks. Homicide detectives, my ass.

Not detectives—"investigators." Now they were all "investigators." At least that's what the business cards said. That's what the brass decided they should be called nowadays. And they did "team policing." Whatever the hell that is. Nobody knew. Four "teams" of "investigators" working their little areas. Teams, my ass. This ain't no football game, Chief. Police work is a whole bunch of decisions you got to make your *own* self out on those streets. Except that every few years the brass had to come up with some new catchword to justify the budget. "Team policing." All it did was add a whole bunch of new chiefs to supervise fewer Indians. Some stations used to get by with one captain. Now they had to have *three*. And a whole fuckin sack full of lieutenants. They were about as useful as Woodenlips Mockett's balls. And Clarence knew *they* hadn't been used in years.

Clarence leafed through Valnikov's reports quickly and said, "You ain't got no bodies in jail. Get your ass on home, I'll cover for you. Shit, you're so full a Russian potata juice you're all swole up like a toad."

"That's real nice of you, Clarence." Valnikov tried to smile, but it hurt. *Hurt* to smile. "I'm okay."

Clarence Cromwell knew better. And it wasn't just the hangover. Valnikov was *not* okay. He was not anything like the detective who worked homicide downtown for fifteen years. That man was quiet and shy, but he was alert. This guy next to him was just some shipwreck victim. Clarence Cromwell pitied him, but he didn't know him.

Clarence looked around at the roar of activity, at the grinding paper mill. Papers everywhere. Take away my gun and car, but *please* don't take my pencils. Nobody noticed yet how extra bad Valnikov looked today: "Val, you got a comb?"

"A comb?" Valnikov looked at Clarence like he didn't understand the word. Like he didn't talk English anymore. "Yeah, Val, you know, a fuckin *comb.*"

Clarence wondered if he could be using drugs. Naw, he thought, a lush like Val don't go smokin dope.

"Here's a comb, Val. I used to ride a old sorrel horse in Griffith Park, had neater lookin hair than you got. Go comb your hair, at least. You look like a skid row blood donor. What're they payin for a pint a blood these days, ten bucks for positive, twelve for negative?"

"Pardon?" Valnikov said.

"Gud-damn, man! Go in my locker and get yourself a clean necktie. Looks like you washed that one in vodka. Git your *shit* together, Val!"

But it was too late. Clarence Cromwell looked up and locked eyes with Captain Hooker, who nodded toward his office.

"There's jist one thing savin your ass, Val," Clarence Cromwell whispered before he stood up. "Me." Then he was gone toward the captain's office.

Valnikov just sat and stared blankly at his crime reports, and trembled, and thought he could hear the voices of a Slavonic choir. Far away. In the frozen Siberia of his mind.

Natalie Zimmerman was furious. She took long-legged strides back and forth, from wall to wall in Captain Hooker's private office. The giant strides were stretching the woolen skirt tight across her thighs.

Well now, old Nat's wheels ain't too bad, Clarence Cromwell thought, as he sat down. Ain't too bad at all.

"I do my job, Captain!" she said, voice shaking.

"I know you do, Natalie. You get straight upper-ten ratings, don't you?"

"Look, Captain, I wanna make Investigator Three."

"You will, I'm sure."

"Not if I work with that . . . with Valnikov. Because I'll get as bad as he is, you make me his partner!" She finally stopped pacing, flopped down in the chair next to Clarence Cromwell and brushed a wisp of frizzy buckskin-colored hair from her forehead.

Clarence Cromwell looked approvingly at Natalie Zimmerman's crossed legs and thought maybe this'll turn out to be a good idea. Might be what old Val needs.

"It's not forever, Natalie," Captain Hooker soothed. He was one of those scholarly looking kind of guys in three-button suits that always made Clarence Cromwell wonder how come they're cops. Hooker was hipless and had to wear suspenders to hold up his pants and gunbelt.

"Did you see him today, Captain?" Natalie pleaded, raising oversized glasses to rub the bridge of her nose. "The sucker's bombed. Let's face it!"

"He ain't bombed," Clarence offered. "He's jist hung over. Jist gotta have some tea, git his shit . . . uh, mind together."

"Why me, why me?" Natalie asked the lock of frizzy hair which usually hung on her forehead. She wore her Friz longer than most.

Captain Hooker studied her, nodding like a condescending headmaster. "You're the best female investigator I've got," Captain Hooker answered softly, hoping Natalie would lower her voice.

"That's great. You've only got two. How about Clarence here? Why can't he work with him? They're old buddies!"

"Uh, well, I, ar-uh, got my team to run," Clarence reminded her. Thinking: Uh-uh, *no* way, baby. I got my own drinkin problem. Me and Val together? Shit! Hose out the drunk tank, Barney, make room for the burglary detail!

"I've known Valnikov for twenty years," Captain Hooker said patiently. "He was only a two-year policeman then. He's always been a fine officer. And always a gentleman, I might add."

"Yeah, well that means this *gentleman's* got twenty-two years on the job, so he can go ahead and retire now and . . ."

"Valnikov is *still* a fine policeman," Captain Hooker said, raising his hand ever so slightly to quiet the passion of Natalie Zimmerman, who happened to catch Clarence Cromwell inspecting her bustline.

Clarence looked up innocently. The old bastard! It was no secret that Hooker did whatever Cromwell wanted. All Hooker was doing was biding his time. Three more months, he would have his thirty in, and would retire to a cushy teaching job in the Police Science Department at Cal State L.A. Everyone knew it. Just like everyone knew that Clarence Cromwell ran the goddamn detective division. Just because his bail bondsman buddy, No-Show Weems, had given him unlimited use of his 53-foot motor yacht with twin diesels and a flying bridge—an *idiot* like Cromwell who couldn't even drive a golf cart!—and Hipless Hooker just had to be the most fanatical deep-sea fisherman who ever lived. And Mrs. Hooker got seasick in the bathtub, so Hipless Hooker could sneak off unattended with Clarence Cromwell on that stinking boat practically every goddamn weekend, probably with some of Cromwell's old wino girlfriends. The evil old spook! He was looking at her tits again!

• ● •

It was true that Clarence Cromwell had unlimited use of a $300,000 motor yacht. It was also true that Captain Hooker asked for Cromwell when he was kicked out of robbery-homicide because Hooker had heard about the magnificent boat. Hipless Hooker may have wondered why a well-heeled bail bondsman like No-Show Weems would be so generous with Clarence Cromwell, but he thought he shouldn't look a gift horse. He was absolutely right.

No-Show Weems was so called because even though he had thriving bail bond agencies all over Los Angeles County, every time the sweating fat man was asked how's business, he'd say: "Terrible. No show. No show. Nobody comes to court. Everybody jumps bail these days. No show. No show."

No-Show Weems had made the disastrous mistake of posting bail for the Moroni brothers, two bank robbers from San Pedro who had shot a bank guard during their last robbery and were awaiting trial, their combined bail set at two hundred thousand dollars. The D.A. had argued against lowering the bail, but the superior court judge had never forgotten Boys Town's Father Flanagan and believed, even before he became senile, that there is no such thing as a bad boy. No-Show Weems knew for sure that the Moroni brothers were bad boys. In fact, he knew it even before Sal Moroni got arrested for throwing a Sicilian cook out the window of an Italian restaurant for overcooking his scallopini.

The old cook swore vengeance after leaving the hospital with a brand-new hip joint, and decided to give the Moroni brothers a dose of Sicilian revenge. She had never heard of it in her country, but since all the American movies did it, Lucretia Pantuzzi, age sixty-eight, began limping up to their door in the middle of the night and leaving reeking bundles of putrid perch and rock cod in the Moroni mailbox. Take that, goatface! A little calling card from Lucretia Pantuzzi!

When the senile judge lowered bail, No-Show bit the bullet and posted it because the Moroni brothers had as an uncle a successful tuna fisherman who signed an agreement to make restitution if the Moroni boys jumped. But two weeks later the old fisherman had fallen from the stern of his trawler and drowned along with six porpoises, trapped in his own tuna nets. A save-the-porpoise environmentalist group threw a bash and offered several hearty toasts and hoorahs for more live porpoises and drowned dagos. The old fisherman's estate went into receivership and a legal battle ensued which tied up his assets.

Meanwhile, the Moroni brothers were getting sick and tired of finding stinking fish in their mailbox. It got so the bank robbers even hated to reach in the box for their welfare checks. And the fact is, they were just plain bored anyway. So they robbed a savings and loan office and cruised south with the migratory gray whales. All the way to Cabo San Lucas, on the tip of the Baja peninsula, in the country of Mexico.

One day Sal and Tony Moroni were lollygagging in the Mexican sunshine, drinking tequila and watching two drunken whores frolic in the surf. They saw a white motor cruiser on the horizon. The chartered cruiser powered ever closer to the beach, anchored some distance back of the surf line and lowered a rubber dinghy into the water. The dinghy had a big outboard engine and the guy in the boat made good time skimming over the swells to the beach.

When he got closer, the brothers saw he was wearing a red knitted cap pulled down almost to his eyes, and a red scarf tied across the lower part of his face. The dumb shit. It was seventy-two degrees on the beach. Then he got even closer. His hands and arms were dark. He was a nigger. A stupid nigger coming from the cool ocean to a warm beach in a red knitted hat and scarf. He looked so goddamn silly the whores joined the Moroni brothers and they all laughed like hell. Then he cut his engine and drifted in through the gentle surf right up to the beach. Dumb nigger probably coming ashore to buy some tequila for his boss on the yacht. He wasn't even looking at the naked whores, but it didn't matter. He looked so silly with his face all wrapped up that they laughed like hell.

And wept when the Moroni brothers, blindfolded and chained together with two sets of handcuffs, were sailing away at gunpoint in the little rubber dinghy.

They were blindfolded all the way, even after leaving the boat. They couldn't identify the boat, the skipper, or the nigger gunman. When they had to eat or use a toilet during the two-day voyage he would take off the handcuffs, but make them do it blindfolded. All they could say about him was that if they yelled or complained he'd put those two big magnums right in their ears and ask them if they saw the movie *Jaws.*

The police were given an anonymous phone tip and found the fugitives, minus handcuffs, gags, and blindfolds, locked in the trunk of an abandoned junkyard car near the Los Angeles County Jail parking lot.

The A.C.L.U. said that if their story were true their civil liberties had been horribly violated. The Mexican consulate said that if their story were true it was an international act of piracy. The L.A.P.D. bank squad said it was all bullshit, made up by the Moroni brothers who had always been poor sports anyway.

Actually, nobody *really* believed the outrageous tale. In fact the Moroni brothers got kidded so much in the slammer about the Scarlet Pimpernel and the Crimson Pirate that they stopped telling the story about the big nigger in the red mask. After a while even Sal Moroni stopped believing it really happened, and Tony had to kick the shit out of him to get his head straight.

And a few months later, No-Show Weems bought himself a 53-foot yacht much like the one the Moronis had seen on the horizon that day, and Clarence Cromwell got to use it just as much as he wanted.

• ● •

Natalie Zimmerman knew part of the story of the motor yacht, but not all of it. Captain Hooker knew all he cared to know.

"Natalie," Hooker smiled unctuously. "Clarence here can tell you what a good policeman Valnikov was, all those years they worked together."

"I worked robbery, the bank detail," Clarence said, melodramatically closing his arm on the twin magnums. "Val was a heavyweight homicide dick, 'cept maybe for one or two other guys he was number one. He ain't always been a . . ."

"Drunk." Natalie finished the statement. Then quickly: "Captain, I've never been put in a position to poor-mouth another officer like this and I don't like it a damn bit but . . ."

"Sometimes a fellow shouldn't work homicide that long," Captain Hooker offered.

"Yeah, I knew a old homicide guy," Clarence agreed. "Started floggin his . . . started masturbatin at a salesgirl in the May Company one day. Had to give the old sucker a psycho pension."

"To continue, Natalie," Hooker said hastily, "when Valnikov transferred in a month ago it was because of a . . . problem. He had some sort of scuffle with a doctor or something and . . ."

"A pathologist," Clarence said.

"Yes, a pathologist. During an autopsy."

"Wasn't nothin," Clarence assured her. "Jist a misunderstandin of some kind. Homicide dicks always get pissed off at those canoemakers at the morgue. Can't never give you enough evidence to make a good murder case, seems like."

"A misunderstanding," she smirked. "The kind you have in a saloon, for instance?"

Damn, this odd broad was one of the world's champion sneerers and smirkers, Clarence Cromwell thought.

"He had a drinking tendency," Hooker admitted. "And after this scuffle or whatever it was, his captain noted he'd been acting a little . . . well, distant for some time. Absent-minded. His reports are a little sloppy and incomplete. A little . . . oh, incoherent."

"He was always sort of a quiet guy, though," Clarence added.

"His captain thought a change of scenery would do him good. Clarence suggested I take him here at Hollywood and I agreed."

Attaboy, Clarence, Natalie thought, smirking.

"He went through a painful divorce a few years ago. Sometimes it makes a man take a drink, and what with . . ."

"Captain, I've been through *two* painful divorces," Natalie Zimmerman said, up again and pacing. "Look, sir, I'm thirty-nine years old. I've been a police officer eighteen years. I can't be expected to . . ."

"Yeah? You *that* old, Nat?" Clarence said.

". . . and I can't be expected to wet-nurse alcoholics."

"Wet-nurse. Hee hee," Clarence giggled. Looking at her tits.

"Nobody said he's an alcoholic," Hooker said. "We don't have alcoholics in the detective bureau!" *That* one made even Clarence Cromwell smirk.

"Look, Captain," she said. "I've been a good police officer. I worked my tail off to get my bachelor's degree and . . ."

"Her tail," Clarence said. "Hee hee." Looking at it admiringly.

"I don't think it's fair!" Natalie said, sneering at Clarence Cromwell, who was obviously behind all this.

The captain started getting gaseous and wished Clarence would just handle the whole matter so he could go shopping and buy himself a yachtsman cap. "Anyway, we . . . *I* think this aimless kind of behavior might diminish if he's not alone so much. He needs a partner. And not a partner who he'll let take charge. Because that's what he has a tendency to be—passive. He needs a *female* partner."

"Ah hah!" Natalie Zimmerman cried, smirking up at the frizzy lock on her forehead.

Now she understood. And with *that,* Natalie Zimmerman couldn't argue. She had been a cop too long to fight with *that* logic.

Natalie Zimmerman had been through it all, through all the humiliating chauvinism in a macho job where women couldn't advance past sergeant until recent years when they magnanimously promoted *one* woman to the rank of lieutenant. Where they used to start the women in the Lincoln Heights Jail until the sheriff's office took over that miserable job. Where Natalie Kelso had begun her police career at the age of twenty-one, still naïve enough to think she would be doing real police work like a real cop.

The Lincoln Heights Jail. Knee-deep in fingerprint ink, vomit, tears, blood. Memories. You've never smelled a stink until you smell the feet in those detention tanks.

"All right, Officer, bring in your next prisoner. Petty theft, huh? What is she, a drunken thief or a thieving drunk? Search her? Can't I just pat her down on the dry spots?" Mean Minnie from Main Street. She just loved to tease a rookie jailor by plucking shitballs from her jockey shorts—jockey shorts!—and flicking them in the rookie's hair when her back was turned.

"Oh, ma'am! Officer! You put me in the cell without money or cigarettes."

"Be glad you don't have any, lady. They'd kill you in that tank just to get them."

"Oh, ma'am! Officer! I found a body crab when I came in here, and it just died."

"Congratulations. You're lucky."

"But a thousand more just came to its funeral!"

"Oh, ma'am! Officer! There's twenty people sleeping in my bed."

"How's that possible?"

"My bed's on the floor."

"But the fifth floor's *full* tonight! There *are* no more beds! Christ! What can *I* do! Take you home with me! Christ!"

A rookie jailor. Still green enough to shake hands with a pregnant Indian drunk from East Fifth Street. The woman had just blown her nose on that hand. *Never* shake hands. Never touch any of them unless you have to. *And don't let them ever touch you.*

Now the women were out on patrol with the men. Wearing men's uniforms, of course. A nasty gesture by the brass to humiliate them since the courts forced the brass to give the women parity. Now they were doing patrol work—the amazons, that is, who were as big and strong as men, as though size and strength were meaningful. But in the investigative divisions they still had them working mostly on juvenile cases, dealing with children and rape victims, doing paper work like glorified file clerks. No, she couldn't argue with Hipless Hooker's logic. If Valnikov were ever going to become an assertive cop, he'd sure as hell do it with a *female* partner. Every one of those *other* chauvinist bastards sure had, even a loanee from patrol she had trained three months ago. She was almost old enough to be the little asshole's mother.

"It ain't gonna be so bad workin with Valnikov," Clarence said, trying hard to come up with something positive for Natalie. Some talent Valnikov could offer. "Looky here," Clarence said. "He's smart. He talks Russian!"

"Wonderful," Natalie said, smirking up at her buckskin Friz. "If we get on the trail of some Communist spies, maybe I can use him."

Five minutes later, Valnikov was sitting in the chair next to Clarence Cromwell. The door was closed and Valnikov was so confused he thought Captain Hooker was telling him he was going to work juvenile with Natalie Zimmerman.

"But I like burglary, Cap," Valnikov said, trying to focus his watery blue eyes on Captain Hooker.

"What I'm saying, Val," Hooker said patiently, "is that I want Zimmerman here to work business burglary with *you*. You've got too much work in your district for one man. You should have a partner."

"Oh," Valnikov said, lips and throat parched. "Could you excuse me for a minute, Captain? I'd like to get a drink."

"Go ahead, Val," Hooker said, while Natalie Zimmerman sneered at her Friz.

Before Valnikov returned, she said, "One more question: Was he bombed or wasn't he, during his *problem* with the pathologist?"

"Argument over a homicide case." Hooker shrugged. "I don't even know the details. Insulted the doctor and got reported. He may have had liquor on his breath at the time. He just needed a transfer, I think."

"And now *we're* going to straighten him out?"

Valnikov scuttled back into the room, his cinnamon hair wet and stringy as though he'd made a half-hearted attempt to comb it. He wore

Clarence Cromwell's green tie instead of his own dirty blue one. The tail of the tie hung three inches too low. It was a half inch off center and his collar button showed. He sat erect and made a vigorous attempt to focus his runny eyes.

"I see you're wearin my tie," Clarence nodded.

"Mai tai?" Valnikov said vacantly. "No, I don't care for exotic drinks."

Then Valnikov looked blankly at Captain Hooker, who laughed, thinking Valnikov had intentionally made a joke.

Natalie Zimmerman knew better. "Oh Jesus!" she said to her Friz.

In the squad room, Fuzzy Spinks had gone out in the field and Nate Farmer had taken over the blackjack game with Earl Scheib Lopez.

The black detective was glowering down at the eleven-year-old who was shaking so much he could hardly hold the cards.

"You think you're bad, Earl?" the detective whispered. "You ain't bad, Earl. Me, *I'm* bad! You hittin or stayin?"

"I'ma . . . I'ma . . . I'ma . . . h-h-h-hitting," Earl Scheib Lopez said, with a king showing and a jack in the hole. Then he said, "I b-b-b-b-busted," even before Nate Farmer gave him his card.

The big cop had won all of Fuzzy Spinks' money back and was into Earl for three of his own bucks while Earl's grandma sat at the table of the other kiddie cop, Irma Thebes, patiently trying to convince Montezuma, in formal Spanish, that *of course* Earl was old enough to be gassed at San Quentin.

5

The Big Sewer

Madeline Whitfield awakened that morning not knowing or caring that it was Russian Christmas. Nor did she care that in two days there would be a football game played within sight of her mansion, just down the hill in the arroyo, just near the base of the San Gabriel Mountains. Nor did she know that the most wistful, desperate dream of her life would be totally demolished by the arm of a left-handed quarterback.

To Madeline Whitfield the day was significant only because it was Friday. And that meant it was only two days from Sunday. And Sunday meant the Winter Show of 1977, sponsored by the elite Kennel Club of Beverly Hills, at the Los Angeles Memorial Sports Arena.

It was perhaps not as prestigious as the Summer Show, and certainly would not compare with Chicago International, or that jewel in the crown, the Westminster Kennel Club Show at Madison Square Garden. But it was an important show and for Madeline, crucial. There would be as many as five major points awarded, and Vickie with twelve needed only three more points to become a champion.

Madeline had agonized with Vickie's handler, Chester Biggs, whether or not to show her now in the Winter Show. Should they bring her in with a coat not quite prime and risk a loss to save the prime coat for New York in February? It was a decision which had to be made weeks in advance. Vickie had never lost yet, and Madeline was beside herself with anxiety. Finally, Chester made the decision by guessing who would judge. He guessed right. The judge was a shrewd old hand, one who could not be bought with expensive gratuities. A judge who knew his business, who would not penalize Vickie because her coat was now not quite prime, who would forgive, knowing that Vickie was being readied for Madison Square Garden and everlasting glory.

Madeline had overridden the vigorous objections of the dog handler by keeping Vickie at home these last crucial days before the show.

"Mrs. Whitfield, I've *got* to keep her for you," he had said. "Owners *don't* keep their dogs at home if they expect to win important dog shows!"

"But, Chester, I just can't bear parting with Vickie. She's never spent a night away from me since I got her."

"Mrs. Whitfield, do you want a pet or a *champion?* This dog is the finest miniature schnauzer bitch I've ever seen. She can win it *all*, do you understand? And I'm not talking about the best of breed, or best of terrier group. I'm talking about the best in show!"

"Chester, I'm sorry," Madeline Whitfield said. "You just . . . well, it's hard to say what Vickie means to me. She's like my child, silly as that sounds."

"It's not silly, Mrs. Whitfield. I've been a handler for a long time. I know how you feel about your Vickie. But you're so fortunate to possess a thing of rare beauty like Victoria Regina of Pasadena." He touched her hand in a gesture of understanding when he said it, thinking how that dumb name made him want to puke. "And you're a generous woman who would want to share Victoria with dog lovers everywhere, like Norton Simon and Armand Hammer share their art. Vickie will never be as beautiful as she *can* be, never show her true perfection, if you don't let me keep her for you. You owe it to dog lovers and to Vickie and to yourself and . . ."

But to no avail. Victoria Regina of Pasadena would sleep between her mother's pearly sheets even the Saturday night before the big show. There was nothing Chester Biggs could do about it but come to the Whitfield home to groom and train the gorgeous little bitch and try to reason with the dowdy big bitch, and try his best to win it all with this little schnauzer and build the reputation of his kennel to where even his stupid brother-in-law could run it and Chester Biggs could get his ass into real estate where he belonged.

• ● •

Chester often said as much during the twelve months he was Vickie's handler. He had said it the night before the Santa Barbara Show last summer. He had said it in the bar of the hotel while drinking with three other dog handlers who discuss dog exhibitors the way thoroughbred trainers discuss horse owners. The conversation generally centered around the richest exhibitors, how much of a bonus had been laid on a handler for winning best of breed, how high the tariff would be if a client was *really* wealthy and competitive and you won him five major points.

Most handlers got only $35–40 a day per dog even when showing a tough breed like a German shepherd. Perhaps $100 a point as a winning bonus. You had to own a kennel to make enough to live on. Handling and showing a few dogs for rich clients simply wasn't enough, unless your client was a crazy Persian like the one who reportedly gave his New York handler a bonus of $10,000 for bringing him a win with his Great Pyrenees bitch.

There were some, like Buck Hickman, who found other ways to collect rich bonuses. Hickman had married a Beverly Hills client and now *he* was an exhibitor and hired his own handlers, and came to dog shows in blue blazers, his silver hair rinsed and back-combed and sprayed just like his dogs, with a rich man's winter suntan, as though born to the purple. That was a secret dream of many handlers who had rich lonely female clients. Women who doted and pampered and spent up to $40,000 a year to show their dogs. Reasonably young and willing dog handlers could hope. There was always a chance, since women exhibitors outnumbered men four to one.

When Chester Biggs sat in the bar that night in Santa Barbara, and talked about the potential of the great young schnauzer bitch who slept in the same bed as her lonely screwed-up owner in Pasadena, there was a handler present who paid more than passing attention, especially when he heard that the owner was rich and available. But he went back to more pressing problems, such as how to convince the cocktail waitress that they might be able to find a little action even in a town like Santa Barbara if she'd meet him when she got off work.

She'd almost laughed in his face because his gray roots were showing and he was tipping only fifty cents a round. "Some other time, highroller," she finally told him.

Philo Skinner had sat there with yet another erection left to wilt. And at his age how many were *left?*

• ● •

Madeline had a minor hangover from the Scotch and Dalmane. In the past she had experienced wretched ones from Scotch and Librium and Scotch and Valium. So far the Scotch and a small dose of Dalmane seemed the best way to sleep.

Victoria was certainly alive enough at eight a.m. She frisked in the kitchen, yapping and wiggling around Yolanda, the housekeeper, formerly a live-in with Madeline, now a day worker on Mondays and Fridays.

"Vee-kee," Yolanda grinned, showing golden Tijuana bridgework in front, a status symbol which, unfortunately, was as much a tip-off to Immigration officers as was the long shapeless hair, the cast-off clothes, the diffident bearing of the illegal aliens.

Vickie started leaping straight up, showing off, barking, begging for the liver tidbits she knew Yolanda would get from the refrigerator.

"Morning, Yolanda," Madeline groaned, shielding her eyes from the morning sun as she shuffled into the kitchen and collapsed at the table, tolerating Vickie's shrill and happy growls.

"Joo wan jus café, Meesus?"

"Please, Yolanda. And perhaps a little orange juice."

"Jas, Meesus," the plump young girl nodded, first giving Vickie another slice of boiled liver, humming with the Spanish music on the radio, too loud for Madeline, who nonetheless tolerated it as she tried to concentrate on the *Los Angeles Times.*

Madeline was distressed to read that one of the city's leading decorators was sick and tired of wicker and rattan and jungle plants and swore that it would be déclassé in six months. Madeline looked around at the white wicker chairs and rattan loveseat, and all the hanging fern which she had bought at great cost six months before when she saw a kitchen in the *Los Angeles Times* done by the same decorator. It was ever thus. She would finally get the courage or the impetus or the money to embrace a style about a month before it was déclassé, whether it be clothes or furniture or hairstyles.

Lord, she wished Yolanda would turn down that radio. The frequent commercials in machine-gun Spanish were unbearable right now. And Lord, she wished she could still afford to have Yolanda live-in and take care of the house as it should be. As it was when Mason was here, before she had to close off three of the upstairs bedrooms, and the guest house, to conserve gas and keep the soaring maintenance costs in check. Many Old Pasadena scions lived on modest trusts and inheritances in mansions remodeled by Sears or Montgomery Ward. Lovely tiles which had been painted, fired, and glazed fifty years before by Spanish, Portuguese, and Mexican artisans now lay side by side with fifty-dollar sheets of formica. Many an eight-thousand-square-foot Colonial or Tudor mansion didn't have enough furniture left to fill a three-bedroom apartment. They settled for leaky gurgling toilets, but kept their expensive club memberships, hence, their identities, intact.

One more year and the trust fund would be finished. As always, her stomach churned when she thought of it. *One* year. Who could have thought about such a possibility when she was Mrs. Mason Whitfield? Not even after the divorce. Her mother had always said the trust was constructed by Madeline's father to endure throughout his only child's lifetime. With "prudent" management, of course. Always, Madeline had thought of the trust anthropomorphically: at first a guardian angel, later a kindly uncle who would always *be* there. Except that when her father designed that trust he didn't consider something as imprudent as a breast cancer which spread to the bone and eventually devastated his widow, her property, her hospital insurance, her Medicare, *and* the trust fund which was to sustain Madeline Whitfield forever.

The medical bills had been truly unbelievable. That was the word. Until you'd been visited by a relentless cancer and all it entailed—chemotherapy, radiotherapy, *four* years of extensive hospitalization, outpatient nursing—the expense was not to be believed.

It was legally difficult, hence expensive, even to break the trust so that the money could be used. Lawyers had to be paid so that Madeline could pay doctors. She often thought bitterly that a physician like Dr. Corey Dills should have known how "imprudent" a raging disease could be, and how a healthy trust fund could decompose like the bones of Madeline's mother.

Toward the end, Madeline's lawyer tried to persuade her to apply, on her mother's behalf, for Medi-Cal. *Welfare*. A word used in Old Pasadena with words like *leftist* and *Socialist*. It was so unthinkable it would have killed the old woman swifter than the disease. The idea of it sent Madeline Whitfield off on the worst Scotch and sedative binge of her lifetime. She continued to pay for a private room and the best medical care possible until the very end. Mercifully, the old woman's bones mortified before the withering trust fund. But the trust was itself terminally afflicted. *One* more year.

There had been a few humiliating attempts to confront the inevitable. Madeline would never forget fearfully approaching the personnel desk of a women's shop on Lake Avenue.

"May I help you?" She was an overdressed woman with green eyelids.

"Yes, I . . . this is a résumé. I understand you have a position available. I'd like to apply."

"A position."

"Yes, as a saleslady. I happen to have a great deal of time on my hands lately and I . . . I'd like to keep busy."

"You'd like to apply as a part-time saleslady?"

"Yes. Or full time, perhaps. Actually, I have a great deal of time on my hands these days and . . . yes, full time."

The woman glanced at the résumé and looked up curiously.

"You live in the San Rafael district?"

"Yes."

"It's lovely up there," she smiled deferentially. "Some of our best customers live in those big lovely homes."

"Yes," Madeline said nervously.

"I see you have a master's degree in history, ma'am," the overdressed woman said. "And these character references, well, some of the most prominent members of the community!"

"Yes, do you think I might . . ."

"Tell me, Mrs. Whitfield, have you done this before? Sales, I mean? There's absolutely nothing here about work experience."

"I haven't been in sales, no, but I think I'd be suitable," Madeline said, face flaming.

"What kind of work have you done, ma'am?"

"Well, I was married, you see, and . . . well, I've been awfully busy over the past twenty years. Awfully busy running my home, and of course there was a great deal of charitable work, and so forth."

"Yes. Tell me, Mrs. Whitfield, have you ever . . . worked? I mean at a job?"

"Not exactly at a job, but . . ."

"Yes, well we have a store policy, ma'am. We, uh, only hire ladies with experience. Actually, ma'am, I wonder if you couldn't fill up this spare time in some other way. A lady of your background, I don't think you'd like being a salesperson. I certainly know what it's like to have free time on your hands. When my children grew up . . ."

"Yes, perhaps you're right," Madeline said, voice breaking. "One gets restless. Yes. Probably I should just increase my involvement in the Junior Philharmonic."

"Yes, that's what I'd recommend," the woman said.

"Yes, I think so. Yes," Madeline said, stumbling out of the office, forgetting her meticulously typed résumé.

• ● •

Madeline looked at her watch and realized that she had to pull herself together. Chester would arrive in forty-five minutes to work with Vickie, and Madeline didn't want to be there for the session today. The anticipation was debilitating.

It was not good to let one's fantasies fly unchecked to New York and Madison Square Garden. To the prospect of owning a national champion.

The exclusive Beverly Hills Kennel Club had only twenty-three members. Well, there'd be twenty-four come this spring. How could they refuse to invite her to join? How could anyone in the dog world refuse her anything if . . . Westminster! Madison Square Garden! Lord!

Madeline scalded her lip with the coffee and decided to get dressed and assuage the tenseness by window-shopping on the west side, to stroll through the boutiques and shops like Theodore's. Not that she was young or brave or slim enough to shop there. Or *rich* enough, since their styles were faddish and you had to be ready to change each season. But it was fun to watch the platoons of voyeurs ogling the nubile young salesgirls who were pantyless and braless, and wore see-through cotton pants and T-shirts.

There was no such shopping in Old Pasadena. In Old Pasadena one shopped for "sensible" clothes, comfortable loafers with low stacked heels in colors to match wool-knit pants and jackets. Scottish plaid skirts would never be out of fashion, nor would cardigans and V-neck sweaters over cream-colored blouses. Sensible.

But if voyeurs went to shops like Theodore's to ogle the salesgirls, most Pasadena Junior Leaguers went there for similar reasons: They squandered money in overpriced west side restaurants, because of (Dare one admit it?) *movie stars*. "Last night at the Ma Maison, I dined next to Barbra Streisand . . ."

Though Old Pasadena deplored the libertine life-style over the hill—the star worship, the "A" tables at Chasen's, the parties upstairs at the Bistro. Though they would never *live* among them: the celebrities, the Jews, the *nouveau riche*—they were *insatiable* celebrity watchers. A proper Pasadena matron might never so much as glance toward the booth in the Palm Restaurant where Jack Nicholson was sitting, but her pulse was racing. And if in the Polo Lounge Warren Beatty said, "Pardon me, you dropped your napkin," to a Junior Leaguer from Old Pasadena, she would look at him blandly in *non*recognition, and say, "Thank you very much," grinding the Neil McCarthy salad thoroughly, with disciplined jaws that wanted to *tremble!*

A maître d' from the Huntington Sheraton Hotel commented wryly that Old Pasadena would dine and drink and dance from seven until midnight, and *grumble* if the check was more than twelve dollars per person. Yet they would gladly *tip* that much over the hill at Matteo's for an "A" table. A restaurateur could get rich off Old Pasadena, they said, if only he could bus in movie stars on Saturday night.

Madeline Dills Whitfield happened to pass the Brown Derby while driving in Beverly Hills that afternoon. She was fantasizing with delicious abandon. She and Vickie would be photographed at the Sign of the Dove in New York. (Did they let dogs in there? Well, *how* could they refuse a champion who had just won at Madison Square Garden?) There was a man with them at lunch. He was a well-known exhibitor from Long Island. He changed variously with her mood. Right now he looked like Paul Newman. Madeline would be pictured with Vickie in *Time* magazine, and the *Los Angeles Times* would do a feature article about the Pasadena dog who conquered New York. Madeline Dills Whitfield would be . . . well . . . *famous.*

In Old Pasadena, family, money, even power seldom got one's picture anywhere but the society page. It couldn't buy celebrity. In Old Pasadena, Madeline Whitfield would soon be as popular as a movie star.

She was so caught up in it she drove down Vine Street without rubbernecking. No matter, there were no movie stars lunching at the Derby at that moment. But if she had looked she might have noticed a gangly, middle-aged dog handler she'd often seen at shows. He was standing at Hollywood and Vine, thinking about a massage parlor on the Sunset Strip.

He was watching the door of the Brown Derby. He was about to commit a crime on a very holy day. But then, only two waiters in the Brown Derby and *nobody* in a Sunset Strip massage parlor knew it was a holy day, that it was Russian Christmas.

Like so many Big Moments in Philo's life, it all came down to a lost erection. Philo Skinner, ever the gambler, tossed a quarter in the air. Heads I drive to that massage parlor on the Strip and give my last fifty bucks to some pimply runaway bubblegummer with undeveloped tits to go down on me. Tails, I snatch the schnauzer from the Rolls-Royce and get *rich.* The blood was surging in his throat, his temples, his ruined chest. He sucked his twenty-ninth cigarette of the day, and flipped the quarter.

Heads. Later, maybe dejection, depression, regret, but now—relief.

Thank God. He hadn't slept five minutes all night. He was suddenly horny as a billy goat.

But she wasn't a pimply runaway. The woman in the massage parlor was a forty-five-year-old professional with lurid eyebrows, who wasn't impressed with Philo's white-on-white leisure suit, and the imitation gold chain dangling on his bony chest.

"I already told you, honey," she said, all business, "I'll give you the standard massage, the businessman's special, or the super massage of the day. The prices are listed."

"Sweetie," Philo Skinner retorted, "I got a picture of General Grant in my pocket, but I'm not about to give him away without knowing *exactly* what I can expect."

"I'll give you the standard massage, the businessman's . . ."

"What's wrong with you?"

"Nothing, Officer."

"Officer?"

"You sound like a cop."

"A cop."

"Last vice cop that tossed me in the slam looked about like you. Can't depend on cops being young and healthy-looking anymore. They dig up some ole bag a bones, give him a Lady Clairol dye job . . ."

"You miserable cunt!"

"Get outta my place of business!"

"Why you old pile a dog shit you got some nerve!"

"Get outta here!" she said, "before I call a *young* cop with a blue suit. I ain't goin for any a your vice cop entrapment."

Philo Skinner was outraged when he roared through the door onto Sunset Boulevard, as limp as linguini. Lady Clairol! With *her* lousy dye job? That old hound had a lot of room to talk!

And it was anger now, more than fear, even more than the *thrill* of it, which gave him the impetus. An amateur was about to make his irrevocable first step into crime.

• • •

Millie Muldoon Gharoujian always had lunch at the Brown Derby on Friday. Just as she always had dinner Thursday at Scandia and Wednesday at La Strada. Millie Muldoon Gharoujian was a creature of habit. It made it much easier to keep her life in order because she had a third-grade education and a 90 I.Q. In her younger days she had a body and bleach job like Harlow which got her out of the uniform of a waitress and into the bed of an Armenian junk dealer who obligingly departed for the Great Scrapyard after his second heart attack, leaving Millie to marry and divorce four young studs in succession and live a hell of a sexy life high up in Trousdale Estates overlooking all the glittering lights of Baghdad. She had owned at various times, in addition to the studs, a pet ocelot, a cheetah, a boa constrictor and a baby alligator named Archie who was accidentally flushed down the toilet. She also had less exotic creatures like a Siamese cat, a standard poodle, and a miniature schnauzer bitch with terrific bloodlines who liked to amuse herself by chewing the hell out of Archie the alligator, who got sick and tired of it and went bye-bye down the john.

The pup's name was Tutu and she later had shown well, twice winning best of breed, until her mistress got bored with dog shows because lots of the young studs around there were geldings. And because Millie got sick and tired of Tutu's handler always sniffing around like *he* was in heat. Millie Muldoon Gharoujian knew a fortune hunter when she saw one. Besides, the dog handler was at least fifty, about twenty years too old for her. Millie was seventy-six.

A lackluster cop named Leonard Leggett was the instrument whereby Archie and Tutu were linked again in the Great Chain of Life. For when Archie took a powder, and found himself tumbling pell-mell in a wild surging torrent right through Millie's new plumbing —while one of the studs in the round waterbed was going through Millie's *old* plumbing—Archie eventually escaped with his life through a pipe vent. Then Archie began an incredible odyssey overland, living on bugs and grasshoppers and french fries which, lucky for him, lay like hordes of dead locusts on the streets of Hollywood. At last, Archie followed his instincts to the Los Angeles sewers, coming to rest in the wonderful, cool, filthy muck below the streets. There was enough tasty fare for a whole battalion of alligators: pastrami sandwiches, beef dips, the ubiquitous soggy french fries, and tons of half-eaten Big Macs and ribs from Kentucky Colonel. And there was plenty of game: rats, snakes, turtles, puppies, human fetuses, a full-term baby or two. Some of it live, most of it dead, the flotsam and jetsam of Los Angeles. People got tired of things very easily in the city and it was adios, down the sewer.

But Archie found that peace and quiet were *boring*. In his dim reptile brain he perhaps remembered the bad old days when he was put upon by the schnauzer, and he became a tyrant in the sewers. He was soon five feet long, nose to tail, and still growing, rampaging around the sewers chewing the hell out of every hapless pet hamster or baby mouse that floated by on a Popsicle stick, right into the gaping maw of Archie the alligator. Then, one day, he made the mistake of chewing the hell out of the leg of Tyrone McGee, a sewer worker from Watts, who was sick and tired of being pushed around all his life and wasn't about to take any crap even from an alligator. Not in *his* sewer, he wasn't.

Tyrone McGee did what he had always done when bullies picked on him. He went and got his big brother. In this case, big brother was Leonard Leggett, the lackluster cop, who reluctantly followed the bleeding sewer worker back down there in the dark and, shaking like a mouse on a Popsicle stick, dispatched Archie to the Big Sewer with three volleys from his Ithaca shotgun, giving Tyrone McGee a chance to grin malevolently at the belly-up sewer monster, and say, "Catch you later, alligator."

That same lackluster cop would make an insignificant bureaucratic decision which would decide the very destinies of four people: Madeline Whitfield, Philo Skinner, Natalie Zimmerman and A.M. Valnikov.

Millie's ex-dog handler, driven by anger for the massage parlor hussy, went for the Rolls-Royce three times. Each time a parking attendant came running by and Philo Skinner was forced to retreat to the safety of the street.

So, as destiny is often decided by tiny vagaries of fortune, the dog was not stolen from the car. If she had been taken from the car, it would have been, technically speaking, a burglary from auto, and would have been handled by the auto theft detail at Hollywood Station. (Policemen, ever the civil servants, have been known to get in screaming battles over who has to work on a crime report which will entail only a phone call, and a notation which reads: "No suspects. Investigation continued.") The parking lot attendant swore to Officer Leonard Leggett that no one got within a hundred feet of that Rolls-Royce, so it was correctly deduced by the lackluster cop that the dog got out of the car on her own. It was incorrectly deduced that the dog got lost. And since lost dogs don't require a written report, Leonard Leggett was about to go lethargically on his way. Except that Millie Muldoon Gharoujian came jiggling out of the Brown Derby with two studs young enough to be her grandsons. And with much more interest in the young studs than in the fact her schnauzer was gone, she said to Leonard Leggett, "Look, kiddo, I got more invested in that pooch than you *made* in the last five years. Now write me out a police report so I can get my insurance company to pay me a *little* dough anyway."

So Leonard Leggett, the lackluster cop, reluctantly penciled out a quick "unknown suspects" theft report to mollify Millie, and since thefts that take place on commercial property such as restaurants are routinely given to business burglary investigators, like Valnikov and Natalie Zimmerman . . . destiny.

The little terrier had spotted Philo Skinner on his first loping, crouching try for the Rolls-Royce. Philo was peeking up over the hood of a red Mark V when Tutu saw him. She hadn't seen her former handler in months and went wild with joy. Tutu had always loved Philo madly.

"Tutu! Hello, Tutu!" Philo whispered, squatting on the asphalt in his sweat-stained, white leisure suit.

Then he had to beat a skulking retreat when he saw another parking attendant coming his way.

After a few moments Philo came slinking back, sweat sticking in his lank dyed hair, all elbows and knees and bony shoulders, crouching behind a gray Mercedes 450 SEL, dizzy in the afternoon sun.

Then still another parking attendant with long floppy blond hair came hotfooting it across the parking lot and Philo began another gasping lope, his imitation gold medallion beating a bruise on his frail chest.

He was determined on the third try, pouring sweat, knees aching from all the squats, eyes raw from peeking over the shiny tops of Jaguars and Cadillacs like a movie Indian. His poor ragged lungs wheezed.

"Tutu! Come, Tutu!" he gasped. "Come to Philo!"

The little dog was berserk now, barking, growling, crying. Leaping up and grabbing the ledge of the open car window, holding herself against the glass, head and shoulders out the window, feet kicking and scratching, only to fall back inside.

Then Philo Skinner eyeballed another one of those tireless frigging kids slapping across the parking lot in his tennis shoes, and he was off again on his last scuttling painful retreat. He knew he was finished.

Five minutes later, Philo Skinner was sitting on the curb at Hollywood and Vine wheezing and creaking, wiping the sweat from his draining face with the sleeve of his ruined polyester jacket. He wanted to cry. He was thinking seriously about giving up this life of crime before it started, when he heard the shrill, ecstatic, *beautiful* bark.

She leaped on his back, nibbling, licking, yapping with purest joy.

"Tutu!" Philo cried.

Philo Skinner hugged the terrier against his heaving chest, and jaded Los Angeles motorists figured it was just another kinky Hollywood freako when they saw a man sitting on the curb kissing a little dog passionately on the mouth.

6

Siberia

"Uh, would you like to drive, Natalie?" Valnikov asked when they finally got their paper work arranged and began to make their calls on burglary victims.

"Hooker didn't even give me a chance to get my pending sex cases together," Natalie grumbled as she opened the passenger door of the stripped-down, tan Plymouth police car. "Just gave *my* sex cases to somebody else."

"We once had a terrible sex case," Valnikov said, sliding in behind the steering wheel. "Spring of 1953. Near the end of the war. The Reds sent in two whores with V.D. Almost wiped out our whole company. They say there's a new strain of V.D. going around now."

Natalie lit a cigarette and sneered at Valnikov's puny humor. But she saw nothing in those red and watery eyes. Nothing. Was he speaking without guile?

That was the thing about Valnikov. Nothing seemed to follow. In his short time in Hollywood Detectives he hadn't made any friends at all. His old crony, Clarence Cromwell, said he was just absent-minded these days. You talked to him and he answered, but you never knew what kind of an answer you'd get from the turkey. They said he was bombed, swacked, bagged. By noon? She wasn't sure if it was booze. She wasn't sure of anything about him except that he was the non-sequitur king of the whole goddamn police department.

"How many calls do we have to make?" Natalie groused, settling on the well-worn passenger seat of the detective car.

"Oh, not too many," Valnikov said affably. His necktie was still askew and his cinnamon hair was fluffing up from the ridiculous combing he'd given it earlier.

"I never thought it would come to this," she sighed, thinking about the new assignment. "Maybe we can have a big day, huh? Maybe we can recover a stolen typewriter table and return it to the owner. Business burglary. Glorified furniture movers."

"I was a furniture mover for a year after I got out of the marines," Valnikov said pleasantly, blinking and wiping his watery eyes on the sleeve of his suitcoat. "Lot of Korean vets looking for jobs then. I was lucky to get a job on the police department. I have a brother, he couldn't find a job for eight months after World War II. He wasn't so lucky."

Natalie lit a cigarette and decided to get the partner-to-partner biographies over with. Ought to be able to dispense with his life history with about three questions. Then she could give hers: two divorces, one daughter away at college. The police department, because it's the best-paying job she could ever have, and she likes it well enough even though the brass does its best literally and figuratively to screw the policewomen every chance they get. And so forth.

She didn't smoke a cigarette, she *sighed* it. Sigh in the smoke angrily, sigh it out sadly, all the time pitying her luck. Why *me?* she asked her Friz.

"I'm divorced. I hear you are too. Live alone, huh?"

"Oh, no," he answered, driving exasperatingly slow through the noontime Hollywood traffic. "I live with Misha and Grisha."

"Your kids?"

"No. I don't live with my kid anymore. He lives with his mother in Chatsworth."

"Too bad. How old?"

"Forty-four."

Jesus Christ! She always had to look at the rummy to see if he was putting her on. He just drove aimlessly, blinking his sad patient eyes.

"My father used to be amazed by all the luxury in Hollywood in the old days. But it scared him because he was an immigrant."

"Is your father still alive?" Natalie said, not really giving a shit.

"No, my father died before my older brother was born."

"What did you say?"

"I said the Hollywood traffic scared him, but the Russian churches are mostly here in Hollywood."

Jesus Christ! The guy's brain is marinated! Shriveled! Sanforized!

But she couldn't smell the booze on him. It must be dope. Jesus Christ! This rummy's a doper!

Natalie snuffed out her cigarette and tried to make it easier for him, as a test. "Valnikov, I wasn't asking how old . . . your father couldn't possibly die . . . never mind that. A moment ago I wasn't asking you how old *you* are. We were talking about . . . you said you live with Misha somebody . . . I thought it was your kid."

"Oh!" he smiled. "No, you asked if I live alone. I said I live with Misha and Grisha. I think that's how you got confused."

"I got confused."

Then he turned right on Gramercy and began humming something she didn't recognize. He drove five miles an hour. He didn't speak. He hummed in a hoarse baritone.

"Valnikov."

"Yes?"

She was turned toward him now, looking and talking to him as carefully as she would to an axe murderer.

"How old are Misha and Grisha? No, wait. Who *are* Misha and Grisha? These people you live with?"

"Oh. Well, do you want me to answer the first question first?"

"The first question. Yes, answer the first question."

Valnikov took the longer tail on Clarence Cromwell's necktie and carefully wiped both eyes. The road was blurring.

"Pardon me," he said when he'd finished. "Well, let's see, Grisha is eight months old. I'm sure of that because I got him when he was a little baby. I fed him with an eyedropper. He used to squeak . . ."

"Valnikov . . ."

"And Misha, I'm just not sure about. I think Misha is older because he was full grown when I got him. Well, I just wouldn't like to say for sure."

"Valnikov," Natalie said, positive now that he was still swacked from the night before, wondering if she should make him drive right back to the station for a breathalyzer exam. They couldn't make her work with him if she could prove he was drunk on duty! "Valnikov, I was asking about . . . you said you have a son."

"Oh, yes. His name's Nick."

"And how old is Nick?" It was a challenge now.

"My Nick is twenty. I never see him anymore."

"Why?"

"I think he doesn't like me. His mother doesn't like me."

"Valnikov?"

"Yes?"

"Do Misha and Grisha like you?"

"Of course! *They* like me a lot. I think Grisha likes me more. Misha only knows one word and I've tried hard to teach him lots of words. He just learned that word when I burned myself on the stove one night and I yelled '*Gavno!*' That means shit. Hard as I tried to teach him other words, he goes and picks up a bad one on his own. Just like a real kid would."

"Yeah. He talks and he's not a kid, right?"

"Of course not," Valnikov said, looking puzzled. "He's a parakeet. Green."

"Uh huh," said Natalie, her mind racing, wanting the day to end in a hurry so she could run to Hipless Hooker with as much of this bullshit as she could remember. He was a doper. He was loaded right now. Speed maybe. Or coke. This was perfect!

"And Grisha is . . ."

"Grisha's beautiful." Valnikov smiled.

"Wait a minute, wait a minute," Natalie said, raising her glasses and massaging the bridge of her nose. "I mean what . . . kind . . . of . . . *creature* is Grisha?"

"Oh, he's a gerbil," Valnikov said. "Didn't I say that?"

"You didn't, Valnikov. No, no, you really didn't!" Then she said, "What's a gerbil?"

"A little rodent, indigenous to southern Russia. I'm indigenous to northern Russia. At least my mother and father were indigenous."

Now she was excited with what she'd deduced. He had had no partners since his assignment to Hollywood Investigative Division. He'd been handling business burglary cases on his own, and keeping to himself. There was a damn good chance that nobody but she knew that he was a doper. Non sequitur, my ass. This dopey bastard couldn't string together one question and answer. They'd put him on the wall. Shake him down. Empty his pockets. Would they find Quaaludes? Or hash? That's it! He was fried on hash oil! He was hearing his own questions somewhere. Who knew from where?

Siberia. The questions today were coming from a frozen wasteland. The Siberia of his mind. This was a bad day. He knew last night of course that if he drank nearly a fifth of Stolichnaya, well, he would have a hard time today linking sentences together, understanding what people said to him. People would say things and he would hear them, but on these bad days it was so very hard to put the picture in focus. There were little motes of light, the shimmering dots when a flashbulb pops. Like when they photograph a corpse. There would be a picture emerging there among the dots. He could almost get it, and if he did, well, then everything would start to make sense. But then someone would say something to him, talk to him like Natalie was talking to him now, and the shimmering sparkly picture would fade. The Great Secret would not be revealed. Not today. Stolichnaya. Too much vodka. But it was almost as bad other times too.

She was talking to him.

"I'm terribly sorry," Valnikov said, smiling that patient, watery-eyed, vacant smile. "What did you say?"

She had removed her glasses. She was pretty without her glasses, he thought. She was pretty with her glasses, he thought. It might be good to have a partner again. He forgot how long it had been. He truly wasn't sure right now if it was one month or one year.

"I asked," she said slowly, "if you were *sure* Misha and Grisha were boys? You refer to them in the masculine gender."

Now that, she thought, was the toughest question she had thrown at him all morning. Let's see how he handles it.

Valnikov's brow wrinkled, and he chewed his lip for a second and scratched the wild cinnamon hair curling over the frayed collar of a white dress shirt. His coat flapped open when he scratched his ribs. Jesus Christ! His inside coat pocket was repaired, not with thread, but with metal *staples.*

"I'm sure that Grisha is a boy," he answered finally. "I'm not really positive about Misha." He looked at her with grave blue eyes and thought that if you look very closely you can see a gerbil's dick, but not a parakeet's peter. But he couldn't say that to her.

"I see," Natalie said.

"Well now," Valnikov said cheerfully. "Shall we make our first call on a burglary victim?"

It was an interminable work day for Natalie Zimmerman. Hollywood had never looked seedier. Even the downtown area, "the sewer" as the cops called it, had never looked this bad to her. She had long since decided that Hollywood is a slum. At least parts of it. The "swells" of filmdom's Golden Age would be shocked: massage parlor girls flaunting their wares in doorways and windows. Dirty book stores. Clean book stores. More dirty book stores. Magazine stands, mostly dirty. Trolling homosexuals, both butch and queen. Jockers in leather and chains. Hustling black pimps. Listless whores, all colors. Paddy hustlers, pigeon droppers, pursepicks, muggers. Don't walk the Boulevard at night and expect to see Robert Redford, baby. Hoo-ray for Hollywood!

Business burglary. She despised it. A public relations job. Ought to hire the Rogers and Cowan Agency. "Unknown suspects broke into victim's place of business using a half-inch screwdriver. Property missing: IBM Selectric typewriters." Sell like hell. Every "honest" businessman in town will lay two hundred on a runny-nosed hype, no questions. Roll of stamps: same thing. Easy to peddle. Got to take a discount but what the hell. Took the office petty cash of course. Maybe took an adding machine if he was big and strong. Those goddamn IBMs are heavy. Same old bullshit, over and over. Why the masking tape? The scumbag dropped it. Uses it to tape the window when he breaks it out to reach inside. No falling glass. Watch out for scumbags who carry masking tape, dearie. They can also tape up your little mouth and eyeballs and then start operating *your* Selectric. (Why scare the shit out of the victim? Because she was so *miserable,* that's why.) Sixty-six thousand burglaries in this town last year, lady. No, that doesn't count car theft. That doesn't count robbery. That doesn't count half a dozen other kinds of larceny. That's just burglary. Just breaking and entering! How many detectives work burglary? Oh, in the whole damn city about two hundred, maybe. How's your math? Two hundred divided into sixty-five thousand is what? Not to mention the other larcenies the same dicks handle. And the arrestees they have to process. And the long days in court. *Solve* the crime! *Recover* your stolen property? How's your math, lady?

A dreary endless slogging death march. That's business burglary with Valnikov. Unknown suspects. Who ever saw a burglar? Like fighting ghosts. And Valnikov. A ghost himself.

Gas stations. A guy doesn't pay for his gas, peels out and beats the proprietor out of eight bucks. Who gets the crime reports? Business burglary. Trouble is there's *always* a suspect. The victims get his license number. Run the license, call the suspect. Where was your car Tuesday night at ten o'clock? Your son, Harvey? Uh huh. And how old is the little zit-faced, coke-snorting, hash-smoking son of a bitch? Seventeen? Yes, well he didn't pay for his gas at Seymour's Shell Station, corner of . . . Yes, that's right, little Hah-vey just didn't pay. (God, she hated transplanted New Yorkers.) No, no mistake. They took his license number. Yes, you take care of it with Seymour and we can close out our report. We won't arrest Hah-vey this time. Thank you very much.

A collection agency. Furniture movers. Paper shufflers. Business burglary. What a thrill. And this was only the *first* day! Why *me!*

But Valnikov didn't mind. He leisurely passed the time of day with every victim of every petty crime report they handled. Natalie was mad enough to spit. Especially, when they were an hour and a half past what should have been their lunch break and he gave twenty minutes to the sixty-five-year-old proprietor of a second-hand store on Western Avenue. She'd been burglarized three times in five weeks. Every time she picked up some decent merchandise, a hit-and-run window smash.

"Sergeant," the Filipino woman said, "I can't go on like this. I can't make enough to pay my utilities even. Do you think I could get a job with the police, maybe?" She brightened and said, "Maybe a crossing guard for school kids. I ain't too old, am I?"

"No, I don't think so. I see lots of old people," Valnikov said. "I can check. I can get an application sent to you."

Natalie was leaning against a ramshackle dress rack, smoking, bored stiff, when she heard the tea pot whistle. She walked over to turn it off and saw a dish behind the hot-plate burner. There was a fork on the plate and what looked like corned beef hash. There was a half-empty can of dog food beside the hot plate.

The woman saw Natalie looking at it and scurried behind the counter, pushing everything back and covering it with a towel.

"My dog . . . my doggie's outside . . . I . . . well . . ."

"Yes, of course, Mrs. De la Cruz," Valnikov said, with his weary nod of the head. "I was telling Sergeant Zimmerman just this morning that every business person around here should have a watchdog. Wasn't I, Natalie?"

And Natalie had a dash of resentment to add to her frustration because a rummy like this saw something quicker than she did.

"I'll be very grateful if you could send me the application, Sergeant," she said to Valnikov, her dentures clicking. "I could dye my hair, pass for fifty-five, if there's an age limit."

"You just let me check on it for you, Mrs. De la Cruz," Valnikov said, patting her hand.

"I used to be an actress," she said to Natalie. "I can play any Asian. Trouble is, not too many good parts for Chinese, Japanese anymore. Lost my SAG card even. No Japanese parts."

Valnikov was reminded of something when she said "Chinese." There it was again. The sparkly flash bulbs. The picture almost formed. An Asian doctor. The morgue? He heard snatches of conversation. Chinese . . . Japanese . . . Japanese parts? Sony? Panasonic? Was her television on the blink?

"It's time to go, Valnikov," Natalie said, grabbing her partner's arm, as Mrs. De la Cruz looked questioningly at the confused detective.

"You won't forget to call me, Sergeant?"

"No ma'am, I won't," Valnikov said over his shoulder. "I think you'd make a super crossing guard."

"I'm getting hungry, what say we grab a bite," Natalie said after they got back in the car. She realized she had almost two hundred minutes left in this endless first day.

"Fine with me," Valnikov smiled. "Where would you like to go?"

"Well, I'd like to go to Sergio's Le Club, but I understand they're having another Save Harry Whatzisface party there today," she snorted. "Every guilt-ridden Hollywood liberal will be there. And that's just about all of them. Or we could . . ."

"Who's Harry Whatzisface?"

"The guy who played in *Deep Throat*. Don't you even read the entertainment section of the paper?"

"No."

"Hollywood folks stomping for our civil liberties and the creative freedom of all artists? You know, so Linda Lovelace can go down on Harry and Harry can go down on Linda and Big Brother can stop repressing us and King Kong can bugger Godzilla? Don't you read the paper?"

"Deep Throat was the guy in the Watergate case, wasn't he?" Valnikov answered.

"Valnikov, have you ever seen a porno movie?"

"No, I haven't been to a movie in, oh . . . When was *Nicholas and Alexandra* out?"

"Several years."

"I haven't been to a movie in several years."

"What do you do with your time?"

"I listen to music. Or I go to a basketball game."

"Start the car and let's go eat, Valnikov."

"Oh, yes, sorry." He started the Plymouth, flicked on his turn signal, gave an arm signal, looked out the window craning his neck, then pulled into traffic at three miles per hour, while Natalie rolled her eyeballs. He turned on the blinker, made an arm signal, changed into the curb lane and stopped. "Did you decide where you want to eat?"

"Well, since we probably can't get an 'A' table at Chasen's and my favorite maître d' isn't at the Rangoon Racquet Club anymore, and since we're six days from payday and I've got about three goddamn dollars in my purse, what say we have a pizza?"

But he was wandering again. The sparkling lights were shimmering. He was trudging across the great trackless Steppes. A wasteland. The picture was dappled, formless. He saw . . . a rabbit in the snow.

"Would you say that again, please?" he mumbled.

"Pizza. Let's get a pizza." She couldn't keep her eyes off him. Couldn't wait to talk to Hipless Hooker. She was positive now that it wasn't speed. And it wasn't barbiturates. His pupils weren't dilated or contracted. No, he was spaced out on some sophisticated drug she wasn't familiar with. Some kind of dope that didn't take his pupils up or down.

Ten minutes later they were parked under a pepper tree near the observatory silently eating their pizzas. Still she watched him. He'd been raised by someone with table manners all right. It was rare to see a man eat anything with such delicacy, let alone a pizza. He chewed small bites thoroughly and dabbed at his lips with a paper napkin when there was nothing there. He was solicitous, asking whether she would like a bit more cream or sugar for her coffee. Whether her pizza was all right. Isn't it going to be a lovely day despite the smog? Then: "Were you married a long time, Natalie?"

"Which time, first or second?"

"Oh," he shrugged. "Let's say the second."

"What is this, a contest?"

"I was married sixteen years," he smiled, careful to swallow his food before speaking.

"Good. You win."

"Pardon me?"

"Never mind," she said, waving at the air. "I was married three years the first time and two years the second time. My daughter's from the first. My second didn't want me to be a cop and tried to make me quit. I stayed a cop. I have a twenty-one-year-old daughter away at college and I don't have a parakeet or a Goebbels."

"That's gerbil," he corrected her gently. "A soft g as in *gentle.* Goebbels was a Nazi who killed lots of Russians. My little gerbil is a Russian rodent. Would you like more cream for your coffee?"

"No, thank you."

"Would you like to see a movie?"

"What?"

"I gather you like movies. I asked if you'd like to see a movie."

"Now?"

"Of course not." Valnikov smiled, sipping at his tea.

It looked ridiculous! He was a hulking man with a broad Slavic forehead and he drank his tea like a grand duchess, for God's sake.

"What movie're you talking about?"

"Oh, whatever you like," he shrugged. "I don't know what's playing. You mentioned *Deep Throat.*"

"*Deep Throat!* You're asking me to go with you to a porno movie!"

"Oh, I thought that's what you liked to see. You don't want to see *Deep Throat?*"

"I *saw* it. Twice. On dates with horny policemen who insisted. Jesus Christ, put a cigarette in your mouth, Valnikov!"

"Pardon?"

"Typical macho cop. A freebie cup of coffee, a cigarette, and a hard-on. I was starting to think you were a little strange. I guess you're normal enough."

"Pardon?" Now Valnikov had lost the thread again. It was unraveled and he hadn't the faintest idea why she was upset, why she was raising her voice.

"You've been working this division one month," she smirked. "We've hardly said more than a good morning before today. We've been partners for, oh, four hours. And you think you can dance me into a porno movie for a nooner?"

"Did I say something wrong?"

"Oh, Jesus Christ!" she sneered, shoving the paper cup into the bag. "Let's finish handling our calls."

Valnikov sipped the rest of the coffee but his lunch was ruined. He knew for certain that he had offended her but didn't know why. He was troubled and didn't know what to say to make it right. The sparkling motes were swimming. He did the only thing he could. He started all over again. "Natalie, would you like to see a movie?"

She whirled in her seat, eyes narrowing behind the over-sized glasses. She viciously brushed back a wisp of frizzy, buckskin hair.

"Do you mean *now?*"

"Oh, no. We're on duty. I meant tonight. Or tomorrow night. Or sometime. It doesn't matter. I haven't seen a movie in . . . I don't know how long."

"You don't know how long."

"No."

"Several years. Since *Nicholas and Alexandra.*"

"Yes, so I can wait. Maybe next month sometime?"

Oh, shit. She turned back and watched the foot traffic sliding by in the shimmering smog. She lit a cigarette. "Valnikov, do you want to take me to a porno? I mean a dirty movie? Is that it?"

"Well, I'd rather *not* see a dirty movie," he said, wiping his watery eyes on his shabby coatsleeve. "But if that's the kind of movie you like, I'm willing. I just thought maybe you were lonely and I felt sorry for you."

"How dare you!" Natalie screamed, in consummate frustration, making Valnikov hit the brakes, almost causing a van to rear-end them on McCadden Place. "How *dare* you say that to me! You don't even *know* me!"

"Did I say something wrong?"

"Wrong! You feel sorry for *me!* You want to take *me* to a porno house!"

"No, I've never even *been* to a porno house. I just gathered that's what *you'd* like. I mean, you said two policemen took you to this dirty movie so I thought maybe you liked it, and, well, if that would make you happy, I just thought . . ."

Natalie was going to scream when they got a radio call.

"Roger that, Natalie," he said, wondering why she was yelling.

"What . . . what . . ."

"We just got a call," he said. "Roger it, please."

"6-W-232 roger," she mumbled into the mike, and now she was looking dazed.

"Western and Romaine, see the vice officer. That was the call, Natalie. Wonder why they want a burglary team? Oh well, that's what makes our job interesting, eh?" He looked at her and smiled and blinked, his cinnamon hair blowing back from the gust of wind as he suddenly "speeded" up the detective car. Now they were going fifteen miles an hour.

The vice cop was about twenty-five years old. He wore his auburn hair in a huge Afro which he had done once a month at a beauty parlor on Sunset where he got a police discount. He was shirtless in a leather vest and wore five strands of beads around his neck. He recognized Natalie but didn't know Valnikov.

"You working burglary?" He leaned in the detective car window from the street side.

"Whaddaya got?" she asked.

"Maybe something for you. There was a pawnshop burglary about three weeks ago. Down on Melrose, I think."

"Western Avenue," Valnikov said.

"Yeah, that's right, on Western," the vice cop said, nodding his shaggy head. "They ripped him off for some shotguns, one a double-barreled custom job with silver inlay . . ."

"Mother-of-pearl," Valnikov said.

"Mother-of-pearl?"

"Yes," Valnikov said.

"Was it your case?" the vice cop asked.

"No, I just remember the report."

"And you remember for sure it was mother-of-pearl?"

"Yes," Valnikov said, wiping his eyes.

"Okay, guess this ain't from that job." He held up a silver-inlaid, double-barreled twelve-gauge, the walnut rubbed smooth from years of loving care. "I'll just book it and let robbery try to make it on some other job. Just thought it might have been from that pawnshop burg, is all."

"What's happening here anyway?" Natalie asked. There was an ambulance in front and a crowd of onlookers from the surrounding homes. There were seven men being loaded into the black-and-whites. "Somebody get shot?"

"No, but he might wish he had," said the vice cop.

"Catch the suspect?"

"Yeah, *he's* the suspect," the vice cop said, pointing to the blanket-covered man being bandaged by a paramedic as two policemen helped lift the gurney into the ambulance. "Thought he was Jesse James. Decided to take down a crap game that floats in this apartment about every Wednesday. We been staking out next door since this morning, and damned if Jesse James here doesn't come crashing in the room just as we were about to make a little gambling bust. He leaps up on the table and fires his twelve-gauge into the ceiling to get all the players' attention. I was next door alone, almost messed my pants. While I'm trying to call on the CC unit for some help, he gets carried away with scaring everybody. He's not satisfied that the players're shaking and begging so he fires *another* round to make them move a little quicker."

"And that's just a double-barreled shotgun," Natalie observed.

"Yeah, and one by one, all the players noticed that too. They say the last thing old Jesse James says is 'Uh-oh.' And that may be the last thing he ever *does* say. They got through with him, his head squirms around like a water bed. Well, does your heart good once in a while to see justice done. Makes you think God ain't dead after all."

When they were back on Vine Street stopped behind a fender-bender traffic accident, Natalie said, "Did you really remember that Western Avenue pawnshop burglary?"

"Yes," Valnikov said.

"You must read hundreds of burglary reports."

"Yes."

"What was unusual about this one?"

"Nothing," he shrugged, at last his eyes starting to clear from the havoc of Russian vodka.

"Then how do you remember?"

"I always remember crime data. I don't know why. I've been a detective so long I just seem to remember."

Memories. Twenty-two years a policeman. Fifteen of them working homicide downtown. Homicide. The first team. The varsity. Shootings, stabbings, rapes, mayhem. Torture murder, extortion murder, kidnap murder, sex murder. Domestic murder: husbands, wives, mothers, fathers. Who said a father never killed his seed? Valnikov knew better. But mothers were more innovative murderers of little children. Lots and lots of child murders. Whodunits, howdunits, whydunits. The Stinker Squad. Corpses. The faces of corpses: bewildered corpses, winking corpses, grieving corpses, laughing corpses, screaming corpses. There was no predicting the expression a corpse would wear to eternity. At times there were just chunks of corpses, slivers of corpses. Sometimes just heads. Remember Homer from Hollenbeck?

Sergeant Ambrose Schultz was the cutup of the Stinker Squad. He loved a good joke. They had been trying to help solve a headless whodunit in Hollenbeck Division for two months. Finally someone informed on a woman who poisoned her unfaithful boyfriend named Homer, and who beheaded the corpse *with a shovel,* which took an hour of relentless hacking but got rid of her tension. Then she preserved the lover's head in a crock of formaldehyde. (Why? they asked. You often discovered the who and the how but less often the why. Who can say why? Why anything?)

Homer's head was hanging around the squad room for a few days after they found it. The preserving fluid had long since leaked, and now Homer's head was putrefied, blackened, engorged.

Homer took with him to eternity the face of a gorilla.

One day Ambrose Schultz happened to notice that clerk typist, Lupe Rodriguez, had made her weekly trip to the panadería and bought four pounds of delicious stone-ground, corn tortillas, handmade in Boyle Heights by Mexican women squatting over brick firepits. Ambrose stole the tortillas out of Lupe's sack when she went to the john, and he left Homer's head inside. Lupe Rodriguez, a perennial dieter and incurable nibbler, was right in the middle of reading a sexy crime report when she reached down inside the sack to nibble. It was odd. The tortillas felt soggy. And *hairy?* They say her shrieks could be heard clear up in the chief's office. It was the best joke Ambrose Schultz pulled that year.

Until Ambrose happened to be handling a homosexual murder wherein one lover strangled the other one and whacked off his penis with a handsaw. Rodney, the demented survivor, said he kept Claude's ragged frontispiece in a fishbowl on his mantel to show his friends at a dinner party he gave after his lover had disappeared. The dinner party was not a success in that the first guest to examine the strange floating fish ran screaming to a telephone. Rodney couldn't understand it because he had spent a fortune on stuffed squab and party favors. He later told detectives he couldn't bear to part with that part of Claude just yet, and besides, he thought the penis in a pickle jar would be tacky, but in a fishbowl it would be a *great* conversation piece. The fishbowl and contents ended up in the care of Ambrose Schultz. Poor Lupe Rodriguez transferred to Personnel Division after *that* one. Memories.

"I said we've still got several victim contacts to make."

"Pardon me, Natalie?"

"I was talking to you."

"Sorry," he said, smiling pleasantly. "We have some more victims to contact, I think."

And that was the way the day went. Almost. The difference being that at 6:00 p.m. that day, when she should have been off-duty—when she should have been home in the bathtub, sipping a gin and tonic, listening to Englebert Humperdinck sing his heart out—she was cowering on a napless carpet of a dingy apartment corridor, trying her best to keep her sphincter muscles tight and her bladder in control. (Oh God, I'm not wearing panties today!) For the first time in her entire police career she was on the verge of being shot to death. And it was all her fault. Not Valnikov's. *Hers.*

The call came at 4:20 p.m. It's never a call exactly, it's a scream. First the hotshot beeper over the radio. Then a shrill voice: "All units in the vicinity and 6-A-39! Officers need help, Lexington and Vermont! Shots fired! *Officers under sniper fire!*"

And then, heaven help any pedestrian or motorist within a hundred feet of a police car. Coffee cups splashing in the street. Dozing policemen jerking upright. Seat belts click and whir tight. Engines roar, transmissions scream. A hundred yards of burning rubber is smeared on Hollywood asphalt, curb, sidewalk. And, all too often, two police cars (one in compliance with regulations, using siren, another in a hurry to be first, *also* using his siren) collide at a blind intersection and never get to the call.

Probably the only Hollywood unit on the street which proceeded in its original direction was 6-W-232. Natalie was outraged.

"Valnikov, didn't you hear the hotshot call?"

"Yes, of course."

"Aren't you going to roll on it?"

"Well, I hadn't planned to. We're over a mile away in heavy traffic. Besides, there'll be plenty of coverage."

"Well that tears it!" Natalie sneered. "Are you a police officer or not!"

"Do you want me to go to the call? If you do . . ."

"Of *course* I do. Jesus Christ!"

"All right, Natalie," Valnikov shrugged. Then to please her, he stepped on the accelerator. They speeded up to twenty miles an hour. Natalie was beside herself.

"Put your frigging foot in the carburetor!" she yelled.

"All right, Natalie. Calm yourself," he said.

Valnikov looked around cautiously, tightened his grip on the wheel, and speeded up to thirty miles an hour. Natalie gurgled and rolled her eyes.

Surprisingly, there were only four radio cars and one other plain-clothes unit at the scene when they arrived. Still, it was bedlam. The radio cars were parked on the curbs, their doors wide open on the street side. Rush-hour traffic couldn't pass down the narrow street and was backed up for blocks. People were on their front lawns, and on balconies of nearby apartment buildings, and hiding behind palm trees. No one wanted to miss the police shooting somebody to death. Or being shot.

One young policeman, hatless, red-faced, was crouching behind his radio car screaming into the uncoiled hand mike. When he was finished he threw the mike into the car.

"Down! Get down!" he screamed at Natalie as she jumped out of the detective car and ran toward the black-and-white, skirt hiked up over her knees, revolver in hand.

"What's going on?" Natalie yelled, eyes ablaze.

Valnikov struggled to get free of his seat belt. He'd never pulled it so tight before. Natalie had startled him into it.

"A barricaded suspect!" the young bluesuit yelled. "Upstairs in the back! He threatened to kill his wife and when she ran out the door he starts popping caps at her! She says he's got an army rifle and three handguns in there!"

"You call for SWAT?" Natalie yelled. They were ten inches apart, screaming into each other's face.

"Yes!" the young cop yelled, spraying her with saliva.

"Is there a sergeant here!" Natalie sprayed him back.

"No!" he screamed.

"Valnikov!" Natalie screamed over her shoulder as he finally got out of the car and came toward them. "Valnikov, you're in charge here!"

"Are you a sergeant?" The young cop sprayed him wetter than Natalie had.

Valnikov couldn't seem to find his handkerchief but he remembered it was soiled from the flow of vodka-induced mucus that morning. He didn't want Natalie to see a dirty handkerchief so he wiped his face discreetly on his sleeve.

"Are you a sergeant!" the young bluecoat screamed again.

"Yes," Valnikov said, wishing everyone would stop yelling. Then he decided he'd better pin his badge to his coat pocket before a young policeman shot him dead.

"Whadda you want me to do, Sergeant!" the young cop yelled.

"Well," Valnikov began, as tactfully as possible, "I was wondering if you could stop spitting in my face? And, Natalie, I think you should wipe the moisture off your glasses. This is a dangerous situation and you've got to be able to see."

"SWAT's on the way, Sergeant!" the young cop screamed. "I've called for detectives and the watch commander! I've called for an ambulance in case we have any wounded! I've . . ."

Valnikov turned away letting the spray strike his left cheek and then he did something Natalie thought extraordinary. He put his hand over the young policeman's mouth. A broad, strong hand. He clamped the lad's mouth shut and held on.

"Please, son," Valnikov said quietly. "I can't hear you because you're hollering so loud. When I let you talk again I want you to try to whisper. Now, whisper to me where the barricaded suspect is."

Natalie watched the young policeman's bulging eyes start to stabilize. His face was reddening, however, because he was having trouble breathing through his nose. He grabbed Valnikov's wrist and nodded. Valnikov released him.

"Thanks, Sergeant, I needed that," he said.

"Oh, Jesus Christ!" Natalie said to her Friz.

"Follow me, Sergeant!" the young cop said, and before Valnikov could grab him again, he was gone, duck-walking across the lawn toward the open door of the apartment building where another policeman crouched, fingering the trigger guard of a shotgun.

"I'm sorry we got involved in this, Natalie," Valnikov said reproachfully as he followed the cop across the lawn toward the ominous opening. Then they heard glass break, which caused everyone, Valnikov included, to fall flat on the pavement by the doorway.

"Son of a bitch aims a rifle out the window every minute or so!" said a craggy cop with a shotgun. "His wife says he's got a semiautomatic rifle and . . ."

"Where's the rest of the policemen?" Valnikov asked.

"Upstairs, second landing," said the craggy cop.

The young cop who screamed so much was crouched behind Valnikov, peeking up at that shattered broken window, his service revolver at the ready. Pointed right at Natalie's temple.

Natalie turned and found herself looking down the black hole of a four-inch Smith and Wesson. She could see the lands and grooves from a glint of sunshine.

"Oh, my God," she said and Valnikov quickly pushed the gun muzzle away. The young cop hadn't noticed a thing.

And then all hell broke loose. PLOOM! PLOOM! PLOOM! A whoosh of air. Windows shattered. A tire exploded.

"Who's shooting?"

"What the hell!"

"The bastard's got a cannon!"

So far, Valnikov noted, nothing unusual had happened. It was a typical barricaded-suspect situation. The kind that rates a small column in the second section of the morning paper, unless a cop gets killed. Then it's front page. So far it was ordinary. Everything screwed up.

A domestic scene. Probably caught his wife cheating. Or she caught him. Maybe the scrambled eggs were too slimy. I love you. I hate you. I love you so much I'm going to kill you. And he tries. He fails. I'm going to kill myself, then. But first of all I'm going to shoot up the goddamn street.

Actually, the berserk gunman yearned for the same things a "sustaining" Junior Leaguer in a Pasadena mansion did: attention, recognition, *celebrity*. He could only get it by playing a scene he'd seen in a thousand movies all his life: He was going out with guns blazing. Watch out, you coppers! Stanley Kravitz ain't going alone!

All of this was going incoherently through Valnikov's mind. Usually, he'd been called in when Stanley Kravitz lay dead, having tired of the game, having put his own rifle in his mouth and fired with his big toe. Valnikov had learned it's hard to fire with the big toe. Sometimes they missed and the side of their skulls cracked off but they lived. On an intravenous diet forever. Never again to complain about slimy scrambled eggs. *Looking* rather like slimy scrambled eggs. Sometimes, like this, Valnikov was there even *before* Stanley Kravitz fired with his big toe. But then a young cop with eyes like balloons would usually put one right in Stanley's ten ring, doing a better job on Stanley than he could have done on himself.

Before Valnikov moved up the stairs toward the upper landing where five policemen with shotguns and revolvers had fired twenty-three rounds through Stanley Kravitz' door, before he tried to quiet down five other policemen with balloon eyes, Valnikov turned to Natalie and said sadly, "Why did you want to come here, Natalie? I *wish* you hadn't insisted on it."

And then Stanley Kravitz (whose real name was William Allen Livingston) opened Act II with an M-14 and pinned everybody inside the building for two hours. And darkness fell.

A command post was set up. The SWAT truck arrived with spotlights. Deputy Chief Digby Bates hovered safely over the building in a helicopter, his teeth clenched in determination, face pressed to the glass, hoping the photographers below had enough light, and telephoto lenses on their Nikons.

It was ten minutes after dark that William Allen Livingston got sick and tired of the noisy police helicopter, and risked leaning out the window to fire up at the chopper. He shot a six-inch shard out of the bubble, causing Deputy Chief Digby Bates to forget about photographers with telephoto lenses and scream: "Let's get the fuck OUT of here!" spraying the pilot with saliva.

And then the situation got totally out of control, and twenty guns responded to the sniper by making a ruin of the side of the building where Livingston had barricaded himself. The police officers trapped inside heard Livingston speak for the first time. He played Act IV the way he'd been taught in Saturday matinees. He said, "I'm coming out, coppers! With guns blazing!"

But before the barricaded suspect could get his guns blazing, a frenzied young cop on the stairwell screamed, "The lights!" And five bluecoats banged away with revolvers at the two wall sconces lighting the narrow hallway now that the sun had set.

Valnikov was momentarily deafened. Natalie was holding her ears. The uniformed cops fired eighteen rounds at the two lights. In the movies one would do. In real life, when adrenaline turns an arm to licorice, eighteen rounds won't do. They were covered with plaster dust. They could hardly breathe from the falling plaster and burning gunpowder. They missed the two lights completely. There was one hole in a lampshade.

They were reloading when Valnikov raised his voice for the first time. He shouted: "Stop it! This is giving me a headache!"

"The lights, Sergeant!" a young cop babbled.

"We're exposed to his fire!" a tall cop added.

"He'll be coming out!" a fat cop promised.

And then Natalie gasped because Valnikov stood, his gun in front of him at the ready, and advanced down the hallway toward the bullet-riddled door of William Allen Livingston, known to Valnikov as Stanley Kravitz, corpse-to-be.

Watching the door carefully, keeping as close to the wall as possible, covered with dust from the bullet-riddled walls and ceiling, Valnikov did something that no one had thought of.

He unscrewed the light bulb.

The hallway was immediately plunged into darkness. One policeman had a flashlight. He trained it on the door when Valnikov returned to his position.

Never one to avoid a cliché, William Allen Livingston yelled again. He said: "I'm coming out coppers and I'm taking some of you with me!"

"Wait a minute! Wait a minute!" Valnikov yelled back. "Let's talk about it. Let me come in and talk to you. I'm sure there's something we can . . ."

When the door flew open, Valnikov threw his heavy body across Natalie Zimmerman. William Allen Livingston lost several ounces of urine and defecation when the fusillade of .38 caliber and .00 buckshot devastated him, but, considering he was struck with twenty-seven lead projectiles, his total weight was increased considerably. The homicide detectives discovered later that the gun he died with was unloaded. He had obviously decided not to take anybody with him. But at least he got one wish. Even though he hadn't shot a cop and didn't rate any more than page thirteen, the siege was so grandiose that it was on the inside front page the next morning.

It made a hell of a flaming explosion, that last volley. One continuous roar in fact, which stayed with Natalie Zimmerman through it all, even while Valnikov, arms around her, led her down the back stairway, through the throngs of policemen, past the reporters, by the command post where Deputy Chief Digby Bates, wearing a flak jacket, was already preparing his statement, his good side facing the television camera crew across the street. Luckily, the detective car was not boxed in by the crowds of laughing, jeering, cheering, Hollywood onlookers who were having a whale of a good time.

There was a Good Humor man double parked beside their detective car selling frozen bananas. He'd busted two stoplights when he heard about the seige on the radio. Last time there was a big deal like this he'd been lucky enough to *be* there when a young rock singer leaped eight stories from the penthouse suite of a record company that wouldn't publish his music. The Good Humor man had strolled through the crowd and made thirty-two bucks selling ice cream and soda pop to all the folks with throats parched from yelling: "Jump, you chickenshit!"

Valnikov waited until the Good Humor man made a triple sale to a guy with two kids. One child sat on daddy's shoulders to see the body better when it was removed.

Natalie got in the car, lit a cigarette and smoked shakily. She couldn't keep her legs still. Nor her chin.

Finally Valnikov said, "Move that ice cream truck. I've got to get out."

"Fuck you, Jack," said the Good Humor man, not knowing Valnikov was a cop. "I'm selling ice cream."

Then Valnikov drew the revolver from his waist holster, pointed it at the astonished ice cream vendor who was holding an ice cream bar in one hand and a fistful of currency in the other.

"If you don't move that truck, I'll put a hole right through your Fudgsicle," Valnikov said.

While the ice cream truck clanked across a driveway with its driver yelling to the bluecoats that he'd found *another* madman with a gun, Valnikov was driving Natalie Zimmerman back toward Hollywood Station.

Finally she said, "Valnikov, where're we going?"

"We're going end-of-watch," he said. "We've had a very long day."

"We've got to go back! We were witnesses! We've got to give our statements!"

Valnikov shook his head and said persuasively: "There were so many policemen, nobody'll even remember us. Besides, what can we say? We didn't fire any shots. Our story isn't important or relevant. A man committed suicide. A dozen policemen witnessed it and helped him do it."

"But . . ."

"Somebody might find out we were at the scene and ask us some questions later. We didn't take part in the man's suicide. Why should we sit up all night while the shooting team interviews and reinterviews, and draws diagrams and takes pictures and . . . well, I think I'm too tired for all that nonsense so I'd just as soon go home, Natalie."

It was a very dark night in Hollywood. For a Friday, the car traffic was not particularly heavy. Of course Hollywood Boulevard and Sunset Boulevard were a mess thanks to the tourists, but Valnikov took the side streets. He drove, as always, ten miles an hour.

Natalie said, "Valnikov."

"Yes."

"I'm sorry I browbeat you into driving to that call."

"Browbeat me?"

"Well . . . we didn't . . . I didn't . . . well . . . you were . . ."

"Natalie, would you like to go to a movie? Not tonight, of course. Maybe next week? Or in two weeks? Maybe you could pick a first-run movie you'd like to see? I haven't been to a movie in . . . I don't know how long."

"Several years," she said, steadying her trembling knees as she smoked. "Since *Nicholas and Alexandra.*"

Then they were on Wilcox, nearing the station. She knew the day-watch crew would be gone home except for the homicide team, there because of William Allen Livingston, deceased. Certainly Hipless Hooker would be gone to get ready for his goddamn voyage with Sinbad Cromwell tomorrow. Even if Captain Hooker were there she couldn't brace him with it tonight. Not now.

Of course, she couldn't go on working with a doper. But she couldn't help thinking of him leading her out through all that horror and chaos when her legs were shaking like . . . and she could not forget his heavy body shielding her from the Big Explosion. He had just thrown himself on her. And never mentioned it. She'd bet the dopey bastard didn't even know he did it. But she knew.

She couldn't tell Hooker tonight. She would have to think about it over the weekend. Tell him thoughtfully, carefully, that Valnikov was unfit for street duty. That perhaps they should make him submit to a search. A terrible, humiliating, degrading search, and find the drug, whatever it was making him behave so . . . so . . .

"Well, I think I'll go home and make myself a Christmas dinner," Valnikov said cheerfully, when they parked at Hollywood Station. "Would you please sign me out, Natalie?"

So . . . crazy!

"But Valnikov, it's January seventh!" Crazy! That's it! Crazy!

"My mother used to bake delicious sweets on Christmas," Valnikov smiled, shambling off in the darkness.

Merry Christmas, she thought. On January 7th. Crazy.

7

The Tragic Muse

On Saturday, January 8th, Madeline Whitfield did something she had never done before: She visited the Huntington Library on a crowded weekend day. She had to do something. It was impossible to sit at home and watch Chester doing his last-minute work with Vickie. She had been over the hill on Friday, prowling through the boutiques, so Beverly Hills was out. It wasn't ladies' day at the Country Club, so golf was out. She had old friends she could visit, but most of their children were home from prep school on weekends and it was . . . awkward. It was always awkward for a single woman. As repugnant as it sounded, she thought about going to the Valley Hunt Club to play some mixed doubles. But no, Saturday the men dominated the courts. A single woman. Discomfiture.

Or she could go to the Hunt Room and *drink*. She opted for the Huntington Library. If only she could have remained thirty-nine forever. If only the Junior League would raise the age limit for *active* members. There had always been something to occupy her there. Dozens of fund-raising projects for everything from planned parenthood to alcoholic rehabilitation.

The library grounds were overrun, not just by the regular crush of tourists and weekend visitors, but by two busloads of children on charter buses. Madeline had to park three blocks away and walk to the gates.

At least the "sustainers" of the Junior League could still be docents at the Huntington Library. Madeline adored taking tenth graders through the art gallery to point out the magnificent collection of French and English works of the seventeenth and eighteenth centuries. She loved to escort even younger children through on the rare occasions it was permitted, children from barrios and ghettos, seeing for the first time idyllic cherubic portraits of children from another time. *The Beckford Children* by Romney. *The Young Fortune Teller* by Reynolds. Children dressed and posed out of period by English artists copying the extravagant whimsical style of seventeenth-century Italians.

The boys and girls from the barrios and ghetto would look at the priceless works of art and follow Madeline through the former mansion of Henry and Arabella Huntington, past Houdon's great bronze, *Diana,* who always disappointed them because the naked woman wasn't built much better than the broad leading them, and what kinda jive-ass bullshit is this when that twat on the statue don't look like no twat I ever seen. And past *Venus,* by Giovanni Bologna (same complaint: nice ass, no twat). Through the main gallery where, voice trembling with emotion, Madeline would show the scruffy band of children the library's most famous painting, Gainsborough's *Blue Boy.*

"A ass-twitchin sissy if ever I seen one," said a young basketball star in a green and yellow apple hat.

Then to Madeline Whitfield's personal favorite, the greatest work of Reynolds and an eternal tribute to the leading actress of the English stage: *Mrs. Siddons as the Tragic Muse.* Madeline would explain to the children in great detail how Reynolds applied his paint to probe and penetrate and reveal the very *soul* of the great actress. Madeline would turn in three-quarter profile when she pointed out the dignity, the nobility in that famous face. Mrs. Siddons staring off with sad dreamy eyes, and pouting lips, and yes, children, some people have even said that if I turn like this, well (Madeline always blushed), that I bear a *slight* resemblance to the lady.

"I kin dig it," the stringbean in the apple hat nodded. "She do look somethin like that dumpy consti-pated broad in the pitcher."

But there'd be no docent tours for Madeline today.

Just a leisurely stroll about the grounds where Henry and Arabella Huntington once lived so sumptuously. Just to make this day pass. Just to avoid thinking about tomorrow, when Vickie would become a *champion.*

Madeline strolled first through the cactus garden where some 2500 species never failed to surprise her though she had come this way perhaps a thousand times. Spined cactus, spineless cactus, giant cactus, creeping cactus. Cactus which flowered at night. *Easter Echinopsis,* with night flowers like trumpets. *Living rock,* a spineless variety which protects through camouflage. *Milk barrel, Cow's horns,* the shaggy *Desert fans,* the massive *Golden barrel* as old as Madeline. The magnificent yuccas, over twenty feet tall.

There was no natural landscape on earth as quixotic as this. An alien landscape. As a child she imagined it as a garden on the moon.

It was *too* other-worldly today. She even passed the Japanese Gardens, wanting to avoid the exotic. She wanted to feel comfortable today. To belong. She headed for the Shakespeare Garden. Madeline needed the reassurance of Elizabethan flowers and the forest of azalea and camellia surrounding the north vista.

Here she felt safe. She'd played hide-and-seek through every path as a little girl, breaking the rules to pluck a pink camellia and pin it in her hair. She could run splashing in the Italian fountain in those days, able to see clear to Mount Baldy every day of the year. That was how she always wanted to remember Old Pasadena: a child doing cartwheels in the grass, surrounded by azalea and camellia, the mountaintops snowy and smog-free and as reassuring as Old Pasadena itself. Before the decline.

There was no place to sit today. Tourists occupied every bench. But there was an escape: Few tourists bothered to walk north by the orange and avocado groves. There wasn't much up there, just the mausoleum, the last vain act of Henry and Arabella Huntington.

Five Japanese tourists were there, taking pictures. She sat on the cool marble bench. It was always cool, the marble of the mausoleum, even in summer. She waited until the tourists left, then climbed the few steps and imagined the pinched dour face of Arabella Huntington, glaring at the world through bottle spectacles, swathed in black, hiding under a black hat anchored by a dozen glinting hat pins. Madeline could imagine Arabella walking these grounds. The incredible story went that she never wanted to see a gardener or servant as she walked, preferring to dream that all the beauty around her was manicured by God. When the hell did they work? As she slept? And there you lie, Arabella. And do you give a damn whether or not Victoria Regina of Pasadena is a champion tomorrow?

Then Madeline Whitfield sat on the mausoleum steps and wiped her eyes because those ghetto and barrio children didn't see a whit of beauty in Lawrence's *Pinkie.* Not a whit. And what would they say if they knew that she would not sleep this night with or without sixty milligrams of sedative, because of an honor to befall a *dog.* Well, it might just make *more* sense to those children than the Gainsborough or Reynolds or Romney she showed them.

They said that Constable's *Salisbury Cathedral* and *View on the Stour* was only the way some old dead white punk *wanted* things to look like, but you know nothin ain't *never* looked like that.

Would her dream for Vickie make any *less* sense to a group of ghetto schoolchildren than Constable's dream? Or Turner's? Or Arabella Huntington's?

Don't laugh at my dream, and I won't laugh at yours, Arabella.

• ● •

On Saturday, January 8th, Philo Skinner spent a frantic, destructive, furtive day at his kennel grooming Tutu and working with her, trying desperately to prepare her in a single afternoon, having to run to the toilet every time the phone rang. No, Mavis, I *won't* be home early. No, goddamnit, there are no little birds here. Call every goddamn one of them. Call Pattie Mae's house if you think I have her here. Call every kid that ever worked for us. Call the fucking chief of police . . . No, wait, just don't call *anybody*. Jesus Christ! I am here *alone* catching up on the book work! And cleaning the shitty kennel because we can't afford Saturday help, and . . . no, don't come, I don't *need* any help. I'll see you tonight. What do I have to do, lay you to prove I wasn't screwing around this afternoon! Yeah, that's right, I *couldn't* do it twice in one day! Bang went the phone on the cradle. He needed an Alka-Seltzer. That cunt! Tongue like a stripping knife. Philo Skinner lit his forty-ninth cigarette of the day and began coughing.

They say the streets of Puerto Vallarta are cobblestone. And that you can see a flower-covered bridge where Richard used to sneak across at night to see Liz when he was still married to the other woman. They say a gringo can live down there like a sultan with a houseful of whores for $200 a month.

"How many months can I live like a sultan, Tutu, with seventy thousand bucks?"

The little dog wagged and whimpered every time he spoke to her.

"I'll tell you, Tutu," he said, trimming her leg furnishings. "Hold still, sweetheart, that's it. I'll tell you, sweetheart, a man can't *live* long enough to spend seventy thousand tax-free American greenbacks. That's how long."

Then he put down the shears and held Tutu's face in his tobacco-stained fingers and said, "I'd take you with me if I could, you know I would."

Then he broke out in a coughing spasm and went to the sink to spit up a massive wad of phlegm. The little schnauzer cried mournfully when he left her side even for a moment. Tutu was the only creature on the face of the earth who *loved* Philo Skinner.

• ● •

On Saturday, January 8th, Valnikov got blind drunk on Stolichnaya vodka. And sat for the better part of the day and night in front of his stereo set listening to Feodor Chaliapin singing the farewell from *Boris Godunov*. When he got too drunk to understand the words he listened to the Osipov Balalaika Orchestra. When he got tired of that he did what he always did before falling unconscious. He listened to heart-breaking Russian Gypsy songs.

Then he lapsed into a deep drunken slumber and dreamed about the rabbit hopping through the snow. He knew there was no escaping the hunter. He knew the hunter would kill the rabbit and cut his throat, and break his jaws, and peel the face back away from the skull with the muscle hissing as it tore in the powerful hands of the hunter. As always, he sobbed while he dreamed.

8

The Cathedral

In many ways the Los Angeles Memorial Sports Arena was not unlike the Russian Orthodox cathedral on Sunday morning, January 9th. Thirty men were crawling all over the arena floor laying a thousand square yards of vivid red carpet and placing stanchions joined by yellow ribbon. Sprays of chrysanthemum and bouquets of carnation and Black Swan gladiolus were for this ceremony as well. Only the incense was lacking. The ikons were certainly there—by the *thousands.*

The ikons wore the faces of Alaskan malamutes, Belgian sheepdogs, Welsh terriers, dachshunds, beagles, Samoyeds, chow chows, pugs and Pekingese.

In addition to ikons there were medals and medallions with the faces of Pomeranians, Dobermans, boxers and Basenjis. Added to ikon and medallion were more secular objects, such as letter openers bearing the likenesses of Vizslas and Brittany spaniels. There were paintings, posters, plaques of bloodhounds, coonhounds, Akitas and bull mastiffs. There were T-shirts, pin-up posters, glow-in-the-dark key chains, cups and plates bearing the faces of collies, poodles, St. Bernards.

The concessionaires were ready for action, all right. One tasteless concessionaire experimenting with plastic rosary beads actually sold several before the sponsors closed him down and banished him. That very day, there were two prayerful exhibitors with those beads, fingering the likeness of a plastic Italian greyhound.

There, in the cathedral of the West Coast dog world, before the light of dawn, with a thousand other souls, was a man infinitely more tense than any dog owner, or any member of the Oakland Raiders or Minnesota Vikings. Philo Skinner had already smoked 13 of what would be a record 105 cigarettes that day.

Philo had been one of the first in line during those brisk predawn hours. But within ten minutes of his arrival, the campers, vans, and motor homes were backed up in a queue of headlights which extended from the west side of the arena to Santa Barbara Avenue. Some of those dog handlers in the trucks chatted breezily on C.B.'s, some sat in the back of their vehicles and drank coffee, read the Sunday *Times*, readied themselves for what would be a long long day for hundreds of people and well over two thousand beasts.

When those vans, campers, and motor homes began roaring onto the floor of the vast arena, Philo Skinner was operating on instinct alone. By rote, he turned off the headlights and drove slowly to his favorite spot on the side of the arena where they showed the terriers. His hands were so slithery he dropped the steel-mesh exercise pens on the concrete floor. A handler next to him offered to help but Philo waved him away, lit a cigarette, sat down in a green canvas director's chair and watched the throngs arriving. There were squads of sleepy janitors who would be kept busy scooping up mountains of dog crap. But where the hell were the food concessionaires? Philo desperately needed some coffee. He was cold. Some judges were arriving already. He'd never been able to figure out why they got there so early. The free-lance photographers who would be snapping pictures all day for the dog magazines were here. The dog owners *paid* to have their pictures taken and *paid* to have them put in the magazines.

The handlers and kennel workers were everywhere. All around him tables and cages were clanging against concrete. Then came the roar of engines as the trucks drove outside after delivering their animals.

Something was different today: a smattering of television sets for Super Bowl XI. Something Philo was counting on if his plan would work to its optimum.

Perhaps the exhibitors were present for something resembling a religious ritual, but the handlers weren't. Many were not about to miss the *other* ceremony taking place across town. In any event, there was not one healthy young giant from Minnesota or Oakland who was as tense, excited and prayerful as the long-legged asthmatic with dyed black hair who was trying to look dog show respectable in a three-button herringbone coat, gray woolen slacks and a paisley tie. Except for white patent-leather shoes, the real Philo Skinner clothing was underneath: the red silk underwear.

Oh, God, *why* didn't he bring another shirt? Philo Skinner, eyes dilated from it all, lungs rattling and creaking, was giving off an odor a whole can of aerosol spray couldn't hide. Philo Skinner had smelled his sweat and the sweat of other men, but the smell he was exuding was something else again: the smell of *fear*.

Somehow, sitting there in his director's chair, mildly paralyzed, Philo seemed more sensitive to the roar of action than he'd ever been. He was detached, drifting, numb, yet his mind was darting about like his dilated gaze. The handler two stations down had a Yorkshire with a touch-up. What would the handler say if Philo were to stroll down there and whisper in his ear, "Okay, dogmeat, lay fifty bucks on me or I'll tell the judge to suck his finger and run it across that bitch's withers. You little shitbag! Think you can pass off that dyed Yorkie? Maybe you can out there, but nothing gets past Philo Skinner! Not today! Philo Skinner's been in this racket thirty years. Philo Skinner's *been* there, baby!"

Better yet, let the Yorkie handler get in the ring, *then* whisper in his ear, "How would you like a suspension for that little dye job? Fuck the fifty bucks. Give me a *hundred,* you stinking little heap of dog shit! Think I don't know? I've *been* there. I'm Philo Skinner, Terrier King."

An exhibitor was sitting with his handler three stations down, frantically ripping through the show catalogue with a pencil, handicapping dog, handler, and judges with as much desperation as any horse player Philo had ever seen at Santa Anita. And here there was no money to be won by the dog owners, only great amounts to be *spent*.

"Hi, Mr. Skinner!" Pattie Mae yelled, clunking across the arena floor in a dead run, lucky she didn't break her dumb neck. Jesus Christ! She was wearing a worn-out cotton blouse, no bra, and a faded, wraparound skirt which barely wrapped around her terrific round ass, pantyless, no doubt. And platform clogs with ankle thongs! Seven goddamn inches high! He had told her not to wear jeans to her first show, to dress *conservatively*. Jesus Christ, she had a *daisy* in her lint-covered hair!

"Gosh, this is exciting, Mr. Skinner!" she said.

"Pattie Mae, take the van out to the parking lot and then come back. It's all unloaded."

"Where do I take it, Mr. . . ."

"Just drive the fucking thing out there and park it anywhere! Lock it up and come back here as soon as you can."

"Yes, Mr. Skinner," she said cautiously, looking at his dilated eyes, perhaps smelling him already.

He was still debilitated by the fear and tension. He lit another cigarette. Every handler around him was already set up. The handlers and their kennel employees were hard at work at the grooming tables. The dogs were being creamed with cholesterol, and the breeds with white coats were being cornstarched. The legs and beards and furnishings were being combed and brushed and trimmed. All around him was the whir of hair dryers, the buzz of electric clippers, the hiss of hair spray. (A no-no but everyone used it with impunity.) The incessant click of scissors and shears. The eleventh-hour show grooming being accomplished.

Then he began to smell the dog shit. The animals were nervous too, and the excrement was runny. Wonder what his own would smell like now? Lucky he hadn't eaten for a day and a half.

This was his *last* dog show, could that be part of it? The last contact with a way of life that hadn't been bad to him. If the truth be known, he loved dogs. Had always loved them, even as an urchin in a Tucson foster home where they ate pinto beans three times a day in the Depression. Even the stray dogs he secretly fed would eat the beans.

From dog shit to the fragrance of roses: white and red and yellow as buttercups. He loved the Santa Barbara Dog Show best. The flowers and grass and gentle loveliness. It reminded him of movies he'd seen. Like the Ascot Races in *My Fair Lady*. He used to dream of marrying a rich exhibitor and showing her terriers at the Santa Barbara show. Wearing a powder-blue blazer and white pants. Sipping from demitasse china. "Mr. Skinner."

"Huh?"

"Uh, Mr. Skinner, shouldn't we be setting up? I mean, we don't have that much time, do we?"

Jesus Christ, she at least could have washed the fucking lint out of her hair!

"Okay," he said, stepping on the cigarette. "Let's go to work and win a few points, Pattie Mae."

Madeline Whitfield glanced at the gangling dog handler with the crazed eyes who babbled ceaselessly to a nervous young girl grooming a Kerry blue. But her eyes passed over them as she strolled around the arena floor, trying to walk off the tension. Many dog exhibitors never saw their animals except at dog shows like these. They spent perhaps thousands of dollars on them and never saw them, because it was infinitely easier to win if the dogs stayed in the kennel with the handlers.

Madeline Whitfield of course was not that kind of dog owner. Not that she wanted to win less—in fact, she was searching for her favorite photographer, prepared to pay anything to get Vickie's photograph in one of a hundred dog magazines—she just didn't like to think of dogs living in a kennel like foster children.

Vickie had the love and care of a real child, and so far it hadn't harmed her chances to win. Madeline was proving that love and maternal care could compensate for the discipline of a kennel-reared champion.

Pattie Mae now had the cowering little whippet on the grooming table. His tail, curled between his legs against his stomach, looked from the side like a second penis. He was so delicate his legs were like fingers. The noose around the trembling animal's neck, attached to the metal arm on the grooming post, was perhaps the only thing keeping him from leaping off the steel table and running through the arena and out the open door. Which of course was what Philo Skinner felt like doing. His voice, almost drowned out by the noises around him, was pitched higher by the fear that possessed him.

"Squirrelly dog, Pattie Mae, that's a squirrelly goddamn dog."

"Yes, Mr. Skinner, I'll just starch his forelegs and . . ."

"Squirrelly! Just like his goddamn owner. I never shoulda said I'd bring him today. I should stick to terriers. He's six months away, training-wise. Look at him cringe. Jesus Christ! Put that dog back in the crate. He's got head trouble. Trouble in his goddamn head. Look at his eyes, Pattie Mae! Look at his eyes!"

But the girl couldn't help looking at Philo Skinner's eyes. They were the same as the whippet's: round, dilated, darting. Shit! The old fart was as scared as the poor little dog. And he smelled. Oh, gross! He *smelled!*

By 8:00 a.m. they'd already started judging the basset hounds in ring number one. The handlers and the low-slung little dogs were queued up tensely as Philo Skinner blundered past in a rush for the men's room. He had suddenly felt as though he'd been given an enema. He wasn't sure he'd make it. He realized he was going the wrong way, turned, and began a lanky loping dash toward the west rest room. He barely made the toilet in time to pass a pathetic little bubble which was all he had in him.

"Get me through the day!" Philo whispered to the god of gamblers and dog handlers. I've been decent to animals all my life! It's got to count for something! Jesus, no one could care for as many helpless unloved dogs as I have and not get *one* break in life. Gimme a break! Philo prayed in that canine cathedral that Sunday morning.

He was so frazzled and numb that when he left the rest room he actually bumped right into a grooming table and was staring eye to eye with an oversized standard poodle done in a continental clip. The enormous lion-colored mane and clipped hindquarters made him resemble a baboon. Philo Skinner was disoriented and giddy and felt for an insane moment that he *was* face to face with a yawning baboon. He tried to get hold of himself when the looming poodle roared in his face, but it was too late. He barely made it back to the toilet to squeeze yet another bubble past his inflamed and screaming hemorrhoids.

By the time Philo Skinner had returned to his grooming area, Pattie Mae had things pretty much under control. She had lost the daisy from her hair and the front of her see-through cotton blouse was covered with dog hair. But she was flush and beaming from the thrill of working her first show.

"Mr. Skinner!" she said when he arrived, looking wan and bleary eyed.

"Yeah, what's wrong?"

"Nothing!" she said, dabbing a little chalk on the beard of the drooling Dandie Dinmont. "It's just that I heard some handlers talking, and did you know that terriers have won three out of the last five Beverly Hills Winter Shows?"

"So what," Philo said, staring at the Dandie like he'd never seen him before.

"Well, jeez, it just shows how popular terriers are with the judges and everybody. I'm so glad I came to work for a kennel that mostly handles terriers and . . ."

"Got a lot a time, Pattie Mae," he said. "Dandies don't show for a while."

"Which ring?"

"Number eight."

It was amazing, he thought, how even now he could rattle off the data of his trade. He could hardly remember his telephone number at the moment, but he knew which ring each terrier breed would appear in and at what time. He was a dog man, for sure. He wondered absently if he'd miss this work just a little bit. He saw the whippet cowering in the corner of the exercise pen. He felt the obsessive need to talk.

"Got to match that dog, Pattie Mae. Match him if I decide to show him."

"Huh?"

"Stick a match up his ass!" he said testily.

"Oh, what for?"

"Jesus Christ, Pattie Mae, look at him! Do you want him to take a shit while I'm showing him in the goddamn ring?"

"How does a match make him . . ."

"Wouldn't *you* want to get rid of a match in *your* ass? Goddamnit, Pattie Mae, sometimes I think you're an idiot!"

But Philo's chastisement of his groomer was interrupted by a panting dog owner from Palo Alto, who was scurrying from one grooming table to the next, eyes more wild and demented than Philo Skinner's. She was over sixty years old, weighed two hundred and fifteen pounds, had a sable fur slung around her red splotchy neck, and wore a flowered hat which was tilted over her nose as she ran. Her voice had risen to a screech when she stopped before Pattie Mae and grabbed the girl desperately by the arm. She held a bichon frisé in her arms. Philo Skinner's expert eye spotted the tiny red spot of menstrual flow under the plumy white tail of the little bitch but Pattie Mae hadn't the faintest idea what was wrong when the puffing woman cried: "Honey, I need help desperately! Do you have a Tampax! Anybody! DOES ANYBODY HAVE A TAMPAX!"

Even before the astonished girl had a chance to reply, the mistress of the bichon frisé was off and running again.

"My gosh," Pattie Mae said to Philo Skinner. "A lady her age? Does she still . . ."

"Never mind, Pattie Mae, never mind. Let's move on to the Kerry blue," Philo said, shaking his head.

And so, with her plumy bottom pointed to the dome of the cathedral-arena, the bichon frisé went bobbing through the crowd in the arms of the owner she hardly knew and whom she was thinking of biting this very minute. A little animal, originally from the island of Tenerife, a darling of the courts, a breed that had led quite a happy life chasing little wooden balls and standing on front paws to the delight of royalty, only to be thrown rudely into the streets and sent rolling along the blood-drenched gutters with the heads of the courtesans. But the bichon frisé had endured. Three hundred years of grit and determination had come down to a search for a Tampax.

Philo Skinner was beginning to wonder. Would it be worth it all down there in Puerto Vallarta? On white sand, under white sun, in white-on-white linen suits? With brown girls, white in the tooth?

With Philo's brown fingers and blackened lungs. He coughed up a frightening gob of phlegm and spit it in a handkerchief which made Pattie Mae want to vomit. Oh, gross! Mr. Skinner, you make me sick! And you think you can fuck me? I'd rather be gangbanged by a pack of Dobermans! Oh, barf!

Then the female voice over the public address system, a voice which was to become familiar and incessant the entire day: "Janitor, ring four. Janitor, ring six. Janitor . . ."

Bring your pooper-scoopers, boys. The dogs are covering the red carpet in a sea of shit. "Janitor, ring ten. Janitor . . ."

Then a crowd of milling bystanders started screaming, and two people were knocked to the floor. A bull mastiff had suddenly gone insane with lust and leaped over his exercise pen, flattening a tiny Norwich terrier bitch. Lunging for all he was worth, the mastiff's huge pink erection overshot the target by a good eight inches. Two groomers were trying to rescue the Norwich, who was doing her damnedest to lift up high enough so the mastiff could get a better angle. If the hot little Norwich could have stood on a box she would have.

"Get that mastiff!" a handler screamed.

"It's not *my* mastiff! It's *your* slutty Norwich!" a groomer cried.

"If that brute hurts my little bitch . . . !" an exhibitor warned.

A matronly dog owner was strolling through with a white toy poodle, minding her own business, when the lust-crazed bull mastiff reacted after the sexy little Norwich was dragged away. He leaped on the woman and began humping her leg for all he was worth while she screamed and threw the fluffy poodle in the air like a soccer ball.

"Get the mastiff!" voices cried.

"Catch the poodle!" other voices cried.

"Knee him in the chest!" a voice from the grandstand advised.

"It always works on my husband!" another promised.

And now the whole west end of the grandstand was having a great time watching the frenzied mob battling the sex-mad mastiff. The woman was down on her back now amid a crowd of handlers wrestling the slobbering brute.

"Don't knee him with *both* knees now, dearie," a hot dog salesman giggled. "Or your next baby might look like J. Edgar Hoover."

The exhausted mastiff finally surrendered to his handler, who carried him out of the arena. This 180-pound champion would live to battle another day, but for now his eyes rolled and tongue lolled and he was carried in the arms of his panting, sweaty handler. The unsheathed pink erection draped futilely over his stomach made Philo Skinner shake his head and sympathize.

"I know how you feel, pal," Philo clucked.

"Is it always this exciting around here, Mr. Skinner?" Pattie Mae asked, blowing dry the Kerry, while Philo looked at his watch and lit another cigarette with the butt of the last.

"Taper the chest hair like I showed you. Damn it, Pattie Mae! You don't want a skirt on a goddamn Kerry blue!"

"Yes, Mr. Skinner."

At 10:00 a.m. Philo Skinner realized he would have to have his mind sufficiently under control to show his first dog in just thirty minutes.

At 10:30, Pattie Mae, her eyes bright with excitement said, "Mr. Skinner, you wanna bait the Kerry with a toy or a ball or some liver?"

"Liver," Philo said, snuffing a cigarette. "This Kerry always works best with liver. Wait a minute, I almost forgot. Check his teeth. That dumbass broad can't resist giving him chocolate cherries everytime she puts one in her own fat mouth."

"Yes, Mr. Skinner," Pattie Mae said, getting the tooth scaler, glancing at Philo from time to time, watching him wipe his sweaty hands on a handkerchief. Unbelievable! Like this was his first dog show!

Philo showed the Kerry like a sleepwalker. He'd always said he could do it in his sleep and he proved it.

"I guess you should always fold the excess lead, huh, Mr. Skinner?" Pattie Mae said as he adjusted his necktie, letting the Kerry smell the liver, preparing to queue up for the show ring.

"Huh?" The voices and sounds of the dog show were a roar in the ears of Philo Skinner. He wiped his forehead and hands again.

"I said, you always fold the excess show lead . . ."

"Yes yes yes. Fold the lead in your left hand, yes."

"By the way, Mr. Skinner, I was wondering, where did the schnauzer come from? Is it a new one of ours?"

"What?"

"The schnauzer bitch."

"The schnauzer bitch?"

"*That* one!" the girl said impatiently, pointing to Tutu, lying unhappily in a crate, looking hopefully at the love of her life, Philo Skinner.

"Oh, *that* schnauzer. Yes, I have a new client. Talked me into . . . into showing the bitch today, but she's not ready, just not ready."

"She's a gorgeous-looking bitch, Mr. Skinner. One of the best I ever seen. What's wrong? Can't she work properly? Gosh, her coat is perfect and . . ."

"Not ready, she's just not ready," Philo blurted. Then he lit his last cigarette before going in the ring. Jesus, this kid! He had to have some kind of plausible story for her. He had overlooked the fact that he'd have someone with him today. It was all so strange, like a dream, this crime business. As though there'd be no one but himself and the schnauzer and the target!

"Pattie Mae," Philo began thoughtfully, "sometimes you have to show fifteen dogs in a day. Sometimes overlapping occurs and you can't be in two rings at the same time. You could actually have to *miss* showing in one of the rings, and that client, that rich client could be sitting up there in the goddamn seats crying in her hankie and threatening to sue, or something. So today, since this is my last . . . since this is your *first* dog show I'm not showing many dogs so I brought along that schnauzer bitch as a favor to . . . it's time to go into the ring!"

"Yes, Mr. Skinner," the girl said quietly, looking into Philo's dilated eyes. "Is there anything I can do?"

"Always remember, Pattie Mae, you communicate with your fingers through the lead. You've got to have great fingers!" He said it as though he were going away and never coming back. "You've got to have great fingers!"

Philo almost panicked for a moment. He couldn't find the huge yellow sign with the red ring number. It was right in front of his face. He almost tripped over a Kerry blue. There was a long file of Kerry blues, yet for a moment he couldn't find the ring! He had to stop and commit a breach of etiquette. He had to smoke one last cigarette just seconds before going in.

A handler he'd never seen before turned and said loftily: "My bitch sneezes from cigarette smoke. Put it out, if you please!"

Philo Skinner had never had a fistfight in his entire life. Philo Skinner was so racked with asthma and incipient emphysema that even Pattie Mae could have beaten him up. Yet he suddenly shocked himself by stepping nose to nose with the other tall handler and saying, "Listen, buddy, if your bitch doesn't like cigarette smoke, then switch to cigars and divorce the cunt!"

Then Philo bumped past the florid handler and was in the ring. Out of the way, you creep! You fag! The *best* go in the ring first. The greenhorns go in last. Out of the fucking way for Philo Skinner, Terrier King!

Then he just toughed it out on instinct. He could hardly hear the applause of the terrier crowd. He concentrated on the Kerry. He wasn't aggressive enough. Maybe if he would growl a little. Christ, the dog was getting old. He had a good steely blue color, though. Where the fuck was Pattie Mae? Keep your goddamn hands off Tutu, you dumb little fucking hippie. Oh, shit, he wasn't even letting the Kerry set its own pace as they walked counterclockwise around the ring. Oh, shit!

He was making the dog move too fast. Another prayer in the dog cathedral. Philo looked up at the steel-beamed ceiling: Let me get through this day and I'll never place another bet! Except maybe on jai alai if they have it in Puerto Vallarta. Do they bet on bullfights?

Pattie Mae meanwhile was fascinated by the miniature schnauzer, and Tutu was dying to get out of the cage and into an exercise pen. She was growling, wagging, hopping around her cage so much she bumped her head.

"Oh, poor thing!" Pattie Mae cried, opening the cage door. "Poor thing. You hurt your little head." And the girl scooped Tutu up into her arms and cuddled her against her face. "You're the prettiest schnauzer I ever seen!"

Then she put Tutu into an exercise pen and gave her a piece of liver which Tutu gobbled gratefully.

The milling throngs of people on the floor of the Sports Arena began flowing toward the food concessions as the morning wore on toward the lunch hour. Philo Skinner was in the ring doing the individual gaiting, "straight-down-and-back." He gaited the dog on his right to correct a slight tendency toward sidewinding. Then he gave an almost imperceptible tug on the lead to bring the head in from the outward line of travel. Even in a state of terror and panic, Philo Skinner was still a dog man.

When the judge trooped the line behind the terrier, Philo, never one to overhandle, reached down and ran his hand over the hindquarter subtly, ever subtly, because this Kerry showed very fine from behind. He noticed that the female handler on the left was staring at the judge. Dumb bitch, he thought. Bad form. Never stare at the judge even if you do have tits like searchlights.

Philo baited the dog subtly with the liver and the dog struck a noble pose. Goddamnit, he was going to get hold of himself and go out with a *win.*

Yet Philo was hardly aware of the burst of applause when his Kerry was named winner's dog, thereby moving closer to his owner's dream of best of breed, for which Philo was promised a $200 bonus.

Two hundred bucks. Best of breed. Shove it, Philo Skinner won't be needing it.

When he got back to the exercise pens, Pattie Mae was leaping up and down on her clogs.

"Wonderful, Mr. Skinner! You were wonderful!"

"Yeah, sure," he mumbled, hardly aware of her young tits jumping, of the look on her face which said: You don't even smell so bad no more, you old champion, you!

Then he saw the empty cage: "WHERE THE HELL IS THE SCHNAUZER BITCH?"

Pattie Mae almost fell on her ass as she whirled so fast in the seven-inch clogs.

"There, Mr. Skinner! I just put her in an exercise pen! She was getting squirrelly and I just . . . There, Mr. Skinner! She's right over there!"

And then Philo Skinner felt all his muscles go limp as he walked over to the wriggling, whining, leaping Tutu. He reached down and scratched her under the chin as the little dog licked and nibbled and whined for the embrace of her Philo.

"Tutu," Philo sighed. "Tutu, sweetheart!"

Then he turned to Pattie Mae, who was by now totally bewildered. "Pattie Mae, take a paper bag. Go out in the van and bring me that bottle of bourbon that's in the drawer under the hot plate in the back. Right away! Go!"

"Yes, Mr. Skinner," she said, and was off, in a clunking run across the arena. The man's a spaz! A total spaz!

"Tutu," Philo whispered. "We'll make it somehow. Somehow!"

Philo Skinner had learned something that all neophyte criminals learn: that it's pretty damn tough to pull your first job (and even your thirty-first) without something to bolster your courage. When Pattie Mae returned, Philo took the paper bag to the men's room, sat on the john and passed another pitiful but painful bubble, polishing off half a pint of bourbon faster than he had ever consumed spirits in his life.

After that, Philo Skinner felt a hell of a lot better about the whole business. The first thing he did was sidle up to Pattie Mae and bite her on the neck from behind.

"Mr. Skinner!"

"Hi, you foxy little kennel groupie, you!"

"Mr. Skinner!"

"Go over on Figueroa and buy me another pint of Jim Beam."

"I'm not old enough to buy liquor, Mr. Skinner. And you shouldn't be drinking . . . should you?"

"Not old enough . . . not old enough," Philo sighed. "Do you have any idea how long it's been since I wasn't *old* enough for something? I'm not *old* enough for social security, and I'm not *old* enough to get into the racetrack at a senior citizen's price, and I'm not *old* enough to ignore the fact that you are not wearing a bra as usual and no panties I bet, and you and me might just go out to dinner tomorrow night and how would you like to go somewhere where the tab for the evening is a hundred bucks? Huh? A *hundred* bucks?"

"Uh, Mr. Skinner, do you think you'd like some coffee? Lemme go get you some coffee, okay?"

"Too young to buy whiskey! Imagine that!"

"How about some coffee?"

"How about some pot?" He was buoyant. Up, down, up, down. Crime was like an elevator. "All you lint-covered, big-titted, flat-bellied chicks with flowers in your goddamn hair smoke grass. Jesus Christ, Pattie Mae, turn me on a little! Gimme a joint. I'll go smoke it in the crapper."

"I don't carry it with me, Mr. Skinner. Where would I carry it?" The girl was looking around nervously at the lone cop she'd seen roaming the arena.

"Not in a bra, that's for sure," Philo leered. "Not in panties either. So go out in your car and bring me back a joint. No, make it *two* joints."

"I don't know what's got into you, Mr. Skinner, but . . ."

"Go *do* it, Pattie Mae. Go out to your car, dig up under the dashboard or wherever the hell you little grasshoppers hide your stash and bring me back some pot! Hear me?"

"Okay, Mr. Skinner," she said. This would be her last show with this grungy old hound dog, that's for sure. Tomorrow she'd start making the rounds of the other kennels. Terrier King, my ass! This old geezer's brain was *thrashed!*

Philo Skinner decided he had half an hour before his next dog was due in the ring. Maybe longer because the show was running long. Philo went staggering around the arena floor, hands in his pockets, cigarette dangling from the corner of his tobacco-flecked lips, grinning, winking, leering at every female handler, exhibitor, or groomer, under the age of fifty. He was suddenly in a jovial *helpful* mood.

A buxom owner and a mousy woman handler were at a grooming table near the grandstand working on a Maltese terrier. Philo stood, hands in pockets, and shook his head.

The Maltese was rolled in oil and tissue paper and tied up with rubber bands so his long hair couldn't drag on the ground and break off. But the Maltese terrier's coat wasn't the problem. His balls were. One was lost.

"What do you *mean?*" the frantic owner demanded, her diamond earrings dancing. "How can you *lose* it! My God, how can you *lose* a testicle!"

"Mrs. Dilfaunt, it happens all the time!" the harried handler explained, while two other dog groomers worked on a pair of bored spaniels who had been through it all too much to lose *their* balls.

"Happens all the time! To *lose* a testicle!"

"You're new to dog shows, Mrs. Dilfaunt," the handler tried to explain. "The dog is monorchid at the moment."

"Monorchid."

"Yes. He's tense, nervous. It's his first show. He's just sucked one testicle up, that's all. We've got to help him bring it down. The judges will reach under there and feel and there *has* to be two."

"My God!" the new owner screamed. "I pay a thousand bucks for a one-nutted dog!"

"I used to get the same way when I was tense," she suddenly heard a voice wheeze in her ear. Then she smelled sour tobacco breath and stale sweat and was staring into the heavy-lidded, boozy eyes of a gangly stranger with blue-black hair. "Tickle the end of my pecker, and I'll drop *my* nut every time!"

"Officer!" the woman screamed, as Philo went slinking off through the crowd. Giggling.

When Pattie Mae returned, she put her hand surreptitiously into Philo's coat pocket and said breathlessly: "One's Colombia Gold, the other's Maui wow-ee."

"Maui wow-ee!" Philo yelled, causing the cringing whippet to defecate for the third time.

And as crowds of the faithful trooped in and out of the Los Angeles Memorial Sports Arena, larger crowds, though not necessarily *more* faithful, began choking the inadequate roads into the Rose Bowl in Pasadena on a brisk, bright, perfect California football day. And if Philo Skinner had previously been ten times more tense than the entire offensive line of the Minnesota Vikings, he was okay at the moment. Okey-dokey. Philo left Pattie Mae with the animals, and went slinking around the outside rings to watch the working and sporting dogs. He had the two joints in his pocket.

He walked right up to a throng of nail-biting owners of golden retrievers and tried an experiment. He deliberately lit a joint with the butt of his Camel. Then he stood in their midst, hands in his pockets, chuckling to himself, smoking the joint right down to a roach. Once he tapped a man in a suede shooting jacket and said, "Your handler is standing the dog on a little hump of turf. He shouldn't face him downhill like that. That dog has a sloping top line and the downhill lie just emphasizes it."

The sport in the shooting jacket turned to Philo, looked him squarely in the face and said, "Sir, that dog is *perfect.*" Then he whirled and turned back to watch the judging with the rest of the nail-biters. Philo was grinning, the stick of Colombia Gold hanging out the side of his mouth. It went unnoticed. Goddamn, it was *fun* being an outlaw!

Philo smoked his Maui wow-ee while watching the German shepherds. He had never found a dog show so funny. The middle-aged handlers were really being put through it by a squinty woman judge who was every bit as tall as Philo but lots tougher. She looked as though she was enjoying their agony as much as Philo was. They couldn't satisfy her. Around and around the ring they ran. The tongues of the handlers were soon dangling longer than the shepherds'. Philo couldn't contain himself. "Atta girl, Granny!" he yelled. "Run their buns off!"

Then for the first time someone noticed. A teenaged boy in the crowd turned, looked at the emaciated dog handler, and said, "Hey, that guy's smoking grass!"

But too late. The outlaw was slithering away through the crowd, the joint cupped in his hand, still giggling.

When Philo was back in the arena heading toward his grooming area, he saw a tight little group of groomers and handlers kneeling on the floor next to a howling Great Dane.

"It's *your* fault," the exhibitor barked.

"It's *not* my fault, Mrs. Von Geldt. *You* had the dog all week!"

"It's *my* fault," a young groomer wailed. "I should have noticed."

"I'm changing kennels!" the exhibitor said.

"That's not helping matters. Just give me a chance . . ."

"Is there a doctor in the house!" the exhibitor screamed.

On a whim, Philo Skinner walked up and said, "I'm Doctor Skinner, what can I do for . . ."

Then he recognized the older dog handler kneeling behind the other one.

"Hello, Philo," the handler said. He was a well-known veteran on the circuit, so Philo's fun was cut short. "Anal glands impacted."

And then, loaded on bourbon and marijuana, certainly not feeling like going up a Great Dane's ass, Philo Skinner bent his gangling frame and squatted. He could never stand to see an animal suffer.

"I thought he had worms, the way he was sliding around on his bottom," the exhibitor cried.

"I think it happened today, Philo," the old handler said. "His eyes still look good."

"Yeah," Philo nodded, and without asking the leave of anyone, rancid Philo Skinner, smelling like thirty days in a dog run, probed the Dane's anus, and with thumb and forefinger—gently, ever so gently—pushed in until he was sure he was behind the glands. Then the dog yelped as Philo squeezed and pulled out and up and the secretion flowed through the anus. The secretion smelled worse than the armpits of Philo Skinner.

"Wash him off, he'll be okay," Philo said.

"Good hands, Philo," the old handler grinned. "You still got those good hands."

But Philo was up and loping sideways as though catching a Kenny Stabler pass. "*Great* hands!" Philo yelled. "Just like Fred Biletnikoff!"

After scoring his touchdown and washing his great hands, he returned to the tense group of people swabbing and toweling the anus of the Great Dane. The relieved exhibitor wearing an orchid carnation had her back to him. She caught a whiff of sweat and tobacco as a voice croaked: "Honey, if you ever need any help with *your* anal glands . . ."

Then he was off and running. It was a hell of a fun day. By God, Philo Skinner *would* miss the dog show circuit!

"Mr. Skinner," Pattie Mae said, shaking her head when he came reeling back to the grooming area. "I see you smoked the Gold."

"You know, Pattie Mae, tell the truth I never liked grass before. I just might switch." And with that he gave her a smack on the bottom. "Damn, I *knew* you didn't have any panties on!"

"Mr. Skinner, I just don't know how you're going to show the Dandie."

He looked at the dogs in the exercise pens. She'd groomed them beautifully. Philo Skinner knew he couldn't have done much better.

"You got good hands too, kid," he said seriously. "And Philo Skinner doesn't toss around compliments very often."

Then he sat in his director's chair and smoked and listened to the buzz of the crowd and the incessant voice on the public address system: "Janitor, ring nine. Janitor, ring four. Janitor . . ."

Endless. It was endless. The world was one big heap of shit. There were those that dropped it and those that cleaned it up. Well, Philo Skinner had scooped up his share of shit and now it was somebody else's turn. He started getting very depressed now and almost felt like crying. It was sad when you thought too much about it. The whole fucking world. Just one big mountain of shit.

Then he heard another crowd cheering. He looked blankly down to the next grooming area. A small television set was being adjusted by the handler there. Jesus Christ, he had forgotten for a minute. Jesus Christ, this goddamn dope boils your brain. The Super Bowl was about to begin! Philo Skinner's heart thumped in his throat. He lit his sixty-first cigarette.

By terrible coincidence they were showing the Dandies in ring number eight just five minutes before the kickoff of Super Bowl XI. Philo Skinner was standing like a zombie and peering through the hair of an English sheepdog on a grooming table trying to see the small television set.

"Mr. Skinner," Pattie Mae said, pulling on his arm. "Mr. Skinner, it's time to show the Dandie."

"Later," he mumbled, glued to the tube.

"Mr. Skinner! It's time!"

Then he turned his drug-dilated eyes to the frantic girl and said, "Pattie Mae, what the hell! Now's as good a time as any. *You* show the Dandie."

"Me! *Me* show the Dandie!"

"You."

"Me!"

"Get hold a yourself. You've been to plenty a dog shows."

"As a spectator!"

"Look, show the Dandie," Philo said, reeling from the effects of marijuana and bourbon. "Show the dog or fuck the dog, I don't care *what* you do with the dog, but leave me alone."

"Mr. Skinner, I'm quitting tomorrow morning. I'm not working for you anymore."

"That's funny. Oh, God, that's funny," Philo croaked, then broke into a wheezy laughing fit that ended in an ounce of black phlegm being gagged into his handkerchief while Pattie Mae blanched. "Listen," he gasped, still chuckling wheezily. "*I* won't be working for me, come tomorrow."

"What?"

"Never mind. Go show the goddamn Dandie. It's good experience for you."

Mrs. Dexter Berryberry had been enjoying the dog show enormously up until that time. And here was the moment she'd been waiting for. She had bought tickets for seven members of her bridge club and they were all chatting excitedly in the grandstand waiting to see the Berryberry Dandie Dinmont do his stuff. Then Mrs. Berryberry began looking concerned. Where the hell was Philo Skinner? She counted one, two, *eight* Dandies. And the fourth one looked like her Pretty Pennie, but who the hell was that kid with the tits leading her Pretty Pennie?

Mrs. Dexter Berryberry wasn't there when her bridge club began the polite applause for Pretty Pennie of Hancock Park. She was hotfooting it down the stairs to the grooming area of Philo Skinner, searching the crowd for that slinky, teased-and-dyed, mangy bastard. She looked everywhere but in the small cluster of sports fans huddled around the television set.

Meanwhile Pattie Mae was knocking them dead in ring number eight. Perhaps not all of them, but certainly the sixty-year-old judge, Landon McWhorter, whose eyes started popping the moment the frazzled girl came bouncing into the ring. He stopped all the handlers once around, except for poor Pattie Mae, jogging along, turning her ankles on those seven-inch clogs. Old Landon grinned more with each bounce and hop, and made the girl do an L away from him, and if that wasn't enough, a T. He made her trot back and forth so much her wraparound skirt was unwrapping.

Unlike most judges he didn't stand his ground as she moved away, but followed along, making furious notes on his clipboard. His notes said: "Brisket flat and muscular. Hock shapely and well defined. Stifle magnificent!" And the dog wasn't bad either.

Mrs. Dexter Berryberry never saw Philo Skinner squatting on the floor in front of that television set smoking his sixty-eighth cigarette. When she returned to the grandstand, her bridge club stood and applauded her win. She accepted it graciously, thinking she must remember to give Philo a bonus for finding a little pigeon with tits big enough to bring old Landon McWhorter back to life.

At 1:20 p.m., early in the first quarter of Super Bowl XI, Philo Skinner, sobering up slightly, decided he'd had enough. He began rooting for the Minnesota Vikings! He only wanted to cover his gambling debts. He was a dog handler and a good one. His life wasn't so bad considering the alternatives. He swore he'd never bet on another horse or another football game if the Vikings could pull it off. So long, Puerto Vallarta! With his luck he'd die of Aztec Revenge anyway, first time he had a Bibb lettuce salad. Or he'd catch clap in some Mexican whorehouse and a swarm of vermin would penetrate his blood and go rushing madly to his brain and . . . Come on, you Vikings!

But at 1:26 p.m. Earl Mann kicked a field goal for the Oakland Raiders.

"Mr. Skinner, we *won!*" Pattie Mae screamed, throwing her arms around his neck. For the first time, she kissed his cheek. "We *won,* Mr. Skinner! The Dandie *won!*"

"That's great, kid, that's really swell," Philo said. "How about going back and getting the bull terrier ready? He's next."

"Sure, Mr. Skinner. I'm so excited. We might win best of breed! My very first show!"

"Listen, honey, maybe you'd like to show the bull too."

"Would I? *Would* I?"

And she was off, running toward the grooming table, deciding to add just another touch of cornstarch.

At 1:42 p.m. the Oakland Raiders scored on a Kenny Stabler pass.

"My God," said Philo Skinner. The pile of butts at his feet had grown.

"Janitor, ring ten. Janitor, ring fifteen. Janitor . . ."

It was all turning to shit. He *would* be a criminal. As sure as there's shit in those shovels. It was Philo Skinner's destiny. He had no control over it. He had no choice in the matter. Fate had brought him here. And Philo Skinner found it as easy to accept a deterministic philosophy as had thousands of criminals before him. Dame Chance was guiding his destiny. His fate lay in the hands of that bearded, left-handed quarterback.

Eight minutes later, Oakland made it 17–0 and Philo Skinner nodded grimly. There was no point waiting any longer. Destiny had made the choice.

"Janitor, ring fifteen. Janitor, ring eight. Janitor . . ."

Pattie Mae didn't do so well with the Staffordshire bull terrier. This judge, a forty-six-year-old fireplug with tits three times bigger than Pattie Mae's, wasn't impressed.

"We didn't have a fair chance," Pattie Mae sobbed to a white-lipped Philo Skinner, who sat in his director's chair, drinking coffee, taking hold, preparing himself for the ordeal to come.

"Yeah, well that's the breaks. Don't worry about it."

"I tried so hard, but she wouldn't even look at us, Mr. Skinner."

"Don't worry about it, Pattie Mae," Philo Skinner said.

"The schnauzers will be going any minute in number seven, Mr. Skinner."

"Schnauzers?"

"Yes, schnauzers." The girl looked quizzically at Philo as she wiped her eyes with a tissue. Then she pointed at Tutu in the exercise pen.

"Yeah, well they're running late. Get her ready. I'll tell you about mini-schnauzers. Cheer up a little, okay."

"Sure," she sniffed.

Now he was once again Philo Skinner, Terrier King. He was still woozy from the drug and the whiskey, but he was taking hold. There was no turning back now. That fucking Kenny Stabler couldn't miss with those passes. Was that Philo Skinner's fault? Was it *his* fault that Jim Marshall and Alan Page couldn't penetrate the Oakland offense and nail that whiskered son of a bitch? Jesus Christ, the Vikings were too old. Too *old!* The whole fucking world was too old! Is *that* Philo Skinner's fault?

"Okay, Pattie Mae, I'm going to give you a little bit on schnauzers while we get this little bitch ready."

"Great, Mr. Skinner," she sniffled, starting to recover from the loss. "By the way, where did she come from?"

"Whaddaya mean?" he said quickly.

"I mean, who owns her? How did we get her today? She's not one a our dogs is she? What's her name? Is she listed in the show catalogue?"

"Goddamn, Pattie Mae, you ask a lot a questions," said Philo, lighting a cigarette with steadying hands. "She's a beauty, isn't she? A little tiger. Schnauzers should never be cute. Growly and feisty, that's the sign of a winner. Know why?"

"Why, Mr. Skinner?"

"They were rat dogs in the old days. Tough little bastards. They could get chewed up by a whole goddamn platoon a rats and still come out on top. You ever wonder how we can strip them down like we do? Pluck them clean as a chicken and they don't feel a thing? The nerve endings aren't near the surface a the skin. That's why you can strip out these double-coated dogs. Strip the wiry jacket *and* the downy cotton. Try *that* with a poodle or Afghan. Just try it."

Philo's hands moved as gracefully as a blackjack dealer's. Touching, scissoring, trimming, combing. Pattie Mae almost forgot that he hadn't answered a single one of her questions.

"Sometimes you get a garbage coat on these schnauzers," Philo said, as he saw an almost microscopic lash protruding from the triangular shade of the schnauzer's shaggy eyebrows. "Sometimes they just grow a crummy jacket and all you can do is strip em out and wait till next time."

Tutu didn't move a muscle as Philo's scissors passed across her beautiful brown eyes. Tutu trusted Philo implicitly.

"Look at that eyeshade, Pattie Mae," Philo said, genuinely admiring the head of the little schnauzer. "You could almost shine that silver, put it in your little hope chest. You got a little hope chest, Pattie Mae?"

"What's a hope chest, Mr. Skinner?"

Jesus Christ. They're all so young. *Young!*

"Those goddamn Kerry blues give schnauzers lots a trouble in shows," Philo said, eyes darting toward the ring where he would *not* be showing this schnauzer. "People really like Kerry blues for some reason, but me, gimme a schnauzer any day. These are little working dogs, is what they are. Not some frigging pet. They reach. You got to learn how to use that lead, make these little tigers *reach.* Like a little Clydesdale horse. Look at the gorgeous furnishings on this bitch!"

"She's the best-looking schnauzer I ever seen, Mr. Skinner."

Second best around here, Philo thought. *Second* best. You'll see the first best later. About the time Fran Tarkenton is sitting on his ass in the locker room wondering what the hell happened. You'll see and even touch the *first* best and you won't even know it! Philo was feeling so much better he even took a peek down Pattie Mae's blouse when she leaned over the back of the schnauzer to comb her leg furnishings.

"She has such beautiful legs. As straight as posts," the girl said, admiring the sturdy silver furnishings, trimmed so that the little black toenails barely showed. "I like the schnauzer better too. More . . ."

"More balls," Philo Skinner said. "You like your dogs with balls and your men with balls. No sissies for you, right, Pattie Mae? Real guys. Hey, Pattie Mae?"

"Sure, Mr. Skinner," the girl sighed, giving Philo the once-over. Six feet three, 145 pounds fully clothed. Hair like an ungroomed otter hound, dyed like a Kerry blue, chest like a cocker spaniel, legs like a whippet, droopy eyes like a beagle. At this moment smelling like one of those barrels of crap the honey dippers are scooping up in the show rings. A *real* guy, Mr. Skinner. Oh, *gross!*

"Janitor, ring number one. Janitor, ring number fourteen. Janitor . . ." The voice was chanting it now. "Janitor, ring number nine." It may as well have been in Latin. "Janitor, ring number twelve." Hail boxer, full of shit. Old age and shit! Philo wanted to cry. A church full of shit clear to the dome! A canine cathedral full of dog shit!

"Mr. Skinner, where did you say this schnauzer came from? What's her name? Who owns . . . ?"

"Here," Philo said, suddenly handing the scissors to the girl. "There's one hair protruding one-sixteenth of an inch from one of the furnishings. See if you can find it and trim it off. Old eagle-eye Skinner spotted it."

And when she took the scissors he let his hand fall against her left breast, the back of his bony knuckles sliding over the large nipple.

Eagle eye, my ass, she thought. Beagle eye, you mean. Beagle-eyed, smelly old fart. Ugh!

He *had* to come up with a story. She had already asked enough to get suspicious. "This little bitch, she, uh, well, I have this client. Oil. Scads of oil. Moved to Tulsa to be closer to her goddamn derricks. I ever tell you about how a savvy handler can give a rich client a champion, without too much trouble?"

"No," she said, looking over every inch of the schnauzer's furnishings for the elusive little hair he had referred to. Where *was* the dumb thing?

"Well, see, Pattie Mae, I can take a dog and pick some shows in Iowa or Oklahoma. Like once I took a Lakeland terrier on the Oregon circuit for a client. We entered five shows in five days and I earned all fifteen points and brought home a champion to mama. In a Lear Jet! Mama's *own* little Lear Jet. She slipped me a thousand bucks from her own little bank account, because daddy was a stingy old bastard. She also tried to slip me something else, I might add." With that, Philo gave Pattie Mae another pat on the fanny.

No pants, Philo thought, sighing.

Sickie! Pattie Mae thought, sighing.

"Anyway, Pattie Mae," Philo continued, "this broad that moved to Oklahoma, she called me and asked could I show her schnauzer. She's been keeping it with a sister-in-law in Malibu or somewhere. So I said okay, for an old client, and went out to Malibu, picked it up and here she is."

Then Philo Skinner stopped, lit a cigarette and stepped back from the grooming table. He held up Tutu's chin and said, "You know what? I still don't think she's ready. Her coat just isn't sharp enough. I don't wanna show this little bitch today."

"Mr. Skinner! I'm no expert, but . . ."

"Remember that!" Philo snapped.

"Yes, but I think this is the finest miniature schnauzer I ever seen! Why her coat looks prime to me, Mr. Skinner."

"To you, Pattie Mae, to *you*. Did you find that protruding hair in the furnishings?"

"Not yet," she said, bending lower, picking up the front paw of the patient Tutu, who panted and looked at Philo. Adoringly.

"Not *yet*," Philo scoffed. "And you think you know when a schnauzer is ready? Gimme those scissors."

And with that, Philo snatched the scissors from the girl's hand and clipped a nonexistent hair from the left front furnishing and said, "*That's* why you're here at Skinner Kennels. To learn. To learn from the Terrier King of the West Coast. This schnauzer is *not* ready and I'm looking out for the best interest of my client by deciding *not* to show her. Christ, there's a thousand other dog shows this little bitch can enter and win. *When* she's ready."

"You know best, Mr. Skinner."

"Believe it, baby," Philo said. Then he reached over and chucked the girl under the chin, once again letting his hand drop and slide across her nipple. "Hey, you did okay today. Who knows? You might win the terrier group with the Kerry."

The fate of the Minnesota Vikings was sealed at about the same moment the miniature schnauzers trotted into the ring that afternoon. Pattie Mae was standing by the ring next to Philo Skinner, who was watching every movement of a bitch called Victoria Regina of Pasadena.

"Look at her!" Philo said to Pattie Mae, whose feet were killing her and who was ready to call it a day.

"Beautiful!" he said. "No crossover in those feet. Tail not set too low. Great neck. Bet she stands thirteen and one half inches right on the nose. See, our schnauzer could never have beat *that* bitch. *That* is a champion."

"I guess so," the girl said, avoiding Philo's tobacco breath.

"I've never seen a finer mini-schnauzer," Philo mused. "Look how those first two schnauzers paddle. Schnauzers shouldn't paddle like toy poodles, for chrissake."

Then, pandemonium. Someone called the stick. Dog showing is a ladies and gentlemen's sport.

"Son of a bitch! The stick!"

"That rotten bastard!"

"Prick bastard!"

"Kick his rotten ass, George. Challenge that dirty scum-sucking rotten little asshole."

"The stick!"

"What happened, Mr. Skinner?" Pattie Mae cried.

At one grooming station they were growling, snarling, lunging toward the ring. The people, that is. The dogs were quietly sitting, or trying to sleep through all the hullabaloo, nuzzling their balls, licking their twats, biting at imaginary itches brought about not by fleas but by the nervousness of the human beings which affected the dogs like poison ivy.

A siren could be heard faintly on Santa Barbara Avenue. The cops were chasing a drunk driver from Minnesota in a Hertz Rent-A-Car. He was careening around the Los Angeles Coliseum convinced that his Vikings were inside kicking the shit out of those pussies from Oakland. He was twelve miles and eighteen points away from the right stadium and the right score. The sirens set the dogs to howling, though Pattie Mae thought the dogs had joined the howling humans because they'd called the stick. Everyone took up the chant.

"He called the stick! The prick!"

Even Pattie Mae started yelling, "He called the stick, Mr. Skinner!" She was caught up in mob frenzy. "The dirty prick called the stick!"

"Pattie Mae, do you know what the stick is?" Philo asked.

"No."

"Calm down for chrissake and I'll tell you."

But it was hard to talk over all the noise.

The humans snarled and the sirens wailed, and some of the dogs in the ring began to howl and move their bowels.

"Janitor, ring number one. Janitor, ring number four. Are there any more janitors on lunch break? All janitors to the arena floor!"

"What's the stick, Mr. Skinner?" she asked when the animals and people stopped howling.

"See that third guy in the ring? The one with the phony dyed red hair?"

Yeah, phony hair, Pattie Mae thought.

"That guy with the phony dyed hair, he's an anesthesiologist from Laguna Beach. A one hundred percent, never deviating, pure-blooded, American Kennel Club registered, prick. He called the stick on that little schnauzer that Billie Jefferson's showing. See the little bitch? Third from the judge's right? Well, she might be a mite under twelve inches at the withers, and that prick, he can spot a schnauzer under twelve inches better than anybody I ever saw. He's called for the stick more than anyone. They used to walk them under a wicket, like a croquet wicket. Poor Billie. That little bitch isn't going to measure twelve inches. She'll be disqualified and Billie knows it. Poor bastard. Been a handler even longer than me. Hustling to make ends meet and some rich doctor from Laguna calls the stick on him. Poor bastard. Bet Billy'd like to put that fucking doctor under the wicket, play croquet on his goddamn phony dyed head. Poor old Billy. Hard to make a living running a kennel, Pattie Mae."

"But if you love dogs, Mr. Skinner . . ."

"Love dogs," Philo said, and looked longingly toward ring number seven. His *last* dog show. "Yeah, I always loved them, true enough. Long as I can remember. When I was a scrawny hungry kid with not enough for me to eat, I always shared with some goddamn dog. Now I'm a scrawny hungry man and . . . aw, what the hell."

And for the first time, Pattie Mae looked at the old bastard with something other than apprehension or loathing. "You're not so scrawny, Mr. Skinner," the simple girl said. "You just smoke too much. And I'd lay off the Colombia Gold I was you, you're liable to lose some clients."

The little schnauzer measured 11 15/16 inches at the withers and was disqualified. The handler's groom at the next station vowed to cut the anesthesiologist's heart out with a stripping knife. And without any anesthetic, the cocksucker.

Then Philo Skinner, with an odd stare that frightened Pattie Mae, turned to her, and said: "Do you know how far people will go to win a show? In Madison Square Garden they cut the eyebrows and whiskers off a Scottie."

"They did! Oh, that's gross!" Pattie Mae grimaced.

"And they poisoned a collie. Poisoned him."

"Oh, my God!" Pattie Mae cried. She couldn't even bear to hear about people who didn't *brush* their animals. She sat for hours with her own Manchester terrier searching for fleas and ticks like a mother chimpanzee.

"I'd never hurt a dog," Philo Skinner announced. "Not for anything. Not ever. I'd rather kill a man than hurt a dog. Can you understand that?"

He was sweating again and starting to smell. The girl just looked at the staring, droopy, beagle eyes of her boss, and said, "Yes, Mr. Skinner."

The time was drawing close. Madeline Whitfield's bitch was certain to take a terrier group first. But she'd never get a chance to win best in show because Philo Skinner had other plans.

Madeline Whitfield was ecstatic when Vickie won winners bitch. She was jumping around on the grandstand seats, banging friends and strangers on the arms and shoulders. Being congratulated, shaking hands, wiping tears from her eyes.

"Get the photographer!" Madeline cried. "Somebody get the photographer!"

Madeline Dills Whitfield was absolutely positive that this was her day. Victoria Regina of Pasadena was now a champion. She wasn't going to stop here, she was going to win best in show. Let them read *that* in the *Los Angeles Times* tomorrow with their all-bran cereal. Let them see who won Best in Winter Show, 1977! Madeline Whitfield couldn't quell the tears of joy. The more she was congratulated the more they flowed. Okay, Beverly Hills Kennel Club, are you ready to increase your membership to twenty-four? Not yet? Well, wait a few weeks. Wait until Victoria Regina of Pasadena wins Westminster! Wait until Madison Square Garden! Screw you, Junior League! She was never so happy in her entire life. All forty-three years had led her to this: her destiny. The pain, the sacrifice, had all been worth it. She was nearly a celebrity!

In thirty minutes she would be one of the most miserable, terrified women in Los Angeles. She would be infinitely more miserable than Fran Tarkenton, who was, at this very moment, caught by the television cameras, sitting on his helmet on the sidelines, wondering what the hell went wrong.

An exhibitor walked by the grooming station of Philo Skinner and said to a companion: "Our bitch is in season. She's not showing well."

Philo Skinner, who had never seen the woman in his life, said, "Yeah, you look a little nervous yourself. Checked *your* drawers lately?"

He was like that. Scared. Bold. Wild. Up again. Is this the way criminals were supposed to feel? It was as though all the conventions, all the regulations of the American Kennel Club had lost their meaning. These were the rules he lived by and they didn't mean a thing. He felt like taking off his Brooks Brothers coat and paisley necktie and yelling, "Janitor! Janitor! Come to Philo Skinner!" He wanted to throw it all into the steaming vats of dog shit. This is what it must be like to blow a safe, to steal a diamond, to rob a stagecoach! He didn't know it, but he was being propelled by the same megalomaniacal force as an eleven-year-old bike bandit named Earl Scheib Lopez. He was a goddamn swashbuckler!

He went to the exercise pens and picked up Tutu, who licked his hands and face as he carried her to her crate. He put her inside and for the first time in his life he did something which would cause great discomfort to an animal. An animal he loved. An animal which was going to let him live the rest of his days like the gentleman he always aspired to be.

"Pattie Mae, go over to the concession stand and get me some coffee. Black."

"Yes, Mr. Skinner," she said, and was off.

He took the syringe from the inside of the herringbone jacket. To be extra safe he removed it from the leather case and squeezed out a few drops.

Philo was still feeling some effects of the bourbon and marijuana. He hugged the little schnauzer to his face and kissed her whiskers. Tutu was delirious with joy because Philo was letting her lick his face. She growled, and licked and nibbled and told Philo how much she loved him.

"I wish I could take you with me, honey," Philo whispered.

Philo Skinner looked around. Most of the crowd was hovering around the ring. A few groomers were stationed at the grooming tables to watch over the animals not in the exercise pens. Nobody was paying the slightest attention to Philo Skinner.

"You and me, we could run on the beach in Mexico," Philo whispered. "If there was *any* way, you know I'd take you. I know you don't like that fat old bitch you live with, but she'll treat you okay. Oh, Christ, I'm sorry, Tutu . . ."

And he jammed the needle into her shoulder.

Tutu yelped and looked at Philo in disbelief. The tranquilizer worked at once, just as they said in the dog books. The dog's eyes filled with pain, then bewilderment. She looked at Philo Skinner like a stranger. She actually growled in confusion at the man she adored. Then she began panting and her eyes drooped and looked glazed over.

"You'll be okay, sweetheart," Philo whispered as he moved across the arena floor, bumping his way through the crowd, "You'll be okay in a little while, sweetheart. Philo's sorry." He forced himself to walk. *Walk* toward the grooming station of dog handler, Chester Biggs.

Philo Skinner had his hand under the chin of the little schnauzer, holding her head upright. Stroking the semiconscious animal under the chin, keeping his eyes riveted on his objective, hoping that he had assessed correctly, and that Chester Biggs, who often discussed sports with Philo Skinner would be . . .

And he was! Chester Biggs was fifty feet away from his exercise pens, watching the degradation of the Minnesota Vikings. Gloating over the humiliation of the Minnesota team by the California team. But there was a dog groomer sitting by the exercise pens, reading a girlie magazine, watching over the eleven animals Chester Biggs was showing that day.

Chester, you should be getting your head together. Your schnauzer bitch could win best in show. If she was my bitch I wouldn't go to the crapper without her. You're a dumb fucking pile of dogmeat, Chester Biggs! You deserve to get ripped off, you dumb fucking pile of dogmeat! Dogs have been stolen before. Dogs were stolen at Madison Square Garden. But you aren't ever going to know about this one, Chester. Never!

The kennel boy, a sixteen-year-old, pimply strawberry blond with half an erection, was looking with disbelief at the enormous fluff of pubic hair on the girl in the skin magazine. He had never seen a real one. Are they *all* that hairy?

He never saw the sweaty, staring, gangling man with a listless schnauzer under his arm, skulking around the exercise pens and cages of Chester Biggs. He certainly never saw the man walk to the crate of Victoria Regina of Pasadena, and stand with his back to the kennel boy for no more than fifteen seconds. And he certainly never saw that Mr. Biggs' champion schnauzer now lay in her cage, eyes half closed and glazed, tongue lolling, panting heavily. The kennel boy couldn't take his eyes off the mound of fluff, tinted and back-combed like the topknot of a Bedlington terrier.

Philo Skinner, felon. From this moment on it was Puerto Vallarta or the slammer. He felt like he was on roller skates. He couldn't stop slipping and sliding and bumping into people as he made his way through the multitudes, toward his grooming station. He was trying to walk with grace and control, perhaps even stealth. Weren't crooks stealthy? Instead his always long, bent-kneed gait became a slinking lope. Philo Skinner was loping through the crowd, all elbows and knees. The schnauzer bitch in his arms was getting very upset and nervous.

"It's okay, baby, it's okay," Philo whispered, stroking Vickie under the throat.

Then he thudded into a handler going the other way with a toy poodle on a lead.

"Watch it, for chrissake!" the perspiring handler said.

Philo thought his goose was cooked. The poodle handler knows the schnauzer! The fag handler letting go with a falsetto shriek! Throw the little bitch in the sissy's face and run for it! Get across the Tijuana border with the three hundred bucks in your checking account before the nigger and Jew with the grooming shears arrive for the circumcision! Jesus!

But the poodle handler didn't even recognize Philo, let alone the bitch. How could he? The goddamn schnauzers were nearly identical. Get hold of yourself. For chrissake, you're Philo Skinner, Terrier King!

Thud! He crashed into a handler named Rosie Lutz, who, luckily for Philo, wore her hair like a Sealyham terrier and couldn't see Philo let alone Vickie. But Philo Skinner panicked. He was skidding and sliding on the slippery floor. He couldn't get traction. Jesus Christ, he couldn't get moving! It was like a bad dream! Does anybody have a skate key? Then he realized he was slipping and sliding in an enormous pile of nerve-runny dog crap, and the offender, a 200-pound St. Bernard, was being chastised by a woman who said: "Bad bad, Cyril! You embarrass mummy."

When he regained his footing, Philo Skinner threw caution to the winds. He stopped trying to be stealthy and just bolted through the crowd while Vickie growled fiercely. By the time he arrived at his grooming area, the little bitch had chewed a half-inch wound in the web of Philo Skinner's left hand without his even noticing it.

"Mr. Skinner, what's wrong!" Pattie Mae said, looking at Philo's white clammy face. "My gosh, the schnauzer's biting your hand!"

Philo looked down and saw Vickie, all spunk and grit, shaking Philo's bony hand around like her ancestors shook dead rats in the mountains of Bavaria. This might be a dog show, and maybe she was trained to let all sorts of strangers pinch and probe, knead and thump her withers and flanks and vagina and anus, and even go into her mouth, but she was an exceedingly intelligent and brave little dog, and sensed that this stranger was up to no good, smelling the fear on him. She wasn't about to let herself be mistreated by someone who smelled like this.

For the first time, Philo noticed her chesty growls. Then he saw the blood running down his wrist. Then and only then was Philo Skinner brought back to shattering reality. *Pain.*

Philo screamed, throwing Vickie four feet in the air, up and down into the arms of Pattie Mae, who caught her like a Kenny Stabler pitchout.

Vickie was howling for all she was worth now, and Philo was sliding around on his still greasy soles, holding his wounded hand by the wrist and making a hell of a commotion which attracted the attention of no more than fifty or sixty people.

"That man got bitten!" a bystander hollered.

"Help that man, he's hurt!" a groomer shouted.

"Is there a doctor in the house?" someone cried.

"Where's the injured animal?" A smallish man in a seersucker suit elbowed through the curious crowd.

"Right here, Doctor!" someone said.

"Oh. That's a man. I'm a veterinarian."

"Yow," Philo Skinner said, wiping his filthy handkerchief around the wound while the veterinarian retreated.

He was hoping the cops would be kind enough to handcuff him in front like they used to do in all the old movies and not in the back like he'd seen real-life cops do on the streets of Hollywood. He was already preparing his defense: I don't know what got into me, Officer. I'd like to plead guilty and go to jail for oh, a year or so, because I owe fifteen thousand, and there's this heartless kike and a nigger with a knife.

He looked around. There were no cops. In fact, there weren't too many people at all. Most had gotten tired of it. It wasn't much of a dogbite after all. Just some skinny guy making a big deal out of a little blood on his hand. What a bore. People went back to watching the various rings where the action was. Or to catch the locker room interviews of the victorious Raiders from Oakland.

"You okay, Philo?" the handler asked.

"Yeah."

"Better get a tetanus shot just to be sure."

"Yeah, thanks," said Philo Skinner as the handler went back to business.

Pattie Mae's nose was wrinkling. She kept backing up and finally bumped into the metal grooming table.

Then Philo smelled it. His shoes were a mess.

Vickie was trembling and whimpering in Pattie Mae's arms. The girl was stroking her, saying, "It's all right, sweetheart. It's all right."

Philo Skinner, criminal, suddenly wished he were a little dog and that a flower child would pick him up and cuddle him to her braless bosom telling him that everything would be all right. He figured Chester Biggs by now was leading a lynch mob across the arena floor. Philo was drenched in perspiration and stained by blood and dog shit. His hand was throbbing like his head. The whiskey he'd guzzled was rising up in his throat, causing his huge adam's apple to jerk around as he swallowed it back. The little schnauzer was staring at him with fear and fury in her eyes. There was only one thing Philo Skinner could do: He lit the seventy-second cigarette of the day. He stood and smoked. No blindfold, please. Bury me deep where the dogs can't dig. I'm Philo Skinner, Terrier King.

He was halfway through the cigarette when Pattie Mae said: "I just don't know what's wrong with the schnauzer, Mr. Skinner. She's acting so strange. Like she doesn't even know us. Gosh, this morning she was licking you and jumping around every time you came near her. What's wrong with her, Mr. Skinner? I think she's gone squirrelly or something."

"Squirrelly," he said. Smoking. Staring off in the distance. Wondering if convicts get to have pets. The Bird Man of Alcatraz. Maybe they'd make a movie about him, his cell full of terriers. It might not be so bad. A few years if he confessed. By then the gamblers would forget. Well, maybe he'd make something from the movie and he could pay them. Get out, start all over. The Dog Man of San Quentin . . .

"Mr. Skinner, you're so pale. I think you're going to faint from the shock of being bit! You better sit down. Do you think I should call a doctor? Sit down, Mr. Skinner."

Philo Skinner obeyed. He stepped woodenly over to his director's chair, sat, and smoked until the butt singed his calloused fingers. Pattie Mae put Vickie in Tutu's cage and said, "Mr. Skinner, since we're through for the day, do you think we could just load up and go home? Honest, I'm so tired I don't even want to stay for the end. I never thought I'd wanna leave early, but I'm so tired I just can't believe it. What a weird day!"

"A weird day."

"Can we go home, Mr. Skinner?"

"Go home."

"Yes, can we? Do you want me to go get the van?"

Philo Skinner looked around at the thinning crowd. The losers were already packing up to go. The bulk of the crowd would of course stay for the final judging, but a good many of the handlers who would not be part of it were folding up the exercise pens and grooming tables.

"Mr. Skinner, damn it, I think you're either in shock from that dog bite or you're tripping on that Colombia Gold. You wanna know the truth you're acting like a re-tard and I'm getting tired of it! Now you can fire me or not, but I'm going home! This is your last chance. Do you want me to get the van and help load up?"

"Get the van and help load up," Philo echoed, and Pattie Mae was off in an ankle-turning jog toward the parking lot.

When they were loading the dogs into the back of the van, Vickie began making a fuss. She started whimpering, and then she began to bark. It was a throaty, frightened bark at first. Then it got chesty and angry.

"Hush. You hush!" Pattie Mae said as they loaded the grooming table, exercise pens, and animals. "Hush now." And then: "Mr. Skinner, what's this schnauzer's name anyhow? You never did tell me. And I asked you ten times!"

"Name? Oh, that's Vic– Tu–" Jesus Christ, he'd almost forgotten he snatched Tutu too. Tutu too. Jesus! "The schnauzer's name is Fred."

"Fred. A bitch named Fred?"

"How the hell should I know why they named a bitch Fred!" Philo was coming around, getting miserable and whiny again instead of catatonic. "It's probably short for Fredricka. Jesus Christ, I know lots of girls named Freddie. I know a guy named Shirley, for chrissake. Handles poodles. At least we call him Shirley, the stinking fag. Goddamnit, is it *my* fault they call her Fred? Let's get the hell outta here. I had enough dog shows to last a lifetime and I ain't woofing."

Fifteen minutes later he was saying good-bye to Pattie Mae in the parking lot.

"You did a great job today, honey," he said as she jumped out of the van and clonked over to her Volkswagen. "Here's a little thank you from Philo. Hope you didn't mean it about quitting. Think it over for a week."

A week. In a week he'd be following the sun and she could have Skinner Kennels, her and Mavis. Maybe before he left though he'd get one last chance to throw this little bitch his bone.

She looked at the five-dollar bill contemptuously. "I paid more than that for the grass you smoked up," she said. "Thanks a lot."

"Wait a minute, Pattie Mae," Philo whined. "I'm tapped right now. You just wait till your next paycheck. There's gonna be a little bonus in there from the boss. You won't be sorry. Just wait till next week. Meantime I'm gonna give you a call tomorrow night, talk about that dinner I promised you."

"Yeah, see you," she said, heading toward the beat-up Volkswagen.

"You wait till you get your check next week, sweetie!" Philo yelled. "Just wait."

Yeah. Wait till next week, he thought. I'll send you a fucking postcard with a dog on it. A chihuahua! Puerto Vallarta, get ready for Philo Skinner!

But Philo Skinner had one bit of unfinished business before the crime was consummated–the letter. He got it out of the glove compartment and checked it over. It was a lulu. Bits of newsprint glued to a piece of plain bond paper, just like in the movies. Only trouble is, he couldn't find names in the newspaper that worked out. He had smoked dozens of cigarettes and sat up until 3:00 a.m. trying to find something that had a *whit* in it. The goddamn L.A. *Times* should print something with a *whit* but they didn't. He found the *field* easy enough. Then he searched futilely for the word *bitch* in a family newspaper. Then he realized he had to cut one letter at a time.

Philo had worn rubber gloves when handling the extortion note. He was doing fine after he got past the *Mrs. Whitfield* except that he smoked a butt too far down as usual, and since the gloves had been soaked in rubbing alcohol which he used to swab a tick bite on a Lakeland terrier, he caught his hand on fire. Lucky for Philo Skinner the basin of foamy water was handy. For once Mavis' failure to clean up didn't rile him. The burning glove barely singed his fingers.

When he finally got the extortion note glued and trimmed and scrawled with crayon, it said:

> Mrs. Whitfield
> By now you know you do not have your bitch. Keep the bitch you have until you get orders from me. You will hear from me by phone. I will get your unlisted number by calling Biggs Kennels tomorrow and telling them I am your friend Richard. You will instruct them to give Richard your phone number. Do not say anything more to Biggs or to the police or you will not see your bitch alive.

The *Richard* was in honor of Richard Burton, whom Philo would do his best to imitate as a retired don in Puerto Vallarta. Wouldn't it be something if Richard Burton's villa was the one Philo finally settled in? Wouldn't *that* be something?

Everything was going just swell until he encountered the residue of the Super Bowl traffic pouring out of the inadequate access roads to the Rose Bowl in Pasadena. Philo almost got catatonic again when a Pasadena traffic policeman waved him to a stop when he entered the area of the Arroyo.

A cop! I'll come peaceably, Officer! I should have realized that crime doesn't pay!

"Can't you go around, buddy? Where you heading, Linda Vista?"

"Pardon?"

"I said, can't you go around? You trying to get up to Linda Vista?"

"Linda Vista."

"Well go around, buddy! Can't you see the traffic's backed up clear to the Bowl? Go around!"

And Philo went around, searching for the address in the dog show catalogue. He went around in a looping circle of ten miles. Philo Skinner ended up on the Ventura Freeway, got off, doubled back, got lost in Glendale, back on the freeway. He rechecked her address, looked at his street map of Pasadena, and was on and off the freeway three more times until he found the Mediterranean mansion.

Philo parked a hundred yards down the road near a score of Canary Island pine trees. Then, after looking in both directions, he moved along the stucco wall and past a wall of oleander, stopping every few seconds to listen for voices or footsteps. Nothing but birds, and sprinklers spraying vast lawns. Nothing but white oaks, pines and eucalyptus. Then he was at the iron gate. Philo stopped, looked both ways again, and broke into a lung-searing lope straight for the front door where he threw the letter. He scuttled back down the driveway, but after fifty yards he stopped. Philo coughed, gagged up a chunk of black phlegm and skulked back to the front door. He picked up the letter, glancing over his shoulder fearfully, and wiped the letter under sweaty armpits to remove fingerprints.

Two minutes later, looking as though he'd run a marathon, he was wheezing, creaking, gasping toward the waiting van where Vickie howled. She knew where she was. Her howls were heartbreaking even to Philo Skinner.

"Please shut up," he begged. "You'll be home in a few days. Please shut your trap. Philo won't hurt you."

• ● •

Madeline was laughing and chatting with her friends and well-wishers, waiting in unbearable anticipation for the last stages of the competition.

"Mrs. Whitfield." Chester Biggs' face was gray.

"Yes, Chester."

"You better come. Vickie's sick."

Madeline Whitfield's nightmare began when she tore her panty hose and cut her leg stumbling down the steps of the grandstand. She didn't remember running with Chester Biggs, banging through the crowds, bumping the stands of concessionaires, almost knocking a photographer on the seat of her pants as she was snapping a Pomeranian bitch for a proud owner who would pay anything to get *her* picture in a dog magazine and to hell with the bitch. It's every girl for herself.

The schnauzer looked as though she were dying. Madeline gasped and picked her up from the grooming table against the advice of a veterinarian Biggs had found.

"Vickie, Vickie! Oh, Vickie!"

"I think this animal's been drugged," the veterinarian said. He put his hand on Madeline Whitfield's arm as she held the schnauzer against her face and cried, "Oh, Vickie! Vickie!"

"Ma'am, I think somebody's drugged your animal."

"That's impossible!" Chester Biggs said. "How could anybody drug Vickie? I've been right here. Right here all the . . ." Then he looked at the kennel boy with the skin magazine sticking out of the back pocket of his jeans. "That's impossible!" he repeated, thinking about the lawsuit she might slap on him. I'll kill that pimply little son of a bitch! thought Chester Biggs.

The schnauzer's eyes were glassy and heavy lidded. She was gasping for breath. Her tongue hung to the side frighteningly. Madeline hardly recognized her.

"The animal's a bit better than she was five minutes ago," the veterinarian said. "I think she's going to be all right."

The kennel boy was already retreating from Chester Biggs, who looked like an English bulldog as he walked toward the horny kid with the magazine, and said, "Come here, Junior, I want to *talk* to you."

Fifteen minutes later, the schnauzer was being rushed by Chester Biggs to Madeline's veterinarian in San Marino, who had been called from home and was in his office prepared to work on the bitch. Chester Biggs had one passing thought while speeding up the Pasadena Freeway. The schnauzer looked different. Almost as though the furnishings were . . . well, it must be her condition. She whined and squirmed around the floor of the crate.

Madeline Whitfield was sent home by the veterinarian, who suggested she see her doctor for a tranquilizer of her own. She wasn't in any condition to drive, and was taken home by the pimply kennel kid. He drove Madeline's Cadillac Fleetwood like it was a hearse, and spoke not a word.

The kid was wondering if he should take a bus clear out of the state. It wasn't *his* fault. It was that yawning fur on the broads in that magazine! But before the pimply kid went pushing, he saw the envelope on the doorstep. It had big newsprint letters stuck on it. It said: "Urgent."

"Mrs. Whitfield," he said, as Madeline fumbled with her keys and dropped them.

"Thank you. Thank you. Oh, I'm sorry." She started dropping keys again.

"Mrs. Whitfield, this letter must be for you. It says urgent."

"Urgent."

"Mrs. Whitfield, give me the keys. I'll open the door."

Three minutes later the pimply kid was high stepping down the road, jumping in the bushes every time a car came by that might contain the murderous dog handler, Chester Biggs.

It took Madeline three minutes to get the letter opened. She was literally bouncing off the walls. There were a good number of chairs, couches, settees in this part of the mansion yet Madeline couldn't seem to find a place to sit. Finally she sat at the kitchen table. She was holding the envelope in her hand, but she was so numb she didn't know what to do. She might not have opened the envelope were it not for Philo Skinner's criminal training at Saturday matinees. The bizarre bits of newsprint brought her around enough to tear it open. She had to smooth it out on the kitchen table. Two of the *b*'s had come unglued and were lying upside down on the table. Coincidentally, both *b*'s were in the word *bitch.* The first sentence read: "By now you know you do not have your itch. Keep the itch you have until you get orders from me."

Madeline began sobbing brokenly. She couldn't understand why someone would send an advertisement about *the itch* in newsprint. Madison Avenue! She was succumbing to hysteria and they wanted her to use their vaginal lotion! Oh, God!

Then the *Biggs Kennels* caught her eye. She got her sobbing under control and started reading from the beginning. She screamed and refused to answer the door when Chester Biggs arrived. It seemed as though he rang for fifteen minutes. Then a short time later the phone rang.

"Mrs. Whitfield!"

"Yes?"

"This is Chester, Mrs. Whitfield. I rang the bell for . . . You didn't answer."

"No."

"Mrs. Whitfield, I want to come up and see you."

"How is she?" Madeline said and she sounded calm to Chester Biggs.

"I'm *so* sorry, Mrs. Whitfield. She died. Vickie just died!"

There was silence on the line and he said, "Mrs. Whitfield, I'd better come to see you. Right now. Are you all right? Do you want . . ."

"No, Chester," she said, staring at the extortion note, reading it word for word again as he spoke.

"Let me come see you, Mrs. Whitfield. I . . ."

"No, Chester, don't come. I'm all right," she said, wiping her runny nose, carefully placing the ugly letter back in the ugly envelope.

"He thinks it was a tranquilizer. Somebody didn't want Vickie to win. Some filthy devil wanted to win badly enough to . . . Maybe it was poison, I just don't know. There'll be an autopsy here and he'll send samples to a lab. I think I should call the police, don't you?"

"No!" she shouted in the mouthpiece causing Chester Biggs' ear to pop. When he stopped grimacing he said, "Why not, Mrs. Whitfield?"

"Vickie is mine. *Was* mine. It's not up to *you,* Chester. I don't want to call the police. If somebody wanted to win so badly as to give Vickie a drug, or poison, or whatever it was, so be it. She's not the first dog to be poisoned at a dog show and it's just pointless to cause more pain to ourselves by having policemen around."

"Whatever you say, Mrs. Whitfield, but sleep on it."

"I'll sleep on it."

"Maybe you'll feel different tomorrow."

"Perhaps, but I forbid you to call the police."

"Okay, Mrs. Whitfield. Well, you try to rest yourself."

"Chester."

"Yes."

"One thing. I was contacted at the show by someone who wants . . . wants a picture of Vickie for a magazine. His name is . . . Richard something. I forgot to give him my phone number, but he knows you're Vickie's handler. He may call you tomorrow. Give . . . give him my phone number." And then she began to weep. He didn't understand a word she said from then on.

"Okay, Mrs. Whitfield. I . . . well, good night, Mrs. Whitfield. I'm real sorry. The doctor's gonna keep Vickie here until you decide tomorrow how to, whether to bury Vickie or let him take care of it for you. Good night, Mrs. Whitfield."

"Wait!" she said.

"What is it, Mrs. Whitfield?"

"I *don't* want any autopsy. You bring Vickie home to me right now."

"Jesus, Mrs. Whitfield, don't do that. She's dead. She . . ."

"Chester, I want her home now. You bring her. I'll call a pet mortuary and arrange for the burial. I want you to bring her body home. Now."

It was nearly midnight before Madeline Whitfield summoned the courage to examine the cardboard carton Chester Biggs had placed on the dining room table.

When she touched the little body wrapped in the white towel, it wasn't as rigid and cold as she anticipated. And she saw almost at once that the dead schnauzer was not Victoria.

Tutu's heart and respiratory system had been overwhelmed by the drug at the end. She had died in pain, gasping for air. Her eyes drooped and the lower jaw jutted forward in the last spasm. With her whiskers and eyeshades soaked and plastered down, and with her lower jaw jutting, she looked like a little bull mastiff.

9

The Black Marble

Monday morning was very tough for Valnikov. It was even tougher for Captain Hooker, who, like Valnikov, had a devastating headache. But whereas Valnikov's headache came from a raging vodka hangover, Captain Hooker's came from problems with his troops. And it was those problems which possibly saved Valnikov's police career for the moment.

When Valnikov came shuffling into the squad room, Captain Hooker was sitting in his office with Clarence Cromwell and staring in disbelief at Montezuma Montez and Rocco Bambarella. Rocco was called Bullets Bambarella after a gas station holdup in which a robber fired eight shots at him and missed. They found an outline of 9 mm. bullet holes in the wall around Rocco Bambarella. It was only his slow reflexes that saved him. Any man with normal reaction time would have jumped left or right and been killed on the spot. Rocco Bambarella, who shot no worse than anyone else in combat situations, also emptied his gun, missed all six, but saved the day by throwing a full quart of 20w engine oil that coldcocked the bad guy and earned Rocco a commendation and something a policeman cherishes much more—a macho nickname. He was Bullets Bambarella forever.

Valnikov managed a smile and said, "Good morning, Natalie. Did you have a nice weekend?"

"Morning," she said, dropping her eyes nervously.

But Valnikov was in no condition to detect body language. He lumbered to his table and sat down, sorting through the mound of weekend burglary reports.

Natalie could hear them all hollering, especially Bullets, who said, "Look, Captain Hooker, I don't care if that Chinaman *does* sue Montezuma here . . ."

"Me!" the Chicano cop interrupted. "Why say Montezuma! I wasn't there with you!"

"You wasn't there with me?" said Bullets Bambarella in disbelief.

"Bullets, git your shit together!" Clarence Cromwell bellowed in total exasperation. "He *wasn't* there with you! You was there with two bluesuits! There was no other detective there!"

"He gave me the tip!" Bullets argued. "Montezuma, *you* gave me the information from *your* snitch . . ."

"*My* snitch! It was an anonymous call!"

"You're just protectin your snitch!" Bullets shot back.

"Please, please!" Captain Hooker begged, feeling the pain shooting across his forehead. Then he looked up at the aging black detective, standing just to the right of him. "Clarence, you're Bullets' supervisor. Can't *you* resolve this so we don't get another lawsuit? The commander said he's never heard of a detective division with so many lawsuits."

"You bring in these fuzz-nutted kids, you git lawsuits is what you git," Clarence snorted. "I told you, Bullets, you wanna play supercop, you and Montezuma and all these young hotdogs, you go work metro or surveillance or some fuckin glory job. You *don't* work divisional detectives!"

"Jesus, Clarence, lemme just explain my side," Bullets whined, since they all knew that Captain Hooker had spent the weekend on Clarence Cromwell's yacht and was unofficially only the bosun around here. "See, Clarence," Bullets explained, "I figured Montezuma gave me straight shit about this Chinaman runnin a printin press for bad checks in the back of his restaurant."

"Bad checks in the back of a Cantonese restaurant," Captain Hooker said vacantly, running his delicate fingers through his sparse gray hair. "Deputy Chief Lichtenwalter's *favorite* Cantonese restaurant."

"Well, anyways," Bullets continued, a bit more uneasy with this latest piece of intelligence. "I wanted to check it out so I called for a few reinforcements."

"Reinforcements," Captain Hooker said.

"And we was staked out in the back by the kitchen where they're throwin all these slimy duck skins out the door. Hit Butch Janowski right in the hat with one, he was hidin behind a trash can." Bullets stopped to laugh at the thought of Officer Butch Janowski getting a greasy duck skin right on his bean. Until he saw nobody else was even smiling. "And then we listen and we listen," he continued soberly.

"You don't work forgery detail," Captain Hooker reminded Bullets, who was starting to perspire.

"I know, Cap, but I thought, Jesus, a Chink printin hot checks there! Well, it sounded like a big caper. So I listen and I hear clickety-click-click."

"Clickety-click-click!" Captain Hooker said, pained.

"Sure!" Bullets explained. "You see, I figure it's a printin press printin up some bad checks. Clickety-click-click. So, bang!"

"Bang," said Captain Hooker.

"I just took positive police action and . . . and I booted the door and it fell right in on this Chink dishwasher, and he does a whoop-dee-doo into the sink and breaks a few . . . well, *several* dishes. And egg rolls and fortune cookies start flyin around and all, and uh, this old Chink that owns the place starts screamin and holdin his chest like he's havin a fit . . ."

"Or a heart attack," said Captain Hooker.

"Yeah, but it wasn't no heart attack, Boss," Bullets said. "It was more a fit, I would say."

"And his lawyer just hung up," Captain Hooker said very quietly, looking ever more like a pale Victorian headmaster. "And his lawyer says two million dollars."

"Two million bucks," said Bullets. "What's that mean?"

"It just means he's suing the city for two million dollars," said Captain Hooker, who startled everyone by suddenly standing and staring at Bullets with glittering eyes and shrieking: "BECAUSE YOU LITERALLY SCARED THE LIVING SHIT OUT OF THE OLD CHINAMAN!"

"Easy, Cap," said Clarence Cromwell, gently placing Captain Hooker back in his chair and squeezing his shoulders reassuringly. "Easy, Boss, it's gonna be okay. Easy does it."

"But I'm retiring in a matter of weeks!" Captain Hooker cried. "You *know* I can't take this kind of tension, Clarence!"

"Easy, Skipper, easy," said Clarence, massaging Captain Hooker's shoulders, which helped the headache a bit. And then Clarence said to Bullets: "I hear those old silky pajamas the Chinaman was wearin really *was* full a shit, Bullets. Butch Janowski told me."

"Hangin right to his knees," Bullets said proudly. Until he looked at Captain Hooker's demented stare again.

"Tell me, Bullets," said Clarence Cromwell, "what was the clickety-click-click sound if it wasn't a printin press makin bad checks?"

"It was a lunch break," the muscular young detective said sheepishly. "A lunch break."

"All those Chinamen was eatin and clickin their chopsticks against their rice bowls. Jeez, it sounded *just like* a printin press makin bad . . ."

"Jam on outta here, Bullets," Clarence Cromwell warned, seeing the insane stare forming in Captain Hooker's eyes.

"Is it gonna be okay?" Bullets whined.

"You guys jist go back to work," Clarence Cromwell said, but he winked subtly, and Bullets breathed a sigh of relief and jammed on out of there.

Natalie Zimmerman thought it was her turn when Bullets Bambarella came out of Hipless Hooker's office glaring at Montezuma Montez, who was giving Bullets a screw-you-too look.

Bullets Bambarella suddenly said icily, "I hear you was at the weight machine the other day braggin how you could pick up the whole station."

"You heard that, huh?" said Montezuma just as icily.

"Bet you couldn't even shoulder press your own weight," said Bullets.

"You got five bucks?" said Montezuma Montez, getting the attention of all the boys and girls who loved macho contests.

"I got *ten* bucks that says *I* can shoulder press my weight," said Bullets.

"All that macaroni you eat? I oughtta make it fifteen bucks," Montezuma grinned at Dudley Knebel of the robbery detail.

"All those tortillas you eat? I oughtta make it *twenty* bucks," Bullets Bambarella grinned at Valnikov of the burglary detail, whose hangover was such that he didn't even know what the two young detectives were talking about.

So while half the squad room got up and followed the two buffaloes into the locker room, Natalie Zimmerman went to see Hipless Hooker and tell him what she had discovered on Friday.

She had gone sleepless last night, deciding to tell, not to tell, to tell. Finally, she knew she *had* to tell. She would have to tell even if he weren't her partner. Even if someone else were stuck with him and she was set free. Because he carried a badge. He carried a gun. He was a sergeant in the Los Angeles Police Department, assigned to Hollywood Investigative Division. And he was insane.

"You're next, Natalie," Clarence Cromwell said.

Goddamn! Clarence Cromwell was actually massaging Hooker's neck when she entered!

"What's your problem today, Natalie?" Captain Hooker sighed, and Natalie looked at Hipless Hooker relaxing under the hands of his sea captain, and she knew there'd be no chance. Still, she tried. "Captain, can I see you *privately?*"

"Oh, God, Natalie!" Captain Hooker said, not opening his eyes. "Do you have a problem too? Do you know how little time I have before I retire and how many problems are stacking up? A little to the left, Clarence."

"It's about Valnikov, Captain," Natalie said, glaring at Clarence Cromwell. "This little experiment of letting him work with a policewoman isn't going to work out. In fact . . ."

"Gud-damn, Natalie!" Clarence interrupted, stopping the massage of Hipless Hooker, who opened his eyes and sipped his coffee and dreamed of being back on Clarence's yacht, cruising into Avalon Harbor, catching fat sea bass and albacore. The Channel Islands. The serene Pacific. Maybe a sailfish. His wife hundreds of miles away in Van Nuys. Landlocked!

"Well, I gave it a try, Captain," Natalie said, "but it isn't going to work out and I have something important to tell you. About Valnikov."

"Yes, yes, what is it?" Hooker said, leafing through the papers on his desk.

"He's crazy," she said simply.

"Yes, what else?" Captain Hooker said absently.

"What else?"

"For God's sake, what's the problem?" Captain Hooker finally demanded.

"I just told you. He's crazy. Bats. Whacko. Do you understand? I'm not saying zany, balmy, or goofy. I'm saying he's psycho. A mental case. Bugs. Loony. A candidate for a pension, a gold retirement badge, and a canvas blazer with wraparound arms!"

"That is the dumbest gud-damn statement I ever heard you make, Natalie," Clarence Cromwell said, coming around and sitting on Hooker's desk, totally blocking him from view, letting Natalie know with whom she must deal in *this* room.

"Clarence, you don't really know Valnikov!"

"What the hell you mean? I worked downtown at robbery-homicide for years and . . ."

"You don't know him *now*. I tell you he's gone nuts. For *real*."

Captain Hooker was trying to listen, but he suddenly found a document on his desk which caused him great displeasure. "Bambarella!" he yelled, forgetting the door was closed, causing Clarence Cromwell to leap from the desk.

"Problem, Captain?"

"Bullets was driving one of our cars sixty miles an hour!"

"But, Skipper," Clarence reminded him. "The speed limit's fifty-five. That's only five miles over. Sixty miles an hour ain't too bad."

"In a subterranean garage?"

"Listen, Captain," Natalie Zimmerman said testily, "you just gotta hear me out on this Valnikov matter."

"Natalie, please!" Captain Hooker said. "Get to the point!"

"You only worked with him one day," Clarence Cromwell said. "He's a little quiet and standoffish, and you say he's gone round the bend. Okay, name *one* crazy thing he did."

"It's not that easy, Clarence. It's a combination of . . ."

"*One* thing," Clarence challenged. "Just one is all I ask."

"One thing?"

"*One* thing."

"Okay, one thing is he said he was going to make a Christmas dinner when we parted on Friday. I believe you'll notice that today is January tenth."

Clarence Cromwell chewed on that one for a moment, then he started giggling. "Well, I'll be gud-damned! Is *that* all it is? Jist sit yourself down and wait a minute, Natalie. I wanna check on somethin."

Natalie was greatly relieved to see Clarence Cromwell charge out the door. Now was her chance to get through to Hooker, if she could get him to stop reading the reports on his desk.

"Captain, there were *lots* of things. Little things. It's hard to get specific. You just put them all together and they spell nut. N-u-t."

"Yes," he said, looking up for a fleeting instant. "I know Valnikov is strange, that's why we put you with him. But, Natalie, really, can't you just work with him for a little while longer . . . God, look at this! Bambarella gets stopped by the security guard while he's speeding around the subterranean garage of an apartment house chasing some blonde in a convertible, and the security guard sees his shoulder holster and says are you a cop and Bambarella says, quote, no asshole, I'm a member of the cozy nostra! End quote. Oh, God! The cozy nostra!"

"Captain, you've got to listen to . . ."

But it was too late. His head was hurting too much. And Clarence

Cromwell came flying through the door triumphantly. He slammed the door and said, "Natalie, do you know what last Friday was?"

"It was January seventh. What the hell do you mean?"

"I mean it was only January seventh to *you!* To him it was Christmas! It was Russian Christmas! *Now* how do you feel?"

"For heaven's sake," Captain Hooker said, actually smiling a little, another crisis averted. "Is *that* all it was! Natalie, why don't you just go to work now . . ."

"I don't give a goddamn if it *was* Russian Christmas. That wasn't the only thing."

"Yes, well, Natalie, this is very juvenile for an officer of your years and experience. I just . . . God, I've got a headache, Clarence!"

"I'll get you some aspirin, Cap," Clarence said, glaring at Natalie Zimmerman, who was looking at her Friz, pushing her oversized glasses back up on her nose. "I'll git you some aspirin, Captain, after Natalie goes back to work with her *partner,* Valnikov."

"Yes, yes," Captain Hooker said. "Look, I know you don't like burglary detail and you don't like Valnikov, but try to get along for a while. And if there's any evidence of, oh, bizarre behavior, report to me and we'll take further action. But do some investigating first, Natalie. Russian Christmas. God! Don't make rash accusations, please! I've got *enough* trouble!"

Clarence Cromwell started massaging the neck of the captain again, while he stared Natalie Zimmerman out of the office.

When Natalie returned to the squad room, Valnikov was sitting, drinking his third cup of tea. Why did he have to drink tea? Why couldn't he drink coffee like every other goddamn cop in the station? She plopped down in the chair beside him in utter frustration and looked at the tea bag on the saucer. She looked at Valnikov. His eyes were red and watery. He wore the same necktie Clarence Cromwell had loaned him. He'd changed his suit from Friday. This one was gray, but even so, it looked just like the other. He *never* looked any different. Watery bloodshot eyes. A faint boozy smell early in the morning. Hair growing every which way, sometimes stuck down by a wet combing, sometimes springing up in a clump of cinnamon cowlicks. He was smiling amiably, that dumb patient smile. Natalie could think of only one thing at the moment. She said, "Valnikov, do you mind opening your suit coat?"

"Pardon me, Natalie?"

"I said, would you please just unbutton your coat, and hold it open?"

"Of course," he shrugged. "If you're afraid that I forgot my gun, no, I'm very careful about such things."

She reached over and flipped open the coat. As she suspected, the inside pocket was repaired like the other suit, not with thread but metal staples.

"I figured."

"Figured?"

"That you'd do all your tailoring with the stapler here on your desk."

"I'm going to sew it. I've been meaning to do that, in fact."

"Doesn't matter," she sighed. "Except you couldn't pass through a scanner to get on an airplane. Not with all the metal you have holding your clothes together."

"Are we taking a flight somewhere?" asked the detective, blinking his watery eyes in confusion. "An extradition or something?"

I'm taking a flight, you dingaling, Natalie Zimmerman thought. I'm flying right over Hipless Hooker's head to the area commander, if I have to. And you're taking a flight right to the police department psychologist. Then she got a pang of remorse as she thought of his heavy body shielding her, keeping her from being hit by flying lead when William Allen Livingston exploded. But goddamnit, he's crazy!

"I've got all our reports logged, Natalie." Valnikov smiled, belatedly realizing she had been joking about the airplane. "I saw you had business with the captain so I got everything taken care of. We can go out in the field now if you like. We've just got one body in jail."

"Let's go see him, get it over with." She sighed.

"Okay, let's handle our case." He smiled.

You handle the case. I'll handle another case, she thought. And from that moment, as Valnikov was nearing what would be his most important case, Natalie Zimmerman decided that *her* case, the only case with which *she* would be concerned, was the case against Sergeant A.M. Valnikov. She was on her own investigation. And she would bring them irrefutable proof. The detective was not eccentric, not a "bit strange." The detective was *mad.*

Just before they got out the door, Clarence Cromwell came laughing out of Hipless Hooker's office and handed Natalie Zimmerman a burglary report. "Here's another one, jist came in, Nat! Somebody stole eighty-three pounds a bat guano from a store in your area!"

"So what's funny?"

"The captain asks me, he says, Clarence, we got a fertilizer store that big in Hollywood? I mean eighty-three *pounds* a bat guano? I say, no, Cap, it ain't no big company or nothin. It's jist some fly-by-night outfit!"

Clarence had to lean against the door, ready to collapse. Even Hipless Hooker had his head on his arms, laughing uproariously. They were in a good mood now from talking about the Channel Island voyage next weekend.

Valnikov didn't get it until Clarence turned and screamed: "Bat guano! Fly-by-night outfit! Git it?"

Then Valnikov got it, and while Natalie Zimmerman talked to her Friz, Valnikov chuckled politely.

• ● •

The body they had in Central Jail belonged to Bernie Mitchell, better known all over Hollywood Station as "Itchy Mitch." So called, because he broke out in hives every time he got busted for a felony, which was, they said, only in the months with *r*'s in them. Itchy Mitch went to jail a lot all right, but since he only stole cars he seldom got more than a few months of county jail time. As a matter of fact, Itchy Mitch only decided to switch to burglary because he was afraid some judge might finally send him to state prison. He had been told that burglary, like auto theft, rarely drew a state prison term, unless you had lots of priors. Itchy Mitch had no prior arrests for burglary, so he decided he might be able to get busted four or five times without getting some judge mad at him.

He was making Natalie itch just looking at him across the table in the jail interrogation room. He was six feet two and weighed less than Natalie, who weighed in very nicely for five feet nine. He had a long fringe of brown hair and only fuzz on top. He was broken out in hives on his arms and neck and on his fuzzy skull. His filthy white dress shirt was torn open from all the scratching. He was sitting across the table from Valnikov and Natalie, looking from one to the other. Both hands were moving ceaselessly. Scratching.

Itchy Mitch scratched his neck, his sunken chest, his back as far up as he could reach, deep in both armpits, his legs. He wanted desperately to scratch his balls, but in deference to Natalie, he didn't. Then he started all over again: the neck, his chest, both armpits . . .

"Never shoulda got hooked up with the broad, Sergeant. Never shoulda," Itchy Mitch whined after they advised him of his constitutional rights, for perhaps the eighty-third time in his life.

"What broad?" Natalie asked mechanically, not really caring what broad. Valnikov had his case to work on, she had hers.

"Always a broad gets an honest man in trouble, Sergeant. Always a broad," said Itchy Mitch, scratching.

"Do you want to talk about the warehouse you were arrested in?" Valnikov asked.

"Shoulda stuck to being a used-car salesman, Sergeant," said Itchy Mitch, reaching clear down to his raw ankles. "Great job, great job. Then one day I'm sitting there looking at this limper. And I done it."

"Limper?" said Natalie, scratching.

"You know, a lemon, a dog. This lousy lemon we took in trade on a Buick. I'm sitting there thinking, who'd miss it? It's just growing hair. A bum stove and organ. Phony white shoes."

"I don't really get it, Mitch," said Valnikov, scratching.

"What?"

"Stove and organ? White shoes?"

"Radio and heater, Sergeant! And whitewalls!"

"Oh, well don't get mad, Mitch, I never worked auto theft detail," Valnikov apologized.

"So I drive it off to Arizona, but I never get there. I just picked the black marble. All my life I pick the black marble. Why me?" he demanded, reminding Valnikov of Natalie, the way he rolled his eyes back. "Why *me?*"

"About the warehouse, Mitch," Natalie prodded, scratching.

"So I'm on my way to unload this limper in Arizona and I decide to stop at a carwash cause I got my girlfriend and I don't want her riding in no dirty car. Imagine that! Sadie's so cruddy I oughtta have *her* washed and polished and I'm worrying about mud on those phony whitewalls. Then up walks a spade, six feet thirteen or something, big moustache hanging down his mouth. I say who's this, Genghis Coon? He tells me who he is, all right. A cop! A goddamn detective, works that bad-cat auto theft detail. Puts the arm on me and I'm in the slammer and my boss won't believe I was just test driving it. All heart, my boss. That lemon wasn't worth five hundred bucks!"

"Uh, can you tell me what that's got to do with this burglary?" Valnikov asked.

"Huh? You don't get it?" Mitch said, scratching.

"I don't get it," said Valnikov, scratching.

"Sergeant, I had to get some money to pay the fine for the auto theft conviction! What the hell could I do? And I get caught inside the warehouse on my first try. That just goes to show I'm no burglar. Any kind a halfass creeper could burgle a warehouse, for chrissake! Do they send burglars to state prison?"

"Not very often, Mitch," said Valnikov, making his last notes on Itchy Mitch's confession.

"That's *some* consolation," said Mitch to Natalie, who had an unbearable itch under her bra strap.

As they were escorting him back to the jailor, Itchy Mitch turned, scratching, and said: "One thing, Sergeant. You been around this world awhile. Tell me something."

"If I can, Mitch," said Valnikov, unbuttoning his collar and loosening his tie to get at an itch on his collarbone.

"Why do some people *always* have to pick the black marble?"

• ● •

Unlike the violent Friday, Natalie Zimmerman found this Monday to be a typical detective's workday, which meant that ninety percent of the day was spent writing reports like a good bureaucrat. Just filing one count of second-degree burglary on Itchy Mitch took four hours, what with cooling their heels downtown in the district attorney's office, along with twenty other detectives. Valnikov was good at waiting. Natalie was miserable. She read the newspaper all the way through. She read every dumb magazine that was lying around, even the sports and girlie magazines one of the cretins had in his briefcase. She paced the halls, smoked, passed some time with another policewoman from Hollenbeck Division.

Whenever she'd return, Valnikov would just be sitting there like a dozing grizzly. He'd open his eyes from time to time for a pleasant nod of the head and a "Good morning" to any detectives who spoke to him, and go back into hibernation.

After the waiting room thinned out, when there were only two other detectives there, both of them nodding in their chairs, Valnikov began to whimper in his sleep. Natalie glanced up from her newspaper at her snoozing partner. He was sweating. Then he started whimpering so loudly he awakened another detective who looked at him and at Natalie and shrugged. Then Valnikov started to *sob*.

It was the rabbit. The wounded rabbit cringing in the snow. The snow, the land, stretched to eternity. Siberia. The hunter's veiny hands slashed the rabbit's throat and gutted him with two swipes of his blade glinting in the frosty sunlight. The rabbit's body jerked around on the log while the hunter pulled the guts out and broke its jaws and pulled on the face until the face was peeled back over the skull. The muscle and tissue hissed as it tore free in the powerful hands of the hunter.

"Valnikov!" She was shaking him.

"The rabbit!"

"What?"

"Natalie."

"Yes, you were sleeping. Having a nightmare or something."

"I was?" Both of the other detectives, strangers to Valnikov, were sitting straight in their chairs staring at him.

"Yes, you were . . . well, you were crying. Sort of."

"That's impossible," Valnikov said, reaching for his handkerchief with hands that trembled. "Impossible."

He wiped his face and was grateful when the receptionist said, "Valnikov and Zimmerman, Mr. Holman is available."

When they were back in their car, bound for Hollywood, Valnikov realized it was lunchtime. "Where would you like to eat today, Natalie?" he smiled.

"I don't care," she said.

It had been a quiet ride. That sobbing. He was crazy and had to be taken off the street, but God, that *sobbing* in his sleep. "Wherever you want to eat, Valnikov. It's up to you."

"Really?" he smiled. She hadn't been so kind to him since they'd been together. How long had it been? He had to stop and think for a moment. A week? Then he realized that it only seemed that long because Friday was the first day and the weekend intervened. The weekend. Lots of drinking this weekend. Stolichnaya. He had to watch that drinking. Some people might think he was an alcoholic.

"Where the hell are you going?" she asked as he suddenly wheeled off the outbound Hollywood Freeway and headed back toward downtown.

"You said we could eat anywhere today," Valnikov smiled. "If it's okay with you I'll take you somewhere a little different."

"Different?"

"You might like it," Valnikov said, looking a bit worried now. "Don't expect too much. It isn't much really. Just something I like to do for lunch from time to time."

"All right, Valnikov, all right," she sighed. "Anything's better than McDonald's. I can't look another Big Mac in the eye."

"Charlie Lightfoot," he murmured. They always said old Charlie Lightfoot was so cranky in the morning the only thing in the world he didn't hate was an Egg McMuffin. Charlie Lightfoot.

"Who's Charlie Lightfoot?" Natalie said.

"Why did you say that, Natalie?" He was stunned.

"Why did I say *what?*"

"I was just thinking about Charlie Lightfoot, and you said his name! That's amazing! Like a psychic . . ."

"Valnikov, you *said* his name!"

"No, I was just *thinking* about old Charlie Lightfoot and . . ."

"And you mumbled Charlie Lightfoot. Jesus Christ!"

"I did?"

Then he started looking alarmed. Like when she'd shaken him awake from his dream. A bull of a man like this. Frightened. She *had* to get evidence. For his own good as well as the police department's. It wasn't just for herself. "I sometimes mutter and mumble, too, when I'm thinking hard about something," she said. "It's no big thing."

"But I wasn't even thinking hard," he said, turning down Spring Street. "I just thought about old Charlie Lightfoot. He was my partner for years at homicide."

"Did you like it there, Valnikov?" she asked, offering him a cigarette as he drove ever cautiously through the heavy downtown traffic, blinking into the smog-filtered sunshine.

"I seldom smoke," he said. Then he thought about her question and said, "Well, I liked homicide work all right. I liked it okay. There's the prestige. You know, everybody thinks you're the varsity if you work homicide downtown. It was okay sometimes. Charlie Lightfoot was the best partner I ever had." Then he added, "Of course *we'll* be good partners, I'm sure, Natalie."

"Why did they . . . *you* decide to transfer to Hollywood dicks?" she asked suddenly.

"Well, I . . . I . . ." He didn't like that question. That was something that scared him lately. If he didn't like a question, if it troubled him, he couldn't quite get the handle. He wasn't even sure what she'd said. There was the murky picture again. All the sparkly shapes, something like a déjà vu experience. Something . . . something was there! If it would only take shape among the sparkly dots from the flashbulbs. If he could just see it once. And then it started to fade, as always. Come back. I almost had you that time!

Charlie Lightfoot. He had been a good partner. The best. A quiet man like Valnikov. Like Valnikov, years with a bad marriage. But a wife who hated him instead of one who drank and played. A child who drifted away. Strange, how they grow and drift and lose their respect for their fathers. The ancient inherited shame of fathers and sons. A good partner. The hardest single logistical task of police work. Find that partner. That good partner you can live with. Then keep him. Especially a homicide detective.

He hadn't answered her question about the transfer. Natalie was turned in her seat staring at him. She knew he had lost his direction. She knew he was somewhere else. Driving, just driving.

"Do you still see Charlie Lightfoot?" Natalie asked quietly. How do you make notes on this? What do you tell the captain? Did he have to go berserk before they'd believe her?

He was driving aimlessly. He'd lost his sense of direction. His whole life in this city and he was lost.

"Tell me about Charlie Lightfoot," she said carefully.

He turned east on Fifth Street and looked at the sign as though he'd never been there. Then he said, "Charlie was old for his age. Twenty-six years on the job when he pulled the pin and went to Arizona. He bought a trailer there by the big river. Charlie was some kind of detective, though."

"What could he do, Valnikov? Tell me about him. What could he do that you admired?"

"Admired," Valnikov said. And now he was looking vague and confused, as confused as when he had awakened from the dream. He was starting to perspire. She noted that. She would remember when she went to the commander. When she described his symptoms to the department psychologist.

"Charlie could get through it all better than anyone," Valnikov said. "Better than me. Do you know how many calls you get from policemen? From the bluesuits and even from soft clothes guys? Do you know how many murders they discover that aren't murders at all?"

"No. How many?"

"Lots. A vice cop finds an encyclopedia salesman dead in a motel room when they're staked out on a whore. He's lying on his back across the bed. His head is down to the floor. There's a pile of blood under his head. The carpet can't soak it all up."

"A pile of blood," Natalie said quietly.

He turned south on Wall Street and unbuttoned his collar.

It's a pile of blood, all right. It's coagulating and you'd need a shovel to pick it up. There's a crimson stalactite growing from his nose to the shovelful of blood beneath him. The vice cop is jumpy and excited. He's discovered a murder victim. Should we call the press, Sergeant? Latent prints specialists? The captain?

No. No press. No prints men. No captain. No murder.

No murder? But, Sergeant. The blood! He's been beaten! Or shot! I didn't touch him. There must be a bullet wound!

No bullet wound. No shot. No murder. And then Charlie Lightfoot found the empty vial under the bed. He had probably told the doctor he needed his prescription refilled for his nerves. The prescription was one day old. His nerves wouldn't bother him anymore. He's swallowed, let's see, forty caps. That's almost two hundred milligrams, right? What did he wash it down with? Ah, yes. Here it is, Charlie. The glass is under the pillow.

But the blood! Sergeant, the blood . . .

. . . is from his nose. See the crimson stalactite? See it ooze and shine in the flashlight beam? There. It's coagulated from his nostril down to the shovelful of waxen blood on the floor. When he lost consciousness he fell back. His head's touching the floor. The blood begins draining, draining, draining. He's a white man but his face turns black. The blood has nowhere to go. It's draining, draining. Finally the blood does what it must, it bursts through his nose.

But, Sergeant! His face, all dark and swollen. I found him belly up. He looks like a . . . like a . . .

The encyclopedia salesman took with him to eternity the face of a turtle.

Are you sure, Sergeant? It's not a murder? The pile of blood?

No, son, it's the law of gravity.

"You were saying about the blood," said Natalie Zimmerman.

He had not spoken for two minutes but he thought he had explained the pile of blood. He went on to conclude his point about Charlie Lightfoot.

"Yes, so you see, Charlie could just cut through. It makes your job so much easier. They call you so needlessly, these policemen. Even the veterans. They just don't know. But Charlie knows. Knew."

"Knew what?" Natalie Zimmerman asked.

Charlie knew. How many murder themselves. God, how many!

First thing, you look for, Officer, did the victim commit suicide.

Suicide? You kidding, Sergeant? There's an old woman in there, stuffed in her closet. Her drawers are down around her ankles! She's been buggered and murdered! Should we call latent prints? Should we call the press? The captain?

No, Officer, it's a suicide.

A suicide! Wait a minute, I've been a cop twelve years!

Did you find it yet, Charlie?

Yes, here it is. She drank a can of Drãno. It unclogged her drain, all right.

But, but, look, she's been sodomized. A rapist. A . . .

A bowel movement, Officer. She discovered pretty quick how fast that stuff unclogs the drain. Of course she wasn't really trying to unclog the drain, she was trying to go down the drain. All the way, and she did. But on the way she had to have a bowel movement. And she's sixty-five years old. And sixty-five-year-old ladies, even on the way down the drain, don't want to have bowel movements in their drawers. So she ran to the toilet but she never made it. And she fell sideways into the closet and that's blood and bile you see coming out her old rectum, all right. But nobody buggered her. And nobody killed her.

But, but, Sergeant Lightfoot. Sergeant Valnikov. I would have sworn. Her face! I would have sworn she was raped and strangled. Her cheeks are puffed up like . . . like . . .

The old woman with the unclogged drain took with her to eternity the face of a blowfish.

"Uh, where are we going, Valnikov?" Natalie asked nervously.

"Charlie Lightfoot used to hate one of the guys from latent prints," Valnikov said, turning on East Sixth Street, past the throngs of derelicts and winos. It was an aimless tour through Skid Row. Past the slave market where eight wretches sat on a bus bench, not waiting for a bus but talking to motorists who would stop. Wanna buy a slave, mister? No homo stuff. Just a day's work. Well, maybe half a day. Mow your lawn, paint your office. Haul your trash. No homo stuff for me, though. And no whips. None a that. Honest day's work. Fifteen dollars? Well, I don't know. Throw in two fifths a bourbon? You got yourself a deal, buddy!

"What guy from latent prints?" Natalie urged.

"This policeman. We called him Goremore. He used to like to fingerprint the corpses for us. Especially if he could find any excuse at all to use the bolt cutters."

"The bolt cutters."

"Goremore loved to cut their fingers off and put them in plastic bags and roll the fingerprints at his leisure back at the office, when he wasn't sitting around the crime lab trying to bring out the dates on buffalo nickles with etching acid. He used to love to go to the morgue and cut off those fingers. He used to say that he gave his wife a three-strand necklace of fingers for her birthday. Some people, some guys at the morgue, liked to joke around with Goremore. Once, on the Fourth of July, they stuck a tiny American flag on a toothpick into the penis of a cadaver. Goremore took a Polaroid of it. Carries it in his wallet to this day, I bet."

"Valnikov . . ."

"Charlie was a good detective. Charlie once caught a strangler who wore rubber gloves when he tortured children. The only clue we ever had was one rubber glove from his fourth murder. When we caught him he had a schoolbook belonging to the little girl. It was a Braille reader, grade two. I'll never forget the title of that book. It was called *Happy Times*. Charlie couldn't get over it: a Braille reader called *Happy Times*."

"Valnikov, I think I've heard . . ."

"Charlie thought of turning the gloves inside out and sure enough they picked up a partial palm print on the *inside* of the rubber gloves. We got a conviction."

He was sweaty now and heading back westbound on the Skid Row street. Lines of bars, liquor stores, fleabag hotels, blood banks, the missions. The flotsam and jetsam which had not yet made it into the Big Sewer with Archie the Alligator.

"Where are you going, Valnikov? Do you know where you're driving?"

He stopped at a red light and wiped his face on his sleeve and said, "Of course. To lunch."

She knew he had no idea they'd been driving aimlessly for nearly half an hour. "Do you still see Charlie Lightfoot?"

"What? I told you when we started this conversation."

"*Told* me?"

"Charlie's dead. He died six months after he retired. I told you. Didn't I? By the Colorado River, they say. It was a hunting accident, they say. But Charlie was a fisherman. He was sitting on a log, they think. Cleaning his shotgun, they think. Somehow he had an accident. A load of twelve gauge square in the face. A hunting accident, they say."

Charlie Lightfoot took with him to eternity the face of a coral sponge.

"I don't think I care for any lunch today, Valnikov. Let's go back to Hollywood."

"No? Well, all right." And then he sat there at the intersection desperately looking around. She knew he was temporarily lost. Then he wiped his face again and said amiably, "Natalie, let's go to lunch. I have a surprise for you." He smiled with that big sincere dumb smile of his that she had come to know so well in just two days.

"Valnikov, I think I want to go back to the station."

"The station? We haven't even called on our burglary victims yet."

"Take me to the station, Valnikov. Please."

"All right," he said.

And that was it. She had made the decision. There was no tangible proof that her partner was insane but she was certain that given an hour of conversation *anyone* could see. That was it. The die was cast. Except it wasn't. As always, fate can intervene. In this case, fate had been trucked into Skid Row in air-conditioned motor homes. Within those motor homes were two very pampered movie stars, reputed to be macho studs, who were portraying detectives on the trail of a whore who had gone underground in the Los Angeles Skid Row.

Every time the director tried to set up a scene the mob of derelicts sitting on the curb, sipping from shortdog wine bottles, started hooting and whistling and jeering: "Fake! Fake! Real cops don't do it that way! Fake! Fake!"

Finally, an assistant director got wise, bought ten fifths of Gallo burgundy from the nearest liquor store, passed it around the thirsty crowd, and they happily gave their blessing to the fake being perpetrated in their neighborhood.

While Valnikov and Natalie were trapped in the intersection trying to get through the maze of studio trucks and cars, vans and buses, they saw something which attracted their attention. There was a boy, fourteen years of age, wearing fifty-dollar, metal-studded jeans, and a T-shirt with the famous logo of a famous motion picture studio emblazoned across front and back, roaming around a group of semiconscious winos in a vacant lot.

"Probably doing a little on-location casting," Natalie said. "Why isn't the little germ in school?"

Actually, the little germ wasn't in school because his producer father hadn't been able to find one this semester which would take him. So poor Dad-o decided to employ Elliott Jr. for a few weeks helping out on his latest epic. To get rid of the little germ, the director promised him fifty bucks to make the location look more authentic.

The little germ took to his job with relish. In no time, he had the vacant lot strewn with bodies, and garbage, and whores. Of course, he promised each of the wretches a double sawbuck which would burn the hell out of the assistant director when he found out later, but no matter. Little Elliott, like big Elliott, wanted realism.

"The way these bums hang around these streets," Natalie muttered with disgust.

"Where can they go?" Valnikov said. "Beverly Hills? They've got nowhere to go."

She looked quickly at him, because it was the first time she ever heard an edge to his voice. Then she followed his eyes to Elliott Jr., who was doing a little set decoration by spray-painting the side of a three-dollar-a-day hotel. On the side of the wall Elliott Jr. had spray-painted: "Santa Claus butt fucks Rudolph the Red-nosed Reindeer."

"Sweet," said Natalie. "I'd like to spray-paint his goddamn head."

"So would I," said Valnikov, who made a sudden southbound turn which threw Natalie against the dashboard. Then he wheeled to the curb, stood on the brakes and was out of the detective car before Natalie could pick up her oversized glasses.

By the time Natalie ran to the vacant lot, Valnikov had Elliott Jr. by the back of the neck with one hand and the spray can in his other. To the amazement of Natalie Zimmerman, and the dismay of Elliott Jr., and the delight of three winos who were not quite unconscious, Valnikov turned the spray can on Elliott's fifteen-dollar haircut and didn't release him until the can of silver paint sputtered and spit.

With Natalie behind the wheel, they raced three blocks before Elliott Jr., dripping paint, reached the wardrobe truck bawling for his father. For two weeks, Elliott Jr. would be the only fourteen-year-old in Beverly Hills with gray hair.

"Wow!" cried a flushed Natalie Zimmerman when they were racing up Spring Street.

"Don't turn here, Natalie," said Valnikov. "Keep going."

"Wow, Valnikov!" she cried. "I hope nobody got our license number. Do you think the little germ knew you were a cop?"

"I don't think so," Valnikov shrugged.

Her glasses were askew and her buckskin Friz was hanging to her nose. She pushed them both up where they belonged and said, "Do you know what you just did?"

"I painted his head," Valnikov said.

"You . . . I . . . I just lived my fantasy! Do you realize how seldom in a person's lifetime that happens? I had a fantasy. I mentioned it to you. And then *you* let me live it!"

"Why not?" he said.

"Wow!"

"Natalie, do you still want to go to the station? Or should we handle our calls first, or what?"

She looked at him for a moment and said, "Let's handle some of our reports first. Let's make some calls. I don't think I have to go back to the station just yet."

Then they were headed back outbound on the Hollywood Freeway. Valnikov stole occasional bleary-eyed glances at the legs of Natalie Zimmerman. She was awfully attractive, he thought. Even with her goofy glasses and dopey hairdo, she was an attractive woman. Valnikov wondered if she might go to the movies with him now that he had sprayed the kid's hair silver.

• ● •

While Valnikov was trying to get up the nerve to ask Natalie Zimmerman again to go to a movie, Madeline Dills Whitfield was sitting in her living room beside the telephone, drinking Scotch and water at noon.

The pet mortuary had already arrived and taken Tutu away.

"We were saddened to hear about your dear Victoria," the balding mortician said.

"Yes, yes, please, just give her a nice burial. Send the bill to me."

"But, Mrs. Whitfield, your dog handler, Mr. Biggs, said you'd probably want to select the casket and . . ."

"Something moderately priced," Madeline said, not trying to conceal the double Scotch. "Something moderate."

"We have some very nice, reasonably priced caskets that . . ."

"Yes, that'll do. Yes."

"As to a burial service, would you like . . ."

"No. No. No burial service. Bury her at once."

"But the grave site, Mrs. Whitfield. You should select her site, and we have to present the body of Victoria Reg . . ."

"Bury her at once, do you hear me! Today. Any grave plot will do. A moderately priced coffin. Take her away now and do it!"

"Yes, Mrs. Whitfield, yes. I understand perfectly. Yes, it'll be done at once. And for the billing, should we . . ."

"Send your bill to this address. Please, I'm not feeling well."

"You have our sympathy, Mrs. Whitfield, and be assured that Victoria Regina . . ."

"Yes, yes, yes."

And now she sat by the telephone, waiting. Finally she called the kennel of Chester Biggs.

"Chester?"

"Mrs. Whitfield?"

"Did that . . . that man phone? The man I mentioned yesterday? Richard?"

"Just a minute, Mrs. Whitfield."

An interminable wait and then, "Mrs. Whitfield, my wife said a man did call, and she gave him your number just as you instructed."

"How long ago?"

"She says an hour, Mrs. Whitfield."

"Thank you, Chester. Thank you. Good-bye."

An hour! Why hadn't he called? Why? Is he trying to make her suffer? Is that it? Are people who do such things sadists as well as common criminals? Do they delight in torturing their victims? Would he torture Vickie for his own perverted enjoyment? Is Vickie being whipped? Or burned? Oh God!

Madeline Whitfield spilled the glass of Scotch on the carpet and leaned across the arm of an old wingback chair, weeping.

• ● •

At that moment, Victoria Regina of Pasadena was reluctantly taking a bite of boiled horsemeat from the tobacco-stained fingers of Philo Skinner, who had been trying to feed her for the last two hours.

"That's it, sweetie," Philo said soothingly. "Philo won't hurt you. Philo loves you. Philo loves all little terriers and you're *so* pretty."

He was at the end of the 175-foot aisle dividing the kennel. The last of thirty-two dog pens on each side of the long, low-roofed building had been reserved for Vickie who spent the first night of her life since weaning outside the bedroom of her mistress.

"Philo loves you, sweetie," he said, tempting the little schnauzer with a chunk of boiled liver. She approached him tentatively as he squatted outside the pen, handing the meat through the mesh.

"That's yum-yum," Philo said, as Vickie accepted her second nibble of meat and wrinkled her nose at the smell of Philo's endless cigarette chain. "You're going to be just fine, sweetheart," Philo said. "Here's another bite of yum-yum, and then Philo's going to call your mommy and your mommy's going to give Philo eighty-five dimes, and Philo's going to send you home wagging your tail. Okay, sweetie?"

After Philo was satisfied that Vickie was eating all right, he went to the office to make the call. Mavis had been hard to get rid of today.

"Philo, I know we're going broke around here, but I can't understand why you gave that Pattie Mae the day off. I mean we still have twenty-five dogs out there in those sixty dog runs, you know."

"Only twenty-five dogs," Philo sighed, trying hard to keep from laughing with joy. "Never been so bad, this business. Just trying to save a few bucks, my love."

"*You* save money?"

"Things are awful tough, my love. I can take care of twenty-five dogs easy."

"Sure isn't like you, Philo," she said suspiciously, "wanting to do all that work. You got something on your mind? Maybe you got Pattie Mae coming back here this afternoon and you don't want me here?"

"Oh, please, please, please!" Philo cried, lighting a cigarette with the butt of the last. "The last thing on my mind is pussy, goddamnit!" And at least *that* was the truth.

"Well, if I ever catch you, Philo, it's all over. You understand? You listening to me, Philo?"

Stripping, stripping, stripping. She never got tired of it. Well, two more days. Wednesday should be time enough. The Thursday flight to Puerto Vallarta would bring him in there just in time for a margarita at sunset.

• • •

She got the call at 2:50 p.m. He was speaking soft and had his voice muffled, like in the movies.

"This is Richard." Burton that is, get it? He was so excited he wanted to giggle insanely.

"Yes? Yes?"

"Have you told anyone? The police?"

"No one, I swear." Madeline, who had been getting desperately drunk, was now sweatily sober.

"I want eighty-five thousand dollars."

The number was so great, she was sure he said eighty-five hundred. She was expecting him to demand more than five thousand, so she wasn't too surprised. "Yes, yes," she said eagerly. "I can get it by tomorrow. Perhaps by tonight if I . . ."

"Shut up and listen to me," Philo said excitedly, speaking with the mouthpiece wrapped in a paper towel. He was in a cocktail lounge, two blocks from Skinner Kennels. The barroom was practically empty midday, but still he jumped at every sound the bartender made.

"Yes, I'm listening," she said.

"I want the money in tens and twenties and no more than two packages of fifties."

"How's Vickie? Is Vickie all right?"

"Listen to me, goddamnit, if you ever want to see your Vickie again."

Then Madeline started to cry and Philo Skinner realized he had to alter his technique. "Damn, lady, calm down. Listen, get hold a yourself. Your bitch is okay. She's fine. Cut it out, will ya?"

"Yes . . . I'm . . . I . . . yes . . . please . . . don't hurt her. *Please!*"

"*Hurt* her! Goddamnit, lady, I'm no criminal! What the hell's wrong with you? I never hurt a dog in my life. Get hold a yourself, lady."

"Yes . . . I'm sorry. All right. I'll get the eighty-five hundred and then where do I take it?"

The line was silent for a moment and Philo Skinner said: "That's eighty-five *thousand*, lady. Eighty-five *thousand!*"

"My God!" she cried. "That's impossible. Eighty-five *thousand?* I don't *have* eighty-five thousand dollars! I wouldn't know where to begin to *get* eighty-five thousand dollars. Please, sir. I beg you . . ."

"You lying bitch!" Philo screamed, then he caught himself and opened the phone booth door to peek at the bartender. "You lying bitch," he whispered. "I know about you. You're rich, goddamn you. Don't gimme that shit, you want your fucking schnauzer alive."

"Please, sir, please . . ." Then Philo had to wait while she wept again. "My God, sir . . . please . . . I beg you . . ."

Philo Skinner was starting to sweat in the phone booth. He lit a cigarette, still afraid to open the door. He began suffocating himself. His eyes were raw from the smoke by the time Madeline stopped crying and was able to talk.

"Lady, I know damn well how much you're worth. I saw your goddamn house. I know you're rich. Rich! I know you can get a measly eighty-five thousand. Now if you care for this bitch a yours, you'll do exactly like I say."

"Listen, listen to me," Madeline begged. "I'd give you anything. I swear. Anything! But you must believe me. I don't have eighty-five thousand dollars. This . . . this big house . . . there's no furniture upstairs. I keep it closed off. I had to refinance it last year. I live on a small trust fund. Please . . ."

"You cunt!" Philo screamed. "You rotten filthy lying cunt! You get the money and have it by noon tomorrow. I'm going to start working on this bitch a yours at noon tomorrow. I'm going to call you at six p.m. tonight and see what progress you made. You understand? And you better have something to tell me, hear? You hear?"

"Yes!" Madeline wailed. "Yes!"

"And one last thing, take care a that little schnauzer bitch you have with you. Keep your handler away from her so he doesn't see she's not your Victoria. I'll give you further instructions on what to do with her when I call you tonight."

Before Madeline could tell him the schnauzer was dead, he hung up.

Philo Skinner was still trembling with rage and frustration when he got back to the kennel. The cunt. The rotten miserable stingy lying *rich* cunt. Imagine, trying to flim-flam Philo Skinner like that. All these rich cunts were alike—stingy. Philo had pampered their goddamn dogs for twenty-five years and they were all alike. Spend twenty grand a year to show a single dog, and throw a Gainesburger to the dog handler. Well, this cunt wouldn't get away with that.

Philo Skinner sat down and began rehearsing his next telephone call. Imagine that, trying to flim-flam Philo Skinner, Terrier King!

Madeline was devastated when the terrifying extortionist hung up. It was a full hour before she could get up from the sofa where she lay, intermittently weeping and drinking.

She didn't pour a second drink. Instead, she began thinking. She surprised herself in that she began formulating a plan. She was filled with dread and overwhelming fear and yet she began to formulate a plan to deal with this extortionist. She found some strength she didn't know she had. The money was totally out of the question. She knew from her year-end audit that her net worth was around forty thousand dollars. That included the surrender value of her insurance policy, a second-trust deed, an inflated value on what was left of the antique furniture, her car, what little equity was left in the house after refinancing, and an arbitrary value placed on the small balance of the trust fund. Until now there was the dream, the fantasy, that after Vickie won Madison Square Garden, a man would rescue her, a widower with a substantial fortune. They would meet at The Sign of The Dove restaurant . . .

Immediate liquidation would take weeks! She would have to explain it to the extortionist when he called again. He'd *have* to listen to reason. Perhaps she could borrow nine thousand. Perhaps ten thousand, at the outside. There was Ariel Wentworth. Her husband was the chairman of the board of . . . which bank was it? Ariel might be able to help her get a loan. A very quick loan. Ten thousand dollars.

The alternative was the police. She was tempted to call them. She went to the phone three times. Each time, she returned to the first plan. The loan. She started to call Ariel. No, first she had to reason with the man who had Vickie. Make him see. Surely, he would see. He wasn't a monster. He said he'd never hurt an animal in his life. She remembered him saying that. It was all she remembered, but he *did* say that. She drank no more that day. She sat in the living room waiting for six o'clock. Waiting for sundown. Waiting for the *call.*

• • •

The rest of the day for Natalie Zimmerman meant burglary investigation, pure and simple. Which meant public relations. An offer of sympathy to the victims who didn't really have any hope for the return of the merchandise. A few tips on how to prevent future breaking-and-entering, a crime report number for the sake of reporting the loss on a tax return or to an insurance company. Was the fingerprint man here yet? He said he didn't get any latent prints? No, they seldom leave prints, even if they *don't* use gloves. Sir, it's very very hard to get good lifts unless a surface is hard, smooth and clean. Yes, I know they get fingerprints in the movies from cotton handkerchiefs. Yes, I know that in the movies the detective caught a rapist by getting a fingerprint from . . . What? From a woman's tit? That's ridiculous!

A typical day for an investigator of business burglaries. They called on six victims and got not a single lead of any kind.

"No clues for the clues closet," Natalie Zimmerman smirked when they finished their fourth victim contact.

"Do you want to stop for some food?" Valnikov asked.

"I'm not hungry," she said. How could she be hungry? How could she get Captain Hooker away from Clarence Cromwell long enough to inform him about today? Valnikov was cracked. Over the edge. Just get him talking about his old homicide cases, Captain, if you don't believe me. Watch what happens to him when he starts talking about *that.*

But what if he doesn't always react the way he did today? A Braille reader. Charlie Lightfoot. Sobbing as he dreamed about some goddamn rabbit. What if he *could* fool Hooker, whose attention span on anything outside of that goddamn boat of Cromwell's was about three minutes? What if he doesn't always go whacko when you make him remember the bad old days?

"Valnikov?"

"Yes?"

"Let's just go stop somewhere, anywhere. Get a cup of coffee and a doughnut, or something."

"How about a deli on Fairfax? I could go for a nice onion bagel," Valnikov said pleasantly. His eyes were starting to clear up, the whites no longer laced with red webbing.

"Okay," she said, and then she said, "Valnikov, do you remember what we were talking about this morning?"

"What's that, Natalie?" he smiled.

She hesitated an instant, took a breath and bit the bullet: "We were talking about Charlie Lightfoot. About murder. Suicide. Dead bodies. Dead children. Your old job."

Corpses. There were stacks of corpses in the morgue. Corpses all around. In the autopsy rooms. In the coolers. In the halls. Tags on toes. Bulges under the sheets.

That one's a woman. Silicone. Look at the boobs. Like twin Everests. Ever rest, baby. What good did all that silicone do you? And that one. Under the sheet and stiff as a catfish. He's got more sticking out than we do alive, eh, Valnikov? And that one. The body's only four feet long. A boy or a girl? Is that the one came through on that West L.A. crime report? You know, the little girl, her mother used to trade for dope? You know the one? The one mom used to loan to the dyke? You know the one? The one the dyke started to sleep with when she was six years old, and then mom started battering when the dyke got tired of her? The one they used to photograph being screwed by the dyke's dope customers? The one mom used to take her empty spike (No heroin today, you little bitch, it's your fault. You could have kept her happy if you wanted to.) and ram the empty spike under her toenails and through her eardrums? You know the one?

Corpses in the morgue. A class of student nurses being taken through the morgue by an orderly who relishes their horror. Goremore is there cutting off fingers.

A little white around the gills, aren't you, girls? If you get tired, don't lay down on those *tables, girls.*

Of course he takes them right into an autopsy about to begin. One he knows about. This fellow loves *his work. He* loves *to take student nurses on tour. Look at that one. A ragpicker the cops found after three weeks in a boxcar.*

Goremore winks. Come closer, girls. Look. He's a black man but his face is white.

His face! His face is moving!

No, it's not moving, girls. It's covered with a swarm of maggots. The maggots are moving, girls. He's a maggot meal ticket.

Grab that girl! Goddamnit, Goremore, she fell on her head, you dumb shit!

And then Goremore says, Fuck it, I ain't no tour guide anyway, just as they jerk on the chin to see if the throat was cut, and the jaw rips loose. Half a pound of maggots sail in a heap and go plop on the tile floor. A second student nurse falls down beside the maggots. The fat and loggy maggots look at her curiously. But in their dim maggot brains they retreat and stay coiled, and writhing, and crawling on top of each other. Even maggots need maggots, after all.

The meal ticket took with him to eternity no face whatsoever.

And then, look out, Valnikov, here it comes! The sparkly flashes. It's the morgue, all right. There. It won't get away this time. Déjà vu. There's a picture *forming*. He's almost got it! It's a pathologist and a . . .

"Valnikov."

Oh, no, it's the *rabbit!* He's bounding through the snow!

"Valnikov. Valnikov!"

"Huh?"

"Valnikov, the stoplight went from red to green to red. Do you hear the horns?"

"Huh?"

Now Natalie Zimmerman was *frightened*. "Never mind, Valnikov. Don't tell me about Charlie Lightfoot. No murder. No dead bodies. Never mind, Valnikov, it's all right!"

"Huh?" Valnikov pulled into the traffic, ignoring the angry motorists behind him.

"What did you say, Natalie?"

"I said, tell me about burglary, Valnikov," she babbled. "Tell me about burglary. I wanna learn."

The picture was gone. Gone again. Valnikov was sweating and trembling.

"Burglary? Yes. As you know, I haven't been working burglary too long, Natalie, I'm an old homicide detective . . ."

"No homicide, Valnikov," said Natalie Zimmerman, her eyes big behind the big glasses. "Tell me about burglary. What have you learned about burglary? I wanna be a good burglary investigator."

"Oh," he said, wiping the sweat from his eyes. "Well, let's see, I've learned that a competent burglar can get through any hole or opening that's big enough for a human head. Isn't that interesting?"

"That's very interesting. Very interesting. Let's go get that coffee and bagel, Valnikov, then we'll be just about finished for the day and we can go to the station."

"All right," Valnikov smiled, the trembling almost stopped.

If only she had a tape recorder. It was going to be hard to explain it to Hipless Hooker. How can you explain it unless you were *there*. But if he didn't understand, she'd go to the area commander. She'd go, goddamnit!

The delicatessen was busy even at this hour. It was one of the oldest in Los Angeles.

One employee knew Valnikov, an old counterman. He had the whiskey voice and puffy eyes of a veteran alcoholic. Takes one to know one, Natalie thought, when he and Valnikov exchanged a warm greeting.

"Hello, Sergeant," the old man said with a wide peg-toothed grin.

Why did all the old people respond to Valnikov? What was his age? Only forty-four? Why did old people treat him like one of their own?

"Hi, Solly," Valnikov said, shaking hands with the counterman, who dried his wrinkled hands on his apron.

"I ain't seen you in I don't know how long, Sergeant," said the counterman. His hair was straight and white and combed back flat. "I was awful sorry about Sergeant Lightfoot. I heard nothing until recently. I was sorry."

"Yeah," said Valnikov. "This is my new partner. I work Hollywood Detectives now."

"A woman you work with?" said the counterman. "A pretty woman. You're lucky, Sergeant."

Then a fifty-year-old busboy came out of the kitchen carrying a metal tray loaded with sandwiches. He was dark, with a flat nose, and shiny black hair, blacker than Philo Skinner's dye job. He was short and squat, with no buttocks, wide hips and skinny legs. He was from the jungles of Sinaloa near Mazatlan, and was known as Indio.

Valnikov smiled at him and said, "Hello, Indio."

"Sargento," the Indian grinned, and there it was: Tijuana bridgework. Gleaming.

"I've been dying for an onion bagel, Solly. What would you like, Natalie?"

"An onion bagel, please," she said.

"Coming up, Sergeant," the old man grinned. "With cream cheese?"

"Of course."

"Lox or herring?"

"Lox for me, Solly."

"That's right. It was Sergeant Lightfoot who liked herring."

"It was," said Valnikov.

Then Valnikov tried to light Natalie's cigarette. "How do you like the smell of this place, Natalie?"

"Smells fine," she said.

"I grew up in Russian Flats," he said. "Over near Boyle Heights.

We were Russians and Jews and Mexicans in those days. I knew Solly's brother, owned a beer bar on Brooklyn Avenue in the old days."

"Is that so?" said Natalie Zimmerman.

"Do you know why the old Russians and Jews got along so well in Boyle Heights?"

"No."

"Because the Russians, like my parents, remembered how it was when they were fleeing the Bolsheviks. How the Jews gave them tea and bread. Not that the Jews were czarists, but they knew that some of the Whites were going to the magical place. To America. When I was a kid in Boyle Heights the Jewish kids used to think borscht was *their* food. Can you imagine?"

"Is that so," said Natalie Zimmerman, drinking her coffee and rehearsing the speech to Hipless Hooker. Look, Captain, if you won't listen to reason, there's always the area commander. I don't like to go over your head, but . . .

Then Solly gave Valnikov his tea. In a glass, Russian style. He remembered the old days too.

"I sure miss Sergeant Lightfoot," Solly said. "You know my grandson? The one I was worried always getting in trouble, that one?"

"Yes," Valnikov said.

"Well, a grand job in a grand place, he's got. A kettle wrench, is what."

"A kettle wrench?" said Natalie Zimmerman.

"A kettle wrench," Solly nodded. "You know, where they punch kettles."

"Oh?"

"He's a cowboy," Valnikov explained.

"Oh."

"The kettles are on a wrench," Solly explained.

"Oh."

"He was always a better boy after you and Sergeant Lightfoot arrested him," Solly said. "Excuse me. I got to go back in the kitchen. We got one dishwasher only today."

"Of course, Solly," Valnikov nodded.

Then another customer at the delicatessen counter said: "My bagel isn't toasted well enough. Take it back." He said it to Indio, who understood by his tone what the man meant. The man was older than the Indian, yet he wore a rainbow T-shirt, a bush coat, and pants carefully spattered with paint. In short, he was five years out of style and thought he was groovy. "Take this bagel back, it's not toasted well enough."

Indio picked up the plate and started for the kitchen.

The man said to his twenty-two-year-old female companion: "That's the trouble with these greaseballs. Let them work in delicatessens, whadda you expect?"

Natalie heard it and ignored it. Indio didn't understand it. Valnikov looked perturbed. In a few minutes Indio brought back the bagel and placed it before the aging hipster.

"It's still not toasted right," the man in the bush coat said. "What's the matter with you? You don't even speak English, do you? What are *you* doing working in a delicatessen anyway?"

Valnikov put down his glass of hot tea and walked over two stools to the man in the bush coat and said, "What's wrong with that bagel? Do you have a color chip to check your bagel with?"

The man looked up at the lumbering man with blazing watery eyes and mumbled something unintelligible to his little girlfriend, who was reading *Variety* and wondering how she got hooked up with this schmuck in the first place.

When Indio sheepishly picked up the dirty dishes and walked past Valnikov, the detective reached over and took the Indian's arm. "Solly," Valnikov said to the old man who spoke all the languages of Boyle Heights: English, Yiddish, Spanish. "Tell Indio for me that when Cortez came to the New World the Aztec emperor put a golden fingerbowl in front of him and the ignorant white man *drank* from it. Tell him that, will you?"

Natalie Zimmerman's mind was racing when they drove back to Hollywood Station. Captain, I have something important . . . something crucial . . . something . . . Captain, could you please excuse Sergeant Cromwell, this is *private*. Captain, if you don't listen to me I'm going to the area commander . . . Captain, sit down. I know you're retiring in a matter of weeks, but this is something you must deal with. Captain, Sergeant Valnikov is a raving lunatic!

Except at that very moment, Natalie Zimmerman's plans were being frustrated by none other than Bullets Bambarella, who was doing nothing more than being himself with an irate and very famous movie star who had come to Hollywood Detectives to complain about the arrest of his seventeen-year-old nephew on a narcotics charge.

"The kiddie cops ain't here," Bullets Bambarella said, hardly looking up from his *Playboy* magazine, which he had concealed inside the Los

Angeles Police Department Manual that he was allegedly studying for promotion.

"Then I'd like to see the boss, whoever that is," said the famous movie star. He had curly dark hair and of course showed beautiful capped teeth. He wore a red-and-white shirtsuit, with the flap pocket bearing his initials. His flared pants bore chalk-white piping around medium bells. He wore kangaroo boots with five-inch heels. In short, he was conservatively dressed for Sunset Boulevard.

The teenage boy with him had dazzling real teeth, and wore a cotton safari shirt and faded jeans with belt loop legs that cost $130, hence were the most popular jeans in Baghdad. On the star's other arm, completing the trio, was a buxom woman with a red bandana over her dark blond hair. She fidgeted with sunglasses which, of course, were on top of her head.

"Well, whom can I talk with about this stupid arrest?" the movie star said to Bullets. "My nephew had a little angel dust. Big deal."

"You can talk to me, that's *whom,*" Bullets Bambarella sighed, closing the book.

"My nephew was arrested two hours ago and . . ."

"Yeah, you said that," Bullets yawned. "And I told you there ain't no kiddie cops here right now. And your nephew ain't here right now. So I guess there ain't much I can do for ya."

"Look, Officer," said the famous movie star. "My nephew was arrested because he was holding this angel dust for somebody else and my business manager was supposed to take care of this and if he doesn't get here soon . . . Margo, take my car and go find that dumb shit."

Bullets watched the buxom lass and the movie star touch cheeks and kiss the air. Then she wriggled off to drive to the Sunset Strip and find the dumb shit.

"I've got an uncle who's a good friend of the district attorney and the chief of police," said the famous movie star.

"I got an uncle who's a notary public," Bullets Bambarella said. "How about givin me a break, fella. Come back later or somethin. Your nephew ain't here."

"Do you know who you're talking to?" said the young companion with dazzling teeth.

"No," said Bullets Bambarella, who was starting to get as pissed off as the famous movie star.

"I don't believe it," the lad said to the movie star. "Do you believe it? I don't believe it." Then he turned to Bullets and said, "Have you ever been to a movie?"

"Don't tell me," Bullets said. "He's an *actor*. I shoulda guessed."

"I'm not wasting any more time with you. Get me your commanding officer," the movie star said.

"He ain't here," said Bullets.

"Where is he?"

"Captain Hooker's off buying a yachting jacket," Bullets said.

"Is he a police captain or a sea captain?" the movie star snickered, causing his young companion to fall against him in a gush of giggles.

"You an actor too?" Bullets asked the young man.

"As a matter of fact he is," the movie star said.

Bullets examined the slender hips and torso of the young lad, who still had his hand on the movie star's arm. The lad had a large head and a small delicate face.

"Yeah, now I recognize ya," said Bullets. "You're one a Charlie's Angels, ain'tcha?"

Now the teenager was livid and looked as though he just might be crazy enough to attack Bullets Bambarella. "Bastard!" he said. "Ignorant bastard! I'll have your badge!"

Bullets then doubled his big fist and said, "Hey leading man, how'd you like me to make a character actor outta ya?"

"You bastard!" the young man screamed, causing Clarence Cromwell to get up and come out from the squad room.

"Bullets, gud-damn it, what're you do-in?" Clarence demanded.

"That bastard!" the young man shrieked while the movie star said, "Quiet down, Buddy, quiet down. Don't let him get your goat. Remember, Buddy, sticks and stones, sticks and stones . . ."

"Yeah and *keep* that in mind," Bullets said, picking up a nightstick.

"Who *are* these people?" Clarence demanded.

"I dunno. Claim they're actors. Look like a couple a interior *dick*-orators to me."

"I'll have his badge, I'll have his badge!" the young man sputtered.

"Everybody quiet down!" said Clarence Cromwell, finally recognizing the famous actor. "You too, Bullets!"

But it was too late. Bullets was having a good old time doing what he did best: causing a riot.

"Hey, Clarence, I just thought a somethin," Bullets giggled. Then he pointed to the movie star and said, "We oughtta book that man for burglary. Look at the age of his playmate. That's illegal entry!"

Captain Hooker came back in the station just in time to see the two actors raging at the reception desk, while Clarence Cromwell did his best to quiet everybody down. He'd had a long day and got the hell out because he recognized the famous actor immediately and started to get a headache thinking of the trouble this would cause him. Oh, God, is *he* the one nominated for an Academy Award?

When Natalie Zimmerman came back and hurried to Hipless Hooker's office, she saw no one but Bullets Bambarella waiting sulkily for Clarence Cromwell. When Clarence finally came storming into the captain's office pointing a finger at Bullets Bambarella, Natalie knew that another day had passed.

She could hear Bullets through the open door saying, "But Clarence, you just can't please some people! Those two fruitcakes came in here and started pickin on me!"

"SHUT UP, BULLETS!" Clarence yelled as everyone signed out quietly and went home, including Natalie Zimmerman, who left talking to her Friz.

And Sergeant A.M. Valnikov had his police career extended for yet another day.

• ● •

The phone call was late. It came at 6:45 p.m. Madeline Whitfield had drunk seven cups of coffee and had not had a Scotch since early afternoon. She was stunned at her reserve of strength. She was cold sober.

"This is Richard," the voice said. Philo Skinner still spoke through a paper towel. Now he was talking from a telephone booth in a service station some three blocks from Skinner Kennels.

"Yes. Yes! How's Vickie?"

"Vickie's fine. When do I get the money?"

"Please, you've got to listen to me, sir."

"When do I get the money?"

"Sir. I've been thinking all afternoon of ways to make you understand. I've got to be blunt and honest. Lots of people like me live in these Pasadena mansions with barely enough to . . ."

"When do I get the money, you lousy cunt!" Philo screamed into the mouthpiece. Then he got hold of himself, and looked around as though he could be heard by the passing cars in the early hours of night.

Madeline was determined to be reasonable and calm no matter how the man terrified her. "Sir, if you could come here and talk to me face to face, I could explain to you. I could show you my financial records. You'd understand how it is. Eight-five thousand dollars! Why it's . . ."

"You rotten stingy cunt!" Philo Skinner was beside himself now. She could hardly understand him. "You want this bitch in one piece? You want this bitch alive? You . . . you . . . don't try to pull that shit on me, you rotten cunt!"

Madeline started to break, but only for a few seconds. The reserve of strength, where did it come from? A word from Edna Lofton at the Valley Hunt Club could set her off on a binge for three days, and yet, this very minute, with Vickie's life in the balance, she could deal with this madman, with this criminal. Madeline Whitfield had some *presence.* Madeline Whitfield was starting to have a little regard for herself.

"Please, listen to me," Madeline said. "Sir, I . . . I'm sure I can get some money for you. I'm sure I can borrow ten thousand dollars. Believe me when I tell you that I have just a little over five thousand of my own that I can get my hands on quickly. I can borrow ten. You'll have just over fifteen thousand dollars. I can get it for you by tomorrow. I can have it for you by the time the banks close tomorrow. I can . . ."

"Okay, now you listen to *me.*" Philo had dropped the paper towel and was croaking into the mouthpiece. "I'm giving you until three o'clock tomorrow. When the banks close I'm calling you. You're going to tell me where I can pick up the eighty-five thousand . . ."

"Sir! Please believe me . . ."

"Shut up!" Philo screamed. "Shut your fucking mouth!"

When it was quiet Philo broke into a coughing spasm. Madeline heard the extortionist spit a wad of phlegm. Then he came back on the phone wheezing, and said, "If you don't have some good news for me, I'm cutting off one toe of your precious bitch and I'm sending it to you." Philo had seen that in a movie. "One toe at a time."

"Oh, please!" Madeline almost broke. Almost. She sat for a moment and took hold and said reasonably, "I'll do what I can, sir. I'll liquidate everything I can as quickly as possible. I'll talk to you tomorrow."

"If you even *think* about calling the cops . . ."

"I won't call them, sir. I give you my word. Don't hurt my Vickie. Please."

• ● •

Philo was a nervous wreck when he got back to the kennel. He was late with the feeding. When he opened the door leading from the grooming room to the long rows of dog pens the animals went crazy.

Jesus. Only twenty-five animals. It wasn't his fault he had to resort to crime. He hadn't so much as cheated on his income tax before now. Well, maybe a little, but he was no criminal. What could a man do? With economic conditions like they were, what could a man do? It wasn't his fault.

Then Philo Skinner prepared the meal for the animals in his care. The bastards ate better than he did these days. That cunt. Lives in a fucking mansion over the Rose Bowl. The servants' quarters probably bigger than the house Philo lived in with all his brothers and sisters when he was a kid. I don't have the money, sir. The cunt! People like her made Philo Skinner what he was. Philo Skinner was a decent human being. Never hurt an animal in his life.

Then he remembered. That stingy miserable cunt got him so upset he forgot to give her instructions about Tutu. He wondered if there was some way he could get Tutu for himself. No, that was stupid. He couldn't risk that. A money drop was one thing. But a schnauzer drop? Tutu would have to go back with that horny cheap old cunt, Millie Muldoon Gharoujian. Too bad, Tutu. He would love to run on the beach in Puerto Vallarta, a rejuvenated man, Tutu by his side.

When Philo Skinner slept that night he had a dream. In the dream he was tiptoeing across a flower-covered rainbow bridge under a subtropical moon. In the dream Philo Skinner looked *just* like Richard Burton.

10

The Fiddler

Hipless Hooker came to work very late on Tuesday morning. He just knew there'd be another personnel complaint on his desk. He'd checked with his wife, who hated boats but *loved* movies, and discovered that the famous movie star he saw screaming at Bullets Bambarella last night had not been nominated for an Academy Award as he'd feared. At least that was *some* consolation. Maybe an actor who wasn't up for an Oscar couldn't cause him as much trouble as one who was. Hipless Hooker tried a glass of milk and it didn't help. He was sure the famous actor would be waiting for him with his attorney and that's why he came to work late.

When Hipless Hooker came in the door he headed straight for his office, tucking his chin under his lapel, hoping that no one would notice him. Natalie Zimmerman leaped up and ran across the squad room but Clarence Cromwell beat her to it. He went into Captain Hooker's office and slammed the door in her face.

"Did the movie star call the press last night, Clarence?" Hooker asked, grimacing at the cup of coffee Clarence had for him.

"No coffee today, Skipper?"

"I've got terrible indigestion," Hooker groaned.

"I took care a both actors," Clarence grinned. "Took them inside, bought them coffee, told them I was personally gonna kick Bullets' ass all over the station. And get this, when they left they was so happy they gave me two tickets to a preview movie at the Director's Guild!"

"You're amazing, Clarence!" Captain Hooker cried.

"Captain? Got a few minutes?" Natalie said, peeking in the door, her Friz hanging down over her big glasses.

"What's the problem, Natalie?" Clarence said gruffly.

"Captain, we've just *got* to talk about Valnikov!"

Then Natalie stood helplessly as both Clarence Cromwell and Hipless Hooker began moaning in unison. "Oooooohhhhh."

"Captain . . ." But she couldn't get a word in edgewise. So Natalie Zimmerman just stood there and sneered at her Friz until the men stopped groaning. When they were finished, Clarence Cromwell said, "Natalie, you said you was gonna work with the guy awhile and give it a fair try."

"Clarence, I gave it a fair . . ."

Then Hipless Hooker started groaning again. But this time it wasn't just *emotional* pain. He felt flame in his stomach that went right up his throat.

"Do you call a few days a fair chance, gud-damn it!" Clarence demanded.

"Oooooooooohhhhhhhh!" groaned Hipless Hooker.

They both stopped talking and looked at him.

"You okay, Skipper?" asked Clarence.

"My stomach!" Hipless Hooker cried. "Ooooooooohhhhhh!"

"Take it easy, Cap. Take it easy!" Clarence said. "Natalie, get me the spare keys. I'll run the boss over to the receiving hospital. What's it feel like, Cap? An ulcer?"

"I don't knoooooooowwww!" cried Hipless Hooker. "It huuuuuuuurts!"

It started to hurt even worse when it turned out that Bullets Bambarella was the one who helped Captain Hooker out the door, and half carried him to the car where Clarence Cromwell waited. "Please, Bullets," Hipless Hooker cried. "Don't get in any trouble while I'm gone!"

"Course not!" Bullets said. The very idea!

"I'm depending on you, son," said Hipless Hooker. "No trouble now. I'm depending on you."

"You can depend on me, Captain!" Bullets Bambarella promised. He was touched.

"Ooooooooohhhhhhhhh!" Hipless Hooker said, when Bullets lifted him into Clarence Cromwell's car and they sped away to the hospital.

Natalie Zimmerman, like Philo Skinner, did not believe in the apathetic Gods. She believed that fate was conspiring against her in the Valnikov matter. Fate was protecting Sergeant A.M. Valnikov. It was getting spooky.

"Well, Natalie," he smiled, when she joined him at the burglary table. "We have a very light workload today."

She looked at him. His eyes were watery, as usual. He exuded a faint odor of booze, as usual. He wore another suit today, the cleaning tags still stapled to his inside pocket, as usual. The suitcoat hung open and the stapled repairs were visible, as usual. He was wearing a polka dot blue and white necktie, and his white shirt was more or less ironed. Frayed like the others, but ironed. So he was looking his best today for whatever reason.

The reason was Natalie Zimmerman. Valnikov had watched every move she made as she ran across the noisy crowded squad room. He watched as she smoked and paced in front of Captain Hooker's office until she was admitted. He watched her walking slowly back to the burglary table, her eyes rolled up in that odd way of hers. Valnikov thought she was pretty even with her dopey hairdo and her big dumb glasses.

Valnikov had deliberately cut his vodka consumption last night and he'd slept better as a result. He wasn't even positive that he'd dreamed about the rabbit, but he guessed he had. The sheets were sweat-soaked. Nevertheless, he felt pretty good today. He sipped his tea and smiled at her.

"I've gotta have another cup of coffee to get my clock started," Natalie sighed when she dropped herself into the chair beside him.

"Let me get it for you," Valnikov said, grabbing her coffee cup.

"Okay," she said. "Thanks."

"Sure," he said, wiping his eyes. It was the first time she'd let him do something for her. He wondered if it was the polka dot necktie and new shave lotion. He'd even combed his hair today. He thought he looked all right.

She thought he looked like hell. Pitiful. Why didn't he make it easy on her and just flip out in front of somebody? Like right now, in front of thirty witnesses? Fire off a round at the coffee maker because it was bitter or something. But he wouldn't even know. He drank tea. What kind of a cop drinks tea?

"All you people listen to this!" said Lieutenant Woodenlips Mockett, who was totally ignored except by Valnikov, who was always respectful of authority. He put Natalie's coffee cup in front of her and gave Woodenlips his attention.

"Sergeant Ballew in patrol got a four-day suspension for an accidental discharge."

"At his age they're all accidental," said Fuzzy Spinks of auto theft, who was older than Sergeant Ballew and knew what he was talking about.

"Sergeant Ballew accidentally fired a round from the Ithaca and it went right through Deputy Chief Digby Bates' car."

"Yeah?" said Dudley Knebel of robbery, suddenly interested because he hated the chief's guts. "Was Bates in the car?"

"Of course not!" Woodenlips Mockett said. "Ballew only got four days' suspension."

"Only," Dudley Knebel said. "That's a pretty tough bail schedule for one lousy shotgun round."

"Yeah, now if the chief had been *in* the car . . ." argued Max Haffenkamp of residential burglary.

"Then I'da gave Ballew four days' pay outta *my* pocket," Dudley Knebel said.

"You men don't take these things seriously enough," Woodenlips Mockett whined.

"Poor old Ballew," Fuzzy Spinks said. "He got ten days' suspension last year for getting drunk and banging his girlfriend on duty."

"On duty!" Woodenlips Mockett cried. "He should've been *fired* for that! Ten days is all he got?"

"Well, it's pretty tough when you figure the whole case was circumstantial," said Fuzzy. "See, they stopped him on the way home for drunk driving."

"Then it *wasn't* on duty," said Woodenlips Mockett.

"Well no," said Fuzzy Spinks, "but it was only fifteen minutes past end-of-watch and his blood alcohol reading was .25 so they deduced it."

"Did they *deduce* the girlfriend too?" Woodenlips Mockett sneered. He sneered as well as Natalie Zimmerman any old day.

"Circumstantial evidence too," Fuzzy clucked, full of sympathy for poor old Sergeant Ballew. "Before they shagged him for drunk driving he smashed into the telephone pole at Gower and Sunset. And when the lousy finks at the receiving hospital took Ballew's clothes off, they found a rubber."

"A rubber!" Nate Farmer of the sex detail was outraged. "That don't prove nothin!"

"Poor old drunk still had it *on!*" said Fuzzy Spinks.

"That's still just circumstantial evidence," said Nate Farmer. "I suppose they checked the scummy thing for his girlfriend's fingerprints, huh?"

"Wouldn't put it past those squints at Internal Affairs," said Montezuma Montez.

Then Woodenlips Mockett gave up because he was the only one who didn't think Sergeant Ballew got railroaded on circumstantial evidence.

"I hear you're a golfer," Bullets suddenly said to Montezuma Montez.

"I play a little golf," said Montezuma without looking up.

"Sissy game," Bullets said. "I never played golf in my life."

"Too clumsy?" said Montezuma Montez, putting down his pencil.

Bullets said, "Any old man on crutches can play that game."

"I'll bet you couldn't hit a golf ball fifty yards," said Montezuma Montez.

"Fifty yards," said Bullets. Now he *had* the wetback! "You heard him, Fuzzy. He said I couldn't hit a golf ball *fifty* yards!"

"If you never played before, I *know* you couldn't hit one fifty yards, Bullets," Fuzzy Spinks said, peeking over his bifocals. "Not on one swing anyway."

Then there was money flying all over the squad room. Bullets was covering all bets. Woodenlips Mockett was whining about gambling in a police station. Everyone was yelling and hollering but Bullets Bambarella covered thirty dollars. Five minutes later there were detective cars squealing out of Hollywood Station speeding to the Los Angeles Country Club where Investigator Nate Farmer could never hope to join, in that he was a black man, but where he could arrange for Bullets to hit a ball on the driving range because Nate's cousin was a caddy there.

• ● •

While half the detective division at Hollywood Station was at the Los Angeles Country Club watching Bullets Bambarella make an ass out of himself by swinging a golf club like a baseball bat and digging up the largest chunk of ethnically restricted turf that anyone had seen in recent memory, and while the other half of the detective division, including Valnikov and Natalie Zimmerman, were handling their routine investigations, a "sustaining" Pasadena Junior Leaguer was doing some detective work of her own. And was surprising herself at how *well* she was doing it.

Madeline Whitfield had not slept but she had vowed over coffee that morning that she was not going to take a drink until Vickie came home to her. And she wasn't going to just wait until that man called.

She checked the lost and found in the morning *Times* and discovered that there were two schnauzers reported lost. The first belonged to a Redondo Beach phone number. The second was a San Gabriel number, close enough to Pasadena to make Madeline hope that this was the owner of the dead animal, and that there might be a connection which would lead her somewhere. Madeline Whitfield made phone calls, prepared to take copious notes. Except that the first missing schnauzer didn't even have cropped ears. The second was pregnant. Madeline Whitfield was thinking that she might have been too hasty in her temperance vow. She was thinking about a double Scotch when another thought intruded. She phoned the Pasadena Police, the Los Angeles County Sheriff's Office, and the Los Angeles Police Department, inquiring about lost or stolen schnauzers.

"But we don't keep reports on lost dogs," said a Los Angeles Police Department clerk who was almost as lethargic as Officer Leonard Leggett.

"Yes, yes, I understand that," said Madeline Whitfield. "But I'm wondering if someone reported a schnauzer *stolen.* You see, this is a very valuable dog. It's possibly a champion, very definitely show quality. Perhaps you have a report of a dog like this being *stolen?*"

"Just a minute, lady," the lethargic clerk said grumpily. Then when the clerk came back he said, "As a matter of fact we *did* get a hit on a stolen schnauzer."

"Yes?" Madeline said.

"Hollywood," the clerk said. "There was a schnauzer reported stolen in Hollywood Division on January eighth."

"Yes! Yes!" Madeline cried.

"Do you want the report number?" the clerk said.

At 11:00 a.m. Woodenlips Mockett received a call at Hollywood Detectives.

"My name is Madeline Whitfield."

"Yes," Woodenlips Mockett said, wishing Captain Hooker would hurry up and get back from the hospital, because with Cromwell there holding his hand, and with the other lieutenant off sick, and with half the troops at some goddamn golf course watching Bullets Bambarella try to hit a golf ball, he was overworked. So far, he had had to make a pot of coffee and answer the phone twice.

"I'd like to inquire about a stolen schnauzer dog," the woman said. "I have a police report number."

"Where was the dog stolen, lady?" said Woodenlips Mockett. This kind of work was demeaning for a lieutenant. Demeaning!

"On Vine Street. The Brown Derby."

"Okay," Woodenlips Mockett sighed, "lemme check for you."

He found the theft report in the control folder belonging to Valnikov and Natalie Zimmerman. "Yeah, wh'adda you wanna know?" Woodenlips Mockett sighed. He intended to take an extra long lunch break to make up for all this work.

"I'd like to speak to the officer working on that case," said Madeline. "Is he there, please?"

"No. His name's Sergeant Valnikov. He'll be back late this afternoon."

"I'd like to talk to him if it's at all possible," Madeline said. "It's important."

"Where do you live?"

"Pasadena."

"Pasadena! Listen, lady, that's a little out of our jurisdiction. Gimme your number, I'll have him call you."

"Could you ask him to call me as soon as he can? I'll be here all day and I'm *most* anxious."

"Okay, gimme your number," Lieutenant Mockett sighed.

Ten minutes later, while driving on Hollywood Boulevard, Valnikov said, "Did you get that, Natalie?"

"Did I get what?" She was lost in a mad plan to go straight to Deputy Chief Digby Bates if she had to. God, what if Hipless Hooker was kept at the hospital? She'd *have* to go over Clarence Cromwell's head.

"We got a call to phone the station," said Valnikov, driving to the nearest call box on Sunset Boulevard.

A few minutes later Valnikov was talking on the field phone to Woodenlips, who was starting to calm down now that three teams of detectives had returned, gloating over all the money they'd won from Bullets Bambarella.

"Some broad in Pasadena gave me the number," the lieutenant said. "She might know something about a case of yours. A dog snatching from the Brown Derby."

"Yes," Valnikov said. "I thought the dog probably ran away. It's a valuable dog according to the report and . . ."

"Yeah, yeah, that's the one," said Woodenlips Mockett. "Call this broad, will you? Get her off my back. I got enough pressure right now."

Then Valnikov couldn't make out the rest because Bullets Bambarella was in the squad room yelling to Montezuma Montez:

"*You* a tennis player! Don't make me laugh!"

"Please, Bambarella," Lieutenant Mockett whined. "I can't hear myself talk. Did you get the message, Valnikov? Call this crazy dog about the goddamn lady!"

"That doesn't make much sense, Lieutenant," said Valnikov.

"Do you think *anything* makes sense around here!" Lieutenant Mockett cried. "How would *you* like to get stuck with all the work while Captain Hooker goes to the hospital for an ache in his tum tum? Huh?"

"Okay, Lieutenant," Valnikov said soothingly. "I'll call her. Don't let yourself get excited." Now now, Lieutenant. Now now.

When Valnikov returned to the detective car he found Natalie Zimmerman dashing off some confidential notes. Observations. About him.

"Natalie," he said, causing her to jump so suddenly her Friz bounced to the top of her head and down again.

"Yes?" she said.

"We got a strange call. Some woman in Pasadena wants us to call her about that dog that was stolen from the Brown Derby."

"What dog?"

"The theft report. You know? The one that came in yesterday morning?"

"Christ, Valnikov. You have time to read theft reports? I mean they give you so many burglary reports you can't even count them, you gotta *weigh* them. And you have time to read plain theft reports?"

"I read *all* our reports," he shrugged.

"And you remember them?"

"I can't help remembering," Valnikov said. "I just remember things about my job. They just . . . I just can't seem to get things out of my mind. Know what I mean?"

"Okay, big deal. We have a major crime about somebody stealing a dog?"

Valnikov shrugged again, and said, "I'll just run over to the gas station and use the phone. See what this is all about."

And while Natalie Zimmerman scribbled furiously, stopping every few seconds to blow her Friz off her glasses, Valnikov searched his pockets and found some small change to make a phone call which would profoundly affect the rest of his life.

"Hello, is this Mrs. Whitfield?" he said.

At first her heart stopped. No, it wasn't him. Richard's voice was high pitched. "Yes," she said. "This is Madeline Whitfield."

"This is Sergeant Valnikov, ma'am. Los Angeles Police Department. You called for me?"

"Oh, yes!" she said. "Sergeant, I live in Pasadena. I found . . . found a little schnauzer. The poor thing was dying. It died just after I found her. I . . . well, I looked in the *Times* and I phoned several police departments and I understand you're investigating a case about a stolen schnauzer?"

"Yes," Valnikov hesitated. "Actually, we haven't had time to contact the victim yet. To tell you the truth I just figured her schnauzer ran away or got lost. That's usually the case, and . . ."

"Can you tell me about the schnauzer, Sergeant?" Madeline Whitfield said quickly. "I know it's a bitch. Does your report describe her?"

"Well, not really, ma'am. Actually, I don't even know what a schnauzer looks like, to be honest."

"Does the report say that she's show quality? A champion perhaps?"

"Yes," Valnikov said. "The report does say she's valuable and has been in various dog shows."

Then the line was dead for a moment as Madeline tried to feign nonchalance. "Yes, show quality. That certainly sounds like the poor little schnauzer I found. Tell me, Sergeant, who is . . . *was* the owner?"

"Let's see, the report's in the car, ma'am. A woman in Trousdale Estates. That's in Beverly Hills."

"Could you give me her name and number, Sergeant?" Madeline said. "I'd like to ask her a few questions."

"I'd better have her phone you," said Valnikov. "We're not supposed to give out a victim's phone number. You understand. Did the dog have a collar?"

"No," said Madeline. "But perhaps the owner could describe the schnauzer. I happen to know a lot about this breed. I have a miniature schnauzer of my own."

"Okay, ma'am, I'll have the owner call you this afternoon. I'll be back in the station about four p.m. and . . ."

"No!" Madeline cried, and then she said calmly, "No, Sergeant. Please. Could you have her call me right away? This is urgent. I . . . I'm a dog owner myself and I know what this means. Please."

"I'll call her right away," said Valnikov.

"Thank you, Sergeant," said Madeline Whitfield.

"You're welcome."

Valnikov was almost out of change. He managed to scrape up enough for the second call. The phone rang seven times. He was about to hang up, when a young man answered. "Yeah?"

"This is Sergeant Valnikov, Los Angeles Police Department."

"Yeah?"

"I'm investigating a theft of a dog. Is this the residence of Millie M. Gharoujian?"

"Just a minute." The line was quiet, then a muffled voice said, "Millie, it's for you. Some cop about Tutu."

"Hello," a husky voice breathed.

"Ma'am, this is Sergeant Valnikov, Los Ang—"

"Yeah, okay," said Millie. "You find Tutu?"

"Well, a lady in Pasadena thinks she might have your dog, ma'am. I'm sorry to say she found a champion class schnauzer that fits the description. But the poor dog died and . . ."

"Yeah, is it my Tutu?"

"I don't know, ma'am. She left her name and number if you'd care to call her."

"Look, pal. What's your name?"

"Valnikov, ma'am."

"Yeah. Listen, pal. I'm seventy-six years old."

"Yes, ma'am," said Valnikov.

"Well, you just interrupted the best . . . Look, I happen to be having a grand time and you have to interrupt it. Is *this* what I pay taxes for?"

"No, ma'am," said Valnikov.

"Okay, now look. My dog was snatched or ran off or whatever, last week. She's a three-year-old schnauzer that cost me upwards a twenty grand before I say, Millie, why you blowing all this dough on a goddamn dog? Get it?"

"Yes, ma'am."

"So look, I already made an insurance claim. If the dog's dead what the hell can I do about it, Sergeant?"

"I don't know, ma'am," said Valnikov. "Could you describe your dog? This lady seems terribly concerned and . . ."

"Jesus Christ!" Millie Muldoon Gharoujian cried. "I got two kids here that look like they were carved by Michelangelo and I'm supposed to worry about a *dog!*"

"She had no identification, I take it," said Valnikov.

"She had one white toenail on her left rear foot," Millie said gruffly. "My ex-dog handler, a jerk named Philo Skinner, used to paint that toenail black before the dog shows. Now please, Sergeant, I appreciate your dedication, but can I get back to *my* business with these boys? Don't you have any respect for senior citizens?"

"Yes, ma'am," said Valnikov. "Yes, ma'am."

"It took long enough," said Natalie Zimmerman when Valnikov returned to the detective car.

"Do you mind if we go back to the station? I have to call this lady from Pasadena again and I'm out of pocket change."

While Valnikov made his call at Hollywood Station, Natalie Zimmerman used the time to phone the hospital. She was told that Captain Hooker had just suffered an attack of stomach gas. He was with Sergeant Cromwell and was presumably resting easily. Natalie Zimmerman put in a call to the area commander, who was out to lunch. Then she returned to the burglary table where Valnikov was talking to Madeline Whitfield.

"That's right," Valnikov said into the phone. "The schnauzer had one white toenail on her left rear foot. What color are they normally? Black? Yes. Did you notice if the dog had one white toenail? You didn't notice. That's too bad. Where's the dead dog now? A what? A pet mortuary? Yes, I know where that is. Do they cremate them or bury them or what? They *embalm* them? Animals? Really? Well, the lady who reported the stolen schnauzer doesn't seem to care very much whether it's her dog or not. That's right. She really doesn't want to bother talking to you. I don't understand either. Yes, I'm a pet owner. I have a parakeet and a gerbil. A gerbil. No, it's a *gerbil.* Indigenous to southern Russia. For now I don't know what else I can do. Yes, that's all right, ma'am. Yes. Good-bye."

After he hung up, he looked at a totally frustrated Natalie Zimmerman.

"Would you like to go to lunch now?" he asked. "I have a surprise for you. A very unusual place to eat."

"What the hell!" she said to her Friz. "Let's go, Valnikov. I'll probably get botulism. Why do I *always* have to pick the black marble?"

He was driving the detective car along Pico Boulevard in a neighborhood she didn't know very well. He'd gone to Vermont and was now heading back west. The Cuban storefronts lined the street. There was Rosario's Boutique. Not like the boutiques in Beverly Hills. Rosario's was a storefront ten feet wide. The most expensive item cost $13.95 and Rosario's did not take credit cards. They passed a liquor store which carried a big window placard advertising *Silox Super-X, Cockroach Control Overnight. Guaranteed!* There was a storefront advertising *Consulto Espiritual,* in case you cared to know the mysteries of the past and future. The present was of not much interest to the spiritualist.

Then thriftshops and wooden buildings which should have been demolished. Vacant lots. Then another Cuban spiritualist who, incredibly enough, offered in addition to herbs and medicines—religion. The sign simply advertised: *Marta's religion.* Natalie Zimmerman thought that was honest enough.

Then past a huge primitive mural on the side of a building depicting dark Latin faces under Mexican sombreros, with eyes like Russian ikons, and letters emblazoned: TIERRA Y LIBERTAD! Leaving Valnikov uncertain as to whether the *tierra y libertad* was the dream of the Cubans of the neighborhood, or the Mexicans depicted thereon. No matter. All Latinos dreamed of *tierra y libertad* regardless of their homeland, and, like the Russians, had seen precious little of it in the course of history.

And then, between Mariposa and Normandie, the import stores which advertised Greek, Arab, Armenian, Persian, Turkish, Italian, Soviet imports. These stores were located strategically near St. Sophia's, the huge-domed cathedral for the Greek Orthodox of Los Angeles. Amidst the food stores there was an international record store which offered tapes and records to the ethnic shoppers.

When Valnikov pulled to the curb and parked, she heard and smelled the exotic.

"I buy my music there," Valnikov said, pointing to the record store from which balalaikas throbbed. Valnikov was beaming. They usually played bazouki because Greek customers far outnumbered Russian.

"Is this a restaurant?" Natalie asked, as Valnikov led her into the smallest of the stores. There were powerful odors of black and green olives, goat cheeses from five countries, oils and wines, pastries and breads, meats and spices from the nations of the Mediterranean. And in this particular store, some foods, some wines, some vodka from the north.

"Andrei Mikhailovich!" a man behind the counter thundered. He wore a meat-stained apron, and a tunic which marked him as a Molokan to those who knew.

"Iosif!" Valnikov grinned, and then a big man came out from the back room. He was wearing a blue sweater and spoke unaccented English. He was close to 280 pounds and stood well over six feet tall. His hair was nearly white but he had the same broad Slavic forehead as Valnikov, and the same kind of ingenuous grin which Natalie decided was more childlike than dumb.

He said, "Where you been for three weeks, you little jerk?" And he grabbed Valnikov, puckered, and kissed him smack on the mouth.

They embraced and bobbed around for a few seconds. Dancing bears.

Then he gave Valnikov a crack on the shoulder and reached out with a sweep of an enormous arm, half crushing the astonished Natalie Zimmerman, and kissed *her* smack on the mouth. "Hello, good-looking," he said. "You smell like a cop to me. And that's a sexy smell!"

"You old devil," Valnikov chuckled.

The big man released Natalie Zimmerman and said, "Now that we're acquainted, how about some borscht?"

"This is my brother, Alex," Valnikov said to Natalie, who was trying to keep her gun from falling out of her purse, her huge glasses from falling off her nose, and her bra from slipping up over her nipple, so quick and violent was the assault of the elder Valnikov. The Molokan butcher was shaking up and down in laughter as he cleavered through a lamb bone like it was salami.

"My partner, Natalie Zimmerman," said Valnikov.

"Ah-hah!" said the elder Valnikov. "I knew she was a cop, but she's not carrying a gun on her person, I can tell you that!"

Which propelled the Molokan butcher into a fit of bouncing laughter.

"We can't stay, Alex," Valnikov said. "We haven't called on a single burglary victim today and . . ."

"Bull! You pop in here once a month and hardly ever come see your nephews and nieces and you can't stay! Bull!"

"How about some tea, Alex?" Valnikov said sheepishly, as though the big man were his father, and indeed he could have been, thought Natalie Zimmerman. He was much older than Valnikov.

"Yeah, some tea *with* some lunch *here!*" Alex Valnikov said.

"Honest, we gotta go," said Valnikov. "How about something to take out? We can only stay a few minutes."

"You know, you're a real pain in the ass, kid," said Alex Valnikov, shaking his head and opening the meat case while Natalie managed to slip the bra back down over the bruised nipple while the Molokan pretended not to notice. "You're a real pain, boy. You must give me an hour of your time. In a whole year!"

"Well, I always mean to stop by," Valnikov apologized. "But you know how busy cops are . . ."

"Sure. Save that for the dummies don't know any better. I know better." Then he turned to Natalie and his eyes, as blue as Valnikov's, creased, and he said, "Now you met Valnikov the bashful. That's me."

"I'm . . . overwhelmed," said Natalie while the Molokan whacked through another lamb shank.

"You didn't even come Thursday night," Alex Valnikov said. "We were all expecting you to at least show up for church."

"I went to church, Alex," Valnikov said, actually dropping his gaze before the chastisement. "I went to the cathedral, that's why you didn't see me. I wouldn't miss on Christmas."

"You'll have lunch with me then?"

"We'll have tea, Alex," Valnikov said. "And if you can, maybe some lunch to take with us."

"If I *can*," the elder Valnikov glowered. "Listen to him. If I *can*."

Valnikov was saved further scolding when an ancient crone with wrapped spindle legs came hobbling into the store. She looked first at the Molokan butcher then back toward Alex Valnikov. Then she recognized the detective.

"Sergeant Valnikov!" she cried.

"Good afternoon, Mrs. Rosenfeldt," Valnikov said, running his fingers through his fluffy cinnamon hair.

"I've been wondering when you'd be back to your brother's store. We was talking about you just recently, ain't that true, Alex?"

"Every day, Mrs. Rosenfeldt," the elder Valnikov nodded.

"I was saying how we need a good cop in this neighborhood, like Alex's little brother. Wasn't I saying that, Alex?"

"You were, Mrs. Rosenfeldt," Alex said. "Every day."

"Come over here, Sergeant, let me tell you what's the latest mischief they're up to. Come over here."

"Yes, Mrs. Rosenfeldt," Valnikov said obediently, crossing by the meat counter while the Molokan swung the cleaver.

"Sergeant Valnikov," she whispered, pulling him down toward her face. She was toothless and smelled of fish. "It's Myer."

"Your husband," Valnikov whispered.

"Yes, they're at it again. I went to visit him in the rest home over in Boyle Heights. You know where that is?"

"I sure do, Mrs. Rosenfeldt," Valnikov nodded patiently, blinking his watery eyes.

"He's been taking up with a hussy there. Name's Ida Schwartz. You won't believe the sex goes on there. It's a disgrace. Of course, Myer's only a man. Him I don't blame. But Ida Schwartz? She should be in San Quentin, that woman."

"Yes, of course," Valnikov agreed. "How old is Mrs. Schwartz now? Eighty?"

"She's eighty-three, the stinking harlot!" Mrs. Rosenfeldt cried. "I don't blame Myer. A man is all he is. And there's just so much temptation a man can take."

"I understand, Mrs. Rosenfeldt," Valnikov nodded, gravely. His runny blue eyes were sad. Earl Scheib Lopez, 11 years old, and Ida Schwartz age 83, San Quentin cellmates.

"Well, what can you do, Sergeant Valnikov?" the old woman demanded.

"It's very hard to put people in state prison," Valnikov explained. "Especially for . . ."

"Adultery!" she cried.

"Yes, especially for adultery. You see, it's not a crime."

"What is it coming to, this world, Sergeant?" Mrs. Rosenfeldt said.

"Now now, Mrs. Rosenfeldt," Valnikov said, leading her over to one of three folding chairs placed for the convenience of aged customers like Mrs. Rosenfeldt. "Just sit down, and my brother will fix you a nice cup of tea."

"Tea. That would be good, Sergeant," Mrs. Rosenfeldt said, with a gummy smile. A wet star slithered from her lashless eyes and followed a jagged course through the creases of her cheeks.

"Did I ever tell you about the samovar we had when I was a boy, Mrs. Rosenfeldt?" Valnikov said, sitting in a folding chair next to the fragile old woman. "Well, my parents carried that samovar and an ikon of St. Sergius and a picture of Nicholas the second across Siberia, all the way to Vladivostok. That's one-fourth of the world, Mrs. Rosenfeldt!"

"Imagine," the old lady said, forgetting about Myer banging that stinking harlot, Ida Schwartz.

"Finally they arrived at the sea, Mrs. Rosenfeldt. Can you imagine how it was then? All the Whites escaping with their families? And at last, with the help of other army officers, and mostly with the help of a fleeing nobleman my father had befriended, they crossed the great Pacific Ocean . . ."

"On a Canadian vessel!" she cackled triumphantly.

"That's right," Valnikov smiled, his sad runny eyes wet not from tears but Stolichnaya runoff. They'd be clearing at about 2:00 p.m. if he could judge by his vodka intake.

"They landed in Seattle!" Mrs. Rosenfeldt reminded him.

"Yes, that's right," Valnikov nodded.

"Is that true?" Natalie Zimmerman asked Alex Valnikov while Mrs. Rosenfeldt picked up the story of the Valnikov odyssey and told it to Valnikov.

"Sure," Alex Valnikov grinned. "They carried one other thing besides an ikon and samovar, and a picture of Nicholas Romanov. They carried *me*. I was two years old when we sailed from Vladivostok in 1922. And I was a one hundred percent, gum-chewing, Los Angeles teenager by the time that baby over there was born in the Depression. Mrs. Rosenfeldt's heard the story a hundred times or so, that's why she's doing the telling. Keeps her mind off her sex problems with Myer. Who died five years ago."

"You mean she doesn't accept that he's dead?"

"In a way she does," said Alex Valnikov, wrapping the cabbage rolls and pumpernickel. "Sometimes she seems to know for sure, then other times . . ."

"Does she come in every day?"

"Just about. And every time she sees my brother it sets her off to telling about how Ida Schwartz should be arrested. I imagine Ida Schwartz is dead by now too. We don't mind it. In fact Iosif looks forward to her stories."

The Molokan heard his name and grinned. One tooth was missing in front. Whack! went the cleaver.

"It's kind of a continuing soap opera," said Alex Valnikov. "My brother has a way with old people. Look at her. She's telling him about his own family who she never met. Have some tea." He served the tea in a glass. "Russian style," he explained.

"Tastes good," Natalie Zimmerman said, sipping the hot tea carefully.

The big man lowered his voice and said, "How long you been working with my brother?"

"Not long."

"What do you think?"

"What do you mean?"

"My brother drinks all the time. He didn't used to do that. Even after his divorce. My brother wasn't a drunk even after the divorce. Now my brother's a drunk. Do all the other cops talk about it?"

"No, I don't think so," Natalie Zimmerman said, putting her glass of hot tea on the meat counter. "Lots of veteran detectives are known to take a drink. I don't think he's known as a particularly heavy drinker."

"My brother started acting different a few months ago." Now he was whispering. "He had a partner, Charlie Lightfoot."

"I know about that," she nodded.

"About the time Charlie died, he started acting . . . different. Sort of absent-minded. Sort of like his mind wanders. Then the *heavy* boozing started. Hell, we never see him anymore! I'm not his only family. We got a cousin lives in San Pedro and we got a cousin in Sylmar. Nobody sees him. We were a close family once. I worry about my brother. I got four kids that can make you stay up nights, all the crap they step in, but I worry most about my little brother."

"I don't think he's a real heavy drinker," Natalie Zimmerman lied, unable to look in the passionate blue eyes of Valnikov the elder. No, he's not a heavy drinker. Just a 14 karat alcoholic, is all. And a 21 karat dingaling to boot. And *I'm* the one fate elected to dispatch the clown with my terrible swift sword.

"Come get your tea, kid," Alex Valnikov said, and the detective got up, patted Mrs. Rosenfeldt's hand, and joined them.

"That's very sad," Natalie Zimmerman said, looking at the old woman who was now telling the Molokan butcher about Myer the whoremonger. That's what philanderers deserve. A cleaver. Whack!

"Well, we don't mind sadness," Alex Valnikov grinned. "Haven't you seen Russian plays? We're only happy when we're sad." He turned to his younger brother and said, "You changed your mind? Staying for some borscht, right?"

Valnikov smiled apologetically and sipped the tea from his glass and his elder brother sighed and handed the heavy paper bag to Natalie Zimmerman.

"It was nice to meet you, hon," the big man said. Then he leaned over and gave her a friendly hug which didn't roll up her bra this time.

"I'll be seeing you, Iosif," Valnikov said to the butcher, who by now was caught up in Mrs. Rosenfeldt's story of sex and depravity in the Jewish Home for the Aged.

"I see you, Andrei Mikhailovich!" the Molokan said, waving his cleaver.

Then Valnikov stopped at the door, where Natalie was taking money out of her purse to pay at the register.

"Don't be silly, honey," the elder Valnikov said. Then he turned to his brother and said, "You come for dinner. Soon. You and me haven't had a talk in a hell of a long time, boy."

"Bye, Alex. Thanks for the eats," Valnikov said, putting an arm around his brother. Then the bears danced for another moment and the elder Valnikov kissed him on the mouth. "You take *care*, Andrushka. You hear me?"

When they got back in the car, Valnikov took the wheel again and headed downtown. "Now comes the best part," he said to Natalie Zimmerman, who was lost in unhappy contemplation of black marbles.

He surprised her by parking at the Music Center. "Follow me," he said with that grin of his. She was sure now after meeting his brother. It was childlike. On Alex Valnikov the big grin didn't look so dumb.

She'd go along with anything on this, the last day. It was the least she could do before . . . before she went to see Hipless Hooker.

He parked on Hope Street and led her up the steps between the Dorothy Chandler Pavilion and the Mark Taper Forum. There were a few people roaming around, mostly coming from the restaurant on the Grand Avenue level. There were tourists taking pictures of the three neoclassical buildings which make up the Music Center complex, and of the enormous contemporary sculpture called *Peace on Earth.* Some decided it was a totem, no, a *pyramid* of bodies, animals and people, piled one on top of the other like a Hollywood orgy.

Valnikov led Natalie past the Mark Taper Forum with its quiet, asexual reflecting pool. It was windy and the snow-capped San Gabriels were visible from Bunker Hill today. Across the avenue was the county courthouse and a sculpted relief of a hopeful knight in chain mail brandishing the Magna Charta.

Then Valnikov beckoned Natalie toward a small cluster of people: tourists, downtown civil servants, pensioners, students, who were gathered around a young man with a full black beard and a war-surplus, navy peacoat, playing "Midnight in Moscow" for all he was worth. He was only worth a few bucks.

"They call him Horst," Valnikov whispered when they were sitting on the steps. "He's a fair musician. Plays here in the afternoons. I've heard he's a medical student."

The bearded young violinist had an old top hat upside down on the pavement. There were a few dollar bills and some change inside, but clearly, today's session was a bummer. Horst Vanderhoof was getting set to trip on home when he opened his eyes and saw that the small audience had grown by two.

"Charlie and I used to listen to him sometimes in the afternoons and have lunch like this. For a while, Charlie wanted to learn something about music."

Valnikov unwrapped a mound of hot cabbage rolls and set the paper plates, plastic forks, and paper napkins in front of Natalie on the concrete steps as though he were waiting on a table.

"Is your brother a caterer?" Natalie asked.

"The best," Valnikov smiled. "That's a big part of his business. He caters Russian weddings and parties. There's always an excuse for a celebration. If it isn't Pushkin's birthday it's Tolstoy's. Or it's the jubilee of the Bolshoi Ballet. Or the jubilee of the day somebody's cousin became an American citizen. Or somebody graduated from barber college. Anything."

"Cabbage rolls," she said. "I had a Polish grandmother made these."

"Oh, you're Polish!" said Valnikov, unwrapping the black bread and little cartons of whipped butter.

"I had a grandmother from Poland and I think a great-grandfather from Germany. Hell, I'm an American. What's that stuff?"

Valnikov held a paper plate stacked with golden pastries and said, "*Piroshki*. They're very light and filled with cheese or meat. My brother usually makes them both ways. And these others are fruit pastries."

"Looks good," Natalie said, as Valnikov presented the array of homemade Russian food.

"I think you'll like this black bread, Natalie," he said. "My mother used to make white bread only on Christmas or Easter. Sometime I'll bring some plastic containers and we'll get some borscht. My brother makes the best borscht you'll ever taste. The secret's in boiling the beef beforehand. And you add *dusha* last. That means soul. Oh, this is lamb, marinated and barbequed. He doesn't have it every day. We're lucky."

"It smells fantastic," Natalie Zimmerman said.

Then Valnikov noticed the music had stopped and he saw Horst packing up his violin case and emptying out the top hat. Most of the onlookers had strolled off.

"Wait, wait!" Valnikov yelled, putting down his plate and scurrying up the steps toward the reflecting pool.

Then Natalie Zimmerman saw him reach in his pocket and give some money to Horst. The kid nodded, took off his top hat again, put down the violin case and opened it up.

When he returned, Valnikov said, "The best part is having music when you eat."

And then came the *pièce de résistance*. Valnikov drew from the bag a half bottle of Bulgarian wine which Alex had uncorked and capped.

"Wine too? I can't believe it!" Natalie Zimmerman said, as Valnikov chuckled and poured into styrofoam cups.

"There's a Russian toast which says, 'If we must die, let's do it with music.'" And then Horst burst forth with five bucks' worth of Rimsky-

Korsakov. Horst could burst forth much better for a tenner, but Valnikov was satisfied.

Then Valnikov said, shyly, "Well, this is the surprise. How do you like it?"

And Natalie Zimmerman pushed terrible thoughts from her mind and concentrated on the wonderful food and the reflecting pool, and the clear sky and the mountains in the distance. She said, "This is the loveliest lunch I've ever had."

"Na zdorovye!" he grinned happily, toasting her with the styrofoam cup.

Jesus, he had fine table manners. The poor doomed bastard. Jesus. Then for the first time, it occurred to her she had never called him by his first name. She didn't even *know* his first name! Sergeant A.M. Valnikov. Val.

"Andrei something, the butcher called you."

"Andrei Mikhailovich," he said, careful to swallow and dab his lips with the paper napkin before speaking.

"But what did your brother call you when he kissed you good-bye?"

"Silly, isn't it? Kissing like that. My brother never really escaped the old ways. He's still an *émigré* in his heart. He's saving to make a long vacation in Leningrad someday. I think this might be the year. Business is pretty good now."

"But what did he call you?"

"Andrushka," Valnikov said softly. "My mother always called me that."

"That's a nice name," Natalie Zimmerman said, looking at Horst the fiddler, who struggled a little, then got hot with Tchaikovsky.

"Do you mean it?"

"Sure. And what would be the Russian equivalent of my name? Of Natalie?"

Valnikov put down the cup and listened to the music for a moment. "The equivalent would be Natalia."

"Natalia," she said. "I've never liked Natalie."

"How about Natasha?" he said, looking deep in her eyes. "It's more endearing. Like Andrushka."

"Natasha," she said, pushing her drooping glasses up. "I like that better."

"Natasha," he whispered. Then he concentrated on buttering his black bread, but his Russian heart was advancing fifteen beats a minute.

• ● •

While Natalie Zimmerman and Valnikov were having a memorable lunch, Madeline Whitfield and Philo Skinner were having a memorable phone conversation.

"It's Richard," Philo whispered into the mouthpiece. He was asphyxiating himself inside a smoky phone booth, in the heat of the afternoon, outside a motel five blocks from his business. It was the motel where he had dreamed of taking Pattie Mae to before she quit on him after the Sunday dog show. The miserable little cunt.

"Yes, I've been waiting for your call," said Madeline, fighting to keep her voice businesslike and unwavering.

"When do I get the money?" Philo croaked.

"You've got to control yourself, Richard, and let me talk," Madeline began. She'd rehearsed it and believed she could even deal with the threats and obscenities.

"Make it quick."

"I've been on the phone all day with my accountant and banker and . . ."

"You *told* someone about this!"

"No, no," she said quickly. "About needing money only. I just told them I had a pressing need for as much as I could possibly get. I even called an old classmate whose husband is chairman of the board of a savings and loan."

"What's the bottom line, lady?" Philo snarled.

"I will have, by noon tomorrow, twelve thousand dollars," Madeline said, and despite herself, her voice broke on the number.

"What did you say? WHAT DID YOU SAY?" Philo began hacking and gagging on the ubiquitous phlegm balls.

Madeline waited until the coughing stopped. When he came back he was wheezing: "Lady . . . lady . . ." Then he gasped and said, "You cunt!"

"Please, Richard," Madeline begged.

"You . . . you rotten cunt. Twelve thousand!"

"Listen to me," she said. "It's not only all I have in the world. It represents borrowed money. I'm looking for a *job*. I've never worked in my life. I'm not qualified for anything but I'm looking for a *job*, and this house was refinanced, and the money's all gone. My mother was sick for four years before she died! Do you know what round-the-clock nursing costs? Do you know what hospital bills are like? Please, Richard. Please!"

He didn't hear a complete sentence she uttered. Twelve thousand. It wouldn't even pay Arnold for the gambling losses. The kike and the nigger would be coming for him with the stripping knife. And he promised Arnold the money by Thursday, plus three hundred interest for waiting past Monday. *Twelve* thousand?

"Twelve thousand," he said, then he felt it grow within him. Philo Skinner had spent much of his life being afraid. He was afraid right now of what the bookmakers would do to him, but he felt the fear being consumed by anger. Twelve thousand!

"I'm cutting off one of that bitch's toes right now. Stay on the line you cunt and you can hear her scream!"

"Noooooooo!" It was Madeline Whitfield who screamed.

"You wanna hear her scream, you cunt!" Philo yelled in the mouthpiece. "You lying, stingy *rich* cunt!"

"Can't we talk face to face, Richard?" Madeline babbled. "I swear I won't call the police. I'll come anywhere. Do anything you want. Oh, please don't hurt Vickie!"

"How's she gonna do in the next dog show, you cunt!"

"Please, please, please. I'll get more money. I swear! Give me one more day. One more."

"I told you I want eighty-five thousand, you . . . you . . ."

"I'll get more! I can get more. If . . . if you let me have Vickie back. I can . . . I can send you five hundred a month until I pay it all. I'm going to get a—" Madeline began weeping brokenly "—job. Please."

"I can't believe it!" Philo said, dropping the paper towel he had wrapped over the mouthpiece. "I can't believe it!" He'd never seen anything like *this* in kidnapping movies. She wanted him to return the bitch and she'd pay the ransom on the installment plan? Ransom by credit card? "Lady I'm gonna cut off a toe," Philo croaked weakly before another coughing spasm made him open the door of the phone booth and hack and wheeze and spit in the motel parking lot.

At which time the motel proprietor, Bessie Callahan, a woman Philo's age, with a surly red face and broken teeth, opened the screen door of the manager's office and yelled, "Hey, fella, go and spit your goopers in the gutter, not on *my* property!"

"Fuck you too, you miserable cunt," Philo barked, which cost him yet another coughing spasm and another gooper on her sidewalk.

"What'd you call me, you scrawny coyote?" Bessie Callahan challenged. "If my husband was here he'd tie you in a knot, you filthy coyote!"

Then, wracked with pain and gasping for breath, and filled with consummate frustration and outrage and anger, Philo Skinner dropped the phone and stepped out of the phone booth, and for the first time in memory challenged someone to a fight. "Step out here, you fat cunt," Philo gasped. "Come out here and I'll punch your fat face in, you fat cunt!"

"Prick!" yelled Bessie Callahan. "Skinny prick! How *dare* you talk to a lady like this!"

And while a trembling Philo Skinner got control of himself, and lit his forty-seventh cigarette of the day, and picked up the phone only to find Madeline Whitfield hysterical because she thought the extortionist was cutting off Vickie's toe, Bessie Callahan had a little surprise for Philo Skinner.

"Control yourself, woman," he ordered Madeline Whitfield. "Get yourself under control and listen to me, goddamnit!"

"Sir . . . sir . . . please don't, please!" Madeline wailed.

"I'm calling you again at six o'clock tonight," Philo Skinner gasped. "Have some good news for me then. I won't cut off any toes until we have *one* more talk. Understand? I won't cut off any toes. Yet."

"Sir . . . sir . . . thank . . . thank you," Madeline sobbed.

"I'll be calling at six. Remember that! Six o'cl–" But he never finished it. He thought he heard running water. Then the door of the phone booth burst open and Philo Skinner was drowning! He couldn't even scream. He swallowed his cigarette butt along with a mouthful of water. He breathed another mouthful into his lungs! He threw his hands out in front of him and fell down in the phone booth. Drowning.

Bessie Callahan, like the sewer worker, Tyrone McGee, had been pushed around all her life, but not by alligators. And certainly not by filthy coyotes who used her telephone and spit goopers on her parking lot. At first she just intended to use the motel fire hose to wash up the wads of filthy goopers he'd deposited all over her sidewalk, but the more she thought of this coyote telling her he'd punch her in the face, and calling her a fat cunt–and heard the coyote screaming over the telephone, calling someone *else* a cunt–the more she decided he wasn't going to get away with it. How about some water for your filthy mouth, you chauvinist prick!

Bessie, her pale eyes bulging with the thrill of it, had Philo helpless on the floor of the phone booth before she knew what she was doing. Still, she kept the fire hose trained on his face. Philo flopped on his belly to breathe. He was finally able to scream but Bessie still wouldn't turn off the hose. Only when she realized what she was doing did she pull the nozzle lever stopping the powerful water jet and hightail it back to her apartment.

"I'll . . . I'll get you for this," Philo croaked, coughing water. The soggy cigarette came up in his throat. He swallowed it down but it came back up with his breakfast. Now Bessie had something else to hose away.

"I'm calling the cops, you coyote!" Bessie screamed through the latched screen door. "You can't attack a woman and get away with it. I'm calling the cops!"

"Cops," Philo gasped. "Cops." He tried to get up but dropped to one knee, retching again. The second of his three polyester leisure suits, this one a cobalt blue, was absolutely drenched. Philo's shoes squished when he got to his feet staggering against the phone booth.

"The cops're coming, you coyote!" Bessie lied. "I hear the sirens. Now we'll see what they do to coyotes that pick on ladies."

"Cops," Philo muttered. Then he was off in a loping, squishy retreat to his El Dorado, which was parked in the alley.

Philo Skinner had driven two blocks before he realized there were no red lights in his rearview mirror. He pulled to the curb and leaned out the window. His tortured lungs were half full of water. He lay back against the leather Cadillac seats and pressed on his scrawny chest trying to give himself artificial respiration. Then he leaned over and out the passenger door, and moaned, hoping the water would trickle out his mouth.

An old pensioner was pushing home a shopping cart full of groceries when he saw a half-drowned man leaning out the El Dorado. The pensioner stopped the shopping cart and shuffled over to Philo, looking down at him curiously. The Cadillac was dry but the man was soaked and dripping.

"Looks like you run yourself through a car wash, sonny," the old man observed. "It's the *car* you're supposed to wash, not yourself."

"Ooooooooooohhhhhh," Philo Skinner moaned, sounding for all the world like Hipless Hooker with a bellyache.

"What's the matter, boy?" the old man said, sucking on a lipload of snuff.

"Ooooooooohhhhhh," Philo answered.

"Well, I gotta go, sonny," the old snuff-dipper said. "I was you, next time I drive through the car wash, I'd call a lifeguard."

• ● •

And while Philo Skinner was wishing he had the strength to start his Cadillac and run over the cackling snuff-dipper, Mavis Skinner was embarked on a little investigation of her own.

That goddamn Philo was acting awful strange lately. She'd bet he was playing around with some little bird at the kennel. Probably had that Pattie Mae coming in every day for some stud service. Probably buying her pretties with what little money the kennel took in. Well, Mavis Skinner wasn't going to put up with any little birds around *her* nest. She decided to pay Philo an unannounced visit.

She was disappointed not to find his car there. She unlocked the office and didn't find any little birds nesting. There was nothing unusual but an uncommonly bad stench coming from the dog pens. Philo hadn't been cleaning them like he said he was. The lazy asshole!

Then a station wagon pulled into the driveway. A man and a woman got out, leading a 110-pound German shepherd. They walked through the door in front of the animal, who carried his ears back and his tail tucked low. The enormous shepherd had an L-shaped scar over his right eye. His snout was crossed by another scar that drew a blue line from his eye to his scarred, curling lip. He had wary amber eyes. Mavis didn't like him one goddamn bit.

"Yes?" she said to the smiling couple who were dressed like a Hawaiian vacation.

"We'd like to board our Walter for two weeks," said the man. "We're going on a Caribbean cruise. The whole family." The thought of it made him grin wider.

"Well," Mavis said, studying the fearsome beast, "we specialize in terriers here."

"You only board terriers?"

"No, we board all breeds, but to tell the truth, sir, that looks like an attack dog to me."

Then the woman stopped smiling and said in a high voice, "Oh, Walter's rehabilitated."

"Rehabilitated?"

"He *used* to be a guard dog, but that was years ago. Why, he's a family pet. Our children ride him like a pony, and box his ears, and kiss him on the nose, and . . ."

"That dog's been mistreated," Mavis said, pointing at the scars. "I dunno . . ."

"Believe me," the man said, releasing Walter's lead, "this dog's perfectly gentle. We've adopted four animals from the S.P.C.A. Walter's our pride and joy. He's been tamed with love. He's a family pet."

But Walter hadn't *always* been a family pet and Mavis knew it by looking at him. He had been seized by court order five years before with thirteen other half-demented brutes, the property of another half-demented brute who owned a guard dog service and "trained" his animals with a three-foot length of ordinary garden hose, loaded with ordinary chunks of lead. Walter had a short unhappy career guarding industrial building sites before the court order brought him to the animal shelter and eventually to the home of the adopted parents who were determined to turn a snarling monster into a lap dog. And they did. He was seven years old now and it was the first time Walter had been away from his adopted family. It was the first time he was to be caged since his hateful formative time in guard dog service. Walter was indifferent to Mavis, but he didn't like cages. Not at all. The bad old days.

"We'll be glad to pay you a premium for taking Walter," the man said, "although he's perfectly safe to handle."

"A premium," she said. The magic word. Oh, what the hell.

So Walter had a new home temporarily. And it was to have a profound effect on Philo Skinner's future. Destiny.

• ● •

When Horst was finished with a very mediocre "Dance of the Comedians" he cleared his throat and Valnikov started to reach in his pocket.

"Wait," Natalie said. "What's he want, more money?"

"It's okay, he's worth it," said Valnikov, but she put her hand on his arm and said, "We've had enough music. Don't spend any more money." Then she turned to the young man and said, "Thanks, kid, it was great."

The bearded young fiddler shrugged and began putting away his instrument.

"He ever play for free?" Natalie asked, devouring her fourth cabbage roll. The bread was incredible with the cabbage rolls and butter.

"Well, no, but it's all right."

"A pre-med student, huh? He's a future sawbones, all right. Get the money before the operation every time. Well, music or no music, it's been a memorable lunch."

"I'm so glad you enjoyed it, Natalie," Valnikov said, gathering up their paper and leftovers. "You know, it's almost end-of-watch. Time passed so fast today!"

Natalie Zimmerman was feeling even more miserable about everything during the drive to the station. Jesus, she *had* to do it. Nothing personal, Valnikov. You're a decent guy. Nothing personal. It's just that you're *nuts*. Turn around now and let Natalie Zimmerman split your skull with a cleaver. Whack! Let your *partner* do it to you. It's for the good of the police department, Captain. Valnikov is insane and anyone can see it if he spends more than an hour with the guy. But you see, sir, nobody spends any time with the poor slob. He's a loner. Not even his brother can get a handle on him. He's off and running, but if you corner him, sit him across the desk, get the doctor to start with the questions, you'll see it. He's on the verge of a breakdown. Hell, he's *already* broken down. He's . . . I don't know . . . he's limping along, Captain.

He can fool you sometimes. Because he's considerate, and thoughtful. Yes, you were right, he *is* a gentleman, and no, not many partners I ever had were gentlemen, and . . . God! She thought of Valnikov talking with the old people. No, she couldn't tell about spray-painting the little germ, because, God help her, she *loved* that. That's the point. A madman can infect people with his madness if you're with him long enough. You get a little crazy too. That's the point!

"That's the point," she said. Damn! Now he had *her* talking to herself.

"What's the point, Natalie?" Valnikov asked pleasantly, driving west on Fountain Avenue, into the sunset.

"Who knows," she muttered. "What's the point? Did you ever figure that out, Valnikov?" Now Natalie Zimmerman felt like crying because she didn't want to do it and she had to do it. "What's the point, Valnikov? All those things you talk about, all the killers you and Charlie Lightfoot hunted. All those murdered children. A Braille reading book. Was there any *point*, Valnikov?"

"There *is* no point, Natalie," Valnikov said matter-of-factly, both hands tightening on the steering wheel, driving as always, fifteen miles per hour. "There's no point and that's the point."

"What's the point?"

"That there's no point, Natalie. That's the point."

"Oh, Christ, Valnikov, let's go home."

"Okay, Natalie, we're home." And he wheeled into the police parking lot at Fountain and Wilcox.

Valnikov was just about ready to ask her to go to that movie when a man in a corduroy sport coat with leather elbow patches walked up to their car.

He was taller and younger than Valnikov. He looked like an average jock, maybe a college football coach. He wore a button-down blue shirt and regimental necktie. He had lots of teeth.

"Jack!" Natalie said. "What're you doing here?"

"You've been wanting to see the musical at the Shubert? Well, guess who has tickets in the orchestra? That means an early dinner, so let's just go from here."

He threw his arm around her and kissed her cheek.

"Captain Packerton, meet my partner, Sergeant Valnikov," she said. "Uh, Captain Packerton commands West Valley Station."

"Pleased to meet you, Captain," said Valnikov, smiling with very sad eyes.

"Valnikov," Captain Packerton nodded, shaking hands perfunctorily. "Let's go, Natalie. Your partner can check you out."

"Jack, I've *got* to talk to Captain Hooker first. I can't leave just yet."

"Yes you can, Nat," Captain Packerton said, and this time he pulled her brazenly into him. "I've already talked to your lieutenant. He knows you have a hot date. Balinkov here will be glad to clean up your paper work, won't you, Balinkov?"

"Yes, Captain, I'll be glad to," said Valnikov, gathering up the work folders and case envelopes which had fallen out of his cheap plastic briefcase. Then the burly detective turned his back and began trudging toward the station. The vent in his old suitcoat had split and his handcuffs were hanging out. The threadbare suit now looked as though he'd taken it out of a washer.

"Jack, I simply *must* talk to Captain Hooker. It's urgent."

"Yeah? What is it?"

"I can't talk about it. A personal problem."

"Yeah? Well, it's impossible anyway. He left with some black detective, I forget his name."

"Clarence Cromwell."

"Yeah, him. Something about a sale on fishing equipment at a discount store."

"Goddamnit!"

"Talk to him in the morning. Let's go to dinner and see the show. Then maybe to *your* place," he grinned.

He swept her along toward his car, which was parked in front of the station on Fountain Avenue. They passed Valnikov, who was shuffling along thinking that maybe he'd buy a bottle of Stolichnaya and pick up a hamburger and listen to some records tonight. Like any other night.

Maybe he'd listen to the great Chaliapin sing the death scene from *Boris Godunov*.

"See you around, Balinkov," Captain Packerton said when they breezed by. He had his arm around Natalie's waist and she was having trouble matching his long strides.

She turned and looked at Valnikov, who smiled his dumb kid smile and waved his plastic briefcase, and lumbered into the station, watching the ground as he walked.

"Phone call came in for you, Val," Max Haffenkamp said when Valnikov sat heavily at the burglary table. Next to the empty chair belonging to Natalie Zimmerman.

"Thanks, Max," Valnikov said, looking at the number which seemed familiar. Of course. It was that Pasadena number he called today.

"Broad sounded like she mighta been crying," Max Haffenkamp said.

"Crying," Valnikov mumbled. A little vodka tonight. A little music. The death of *Boris Godunov*. Natalie seemed genuinely to like the music today. She could learn about music very quickly. She had a good mind and was a sympathetic person, you could tell. She and that Captain Packerton made a handsome couple. They were probably going to get married or something. Stolichnaya.

"She said the call was very important, Val," said Max Haffenkamp.

"Sure," Valnikov said. "I'll call her right away." He misdialed the number twice. He couldn't help thinking of how Natalie looked when she smiled. She had only smiled twice in the three days they'd been partners. She didn't smile much, but when she did . . .

"Hello?" the voice cried.

"This is Sergeant Valnikov, ma'am."

"Sergeant!"

"Yes."

"I have to see you at once!"

"At once?"

"Sergeant, I'm in trouble. Terrible trouble. I haven't been honest with you. Oh, God!"

"Trouble?"

"Sergeant, you have to come to my house. I lied to you. My schnauzer, my Vickie, was stolen from me Sunday at the dog show. And a man has been calling me. He wants a great amount of money to return Vickie. Please come!"

"How much does he want?"

"Eighty-five thousand dollars!" she cried.

"For a *dog?*"

"Yes," she cried. "It's insane. I mean I don't have it. If I had it I'd give it to him."

"You'd give him eighty-five thousand *dollars?*"

"Yes! Yes! But I don't have it! I don't . . ."

"One moment, please," said Valnikov. He opened his work folder to the theft report from the Brown Derby. It was getting confusing. "Ma'am," he said. "I have a theft report from a restaurant in Hollywood. You say your dog was stolen at a dog show?"

"Yes!"

"Where was the dog show?"

"The Sports Arena!"

"That's in Southwest Division, ma'am."

"I don't know about such things," she cried. "Please, I need help!"

"Yes," Valnikov said. "I'll get you some help, but first I have to know who to call. Let's see, your dog was stolen in Southwest. A man is extorting you by telephone at your home?"

"I thought about the F.B.I., Sergeant!"

"Yes, well they *do* get involved in kidnapping, ma'am. But I don't believe the Little Lindbergh Law applies to Scotties."

"Schnauzers."

"Not even to schnauzers, ma'am," Valnikov said patiently.

"I NEED HELP!" Madeline wailed.

"Let me call you right back, Mrs. Whitfield," said Valnikov. "Just stay calm and I'll call you right back."

When Valnikov did his best to explain the complicated problem of Madeline Whitfield to Woodenlips Mockett, the lieutenant started to get a stomachache like Captain Hooker's.

"Could you go over the whole thing one more time, Valnikov?" said Lieutenant Mockett, feeling the stomachache worsen. "Start with the dog theft at the Brown Derby."

And he did. Again. When Valnikov was finished with the story, Lieutenant Mockett showed his expertise at civil service. He could pass the buck with the best of them.

"It's simple. We don't have to handle it!" Lieutenant Mockett cried, and his woodenlips almost grinned in triumph.

"I realize, Lieutenant, that the dog theft took place at the Sports Arena," said Valnikov slowly.

"That's Southwest Division. They can handle it," said Lieutenant Mockett quickly.

"And the extortion took place in Pasadena. At least the calls are *received* in Pasadena."

"Let Pasadena P.D. handle it," Lieutenant Mockett said quickly.

"Except that the jurisdiction from where the *original* crime emanates should handle the entire crime," said Valnikov.

"That's Southwest Detectives. That's Southwest!" Lieutenant Mockett cried. "The dog was snatched from the Sports Arena!"

"Yes, sir," Valnikov said, blinking patiently, "but this lady seems to believe that the dog they switched on her was definitely of championship caliber. And there's only one dog like that reported missing in the entire Los Angeles basin. And that's the dog that was stolen from the Brown Derby. So maybe Mrs. Whitfield is on to something. Maybe the extortionist *did* steal Mrs. Gharoujian's schnauzer as the *first* step in his extortion plan. If so, Hollywood Detectives would probably be the jurisdiction to follow through on the entire investigation. And that dog theft at the Brown Derby belongs to me."

Lieutenant Mockett was quiet for a minute as the psychosomatic stomachache worsened. Then he said, "You actually *want* to handle the case, Valnikov? A dognapping? Don't you have *enough* to do?"

"Well, I've been involved on the periphery and . . . well, the poor woman sounds so desperate."

"A dognapping. And you want to handle it," said Lieutenant Mockett, who could not understand why anyone under *any* circumstances would want to do work he didn't have to do. "You must be nuts, Valnikov."

And at last, someone agreed with Natalie Zimmerman, who was not present to hear it.

"Well, sir, I don't have anything else to do tonight."

"No overtime, Valnikov," Woodenlips Mockett warned. "The commander's been bitching about paying overtime. No overtime. That's out."

"I won't put in for overtime, Lieutenant," Valnikov promised.

"You won't put in for overtime?" cried Woodenlips Mockett. "You *must* be nuts, Valnikov!"

"Yes, sir," said Valnikov. "So if it's okay, I'll drive to Pasadena now and be present when the extortionist calls."

"I got a feeling we shouldn't get involved in this. It's always best never to get involved in cases unless you're absolutely sure you can't get out of it. I just wish I knew for sure the dead dog is the one stolen from Hollywood."

"Tell you what, Lieutenant. I'll find out somehow. And if it turns out the dead dog isn't the one belonging to Mrs. Gharoujian, I'll turn the case over to Southwest Detectives."

"Okay, okay," Lieutenant Mockett said, holding his psychosomatic stomach. "Do you have an Alka-Seltzer? Does *anybody* have an Alka-Seltzer? Ooooohhhh!"

It was the first time Valnikov had ever driven on the Pasadena Freeway during rush hour. It was the oldest freeway and showed it, being too narrow to accommodate the flow of cars in 1977. The turnoff lanes were inadequate and a stalled car could stop traffic for miles. Valnikov passed time in bumper-to-bumper traffic and eye-burning air pollution by thinking about this day.

It was his best day in recent memory. He used to have some good days when he worked with Charlie Lightfoot. But today . . . today was the best day in years. He thought of Natalie's brown eyes smiling through those big glasses as she drank red wine. Was she drinking wine tonight? French wine out of crystal and not styrofoam? They were a good-looking couple, no doubt about it. *Na zdorovye,* Natalie. Still, it was harmless to dream. To pretend. It seemed as though he had lived alone all his life. He suddenly wanted to stop and buy some vodka. But only better-class liquor stores carried Russian vodka and he couldn't stomach American vodka. Then he thought of Madeline Whitfield. She didn't deserve that. She was a desperate woman in trouble and deserved a clear-headed policeman to help her. The vodka could come later.

He used his map book and found the house without much trouble. It was more beautiful than the old Spanish homes in the Los Feliz district. Valnikov admired the vast numbers of ancient oaks. The trees were all well over a century old. And camellias were everywhere. And eucalyptus and pine and azalea. Her driveway was circular and private. What would it be like to live in a house like this? Valnikov was certain a butler in livery would answer the door. He was excited. The Great Gatsby.

Madeline Whitfield answered the door. She'd touched up her makeup and combed her hair and hadn't had a drink, and she looked awful. Her eyes were swollen and raw from crying. She wore a white blouse and tartan woolen skirt. The blouse was stained by coffee. It was very hard to hold things steady in those hands.

"I'm Sergeant Valnikov," he said to the big woman. He guessed she was about his age. A little overweight but not bad-looking if it weren't for a rather heavy layer of hair under her nose.

"He said he'd call at six, Sergeant," she said with a great effort at control. "He's usually very punctual. Would you like some coffee while we wait?"

"No, thank you, ma'am," he said standing in the large foyer.

"Tea?"

"Yes, tea would be nice. Thank you."

"I'm ever so grateful to you, Sergeant," she said. "Please sit down and excuse me for a moment."

"I just hope we can help you," he said, looking at the quarry tile floor, done fifty years ago when craftsmen cared. And there was a beamed ceiling with something he'd never seen: ceiling boards painted by artisans in Moorish designs and Mexican colors, the most impressive residential ceiling he'd ever seen. The paint was kept vivid by nothing more than linseed oil. There was a sunken living room which was the style when great Southern California architects were having their heyday in Pasadena and Beverly Hills. The windows were too small, as was the style then, but were finished with mahogany frames and leaded glass. Privacy was more important than a view in 1927, but on the arroyo side, the windows had been enlarged over the years and there was a panoramic view of the Rose Bowl and the defunct Vista del Royal Hotel glowing pink and dusty gold in the setting sun. And in the foreground, the ominous old Suicide Bridge where many tormented souls had plunged to their deaths while looking at the lovely San Gabriels, and at the splendid old mansions dotting the hillside over the arroyo among the pines and camellias.

Madeline Whitfield returned, her face wet where she had been dabbling at her swollen eyes with a cold cloth. She carried a tray bearing English silver service given by a guest at her grandmother's wedding. There weren't many of the old things left. Not many at all.

"In here, please," she said and put the tray on the table in the library. It was a masculine heavy somber library, but sparsely furnished. She understood how impressive it must be to him.

"A grand old house, isn't it?"

"It certainly is," Valnikov said. He wished Natalie were here to see it.

"I have no help except for a girl who comes in two days a week for four hours a day."

No butler in livery? Not even an upstairs girl? No groundskeeper?

She saw it and smiled and said, "I'm broke, Sergeant. Very nearly broke. I couldn't pay that monster if I wanted to. And I *do* want to.

But I can't. That's why I have no choice but to ask the police to help me."

"I'm sorry about you being broke," he said. "And I'm sorry about your troubles. But I'm glad you called the police. I'll just have my tea plain, thank you."

"Behind lots and lots of these winding driveways and oak doors it's the same story, Sergeant," she said. "No romance of old money. Just people like me holding on."

"Yes, ma'am," he said, sipping his tea noiselessly.

The dusk was settling fast. It was twenty minutes until six. "Would you mind if I didn't turn the light on just yet?" she said. "I have a ripping headache. The dark soothes sometimes."

"I don't mind at all, Mrs. Whitfield," he said. "I've noticed the same thing."

"What will I say when he calls?"

"I really don't know, Mrs. Whitfield," he said. "That's up to the extortionist. Just let him talk. The main thing is that you and I both pick up our phones together and that you stall for at least another day."

"Should I tell him the schnauzer is dead?"

"No, I don't think so."

"Why?"

"Let's not give *him* any information. Let him give *us* information."

"Should I promise him the eighty-five thousand tomorrow?"

"I don't think so," Valnikov said. "Just promise him you'll do better tomorrow. That you'll have some money soon. I've got to have time to work."

"Of course," she said. "I've been wracking my brain. I think I can get a few thousand more. I think I can raise seventeen thousand by tomorrow afternoon," she said.

"I wouldn't like you to pay anything, ma'am," Valnikov said. "But that decision's up to you."

"Vickie's like a child to me, Sergeant," she said. "Look around you. I live in this house alone. There's only Vickie."

"Alone. Yes. I can understand how you feel. Yes."

"How could that woman whose dog was stolen from the restaurant, how could she not care? Does she have a family living with her?"

"I rather doubt it, ma'am," said Valnikov, sipping. "She said she's seventy-six years old."

"And she doesn't care about her beautiful schnauzer? Does she have other pets?"

"You might say that, yes, ma'am," said Valnikov, blushing.

"At first Vickie was just to be a pet. I was lonely. And then people who knew, told me how exceptional she was. I began getting involved in showing her. I entered a whole new world of dog shows. The sport. The parties. The awards. Our picture was in the *Times.* Vickie opened up my life, you see."

"Yes, ma'am."

"And she *is* truly like my . . . it sounds foolish . . . like my child. That man said . . . said he'll cut off her toes. He may be doing it now."

"I don't think so, ma'am," said Valnikov.

"He sounds as though he would," she said and her voice broke. "He sounds so wicked. I can't help it. I have a dreadful premonition of this man holding Vickie on a table. With a knife!"

A knife. Valnikov was leaving her. Drifting. He was going after it! There it was! A little schnauzer dog. The big strong hands of the hunter. No! The *extortionist* with a knife. He was going to disembowel the little dog. The picture was there in the darkness. There was only moonlight now and he could almost see the doctor in the bloody smock cutting the rabbit's throat. He almost had it! Then a voice. Valnikov's own voice cried out and the rabbit bounded off through the snow and escaped.

The detective sat there trembling in the dark, on the damask wingback chair. He spilled some tea on his trousers. He didn't notice. Madeline Whitfield didn't notice either. She was lying across the sofa sobbing so hard she could scarcely breathe. Those pathetic sobs brought Valnikov back from Siberia.

"That's all right, Mrs. Whitfield," he said, when his own fear subsided. "Go on and cry. It's all right."

She cried for a long time. Whenever she tried to stop she would burst forth again. Valnikov sat quietly in dusky shadows, among leather-bound books and glossy old wood, in the lonely wingback chair. He watched the woman weeping on the sofa. It had been a long time since he'd heard such sounds of grief. Valnikov sat in brooding darkness and vowed he would find her little dog. Nothing would stop him.

• ● •

Philo Skinner was not punctual. He didn't call until 6:15 p.m. He had gone home and changed into the last of his leisure suits. He couldn't explain why, but somehow he had a need to be well dressed when he consummated his crime. He didn't want to look like a bum even though no one would see him. He never wanted to look like a bum again. When he stripped off the soggy leisure suit he threw it in the trash can. Then he went back to the kennel to feed the dogs. It was getting harder to keep Mavis away from the kennel. By tomorrow she'd insist on coming in and might see the little schnauzer bitch. He had to get his money and return the dog tonight. Then it occurred to him: He hadn't yet given the rich broad her instructions on what to do with Tutu. Oh, well, Tutu was probably having a better time in the Pasadena mansion than she ever did with that stingy sex maniac, Millie Muldoon Gharoujian.

He wondered if old Millie still kept a couple of studs and a cobra, or mongoose, or whatever the hell. Once when Millie was still interested in dog shows he had come early and found the door open and there they were: a pile of bodies snoozing in Millie's water bed. The pile included Millie, two or three boys, a leopard or something, and incredibly enough, a goddamn baby alligator! Perverted old cunt!

• ● •

Valnikov was on the phone extension in the library. Madeline was in the living room. The lights were on now and Madeline was shaky but controlled. After two rings, he nodded and they picked up the phones together. "Hello."

"It's Richard." He didn't bother with the paper towel anymore. And he'd returned to the cocktail lounge where he'd made the first call. Philo was getting bold. And desperate.

"Yes," she said.

"Do you have the money?"

"Not all of it."

"How much do you have?"

"Tomorrow I'll have more."

"How much do you have?"

"Tomorrow I'll have seventeen . . . no," she lied. "I'll have twenty thousand for you!"

"You cunt!" Philo screamed. "You owe me eighty-five thousand. You rotten cheap cunt!"

"Wait, please, Richard!" she said. It was much easier with Valnikov present. The extortionist didn't scare her so much anymore.

"Don't you please Richard me, you cunt," Philo wheezed. "You ain't gonna welsh on me. Not if you want your bitch alive. I'm sick a playing games with you. I been too nice to you, that's my problem. Well, no more Mr. Nice Guy!"

"Please, Richard, twenty thousand is a lot of money. I can get that much by this time tomorrow. That's a lot of money, Richard."

The line was quiet for a long moment. Twenty thousand. But he owed Arnold $15,200 as of today, and an extra hundred tomorrow! Puerto Vallarta *for life* on less than five thousand? Could she be telling the truth? But how *could* she be? That goddamn house she lived in? She had it, the cunt!

"I'm getting your bitch," he said. "And I'm calling you back in five minutes. And I'm going to cut her toe off while you listen to her scream. You ready for that?"

Madeline nearly dropped the receiver. She almost collapsed. But she looked at Valnikov, who just shook his head slowly at her. The husky detective stood like a rock, his cinnamon hair rumpled, his tie askew. A slouching man who might have never stood straight in his life. But he had a broad earthy strong face. And he sustained her by just shaking his head slowly, telling her not to break. She didn't.

"That won't help you at all, Richard," she said, her voice so controlled it surprised her. "If you hurt Vickie, she'll be worth nothing in a dog show. That's the only reason I bother, you know, to show her and win. Without a toe she's worth nothing. Injure her in any way and she's worth nothing." She held on, held on, closed her eyes. When she opened them, Valnikov was nodding. He seemed proud of her.

Philo was beside himself. He started yelling so loud that the bartender came over, banged on the door, and said, "Hey fella, there's ladies in this joint! Watch your language."

And Philo almost yelled something at the bartender, but he remembered what happened to him today in a phone booth when he popped off, so he bit his lip and kept quiet. When he came back on the line he said, "You have *thirty*-five thousand for me at this time tomorrow night. *Thirty*-five and that's my last offer. You understand? I'm calling you at six o'clock tomorrow night and you're going to tell me you have the dough or I'm going to hurt that bitch. I never hurt an animal in my life, lady, but I swear I'll hurt your bitch if you don't have the dough for me by tomorrow night."

"All right, Richard, I'll have it," she said. "Good-bye." And she hung up the phone, walked back into the drawing room, threw herself on the couch and wept.

Valnikov sat quietly and watched her cry. He blinked patiently from time to time.

Finally, she said, "I . . . I've been try . . . trying to get a . . . a job. I've never . . . never *worked.* This house . . . this . . . I'll have to be out in a year. I have . . . have enough in a trust fund to last till then. But I can't *get* it. I'd give it all to him. But I can't *get* it! It took a court order to get . . . to get it for my mother's . . . her hospital expenses. Her funeral. I can't get . . ."

"Now now, Mrs. Whitfield," he said, sighing deeply. His eyes were sad and red. "Now now."

"How does one find a *job,* Sergeant? Can . . . can you tell me? Where . . . what can I . . . what . . ."

"Now now, Mrs. Whitfield," Valnikov said softly.

Then he switched off the light and lumbered to the couch and sat down. He started patting her on the back. Now now, Mrs. Whitfield. Now now.

She didn't feel his hand at first, though it was a meaty hand. When she did, she sat up, but couldn't stop the tears.

Then Valnikov put his arm around her and it startled her. Still she couldn't stop weeping. Then Valnikov put both arms around her and she wept on his chest. He kept patting her back, rather solidly, as though he was trying to burp her. Then she relaxed and he began patting her softly. Then he was holding her, rocking her, patting her ever more gently and she was catching her breath.

Then she put both arms around Valnikov's neck and sat there crying in the darkness. Valnikov looked almost as sad as she. Now now, Mrs. Whitfield. Now now.

Then, instinctively, Valnikov began kissing Madeline Whitfield on the salty cheek. Now now. Now now. And she tightened her grip on his neck and let him.

Of course Valnikov could not have known that this woman had not felt a man's body in five years. He was only vaguely aware that he hadn't felt a woman's body since Thanksgiving weekend when he got drunk in a Chinatown bar and picked up a clerk typist from the police academy. Madeline turned her tear-drenched face to the detective and kissed his mouth. Valnikov responded. Then they were groping in the darkness on that damask sofa and she was saying, "Sergeant, Sergeant!" And he was replying, "Mrs. Whitfield, Mrs. Whitfield!"

"Sergeant! Oh, Sergeant!" she cried.

"Mrs. Whitfield," he cried. "I'll find your doggie, I swear!"

"Sergeant!" she cried, and unhooked his gun belt.

When he left her an hour later, he was filled with pity for this woman. She was sleeping soundly in her bed for the first time in days. He paused in the door to look at her naked body. She was a fine woman. He wished she could find someone from her station in life. She needed someone to care about. Something useful to do.

Valnikov went home and before he slept he renewed his vow to find this lonely woman's dog. Then he went to sleep and dreamed of the rabbit.

11

The Dog Lover

Valnikov felt very strange when he awakened Wednesday morning. At first, he didn't know what it was. He got up, boiled water for the tea, fed and watered Misha and Grisha, cleaned their cage. He brought the morning paper in, sat down to read. Then he looked around the bachelor apartment. Nothing had changed. He still had the same clothesline strung from the animal cage to the nail he'd pounded into the top of the door frame. Several pair of underwear and socks still hung on the clothesline. There was still a pile of dirty dishes on the sink which he washed one plate at a time when he was hungry. There were still stacks of records and album covers strewn around the room. But something was different. Then it dawned on him. There was no empty bottle of Stolichnaya either on the kitchen table or on the walnut veneer coffee table. And that gave him the *big* clue as to what was totally different this morning: He had no hangover!

He had worked, and kept company with Madeline Whitfield until midnight. He had come home and gone to bed. He had not had a single glass of vodka. Remarkable! He got up, went into the bathroom, tossed two hand towels off the metal arm that dangled in front of the medicine cabinet. He examined his eyes. They were slightly red but *dry*. He looked well. He felt well. He celebrated by making himself two scrambled eggs and rye toast. He drank three cups of tea and had a glass of orange juice. Then he took a shower and ironed a clean shirt. He tied his tie carefully so the collar button didn't show. He put some tonic on his hair and combed it, careful to get a straight part.

He felt like a new man when he walked out that door. He couldn't wait to tell Natalie. They were going to catch a *criminal.*

When Valnikov got to the station, things were about to get tense. Bullets Bambarella had lost two weeks' pay in the last two days by making bets with Montezuma Montez. Aside from that, Bullets had had a lousy night with a cop groupie from downtown.

Bullets had Clarence Cromwell cornered at the burglary table when Valnikov got himself a cup of tea. Bullets was saying, ". . . so I take this broad home. You know her, Clarence?"

"Yeah, yeah, she works the D.A.'s office," Clarence sighed. All these young kids got woman troubles and who do they bring them to? Clarence Cromwell, that's who. "Bullets, do I look like the fuckin Ann Landers of Hollywood Detectives, or somethin?"

"But, Clarence, listen! She's a sicko. Some kinda fruitcake or somethin. She plays with her own clit when I'm lovin her up. Can you believe it? Then . . . get this . . . she starts suckin on her own big tit! I says to this freako, I says, 'Hey. Whadda you need *me* for?' She says, 'Come to think of it, dummy, I *don't.*' "

"Yeah, this is very interestin, Bullets. I mean, there ain't nothin I'd rather do than talk about your sex life but . . ."

"Then I done it!"

Suddenly the scowling black detective stiffened and said, "You done *what,* Bullets?"

"Nothin much. I just got mad. I just threw her in the swimmin pool, is all."

"Jesus! You had me scared for a minute. I can't be coverin for you anymore, Bullets!"

"I know, Clarence, and I just wanted you to know how it was."

"I don't think she can bitch too much, you just threw her in a swimmin pool."

"Thanks for bein so understandin, Clarence," Bullets breathed.

"Nothing but whackos in Hollywood anyway," said Montezuma Montez, overhearing Bullets' problems. "Over in East L.A. you pick up a Mexican chick, you buy a six-pack a beer and have a great old time in a drive-in movie. In Hollywood you pick up a broad you gotta spend thirty bucks on dinner. Then to satisfy her you gotta go down to Western Costume and rent a werewolf mask and spend the night whopping each other over the head with live kitty cats. I wanna transfer back to Hollenbeck," said Montezuma Montez.

But Bullets was ready for trouble. "Yeah, that's just like a spic to say that," Bullets sneered. "You get the wrong hole with those Mexican broads you end up with a blister on your joint, all the chili seeds they eat. I'll take a Hollywood girl any old time."

"Oh, yeah?" Montezuma said. "Well lemme tell you about this *Hollywood* lady I picked up the other night. Said her folks were from Venice. Not Venice, California. Venice, *Italy*. Had her little two-year-old spumoni sucker *in the car* when I picked her up at the tennis court," said Montezuma.

"That's a filthy lie," said Bullets Bambarella, and Clarence Cromwell finally said, "Will you two please shut up!"

"It's *gotta* be a lie, Clarence," Bullets argued. "You think a spic can play tennis?"

"Better than any dago I ever seen," said Montezuma Montez.

Then Bullets turned to Montezuma and said, "I never played tennis in my life and I could probably beat you."

"I could beat you left-handed," said Montezuma Montez.

"Gotcha covered, dummy!" Bullets yelled in triumph and suddenly Montezuma Montez was looking down at forty borrowed dollars, thinking he may have gone too far.

Then money was flying all over the squad room and Lieutenant Mockett was whining to no avail about illegal gambling, and four cars full of detectives went speeding to Hollywood High School for a bizarre one-set tennis match in stocking feet, suits, and ties, between two clumsy buffaloes, one of whom was playing with the wrong hand.

Natalie Zimmerman, wearing a new side-pleated skirt and matching cardigan jacket, came to work five minutes late, and was almost knocked to the floor by the thundering herd charging out of the station to the tennis match.

She was relieved to see that Hipless Hooker was also late. She was not going to fail today. She was going to grab him by the goddamn throat if she had to, the minute he came in the door. And then she was going to walk him into the office and put a chair in front of the door to keep out Clarence Cromwell. Then they were going to talk about Valnikov.

The reason she was late was that she had only gotten three hours' sleep, what with Captain Jack Packerton jumping on her every two hours or so to prove he still had it even though he'd just turned forty. She felt like telling him it would be the last all-nighter until he accepted impending middle age. And all the time he didn't know that Natalie Zimmerman had much the same fear because she had failed at orgasm the last *five* times.

What the hell, Jack, let's just live together. I've been divorced twice now and . . . Live together? Natalie, I'm a captain! Have you read the latest memorandum from Chief Digby Bates about moral rearmament? Do you know what would happen if a captain was found living in sin? Christ, I'd rather risk another divorce than face the alternative! Do you know that I stand a very good chance of being a deputy chief someday? What're you trying to do to my career? *Live* together? Without benefit of clergy? I WANNA BE A DEPUTY CHIEF!

And all she wanted to be was an Investigator III who wasn't lonely and who could have an occasional orgasm. Yet she was an Investigator II, and hadn't had one lately, and was working with a closet madman, and there was no help on the horizon.

She was telling all this silently to her Friz when Valnikov set a cup of coffee in front of her. He was looking all spruced up today for some reason. Just her luck. The day she vowed to expose him is the day he picks to get all gussied up and comb his hair. Well, it didn't matter whether he *looked* like a madman or not. He couldn't fool anybody if they just pushed the right buttons. Tell me about your dream, Valnikov. Is it Bugs Bunny? Peter Cottontail? Tell me about a rabbit that makes you cry. Jesus, he was smiling that big goofy kid smile.

"We have a real case to work on, Natalie," he said. "Would you care for a little cream or sugar?"

"No."

"I just finished telling Clarence about it."

And hearing his name, Clarence Cromwell came over and sat on Valnikov's table. "Mockett wants to know if you're putting in overtime for last night."

"No," said Valnikov.

"Okay, that'll keep him happy. I'm gonna have Max Haffenkamp handle your cases for today and maybe tomorrow. I might go out and help him. But that's *it*. We can't be makin no major crime outta this extortion."

"Extortion?" said Natalie.

"I'll tell you all about it," Valnikov said. "It's a pretty big one. Eighty-five thousand dollars."

"Yeah, but it's over a dog, Val. Keep that in mind. It's only a guddamn pampered *dog*."

"I appreciate your handling my regular workload, Clarence," Valnikov said, and Natalie was shocked to see that even his blue eyes were clear this morning.

"One thing you gotta do first, Val," said Clarence. "Mockett says you make sure that dead dog is the one from the Brown Derby. Go to the pet mortuary and see if they haven't disposed of it yet. Have that broad from Trousdale . . . what's her name?"

"Millie Gharoujian."

"Yeah, you have her or somebody identify that dead dog. If it ain't from the Brown Derby, you turn the whole thing over to Southwest Detectives or Pasadena P.D. Them's orders from Mockett. First order he gave this month. We gotta humor him."

"Okay, Clarence," Valnikov said. "Let's go, Natalie."

"Wait a minute," she said, brushing her Friz out of her eyes. "Clarence, where's the captain? I have to talk to him and I'm not going anywhere until I do!"

"Gud-damn, Natalie!" Clarence sneered, standing up and putting his fists on his hips, the twin magnums dangling impotently beside his barrel chest.

"Gud-damn, what!" she sneered right back. A black General Patton!

"Is it that same thing you been complainin about the last three days, Natalie?"

"Yes it is," she said, looking involuntarily at Valnikov, who busied himself with a follow-up report, too polite to pry.

"Well, this is a hell of a time," Clarence snorted. "You got an extortion to work on and you wanna go runnin to . . ."

He was interrupted when Natalie jumped to her feet. She jumped because Hipless Hooker came flying through the door and ran across the squad room. He was holding his stomach and was followed by a young woman in a yellow pantsuit, walking like a robot, wearing a neck brace.

"Clarence!" Hipless Hooker cried, but Natalie Zimmerman beat Clarence to the captain's office.

"I just gotta talk to you today, Captain!" Natalie cried.

"Not *now*, Natalie," Hooker whimpered. "Clarence, this lady was waiting for me at the desk when I came in. She claims she was out on a date with Bullets Bambarella last night. She works for the district attorney's office. She wants to sue us for half a million dollars!"

"Let's all go in and quiet down," said Clarence, smiling at the woman in the neck brace.

"Bullets told me about it, miss," Clarence said placatingly, "but I didn't know he hurt you. He said he just pushed you into a swimmin pool."

"He did!" Hooker cried. "But her apartment was two floors up!"

"I got a whiplash," the young woman said, "and Bullets is *not* gonna get away with it."

"Oooooooooohhhhh, my stomach," Hooker suddenly moaned.

"And I was wearing a good wristwatch and my contact lenses at the time," the girl said, sitting down gingerly.

"Yeah, well I think we can clear this up," Clarence said as he closed the door in Natalie's face. "You see, Bullets really *cares* about you a lot. He told me."

• ● •

It was starting to seem like a dream to Natalie Zimmerman. Destiny and Bullets Bambarella were conspiring to save Valnikov from his fate. And here they were driving up the hill, high to the top of Trousdale Estates, overlooking Hollywood and Beverly Hills. Natalie Zimmerman was starting to believe she would never be rid of the man next to her, driving all of fifteen miles per hour.

"It's beautiful up here on top of the smog, isn't it?" he said amiably, as she sat and smoked and thought about sex without orgasm. And the black marble.

"Yeah, beautiful."

"Mrs. Gharoujian must be very rich."

"Jesus!" said Natalie, coming out of her funk when she saw the contemporary home of Millie Muldoon Gharoujian on the cul-de-sac overlooking all of Baghdad. There was a Silver Shadow Rolls-Royce in the driveway, and a chauffeur in a black cap. He was nineteen years old and had shoulder-length blond hair hanging from under his cap. He got out of the car when they pulled up to the gate.

Valnikov held his badge out the window and the chauffeur nodded and opened the gate. There was a granite fountain in the center of the circular drive. On it was a plaster sculpture of David. With an erection. A stream of water flowed from the erection. In the fountain, a boa constrictor writhed and rubbed his scales against the granite bowl and got a suntan, compliments of Millie Muldoon Gharoujian.

When Natalie pushed the doorbell, the chime played a chorus of "Roll Out the Barrel." Then the door was opened by a houseboy with a 29 waist and 19-inch arms. The houseboy was eighteen years old and was a runner-up in a Mr. California contest.

"Mrs. Gharoujian is expecting you," he said, admitting them into the living room overlooking the cantilevered, clover-shaped swimming pool.

The living room was white. White sofas filled seventy square yards of room. White wall-to-wall carpet buried Natalie's heels. White slumpstone fireplace. White baby grand ingeniously built so that it could play as well as any upright player piano when Millie wasn't too tired to pump the white enamel foot pedals.

The white walls of the living room were covered with gilded antique mirrors and paintings of nudes, men and women. Over the fireplace was an enormous painting of a reclining Millie Gharoujian when she was thirty years old and still looked like Harlow. The painting was done in 1932.

Then the east wall, which was all mirrors, opened. Millie came briskly through the mirrored door. She had had five face lifts over the past twenty-five years, and in a huge silk kimono barely covering the breasts which hung like twin punching bags, she looked not a day over seventy-two. She was perspiring and red-faced and petulant.

"Sergeant, I told you on the phone, I already reported that schnauzer to my insurance company. It's a closed incident, far as I'm concerned. I appreciate you're a good cop and all that, but why don't you gimme a break? I got something in there hung like . . ."

"Yes, yes, yes!" Valnikov cried, not wanting Natalie to hear about Michelangelo penises. "But, Mrs. Gharoujian, if you could just come with us. The pet mortuary is only twenty minutes from here and we'd bring you right home as soon as you say if it's your Tutu or not. And . . ."

"Leave here? Now? Sergeant, you gotta be kidding! With what I got waiting for me on that water bed in there?"

"Uh, yes, I understand, ma'am," Valnikov said quickly, as Natalie moved a few feet to her left to try to see what Millie had on her water bed.

"Damn, you're a tough man, Sergeant," Millie sighed. Then she picked up a cigarette, put it into a ruby-studded holder, and said, "You married, Sergeant?"

"No, ma'am," Valnikov said.

"Hmmm," said Millie. "Well, some other time maybe. Right now, I gotta get back to business."

"Is there anyone else here . . ."

"Anyone else here! You kidding! I got two kids in there with . . ."

"Yes, I mean anyone who could come with us and look at the dead schnauzer," said Valnikov. "It might save everyone a lot of trouble."

"Hey, Twinkles!" Millie yelled, and the houseboy returned from the kitchen with a plastic mixer full of banana daiquiris.

"Yes, Millie?"

She patted his buttocks and sighed, "If only you were Japanese, sweetie. Maybe we could get your eyes fixed. Listen, go with these cops, will ya? Have Buttons drive you in the Rolls. Look at this dead dog they wanna show you and see if it's Tutu or not. Then get your ass right back here. These two in the bedroom are already tired out." Then to Valnikov, "The youth of America ain't what it used to be, Sergeant. The President's Council on Physical Fitness oughtta listen to *me,* sometime. I could tell em."

"Yes, ma'am, and thank you," said Valnikov as he and Natalie followed Twinkles out the front door, getting a fair glimpse into Millie's boudoir. There was a huge hairy creature lying on the floor. Alive!

"There's a goat in there, Valnikov!" Natalie cried when they were outside.

"It's a baby llama," Twinkles said. "Millie's keeping it for a friend. And I'm getting sick and tired of cleaning llama shit all day, I can tell you." Twinkles peeled off his waistcoat and revealed a torso that actually split the shoulder seams of his starched white dress shirt. He rolled up the sleeves over bulging forearms with tendons like pencils. "We'll follow you in the Rolls," he said. "If it's Tutu, I'll know her."

There was a wake going on when they arrived at the pet mortuary. Three women and two men were weeping inconsolably and saying adieu to a raccoon who lay in state in a little walnut baby coffin. It had a fawn satin lining with black ruffles to match the tail stripe and mask on the eyes of the dead animal. The coffin had a double lid and the lower half was closed, revealing only the head and torso of the deceased. There was soft music drifting over the intercom, instrumental strings playing "My Buddy." The deceased had never looked better. His fur was brushed with lanolin. His black raccoon mask was touched up with shoe dye. His little raccoon hands were folded on his chest, as though in prayer, artfully kept in that position by driving a cobbler's needle clear through his chest and sewing them in place. In this prayerful pose the raccoon looked anything but dead. The raccoon could have been playing possum.

They were greeted by a balding man in a somber gray suit with a white carnation in his lapel.

"May I be of service?" he asked.

"Mr. Limpwood?"

"No, he's conducting a graveside service at the moment."

"I called him. I'm Sergeant Valnikov from the police department."

"Yes, he said to show you to the cemetery. He'll be finished shortly. It's a private graveside service for the immediate family."

Valnikov and Natalie walked outside and saw Mr. Limpwood consoling a tearful couple. He tried in vain to scratch the arched backs of the immediate family of Siamese cats. Then he walked jauntily along the cobbled path among tombstones and granite sculpture of all sizes and description which said things like: "Our beloved Duchess, lest we forget!" and "Farewell, Happy Oliver! Till we meet in the Great Beyond!"

He was dressed similarly to the other mortician, but was much shorter and more bald. He wore a white carnation. "May I be of service?"

Valnikov showed his badge and Mr. Limpwood registered disappointment. It was the best week since he'd been in business: fourteen dogs, ten cats, a chimpanzee, two ocelots, a piranha from Pomona (Not all freakos lived in Hollywood.) and a raccoon. There was a rumor that they might get an Arabian gelding, which had them all excited. (Eleven plots of ground to bury that baby. Eleven! And the embalming cost!) But these were just cops not customers.

"You know, Sergeant, I tried to call you this morning but you'd just left. I'm terribly sorry, but the deceased was buried last night. I thought we still had her set for burial this morning, but as you know, there was no bereaved, only dear Mrs. Whitfield, who kindly arranged for the burial, bless her heart."

"Where's she buried? Let's dig her up," said Valnikov.

"Dig her up? Sergeant! Exhume the body? I've never been asked . . ."

"I think that only applies to people bodies," said Valnikov. "Is it that fresh grave over there? By the shovel?"

"Yes, but I don't know! I don't want to be sued, Sergeant! In the event the deceased's next of kin is determined!"

"We can't determine anything until we look at the body," said Valnikov.

"Millie wants me back on time and she means business," said Twinkles suddenly, and Valnikov didn't doubt that at all. Then the giant kid strode over to the half-filled grave, stripped off his dress shirt, showing a black silk bodyshirt that Millie had bought him, and started swooping up earth like a steam shovel. He had the shallow grave uncovered in fifteen minutes.

"I don't want to be responsible," Mr. Limpwood cried. "I'm getting out of here." And he took off in a hurry while Twinkles pulled the box out of the ground with one hand. (It was a cheap pine box and not the walnut that Madeline paid for.)

The lad used the shovel blade and cracked it open easily. Then he grimaced. "Oh!" he said. "Oh, I don't think that's a schnauzer!"

"It's a schnauzer," Valnikov said, with little admiration for Mr. Limpwood's art. (When there's no bereaved, save a buck where you can.)

The young giant was unaccustomed to death in any form. "Tutu was so beautiful!" he said. "I don't know!"

"Mrs. Gharoujian said something about a white toenail on the rear foot. Do you remember that?"

"Do dead things look so . . ."

"Yes, they do," said Valnikov. "Now look at the back foot. You can just reach in there."

"I couldn't," the kid said, getting pale. "Is her body hard?"

"Rigor has come and gone," said Valnikov. "Let's see." And he reached in the coffin. "Yes. There *is* a whitish toenail. I think this might be Mrs. Gharoujian's Tutu."

"But the face!" the young man cried. Then he sat by the grave site and dropped his head. "I loved Tutu." His eyes were filling. "Millie never cared about her."

"Listen, son," Valnikov said, squatting beside the tearful body builder, "who would be able to positively identify this schnauzer by her markings? Who knew her best?"

"There are so many guys that come and go at Millie's," said the young man. "Everybody played with Tutu. So *many* guys."

"Mrs. Gharoujian mentioned her dog handler," said Valnikov. "Would he know her markings?"

"He might." The kid nodded, taking a look at the contorted mastiff face on the dead animal. "That *can't* be Tutu! Is *this* what death does to you?"

"Sometimes," said Valnikov. "What's the dog handler's name?"

"Philo Skinner," said the lad, looking in the grave. "She got tired of dog shows. Millie gets tired of everything. Maybe it *is* Tutu. I just can't say. I had no idea this is what it does! God, I'm sorry!"

"That's okay, son," said Valnikov, patting the enormous shoulder of the young giant. "Thanks for your help, anyway."

"Maybe it *is* Tutu," the boy said softly, stealing his last glance into the pine coffin at the jutting mastiff jaw.

Tutu in her final agony took with her to eternity the face of J. Edgar Hoover.

When they got back to the waiting Rolls, Natalie said, "Buttons, give Twinkles a chance to get himself together. He'll be out in a minute."

"I ain't in no hurry to get back," the blond chauffeur shrugged. "No hurry at all."

And no wonder, Natalie Zimmerman thought, as she and Valnikov waved to Mr. Limpwood who was calling his lawyer to make sure somebody couldn't sue him for letting them dig up a stiff schnauzer. His lawyer wasn't in, so he looked at Valnikov's business card and called Hollywood Station just to make sure this was an authorized police investigation.

The phone was answered by Bullets Bambarella, who was back from the tennis match, dead broke, thinking he'd be eating grass in Griffith Park if this kept up.

"Good morning, Hollywood Investigation, Investigator Bambarella speaking, may I help you." Bullets gave the rote greeting sullenly, then he listened with only half his concentration. He was worried sick. He took a look at the captain's door. Thank God the groupie with the neck brace was gone. He knew he'd be facing Clarence Cromwell's wrath soon enough over this one. Jesus, Clarence, what I gotta do to make up? Marry the broad or what?

Then Bullets heard something which popped his eyes wide. "Just a second, Mr. Limpwood!" Bullets cried, punching the phone button and putting him on hold. Someone was in *lots* more trouble than he was! Bullets ran to the captain's door, knocked, and jerked it open.

"I ain't ready for you yet, Bullets," Clarence Cromwell said with murder in his eyes.

"But this is important, Clarence!" Bullets cried. "Captain! There's a guy on the phone. From a cemetery! Guess what Valnikov done! He dug up a grave! Some stiff named Schnozzle! And the mortician wants to talk to you right now!"

They said that Captain Hooker's moan set a new record for police department moaners. He was taken to the hospital with a gas attack severe enough to require an ambulance. Bullets Bambarella loyally accompanied his captain to the ambulance, saying, "Gee, Skipper, if you could just loosen up and fart you'd feel lots better."

"Ooooooohhhh," said Hipless Hooker.

It didn't help when Clarence Cromwell phoned the hospital later that afternoon and tried to explain that it was only a dog's body. The medication they gave Hipless Hooker kept him belching and farting and off-duty all afternoon.

Which meant that Valnikov's career was secure another day.

"So what do you have in mind now, Valnikov?" said Natalie Zimmerman as they drove toward Pasadena on the freeway.

"I think we proceed on the assumption that the dead dog *is* Tutu."

"Where does that leave us?"

"With the responsibility to handle this case," said Valnikov. "It's *our* extortion. First thing to do is be there when he calls at three o'clock. What do you think?"

"I don't know what to think," Natalie sighed. "Maybe we should just turn the case over to Pasadena P.D."

"I feel a . . . responsibility," Valnikov said. "I want to help Mrs. Whitfield."

"It's only a dog, Valnikov."

"The extortionist calls her a bitch," Valnikov mused.

"Mrs. Whitfield?"

"No, the schnauzer. He always says the word bitch, never the word dog like you just did."

"So?"

"He's familiar with dogs. He uses the right terminology when he refers to Vickie. He knew Tutu would fool them long enough that he'd be home safe before they guessed. He's a dog lover."

"So?"

"Nothing. Something. I don't know. Another thing. He said, 'I've never hurt an animal in my life.' That was important to him."

"So?"

"I don't think we should let him know Tutu's dead. When we're out of possibilities, we can tell him he's killed Tutu. See how he acts."

"You think it was one of Millie's playmates?"

"That's what I'm thinking," Valnikov nodded. "If we could just get that woman's undivided attention for fifteen minutes."

"Impossible, what with the people, aardvarks and lizards in her bed."

"If we could get her thinking, I'll bet there're three or four guys who lived with her when she was involved in dog shows. I'll bet it's one of those guys."

"She's a chickenhawk!" Natalie sneered. "These kids come and go hourly through her zoo. Sunset Strip one week, Haight-Ashbury the next."

"Except that this one's in town. Only thing bothers me is the voice. That voice, even if he was an actor, that wasn't a youngster's voice. And Millie likes *boys.*"

"So you think there were two."

"Or more," Valnikov nodded. "Would probably take two anyway. Millie's former friend takes Tutu from the restaurant. Maybe one or both take the dog into the show and switch schnauzers. Then the other one calls Mrs. Whitfield, the older man."

"A dog lover," Natalie sighed. Her police career had come to this.

"A dog lover," Valnikov said. "Yes. Not an ordinary thief. Not a burglar, certainly. Her address is in dog show catalogues, I'm sure. It wouldn't be hard to find. This is someone who was much more *comfortable* committing a theft in the presence of thousands of people at a dog show than he would be shimming her back door, or prowling her neighborhood. This wasn't an ordinary thief, or he'd have stolen the dog from *here*." And as he said it, Valnikov stopped by the iron gate overlooking the winding cobbled driveway into Madeline Whitfield's fifty-year-old Mediterranean mansion.

"Wow!" Natalie said. "I see why he picked her!"

"He picked the wrong victim," Valnikov said, wheeling into the driveway. "She's almost broke."

"How could you be broke and have a house like this? And squander money on a show dog?"

"That's what the extortionist can't understand," said Valnikov. "It's a long story."

Madeline Whitfield was on the steps when they got out of the detective car. She looked at Natalie curiously and smiled at Valnikov like an old friend.

"This is my partner, Sergeant Zimmerman," Valnikov said. "Mrs. Whitfield."

"Come in. I'm glad you came early. The waiting is hard."

"We're pretty sure the dead dog was the one belonging to Mrs. Gharoujian," said Valnikov. "I wish we knew for certain, though."

"Does that help you?" Madeline asked, and Natalie Zimmerman, a fair detective herself, noticed that Madeline Whitfield held Valnikov's arm all the way into the sitting room. And that when she said, "I'll get you some tea, Sergeant," she fluttered like a pigeon and *squeezed* his arm.

Natalie strolled around the room, admiring the view of the Rose Bowl. "How long did you stay here last night?"

"Pardon?"

"I said, how long did you stay here last night?"

"Uh, well, the extortionist called just after six."

"She lives all alone in this big house?"

"All alone," Valnikov nodded and his reddening face was not lost on Natalie Zimmerman.

"If she'd lose twenty-five pounds. And shave . . ." Natalie smirked.

"She's a fine lady," Valnikov said, a bit too quickly. "She's loving . . . of her Vickie. She's educated. She knows music. You should see her record collection."

"Really?" Natalie said. "I thought you were busy with an extortionist."

"I . . . uh, listened to a few records with her."

"Did she play? Music, I mean?"

"And she's very smart. After all, she's the one who first discovered that the dead dog was Mrs. Gharoujian's."

"Which we're not sure of at all," Natalie reminded him.

When Madeline returned, she said, "Sergeant Zimmerman, how would you like your tea?"

"Well, actually," Natalie said petulantly, "I'd prefer some coffee. Most *ordinary* cops drink coffee."

"Of course," she said. "It'll just take a minute." Then she poured for Valnikov and handed him the cup and saucer, and met his eyes, and smiled demurely, touching his arm before leaving for the kitchen again.

"Oh, horseshit!" Natalie said to her Friz.

"Pardon, Natalie?" said Valnikov.

"Nothing. Nothing at all," Natalie smirked. "It's not *my* business."

"What?"

"Nothing, for chrissake!"

"Sorry," said Valnikov, sipping. "Very good tea."

"Of course it's good tea. She probably has it imported from Bombay. From the plantation of a retired rajah, for chrissake."

"Sorry," said Valnikov, wondering why she had him apologizing.

"Did you ask *her* to go to the movies?" Natalie smirked.

"Why, no."

"Why not take her to see *Deep Throat?*"

"I told you I'd rather not see porno films, Natalie," Valnikov said. "But if you need an escort and you have to see it again, I'll be glad . . ."

Madeline's return interrupted Valnikov's offer and Natalie's impending outburst. Madeline put the coffee down and said nervously: "What should I tell him? Should I tell him I have the money?"

"I think it's time to say just that," Valnikov nodded while Natalie glared coldly at Madeline Whitfield, unable to fathom this overwhelming anger.

"I *do* have money for him, Sergeant. And as we discussed last night, it's *my* choice. I've decided today that if he'll promise to release Vickie unharmed, I'll give it all to him. I've managed to borrow and raise twenty thousand dollars!"

"That's stupid!" Natalie Zimmerman said.

"Please, Natalie," Valnikov said. "Natalie didn't mean that harshly, Mrs. Whitfield."

Now he was apologizing to this dowdy broad for his *partner's* manners! Him! A certified dingaling and a drunk apologizing to this Pasadena dog freak about Natalie's manners! Natalie was ranging from fury to contempt. For the both of them.

"I can understand that it might be hard for you to comprehend," Madeline said carefully to Natalie Zimmerman.

Don't patronize me, Dame Whitfield. Don't patronize Natalie Kelso Zimmerman or you'll be wearing a fat lip under that goddamn moustache!

"I can't understand *ever* giving in to kidnappers and extortionists," Natalie said. "For solid professional reasons *you* couldn't comprehend, Mrs. Whitfield. And I don't think many people, cops or civilians, could comprehend laying out twenty thousand in ransom for a *dog*."

"Sergeant Valnikov understands," Madeline said, looking at him with *that* look again while Natalie muttered to her Friz.

"I *do* understand, Mrs. Whitfield," Valnikov said, patting her hand. Now now. Keep your chin up, Mrs. Whitfield. Now now.

Natalie Zimmerman felt like screaming. Or getting sick. A *nut* who shouldn't even *be* a cop, and a woman maybe crazier, who's willing to shell out twenty grand for a pooch, and they're sitting here patty-caking and feeling smug and condescending toward the one who just can't understand. The *only* sane person in the goddamn house. What am I doing here! Why does everything happen to me? The black marble!

"What I'm hoping you might consider," Valnikov said, "is going along with a money drop. But trusting us to handle it for you. I want you to tell him you'll give him the money tomorrow. Tell him how much you have and that you'll be able to make the delivery tomorrow afternoon. Then we'll take over. We have helicopters and surveillance people who're expert at this sort of thing and . . ."

"I don't know. I think I'd just rather not risk it," Madeline said softly. "I *want* to let you catch him but . . ."

"I thought that if you trust me, personally, I could coordinate the operation," Valnikov said. "If you trust my judgment I'll promise not to let anything happen to scare him off and endanger Vickie. I won't risk

Vickie's safety. If I'm positive we can take him, we'll take him. If not, we let the money go. What do you say? Do you trust me?"

She squeezed his forearm again, this time with both hands and whispered, "You *know* I do."

"Oh, *shit,*" Natalie muttered aloud.

"I give you my word I'm going to return Vickie to you. I promise," Valnikov said.

Then Madeline got tearful in spite of her best efforts, and Valnikov said, "Here, let me fix you some tea. Now now, Mrs. Whitfield. That's a brave girl. Now now."

"It's a dog."

"Pardon, Natalie?" Valnikov said.

"It's a dog," said Natalie Zimmerman to no one. To everyone. "It's a dog we're talking about."

"It's an extortion," Valnikov reminded her. "A felony."

"It's a *dog* you two are talking about," Natalie Zimmerman said stubbornly. "You two have *never* been talking about an extortion. You two are talking about a *dog*. I'm not running into a burning house to rescue a bowl of goldfish. And I'm not going to sit here and let you two make me so . . . make me forget that we're all talking about a *dog*. A dog! Do you hear me!"

But they didn't. Because Madeline Whitfield's tears had gotten the better of her and she was weeping on Valnikov's shoulder and Valnikov was patting her and saying, "Now now. I understand. You can be sure that I understand. Now now."

At which time Natalie Zimmerman got up and stalked out the front door to pace in the driveway and smoke, and watch the sun set pink and gold on the defunct hotel over the arroyo, over the picturesque Suicide Bridge.

Natalie felt a twinge of shame and then a rush of remorse as the anger ran out of her. Jesus, she couldn't even manage a little bile at a time like this? She was letting a brace of loonies make *her* ashamed for not being like them? Ever since she had been teamed with Valnikov, nothing made any sense. Before Valnikov, she knew who she was and where she was going. In that short time she'd seen a man shot to pieces, seen a kid's head painted silver, dug up a dog that was buried next to a goddamn koala bear, or a yak, or whatever the hell. And everytime she tried to tell someone, another mental deficient, like Bullets Bambarella, would do something and they wouldn't listen to her. *Nobody* would listen to her. Now, Valnikov was talking about being a party to a money drop of twenty thousand dollars. For a *dog*. Explain *that* to the promotion board on your next oral exam, Natalie. Yes, sir, it just seemed like the thing to do at the time. Why did we willingly give the extortionist twenty thou? Because we didn't *have* eighty-five thou. If we had eighty-five thou like he demanded, we would have given him eighty-five thou. Because Valnikov and Mrs. Whitfield *understood* each other, that's why.

Natalie scraped her shoes and coughed and made some discreet noises before she went back inside. Just in case the two psychos were relieving each other's tensions on the floor. Like schnauzers. Like they probably did last night. I understand you, Mrs. Whitfield. Sure.

When she came back in the sitting room he had his suitcoat off and his tie loosened. Pretty chummy. Pretty goddamn chummy. Impulsively, she stepped back in the foyer and eavesdropped.

Valnikov was saying, "I've thought about it a lot and I truly believe a person can come out of something like this a stronger person."

"If I just get her back, Sergeant. If I just . . ."

"You will, I promise you," he said, taking her hand. "And about the other thing. Losing this house. Working. Listen, do you realize that in one year you could pick up enough college credits to get your state teaching credential?"

"Teaching credential?"

"Sure. With your fine education and sensitivity and intelligence, why you'd make a wonderful schoolteacher, Mrs. Whitfield. Just wonderful."

"It's true I've always enjoyed the children at the Huntington Library," she mused.

"That's the answer. Teaching," Valnikov said, her hand in both of his.

"Teaching. It *is* a possibility," she said eagerly. "Yes, it *is!* But . . . I wonder. Could I stay in this area? Would I be . . . embarrassed, moving, say, to a small apartment?"

"I think you should stay, Mrs. Whitfield," he said quietly. "From what you've told me, Old Pasadena isn't a place. It's a way of life. *Your* way of life. Maybe being a Russian I can identify in some ways. There's tradition here. Manners. Gentility. Order. Where else in Southern California are you going to find all that in these times? Old Pasadena is a *good* way of life for someone like you. My mother would have liked it. I think I'd like it too."

"If I'm interrupting anything I can go back outside," Natalie said to her Friz, causing them both to jump apart. Pretty chummy. Pretty goddamn chummy.

"Come on in, Natalie," Valnikov said. "It's almost time for him to call."

"You do the listening," Natalie said, sprawling on the settee, determined at least to demand overtime pay for all this.

"I think we should both listen," Valnikov said. "There's another extension in the bedroom."

Ah-hah, you son of a bitch! How do *you* know about the bedroom? Then remorse again. *Why* was she letting this lunatic liaison get her mad? Simple. Valnikov infected everyone. You're around him awhile, you start getting as nutty as he is. The hell with it. Now, she'd feel no guilt when she told them about his mental condition. None at all. Sorry, Valnikov, but it's simply a matter of survival. Natalie Zimmerman's!

"Okay, I'll listen on the bedroom phone," Natalie smirked. "Unless *you'd* rather use the bedroom, Valnikov?"

• ● •

Philo Skinner at that very moment was answering the extension in *his* bedroom. He held his hand over the receiver and whispered in desperation: "Arnold! You shouldn't call me at home!"

"That's exactly what I told *you*, Philo," the voice said. "Last week when you called me at home and talked me into letting you get down on the Vikings, and now it's Wednesday and I still ain't got my fifteen dimes."

"I *told* you the escrow money won't clear until Thursday, goddamnit!" Philo croaked. "I agreed to bump you a hundred a day. You want my blood?" You want my foreskin, you murderous fucking kike!

"I want your *balls,* Philo, you don't pay," he said.

Philo was right! The nigger with the knife!

"Why do you talk to me like this, Arnold?" Philo whined.

"Because it's Wednesday. And tomorrow's Thursday. And I carried you so far I need a head doctor, is why."

"So tomorrow I pay. Goddamnit, Arnold, I thought we were friends?"

"*Business* friends, Philo," the voice said. "Business friends. Tomorrow a man's coming to your house in the afternoon to close our transaction."

"Not my house, Arnold! Not my house!"

"The kennel, then," said the voice. "In the afternoon."

"Make it after two," Philo whined. "Make sure Mavis is gone. After two o'clock?"

"We are gonna close our transaction tomorrow afternoon, Philo, one way or the other."

"I know that, Arnold. I know!"

"Good night, Philo."

Philo cut himself twice while shaving. He gave up and wiped the lather off his chin stubbles. He doused on half a can of baby powder but it couldn't dry the sweat pouring from his bony torso. Philo put on his polyester suit and a tapered orchid shirt. He hung his gold chains around his neck and teased his blue-black hair and started for the door.

But Mavis said, "Philo, I think I'll go to work with you tomorrow. I'm getting sick a soap operas all day. Maybe I'll do some book work."

"Christ, Mavis!" Philo said. "What kinda bookwork you think we got with twenty-five lousy dogs in the whole kennel? I told you there ain't enough work for even one kennel girl the way things are these days. Christ, I can't even keep busy with the grooming. Why you wanna hang around and go crazy too?"

"Just to be together, Philo. You're so jumpy lately. I know business is eating at you, but things'll work out. Business is funny."

"Yeah, well, I gotta run out get a few packs a cigarettes."

"Why you getting dressed up to buy cigarettes?"

"Christ, just cause I'm living like a bum don't mean I gotta dress like one. Get off my case, Mavis!"

"You been acting awful funny the last several days, Philo," Mavis said, turning down the television volume with a remote control. "If I didn't trust you I'd think you were maybe nesting with some little bird."

Then Philo lost his temper. "That does it! I'm going out to buy cigarettes. I'll be back within twenty minutes. You time me with a stopwatch. You and me been married six years. You tell me, can I run out of this house, drive somewhere, for five or ten minutes, meet some bird, take her to a motel, and come back here in twenty minutes? You tell me that's possible, you dumb shit!"

"I guess not," she said sweetly. "You couldn't even get a hard-on in half a day, come to think of it. In fact I ain't seen one in three months!"

Thank you, Mavis, he thought when he squealed out of the driveway in his El Dorado. It all comes down to an erection. I'll remember that in Puerto Vallarta when I'm screwing their serapes off, you miserable cunt!

• ● •

The call was late. It came at 6:25 p.m.

"Hello."

"This is Richard. I want the money tonight. Get a pencil and paper. Here's the instruc–"

"I don't have the money tonight. I'll have it tomorrow."

"What!"

Very quickly she said, "I'll have the money tomorrow afternoon. I'll have it then but it's only twenty thousand dollars. I won't lie to you, that's how much I was able to borrow. I'll bring it wherever you say."

Twenty thousand dollars. He was stunned. Twenty thousand. Enough to pay off Arnold and five left over. Five thousand wouldn't begin to pay off his El Dorado! Five thousand wouldn't begin to pay his *delinquent* payments on the kennel! Five thousand wouldn't pay the balance of his income tax! (None of which he planned on paying anyway after he got the ransom.) Five grand! How long could he live in Puerto Vallarta on five grand? He was stunned.

It was fortunate that he had picked a remote telephone booth beside a service station that closed early on Wednesdays because he was screaming: "YOU CUNT! YOU WON'T GET AWAY WITH THIS! YOU WON'T! YOU CAN'T TREAT ME LIKE THIS! I WON'T LET YOU GET AWAY WITH THIS! YOU WAIT! I'M GOING TO CALL YOU BACK IN TEN MINUTES!"

Then, Philo Skinner, hardly aware of what he was doing, was speeding through alleys in his El Dorado, throwing up sparks in the night, clanging over holes in the asphalt and bumps in the pavement, roaring through backstreets toward Skinner Kennels. Philo screeched to a stop in the parking lot, stumbled from the Cadillac, ran to the door with his jangling keys, and in a moment, was gasping and wheezing through the grooming room loping toward the kennel where twenty-five dogs went mad with joy, anger, or fear, depending upon their dispositions.

Philo unlocked the last dog pen but nearly lost Vickie, who went running toward the rubber doggie door and the gravel dog run outside, which was littered with defecation now that Philo Skinner was too busy being a criminal to clean up dog crap.

He grabbed her as she was almost through the doggie door and she growled but did not bite him, having gotten used to his rancid tobacco smell these past days. Then Philo ran to the office beside the grooming room, and throwing caution to the winds, picked up his own telephone.

• ● •

Valnikov knew that Madeline's conversation had driven the extortionist to some desperate move, but he also knew that there was nothing to do but wait.

"Can't we trace the next call, Sergeant?" Madeline said fearfully. "He's going to do something terrible!"

"They can only trace calls easily in the movies," Valnikov said. "A phone trace is terribly complicated and has to be set up well in advance. We just have to wait."

They didn't have to wait long. She picked it up on the first ring. "Yes."

"Okay, you cunt," he snarled. "Now listen to this." And Philo Skinner held Vickie's mouth to the receiver and pinched the tender flesh around her vagina.

The little schnauzer yelped and began to whine.

"That's your Vickie, mommy. You recognize her voice, you cunt?" He had to drop the phone and cough until he spit a wad of phlegm in the wastepaper basket.

Madeline was trying to suppress a scream and it was only Valnikov's strong steady gaze and his reassuring nod that kept her from doing it.

"I . . . please . . . I don't know what Vickie sounds like . . . on the phone."

Which caused Natalie Zimmerman to put her phone down on the bed and walk downstairs to the drawing room, because she was absolutely certain now that she was the only sane person left in Los Angeles County. They were talking to the kidnapped dog.

"Listen, mommy, you miserable cunt!" And he pinched the animal brutally and Vickie yelped louder and began to cry.

"I take your word!" Madeline cried. "I believe you! I believe it's Vickie! Please don't!" And Valnikov couldn't hold her back this time. She began sobbing. But she was still holding the phone. Still listening and trying to answer.

"YOU LIED TO ME!" Philo shrieked. "Twenty thousand! You miserable cunt. It ain't enough. It ain't enough to get me *anywhere*. I'm going to do it. I swear to you I never hurt an animal in my life but I'm going to kill this bitch. NOW!"

Madeline said, "Wait! Wait! You've already killed once. Don't do it again. The little schnauzer you drugged. It's dead. Don't hurt another one!"

Then Philo gasped and had to cough and wheeze and catch his breath. And Valnikov listened.

"You're lying!" Philo finally said.

"I'm not," Madeline said. "The drug you gave her was too much. She died. There was nothing I could do."

"Dead?" Philo mumbled. Tutu was dead? The only creature in the world who loved Philo Skinner?

Valnikov was astonished. He motioned Natalie over to his phone. They stood together cheek to cheek and listened. The extortionist was crying!

"You rotten lying welsher," he sobbed. "You lied to me. You been lying to me all along. You been lying to me!"

"Please . . ." Madeline said. "Please!"

Philo Skinner threw the phone down on the desk, and still holding the whimpering schnauzer in his arms, ran crying into the grooming room and pinned Vickie on the metal table. The plucky little animal sensed danger and began to growl fiercely. When he removed one hand she bit him on the other and hung on. But Philo felt little pain, only rage. He reached for the instruments on the counter as Vickie snarled and chewed. He tried for the stripping knife. He couldn't reach it. He got his hand on the straight razor. Vickie growled in panic now, and still sobbing, Philo Skinner aped notorious kidnappers of recent history. Philo Skinner was a copycat.

He held Vickie's head on the metal table with his bleeding arm and sawed through the gristly flesh of her right ear. The gristle crackled when the razor sawed through. Vickie released her bite involuntarily and blood from Philo's hand ran down her throat as she screamed at the incredible pain. Philo didn't stop sawing until the razor was screeching across the stainless steel of the table. Then he looked down in horror at the bell-shaped schnauzer ear lying in blood.

Philo threw Vickie off the table and she hit the tile floor, still screaming, getting up, listing, staggering, falling to one side, instinctively trying to rub the devastating pain away on the slippery tile floor, leaving a trail of blood across the tile as she flopped like a fish on her bloody head. When she found herself in the corner of the room she rammed her head against the wall several times trying to escape. She let loose with a whine so loud and shrill that Philo had to hold his wounded hand over his left ear when he picked up the telephone. Then she balled up and tucked the amputation far beneath her as though she were ashamed of it.

Philo Skinner was panting and sobbing and gasping for air. "I . . .

did it, you miserable woman!" he said. "I . . . you . . . you *made* me do it!"

"Vickie's dead. You killed Vickie," Madeline said, knowing it wasn't true, able to hear a dog screaming in the background.

"I cut off her ear!" Philo Skinner cried. "You *made* me do it! It's *your* fault!"

"Spare her *life!*" Madeline begged, and even Natalie Zimmerman was impressed. Madeline Whitfield was on her feet, wiping her eyes. She was gaining control and the extortionist was going to pieces.

"Spare her *life*, Richard," Madeline repeated. "I'm going to take the twenty thousand dollars tomorrow. Tonight. Wherever you say. I don't care when. I'll pay it for Vickie's life. Where shall I take the money, Richard?"

Philo couldn't think. His hand hurt like hell. He was afraid for a moment that the tendon was severed, but he saw he had good finger movement. Vickie was still screaming piteously and Philo slammed the office door shut. Still she screamed.

"No, not tonight," he said. "Not tonight. Tomorrow. I'm going to call you tomorrow morning. Eleven o'clock. I'll tell you then. Bring the twenty thousand then."

"Yes, Richard," Madeline said, nodding at the mouthpiece. "Yes. I'll be here. I have the money. I'll do whatever you say. Yes."

When the phone went dead, Madeline sat down. She stared at Valnikov. Then at Natalie. Then at the phone.

Valnikov said, "We'll be here at nine a.m. with some other officers. Tomorrow he'll want the money. He'll decide that twenty thousand is better than nothing. In any case, you can observe the precautions we're going to take, and then you can decide whether or not to let us keep you under surveillance when you make the money drop. It'll be up to you. I promise." When he finished talking, Valnikov walked over and knelt in front of Madeline. "Do you understand me, Mrs. Whitfield?"

"Yes, Sergeant," she said.

"I'll be with you tomorrow morning. Don't be afraid."

"I'm not afraid," she answered bleakly.

"I know that." Valnikov patted her hand and said, "You're a very strong woman. Do you hear me?"

"Mrs. Whitfield," Natalie said. "If what we heard was . . . well, if he did what he said, then your dog is . . . mutilated. She's no longer a champion show dog. My God, Mrs. Whitfield! You don't want to give him the twenty thousand *now*, do you?"

"I want to give it to him even *more*," Madeline Whitfield said. She looked evenly at Natalie. "I'd give him the eighty-five thousand if I had it. I'd give him anything. Now more than ever."

"Now more than ever," Natalie echoed.

"You don't understand," said Madeline Whitfield.

"I understand, Mrs. Whitfield," Valnikov said, patting her hand again and standing up. "I understand perfectly. Good night, Mrs. Whitfield."

• ● •

Like Madeline Whitfield, Philo Skinner had to sit and stare for a while after hanging up the phone. But the worsening pain in his hand brought him around faster. He took off his bloodstained polyester jacket. The *last* of his polyester leisure suits would end up in the trash-can this night. Vickie was no longer screaming. He opened the door to the grooming room. She was whimpering quietly in the corner.

Philo Skinner ran to the sink and began tearing out paper towels to wipe the grooming table and the floor. There was too much blood. He went to the closet and got the mop and pail. Then he cursed when he saw that he trailed his own blood to the closet and back. First things first, Philo! He went back to the sink and rolled up his sleeves and washed the blood from his hand. Vickie had really ripped him this time. He could close it with a butterfly bandage, though. No doctors. This one looked too much like a dog bite. No doctors. No explanations. He poured disinfectant over the wound and cried out in pain. His voice made Vickie whimper louder. He wrapped his hand in gauze for now. The butterfly bandage could come later.

He had the room cleaned in ten minutes. Except for the table. He hadn't touched the table yet because of the ear. Now it was time. He was dizzy. For one nightmarish second he imagined that it moved! That the frayed bleeding nerve ends made it twitch. He could hardly bear to look at it, but it was time. He got a paper towel. Then another. Then three more. With the padding between his fingers and the ear he reached for it. The ear slipped out of his grasp. It slapped on the table and splashed drops of blood.

"Oh," Philo said. "Oh."

Then he picked it up again. He held it away from his body like a poisonous snake. He ran for the toilet and threw it splashing into the bowl. He flushed the toilet and balled the paper towels up in a wad. The ear refused to go down in the Los Angeles sewers.

Philo looked in horror at the ear floating in the toilet bowl. Then it sank slowly. Then it bobbed up when the toilet gurgled.

"Oh!" Philo cried, holding his wounded hand to his mouth. "Oh!"

He ran back into the grooming room. He sloshed water on the bloody grooming table and washed it clean. He waited until the toilet filled. He ran back into the rest room and without looking in the bowl flushed the toilet. Then he staggered back in the grooming room and lit a cigarette. He washed his hands once, twice, three times in the deep sink. He washed them in water as hot as he could stand.

Then he felt a tingling around his skull, at about the hairline. The tingling wouldn't stop. He was wheezing and put the cigarette in the ashtray. His face started burning. He went back to the toilet. The ear was floating in the water.

Philo cried out and backed into the door, almost falling down. He flushed the toilet again and again. He stood over the toilet and watched it.

He watched it go down and disappear from sight while the toilet swooshed and gurgled. Then he watched it come back up.

It floated on the water like a dead bat.

"Oh," Philo said, then he started crying again. He was getting sick. He went back to the deep sink. He pulled out ten paper towels from the dispenser. He took the handful of towels and ran back to the toilet. He fished up the ear. He held it in front of him in horror, an arm's length from his body. He felt a bat crawling up his spine, clinging to his neck.

He loped out of the kennel, heading straight for the street. A car slammed on his brakes when he caught Philo in the headlight beams. The driver cursed and drove on. Philo ran shuddering to the sewer by the curb and threw Vickie's amputation down the black hole.

Philo was holding his arms and shivering when he came back inside the kennel. He couldn't stop shivering, but there was one task remaining. One more unbearable job to do. Philo looked fearfully at the bloody bundle in the corner. Philo had been unable to look there. Had been avoiding that corner, but now it was time.

He thought she would try to bite him for sure when he reached down beneath her. She didn't. The overwhelming pain from the razor had cut away her courage. Vickie whined and cried when he picked her up in his arms. Vickie's blood put stains on Philo's orchid shirt. She cried and licked Philo's tobacco-stained fingers.

As he bandaged her head, Philo Skinner was bawling louder than Vickie. Philo took her back to her dog pen and left more boiled liver than she could possibly eat even if she didn't vomit at the smell of food. He poured some warm milk in her bowl and even the smell of milk made her bilious. Still crying with her, Philo placed her gently in her bed and tried desperately to get her to accept a codeine pill in some ground beef. She retched when the food touched her whiskers. Then Philo started to retch. Philo Skinner slammed the chain-link gate and upchucked outside Vickie's pen. All twenty-five dogs began barking in joy, excitement, or fear, depending upon their dispositions, as their keeper crawled on all fours and vomited. Sick as a dog.

12

Charlie Lightfoot

It was eight o'clock by the time they were driving back to Hollywood Station.

"We've got a lot of work to do tomorrow morning before he calls," Valnikov said.

Natalie was riding silently, smoking, looking out at the headlights on the freeway.

"I think a phone trace for tomorrow would be useless even if we *could* arrange it," he said. "It's payday for him and he'll be careful. I think we should have three surveillance teams. If we can't get them from downtown our own guys'll have to do. We'll have a chopper standing by and one of our own people riding shotgun."

She shrugged without comment and Valnikov continued: "I just hope he's not too fancy with his money drop. I want to get him, but we can't endanger Vickie."

"Valnikov . . ."

"I *really* want to get this guy."

"Valnikov."

"Yes?"

"Vickie is a dog."

"Yes."

"I just have to keep saying that for my own benefit more than anyone's."

"You know, Natalie, I'm convinced the dead schnauzer is Tutu. And that's our only lead, really. I think that after we get the surveillance set up at Mrs. Whitfield's tomorrow we might call that kennel owner. What's his name? Skinner? If he knew Tutu that well, I'm going to ask him to come to the pet mortuary and make a positive identification. Then after that, I'm going to take him to Mrs. Gharoujian's if he's willing to come, and maybe between the two of them they'll have some idea which one of Mrs. Gharoujian's present or former house guests is capable of all this. You know Mrs. Gharoujian wouldn't bother with Tutu, so some of her boys must have worked with the animal. Some of her boys are very familiar with the world of dog shows. This man, Skinner, just might give us a lead as to which one."

• ● •

Philo Skinner was late getting home. He came in the back door, wearing a grooming smock instead of the shirt and jacket he left with. He was relieved to see that Mavis was in the bedroom undressing for her bath. He got a windbreaker from the hall closet.

"That you, Philo?" Mavis yelled. "Twenty minutes, huh? Where you been, Philo?"

He zipped up the jacket and headed for the door again. The butterfly bandage hadn't closed the wound as well as he thought. The gauze was spotting red on the back of his hand. He banged noisily through the kitchen until he found the fifth of Canadian bourbon he'd bought for Christmas guests. It was still nearly full. Drinking was not a Philo Skinner vice. As he slammed out the kitchen door, Mavis yelled: "Philo? That you, Philo? You can't tell me you ain't nesting with some young bird! Philo!"

She opened the front door in time to see the Cadillac roaring out the driveway. Philo made a screeching right turn at the bottom of the street, driving back to the place he loved and hated. The only place he belonged: Skinner Kennels. Home of the Terrier King.

• ● •

"How about stopping for dinner before we go back to the station, Natalie?" Valnikov said, impulsively.

"Dinner?"

"Sure. You have to eat. Why not let me buy you dinner? Any place you like."

"I can buy my own dinner," she said. Then she added: "Funny

thing, I'm not even hungry. I haven't eaten in twenty-four hours and I'm not even hungry."

He drove silently for a moment and said, "Did you have a nice dinner last night? With your captain friend?"

"Yeah," she said, looking at him sharply. "Did you have a nice dinner with Mrs. Whitfield?"

"We didn't have dinner," Valnikov said, looking at Natalie in surprise as he took the Hollywood Freeway outbound, creeping into the slow lane.

"Didn't have time, huh?"

"Time?"

"Never mind."

They were quiet again until he said, "I know a Russian restaurant overlooking the Sunset Strip."

"The Strip," she scoffed. "They have an entertainment license?"

"Entertainment?"

"Sure. For the freak show while you eat."

"It's on the hill *over* the Strip. None of the Strip people come there. It's a family place. How about it, Natalie? Let's have a bite to eat. Their borscht is good. I guess I just don't feel like being alone tonight."

"Neither does Mrs. Whitfield, I'll bet," said Natalie.

"No."

"It's only a dog, Valnikov. Try to remember. It's only a dog."

"Yes."

"You feel sorry for her."

"Yes, very sorry."

"You feel sorry for lonely people."

"Yes."

"You think *I'm* lonely, is that it? You want to take me to dinner because I'm lonely."

"No."

"Because *you're* lonely."

"Yes."

"Okay, Valnikov, I just wanted to get it straight. Now let's go have some borscht. And I'll pay for my own."

"Swell!" he said, with a wide grin in the darkness, driving forty miles an hour for the first time.

"I have a daughter, Valnikov," she said. "My daughter goes to Colorado State and has a great old time. She majors in skiing and ski instructors, thanks to mom's monthly checks. But I *have* a daughter, and she loves me very much."

"That's swell, Natalie," Valnikov said. "I have a son, but I don't think he loves me at all. He turns down all my invitations and . . ."

"I also have a boyfriend, Jack Packerton. He'll probably be a deputy chief someday."

"Yes, I don't wonder," Valnikov said.

"What I'm saying is, I don't get dogs and people mixed up. I don't have a schnauzer or a parakeet or a gerbil. I don't want you to get me and Mrs. Whitfield mixed up. Not in *any* respect, do you understand?"

"Of course," he said. He couldn't seem to understand his partner even when he didn't have a hangover.

"I'm not at all like you and Mrs. Whitfield, Valnikov."

"Like me and Mrs. Whitfield?"

"Forget it," she said, brushing her hair off of her glasses. "I don't even understand myself anymore. I didn't get enough sleep last night I guess." (Failed orgasms on top of all this shit!) "I don't know what I'm babbling about, I guess. Or why. This crazy investigation is giving me a headache."

"You'll feel better after some borscht," Valnikov said, smiling again. "My mother always said that."

"After some borscht," Natalie sighed.

Valnikov turned off the freeway at Highland Avenue and drove out the Strip. He parked on the steep street in front of the restaurant, careful to cut his wheels in. Lose your car on this hill and it wouldn't stop until it squashed three cocaine peddlers, two pimps, and a Krishna chanter eating pumpkin seeds on Sunset Boulevard below.

Valnikov was disappointed that the proprietor wasn't in. He seldom got a chance to talk Russian these days and the Armenian waitress knew not a word. The restaurant wasn't doing much of a business on this chill Wednesday night. They took a seat by the window to look at the cascade of monster billboards on the Strip. An arabesque of color and blazing neon advertised famous rock stars Valnikov had never heard of.

"You know, Natalie," he smiled when they were seated. "I haven't had a vodka for two days."

"That must be a record," she said. "I think you should have one tonight."

"Well, would you like to join me?"

"Do you have any gin and tonic?" Natalie said to the young waitress.

"Have you ever tasted Russian vodka?" Valnikov said.

"What's the difference between Russian and American?" Natalie shrugged.

"The whole world," Valnikov said. "Will you try Russian? Just one?"

He looked at her with those serious, no *sad* blue eyes of his and his shy kid smile and she said, "I'll try Russian. *Once.*" When she said it she changed her mind immediately, but the tired waitress was gone.

"I'm so glad you came, Natalie," Valnikov said. "I'm so *very* glad."

The girl returned quickly with the two double shots. Valnikov beamed and raised his glass: *"Na vashe zdorovye!"* he said. "To *your* health, Natalie." He downed the entire glass and closed his eyes blissfully.

Natalie was nothing if not plucky. She figured it would taste like American vodka, which always tasted to her as she imagined gasoline would taste. What the hell. Let him laugh his ass off when she did a backflip over the chair.

"Cheers," she said and downed the double shot. The heat flooded through her, and there was a not unpleasant taste from the bottom up, and then, "Mellow!" she cried. And it was. "That's not like *any* vodka I've ever tasted."

"It's Russian," Valnikov chuckled. "There's a *world* of difference. It's east and west. It's Igor Stravinsky and Bob Dylan. It's . . . Russian. Want another?"

"What the hell," said Natalie Zimmerman.

"What the hell," she repeated after their second.

"What the hell," she giggled after the third. And then her nose was tingling and her fingers were getting numb.

"Na zdorovye," she said when they drank that one.

"Maybe you should sip it," Valnikov said. "Some people put pepper in it."

"It's so mellow!" she cried. *"Na zdorovye!"* She was flushed and glowing. Her Friz was drooping.

"Want some borscht now, Natalie?" Valnikov asked.

"Who needs borscht?" she said. *"Na zdorovye!* I like this place. I might bring Jack here."

"It's a nice quiet place," Valnikov said. "Sometimes there's a gypsy violin. That's when I like it best."

Natalie Zimmerman insisted on a fourth. She took Valnikov's word that the borscht was pretty good tonight. She let him ladle sour cream into it and she noted that it had a nice consistency going down. The black bread and butter also had a very nice texture, but she had to take his word on that, too. Because all she could really taste was the vodka, and she wasn't really tasting it. She was experiencing it.

"I don't think you should have another," Valnikov warned. "Five double vodkas! That's a lot when you're not used to it."

"I can buy my own, Valnikov," Natalie said with a toss of her buckskin Friz.

"Two more," Valnikov said to the waitress. "Do you always drink so much?"

"Do *I* always drink . . . do *I* always . . . Valnikov, you're driving me crazy, do you know that?"

"I am?"

"I hardly drink at all!"

"Oh."

"I'm a social drinker."

"Sorry," he said.

"And I *hate* porno flicks."

"Yes, of course," he said, dabbing at his lips with a napkin.

"And I never saw a man with such impeccable goddamn table manners. Why the hell don't you slurp your soup like Jack does!"

"Sorry, Natalie," Valnikov said, looking over his shoulder to see if her yelling was disturbing the other diners.

"Sorry. That sounds like you. Sorry. Quit being so considerate or you'll bore me too."

"Sor— Natalie, have a little more bread."

"I'd like a little more vodka."

"Oh, no. I wouldn't advise that."

"I'm thirty-goddamn-nine years old. I oughtta know how much I can drink."

"May I butter you some more bread, Natalie? This pumpernickel is very tasty, don't you think? It's so . . ."

"Russian," she said.

"Yes," he said. "Please try to eat some more. Lots more."

When the check came, Natalie Zimmerman was slightly more sober. At least she'd stopped yelling.

"Wasn't the pastry good?" he said, counting out a fifteen percent tip for the girl. Natalie was too drunk to object when he paid.

"Sure," Natalie said, lighting a cigarette with a match that missed the flame twice. Valnikov had given up trying to light them when she informed him that no cop should be lighting another cop's cigarettes, goddamnit!

"Will you have a little more tea before we go?" Valnikov said. It took lots more than five double vodkas to put him away. Maybe twice that many, and then—oblivion. A wasteland. Siberia.

"A little more tea," Natalie said, smoking, examining his face. Finally she said, "It's only a goddamn dog, Valnikov."

"I know," he said softly.

"It's *your* case. I'm just along for the ride."

"No, we're partners," he said.

"It's *your* case. I'm working on a case of my own," she blurted. Her words were slurred and her voice was getting loud again.

"What case is that?"

"The case of Sergeant A.M. Valnikov." She sighed the smoke out. "That's *my* case."

"I don't understand."

"Never mind," she said. "Tell me about your childhood."

"My childhood."

"Yeah, tell me about it. I told you about mine, didn't I? I got married in my childhood. To a dirt bag. Then I had a baby. Then I got rid of the dirt bag and became a cop to support my Becky. Then I married another dirt bag who didn't know he hated cops till he married one. Then I got rid of that dirt bag. And I did a hell of a good job raising a kid."

"I'm sure she's a fine girl," Valnikov said, sipping his tea.

"At least I don't think she's going to get herself knocked up like her mom did, because I don't think she'd take her skis off long enough to hop into bed with a guy. Can they do it on skis? God, I miss that kid. Do you ski?"

"No, I don't have any talents," he grinned. "My mother wasted money on piano lessons but I just didn't have the talent."

"You have talent," Natalie said, elbows on the table, her chin propped by both hands, her big glasses slipping down her nose.

"What talent?"

"You can catch felons," she said. "I just bet you caught lots and lots of felonious bastards when you worked homicide."

"I'll tell you a secret," he said. "My mother got me piano lessons but do you know what she *really* dreamed for me?"

"What's that?"

"She wanted me to be a ballet star."

This time the other diners *did* turn and look at the drunken broad with the big frizzy hairdo and the four-inch glasses who was doubled up in snuffling giggles and falling off her chair.

"A . . . a . . . ballet dancer!" she screamed. "You! Smokey the Bear in leotards!"

When she quieted down, Valnikov said, "My mother was always appalled by the lack of culture in America. To the day she died she couldn't believe that Americans found batting averages more important than ballet. But I was never quite . . . delicate enough to dance. And my big brother weighed two hundred pounds when he was thirteen years old, so it was hopeless."

"Did she teach you to eat the way you do?" Natalie asked.

"How do you mean?"

"I'll bet she was awfully big on table manners."

"*She* could dance, my mother!" Valnikov said. "Do you mind if I have just one more Stolichnaya?"

"Only if I can have one," Natalie said. She was still propping her chin in her hands, staring into Valnikov's blue eyes which were getting watery.

"Two," he said, holding up the vodka glass to the waitress.

"I just wish my mother could have seen the Moiseyev Dance Group. She could do all the national dances: Georgian, Crimean, Ukrainian. And remember, she never lived in a country called U.S.S.R. They'd fled before the Whites were really finished."

"They were from Leningrad?" Natalie said.

Valnikov nodded and said, "Petrograd, to them. Do you know that the city is filled with cottonwoods? Do you know that in late summer the flowers set seeds by the billions! It's extremely fine and silky. It fills the air. It piles up against the buildings like snowdrifts. You can imagine that it's snowing under a hot August sun. What a place!"

"You ever been there?"

"No. I'll go someday. When I save enough. My ex-wife's remarried. My child support officially stopped two years ago but I still send money. Nick doesn't return it so I guess he's using the money. I'll save enough one day, then I'll go there."

"Sounds like you could get a bad case of emphysema, all that milkweed blowing through the air," Natalie said, smiling at the waitress who set the last vodkas before them.

"Maybe," he said. "But, Natalie, the Paris of the North! Imagine a place with streets full of silky snowdrifts! In the hot August sun."

"I'm sure it's fantastic," she smiled, the warmest smile she had ever shown him, and it set his heart pounding. "*Na zdorovye!* That's mellooooooow!"

"Ah, yes," he agreed when the vodka was flowing through him.

She looked at his dumb kid grin and said, "Why did you say your father died before your brother was born? That's impossible, you know."

"I didn't say that."

"Yes, you did. The first day we worked together. You've been . . . okay today. But sometimes you say things like that."

"Did I say that?"

"Does vodka drinking make you . . . *confused* the next day?"

"I don't think so."

"When did your father die?"

"In 1941. I wasn't quite eight years old."

"What did he do in this country?"

"Anything he could," Valnikov shrugged. "He never really learned much English. He had been a career soldier. He was a young captain in the czar's army."

"I see," Natalie said, feeling her speech getting thicker. "Do you think you meant his *spirit* died before your brother was born? Maybe during the Revolution when his whole world was going to hell?"

"I don't know. I don't remember saying that."

"Do you ever notice your mind wandering? Maybe find it tough to understand or answer questions?" Natalie's elbow slipped off the table and her face almost went in her plate.

"I think you've had enough vodka," Valnikov observed.

"You got *your* case to solve, I got mine," she said belligerently. "Let's go to my place."

"*Your* place!"

"No, on second thought, I can solve my place, I mean, case, better at your case, I mean place. Let's go to your place."

"My place?"

"You got any Russian vodka at your place?"

"Yes, but I don't think you should have any more."

"Okay, but I wanna go to *your* place. You gonna refuse a lady?"

Valnikov drove bleary-eyed down the hill to the Sunset Strip, careful not to run over any kids eating raisins and nuts. He spotted a flower child in bib overalls and rubber fishing boots. The flower child was doing what flower children so often do on the Strip—selling flowers. Little bunches of forget-me-nots and violets.

Valnikov weaved to the curb and jumped out of the car. When he came back he had a bunch of violets in his hand.

"Maybe you won't let me light your cigarettes, but you can't refuse me this," he said. "I'm not being chauvinistic or anything. Honest. It's just that Russians *love* to give flowers."

"Valnikov," she said, shaking her head and pressing the violets to her face. "You're a crazy crazy man, do you know that? I'll bet you *would* run into a burning house to save a bowl of goldfish."

When they were parked in front of Valnikov's furnished rooms on Franklin Avenue, he got thinking how the bachelor apartment looked. The daybed was, of course, unmade. The underwear and socks were still strung from the cage to the door. The pile of dishes in the kitchen. My God! Were the toilet and sink clean?

"Uh, Natalie, could you just sit here for a minute and finish your cigarette? Give me a couple minutes to straighten things out."

"You live upstairs, Valnikov?" she asked, a bit anxious about negotiating any stairway at this time. Now her fingers had feeling, but her toes were numb.

"Number twelve, right at the top of the stairs and turn left. Just give me two minutes, okay?"

"Two minutes," Natalie said, rubbing her nose which also had lost feeling. Stolichnaya. Siberia. Oblivion.

Valnikov didn't take the stairs any too gracefully himself. He had lots of trouble finding the lock. Then he was in and running through the apartment, grabbing underwear and socks and dirty dishes. He tossed the underwear and socks in the oven and the dirty dishes in the refrigerator. He picked up dozens of loose records off the floor and stacked them on the tired and shabby coffee table. He pulled up the cover on the daybed, smoothed hastily over the lumpy sheets, tossed the sleeping pillow under the daybed and arranged some throw-pillows for atmosphere. Then he saw that two of the pillows had tomato soup on them. He put them on the floor and kicked them under the daybed too. He heard Natalie climbing the stairs with no little effort. He dashed in the bathroom and inspected the toilet, shower, and sink. Okay except there was toothpaste smeared all over the sink. He grabbed a bath towel, did a quick wipe of the sink and ran into the kitchen, tossing the towel in the refrigerator with the dirty dishes. He was out of breath when she knocked.

Then he panicked for a second and ran to the seven-foot animal cage. Thank God! It didn't look too bad.

"*Gavno,*" said Misha to his master, who was indeed thinking about *gavno* on the cage floor.

Valnikov threw open the door and held the screen door for her. "Welcome, Natalie," he puffed. "I don't get too many visitors, I'm afraid. But welcome!"

Natalie weaved sideways as she crossed the room and sat on the only upholstered chair, cracking a loose record in three places.

"Oh, sorry!" Valnikov said, when she jumped up. He picked up the broken disc and said, "Mussorgsky. Not one of my favorites anyway."

"That's a lumpy-looking couch," she said.

"That's a daybed," said Valnikov. "Let me smooth it out."

"Why?" Natalie said suspiciously, missing the cigarette with her match again. "You think I'm going to lie on your *bed?*"

"No!" Valnikov cried.

At which time Natalie got up and sat on his daybed. "Lumpy," she complained.

"I can smooth it out," he said quickly.

"Not with *me* in it, pal," she said.

"Of course not!"

"For chrissake, Valnikov, sit down!"

"Would you like some tea?"

"I'd like some vodka. Russian vodka."

"How about some tea?"

"Well shove it, then! I can get vodka somewhere else!"

"I'll get you some vodka," said Valnikov, disappearing into the kitchen.

"How about some Gypsy music?" Natalie said, knocking the sparks from her cigarette all over his napless carpet. "Whoops!"

"Voice or violin!" Valnikov yelled from the kitchen.

"Both! Shoot the works!" Natalie said imperiously.

While she brushed off the sparks from his daybed, Valnikov poured the vodka and selected the records. First balalaika. Why not? Then some folk music. Happy music. Then . . . Gypsy.

When the first record played, Valnikov suddenly felt giddy and whimsical. He couldn't remember when he'd had so much fun! He was standing in the middle of the floor with a half-empty vodka glass in his hand.

The Russian baritone began with a lively song. Valnikov said, "It's called 'Kogda Ya Pyan.'" Then to her astonishment, Valnikov began a dance for her, translating the Russian lyric as he hopped and whirled.

First the Russian baritone, followed by Valnikov translating: "I shall drink and drink . . . and I am always drunk . . . there is nothing I am afraid of . . ."

"Sing it, Valnikov!" Natalie yelled, clapping her hands as Valnikov danced.

The Russian and Valnikov sang: "There is nothing I am afraid of!"

"Sing it, Valnikov!" Natalie ordered, spilling her vodka and pouring some more.

Valnikov danced with his vodka glass tight in his teeth, no hands. Then Valnikov fell down on the daybed next to Natalie.

He stripped off his suitcoat and unbuckled his gun belt. The gun and belt went flying into the overstuffed chair.

"Wait a minute, Valnikov," Natalie Zimmerman warned. "Keep the rest of your clothes *on!*"

But Valnikov wasn't even listening. He was up again. He loosened his tie and threw it off. He rolled up the sleeves of his white shirt. Like many burly men, Valnikov was light on his feet. He began dancing to the lively beat of "Kak U Duba Starovo."

"Dance, Valnikov!" Natalie giggled while she clapped. When the song ended he fell on the daybed again.

"That was terrific!" Natalie yelled. "*You're* terrific!"

"I am?"

"You're a terrific dancer!"

Then a Gypsy woman, who sounded like a man, began singing. Valnikov turned serious and poured more Stolichnaya for both of them. Gypsies. God help us. Gypsies.

"What is it, Valnikov?" she said.

"I don't know. I just get sad with the Gypsies."

"But why?"

"Because I'm supposed to, probably."

"You're a lousy American, Valnikov."

"Listen to this!"

A Gypsy baritone began singing "Starinye Vals," The Old Waltz.

"That's the most beautiful waltz I've ever heard," said Natalie Zimmerman.

"Do you waltz?" Valnikov asked.

"Yes."

He went to the turntable and moved the arm back to the beginning of "Starinye Vals." The Gypsy sang. Valnikov bowed and extended his arms. Natalie Zimmerman stood unsteadily and leaned toward him. He was a powerful leader. He led her gingerly around the debris in the tiny cluttered apartment while the Gypsy sang.

"The snowstorm howls behind the windows," Valnikov said, translating the lyric. "And no sound of the waltz is heard."

"Valnikov!" she said, and pulled away from him, sitting down on the lumpy daybed. "What's happening to me!"

"And I was young." He translated the Gypsy's lyric.

"Valnikov!"

"And I *loved* you so much!" he said, translating the lyric.

"Do you have any more vodka? I'd like some more vodka!"

"Of course," he said politely, and disappeared into the kitchen.

"Is the bathroom through this door, Valnikov?" she yelled while he was pouring the drinks.

"You can't miss it in this place," he said. "It's to the left."

She rinsed her face in cold water, dried, put on fresh lipstick and examined her watery eyes. My God, what's happening to me? Valnikov's a madman. But what's the matter with *me?* When she returned a Gypsy woman was singing as though her heart were breaking. Valnikov was dancing drunkenly in the middle of the floor.

"Valnikov, you're so funny," Natalie said while he swayed with the music. She was nearly as tall as he. "Stand up straight for once, why don't you?"

"I don't care about standing straight," he said, swaying to the music, eyes closed.

"You'd be almost six feet tall if you'd stand straight," Natalie said. "And you must weigh 220 pounds. You should be taller."

"I don't care if I'm six feet tall," Valnikov said, squatting on his haunches, trying some prisiadka kicks that put him temporarily on his ass.

"Valnikov!" Natalie shrieked. "This is hysterical!"

"The nightingales sang in the raspberry bushes!" Valnikov cried.

"What?" She poured his glass full of vodka as he got up, dancing.

"I said the nightingales sang in the raspberry bushes," Valnikov said. "Who but a Russian would write a lyric like that?"

And while a Gypsy baritone sang, Natalie smiled and said, "Is that what the song says?"

"The leaves of the poplars rustled," Valnikov translated. "In the leafy forest young girls greeted the horsemen with song."

"That's what he's singing?" Natalie demanded.

Valnikov nodded and danced with his eyes closed.

He opened his eyes when the Gypsy stopped singing. Valnikov replayed the Old Waltz. She stood before him with her arms beckoning. He took her and they waltzed, careful to avoid the cage and coffee table.

"Tell me what the lyric says," she whispered.

"On a spring night an unknown voice sang the beautiful melody." Valnikov talked while the Gypsy sang.

"This is a *lovely* waltz," Natalie whispered, as they whirled slowly in the tiny apartment.

"Gavno!" said Misha, watching the dancers.

"And I was so young," Valnikov translated. "And I loved you so much!"

"I'm awful mad at you for laying Mrs. Whitfield last night, Valnikov," Natalie whispered as they waltzed.

"You are?" he said, light-headed, dizzy.

"Yes, I'm goddamn mad."

"Why, Natalie?"

"Because you're a police officer," she snapped. "It reflects badly on the whole police department, damn it. Screwing on duty!"

"I'm sorry, Natalie," he said. "That was a very unusual night for me."

"I forgive you," she said in his ear while the Gypsy sang. "What did that Gypsy say about nightingales, Valnikov?"

"That the nightingales sing in the raspberry bushes," Valnikov murmured against her cheek.

"Damn right they do," said Natalie Zimmerman, blowing her Friz out of her eyes. And suddenly kissing Valnikov's burning earlobe.

He was ecstatic. He never dared dream. "Natalie!" he cried.

Then she cried: "Andrushka!"

"What! *What* did you say!"

"Andrushka!" She kissed him and bit his ear.

The sound of her saying it nearly moved him to tears. "Natasha!" he cried.

He was the most tender and unselfish lover she had ever known. He kissed her body everywhere and endlessly. He caressed her everywhere and endlessly. He whispered to her in Russian and English. She didn't know if the words were his or the Gypsy's who sang to them through it all. Natalie Zimmerman had *four* orgasms, only one less than she *didn't* have all week with Captain Jack Packerton.

Every few moments she cried: "Andrushka!"

"Natasha!" he replied. "Oh, my Natasha!"

"Andrushka!"

• ● •

At about the same moment that Natalie Zimmerman was having her fourth orgasm, Philo Skinner, who hadn't had one in three months, was sitting in the little office beside the grooming room, drinking Canadian bourbon by the light of a desk lamp, doodling on a note pad, staring at the telephone.

The whiskey was helping him to stop thinking about what he'd done. He wondered if she was able to sleep but he couldn't bring himself to go back in the kennel and look at her. He had arrived at a decision.

His Mexican tourist card had long since been arranged. There was a daily Mexicana Airlines flight at 3:00 p.m., a flight which would have him gliding over the subtropical paradise, over white beaches and warm ocean just after sunset, as he'd dreamed it. He wouldn't have seventy thousand dollars as he'd dreamed it, but he wouldn't have five thousand either. He was going to have *twenty* thousand. He was going to stiff Arnold and take the bundle and run. He smiled grimly and hoped the other bookmakers cut *Arnold's* balls off. Let the kike and nigger come looking for Philo tomorrow afternoon. At about that time he'd be high over the Gulf of California. Drinking margaritas.

Of course he could never come back to his country. That made him sad. But then, never is a long time. Maybe Arnold would die, the bloodsucker. Philo Skinner might be back one day. He'd take that twenty K and run it up ten times that much in two years. There were investments to be made in a country like Mexico, and he could outsmart any greaseball that ever lived. Philo Skinner would probably *own* half of Puerto Vallarta before long.

Then as Philo drained the paper cup and started to pour some more bourbon he had a terrifying notion. Christ, what if she had second thoughts? What if she decided a one-eared dog was worth nothing to her? What if all that talk about Vickie being like a kid to her was *just* talk? What if she was really a celebrity-hungry cunt like most of them, who didn't give a schnauzer's shit about their animals as long as Philo made them win? Twenty thousand for a maimed animal? Why did he tell her he mutilated the schnauzer? Why *did* he mutilate the schnauzer? He'd never hurt an animal in his life!

Before he'd made a conscious choice, Philo had the phone in his hand and was dialing the number he knew so well.

She lay awake in the moonlight, on satin sheets damp with tears. She sensed who it was. Their conversation was grimly subdued this time. They were both exhausted.

"Hello."

"It's Richard."

"I know."

"Get dressed if you're not. Get the money."

"All right."

"How big is the bundle?"

"Not large." It was surprising what a small bundle twenty thousand dollars made.

"Can you put it in a shopping bag?"

"Yes, easily," she said.

"Okay, put it in a shopping bag. No, a plastic bag. Do you have any plastic trash bags?"

"Yes, I think so."

"Put it in the plastic bag. Wrap the bag good and tape it shut. Make a neat bundle."

"Yes."

"Drive . . . let's see . . . drive east on the Suicide Bridge. Drive slow."

"Yes."

"When you get to the east end of the bridge, toss the bundle out the passenger side of the car. Carefully. So it falls in the street."

"Yes."

"There shouldn't be a single car on that bridge at this hour. Don't most of you people in that area use the freeway instead of the old Suicide Bridge?"

"Yes. There won't be anyone on the bridge."

"If there is, if you see another car's lights, don't drop the money. Go home and wait for my call. Understand?"

"Yes. When will you bring Vickie home?"

"I won't *bring* Vickie home. You'll get a call from me tomorrow at noon. I'll pick a safe place for Vickie near your home. Maybe a church or a public building. I'll tie her up there and I'll call you and tell you where."

"How is she?" Madeline stifled a sob, remembering the horror of that last call.

"She's all right," Philo said bleakly. "That wasn't my fault. I never hurt an animal before. That was *your* fault."

"Yes. I'll do as you say. Shall I go now?"

"Wait exactly thirty minutes. In thirty minutes you better be driving east on the Suicide Bridge. And there better not be any cops around."

"There won't be."

Then Philo lied and said, "Because if there are . . . if there are, my friend is ordered to cut the schnauzer's head off."

"Oh, my God," Madeline said.

Then Philo told the truth and said, "Do you know *why* I decided on the Suicide Bridge?"

"No."

"Because," he said, "if there *are* any cops waiting for me, I'm going to *jump* off that bridge."

"There won't be, I swear."

"I'll be dead and so will your Vickie."

"Yes, I understand."

"This is *not* the way I planned it, lady. I'm not stupid enough to plan it like this. I'm desperate, do you believe me?"

"I believe you," she said.

"So we're going to just *do* it. In thirty minutes. And trust each other. I get the money, you get Vickie. Or I jump. Right now, lady, I want you to believe that it don't make much difference to me."

• ● •

There was a range light burning in the kitchen, otherwise the cluttered apartment was dark. They lay in Valnikov's daybed with only a coverlet over them. She had her face on his hairy keg of a chest listening to his heart. He had a heavy slow heartbeat now. He wouldn't stop caressing her. Her head, her shoulders, her neck, her arms. Natalie Zimmerman was purring like a cat. In fact, Misha and Grisha were getting nervous just listening to her.

"Andrushka?" she said.

"Yes, Natasha?"

"It's been a good night."

"The best of my entire life," he said.

"Andrushka?" she said.

"Yes?"

"Nothing. I just love the sound of the name."

They were silent for a moment and he said, "Natasha?"

"Yes?"

"Nothing. I just love Natasha."

Suddenly it troubled her. She said, "The name? You mean you love the *name*."

But he was silent. So she said, "This is just a crazy night. We're just drunk and having a hell of a good time and . . . this is just a crazy night that's resulted from a crazy day and the craziest investigation of my life and . . . well, you mean you love the *name* Natasha."

His silence troubled her more. It made her remember the case *she* was working on. Reporting his madness was now out of the question. In fact, it was past changing her burglary assignment. She was going to demand a transfer from Hollywood Detectives immediately. She didn't want to be there when somebody *else* discovered the truth about Valnikov. But mental aberration wasn't incurable. It wasn't irreversible, for God's sake! And though she had to get away from him, there was no denying how much she liked him. You *had* to like anybody born and raised in Los Angeles, twenty-two years a cop, who was as corny and old-fashioned as he was. And so crazy. And that, she reasoned, was probably what brought on the orgasmic bursts. Some perverse streak in her she wasn't aware of. Making love to a madman.

"So it's been the best night of your entire life," she said.

"Yes," he said, still stroking, caressing, as he listened to the Gypsy violin and stared at the darkened ceiling.

"Tell me more about your entire life," she said.

"How can I tell you about my entire life?" he chuckled.

"Tell me about your old neighborhood."

"Boyle Heights? Well, it was Russian and Jewish and Mexican, and old. It's a very old neighborhood. Now of course it's almost all Mexican."

"Were you a happy kid?" she asked, propping herself up on an elbow, looking at his eyes, wet in the darkness.

"Sure I was happy," he said. "Of course it was tough after my father died, but Alex was much older and he supported us just fine."

"Did you go to church?"

"Of *course* we went to church," Valnikov smiled. "Our lives centered around the church. Our *batushka* was there. Our professor was there. We went to services and to Sunday School and to Russian school all there in the church. All of us had to learn to read and write the language from our professor."

"The Russian language?"

"The *only* language as far as our mothers were concerned. They were monarchists, you see. They truly believed they were going back one day. Every single one of them dreamed of at least having their bones sent back someday when the Bolsheviks were overthrown. Do you have any idea how impractical they were, those immigrants? How they dreamed? How mystical they were?"

"But you kids were happy?"

"Of course we were happy. It got a little tough *after* World War Two when it wasn't fashionable to be a Russian anymore. In fact, when I graduated from high school it was very unfashionable. We were in the Korean War, and kids used to call us Communists and Reds. The new immigrants from the second immigration had it worse. They actually *were* Soviets and got it from all sides. If you didn't go to church even the old Russian people called you a Bolshevik. The American kids didn't know the difference. We were *all* Bolsheviks, even though every single house of the first immigration had a picture of Nicholas Romanov displayed as reverently as an ikon. You could depend on it. Nicholas, then the Virgin, then *Khristos.*"

"Did you think in Russian?"

"Only until the fifth grade or so. Then I started to think in English. My Russian got terrible. But my mother lived long enough to hear Khrushchev on television and she said her Andrushka would always speak Russian better than that ignorant Ukrainian. She used to say that when that peasant farted you could hear it from Moscow to Malibu." Valnikov stopped to laugh and wipe his eyes at the memory.

Natalie Zimmerman got up suddenly and walked naked to the kitchen and he heard her pouring something. He thought it was water but she returned with a tumbler full of vodka.

"Here," she said.

"I don't want any more."

"Please have some more. I'd like to talk."

"But I don't need vodka to talk."

"You might."

"But I'm trying to cut down on my drinking."

"Do it tomorrow. Tonight drink for me. I'll help you."

Valnikov pulled himself up on the daybed and let her prop a pillow behind him. Then Natalie slipped under the sheet again next to him.

"Drink," she said. And he drank.

"I want to hear more about your old partner."

"Charlie Lightfoot?"

"Yes. Why was he such a good homicide detective?"

Valnikov drank now without prompting. "Good? He was good. He could cut through it all."

"Yes?"

"Like the old black woman they found decomposing in her bed. The neighbors called to complain about the bad smell coming from her little cottage." Valnikov stopped to drink again. "And the officer that got there discovered the glass was smashed out of a side window. And then he discovered a pane broken out of the back door. And then he discovered a burnt match on the back porch. And another in the kitchen. And another in the hall. And another . . ." He drank more vodka. Ah, what does Natalie call it? Mellow. Yes. "And another and another. Burnt matches leading all over the house and finally into her bedroom, where the trail stopped. And there she was. Charlie used to keep the crime lab photo. You see, the patrol officers had called the crime lab and latent prints and photo lab and their watch commander. Her hair was white and electric. It fanned out electric around her skull. She was so decomposed her eyes were silver sockets and her lips were mostly gone showing all her teeth clear up past where they should have been tissue and wasn't. Charlie took one look and said, No murder. No murder! they yelled. No murder? The house has been broken into. A burglar broke in and murdered her in her bed! I'll bet they'll find a knife wound! the patrol officers yelled. Maybe she was strangled. Oh, everyone was raising hell over this one."

"And *was* it murder?" Natalie asked while Valnikov sipped at the glass.

"No murder," Valnikov said. "Charlie got all the bluesuits together and showed them how it happened. The burglar came to the house at night. He broke out the pane in the back door. The glass is on the floor inside. He starts lighting matches, going around the house, pleased as punch, wondering how he's going to cart all this stuff away. Maybe there's a bad smell coming from the bedroom. Maybe he's got a cold and doesn't smell it. Anyway, the trail of matches tells us that he goes in there last. He's maybe singing to himself. She's got a TV set, a nice transistor radio, some money in a kitchen jar. He's going to make enough to buy some dope. He lights the very last match at the foot of the bed. Then he sees the corpse I described to you. The bedroom window is busted from the inside out. He yells and goes through the glass head first. He's still running . . ." Valnikov was shaking the daybed with his laughter. "She was ninety years old and died a natural death, the autopsy showed. He's still running . . ."

Valnikov, incredibly enough, almost had the tumbler emptied. *He* wouldn't die a natural death, she thought. Not if he continued to drink like that. Which of course she wasn't helping.

"Why did Charlie Lightfoot shoot himself?" she said suddenly.

Valnikov drained the glass. "They said it was a hunting accident."

"Charlie Lightfoot was no hunter," she reminded him.

Valnikov said, "He never should have retired. He had his work, at least."

"Did he like his work?"

"He was old. He was very old for his age. He thought the world was draining into a sump hole. The Big Sewer is how he referred to everything. Gone down the Big Sewer, Charlie would say about a dead body. He was an atheist, Charlie was. And human beings were nothing more than . . . than something to rush down the Big Sewer."

"He was your friend. He liked you, didn't he?"

"He did," Valnikov nodded. "Except toward the end. He didn't care about anyone, especially not himself. I think I started drinking on duty then. I'd been a policeman twenty-one years, and even as a detective I never drank on duty. When all the other dicks had martinis and bourbon for lunch, I never drank on duty. We both started drinking a lot then. On duty, off duty." Valnikov sighed. "When Charlie pulled the pin and went to be a mountain man I knew it wouldn't work out. We were both in the habit of daytime drinking then. We'd had the worst time either of us ever had then."

"The worst time?"

"*Five* child murders in a month! Nobody ever had to handle that many so quickly. And we were only supposed to assist divisional detectives on their unsolved murders, on their whodunits."

"Did you get the killer?"

"Killers!" Valnikov cried suddenly. "That's just it. They were unrelated killings. Five in a row, all under ten years old. Three by their mothers, one by a father, one by a mother *with* a father. They weren't whodunits. The divisional detectives should have been able to see the marks of old torture. Five in a row we had. That was too *many.*"

He dropped the water tumbler. It didn't spill. It was empty. "Here, let me get you some more," Natalie Zimmerman said. And she was up and hurrying to the kitchen again. Let old Natalie help you. Sure. Let Natalie do the torturing. God, Valnikov could make you hate yourself. He had that way about him. She poured the glass half full of Russian vodka. Have a shot of oblivion, Valnikov. Kiss your liver good-bye. Compliments of your good old partner, Natalie Zimmerman. Let your partner turn your head into *piroshki.*

When she handed him the vodka his hands were shaking. He drank with both hands. He was perspiring and his teeth were chattering. She pulled a blanket up over them and got under the covers.

"What made you get in the fight with the doctor?"

"Doctor?"

"They kicked you out of homicide. They transferred you to Hollywood Detectives, didn't they? Was it drinking? There was some problem. At an autopsy."

"Doctor," he mumbled. And there it was! The sparkly dots beginning to shape into . . . a doctor! There was an Asian doctor. No, a Caucasian doctor. *Two* doctors.

"What is it, Valnikov?" she demanded.

He drank vodka. It spilled down his chin onto the curly cinnamon hair on his chest. "Sometimes I get a picture," he said, staring off in the darkness at the picture forming. Siberia. Snow again. "The picture just gets . . . away."

"Does it come every day?" Natalie Zimmerman was sitting up in the daybed, white flesh in the darkness.

"Every day," Valnikov said. "If I could just get it once. It's like . . . déjà vu."

"Déjà vu," she said.

"It's déjà vu. But the most . . . intense kind of déjà vu. I . . . I know that if I could just get it clear and see it . . ."

"Does it come at night? In a dream?"

There it went. The sparkling dots were swimming and losing form.

"Do you dream about a rabbit?" she pressed.

Now it was coming back. Now, by God! The rabbit was hopping through the snow.

"The rabbit!"

"Do you dream about a rabbit?"

"Yes!" he cried.

"Take it easy," Natalie said. "Drink a little vodka."

Valnikov drained the water tumbler. She didn't know anyone could drink that much and stay conscious.

"What's the last autopsy you remember? It must have been the one where you got in trouble."

"Last autopsy?" he said, watching the dots lose their shimmer. Watching the phantoms retreat in the darkness.

"How many autopsies have you attended?"

He looked at her and said, "Hundreds, I guess. I don't know."

"And the *last* one. Who was dead?"

"The last one," he muttered.

Was that the one with the pretty teenager who had died of a barbiturate overdose? Yes. No.

How about this one, Valnikov? This little chippy and her boyfriends, they have a pill-popping party and she . . . get this . . . she dies of an overdose. Look.

The man plunges the turkey skewer into her flawless young belly. The steel dart squeaks when it goes in.

Get this: The liver temperature says she was dead all the time the boys were gangfucking her last night. Imagine that? They banged a corpse! Know what one doper says when they told him that? He says, well, she always was a dead piece a ass. I didn't notice no difference. Isn't that a scream?

A scream.

The little boy used to scream, Sergeant.

Then why didn't you call the police, damn you!

But I didn't want to get involved.

Involved! How long did you hear these screams in the night? How long?

Three weeks, the neighbor answers fearfully.

Three weeks! Three weeks! If there's a hell, lady, you'll burn there! If there's a hell!

There is no hell, Charlie Lightfoot says. There's no heaven either. There's just the Big Sewer.

Tutu was there. Charlie Lightfoot was there. The rabbit was there.

"The rabbit!" Valnikov cried out. He had been drifting asleep and Natalie Zimmerman, who by now decided that it was very dangerous playing Dr. Jung, decided to let him.

He sat up straight in bed, dripping sweat and cried: "The rabbit!"

"What's the rabbit doing, Valnikov?"

"The hunter's gutting him," Valnikov cried. "With a big knife. A butcher knife with a white handle like bone!"

"Try to remember, what did the hunter do then?"

And it came. For the first time in the months that it had been tormenting him it started to come. The picture was forming on the ceiling, among the sparks and motes and shimmering dots. "He's gutting it like a fish! He's reaching inside the throat that he's slashed open. It's like holding a fish by the gills. He just reaches clear inside and the little fish body jerks upward. He jerks the little body up with his strong hands."

"The fish? The fish?" Natalie demanded.

"The rabbit!" Valnikov cried. "The neck is limp and the little head is thrown back because he's got it under the throat. *In* the throat. He's got the jaws. His big hand is clear inside. The little head is thrown back on the . . ."

"On what?"

"On the wooden pedestal. The light . . ."

"What kind of light?"

"Sunlight!" he cried. "And snow. The doctor must have caught the rabbit in the snow!"

"And then what?"

"It changes," Valnikov said. "The picture changes but I still see it. I . . . I had to keep looking at the little arms and hands to remember it's still a rabbit. Because the face was all swollen and deformed from the beatings . . ."

"Yes? Yes?"

"He starts skinning it then. He tears the face right back over the skull. The face is pulled inside out, the little swollen deformed face. The hair is fine because it's so young. The hair goes inside out too!" Valnikov sobbed.

"Yes," Natalie said. "What then?"

"I have to keep looking at the arms and hands to . . . to remember it's a rabbit! I think its a *fish* he treats it so brutally."

"The hunter?"

"Yes. He says the anus is still open. After death!" Valnikov was crying now.

"Yes. Go on."

"I know what that means. I've investigated hundreds, *hundreds*. I just had four others. This is too *many!*"

"What does it mean? The anus being open?"

"Sodomy after death," Valnikov cried. "I thought it was *only* the mother! I *believed* the father because he seemed so pathetic. He said he'd been away. He cried so much I believed him. But there was semen in the anus. The neighbors didn't want to get involved. He screamed in the night. Five in a row. That's too *many!*"

"Was Charlie Lightfoot there?"

"Huh?"

"In the dream? Is Charlie Lightfoot there when the . . . rabbit is skinned?"

"No, Charlie was dead. Charlie had been dead for a month."

"Did you attack the hunter in the dream?"

"I wanted to," Valnikov said. "I wanted to. I wanted to kill him with his own knife with the bone handle. There were granules under the tongue. He said maybe it's some toxic substance. He had a swab right there. He could swab out the granules for the lab. But he just . . . just took the bone-handled knife and sliced off the little tongue! I wanted to kill him then," Valnikov said. Then he started crying again.

"What happened?" Natalie said. She was crying too.

"He said, 'Are you crazy? What's wrong with you?' I said, 'You could use the swab! You don't have to treat it so brutally. You don't have to. Hasn't it had enough? Isn't the torture, isn't a gaping anus enough! Look at him! You've turned his face inside out like a surgical glove! Isn't that enough! His face is like a doctor's glove hanging inside out!' "

The little rabbit took with him to eternity a face like a rubber glove.

"He said, 'I *thought* you looked drunk! I smell the booze on your breath!' I said, 'I'd like to punch your face in.' He said, 'You're drunk, I'm going to report you to your commander.' And I . . . I looked around. I'd been there hundreds of times. Hundreds. I saw an orderly helping an Asian pathologist on another one. They weren't paying any attention. They were cutting through yellow fat with a bone-handled knife. They were cutting a skull off with a power saw. The orderly was pulling out the intestines in a big heap and piling them on the knees. There was an enormous brain tied with a blue string. You'd never believe it could fit inside a skull it was so big. The orderly was putting a piece of meat in a jar. He was eating a jelly roll."

"Did you hit the doctor?"

"No." Valnikov sighed again and again. "I just realized at last that . . . that Charlie Lightfoot was right. I stopped going to church. It's nothing more than a Big Sewer and it's nothing more than gutted fish in the end. Or a . . ."

"A rabbit," Natalie said.

"Yes. Or a . . ."

"A schnauzer," Natalie said.

"I just realized that there's nothing more than the Big Sewer. Anything else is . . ."

"Is what you make of it," Natalie said: "What *we* make of it." She held him in her arms. He was wet and cold and shivering.

"I don't want to be like Charlie Lightfoot," Valnikov said, burying his face in her naked breasts.

Natalie rocked him and said, "You're *not* like Charlie Lightfoot. You're not *anything* like Charlie Lightfoot."

"I'm afraid," he said.

"Hush," she whispered, kissing his head. "You're not anything at all like Charlie Lightfoot. Hush, Andrushka," she whispered. "Go to sleep and dream of . . . of those Russian nightingales singing in the raspberry bushes."

She rocked him and was covered by his sweat. She threw off the clammy sheet and drew up the warm blankets. He was so devastated by the vodka and the tears that he fell unconscious almost at once, his face pressed against her. Natalie Zimmerman still rocked him and caressed his burning body until she fell asleep.

13

Suicide Bridge

Valnikov didn't dream of nightingales singing in the raspberry bushes. And he didn't dream about a rabbit. He dreamed he was waltzing with Natalie Zimmerman. In the squad room of Hollywood Detectives. Hipless Hooker yelled about a tummyache and Clarence Cromwell said they were crazy but he didn't care. They danced to the "Starinye Vals."

And while Valnikov dreamed his fantasy, Philo Skinner *lived* his. He was sitting in his El Dorado, west of Suicide Bridge, in the darkness. He was terrified that a cop would come by, but in a Cadillac El Dorado he hoped he could reassure a cop. Waiting for a girlfriend, Officer. Please don't pry. She's a married lady and you know how it is. Only in the middle of the night, Officer. Gotta take it when we can. When the old boy's asleep. Hah-hah!

He saw her Fleetwood right on schedule. His heart was banging in his ears. She drove past his El Dorado without looking. She started across Suicide Bridge. He saw headlights in the distance, but the headlights turned toward the freeway. Madeline began crossing the bridge, toward the ghostly looming old hotel. Her brake lights went on when she reached the east end of the bridge. Philo started his engine but kept his lights out. Madeline's brake lights went out and her Fleetwood continued to Orange Grove Avenue, which two weeks ago was jammed with Rose Parade flower floats. Then she was gone.

Philo Skinner drove drunkenly, dangerously, recklessly, east over the bridge. He panicked when he reached the end of the bridge. It wasn't there. No, it *was* there! It was in the gutter! He slammed on the brakes and leaped out of the Cadillac. He twisted his ankle and fell, tearing the knee out of the polyester trousers. He picked the bundle up. It was small. Could twenty thousand dollars be contained in such a small package? He ran back to the car. He jammed it in low gear and sped toward Orange Grove Avenue.

Philo broke into a coughing spasm on the freeway. His eyes filled and clouded and he was gagging on an enormous wad of phlegm. He desperately groped for the electric window buttons until he had every window in the car open. He didn't realize for a moment he was hyperventilating. When he realized it he hacked the phlegm from his ragged lungs and spit out the window. It blew back with a smack on the side of his El Dorado. He deliberately exhaled until he was able to breathe again. He was wheezing and creaking, but he was able to breathe at last. He tore open the plastic as he drove. He switched on the map light. He looked at the thrilling pictures of Ulysses S. Grant and Benjamin Franklin. Hundreds of pictures. He spent the night in the kennel office caressing them, fondling them, caressing them again and again. Philo Skinner made noises that were half laugh, half cry. He was sick and exhausted but now he wanted to live. He hid the money in the supply closet and slept curled up on the grooming table. He dreamed of a white sand beach and a puppy frolicking in the surf. The puppy, of course, looked like Tutu.

14

The Assassin

Natalie was awakened at dawn by Misha expressing his opinion of it all: *"Gavno"* the bird cried. *"Gavno. Gavno."*

Then she heard the shower turning off, and Valnikov, wearing an old flannel bathrobe, tried to tiptoe quietly to the kitchen. She sat up in bed.

"Oh, sorry. Did I wake you?" He was drying his hair. "I wanted to get your breakfast before you had to get up."

"What time is it?" she asked, pulling back a taped window shade to peer out at the street lights.

"Five thirty."

"Five thirty!"

"We'll have to get an early start. I've already called Clarence Cromwell at home. He'll meet us in the office at seven so we can get started. He's going to arrange for the helicopter and the surveillance cars. I hope we don't have to use our own guys, but if we do, I think Fuzzy Spinks might be a good man on point. What do you think?"

Think? Think? Who could think anything about the past days. My God, she'd lost her ability to think or she wouldn't be lying here! With a pathetic tormented crazy man and a bird that yelled shit in a foreign language and a goddamn Russian rat that kept trying to keep the bird off his head. What a night! What a week! *She'd* be the one they retired. Give old Natalie Zimmerman a medical pension and a party and six months in Camarillo State Hospital with a live-in psychiatrist.

"How do you like your eggs?" Valnikov smiled. "I'm a pretty good cook."

"Please, Valnikov," she said, sitting up and wrapping the sheet around her. "Please don't."

"Don't what, Natasha?"

"Don't cook for me. Don't do anything for me. And *don't* call me Natasha."

"Sorry," he said.

"And don't say you're sorry. I'm sorry for *you.*"

"For me?"

"Never mind. Let me shower and get dressed. We'll have some coffee."

"You wouldn't like tea?" he said. "In a glass?"

"I'll have coffee. In a cup."

"Coffee, sure," Valnikov said, losing his buoyancy, shuffling into the kitchen to look for the coffee pot. He hoped he had some coffee. He hoped he could come to understand Natalie Zimmerman.

Twenty minutes later they were both dressed and sitting at the tiny kitchen table. He drank tea from a glass. She drank coffee from a cup. East and West.

His hair was carefully parted and combed, but still a cinnamon cowlick popped up at the crown. She watched him sip his tea. Noiselessly, just as his mother had taught him.

"Do you have a hangover?" she asked, breaking the silence.

"A little." His sad blue eyes were watery and bloodshot. His necktie was off center. Another cowlick popped up as he sipped the tea. He looked ridiculous.

"Valnikov."

"Yes, Natash . . . Natalie?"

"Do you ever think of retiring? After all, you have twenty-two years' service. You could retire now with almost half your pay. You're still young. You could find an . . . easier job to make up the difference. Do you ever think about retiring?"

"I think about it sometimes," he said. "I think about it, but I'm forty-four years old and I don't know anything but police work."

"I'll bet your brother'd take you in business with him. He's crazy about you, your brother."

"I don't want to work for Alex," Valnikov smiled. "He's too much like a father. Besides I'd just get in his way. I don't know his business. But I did think about something."

"Yes?"

"Well, I know something about music. Not so much about pop or rock, but do you know there aren't many good record stores with imported records? Not in a good location. I think that if someone opened a foreign music store in a good location, like here in Hollywood . . ."

"Holly-weird. Ugh!"

"Yes, it's not the greatest place to live anymore, but to do business with Russians, and Greeks, Armenians, Persians, Arabs, and so forth, well, they *like* Hollywood. It still represents the magic of America. The Good Life."

"Do you have any money for a business?"

"I have a few thousand saved," he said, pouring some more coffee for Natalie. He was pleased that she didn't seem angry anymore. Maybe it's when she just wakes up, he thought. "And I could go to my brother for a loan. And I guess I could borrow some from a bank. I could start on a shoestring. After all, I'd have my police pension to live on."

"Are you going to do it?"

"Well, I never had any reason to make a move before now."

"Before now."

"Yes," he said, blinking his sad eyes, wiping them with a napkin. "Sorry. Too much vodka always does this to me."

"I noticed," she said. Then, "Tell me, Valnikov, did you ever feel like you always pick the black marble?"

"The black marble?"

"Yeah, remember Itchy Mitch?" she said, scratching under her bra strap. "The black marble."

"No, I don't think I ever felt like that," he said.

"You don't expect much, do you?"

"I don't know, Natash . . . Natalie," he said.

"Why did your wife leave you?"

"Oh, she said I bored her stiff. She said I was . . . well, you said it too. Out of date."

"I didn't mean it like that, Valnikov."

"It's all right. I am."

"Not like that. Not like she meant it."

"Well, she liked to go out a lot. And I thought we should stay home with our son more. And besides, I couldn't afford to take her to the Polo Lounge for lunch and Chasen's for dinner and . . ."

"You don't see the kid?"

"No," he sighed, standing up, getting more hot water for his tea. "I don't know, maybe I bored him too. He got in lots of trouble. Three arrests for smoking pot before he was fourteen. And twice they let him go because his dad was a cop. He finally said he hated cops. *All* cops. Well, I don't know."

"How old is he now?"

"He's twenty. Just twenty."

"He's young," Natalie said. "Kids change when they grow up."

"Yes," he sighed. "They change."

"Tell me," she said, lighting a cigarette. "When your wife and boy left, when Charlie died, when you were working those homicide cases, when the drinking was very bad and you were having those bad dreams, tell me, did you ever say to yourself, why do I *always* pick the black marble? Haven't you *ever* said that?"

"I don't think so," he said.

"Why?"

"Why?"

"Yes, I wanna know why."

"I don't know," he shrugged. "My mother always said . . . you see, my mother and father, the people from the first immigration, they didn't come to America *for* the Good Life. America was the *end* of the Good Life for them. Until the day she died she never stopped talking about her home in Petrograd. That's why I guess I seem so . . . old-fashioned, maybe. Even though I was born and raised in Los Angeles, I heard so much about the suffering of Mother Russia, and the sorrow of life, and . . . well, I never expected much, I guess. I don't know." Valnikov sipped his tea and dabbed at imagined moisture on his lip and said, "Maybe my father . . . I didn't know him well, of course, but maybe before he died, maybe when he was here in Los Angeles during the Depression trying for jobs he couldn't get, never speaking this foreign tongue, maybe my father wondered about the black marble. I'll bet he did. I'll bet that when his entire world had been destroyed he said to himself: Mikhail Ivanovich, why do you always have to pick the black marble?"

"Valnikov."

"Yes, Natalie."

"I'm asking for a transfer."

"From the burglary detail?"

"From Hollywood Detectives."

"Oh? Is it because . . ."

"Look, Valnikov, I don't know what happened last night. I don't understand anything anymore, so help me. I mean, I'm running around looking for a one-eared dog like it's the Patty Hearst kidnapping. I mean, I'm calling myself by another name, even."

"Natasha," he smiled.

"Don't call me that. This isn't a goddamn Chekhov play."

"Sorry."

"Valnikov, doesn't it seem that things have become a bit too much for you? The dreams?"

"I didn't dream about the rabbit last night." He wanted to tell her what he dreamed about.

"Yes, but it seems you've been undergoing a kind of . . . mental breakdown. You *must* know you haven't been yourself for quite a while now. For several months from everything I can understand. I mean the incident in the morgue? When you threatened the doctor? I mean, you have some *problems* to cope with."

"I can cope with them . . . now."

"Oh, please don't say that to me, Valnikov. Last night was last night! I don't understand last night. If our . . . *talking* last night was helpful, I'm very glad. So help me, I am. Look, do you know what I've planned for next month? Jack Packerton and I are flying to Honolulu. Then we're going to Kauai where we're renting a bungalow in Hanalei Bay. It's supposed to be a paradise."

"A paradise," Valnikov said.

"Jack's going to be a deputy chief of this department."

"Yes, you said that before."

"Yeah, well what I'm saying is, I've got a routine. My life's in *order*. Yours is a mess. Do you understand?"

"I guess so," he said.

"Hell, Jack's been wanting to get married for the past six months. I wanna just live with him but he has this phobia. Deputy Chief Digby Bates gets tight-jawed when unmarried officers live together. Did you read the moral rearmament bulletin from that Jesus Freak?"

"No," Valnikov said.

"Anyway, that's where *my* head is. I don't want to be always picking the black marble!"

"Well," Valnikov sighed, dabbing at his lips, "I guess we'd better get going. Clarence Cromwell's going to wonder where we are."

"Yeah, let's get it on," Natalie Zimmerman mumbled miserably.

Valnikov fed and watered Misha and Grisha before they left. Then he went into the bedroom and strapped on his gun belt and got his suitcoat with the stapled pockets. Natalie could hear his heavy sighs from the other room. She watched the little creatures in the big cage.

"Whadda you think of it?" she said to the parakeet, knowing what his answer would be.

He did a forward fall, looked at her while hanging upside down, and said, *"Gavno."*

• ● •

Clarence Cromwell was on his second cup of coffee when they arrived.

"Glad you could finally make it," he growled, "after you git me outta bed at some ungodly hour!" Then he looked at Natalie and noticed she wore the same clothes as the day before. She never did that. And her Friz was a little unfrizzed. And she came in *with* Valnikov. Clarence hadn't been a detective twenty years without being observant.

Natalie saw him grinning at them. The evil old spook!

"Are we getting the chopper?" Valnikov asked, gathering his paper work from the report box while Natalie headed for the coffee.

"Got it," Clarence said. "Okay on the surveillance teams too. Gonna have quite a show. Hope the dognapper shows up."

"The extortionist," Valnikov said.

"Yeah. Hope he shows up."

Then the phone rang and Cromwell grabbed it. "Yeah," he said. Then to Valnikov, "For you."

"Valnikov," he said, picking up his extension and punching the first line.

"Sergeant, this is Madeline Whitfield," she said, very tentatively.

"Mrs. Whitfield!" Valnikov said. "What happened? Did he call?"

"He called. Last night. At about two a.m. I . . . Sergeant, I'm sorry. I took him the money. He told me to drop it off on the bridge by my home. I did it. I assume he picked it up. I went back at daybreak and it was gone. I haven't slept a minute. I guess he got it. I . . ."

"Do you have Vickie?" Valnikov said and got Natalie's attention at once. He held his hand over the phone and said, "She dropped the money on him during the night."

"No," she said, her voice cracking. "He said he'll call me today. He promised he'll release her today. I just have to wait. I'm sorry, Sergeant. Well . . . I wanted . . . I know I probably did the wrong thing. I *wanted* to do it your way. Well . . . she's all there is in my life. Well . . ."

"Don't cry, Mrs. Whitfield," Valnikov said softly. "I do understand. I don't blame you for anything. I do understand. Don't cry. Now now, it's going to be all right, I promise you. There'll be someone here all day who can get in touch with me. You call the moment you hear from him. Yes. Don't cry. I promise you it'll be all right."

When he hung up, Clarence took a drink of coffee and said, "I'll cancel the chopper and the surveillance teams."

"She doesn't have Vickie yet," Valnikov said. "Why didn't I think of that? Why didn't I anticipate that he might call during the night?"

"Because this guy doesn't do anything orderly," Natalie said. "He's erratic and messy and crazy and you can't figure him because of it. Don't worry about it. It's not your fault. You've done all you can do."

Valnikov was on his feet. "It's almost eight o'clock," he said. "I'm still going to contact Mrs. Gharoujian's dog handler. That man Skinner. I'm going to have a talk with him about all the guys who lived with Mrs. Gharoujian when he was showing Tutu. He's the only hope there is now. He's got to come up with a few names for us."

"Valnikov, it's over, forget it!" Natalie said. "She *chose* to pay the money. He'll probably release the dog like he said. Or maybe the dog's dead. In either case, you've done all . . ."

"I'm going to Skinner Kennels," he said, looking through the phone book.

"Well, sit down awhile at least," Clarence Cromwell said. "It ain't even opened yet, if it keeps regular business hours. Sit down and drink your tea and relax a little bit. This ain't the Patty Hearst kidnapping."

Which caused Natalie Zimmerman to say, "*That* is maybe the first time I ever agreed with *anything* you ever said, Clarence."

As the other detectives straggled in for the day, and as Natalie Zimmerman did their routine paper work and filing of crime reports, Valnikov drank tea and made secret notes and drew pictures of a schnauzer and a bird.

Natalie glanced over at the pad and recognized the dog. "What's that, your parakeet?" she asked.

He almost told her it was a Russian nightingale in a raspberry bush, but he looked up with sorrowful runny eyes and said, "Yeah, my parakeet."

Captain Hooker arrived rather early. He had a paper bag in his arms. It contained three bottles of Maalox. He figured that would keep his stomach quiet for a couple of days at least. But he was wrong.

First of all, Bullets Bambarella usually had a Twinkie with his morning coffee but couldn't afford one now, so he was grumpy. He had exactly two dollars and fifty cents to last until payday thanks to the bets he'd lost to the smirking Mexican, Montezuma Montez. Bullets was looking for trouble, right off the bat.

"How about lendin me ten bucks till payday, Clarence?" he whispered to the grizzled black detective.

"What for? You got some other bet you wanna lose to Montezuma?" Clarence snorted.

"Listen, Clarence, you ever hear of a good Mexican heavyweight? There *ain't* any. I think we could go up to the academy, get some boxing gloves and . . ."

"I don't want any of my men boxing," said Woodenlips Mockett, overhearing it. "Somebody'll get hurt."

"I could lick him, Clarence," Bullets whined. "You could make some money bettin on me!"

When Bullets had gone back to the residential burglary table Clarence said, "Humph! Young coppers around here, they jist wear me down, is what they do. I see them smart-walkin all over the Chinatown barrooms these days. Their gud-damn guns hangin out so all the girls know they're cops. Shee-it. They probably drink High-waiian punch on the rocks. They jist wear me down."

Then Frick said to Frack, "Who smells so good, you or Irma?" And he bit the giggling policewoman on the shoulder.

"Me," said Frack, "and I don't know how to control it, neither."

Then Bullets interrupted them with an important announcement: "Italian food is the best in the world. Italians are gourmets. Mexicans eat horsemeat tacos."

"Bullets, is your mind gone, along with your paycheck?" said Clarence.

"I just heard that Montezuma is making enchiladas for the detective party next week," said Bullets.

"So what's it to you?" said Montezuma Montez, and all the telephone calls stopped as the squad room got ready for a fight.

"I won't have my men boxing," Woodenlips Mockett whined to Clarence Cromwell.

"Well, I don't wanna go to no party where I gotta eat horsemeat enchiladas," said Bullets glaring at Montezuma Montez.

Frick and Frack were now grinning back and forth from Bullets to Montezuma. There were secret bets coming out under the tables. "They're gonna fight, Clarence! You stop them!" Woodenlips Mockett cried.

Then Bullets said, "Italians are gourmets. Chefs. You probably never heard of eggplant parmesan."

"I heard of it," Montezuma said.

"Put my eggplant and your enchilada side by side, your enchilada's gonna taste like horseshit."

"I'm somewhat of a gourmet if I do say so," said Dudley Knebel. "I'd like to try them both."

"So would I," said Irma Thebes.

"Could you be a fair judge, Dudley?" Bullets challenged.

"Perfectly," said Dudley Knebel.

"Me too," said Irma.

"I think I could go for it too," said Nate Farmer. "But I think we should be able to write our opinions secret, so no hard feelins later."

"I'll read the findings," said Max Haffenkamp, "and just say which dish the judges picked."

"Okay," said Bullets. "Clarence, will you loan me twenty bucks?"

"I'll take five a that," said Frick.

"I'll take five," said Frack.

"Who wants *thirty* bucks?" said Bullets. "Payable on payday?"

"Covered!" said Montezuma.

"Well, that does it!" said Clarence Cromwell with utter, lip-curling contempt. "You don't have to worry about a fist-fight no more, Lieutenant. It's down to a fuckin bake-off!"

Captain Hooker came out of the office, heading for the hot plate. He was going to pour some water into his powdered chocolate.

"Everything going smoothly, Clarence?" he said, mixing the brew.

"Fine, Skipper," said Clarence.

Dudley Knebel said, "Oh, Captain. You know that market they robbed three times this month? The one on the Boulevard? Well, the commander called and suggests we stake it out this Thursday. Maybe the computers told him."

"Now if the computer could jist *do* the stakeout . . ." Clarence grumbled.

"Clarence will coordinate it for you," Hipless Hooker said. He didn't have time for any of this. He had to go buy a new pair of deck shoes, the kind real yachtsmen wear.

"Yeah, but Captain," Dudley Knebel persisted, "the commander says we should put an undercover cop behind the counter. You know, dressed like one a the clerks? Because they pistol-whipped the last three clerks and he figures a cop should be there."

"Great," Clarence Cromwell snorted. "Let a cop get pistol-whipped instead of a clerk."

"Yes, yes," Hipless Hooker said impatiently. "Well, just pick someone to masquerade as the clerk. Police work entails some risks once in a while."

"Yes, sir," said Knebel. "But the crooks been in there three times. They *know* all the clerks. The commander said to put in a guy who actually resembles the oldest clerk and let the poor clerk work another part of the store."

"Well for heaven's sake, can't you find an officer who resembles the old clerk?"

"Yes, sir," said Dudley Knebel. "The commander says that you look just like him."

Captain Hooker had to go home that morning with a dreadful tummyache. Which in no way affected Valnikov's police career this time. Valnikov's destiny was in other hands.

At 9:15 a.m. Valnikov finished drawing his eighth nightingale in a raspberry bush. By now Natalie guessed that he was not drawing parakeets.

Valnikov jumped up and said, "Clarence, I'm going to that kennel and talk to Mr. Skinner. I just can't sit around. If Mrs. Whitfield calls, get me on the radio or call me at the kennel. I wrote the number down on my note pad." Then without looking at her he said softly, "Natalie, maybe you wouldn't mind staying and doing our paper work this morning? I won't be . . . needing you."

"I wouldn't mind," she said, not looking at him either. And all the non-looks and averted eyes were not lost on Clarence Cromwell, who just shook his head and said, "Gud-damn! Don't *nothin* ever work out right for *nobody* in this gud-damn world!"

"What?" Woodenlips Mockett said.

"Nothin," Clarence Cromwell grumbled. "Nothin, gud-damnit!"

• ● •

Philo Skinner had not been able to sleep for a day and a half. Nor had he shaved. He was wearing a pair of brushed denims and a striped turtleneck sweater. He hung his new imitation gold chain outside the sweater. He had bought the clothes this morning the moment the stores opened. He had a battered suitcase, which usually stored dog powders and lotions, packed with new clothing. He wasn't even going home. He also packed a hair dryer which had dried a thousand dogs but never a human head. He couldn't find another thing he cared to take. He was sure he could outfit himself in a fancy Puerto Vallarta hotel cheaper than here. That peso devaluation was going to make his twenty thousand look pretty good. Pretty damn good! He glanced in the mirror and his spirits fell for a moment. He looked terrible: eyes baggy and sunken, cheeks hollow and gray and bristling. Hands gray and scaly. The tension had taken a great toll on the Terrier King.

He had thought about driving the El Dorado across the border and trying to sell it in Tijuana to some Mexican crook. He quickly dismissed that idea, having heard about gringos being robbed and murdered down there these days. Just his luck to have them discover he was carrying twenty K and cut his throat.

He couldn't stop trembling, more from exhaustion than excitement. Mavis said yesterday she would be in this afternoon. Well, let her come. He wanted to leave her a note but couldn't think of anything sarcastic enough. He parked the El Dorado in the rear of the kennel, out of sight. He didn't want any new customers today.

Only one thing left: the schnauzer. Philo had to take the bitch and drop her someplace and phone the Whitfield broad. Then he was going to the airport. They'd find the car in a few days. They'd probably find out he took a Puerto Vallarta flight. So what? A guy with lots of debts bugs out. Happens all the time. There was absolutely no connection with the dog snatching so there'd never be a cop looking for him. And Mavis could find some other sap to work the kennel, to slave like a goddamn sled dog. Of course Arnold might find out Philo had booked a flight to Puerto Vallarta. So what? That was a long way from here. Arnold was a two-bit bookmaker. The kike and the nigger with the knife wouldn't dare try anything on the Mexican Gold Coast. They don't put up with crooks down there. Let Arnold try. Philo'd have the *Federales* on him. Dig a grave, smoke a cigarette, and adios, Arnold, you fucking vampire.

Then he heard a car door slam. The door of the detective car slammed shut on the dream of Philo Skinner. He looked out and didn't see a detective. He saw a burly man with wild cinnamon hair and a slouchy walk, coming right for the front door.

He knew who it was at once, this brawny stranger! He was the nigger and the kike! It was Arnold's gunsel. Arnold crossed him up, that slimy bloodsucker. He said a man would come that *afternoon*, not morning! Philo peeked through the shade and the man got closer.

This gorilla wouldn't listen to reason! They *never* do in the movies. He'd just start tearing the place apart looking for money. He'd find the flight bag with the twenty K. *After* he cut Philo's throat! Then Philo tried to calm himself. No, it's just a customer, that's all it is. Just someone who wants Philo to take care of his fucking Irish setter for a couple weeks. That's all it is. The man was at the door now. He was knocking. Philo peeked through the blind and looked for a telltale bulge under his arm. The suit hugged his husky torso pretty well. There was no bulge. Philo was imagining things. Jesus! He had to keep his mind together. He'd be on that plane in a few hours. Then the man knocked again. Still Philo peeked. Go away, asshole. Take your fucking Irish setter and . . . Then the man pulled open his jacket to get a notebook. Philo saw it. It was on his belt. A gun! It *is* one of Arnold's gunsels! He *won't* cut Philo's throat! He'll shoot his balls off!

Philo Skinner knocked the metal grooming table clear across the room when he ran for the office. The table clashed to the tile floor and knocked bottles smashing against the wall. Philo grabbed the suitcase and the flight bag with the money. He slipped on the shampoo, which was all over the floor, and fell hard, cutting his hands before he got to the kennel door.

Valnikov heard the commotion and tried the door. It was locked. He heard the dogs barking and howling and heard someone running in the kennel. He thought that he had stumbled into a burglary in progress! Someone was ransacking Skinner Kennels! Then he heard another crashing sound as Philo Skinner slammed into the steel-reinforced back door, double keyed on *both* sides. Security, Philo. There's lots of thieves in this world. And you just caught one, Mavis. Thanks for *everything*! You cunt!

"YOU CUNT!" Philo screamed, and twenty-five animals went mad. A Welsh terrier began barking. A Great Dane started bellowing. A malamute howled like a wolf. Then other voices joined the chorus. Mavis couldn't have heard Philo's hysterical obscenity if she were in the grooming room.

Neither could Valnikov. All he heard was a burglar trapped inside, trying to get out. Perhaps more than one burglar. He drew his revolver and kicked the door beside the lock. The jamb splintered but it didn't open. He backed up, took a step and kicked again and the door fell off the hinges and crashed on the overturned grooming table. The clashing crashing splintering sound made Philo and the dogs howl all the louder.

Philo dropped his suitcase but clung to the flight bag. He ran desperately back, back toward the grooming room. There was only one potential weapon in the kennel, and it was 100 feet back down the narrow aisle between the pens full of bellowing beasts.

Philo Skinner was holding his chest, fighting back a coughing spasm.

He felt a ball of phlegm as big as a fist ripping free from his lungs and rising in his throat. Yet he couldn't make a sound. Arnold's enforcer was creeping through the grooming room. Philo could hear his quiet steps on the broken glass. Philo held his breath as much as possible. The wheezing sounded deafening to him even in the din from the frightened animals. Philo removed a small fire extinguisher from the wall and backed into the shadows, into an alcove near the side door leading to the fenced exterior aisle on the periphery of the dog runs. Philo almost kicked over a mop and pail of water. The chunk of black phlegm was rising, rising, choking him. Please! Just a few seconds more!

Then Valnikov cautiously opened the door to the kennel. The dogs in the near cages saw this stranger with a gun. A Doberman started going berserk, slashing at the chain link with his teeth. Philo Skinner backed against a concrete wall, saw the gun of Arnold's enforcer, and thought he would strangle before the bullets tore through his tortured lungs.

Valnikov saw a T-shaped aisle at the far end of the kennel where Philo had dropped his suitcase. Valnikov started to move toward the suitcase when Philo's survival instincts took over. Valnikov saw a blur from the corner of his right eye. He turned but not fast enough. The fire extinguisher caught him on his broad forehead, over his right eye. Philo had swung with all his strength. It was enough. Valnikov fell back heavily against the first dog pen and went down on the concrete floor. He dropped his gun, but instinctively fell on top of it.

Philo Skinner was stopped by the chunk of poison in his throat. He started to gag and cough and gag some more. He leaned against the wall and gagged it out. A hunk of phelgm like a black golf ball splattered on the concrete floor. Valnikov was groaning and flopping on the floor like a beached baby whale.

Both men were acutely aware of their danger and both tried to recover first. It was Philo who at last caught some life-saving oxygen in those creaking lungs. He took as many sweet breaths as he dared and leaped forward. He picked up the fire extinguisher. He raised it over his head and Valnikov was just able to raise his left arm in time. It cracked down on his forearm and Valnikov cried out.

The dogs were by now frothing and screaming and running in circles, sensing a death struggle in their midst. The Doberman was past madness. His foam white lips and gums were bleeding from gnawing on the chain-link dog pen. Without knowing why, the Doberman lusted to be part of the kill. He was not an attack dog, but smelling blood and seeing the frenzied thrashing of two men at his feet, he wanted to kill without reason.

Philo wheezed and gulped and raised the fire extinguisher again. Valnikov held up the wounded arm but the fire extinguisher crashed into the arm *and* his head, near the temple. The cowlicks immediately became matted with blood as the vessels burst. Blood was running down Valnikov's face and neck. He bellowed like the Great Dane and rolled over on his stomach, on top of the gun. He groped under his stomach for the gun when Philo attacked again. Philo missed Valnikov's head this time but the fire extinguisher smashed into Valnikov's right shoulder and his fingers became paralyzed for a moment. He couldn't pick up the gun.

Philo had now fallen on top of Arnold's assassin. He couldn't move the heavy man, but he punched at the broad head weakly with his bony fists. He thrashed and whimpered and pulled on the assassin's bloody hair but there was no moving a man who weighed more than a St. Bernard. Philo then reached under Valnikov, under his belly. Valnikov's half-paralyzed fingers and Philo's tobacco-stained fingers fought over the revolver.

Philo was whining and whimpering louder than any dog in the kennel. Then he started growling like the Doberman. He buried his stained teeth in Valnikov's shoulder, but the bulky flesh was too hard. Philo bit Valnikov on the bloody neck. Still he couldn't get the gun.

Then Philo fell on his stomach and put both hands beneath the detective and with all his strength moved the body. Philo reached under and jerked backward and rolled over against the door to the grooming room. The gun was in his hand.

Valnikov and Philo lay prone for a moment staring at each other across four feet of bloody concrete floor. The dogs were running in drooling circles. A Sealyham terrier was lying on her back kicking her feet. She was crazier than the Doberman by now.

Valnikov was shaking his head like a wounded bull, moaning in pain as the initial shock decreased. He thought he was going to die. He watched the burglar's eyes.

Philo knew he had hurt the assassin. Still, he was infinitely stronger than Philo even in this condition. Philo Skinner had never considered that he might have to kill a man. He kept the gun pointed at the assassin's bloody face. He wasn't absolutely certain whether you had to cock this revolver but he guessed you didn't. He was trying to get up the strength and courage to do what he had to do. But he had never in his life hurt an animal. How could he kill a man?

"You . . . you . . . turn around." Philo stopped to cough and spit on the floor but he never took his eyes off Arnold's assassin. "Crawl on your stomach. Crawl . . . back. Back! Crawl back or I'll kill you."

Valnikov hesitated for a second. Then, on his stomach, his suitcoat torn in three places, he began wriggling back along the floor.

"Back!" Philo commanded. "Crawl back! Further! Further!"

Valnikov inched back, wiping blood from his face, never taking his eyes off the burglar.

When Valnikov was lying beside an empty animal pen on the west side of the kennel, Philo said, "Stop." Only then did Philo Skinner struggle to his feet and walk carefully along the pens to his right, just avoiding the Doberman who was desperately trying to get his nose through the mesh and grab Philo's skinny thigh.

Philo stood over Valnikov and said, "Put your face down on the concrete." Valnikov did, and waited for the bullet to crack through the back of his skull. He wanted to roll quickly to the right, to die fighting for his life, but the pain had weakened him. Pain, more than anything, made him obey when he was sure it was the end. He thought of something to take with him to eternity. He thought of nightingales singing in a raspberry bush.

But Philo said, "Don't move or I'll kill you." And he heard Philo fumbling with a set of keys. Then Philo turned the lock on the door of the empty dog pen. He pulled the door open. "Now crawl in there on your stomach," Philo wheezed. "Stay on your stomach. Don't try to get up or you're dead."

Still, Valnikov had not spoken a word. He began crawling. He pushed a large feeding dish out of his way. He crawled past a mound of feces. A very *large* mound. He heard a low rumbling just beyond the doggie door leading to the gravel dog run outside.

Philo, standing in the doorway of the pen, didn't hear the rumble that Valnikov could hear at floor level. Philo couldn't hear anything in that howling, barking, growling, whining, yapping canine bedlam.

And then, Philo Skinner, who had been beaten up by every half-assed bully all through his miserable childhood, Philo Skinner, who had been punched around by half the redneck squirts in his army platoon before his medical discharge for asthma, Philo Skinner, who for the first time in his life had bested another human being in a physical encounter, couldn't resist a victorious howl or two. Like a wild dog standing over his helpless prey.

"Tell your boss," Philo croaked triumphantly. "Tell that bloodsucker that Philo Skinner said adios! Tell him next time to try it himself, he wants to take Philo Skinner!"

Philo was enjoying himself so much he did not see the maniacal amber eye on the other side of the slit in the rubber doggie door. Valnikov saw that frightful eye. Valnikov heard the rumbling, which at floor level sounded like an earthquake beginning, or a cyclone on the horizon.

Walter, the German shepherd, didn't like being away from his adopted family. Walter didn't like the pen they had put him in, the first time he had been caged since those bad old days as an attack dog. Walter didn't even like the delicious horsemeat and liver that Mavis had tried to feed him yesterday. But most of all Walter didn't like *guns.*

In fact, Walter had been trained by his former owner to hate guns. And to rip into tiny pieces of hamburger any human being who *dared* to point a gun at him. Walter's former owner taught all his doggies very special tricks with his lead-filled rubber hose. The tricks made his guard dogs very popular with his clients. Walter's former owner, who loved his work as much as his animals hated theirs, wore special equipment for his demonstrations. The special equipment included a steel-mesh apron. Strapped outside the apron was a Little League groin cup, covered with sponge rubber. Something a crazed animal could get his teeth into.

The potential clients invariably laughed like hell when they saw that *these* dogs weren't so stupid as to let someone "feed them the arm" like most attack dogs. Walter and his thirteen wretched pals were taught to feint for their master's padded forearm and then dive straight for the Little League cup and tear it off the apron. One of Walter's chums was so crazed by the "training" that he once tried to *eat* the groin cup. The clients laughed like hell at the demonstration. These dogs would attack a burglar right where he *lived.*

Philo Skinner was enjoying this moment of triumph too much to see anything. He was so busy gloating over the fallen assassin, he didn't notice the huge mound of feces in the "empty" pen. He didn't see the amber eye of the cyclone. He never heard the roar.

The roar.

Valnikov covered his face when the cyclone roared over him. The black-and-tan cyclone bashed Philo into the steel post holding the seven-foot gate of the pen. Philo's head striking the post hardly bothered him. What did bother him was that this cyclone had him pinned up against the chain-link wall trying to chew his groin into hamburger.

Valnikov struggled to his knees and crawled away from the snarling slashing frenzied beast, while every dog in the kennel increased the roar by several decibels, totally drowning out Philo Skinner's screaming. The dog lost his first grip and settled on the extremely sensitive flesh on the very top of the inner thigh of Philo Skinner. The dog plunged his teeth into this tender meat just as the first two explosions erupted his flanks. The dog jerked his head around and snapped at his own flesh like a shark, amber eyes wide with the same surprise Valnikov had shown, the shock of unbelievable pain. Philo was backed against one side of the pen and Valnikov the other. Both watched the shepherd thrashing and then Philo pointed the gun and an explosion splattered through the shoulder of the dog and he fell on his back kicking his feet.

Philo Skinner looked down at the blood spreading over his crotch and he screamed like a woman. Valnikov at last felt the full effects of the concussion and started to get dizzy and very sick. Valnikov was crawling on his stomach getting sicker and sicker when he saw in amazement that the dog had gotten his feet under him and was coiled again. The last thing Valnikov saw of the dog in life was the look on his face. The look of consummate hate and outrage as he made his last pain-wracked leap at the terror-filled face of Philo Skinner.

Philo was coughing and spitting when he fed his arm to Walter and fired three rounds into the chest of the monster, and this time the echoing explosions drowned out the animal din.

Then Valnikov was swallowing back the vomit and kneeling on all fours watching the shrieking dog handler try to throw the body off himself. Valnikov didn't know that Philo had fired all six rounds, and made a lunge for the gun while Philo fought with the dead animal.

Philo didn't know that he had fired all six rounds and the gun clicked impotently three times in the face of Valnikov as he lunged forward. Then the three of them rolled on the floor, through blood and feces. Two wounded, weak, desperate men with a dead dog between. Two bodies thrashed and punched and kicked and rolled in slow motion. Walter lay dead, pressed between them, a shepherd sandwich.

Philo hacked at Valnikov with the gun, hitting him once on the shoulder, but Valnikov slid free and Philo only hit the dead dog with the next blow. Philo whimpered and sobbed and threw the gun at Valnikov, striking him in the chest. Then Philo got to his knees and crawled for the open gate. He grabbed the metal post, pulled himself upright and was one step out of the cage when Valnikov grabbed his legs in a bear hug and held on.

"You bastard!" Philo shrieked. "Let me go!"

The dogs answered with ear-splitting howls.

Valnikov gradually pulled himself to his knees, trying not to vomit, holding Philo around the legs.

Philo held on to the gate post and yelled "YOU BASTARD!" as Valnikov, with nearly a hundred pounds more weight, locked around Philo's bloody hips and pulled him back into the pen.

"BAST—" Philo sobbed and grabbed the cage gate while falling, and it clanged shut as the two sick and wounded men fell on their backs next to Walter.

Philo looked at the locked gate and started crying. Valnikov looked at the locked gate and started throwing up. Walter looked at the locked gate with dead eyes.

When Valnikov stopped vomiting, the concussion played a trick on him. His head started falling on one shoulder, then the other. It felt like his head had ballast attached, or that his thick neck had lost its strength. He couldn't keep his head straight.

Philo Skinner looked at him and got to his feet. The gate in front of him went clear to the ceiling. He thought about crawling through the doggie door but the outside dog run was completely fenced up to eight feet, and then the chain link had been stretched over the top. Skinner Kennels has the best of security for your pet. Thanks, Mavis.

There was only one thing to do. The side walls of chain-link fence in each dog run stopped one foot short of the ten-foot ceiling. But there were eleven dog pens between Philo and the aisle to freedom. Eleven dog pens full of terriers. There were seven dog pens the other way. Full of huge beasts like Walter. Philo Skinner, Terrier King, started the climb the long way.

He was wheezing and gasping and slippery with sweat and blood when he reached the top of the first chain-link wall. He took as large a breath as possible without coughing, and heaved his lanky frame up on the top bar and hung scrambling down the side. He fell to his knees when he dropped. He looked at his crotch. It was throbbing but the spreading stain had stopped. Oh, please, God, let me have a cock when I look, Philo prayed. I'll *need* it in Puerto Vallarta. Please God!

While Philo scrambled up the next wall of fencing, Valnikov concentrated on staying conscious. He lay face to face with the shepherd and tried to think of other things. He was clammy over his whole body and knew he had to lie still for a moment if there was any possibility of avoiding unconsciousness. He stared into the dead eyes of Walter. Courage had not been enough. Three bullets weren't enough to overcome that bravery and rage, but six had done the trick. Walter's death mask was frozen in a look of . . . what was it? The snarl had been replaced and he looked lonely and hopeless. He had probably sensed it was futile at the end. Valnikov found that look of despair truly unbearable.

Walter took with him to eternity the lonely hopeless face of Charlie Lightfoot.

Then Valnikov tried to sit up. He was careful and tentative. He used the chain link to support him. He looked up at the burglar, moaning and scrambling over the second bar of steel. The burglar dropped down heavily into the next animal pen and fell on top of a whining Kerry blue terrier. Now there were two dog pens separating them.

Three minutes later, both men were trying the wall of chain-link fencing. Valnikov was not so dizzy now, but still feared falling unconscious from a height of nine feet.

Philo Skinner was so exhausted he wasn't thinking of anything but breathing. One breath at a time, Philo. One breath at a time through raw crusty lips.

The pursuit through the dog pens lasted one hour. Panting, moaning, crying out. Up nine feet of fence, balancing precariously on the top until the feet were over the side, scrambling for toeholds, flesh tearing, sliding down into the next pen, falling in little piles of terrier feces.

The sick and wounded pursuer was never able to gain on the sick and wounded quarry during the funereal chase. They watched each other wordlessly through two walls of steel mesh and by unspoken agreement took their rests together. Usually it was Valnikov who signaled the rest break was over, by heaving his heavy bulk upright, and stretching his broad bleeding fingers over the steel mesh and hoisting himself up. Sweat scorched their eyeballs and flowed painfully into the numerous wounds on their tortured bodies.

When Philo was two cages from the aisle he had a horrible siege of giddiness. He had to sit down, right in a puddle of yellow diarrhetic Dandie Dinmont dog shit, brought about by the hysterical hour the animals had endured. But dog shit was the least of Philo's worries. He stared in disbelief as the bullish assassin didn't seize the opportunity to rest himself. Philo watched in horror as the assassin went up the next wall of steel, like a giant crab, two inches at a time. Philo watched in terror as the bloody assassin, his clothes in rags, hung for a second on the bar nine feet over the concrete floor.

"Fall, you bastard. Break your fucking neck!" Philo croaked, but the giant crab gripped the side of the chain link and scuttled down the other side. Now there was only one wall of fencing between them.

The assassin staggered over to that fence and stared Philo straight in the eyes. Then he tried to climb. But he couldn't. He fell to his knees and groaned almost as painfully as Philo Skinner. Then an astonishing thing happened while a terrified Yorkshire terrier crawled over to the assassin and curled up in a gesture of total submission. The astonishing thing was that when the assassin tried to nudge the terrier out of his way his tattered coat sleeve caught on something on his belt. The assassin reached back to pull the coat free and a pair of handcuffs clattered to the floor.

Handcuffs? On a hired thug? Philo Skinner wiped the sweat from his face with what was left of his turtleneck sweater. His imitation gold chain hung clear to his bloody crotch and he jerked it off his neck and tossed it aside. A hired killer with handcuffs?

"Who . . . who are you?" Philo croaked.

"Who . . . who are *you?*" Valnikov gasped.

"I . . . I asked you first," Philo croaked.

"I . . . I'm . . . Valnikov, Los . . . Los Angeles Police Department. And you . . . you're under arrest!" Valnikov gasped.

"You . . . you . . . you aren't gonna *kill* me?" Philo wheezed.

"I'm . . . I'm going to . . . *arrest* you!" Valnikov panted.

And then Philo realized. A cop! Somehow they'd solved it already. Somehow he'd left a clue for them. They'd traced that last call he was dumb enough to make from the kennel when he was desperate. When he'd cut the bitch's ear off and wasn't thinking clearly anymore.

"I never hurt an animal in my life!" Philo whined. "That cunt made me do it!"

"Made . . . made you do what?" Valnikov panted.

"Cut . . . cut the ear off!" Philo cried. "I'll give the money back! I never hurt an animal in my life!"

Then Valnikov wiped his sweaty face with his sleeve and stood up, holding on to the chain link. He tried to get his head clear. He followed Philo's eyes to the last pen, the one beyond Philo Skinner. To the little schnauzer curled up in a corner, trembling and whining softly. A little schnauzer with her head wrapped in gauze bandage.

"You! *You* stole the dog!" Valnikov cried.

"Well, what . . . what did you think?" Philo said.

"That you were a . . . a burglar!" Valnikov said.

"You what?" Philo got even more pale and pulled himself painfully to his feet. "Why . . . why'd you come here?"

"To ask . . . to ask about Mrs. Gharoujian's Tutu. I . . . I hoped you might be able to tell me if someone . . . if one of her boyfriends could have . . ."

"How did you *know* the dead schnauzer was Millie's Tutu?" Philo cried.

"I *didn't* know for sure," Valnikov panted. "I was here to ask you to look at it."

"NOOOOOOOO!" Philo howled, and some of the dogs who had been quieting down started howling again with Philo Skinner.

And while Philo was busy howling, Valnikov took the opportunity to begin scaling the cage which separated them. Philo finally stopped howling when he saw the detective halfway up the steel mesh, and then he yelped and turned and began a desperate climb up the penultimate fence of steel.

Philo was cursing and whining at the top, seemingly without the strength to pull his bony body over the bar. Then he heard the detective's heavy body thud to the floor below him. Valnikov grunted, slipped in feces and fell, his head thudding on the concrete.

Then Philo was over, down into the last dog pen. Into Vickie's pen. The little schnauzer squirmed deeper into the corner, as far as she could get from Philo Skinner. She was trembling so hard her toenails were wearing down on the concrete floor.

Valnikov was on his back, groaning. He didn't know he'd been unconscious until he looked up and saw Philo Skinner, with one last effort, pulling himself up the nine feet to the last bar. Valnikov was on his feet then and climbing. Both men were sobbing, more from exhaustion than the pain, which was anesthetized by the fatigue. Valnikov somehow reached the top of the horizontal steel bar when Philo Skinner reached his.

Philo Skinner looked over at the detective perched like himself nine feet over the floor and he cried, "You didn't even *know* I did it! You came to have me look at Tutu! Why does everything happen to me! *YAAAAAAAAAAAA!*"

And after Philo Skinner's primal scream, he let go and fell scrambling down the steel mesh to the floor. He was in the aisle. He had made it. He was free.

Valnikov fell, landing on one knee. He heard something pop and cried out in pain, but he crawled across the cage and pulled himself upright. He was standing face to face with Philo Skinner between the last strands of steel.

Then the whimpering beside him made him look down at the mutilated schnauzer. "You . . . you're under arrest," Valnikov gasped.

"You . . . you catch me first," Philo wheezed, picking up the suitcase, shocked to discover that he couldn't lift it with one hand now.

"Don't . . . don't," Valnikov said, feeling himself getting dizzy again. "Give up, Skinner. Give up."

Philo almost vomited again when he looked at his bloodstained crotch. Please let it be there, God! Oh, please! He found that he could pick up the lightweight suitcase if he used both hands. The last thing he said to Valnikov was: "You tell them . . . tell them that Philo Skinner never . . . never hurt an animal in his *life!*"

Then while Valnikov tried to scale the last wall of steel mesh, he heard Philo in the doorway grunting and wheezing as he picked up the flight bag, dragging the suitcase with one hand. He heard glass breaking as Philo made his way through the debris in the grooming room.

Valnikov was sick and reeling from vertigo when he reached the top bar. He knew he had one surge left, only one. He yelled and felt like the blood would burst from his nose as he pulled his heavy body up, up, until his bloody fingers gripped. He kicked and lunged and got his toe hooked over the top. He couldn't rest. He had to keep the momentum of the last surge. It helped to yell, with the bellowing dogs, and then he was balancing on the top. But there was nothing left. He couldn't climb down, he couldn't hang and drop, he just had to risk it. He let his feet fall and followed with the rest of his bulk and dropped stiff-legged, sending a shock through his skull. Then he fell on his back and lay there.

The dogs seemed quieter now, and then he heard the engine of the El Dorado grinding. Philo Skinner in his panic had flooded the engine. Valnikov looked at Vickie still huddled in panic and terror. Poor thing, he thought. Poor tortured little . . .

"Now now, Vickie," he said. "Now now. You're going *home.*"

Philo Skinner sobbed in desperation, turned off the key, and forced himself to sit while the carburetor drained. He looked at his face in the rearview mirror and couldn't believe what he saw. He'd seen starved scabby mongrels that looked better. The mucus clotted in his windpipe and he gagged.

Valnikov staggered down the long aisle between the animals, determined not to faint, forgetting for a moment who he was pursuing and why. He reached the door before Philo tried again. If Philo had turned and seen the detective, with his trousers flapping in shreds, one coat sleeve totally gone and the other hanging from the elbow, the detective with his face grimy and caked with blood and dog food, Philo might have panicked and flooded the El Dorado again. But he didn't even see his pursuer staggering toward his Cadillac. He looked at the ignition and turned it. The engine roared.

Philo screamed with joy and squealed away, never seeing the relentless bloody crab falling on his face in the parking lot of Philo Skinner, Terrier King.

15

Paradise

Philo Skinner was halfway to the airport before he had even a remote idea of what he was doing. It wasn't the incredible exhaustion, nor the horror, nor the pain that revived him. It was the smell. The smell of stale sweat, the smell of blood and fear. Mostly it was the smell of dog shit. Philo Skinner had excrement in his hair, on his pants, on his bare chest. It was mashed into the hair of his armpits where the clothing was torn away. It was even in his pockets!

Philo turned off the San Diego Freeway and drove aimlessly for twenty minutes in an area he didn't know. Then he found a public park. He circled the park several times until he found a rest room. He parked the car in the shade of an elm tree and when there were no passersby in sight, he got out of the car and hobbled across the green expanse toward the park rest room, dragging both suitcase and flight bag.

Five minutes later, Philo Skinner was standing stark naked in the rest room, bathing himself with paper towels and harsh hand soap in one of two rusty sinks. He cried out often and sobbed in relief when he got all the dried blood off his wounded genitalia and saw it was still there. But it would be out of action a long long time. The foreskin was ripped and already swollen purple. His testicles were still intact, but his upper thighs on both sides were mangled and still bleeding. He knew he needed suturing. Philo Skinner had doctored many injured dogs in his time and had a very good idea of what dog bites could do. His hands were a bloody mess, as were his knees and chest. One eye was blue and green and swollen shut and he knew he would need more sutures behind his ear where he could hardly stem the flow of blood.

Philo urinated in the sink and cried out in pain. Then he opened the suitcase and used two of his brand-new thirty-dollar body shirts as *diapers.* He couldn't afford to arouse suspicion by bleeding all over the seats in the airport lounge. He tied both shirts around him like loincloths, put on the new pants and cursed because he had bought them so stylishly tight. Like everything else it had seemed like a good idea at the time. He put on the jacket of his new leisure suit and planned to keep it buttoned since both new shirts were wrapping his groin. This left him without shirt, socks and shoes, as there was no way he could use his time and waning energy to clean the blood and feces from his imitation alligators.

Fifteen minutes later, a clerk in a men's store just off the San Diego Freeway was surprised to see a man who looked like he just played goalie without a mask stroll into the store barefoot and shirtless. The customer was easy to please, and didn't even care that the patent-leather shoes failed to coordinate with the leisure suit.

The clerk noticed that the man's flesh was gray where he wasn't bruised, and that a trickle of blood leaked down behind his ear. Philo noticed too and bought a dozen handkerchiefs which he jammed in his pockets. He paid in cash and limped out of the store, pausing in the doorway to double up in pain. Then he went next door to a liquor store and bought four packs of Camels which he figured would see him through the next twelve hours.

At 2:00 p.m. Philo Skinner was limping up to the Mexicana Airlines desk at Los Angeles International. He dabbed often at the flow of blood behind his ear. It would stop temporarily and then start leaking. He felt soppy between his legs and knew he was bleeding again down there. Philo Skinner knew he was *hurt.*

When he put the flight bag through the x-ray he panicked for a second. Did he leave his ballpoint pen in there? Was there any metal in there which might cause them to open it? He was ready to faint when he got through the x-ray check. A woman in a uniform handed him his flight bag.

Each step was agony now. Philo was limping to his terminal when he spotted a skycap carrying some bags toward the front.

"Hey, pal," Philo croaked. "If you'll run quick and get a wheelchair and help me to my gate, I'll give you twenty bucks."

The skycap looked at Philo's battered, sweaty, gray face and said, "Man, you're hurtin. You better let me git you a doctor!"

"Hey, I just had a little traffic accident, that's all," Philo wheezed. "I been checked and I'm okay. Look, get that wheelchair and it's worth *thirty* bucks."

"Okay," the skycap said. "Be back in five minutes."

Philo sat and waited and watched passengers being checked for guns and bombs and wished *he* had a gun or bomb. He'd come this far. He had a feeling he wasn't going to make it. He'd rather be dead than go to prison. He felt so sick he thought he might die. He wanted to die in Puerto Vallarta. To die with his dream. In paradise.

"Ready, mister?" the skycap said and Philo opened his eyes. The skycap was standing there with a wheelchair.

"Yeah," Philo said. "Could you do me one more favor? Light me a cigarette. I ain't got a match."

The skycap wheeled Philo, smoking and coughing, through the terminal to his gate. The skycap was reluctant to leave Philo.

"Hey, you sure you oughtta be takin this flight?" the skycap said. "They ain't gonna let you on this flight, bad as you look. Not if you can't make it on your own."

"I'll make it," Philo said, giving the skycap two twenties. "Keep the change," Philo said. It was the biggest tip he ever gave in his life.

"Anything else I can do, mister?"

"One more thing, pal," Philo croaked. "Use a couple bucks a that tip and bring me a drink. Straight whiskey. Put it in a paper cup or something so you can get it here."

"You got it, mister," said the skycap, who was gone and back in five minutes.

Just a moment before the public address system announced that the 3:00 p.m. Mexicana Airlines flight was boarding, Philo Skinner had stemmed the blood behind his ear. He had dabbed at his face with what was left of his dozen handkerchiefs. The sweat would alert them to his condition more than the swollen battered face. He put on his bubble sunglasses and looked down, frightened to see a tiny bloodstain starting on the crotch of his polyester pants. Why had he picked a cream-colored suit? Why couldn't he have picked red? Why couldn't he have done a lot of things?

Why did he always have to pick the black marble?

When he hobbled toward the Mexicana jet, he said, as casually as possible to a young man who looked like a student on holiday, "Hey, pal, how bout letting me just lean on your arm when we board this plane? See, I had this car accident and I'm not feeling too good."

The stewardess assigning the seats said, "Are you all right, señor?"

The handkerchief, wiping his face every few seconds, couldn't keep it dry. The pain was so terrifying that the sweat poured with every step. "I'll be okay, soon as you fix me a margarita," Philo grinned. "I had a car accident this morning but the doc says I'm fine. Just bring that margarita as soon as you can."

"I'm sorry, señor, but we are out of margarita mix."

"No margarita?" Philo croaked, limping down the aisle to his seat in first class.

"I can feex you a nice Bloody Mary," she smiled.

"Blood," said Philo. "Just a bourbon and water."

"Right after takeoff, señor," she said.

"Right after takeoff," said Philo Skinner, his mouth as dry as a tomb.

• • •

Valnikov was never fully unconscious. He was never fully conscious either. He saw Clarence Cromwell in the hospital room. And Hipless Hooker. He didn't see Natalie. They were talking to him. He couldn't understand everything they said. Clarence kept grinning and patting Valnikov gently on the arm and saying, "They don't make em like this no more. Fuckin kids with peanut balls think they're cops!"

Then Hipless Hooker left, but Clarence stayed.

"Did you get Skinner, Clarence?" Valnikov said, coming out of the sedative mist. He had been in some trackless wasteland, it seemed. But at least it wasn't Siberia.

"We'll git him, Val," Clarence said. "Don't you worry, we gonna git that sucker. The little dog's back with her momma at least. She called about you, maybe ten times. Wants to send you flowers and visit you and have the chief give you a medal or a ticker-tape parade or somethin. Last time she called she said for me to say to you that Vickie's gonna be okay and that she's gonna be okay too. Whatever that means."

"I think she *will* be okay," Valnikov nodded. "Did Natalie call?"

"She, uh, she sends her . . . wishes for uh . . . you to git well. I called your brother, but the doc says no visitors till tomorrow. I figured I ain't exactly a visitor and I knew you'd wanna know what's goin on when you came around."

"Do I have a phone in here, Clarence?"

"Course you got a phone, fool!" Clarence grinned. "You think I'm gonna let them put a ace detective in a room without a phone?"

"Dial Natalie for me, will you?"

"I don't know her number."

"Sure you do. You have all our phone numbers in your little notebook. The one in your coat pocket."

"Oh, yeah," Clarence said glumly, taking out the notebook.

While he dialed, Valnikov touched his head. It was swathed in a bandage that covered his left ear. Some hair stuck out on top. He had some pain in his knee, and his shoulder and ribs hurt, but he didn't really feel as much pain as he expected.

"Natalie?" said Clarence, scowling. "This is me, Clarence. Jist a minute."

He handed the phone to Valnikov, who took it and said, "Natalie?"

"Valnikov!" she said, "I was worried! How *are* you? They said for us not to visit you until tomorrow! I would've come!"

"I know you would, Natalie," Valnikov smiled. "How are *you?*"

"We heard you have a concussion. And there was gunfire! A dead dog. Did you shoot him?"

"No, Skinner did. Natalie, are you . . . well, when do you leave for Hawaii?"

"Valnikov," she said softly, then the phone was quiet. In the background Valnikov heard the voice of Captain Jack Packerton saying, "Who's that, Natalie? Who're you talking to?"

"My partner," she said. Then to Valnikov: "We moved up our plans. We're going tomorrow. We had our reservations changed. It was tough to do, but we were told that in two weeks there might be too much rain in that part of Kauai. Rain would ruin our vacation."

"Yes, of course," Valnikov said.

"Clarence Cromwell fixed it so I could leave tomorrow."

"Yes, he's a good man to work for," said Valnikov.

"I wouldn't have gone without checking on you though. I was going to stop tomorrow to see you. Our flight isn't until tomorrow afternoon."

"Yes, that's the best time to fly," said Valnikov.

"Well, I better let you rest. You take care, huh? Would you like to have visitors tomorrow? I could bring some books or . . ."

"No, I don't think so, Natalie. I think I'll just rest tomorrow. You have a good time in Hawaii, okay?"

"Okay, Valnikov. Be seeing you."

"Be seeing you," he said, handing the phone to Clarence, who hung it up.

Clarence said, "Hey, guess what? I decided I'm gettin sick and tired a sittin around on my ass runnin that division. I wanna do some detective work again. I was hopin you and me might team up a few days a week. Couple a real ball-bustin cops! How bout that!"

"Great, Clarence," Valnikov mumbled. "Sounds great."

"Okay, you git some sleep now, hear? I'll come see you tomorrow. Doc says he's on'y gonna keep you maybe a day or so. Git some sleep, hear?"

"What time is it?"

"Ten o'clock," Clarence said.

"Night or morning?"

"Night. This is still Thursday. All you lost is an afternoon."

"That's all I lost," said Valnikov.

• ● •

Philo Skinner didn't come soaring in over white beaches and crashing surf at sunset. It was after dark when they touched down, but it wouldn't have mattered anyway. Philo Skinner was slumped in his seat, with his head on a bloody pillow, trying to keep from vomiting. He was burning with fever and making all the first-class passengers around him sick by coughing up endless phlegm balls and spitting into a towel.

The stewardess had not noticed the serious condition of the gray feverish man until they had passed the point of no return. She advised the pilot, who came back to talk to him.

Philo nodded in answer to most of the questions. "I got in a car accident yesterday. Been in the hospital but I'm okay. I'm okay, goddamnit!"

At one point, while Philo slept fitfully, moaning in pain, the stewardess gently removed the flight bag from his lap and put it on the floor under him. The battered man had not released his death grip on the flight bag since boarding. She was afraid of it. Some sophisticated explosives could get by the detector. She opened the flight bag and then closed it quickly and took it forward to the captain, who asked that a radio message be relayed to Los Angeles. The captain believed they had a wounded bank robber aboard.

There was an ambulance waiting when the plane touched down. At about the same time that Valnikov lay staring at the ceiling in the police ward at Central Receiving Hospital, Philo Skinner was being admitted to the Hospital Seguro Social. Philo had not seen the beach and surf nor even the sunshine in Puerto Vallarta. Philo's fever was more than 104 degrees, though they measured it in centigrade and only translated it to Fahrenheit when he demanded to know. Philo Skinner requested that someone from the American consulate be brought to him immediately.

Philo had been asleep for hours but was awakened by a throbbing in his penis. The throbbing became warm, then white hot. He cried out and a young man walked in. The man was in street clothes. He was short and slender, had a small moustache and black hair bright and shiny under the white light.

"I am Doctor Rivera," he said in nearly unaccented English.

"It hurts," Philo sobbed. "Down here." He had to reach with his right arm since the other contained an intravenous needle. He patted the bandages between his legs. "Is it . . . Oh, please! Is it . . . ?"

"Still there?" the doctor smiled. "It is still there, Mr. Skinner. But you have been mauled pretty badly. You won't be having much of a sex life for a while, but yes, it is all still there."

"Thank God," Philo sobbed. "Doctor, I hurt!"

"You are urinating," the doctor said. "I had to put a catheter in you. You are a sick man, Mr. Skinner."

"Where's my . . . my flight bag?" Philo croaked.

"Mexicana Airlines has seized your flight bag, Mr. Skinner," the young doctor said. "There is a receipt for almost twenty thousand dollars from Mexicana Airlines. They have seized your flight bag pending an investigation with the American authorities."

"Oh, God!" Philo cried.

"Tell me, Mr. Skinner," the young doctor said, curiously, "are you a bank robber or what?"

"Oh, God!" Philo cried.

"You may as well satisfy my curiosity," the doctor shrugged. "I am sure the Los Angeles Police or the F.B.I. or someone is after you. A man with animal bites and multiple contusions and lacerations? A man with a bag full of money? We have a little . . . how do you say . . . lottery going on. Some of the doctors and nurses think you are a bank robber. But I don't think banks employ police dogs in Los Angeles. I went to Loma Linda University and I never saw a police dog in a Los Angeles bank."

"Oh, God, a *lottery!*" Philo cried. He who lives by the bookmaker . . .

"I think you are a safe . . . how do you say?"

"Cracker," Philo croaked.

"Yes, a safecracker. I think that you were cracking a safe and a watchman turned a dog loose on you and . . . tell me, Mr. Skinner, did you kill someone? A watchman maybe?"

Then while Philo was looking around the little hospital room at the Friday morning sky over Puerto Vallarta, at the smiling young doctor with eyes as brown as a dog's, with eyes as oval and brown as . . .

"I killed Tutu," Philo said.

"You what?"

"I KILLED TUTU!" Philo wailed, hollow-eyed and frightful. "And I cut Vickie's ear off! And I shot . . . I shot . . ." But Philo couldn't continue. His tears were scalding. Philo Skinner's long bony frame was heaving and shaking the bed. Philo Skinner only stopped crying when he broke into a coughing spasm that almost strangled him.

A nurse came running in and the doctor said something in Spanish.

"Lean forward, a little, Mr. Skinner," the doctor said. "Here, spit the phlegm in this tray."

When Philo lay back on the pillow he could hardly see them through the tears. The nurse wiped his eyes and his mouth and said something in Spanish to the doctor.

The doctor's oval eyes were round and electric now. Nobody was going to win *this* lottery! A mass murderer!

"Do you want to tell me about it, Mr. Skinner?" the doctor said. "You killed *how* many? And you cut off an ear?" The doctor couldn't wait to tell the staff. The skinny gringo was another Charles Manson!

"Please, Doctor," Philo sobbed. "I don't wanna die here. I don't wanna die in this foreign country."

"You are not going to die, Mr. Skinner."

"I don't wanna *live* in a foreign country!" Philo cried.

"You are full of infection and you have lost blood and I believe you have a fairly serious lung disorder, but . . ."

"I wanna go home!" Philo wailed. "Call the Los Angeles cops, Doctor. Tell them to get me home."

"Yes, but about all those you killed, can you tell me . . ."

"I'm an American," Philo Skinner sobbed. "I wanna go *home!*"

16

Byzantine Eyes

On Friday, Valnikov got out of bed before noon and walked unsteadily around the room. Then he phoned his brother and told him to go to the apartment and bring him some clothes.

At 1:30 p.m. Alex Valnikov had come and gone, and his younger brother was walking around the ward in poplin slacks and an old sport shirt.

At 2:00 p.m. a nurse complained to a doctor that Sergeant Valnikov was checking out of the hospital whether they liked it or not.

At 2:30 p.m. Hipless Hooker called Valnikov's room and ordered him to listen to his doctor.

At 2:33 p.m. Sergeant Valnikov informed Hipless Hooker politely that he had just retired from the Los Angeles Police Department and that Captain Hooker could start processing his retirement papers.

At 5:30 p.m., just after a blazing winter sunset in Los Angeles, Valnikov was sitting on the steps by the reflecting pool at the Los Angeles Music Center, listening to Horst, the fiddler, play Rimsky-Korsakov. Fifteen bucks' worth.

Horst was getting tired. There was no one left at this time of day except this guy with the turban bandage who wanted Russian music. Horst asked him what happened to his head, but the guy just said, "An accident."

Horst was happy to take the guy's bread, but the fifteen bucks' worth had just about run out and Horst had exhausted his Russian repertoire and didn't want to start over again.

Valnikov sat with his back to Hope Street. He listened to a Gypsy violin and stared at the melancholy tableau of a fiddler, and beyond, in the dusk, the courthouse and the knight in chain mail with his hopeful document wrested from King John.

Then Valnikov heard a familiar voice: "They tell me it's raining in Kauai."

Valnikov turned and cried: "Natalie!"

"Sit down, don't get up," she said. "Oh, he hurt you! Oh!"

"Hurt? Hurt?" Valnikov cried, with the biggest dumbest smile she'd ever seen on him. "I'm fine! I'm swell!"

Then Natalie walked over to Horst, the fiddler, and said, "Your motor still running, Horst?"

"Huh?"

"We got any music left for the loot he's laid on you?"

"This is it, lady, I gotta go home."

Natalie Zimmerman took a twenty out of her purse and said, "Rev it up, Horst. Until this is gone."

"Okay, lady," Horst grinned. "Whadda ya wanna hear?"

"Gypsy," she said. "Russian Gypsy."

"Jesus, more Russian? Does it have to be *Russian?*"

"If you want the grease for your crank," she said, brushing her Friz out of her eyes.

"How about 'Ochi Chornyia'?" Horst suggested. "You know, 'Dark Eyes'?"

"Okay, Horst, give us a shot of 'Dark Eyes'," she said, going back to Valnikov, who was standing on the steps, looking like a quiz show contestant.

"Sit down and rest yourself," Natalie said, forcing him down on the steps. "You shouldn't even *be* here. I heard you walked out of the hospital. I heard you retired. Was that for real?"

"I've had enough," he said. "But you? You're *not* going to Hawaii?"

"Waste of money," she said. "I think I'd rather invest my savings in a music store or something."

As Horst burst into twenty bucks' worth of "Ochi Chornyia," Natalie moved close to Valnikov and said, "Do you know the lyrics to this one?"

"I can speak them to you," he said. "I'm not in very good voice but . . ."

Then Natalie moved even closer. He looked at her big goofy glasses, at her brown eyes behind them, and translated from the Russian.

"Dark eyes, passionate eyes, fiery and beautiful eyes. How I love you . . ."

"Yes," she whispered. "Go on."

"The rest of the song is sad, like all Gypsy songs," he said joyfully.

"Then don't tell it to me," she said. "We'll settle for that part."

"You have eyes like the Virgin on the ikon," he said. "The Byzantine eyes. The *sweet* Byzantine eyes!"

She put her head on his shoulder and those Byzantine eyes started to fill up while Horst played and eavesdropped.

"I thought I'd picked the black marble," Valnikov said.

"I don't wanna be like Charlie Lightfoot," Natalie said.

"You're not *anything* like Charlie Lightfoot," Valnikov said.

"Andrushka!" Natalie said, and it melted him.

He kissed her gently. She kissed him passionately. Then they lay back across the steps while Horst pretended to look elsewhere.

They faced Hope Street and kissed to a Gypsy violin.

"Andrushka!" she cried.

"Natasha!" he cried.

Then Horst got awfully nervous and started looking around. It was dark now, thank goodness. Good thing there weren't any bystanders around. Still, there was a lot of light from the reflecting pool.

"Hey, lady, I can't afford to get in trouble with the management around here," said Horst.

Natalie broke the kiss to say, "Keep it in gear, Horst."

Horst thought of the twenty scoots and kept playing. But finally they were getting *too* playful.

"Hey!" he said, stopping the music. "Why don't you two go to a motel or something? I'll refund part of your money."

Valnikov didn't even hear him. Valnikov was hearing nightingales singing in the raspberry bush. Natalie didn't break their kiss but she felt for her purse. She pulled out her service revolver and put it on the step beside her. Then she broke the kiss.

"How would you like a hole in your fiddle, Horst?"

"My God, lady! My God!" Horst cried. "That's a gun! Hey, lady! I don't want any trouble! Hey, lady!"

"Then you better crank it on, kid," Natalie said, tapping the revolver, biting on Valnikov's lower lip until they were lost in another interminable kiss.

Horst was so scared he could hardly finger the violin. His fingers were so sweaty they were slipping off the strings. Every time he thought about picking up his top hat full of money, and the violin case, and folding chair, and running like hell, he'd look at the gun lying there beside the two lust-crazed maniacs.

"Hey, lady!" Horst cried, playing an off-key "Ochi Chornyia." "Gimme a break!"

Then he looked in the shadows and saw their hands roving, caressing. Heard the kisses and moaning.

"Oh, Andrushka!"

"My Natasha!"

"You two oughtta be ashamed!" Horst whined, still playing. "A cop might come along and think I'm involved in this." Then he looked at the gun. "In fact I wish a cop *would* come along!"

"Andrushka!" Natalie cried.

"Natasha!"

"And they say *my* generation's going to hell," Horst whimpered.

Horst stole one last glance at the gun, gleaming malevolently by the light from the reflecting pool. Horst suddenly felt he might wet his pants. Why is there *never* a cop in this town when you need one? Horst looked at the madman with her. Christ, his head was all swathed in a bandage turban. He probably just had a lobotomy. No sense even *trying* to talk to him. And the female thug with the gun was obviously *more* dangerous.

So there was nothing to do but play "Ochi Chornyia" until they either shot him dead or let him go. Horst locked his knees and concentrated on controlling his bladder and played his violin gamely.

All he *ever* wanted to do was become a doctor and help people. And maybe make twenty grand a year on unreported fees he didn't have to claim on his income tax so he could buy a Porsche Turbo. And maybe pad the medicare statements here and there to make enough to buy a ski boat with a 454 Chevy engine. Jesus, he was a humanitarian!

His bladder was about to explode. Horst groaned and looked at the night sky and concentrated on one brave star which had penetrated the smog. Horst whined aloud to that hopeful star. Horst asked the timeless, universal, unanswerable question. "Why do I *always* have to pick the black marble?"

The lovers never heard him. They heard a Gypsy violin, and Russian nightingales and their hammering hearts.

"Andrushka!"

"My Natasha!"

"Oh, Andrushka!"